Seventh Edition

Effective Communication In Business

Morris Philip Wolf, Ph.D.
Formerly Professor of
Business Communication and Chairperson,
Department of General Business Administration,
University of Houston

Dale F. Keyser, Ph.D.
Professor of Business
Delta College
University Center, Michigan

Robert R. Aurner, Ph.D.
President, Aurner and Associates Corporate Counsel
Vice President, Management Consultant Division
Scott, Incorporated
Formerly Dean of the College of Commerce
United States Army American University
Biarritz, France
Professor of Business Administration
University of Wisconsin

Published by

E52   **SOUTH-WESTERN PUBLISHING CO.**

CINCINNATI   WEST CHICAGO, ILL.   DALLAS   PELHAM MANOR, N.Y.   PALO ALTO, CALIF.

ISBN: 0-538-05520-0

Library of Congress Catalog
Card Number: 77-92288

1 2 3 4 5 6 7 8 K 6 5 4 3 2 1 0 9

Printed in the United States of America

Treat this book with care and respect.

It should become part of your personal and professional library. It will serve you well at any number of points during your professional career.

Preface

This book is a product of many disciplines: of physical and social sciences, of liberal and communicative arts, of career-oriented education and of real-world business practices. The seventh edition provides updated concepts, methods, and guides for developing student awareness of—and competence with—the business of communication.

Like its six predecessors, this edition is both traditional and innovative. It is traditional in continuing the study of values, principles, and techniques which have guided human behaviors through trial and error to emerging expertise. It is innovative in reinforcing that study with modern insights to a quickly changing world, a world in which management is inseparable from communication and in which business directly or indirectly affects every person. Whatever their academic "majors" may be, students can gain personal as well as professional benefits from *Effective Communication in Business.*

Organization. The seventh edition is arranged in nine main parts which identify, describe, explain, and illustrate the following:

1. Communication concepts, goals, skills
2. Communication planning, organization, development, tone, formats, media
3. Multipurpose business messages for frequently recurring situations
4. Research and creativity for employment opportunities and career advancement
5. Research and creativity for sales and other persuasive communication
6. Responsibilities and techniques for claims, adjustments, credit and collection messages
7. Methods and guides for research proposals, research plans, research reports
8. Advanced communication exercises
9. Review of basic language skills

Special Features. The seventh edition has these characteristics:

1. Demonstrates communication methods of conveying sexist as well as ethnic equality through language and through illustrations
2. Sets the study of business communication in individual, organizational, and worldwide communication contexts
3. Merges communication theories and practical applications
4. Describes innovative and traditional approaches to successful management through effective communication
5. Emphasizes applications of behavioral science in planning, composing, transmitting, and evaluating business messages
6. Includes new material on multimedia communication—written, oral, and nonverbal—with opportunities throughout the book for practice
7. Conveys updated information through the revision of style as well as data for every chapter
8. Provides introductions for every main part and topic outlines for each chapter, helping students to preview and review assignments
9. Supplies comments at the end of every chapter, helping the student to summarize what has been read and to anticipate the next reading unit
10. Includes abundant discussion questions and exercises which give the teacher flexibility in varying assignments from class to class and from term to term
11. Provides new minidramas, scenarios, and case narratives as integrating exercises
12. Is accompanied by correlated publications (teacher's manual, student's workbook, and comprehensive examination)

The seventh edition reflects suggestions from those who have used its predecessors—suggestions from students, teachers, researchers, administrators, employers, and employees. Believing that effective communication is indeed a reciprocal process, the authors invite your comments concerning this book and your recommendations for the next edition.

Morris Philip Wolf
Dale F. Keyser
Robert R. Aurner

Acknowledgement

Many people, each in special and valuable ways, have earned our gratitude. We acknowledge our indebtedness

—to students, those we serve personally in the classroom or office throughout the world

—again to students, whom we have the privilege of teaching and with whom we keep searching

—to teachers, whatever their titles or work descriptions, especially those who teach people rather than subjects and who, thereby, continue to learn about themselves

—to researchers, who disclose what had been unperceived or forgotten, especially to those who communicate their discoveries effectively

—to administrators—supervisors, chairpersons, other managers, and their staff members; especially to those who interpret "administration" as *service* through leadership

We are grateful to South-Western Publishing Company for its investment of resources in this book. And we thank *you* for reading, and hopefully for *using, Effective Communication in Business.*

Table of Contents

PART ONE

Business People as Communicators

The needs of modern life are food, clothing, shelter—and communication. Yes, misunderstandings occur. But where there are communication gaps, people can build bridges.

Those bridges are necessary now. More than ever before in history, human beings must work together to share products, services, and peace. The profit motive remains strong. But today profit transcends cash value. Profit includes understanding. And understanding requires communication.

Surely your own life proves this fact: To be human is to have urgent communication needs. So that you can identify opportunities of fulfilling those needs, Part One provides a three-chapter study unit. Chapter 1 introduces personal and organizational approaches to the exchange of business messages. Chapter 2 identifies goals and skills of effective business communicators. Chapter 3 describes techniques and traits of those communicators.

Every chapter in this book has discussion questions and application exercises. Use these materials, with the guidance of your instructor, to develop your own communication abilities. And as you do so, consider: Unless you communicate effectively, how can you expect—whatever the marvels of modern technology—to share the evidence of your ideas and feelings, the proof of your being a person?

Personal and Organizational Concepts

Capable of reasoning, people act irrationally. Capable of emotion, people conflict with themselves, their environments, and their fellow creatures. How do these insights pertain to you and to communication?

SELF AND OTHERS

Although similar to other human beings, you are unique. You are yourself. Yet you must live and work with others, who also are unique. They too are striving to fulfill their individuality. At the core of modern life is an obligation to fulfill oneself within the requirements of nature and society. This obligation confronts families, business organizations, and governments. It confronts individuals, certainly including you.

As you attempt to fulfill yourself, your brain enables you to identify, classify, relate, and solve. But in responding to your environment, which includes the actions and messages of other people, you generate emotions as well as ideas. You feel as well as think.

What happens, for instance, when a fellow student or a co-worker offends you? Your sense organs perceive and your brain recognizes what is happening. Your heartbeat accelerates. Adrenalin and sugar rush through your body. You feel anger or fear. Fortunately, anger and fear are not your only emotions. What happens when your professor or your employer praises you? Your perceptors, your brain, and your emotions respond; you feel gratification or pride. Through such experiences you continue adjusting profitably to yourself, to other people, to the environments in which you and they live, cooperate, and compete.

Since you are rational, you create ideas. Since you are emotional, you modify your ideas with egotism and generosity, with fear and courage, with hatred and love. The combinations and conflicts of these personality attributes are to be expected; all people, including you, are emotional-rational beings.

You, however, are gearing your efforts toward a business career. And since modern business directly or indirectly affects virtually every human being, you are assuming an important obligation. It is the obligation of striving ethically and efficiently to *use* thoughts and feelings, ideas and emotions, actions and reactions, in conducting yourself, your life, and your work.

The following chapters of this book deal extensively with *how* you may meet that obligation. This chapter concerns itself mainly with *what* is involved and *why*.

MANAGEMENT THROUGH COMMUNICATION

As a student or an employee, you help to bring resources and objectives together. You thereby participate in management, which is the achievement of efficiency through intelligent decisions and actions. Simultaneously you participate in communication, which is the sharing of information through symbols, including "words" and "messages." Management and communication are inseparable. In business contexts, messages are instruments for influencing human beings. When you write a letter, compose a report, or communicate through oral/visual language, you affect not only things but also people. You know that your success requires useful messages that produce appropriate actions. You know that without effective writing, speaking, reading, and listening, even the best decision may produce the worst action. But do you know the approaches, purposes, and functions associated with management through communication?

Organizational Communication: Systems Approach

A "systems" approach to management emphasizes that organizations consist of interdependent, interacting parts. With this approach, managers view decisions, actions, and messages in terms of effects upon the total organization. For example, what an accountant does is important to his or her department *and* to the entire company. A marketing decision affects advertising *and* production, distribution, sales, collections, etc. Accounting, marketing, and other specializations become information processes for decisions at advanced management levels. And a business organization becomes a communication network.

Modern scientists have tied the systems approach with the study of human behavior.[1] The late Douglas McGregor theorized that individuals

---

[1] These landmark publications describe behavioral science applied to management theory:

Douglas M. McGregor, "The Human Side of Enterprise," an address reprinted from "Adventures in Thought and Action," proceedings of the Fifth Anniversary Convocation, School of Industrial Management, Massachusetts Institute of Technology, Cambridge, Mass., April 9, 1957. Also McGregor's book *The Human Side of Enterprise* (New York: McGraw-Hill Book Co., 1960). For a discussion of the human "hierarchy of needs," upon which McGregor largely based his views, consult Abraham H. Maslow, *Motivation and Personality* (New York: Harper & Brothers, 1954).

can fulfill increasing responsibility for planning and evaluating their contributions to group aims. According to McGregor, employees would place controls upon themselves while meeting their own needs and those of the organization.

One wonders sometimes whether ideas change quite so much as do the words that stand for them. More than half a century ago, for example, management experts wrote these statements: "Industry is not a machine; it is a complex form of human association." And industry "designed to meet the needs of our life—physical, mental, and moral—must be living. The aim of management must be to render industry more effectively human. . .all these factors are interdependent." [2] Those words, appropriate to the 1980's, were published in 1923, as were these: ". . . the ultimate motive of industry should be that of service to the community . . .the art of leadership will develop with the growth of the science and social responsibility of management. . . ." [3] Like the arts and sciences that are its parents, business administration involves the need to understand, to influence, and to communicate effectively.

Organizational Communication: Traditional Approach

Purposes. The historical *purposes* of management basically are these: to decide and to achieve.

Functions. These traditional, or classical, purposes usually involve at least four *functions*:

1. Planning—using facts, inferences, and assumptions as guides to appropriate action;
2. Organizing—unifying people, ideas, materials, and circumstances to pursue appropriate action;
3. Activating—energizing plans, organizations, people, and equipment into appropriate action; and
4. Controlling—identifying, observing, evaluating, and adjusting standards as well as performances to achieve appropriate action.

How do these management functions apply to communication?

Planning. The management-communication function of planning involves you in a creative process. You participate in determining objectives. You assist in formulating or revising concepts, enhancing policies, introducing improvements. With conferences, interviews, conversations, demonstrations, reports, memorandums, and letters, you accommodate company objectives. Plan your messages according to management purposes.

---

[2] Oliver Sheldon, *The Philosophy of Management* (Englewood Cliffs: Prentice-Hall, 1923), pp. 27-30.
[3] *Ibid.*

Planning contributes to unity of purpose and efficiency of method. *Planning* stimulates orderly action based upon orderly communication.

Organizing. Planning requires identification of an objective and formulation of means to attain that objective. Organizing, which builds upon planning, requires the integration of resources. Organizing is the bringing together of people, equipment, materials, processes, and company objectives.

How does this function of *organizing* affect you as a communicator? Surely you need to become familiar with your company's role and scope. You need to learn its past, current, and future goals; its structural units and operating methods; its assignment as well as its exercise of authority and responsibility. Such familiarization is necessary to the proper composition and routing of your messages. And it guides you in answering this basic communication question: "Why should I say what—when, where, and how—to whom?"

Organizing aligns plans, resources, actions, and goals. *Organizing* unifies words, sentences, paragraphs, and entire messages according to the manager-communicator's purposes.

Activating. You probably prefer to motivate yourself and stimulate your co-workers rather than to compel action by commands. Indeed, directives and instructions have greatest use when they are clearly stated in terms of employee benefit through company benefit. You recognize personnel as individuals who need explicit guidance and encouragement as well as tactful supervision and correction. You therefore communicate not to tyrannize people but to transform ideas and emotions into appropriate actions.

Activating requires the communication of what you and your fellow workers rightly expect of one another. It involves the sharing of honesty, reliability, creativity, cooperation, and productiveness. *Activating* applies skills, energies, and values to what has been planned and organized.

Controlling. So far we have traced the process whereby your planning and organizing produce action. Action, in turn, involves supervision. As a successful business person, you remind yourself and your associates continually of the goals that you and they share. The development of personal identity and of identity with the company reinforces goal sharing. Your function of controlling thereby becomes largely that of explaining, which, in turn, provides reasons for others to do as you say.

In business, however, "doing" is not enough; what is done must also be appraised. Perhaps no management task is more significant than that of justly determining and communicating relative success or failure. You therefore do not limit evaluation to mere praise or blame. You *use* evaluation to measure performances against standards, to remedy deviations from company goals, or to set newly appropriate standards and goals. **As an effective communicator, you** evaluate your own performance in terms of what your messages produce. "Feedback," or reaction to what you communicate, is your major instrument of control. Planning, organizing, and activating (that is, transmitting) messages are not enough. You need also to assess the results and revise your ongoing communications.

Founded upon planning, organizing, and activating, *controlling* relates performances to standards. *Controlling* is the art of using feedback appropriately to influence human behavior.

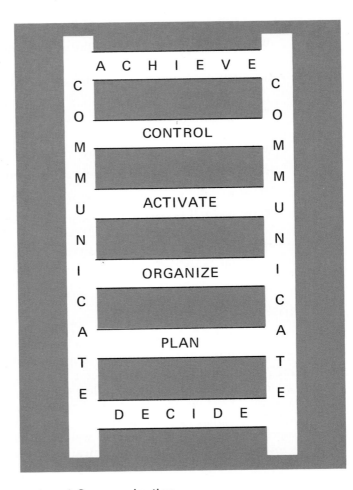

Management and Communication

To decide and to achieve are management purposes. Planning organizing, activating, and controlling are management functions. Communication implements those purposes and functions.

The real business world ties together those management approaches, purposes, and functions that we have mentioned. The purposes of business communication and of business management actually interlock; their functions coincide. The effective manager-communicator plans, organizes, activates, and controls so that he or she may decide and achieve. The effective manager-communicator constantly asks: "WHO? WHAT? WHERE? WHEN? WHY? HOW?"

WHO are the senders/receivers of this communication?

WHAT is the corethought—the key idea, the main point—of this communication?

WHAT relates the corethought to both the senders' and receivers' purposes?

WHERE does the message reinforce relationships between senders and receivers?

WHEN was the message sent and received (or when will it be sent and received)?

WHY was the message (or why will it be) sent?

HOW does the message use sources and information?

HOW was the message (or how should it be) worded?

HOW was the message (or how should it be) transmitted?

Those questions and their answers provide valuable guides for managing your business messages inside and outside your company.

Internal Communication

Advocates of the systems approach emphasize *information* as an essential ingredient of administration. They view business communication as a reciprocal, multidirectional process. As sketched by the following diagram, communication does not flow simply upward or downward or along a single level of the business organization. Communication involves stimuli originating anywhere in the organization (messages and actions represented by the solid lines) as well as responses (messages and actions shown by the dotted lines) in vertical, horizontal, and diagonal directions. The responses themselves often act as new stimuli, thereby continuing organizational interaction by communication. The communication guides that follow the diagram can help you perform successfully in roles at subordinate, superior, and peer levels of organizational communication.

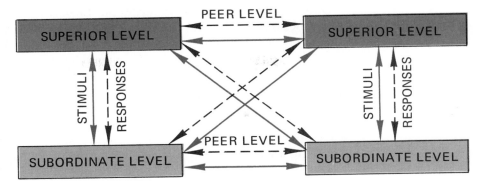

Guides for Subordinate-to-Superior Levels. When you communicate with an executive of your company, your job is mainly to supply appropriate information for decision and administration. By doing this informative job efficiently, you assist the executive; by assisting the executive, you aid the company and thereby yourself.

To insure that the information you present is accurate, verify data before including it in your message. Unless your information is currently correct, you may hinder the manager's efforts to decide and to administer intelligently. Therefore evaluate validity, reliability, timeliness, and pertinence of your data.

To insure that your message is properly transmitted, send it through recognized organizational channels unless special authorization or extraordinary circumstances compel you to do otherwise.

To insure that your message is properly received, remind yourself constantly that other written or oral communications probably will compete with yours for the executive's attention. Use the techniques described in the following chapters to make your messages thorough but brief, courteous but rapid, interesting but unpretentious. Keep reminding yourself of what the executive has requested; anticipate what the executive will need. His or her work monitors *your* business success.

According to these insights, are you ready now to contrast the following examples and to render your own messages more nearly effective than they would otherwise be?

ACCURATE AND CLEAR?	ACCURATE AND CLEAR!
1. That merchandise didn't last long.	1. The Biasi L500 valves sold fast.
2. Our West Mall store is open late on Mondays.	2. On Mondays our West Mall store closes at 9:30 p.m.
3. Check those cartons before shipping them to the Lenno Company.	3. Be sure that every carton for the Lenno Company has a dozen K41 Kits.

Guides for Superior-to-Subordinate Levels. Communication, like other processes, undergoes shifting emphases of which you should be aware. For instance, while composing messages for employees at levels subordinate to yours, remember that a person needs to know work requirements as they relate to organizational policies and to job security. Worded from that person's viewpoint, the communication questions deserving answers include these:

1. What, where, when, why, and how does my company expect me to perform?
2. What, where, when, why, and how will my work benefit my company and me?

Notice that a *who* element also runs through all work requirements and company relationships, especially those concerning job security. Your messages should enable your readers or listeners to identify *themselves* constructively within the context of what you write or speak. Your words should bring yourself and your receiver together through a sharing of organizational objectives.

Emergencies, of course, may postpone immediate answers to key communication questions. Urgent matters may necessitate direct orders unaccompanied by statements of reasons. In this context, management research confirms these findings:

1. Direct orders are effective with loyal personnel.
2. Appropriate explanations, identifying genuine reasons for direct orders, sustain loyalty.

Those statements complement, rather than contradict, each other. They suggest that, at best, explanation should precede or accompany the order; at less than best, explanation should follow the order quickly. In business, as in other planned and orderly activities, one person must tell another what, where, when, and how to do something. But in modern American business, the mind of the clerk as well as that of the board member asks: "Why?" In our democratic society, people expect reasons for the use of their energy and talent. And people work efficiently when they understand that fulfilling their employer's justifiable objectives helps to fulfill their own.

Guides for Peer-to-Peer Levels. Adapt the preceding guides when you exchange messages at organizational levels similar or equal to yours. Assume that your peer receiver needs appropriate answers to key communication questions and that his or her cooperation involves fulfillment of that need. Assume, too, that your peer receiver will interpret those questions and answers from *his or her* viewpoint, as follows:

1. What, where, when, why, and how does my co-worker expect me to perform my duties?

2. What, where, when, why, and how will cooperation with my co-workers benefit my company and me?

As with other communication levels, your messages to peers should enable those people to identify *themselves* constructively within the context of your message. With superior, subordinate, and peer levels of communication, strive to have your words and your actions bring yourself and your receivers together through a sharing of organizational objectives.

External Communication

What modern company can long afford to ignore public demands? The "public" is all of us who need goods and services. Except for monopolistic situations, if Company A ignores your preferences, you will deal with Company B, which seeks to serve you well. And millions of other customers—including business people, who are buyers as well as sellers—will do as you do.

Modern business people engage in an extensive contest of communication. Making available a product or a service, whatever its excellence, is seldom enough for success today. Management must inform the public; management must communicate so that people will motivate themselves to buy.

But to motivate is to impel, not compel. To motivate is to arouse incentives within a person, prompting action. Even with mass communication media, management may persuade but cannot force the public to act. A free-enterprise economy is a communication system. It is built upon plans, performances, and follow-ups communicated by reports, letters, publications, radio-television broadcasts, poster announcements, conferences, and conversations. Not action alone but action-plus-communication helps modern people to motivate themselves. Of the many ways to benefit a company, probably the surest today is to serve the public and to communicate that public service well.

SCOPE AND COST

As an effective business communicator, your needs are tied to those of other people. Whether you share the evidence of ideas and feelings with employers, co-workers, customers, or the general public, you constantly analyze yourself in relation to others. You select words and actions that represent yourself as you intend other people to know you. You strive to understand—moreover, to *use* your understanding of—the words and actions that represent other people to you. Improving your communication performance certainly can expand as well as enrich your business career, enabling you to succeed with these tasks:

1. inquire, reply, announce, advise, invite, acknowledge, appoint, recall, direct, buy, and sell;
2. request, grant, decline, thank, praise, encourage, congratulate, censure, correct, introduce, and recommend;
3. identify, describe, demonstrate, explain, entertain, persuade, adjust, compromise, solve, and collect; and
4. investigate, analyze, synthesize, implement, supervise, unify, evaluate, and report.

Your job as a business communicator is truly challenging, and this book is intended to help you do your job well. But what is the size of the challenge that faces you? What is the cost of business communication?

Replying to a recent inquiry by your authors, Mrs. Rita Moroney, Research Administrator/Historian, Office of the Postmaster General, reported these startling facts:

1. Americans represent about 6 percent of the earth's population, but United States mail volume is 50 percent of the entire world's.
2. Americans produce 89.7 billion pieces of mail in a single fiscal year.
3. More than 75 percent of United States postal volume consists of business mail.

Using these figures, you see that Americans mail at least 67 billion business messages yearly. Assume, very conservatively, that a third of 67 billion represents personally dictated business messages. Also very conservatively, consider that a personally dictated message costs about $5. [4] A third of 67 billion gives us about 22.3 billion business messages. At $5 each, the cost is at least *$111.5 billion in a single year*. If we improve business correspondence so that we cut its cost merely by 10 percent, we can save more than *$11 billion annually*. Management certainly can use this enormous saving (eleven times a thousand times a million dollars a year) to improve operations, products, and services, thereby benefiting the company, its employees, and the public.

As you continue studying this book, visualize the time, energy, and money we can conserve by reducing verbiage (but not information) from three pages to two, from two pages to one page, or from verbose phrases and clauses to single, equivalent words. As you study the chapters that deal with oral and with written messages, recognize that one of your goals in becoming an efficient communicator is conciseness—the combination of thoroughness and brevity—when you write or when you speak.

---

[4] The Dartnell Institute of Business Research has tabulated annual costs of business letters since 1953. The May 11, 1978, issue of the *Wall Street Journal* reported the average cost of a business letter as $4.77. This indicates a 30¢ increase, approximately 6% above the 1977 cost figure of $4.47. Cost factors, continuing to rise, include payment of secretarial work, dictator's work, fixed overhead, nonproductive labor (compensated vacations and sick leaves, coffee breaks, etc.), filing materials, and mailing expenses.

REVIEW AND TRANSITION

The Introduction to Part One provided insights of communication and management involving your life and your career, identified personal as well as worldwide contexts for communication, and emphasized the abundance of attention being given to communication today. Supporting the communication-management theme, Chapter 1 presented these topics: interaction of ideas and emotions; interrelationship of communication and management with consideration of approaches, purposes, functions, and implications; general guides for communicating inside as well as outside the company; and consideration of communication scope and cost.

Now you have opportunities for feedback to the Introduction and to Chapter 1. As with other units of this book, the following Discussion Questions and Applications are designed to help you *use* information in developing your own communication proficiency with other students and professors, with co-workers or employers, and with other people whose lives your life will touch.

Continuing the Part One theme of relating communication/ management to your career, Chapter 2 offers you additional information concerning goals and skills of effective communicators.

DISCUSSION QUESTIONS

A. Within the context of Chapter 1, what are appropriate definitions and illustrations for these terms:

1. communication
2. "systems" approach
3. planning
4. organizing
5. activating
6. controlling
7. subordinate level
8. superior level
9. peer level
10. media

B. What challenging opportunities as well as urgent needs do you see for business communicators?

C. In what ways does your self-concept help and hinder you when you try to communicate with other people?

D. Chapter 1 asserts that as a business person, you assume an obligation which directly or indirectly affects every human being. What is that obligation, as you see it? Which of your strengths and weaknesses do you recognize as influencing that obligation? In what ways do you expect this textbook to help you reinforce those strengths and minimize those weaknesses?

E. Why is effective communication necessary to efficient management? Having studied Chapter 1, what do you mean by "effective communication"? by "efficient management"?

F. Why should you concern yourself with messages themselves *and* with their effects upon people? In what ways can you observe the communication of personalities through business messages?

G. From your own experience, what examples confirm or contradict this statement: "One wonders sometimes whether ideas change quite so much as do the words that stand for them"?

H. In what ways do management purposes and functions affect your composing, transmitting, interpreting, or evaluating a written message? an oral-visual message? a nonverbal message?

I. From your own experience with superior-to-subordinate communication, what real incidents show that these statements are complementary:

  1. Direct orders are effective with loyal personnel.

  2. Appropriate explanations, identifying genuine reasons for direct orders, sustain loyalty.

J. From your own experience with peer-level communication (for example, communication with other students or with co-workers), what real incidents show the need for answers to these questions:

  1. What, where, when, why, and how does my peer expect me to perform?

  2. What, where, when, why, and how will cooperation with my peer benefit my company (or group) and me?

APPLICATIONS

1. In a written message of not more than 400 words, introduce yourself to your professor and the class. State this data about yourself:

  a. Name and birthplace

  b. Educational background

  c. Work experience (paid or unpaid)

  d. Community participation (civic, professional, social, or other public service)

  e. Educational and career goals

  f. Avocational interests and activities

2. In a postscript, explain how you applied the communication-management functions to your message of introduction; that is, explain how you planned, organized, activated, and controlled this communication activity.

3. In another written message, ask your professor to evaluate the apparent accuracy, clarity, conciseness, and courtesy of your written introduction.

SPECIAL NOTE: Keep the materials that you prepare for Applications 1-3, and keep your professor's critique also. You can use those items for revision exercises and for oral-visual presentations later in your course.

4. Using appropriate library resources, write a summary of major contributions to management theory by at least one of these behavioral scientists: Mason Haire, Rensis Likert, Douglas McGregor, Abraham Maslow.

5. Write an explanation of why the following statements are likely to cause miscommunication:
   a. I have no time to give you reasons; just do as I say.
   b. I know you're against this project, but let's go ahead with it anyhow.
   c. Nothing you say can change my mind.
   d. Driving through the main gate, the parking lot is on your left.
   e. The accountant who prepared those reports promptly was promoted.
   f. Looking through her office windows, the East River can be seen.
   g. Of our top account executives—I mean Liz, Alfredo, Gus, and Stella—she has the best record; but his is a close second.
   h. All you need to know is that it behooves us to delay action on your recent recommendation.
   i. I don't like your marketing proposal. Don't ask me why. Just come up with something better. Pronto.
   j. Since we must work together on these reports, why cant you be accrate?

6. Now write appropriate revisions of the items listed in Application 5.

THE BORN LOSER   **by Art Sansom**

© 1973 by NEA, Inc., T.M. Reg. U.S. Pat. Off.   7-10

© 1973 NEA, INC.

Do You Unfairly Shift Communication Responsibility to Your Reader or Listener?

CHAPTER 2

Basic Goals and Fundamental Skills

I. BASIC GOALS
- A. To Gain Goodwill
  1. Convey Justification
  2. Show Relevance
  3. Develop Tone
- B. To Inquire
- C. To Inform
- D. To Persuade
  1. Overall Guide: Elicit Favorable Response
  2. Address a Person
  3. Identify a Need or Desire
  4. Explain Pertinent Details
  5. Encourage Visualization

II. FUNDAMENTAL SKILLS
- A. Perceiving
  1. Observe
  2. Read and Listen
- B. Interpreting
  1. Analyze
  2. Synthesize
  3. Use Logic Carefully

III. REVIEW AND TRANSITION

As a business person, you deal with inquiries, special requests, and replies. You process employment applications and personal résumés. You encounter sales promotions, claim and adjustment messages, and credit and collection systems. You communicate through interviews, conferences, telephone conversations, written messages, and multimedia reports. You learn that communication efficiency requires useful answers to *who? what? when? where? why?* and *how?* The answers to those questions involve basic goals of business communicators.

BASIC GOALS

For written, visual, or oral communication inside or outside a business firm, these basic goals recur:

1. To gain goodwill
2. To inquire
3. To inform
4. To persuade

Message composition and format to reach these goals are discussed later. First we shall examine the goals themselves.

To Gain Goodwill

Goodwill in business is appreciation that a company or an individual acquires beyond the value of what is sold. Goodwill represents an attitude and a commodity: the attitude of business friendship, the commodity of business reputation.

Goodwill is so important to business that a complete chapter (Chapter 8) is devoted to that single topic. To help prepare you for that chapter, here are five introductory examples of how almost every business situation can be used to generate goodwill messages.

As the writer of Example A, you would be cordially acknowledging a successful transaction—*and* you would be promoting future business as well. If you wrote a message resembling Example B, your concise review of contractual terms and your concern for customer satisfaction would again promote a continuing business relationship. With Example C you would appropriately recognize outstanding performance, reinforce employee loyalty, and highlight future prospects. With Example D you would convey gratitude for a service, offer a counterpart of that service, and stimulate continuing cooperation. Example E shows how goodwill can help you gain an employment opportunity. Because job interviews are especially competitive today, be sure to study the additional comments that follow Example E.

EXAMPLE A: GOODWILL AFTER A SALE

Thank you for having scheduled your recent sales conference at the Leta Hotel and Convention Center. Accommodating you and your conferees was more than a business transaction. It was a pleasure.

Inez Bolivar, your program coordinator, assures us that your guests enjoyed their Leta visit. We are grateful for Ms. Bolivar's report and appreciate the privilege of serving your organization.

The entire Leta staff remains at your disposal. Please call on us again.

EXAMPLE B: GOODWILL IN FULFILLING AN OBLIGATION

As you know, an important feature of your ETM Display Sign contract with us is regular cleaning and maintenance. For three years from the purchase date of your ETM sign, this service is provided at no additional cost to you.

So that our seasonal service visit will be convenient to your business needs, please notify us of the dates you prefer for this maintenance work. Just complete and mail the enclosed postage-paid card.

EXAMPLE C: GOODWILL IN RECOGNIZING ACHIEVEMENT

The keynote of this message is . . .CONGRATULATIONS, LAURIE!

Your achievement will be highlighted in the next issue or our corporate newsletter. The $1,330,000 you have marketed in added protection for personal, estate, and corporate insurance needs has made you our Number One C.L.U. And you can be certain of receiving the appropriate recognition you merit.

A.J. Metz, president of our firm, will be in touch with you soon, Laurie. A.J. wants to congratulate you personally and discuss your career advancement.

You have our confidence in your continuing success.

EXAMPLE D: GOODWILL IN ACKNOWLEDGING COOPERATION

Thank you for promptly supplying the agribusiness research data which I requested June 28. Your field studies confirm the findings of our agronomists and are valuable to the entire Planning Division. In exchange for your courtesy, please accept the complimentary copy of our *Farm Census Abstract* which accompanies this note. Your research team may be especially interested by these facts, documented on pages 42-43 and 49 of the *Abstract:*

1. Sales of U.S. farm products last year exceeded $80 billion.
2. That amount pertains to food and fiber, not to farm machinery and farm chemicals.
3. Within the Central Savannah River Area, Emanuel County's 533 farms averaged 317 acres apiece; Screven County's 589 farms averaged 442 acres apiece.

Thanks again for sharing your information with us. We gladly offer our cooperation to you.

EXAMPLE E: GOODWILL FOR AN INTERVIEW REQUEST

Do you need new management trainees whose education, experience, and energy can keep pace with Metrico's expansion?

The enclosed résumé includes a description of work experience during my business management studies at Arista College. Following commencement ceremonies on June 3, a complete academic record will be available for your review. I enclose the résumé now as interim evidence of genuine interest in a Metrico career.

An opportunity to discuss Metrico's employment needs will be welcome. Please write or telephone me (317-633-8440 days, 317-633-9085 evenings) for an interview appointment that is convenient to you.

With your very first message to Metrico, you succeed where other applicants fail. Your message establishes *rapport*—an active, positive association—with your reader. Your message concisely and courteously conveys accurate, pertinent information. You relate that information not only to your own needs but also to your reader's. Thereby you empathize, and empathy is essential to goodwill.[1] Read your message (Example E) again. Notice that it enables you to do the following in establishing goodwill, through empathy, with your reader:

1. To convey justification for your sending, and for Metrico's reading, your interview request;
2. To show relevance between your interests and Metrico's; and
3. To develop tone—evidence of personal attitude—that is appropriate to yourself and your reader.

---

[1] *Empathy* is often defined as the psychological projection of oneself into another person's circumstances. Realistically, however, empathy seems to be a communicator's use of symbols, including words, whereby he or she virtually senses the feelings of another person. Apparently, empathy is a communion of emotional and mental sensation.

Let us consider more closely those three highlights of goodwill.

Convey Justification. As an effective business person, you determine *why* you send, or respond to, a message. Balancing ethics and desires, you convey reasons for bringing sender and receiver together. Your Metrico request, for example, conveys your career ambitions and acknowledges Metrico's expansion program. With your message you assert but do not exaggerate justifiable confidence in your prospective employer and in yourself. Thus justifying your interview request, you begin to establish goodwill. Your next communication step is to show that every part of your message pertains to a corethought (also called gist, main point, or key idea).

Show Relevance. Besides conveying justification, you tie the parts of your message to the corethought that you intend to share. Your corethought statement has a double function: (1) to serve the reader or listener, (2) to serve the writer or speaker. Every part of an effective business message supports the corethought statement. Notice that every part of your message to Metrico pertains logically to the corethought of gaining an interview. Having conveyed justification and shown relevance, you also need to represent appropriate attitude by your tone.

Develop Tone. Tone is evidence of a communicator's attitude toward a message and its receiver. The evidence includes word choice, paragraph structure, and punctuation. These devices are not merely decorative; they actually influence your reader's judgment and response. The tone of Example E implies justifiable confidence and willingness to serve the reader as well as yourself. Communicating sincerity, courtesy, and readiness, your tone helps you to earn an interview and ultimately a job with Metrico.

Conveying justification, showing relevance, and developing tone can move you toward this basic communication goal: *to gain goodwill*. By establishing and reinforcing goodwill, you can attain these goals also: *to inquire, to inform,* and *to persuade*.

To Inquire

When you inquire, you seek to learn by asking. If your questions are vague or needlessly wordy, your respondent—although willing to cooperate with you—will hardly know what to say. If your questions are specific, clear, and concise, the answers are more apt to be definite and useful. Techniques and examples of precise inquiry, presented later in this book, show that effective asking is a form of communication art. At this point, we merely identify the need for precision, especially precision in conveying the corethought of your inquiry.

To Inform

This brief introduction of goodwill and of inquiry leads to a third communication goal. *To inform* is to acquire knowledge and share it with other people.

This section of Chapter 2 uses identification as an informative device. These paragraphs merely name goals and concepts which later pages develop in detail through other informative devices. The devices include illustrations, explanations, discussions, and exercises.

To Persuade

Three basic goals of business communicators are *to gain goodwill, to inquire,* and *to inform.* A fourth goal is *to persuade*; that is, to have your receiver think or act as you propose.

Overall Guide: Elicit Favorable Response. Using techniques described in Chapters 8-10 and 13-14, you can stimulate favorable feedback to your persuasive messages. And you can guide yourself as well as your receiver by using answers to these questions:

1. What are my receiver's needs?
2. What are my needs as company communicator?
3. In what ways should this message associate the receiver's needs and mine?

A slight rewording of those questions clarifies their relevance to "customer" rather than to "general public" communication:

1. What does the customer need?
2. What can my company do to satisfy the customer's need?
3. In what ways should my message relate satisfaction of the customer's need to what my company can provide?

What does the customer need? A customer indicates awareness of needs by an inquiry or an order. Then management's task—and yours as a business communicator—is this: Make available what the customer requires, where and when requested, on mutually acceptable terms. A corollary task is to share pertinent information with the customer, often persuasively.

When a customer is unaware of her or his needs, management's tasks—and yours—become the following:

1. Attract the customer's attention.
2. Focus upon the customer's self-concern.
3. Identify needs that the customer has not recognized.
4. Stimulate the customer's visualization of benefits from what your company offers.

5. Persuade the customer to act—to order or at least to demonstrate interest in what is offered.

What can my company do to satisfy the customer's need? Analyze your company's product or service in terms of customer benefit; analyze the customer's ability to pay for what your company supplies. This dual analysis enables you to communicate appropriate, genuine reasons for a mutually profitable transaction. Such a transaction earns the buyer's continuing interest, confidence, and patronage.

In what ways should my message relate satisfaction of the customer's need to what my company can provide? Stimulating favorable customer response often involves "subjective" as well as "objective" values of the proposed purchase. Objective values emphasize physical and logical factors of size, shape, color, mechanical specifications, price, terms, shipping, and maintenance. Subjective values emphasize your ethical interpretation of the physical and logical factors in terms of *customer* motives. Conveying those values involves vivid explanation and persuasive description to answer the customer's inevitable question: "How will it benefit me?"

To elicit a favorable response is an overall guide. What related guides can help you persuade? The following often are profitable, especially in representing business firms to the public:

1. Address a person instead of a mass.
2. Identify within the person a need or a desire that you, as company spokesperson, can satisfy.
3. Explain how you and your company ethically can satisfy the person's need or desire.
4. Encourage the person to visualize benefits of what you and your company offer.

Address a Person. Although group behavior can differ from one person's actions, "the public" does consist of many *individuals*. Therefore, even when you use mass communication media, realize that you are presenting your message to individuals. Consider the *person* and his or her motives. Those motives include health, comfort, and social acceptance. They also involve efficiency of effort, economy of time, and variety of experience.

Identify a Need or a Desire. To personalize your messages, determine a problem that affects people individually and that your company can help solve. Is your message to be part of a published corporate report? Then stress facts that justify a person's confidence in your firm. Are you announcing a new product, location, or enterprise? Then emphasize how it will serve the individual customer. Make valid promises, only those that you and your company expect in good faith to fulfill.

Explain Pertinent Details. Particularly in business communication, explanations influence human behavior. In this Communication Age employees and customers expect answers to these questions: What is happening? Why is it happening? How can it affect my life? Inflation, unemployment, and consumer advocacy have made buyers especially cautious about purchase decisions. Although sometimes motivated by impulse, modern customers increasingly require valid, appropriate reasons for a purchase. They want to know specifications of the product, terms of the sale, and conditions affecting those terms.

For example, if as a seller you reduce price to increase your profit on volume, you gain and the customer saves money. But people know you probably would not lower prices if losses resulted. Certainly your customers are interested in benefits to themselves. Remember, however, that they are concerned also with reasons for your actions. Your work includes defining, describing, explaining *what* you do and, often, *why* you do it.

Encourage Visualization. You know that logical explanation can be powerful. You know also that people are emotional as well as rational. As a business communicator, you deal with ideas *and* feelings. You use words, illustrations, demonstrations that convey pictures of the advantages you propose. For example, describing a new automobile may seem interesting. But using words that cause people to see themselves as the owners of that car can do more than explain; it can persuade.

FUNDAMENTAL SKILLS

You have identified four goals of effective communicators: to gain goodwill, to inquire, to inform, and to persuade. Reaching those goals requires you to develop fundamental communication skills:

1. Observing, reading, and listening are "input" skills. They enable you to *perceive* data.
2. Analyzing and synthesizing are "processing" skills. They enable you to *interpret* what you perceive.
3. Writing and speaking are "output" skills. They enable you to *apply* what you interpret.

The rest of this chapter focuses upon "input" (perception) and upon "processing" (interpretation). Later chapters deal with details of "output" (application).

Perceiving

Through your physical senses of sight, hearing, touch, etc., you input data about yourself and your universe. You extend your physical senses by using telescopes and microscopes, earphones and amplifiers, meters and gauges. Thereby you enlarge the quantity, quality, and variety of stimuli that activate your brain. This process of detecting stimuli, of inputting data to the human being, is what is meant by *perception*.

Like other processes, perception has limitations. Your sensory organs and their mechanical extensions are imperfect. Presumably there are "sights" and "sounds" which people and machines do not detect. But you may unnecessarily restrict your perception by sometimes mistaking the undetected for the undetectable. Furthermore, your mind defensively screens and sifts stimuli. In effect, except for stimuli whose force is irresistible, your mind admits only that data you choose to recognize.

How do these comments pertain to you as a communicator? What is the benefit of acknowledging that you cannot perceive *every* aspect of a person, an object, a process, a message? Ironically, the admission of imperfection can improve your communication ability. Awareness of the fact that you may easily "miss" important details of a communication event can put you on guard. That awareness can help you become a careful observer, reader, and listener.

What you perceive becomes part of you; the data passes through your sense organs to your mind. Conversely, you are part of what you perceive; by selecting some stimuli and excluding others, you create your own world.[2]

Do you expect other people to have your own traits and attitudes? Do you reject contradictions of your prejudices or habits? Those human tendencies further limit what and how you perceive.

For example, assume that you particularly enjoy the study and practice of accounting. If so, you are motivated to learn more about that business specialty than would someone interested in another field. Consciously and unconsciously, you set your senses to input and set your mind to process accounting data which other people, who do not have your motivation, exclude from themselves. That data becomes part of you. And because of their importance to *your* needs, you may expect other people to share your accounting values. In turn, you may not share someone else's appreciation of an advertising layout, a textile design, a symphony, or a poem. What seems obvious to you may not be perceived by someone else, and vice versa. Through individual perceptions and interpretations, all of us create our own realities.

---

[2] Compare Alfred Tennyson's and John Milton's statements:
"I am a part of all that I have met . . . ."
(*Ulysses*, line 18.)
"The mind is its own place and in itself/Can make a heaven of hell, a hell of heaven."
(*Paradise Lost*, Book I, line 254.)

But if you develop your personality by enlarging your experience, your perception can become keener and more nearly precise. How may you, as a business communicator, "enlarge your experience"? Observe. Read Listen.

Observe. A successful communicator is an expert noticer. Consider those people whose writing or talking bores you. At best they *express themselves*, but they *do not communicate with you*. They vent their egotism (which often disguises emotional insecurity) or their timidity (which often masks egotism). They relieve themselves by verbal catharsis. But they do not notice—or they notice and disregard—the feedback to what they do. Your drooping eyelids and fidgeting motions should signal such people that they are expressing themselves but are not sharing ideas and feelings with you. Expression is one-way relief; communication is reciprocal participation.

To communicate effectively, *notice* what less careful people overlook. Search for internal and external cues that signal the *who, what, when, where, why,* and *how* of messages. Welcome opportunities that can complement your personal observations by careful reading and listening.

Read and Listen. When you observe an event, you perceive stimuli as they exist in the real world outside yourself. For instance, you can see a real-world typewriter, hear its real-world keys strike, touch its real-world space bar. But when you read or listen, you perceive stimuli which *stand for*, which *represent*, actual objects or events. For example, when you read (or listen to) the word "typewriter," you *perceive* a set of ink marks on paper (or a pattern of sounds in the air). What you then "see" in your "mind's eye," is the machine represented by those marks or sounds. Your "mind's eye"—your perception—can be enlarged by using the following suggestions.

To improve your reading, first become aware of the rate, or speed, at which you detect stimuli (ink marks). The reading experiment described in the Applications section of this chapter will help you. If you read slowly, your eyes probably stop, or "fixate," more often than necessary on a line of words. To read faster, fixate your eyes only three times on a line (near the beginning, at the middle, and near the end of the line). A little practice will make this three-stop-per-line rhythm comfortable for you. Then you can reduce the fixations to two or perhaps even to the speed-reader's goal of one per line. Your reading rate will accelerate, and your comprehension will be effective.

Try to avoid moving your lips and your throat muscles as you read. If you silently pronounce or whisper the words, you will slow your reading rate. With deliberate practice you can reduce and then eliminate "lip-reading" or "vocalizing" tendencies.

Also, vary your reading techniques according to your particular purposes. Three of those techniques—skimming, scanning, and study-reading—are described here:

1. *Skimming*. Is your purpose to identify general topics rather than details? to review what you have already read? or simply to be entertained by amusing literature and personal correspondence? Then *skim*. Read quickly, but notice these aids to your comprehension: headings and sub-headings; introductions, transitions, and summaries; corethought statements. Other aids, especially for skimming a book or a report, are title pages, prefaces, tables of contents, illustrations, appended materials, and indexes.

2. *Scanning*. Is your purpose to discover or to verify a specific item—for instance, a name or an address? a date? a word, statistic, or fact? First skim the message to locate the section(s) that pertain to your purpose. Then read those particular lines attentively. Scanning, you see, is skimming with a specific target of information in mind.

3. *Study-Reading*. Is your purpose to absorb virtually all of a message? every fact and implication? every nuance of style as well as of data? Then skim, scan, and study-read. Summarize the message, and its parts, in your own words. Test your summaries, notes, and comments against evidence in the message itself. Ask and answer appropriate questions concerning the evidence, its presentation, your perception, and your interpretation. For example, are you perceiving words and numbers as they actually appear in the message? Are you reacting to the message itself? to your impressions of the writer? to the appearance and format of the message? to data presented by the message? to data within yourself but not presented by the message?

As reading is an application of vision, so listening is a use of hearing. To listen is not just to hear; it is to understand what you hear. Effective listening requires you to use your ears and your brain, with such additional insights as these:

1. Recognize that compulsive talkers—people who constantly monopolize speech—block effective listening and exclude valuable feedback. Notice that those talkers defeat themselves by obstructing the exchange of information that they and others can use. Observe that when everyone talks, few hear and none listens. Speak when necessary and appropriate for you to do so. But use an active and effective listening attitude; your attitude affects what you hear.

2. Develop your listening attitude by following these suggestions:
   a. Focus your attention upon the oral message and the speaker.
   b. Respond with pertinent questions or comments concerning the data and its intended interpretation.
   c. Reinforce rapport by your own behavior. Your listening posture, facial expressions, and gestures are parts of feedback language.
   d. Participate in the communication event. Instead of being passive, respond vocally, in writing, or with silent but mental reactions. The more active your participation as a listener, the more informative your listening is likely to be.

3. As you develop your listening attitude, you will become aware of these communication insights also:
   a. Effective listening to data and to style of presentation acquaints you with interests, needs, and values of associates or customers.
   b. Effective listening provides cues to personalities, biases, abilities, and resources.
   c. Effective listening thereby enables you to deal more profitably with co-workers, with customers, and with competitors than you might otherwise do.

Let others bypass opportunities for such listening. *You* listen to learn and to use what you learn. To enlarge your world, read and listen—but not simultaneously. Reading and listening skills require separate attention, although they pose these questions mutually:

1. What is the corethought of the message?
2. What evidence supports the corethought?
3. What is implied as well as stated?
4. What response does the message elicit?

The following suggestions are useful in answering those questions.

READING

Concerning the Message

1. Notice the name of the sender and the date of the message.
2. Benefit from structural devices (letterhead, subject or reference line, table of contents, list of illustrations, bibliography, index).
3. Read quickly to identify the corethought of the message.
4. Notice signals of emphasis (indention, capitalization, underlining, italics, lists, illustrations, colors).
5. Note mentally, or in writing, the data that you receive from the message.
6. When permissible, underline or encircle key units of the message.
7. When permissible, write marginal summaries of the data and of your response to that data.

Concerning Yourself

1. Attend to the message. You deceive yourself if you think you can simultaneously speak-read or speak-listen. Focus your full attention upon the message you are reading.
2. Read silently. Avoid shaping your lips into sounds.
3. Read progressively. Do not begin a new line and then look back at the preceding line.
4. Focus upon word *groups* rather than upon individual words.
5. Guard against "seeing" only what you expect instead of what is actually written.
6. Concentrate upon your reading. Minimize interruptions as you read.

LISTENING

Concerning the Message

1. Since thought is faster than speech, your mind may wander from what is being said. Use the time lag: Review what you hear. Anticipate what you may hear next. Make pertinent notes.

2. Detect whether the speaker goes from general statements to specific examples or vice versa. Identifying message structure helps you to listen.

3. Determine the corethought. Note transitions; often they signal changes of data and restatements of corethoughts.

4. Notice changes of volume, resonance, intensity, and rate. They are signals of emphasis.

Concerning Yourself

1. When possible observe the speaker's facial expressions, gestures, and other mannerisms. During telephone conversations, try to visualize the speaker. Your listening will improve as you mentally perceive the *person* who is speaking instead of a disembodied voice that you happen to hear.

2. Discern the speaker's patterns of breath groups, sounds, and pauses. They are the punctuation of speech.

3. Guard against "hearing" only what you expect instead of what is actually said.

Effective reading and listening require awareness of what we perceive and of the responses produced by perceiving. To improve your awareness, a communication "diary" may be valuable. For example; here is a listening diary format:

SITUATION: Sales Conference, March 5, 19--, 1:30-5:45 PM

PRINCIPAL SPEAKER: E. L. Soo, Marketing Coordinator, Region 5

CORETHOUGHT:

DETAILS:

MY RESPONSES:

GROUP RESPONSES:

And here is a reading diary format:

MESSAGE:

        Quarterly Merchandising Report, dated _____, received _____

SENDER: E. L. Soo, Marketing Coordinator, Region 5

CORETHOUGHT:

DETAILS:

RESPONSES:

We have described how you perceive data by observing, reading, and listening. But what happens to data after you perceive it? How is data processed, or interpreted, by your mind?

Interpreting

Interpretation is the assignment of meaning. Interpretation requires logical reasoning, the analysis and synthesis of data.

Analyze. When you analyze, you identify elements; you separate a whole into its parts. When you analyze a message, for instance, you identify the elements of structure, format, and tone. Analysis provides ingredients for interpretation.

Synthesize. Often, however, you are confronted not by an organized presentation (a complete message) but by apparently miscellaneous parts (by words, punctuation marks, ideas, and feelings). Your job then is one of synthesis. You combine elements into a significant pattern; you combine words, punctuation marks, ideas, and feelings into a measure. Analysis and synthesis are complementary. They are tools of interpretation through logical reasoning.

Use Logic Carefully. When you reason from specific instances to a generalization, your form of logic is *induction*. When you reason from the general to the specific, your form of logic is *deduction*. Here is an example of how induction and deduction work in a business research situation.

Assume that your employer asks you to participate in a marketing survey. You use questionnaires to collect data. You perceive before you can interpret; you note the responses on every questionnaire returned to you before you can analyze and synthesize those responses. You are using induction at this point. You are using specific instances (individual responses to questionnaire items) for deriving a generalization. You reason from the particular answers of Mr. A, Mrs. B, Miss C, Ms. D, and the other people questioned, to this generalization: "The responses indicate that we should [or should not] market our product as proposed."

Deduction is often stated as a *syllogism*. The basic form of a syllogism has three parts: a large assumption (or "major premise"), a little assumption (or "minor premise"), and an inference (a logically inescapable conclusion) derived from the assumptions. Here is an example of deductive reasoning in the form of a syllogism:

MAJOR PREMISE: All Metrico employees are reliable.
MINOR PREMISE: You are a Metrico employee.
CONCLUSION: You are reliable.

The syllogism can persuade as well as inform (for example, when used with requests and adjustments, Chapter 15). But the syllogism requires careful use. If the premises are true, the conclusion will be true. If even one of the premises is false, the conclusion must also be false. Syllogistic reasoning can be logically correct but untrue. Consider this example:

MAJOR PREMISE: Every Metrico employee is honest.
MINOR PREMISE: This thief works for Metrico.
CONCLUSION: This thief is honest.

Briefly reviewed, induction is reasoning from particular instances to generalization; deduction is reasoning from premises (often one general and one particular) to an inferred conclusion. The results of induction may become the premises of deduction. Induction helps you *synthesize* data; deduction helps you *analyze* data.

Unless you are careful, however, you may mistake logic for truth. Logic imposes order upon otherwise miscellaneous data. What you choose to do with logic may, or may not, yield truth. For example, the following fallacies, or errors of reasoning, are common. Several of them still have Latin names reflecting their antiquity. But instead of weakening with age, these fallacies remain potent today. They substitute emotions for ideas.

Argumentum ad hominem is illogical reasoning that distracts attention *from* an idea *to* a personality associated with the idea.

Examples: 1. "Maybe we should open a branch office. But I'm against the idea because Lee Fong proposed it. He probably wants to manage the branch, and we need somebody with a name like Smith or Jones to rely on. Besides, Fong comes from a rich family, so why make him richer?"
[What happened to the topic of whether to open a branch office?]

2. "This purchase request was submitted by Ethel Levy. Ethel is a woman, and you know that women just like to buy things. So her purchase request is bound to cost our company more than we need to spend. Turn it down."
[What is the topic: approval or disapproval of a request? women's lib? male chauvinism?]

Argumentum ad populum is illogical reasoning that distracts attention *from* an idea *to* the desire for group approval.

Examples: 1. "Every reasonable person can see the sense of what I'm saying. You're a reasonable person, so you must agree. Join the rest of us. Why be alone in your thinking?"
[Agree about *what?*]

2. "Maybe Paula should get this promotion, but everybody expects Carmen to move up. Let's recommend Carmen."
[Facts, please: Which candidate has merited promotion?] [3]

Post hoc, ergo propter hoc is illogical reasoning that distracts attention *from* cause-and-effect proof *to* the simple passing of time. *Post hoc* insists that if A precedes B, A must have caused B.

Examples: 1. "We didn't have these personnel problems before Stanislavsky was hired. He must be causing them."
[Maybe, maybe not. What other causes are possible?]

2. "For years this company was losing money. Then I became general manager. We're making a profit now. The reason is obvious, but I'm too modest to mention it."
[Could "the reason" have been the work of other people? improvement of the national economy? coincidence with changing market demands?]

Non sequitur is illogical reasoning that asserts a conclusion not derived from the given premises.

Examples: 1. "Yes, we need to increase sales; and this is the best advertising proposal I've seen, so it will do the job for us. Let's adopt it right now."
[How many proposals have you seen? What kinds? How can adopting this proposal *guarantee* increased sales?]

---

[3] Notice how *argumentum ad hominem* and *argumentum ad populum* use the persuasive devices known as "name calling" and "transfer." Name calling stimulates bias by attaching emotion-arousing *labels* to ideas or to people. Transfer (known also as *argumentum ad vericundiam*) associates psychological *appeals*—prestige or glamour, hostility or fear, etc.—with ideas or people.

2. You've been a computer programmer for five years, and your work has been excellent. Therefore you should become head of the Personnel Department.
[Do five years of computer programming qualify me to head the Personnel Department?]

Begging the question is illogical reasoning that offers restatement instead of proof.

Examples: 1. Your work is shoddy because it is inferior. Since it is inferior, it's not satisfactory. And since your work is unsatisfactory, why should I pay for it?
2. We should adopt this policy because it is what we need. Furthermore, since this policy is what we need, let's adopt it.
[In both of those examples, repetition is not a logical substitute for evidence.]

Self-contradiction is illogical reasoning that asserts incompatible data. The ideas presented are such that if one is true, another must be false.

Examples: 1. This report does not have the information you requested. But I've worked overtime on it, so you ought to accept it.
[Why should I reward you for *not* providing what I need?]
2. Our office always closes at 5 PM. It will be open today until 6.
["Always" at 5 is not "today" at 6. Your confusing statement tempts me to do business elsewhere.]

Hasty generalization, or *jumping to conclusions*, is also illogical reasoning. It asserts that what *may* be true of a few cases *must* be true always or almost always.

Examples: 1. Olsen left the office early yesterday. Schultz and D'Agostino left early today. Those three people are in the Warehouse Division [which has 30 employees]. Warehouse employees leave work early.
[Is it logical to judge 27 employees by the actions of three?]
2. On June 7 and 14 we wrote Gomez about his overdue payments. He didn't answer us then, so he won't respond if we ask him again.
[Maybe your messages or Mr. Gomez's payments have gone astray. Perhaps you can prove that the payment has not reached you, but you have not proved anything else.]

All too common are the seven fallacies, or errors of reasoning, that we have discussed: *argumentum ad hominem; argumentum ad populum; post hoc, ergo propter hoc; non sequitur; begging the question; self-contradiction;* and *hasty generalization.* They can cause the loss of jobs and of customers.

Here is the corethought of this discussion: When you use analysis and synthesis to interpret data, *recognize* the advantages and the limitations of logic. Also, guard against fallacies, which introduce inaccurate, irrelevant, or incomplete evidence. Fallacies often are fed by emotions. Fallacies are unacceptable substitutes for logical reasoning.

REVIEW AND TRANSITION

The basic goals of an effective communicator are to gain goodwill, to inquire, to inform, and to persuade. Those goals involve perception by observing, reading, and listening. Those goals involve interpretation by analysis and synthesis. The skills of perception *input* data to our minds; the skills of interpretation *process* the input data.

Succeeding chapters deal with another set of communication skills—those of application by writing and by speaking. Chapters 1 and 2 have been offered as an introduction, emphasizing answers to *who? where? why?* The following pages explore *what? when? how?*

DISCUSSION QUESTIONS

A. Within the context of Chapter 2, provide appropriate definitions and illustrations for these terms:

1. goodwill
2. rapport
3. empathy
4. justification
5. relevance
6. tone
7. corethought
8. induction
9. deduction
10. interpretation
11. analysis
12. synthesis
13. syllogism
14. premise
15. conclusion
16. inference
17. assumption
18. fallacies
19. *argumentum ad hominem*
20. *argumentum ad populum*
21. *post hoc, ergo propter hoc*
22. *non sequitur*
23. begging the question
24. self-contradiction
25. hasty generalization

B. Stated in your own words, what is the corethought of Chapter 1? of Chapter 2? In what ways do those corethoughts reaffirm the Introduction to Part One?

C. In what ways do these statements support the corethought of Chapter 2:

1. "In effect, except for those stimuli whose force is irresistible, your mind admits only those data that you choose to recognize."
2. "I am a part of all that I have met . . . ."
3. "The mind is its own place, and in itself/Can make a heaven of hell, a hell of heaven."

    D. What incidents from your own experience illustrate the effects of goodwill in business situations? To what extent did justification, relevance, and tone affect those incidents?

    E. Chapter 2 identifies four goals of an effective communicator: to gain goodwill, to inquire, to inform, and to persuade. Why is goodwill necessary to attain the three other goals?

APPLICATIONS

1. To discover the kind of reader you are, try the following experiment. The materials needed are one book, one desk or table, and one mirror for two people (yourself and a partner).

   Sit at the desk or table. Place the mirror against one page of the open book, but read from the opposite page. Have your partner stand behind you. Ask your partner to arrange the mirror so that he or she observes your eye movements as you read. By looking at the mirror, your partner counts the number of eye fixations that you make per line. After verifying and reporting your reading rate to you, your partner exchanges places with you. You then test your partner's reading habits. Use a new page of the book for each test. Keep retesting to increase reading speed. Comprehension can be determined when you and your partner discuss the corethought and supporting details of what each of you has read.

2. Guided by the Chapter 2 discussion of goals and skills, write appropriate revisions of the following items. Justify every revision.

   a. You are industrious because you work hard.

   b. I want you to learn something about the way we do things.

   c. I worked hard to complete this assignment, so you should raise my pay.

   d. As I walked into the office, you and Osaki stopped talking. The two of you must have been discussing me. What have I done wrong now?

   e. Sensible people agree with me. You're sensible; agree with me.

   f. I don't know if you are the proper person to receive this operating manual. If you're not, will you please dispose of it through channels?

   g. Mail your travel reports to me at our Chicago headquarters or to MacKellar at the New York office. But if you send them to MacKellar, let me know and vice versa. Check?

   h. We have written to you twice about your unpaid balance. Why do you refuse to pay what you owe?

   i. Since you're intelligent, you won't mind this criticism.

   j. Before you joined this project, we were on schedule. Now we're a month late. How could you have caused the delay?

   k. Povatong, Costello, and Duval were interviewed for this job. Of those three, she is best qualified because her résumé is the longest.

   l. Our products are advertised nationally, so you can always buy with confidence.

   m. You better buy *now*. At these bargain prices, this merchandise won't last long.

   n. During this special sale, all of our denim jeans are half off.

   o. Immediately after the safety lecture, there was an accident in Area 27. Those lectures must be worthless.

    p. Prepare the memo first. But before you do, take your coffee break and deliver this report to the accounting office. Then phone me. I'll be in conference with Sharif in Russo's office.

    q. I know you have only an hour to do that report, but let me tell you about something really funny that happened to me yesterday. Or was if the day before yesterday?

    r. Dear Sir or Madam: Your merchandise is unsatisfactory. I want my money back. Cordially yours, J.J. McNair.

3. Reread the illustrations of goodwill messages in Chapter 2 (Examples A-E, pages 18-19). Then, in a written message addressed to your professor, answer these questions:

    a. Stated in your own words, what is the corethought of Example A? In what ways does every paragraph support the corethought? What words particularly reinforce goodwill? What impression does the writer's repetition of *you* and *your* convey? What other evidence in Example A confirms or contradicts your impression of the writer?

    b. Stated in your words, what is the corethought of Example B? In what ways do every sentence and paragraph support the message corethought? What evidence conveys the writer's goodwill? Which words particularly reinforce the goodwill tone?

    c. In what ways does Example C differ from A and B? In what ways is Example C similar to A and B? Stated in your words, what is the message corethought of Example C? What evidence supports that corethought?

    d. Stated in your own words, what are the corethoughts of every paragraph in Example D? What is the message corethought? Which items especially convey or reinforce goodwill? What is your impression of the person who wrote Example D? What specific evidence confirms or contradicts your impression of the writer?

    e. Which aspects of Example E impress you favorably? Why? The first paragraph of Example E is a single sentence in the form of a question. What effect does that form produce upon you as a reader? How often is the personal pronoun *I* used as a grammatical subject in Example E? What word is grammatical subject of the very first sentence? How does the writer's use of grammatical subjects relate to the tone of Example E? What is your impression of the person who wrote Example E? What specific evidence in that message confirms or contradicts your impression of the writer?

Perception and Interpretation Vary From Person to Person

CHAPTER 3

Criteria for Effective Business Messages

I. THE FIRST CRITERION: ACCURACY

II. THE SECOND CRITERION: COHERENCE

A. Coherence by Planning
B. Coherence by Emphasis
1. Emphasis by Word Order
2. Emphasis by Balance, Contrast, Comparison, Repetition, Restatement
3. Emphasis by Subordination
4. Emphasis by Typographical and Visual Aids
C. Coherence by Linguistic Usage
D. Coherence by Transition
E. Coherence by Modification
F. Coherence by Parallelism

III. THE THIRD CRITERION: CLARITY

A. Clarity by Word Choice
1. Word Choice by Empathy
2. Word Choice by Definition
3. Word Choice by Explanation
4. Word Choice by Description
B. Clarity by Complete Comparison
C. Clarity by Grammatical Agreement

D. Clarity by Pronoun Reference
E. Caution: Sentence Fragments
F. Caution: Unnecessary Connectors
G. Caution: Omitted Words

IV. THE FOURTH CRITERION: CONCISENESS

V. THE FIFTH CRITERION: COURTESY

A. Courtesy through Empathy
B. Stereotyped Miscommunicators
1. Information Hog
2. Chatterbox
3. Vague Referencer
4. Twister
5. Thunderer
6. Mumbler
7. Scarecrow
8. Laugher
9. Chronologist
10. Wanderer
C. Courtesy in Speaking and Writing

VI. REVIEW AND TRANSITION

By what standards will your professor or your employer judge your business messages? This chapter presents five suitable criteria: accuracy, coherence, clarity, conciseness, and courtesy.

THE FIRST CRITERION: ACCURACY

Although total freedom from error is not always attainable, these question-guides can help you reduce the number and kind of mistakes you might otherwise make: To what extent does your data represent observable, measurable, real-world evidence? How nearly valid, reliable, and complete is your data? Does your data *presentation* fulfill appropriate message format? How appropriate are your word choice, grammar, spelling, and punctuation?

INACCURATE	ACCURATE
A $35 price discounted by 10% is $3.150.	A $35 price discounted by 10% is $31.50.
Of 480 questionnaire respondents, 40%, or 129 people, had seen the Metrico TV commercials.	Of 480 questionnaire respondents, 40%, or 192 people, said that they had seen the Metrico TV commercials.
Management, and communication are inseprable.	Management and communication are inseparable.

INCOMPLETE DATA	UNRELIABLE DATA
A magazine publisher mails 250,000 copies of a subscription invitation. The envelopes have complete names and addresses. But to save costs, those names and addresses do not appear on the invitations themselves. The message closes with "Just initial and return this invitation. I'll send the January issue to you immediately." Nine thousand invitations are returned—neatly initialed, entirely anonymous, and altogether worthless. Having elicited incomplete data, the publisher cannot know whom the initials represent. What should have been profitable communication is an expensive failure.	A farmer in a remote location selects much-needed equipment from a catalog and mails a check with the order. But the catalog is outdated; prices have risen considerably since its publication. Costly frustration of that farmer's livelihood is almost certain. A typist or punch-card operator inadvertently adds a zero to a claim. What should be $1,000 appears as $10,000 on the settlement check. The claimant detects the error; the correction costs time, money, and goodwill.

Many people produce messages that may be understood. Effective business communicators strive to produce messages that cannot be misunderstood. Accuracy therefore is a primary communication criterion. And a complement to accuracy is coherence.

THE SECOND CRITERION: COHERENCE

To make your messages understandable, unify their sentences and paragraphs into a whole. You can achieve that coherence through planning, emphasis, linguistic usage, and transition.

Coherence by Planning

Do you design your sentences so that every word pertains to the sentence corethought? so that every sentence in every paragraph supports the paragraph corethought? so that every paragraph reinforces the corethought of the entire message? Subsequent chapters of this book present message-planning techniques in detail.

Coherence by Emphasis

Do you highlight key thoughts and feelings by deliberate, appropriate word order? by balance, contrast, or comparison? by repetition or restatement? by subordination of minor items? by typographical, visual, or oral aids? The following paragraphs discuss those methods.

Emphasis by Word Order. The beginnings and endings of sentences and of whole messages attract special attention *unless* those positions are filled by needless words. Do you emphasize key data by stating it at the beginning or the ending—rather than in the middle of—what you write or speak? Word order and word choice are intimately related, as shown by these examples:

UNEMPHATIC	EMPHATIC
It will be appreciated if you complete and return the enclosed form immediately for prompt processing of your claim in this matter.	For prompt processing of your claim, please complete and return the enclosed form immediately.
I have the pleasure of informing you of your selection as Salesperson Of The Year, Lee, and of offering my congratulations on this auspicious occasion.	Congratulations, Lee—you are Salesperson Of The Year!

Emphasis by Balance, Contrast, Comparison, Repetition, Restatement. When you *balance*, you emphasize items equally. When you *contrast*, you emphasize differences. When you *compare*, you emphasize similarities. With *repetition* you emphasize by presenting an item verbatim at least twice. With *restatement* you emphasize by presenting an item and then using synonyms to present it again.

Emphasis by Balance

Aldo is the recruiter; Ponti, the personnel manager.

Emphasis by Contrast

Whereas Aldo is the recruiter, Ponti is the personnel manager.

Emphasis by Comparison

As Aldo is to recruitment, so Ponti is to personnel management.

Emphasis by Repetition

Ponti is the personnel manager. Remember, please: Ponti is the personnel manager.

Emphasis by Restatement

Aldo is the recruiter, the talent scout of prospective employees, the one who finds new applicants.

Emphasis by Subordination. Sentences may present data of equal rank or value; this compound sentence is an example of that fact. Often, however, a sentence may emphasize one item more than another, as this sentence illustrates. Key data is conventionally conveyed by independent clauses, minor data by dependent clauses.

COORDINATE AND UNEMPHATIC	SUBORDINATE AND EMPHATIC
The shipment was prompt, and the customer reordered.	Because the shipment was prompt, the customer reordered.
Sales of the Metrico KB Turbine doubled, for Metrico had modified the KB six months earlier.	Six months after Metrico had modified its KB Turbine, KB sales doubled.

Emphasis by Typographical and Visual Aids. Almost every page of this book shows examples of mechanical aids for emphasizing typewritten or printed messages. Those aids include formats and layouts; sizes of type, print, or script; headings and subheadings; underlinings or italics; capitalizations of whole words or of word groups; varied spacings, margins, and indentations; colored inks or papers. Emphatic visual aids include illustrations, tables, graphs, and similar figures.

FOUR TECHNIQUES FOR EMPHASIS

1. Place the item in a prominent position.
2. Support the item by comparison, contrast, or subordination.
3. Repeat or restate the item.
4. Use—but do not overuse—typographical and other mechanical aids.

Coherence by Linguistic Usage

Consult Part Nine of this book for detailed review of linguistic usage. But here are a few general insights concerning conventional spelling, punctuation, and grammar.

English has twenty-six symbols (alphabetical letters) representing about forty-five sounds. American English spelling reflects the influence of Noah Webster, whose publications changed *flavour* to *flavor*, *centre* to *center*, etc., supposedly to match spelling with pronunciation. Other phonetic reforms of our spelling have generally failed. For example, we have rejected *tho* for *though*, *thru* for *through*, and *biznis* for *business*. We use several spellings for one sound (e.g., the vowel sound in *to*, *two*, *too*, *shoe*, *flew*, *flu*, *flue*, *lieu*). And we represent several sounds by one spelling (e.g., the spelling *ough* in al*though*, b*ough*, *ough*t, and r*ough*). Current dictionaries are therefore necessary office equipment. We emphasize *current* dictionaries because, like other features of a "living" language, spelling changes. What once were *bysig* and *wela* have become *busy* and *wealth*. *Catalogue* is changing fast to *catalog*, *cigarette* to *cigaret*, and so on.

Punctuation, like spelling, is an integral part of written communication. Notice how easily punctuation, not necessarily word choice, can change interpretation of a message:

VERSION A	VERSION B
Send this report to Lynn Ray.	Send this report to Lynn, Ray.
Raise the gear-release lever.	Raise the gear. Release lever.
I think so; do you?	I think. So do you.

Punctuation marks are useful communication symbols. Part Nine, Section 14, of this text reviews them in detail.

Besides spelling and punctuation, grammar enhances communication. Centuries ago, English grammar was much more intricate than it is now. A noun, for example, had separate signs for naming, possessing, receiving, etc. Adjectives and pronouns reflected masculine, feminine, or neuter gender. Personal pronouns had singular, dual, and plural number. Today the signs of a noun's function are minimal: one for possession (e.g., per*son's* or its prepositional alternative *of the person*), one for other grammatical cases (the *person* writes, write to that *person*, hire that *person*). Also, modern English pronouns have two instead of three grammatical numbers.

The alleged complexity of modern American English grammar is largely a myth. But this is a fact: Departure from conventional grammar can obscure messages, weaken business reputations, and lose sales. Therefore study and occasionally review Part Nine, as you continue your work with this text.

You have identified planning, emphasis, and linguistic usage as aids to achieving coherence. Transition, modification, and parallelism also merit your attention.

Coherence by Transition

With words, phrases, sometimes even whole paragraphs, carry your reader or listener from one unit to the next in your message.

REPEAT KEY WORDS AND KEY PHRASES

You've tried. You've tried to find a *home.* But *have you tried to find your home* at *New Town? New Town*, conveniently located where Jordan Highway crosses West Road, offers spacious *garden apartments* and townhouses. The *garden apartments* are . . . .

USE LINK WORDS AND LINK PHRASES

Plant #3 employs only 1,137 people. *Moreover*, new contracts probably will require at least six additional machinists and eight additional office workers at Plant #4 during the next quarter. Plant #5, *however*, can meet its quarterly production schedule with its present work force of 1,750 employees. Supporting data is documented *in the next section of this report.*

Coherence by Modification

Modifiers are words, phrases, and clauses used to influence the interpretation of other sentence elements. For coherent communication, generally place modifiers next to the element you intend them to affect. Notice that you change interpretation by shifting the position of a modifier:

1. *Only* you have invested $8,500 in Project X.
   (You alone have put that sum into the project.)
2. You have *only* invested $8,500 in Project X.
   (You've participated financially but in no other way.)
3. You have invested *only* $8,500 in Project X.
   (You've put neither more nor less than that sum.)
4. You have invested $8,500 in Project X *only*.
   (You've put that amount into no other project.)

Position your modifiers so that they show a logical connection with the words they are intended to affect.

ILLOGICAL, INCOHERENT	LOGICAL, COHERENT
The price is $12, but I *just have* $10. (Do you just *have* $10? Or do you have *just* $10?)	The price is $12, but I *have just* $10.
Arriving ahead of schedule, it was necessary for the cartons to be stored. (Did *it* arrive early?)	*Arriving ahead of schedule, the cartons had to be stored.*
Schwab put a fabric on the cutting table *which was a blend of cotton and dacron*. (Was the *table* really made of cotton and dacron?)	Schwab put *a cotton-and-dacron fabric* on the cutting table.

Coherence by Parallelism

When two or more pieces of data share the same relation to a main thought, state them in identical grammatical form. By communicating their parallelism, you can reinforce understanding of the sentence.

NONPARALLEL, INCOHERENT	**PARALLEL, COHERENT**
Stiegler enjoys *writing* and *to illustrate* sales brochures. (*Writing* is a gerund; *to illustrate* is an infinitive. The construction needs two gerunds or two infinitives.)	Stiegler enjoys *writing* and *illustrating* sales brochures. (Gerund and gerund.) Stiegler likes *to write* and *to illustrate* sales brochures. (Infinitive and infinitive.)
These guides are useful *for coherence* and *to enhance clarity*. ("For coherence" is a prepositional phrase; "to enhance clarity" is an infinitive phrase. The construction needs two prepositional phrases or two infinitive phrases.)	These guides are useful *for coherence* and *for clarity*. (Two prepositional phrases.) These guides are useful *to achieve coherence* and *to enhance clarity*. (Two infinitive phrases.)
The job includes *scheduling mechanical maintenance* and also *that you should dispatch the delivery vans*. ("Scheduling mechanical maintenance" is a gerund phrase. "That you should dispatch the delivery vans" is a dependent clause. The construction can be made parallel by two grammatically identical phrases, by two gerunds, or by two grammatically identical clauses.)	The job includes *scheduling mechanical maintenance* and involves *dispatching the delivery vans*. (Two gerund phrases.) The job includes *scheduling mechanical maintenance and dispatching delivery vans*. (Two parallel gerunds in one phrase.) In this job *you schedule mechanical maintenance, and you dispatch delivery vans*. (Two independent clauses.)

You have gained insights to two communication criteria: accuracy and coherence. Now consider another criterion: clarity.

THE THIRD CRITERION: CLARITY

Communication was relatively simple when a business could be managed directly by its owner. In those days the "proprietor" personally supervised employees. If a message seemed vague, someone asked "What do you mean?" and often received on-the-spot clarification. In the daily conduct of modern business, an owner or executive cannot speak individually to everyone on the payroll or to every customer. Therefore, the need for clarity of communication is urgent.

As a business communicator, your data may be accurate and coherent, thereby meeting two criteria of effectiveness. But accurate and coherent data may be vaguely *stated*. Appropriate word choice, complete comparison, grammatical agreement, and suitable pronoun reference can help you meet a third communication criterion: clarity.

Clarity by Word Choice

If mental telepathy exists, business people have yet to learn its nature and use. But clarity of business messages *can* be attained through word choice involving empathy, definition, explanation, and description.

Word Choice by Empathy. Even familiar words do not represent exactly the same idea or feeling in various minds (or in one mind at various times). To narrow or bridge communication gaps, your knowledge of other people and of yourself should influence your word choice. For example, "Illumination is required to be extinguished before departing these premises" is not nearly so empathetic or so clear as "Turn out the lights before you leave."

Word Choice by Definition. To clarify your messages, assume that words are meaningless. Meaning exists within people, not within words.[1] A word stands for but *is not* an idea, a feeling, or a physical object. Especially when you choose a term that is unusual to your receiver, state not what the term "means" but what *you* mean by using it. Do likewise when you use a familiar term in an unfamiliar way. For example, "quark effect" may be a common term to certain scientists but needs definition in messages to nonscientists. And "hard rock" signifies one thing to an oilwell driller but something else to a popular-music fan.

Word Choice by Explanation. To satisfy *logical* needs, choose words that help your receiver understand, identify, compare, contrast, remember, or apply what your message represents. For example:

> Noah expected a deluge. But a springtime blizzard has caught J&L Transport Company—and all of Denver—by surprise. Except for emergency vehicles and mail trucks, traffic is almost at a standstill here.
> The Weather Service and the Highway Department expect clear skies, not in forty days and nights but by the beginning of next week.
> As soon as streets are passable, J&L will "hit the road" again. And yours will be among the first shipments to leave our terminal.

---

[1] For discussions of general semantics, see S.I. Hayakawa, *Language in Thought and Action* (New York: Harcourt Brace Jovanovich, 1972); Charles K. Ogden and Ivor A. Richards, *The Meaning of Meaning* (New York: Harcourt Brace Jovanovich, 1959); Alfred Korzybski, *Science and Sanity, An Introduction to Non-Aristotelian Systems & General Semantics* (Lakeview, Conn.: Institute of General Semantics, 1958.)

Word Choice by Description. *To satisfy psychological* needs, choose words that help your receiver experience *feelings* of seeing, hearing, tasting, touching, smelling, enjoying, or profiting from what your message conveys. For instance:

> See yourself in the new XR Landau, designed for your comfort and engineered for your safety. Drive confidently through city traffic. Feel your XR respond eagerly, efficiently, dependably. Explore the countryside; relish the fresh air of hilltop and seashore. Wherever you go, rely on your XR. And enjoy driving again.

Here is another example of word choice by description:

> Easylife Textiles will have you and your customers "lookin' good" next season.
>
> Please test the enclosed sample of Easylife Doubleknit. Feel its lightweight yet luxurious texture. Twist the sample. Crumple it. Crush it in your hand.
>
> Now examine that sample again. Your eyes prove that Easylife is snagproof and wrinkle-free. Touch the sample one more time. Your fingers prove that Easylife stays smooth and comfortable.

Clarity by Complete Comparison

To reinforce clarity, state *all* of a comparison. For instance:

INCOMPLETE, UNCLEAR COMPARISON	COMPLETE, CLEAR COMPARISON
Engine 44 A uses less fuel. (Less than what? How much less? To do what?)	Engine 44 A uses 15% less fuel than does Engine 43 B in operating a 3,000-pound, standard-shift car.
WBI's Flight 319 is ten minutes faster. (Faster than what?)	WBI's Flight 319 is ten minutes faster than its Flight 535.

Clarity by Grammatical Agreement

Another way to clarify your messages is through consistent grammar.

GRAMMATICALLY INCONSISTENT	GRAMMATICALLY CONSISTENT
For all of *your* help, we thank *them*.	For all of *your* help, we thank *you*.
Unless you plan your messages, *it* wastes time and money.	Unless you plan your messages, *you* waste time and money.
	Unless business messages are planned, *they* waste time and money.

Do this *machine cost* $950?	*Does* this *machine cost* $950?
Here *is* the *contract and* your *memo*.	Here *are* the *contract and* your *memo*.
When *was* those *circuits* tested?	When *were* those *circuits* tested?
Schools for all sorts of training *is* needed.	*Schools* for all sorts of training *are* needed.

Clarity by Pronoun Reference

Antecedents are those words which pronouns represent. For clarity, make antecedents obvious when you use pronouns, and avoid using whole clauses as antecedents.

UNCLEAR REFERENCE	CLEAR REFERENCE
When *Ms. Duval* and *Mrs. Rhys* discussed that decision, *she* emphasized production schedules. (*Who* emphasized?)	When *Ms. Duval* and *Mrs. Rhys* discussed that decision, *Ms. Duval* emphasized production schedules. (Noun repeated for clarity.)
	When *Ms. Duval* discussed that decision, *she* emphasized production schedules to Mrs. Rhys. (Pronoun clearly represents Duval.)
Van Dorn requested a special *discount, which* arrived after the goods had been billed. (*Which* refers to *discount* or to the clause that begins with *Van Dorn*. But the request arrived late.)	Van Dorn's special-discount *request* was late; *it* arrived after the goods had been billed. (Pronoun clearly represents *request*.)

Caution: Sentence Fragments

A completely stated sentence requires at least one independent clause. Incomplete statements, called "sentence fragments" or "fragmentary sentences," may be common to informal writing and to speaking; but they can cloud communication. Generally, effective business writers do not present dependent clauses as if those clauses were complete statements.

FRAGMENTED	COMPLETE
When did you receive the Jeffers order? The one which I mentioned to you yesterday afternoon?	When did you receive the Jeffers order that I mentioned to you yesterday afternoon?
This collection procedure is customary. Although you can modify it when necessary.	Although this collection procedure is customary, you can modify it when necessary.

Caution: Unnecessary Connectors

To enhance coherence as well as clarity, use connectors (*and, or, but,* etc.) only when they are required to complete a thought.

UNNECESSARY, UNCLEAR	NECESSARY, CLEAR
This collection procedure is customary; but you can modify it, yet only when justified.	This collection procedure is customary, but modify it when justified.
Send two cartons to Metz and also to Ramos and an additional two to Stern today or tomorrow afternoon.	By tomorrow afternoon send two cartons apiece to Metz, Ramos, and Stern.

Caution: Omitted Words

Include every word that is necessary for understanding your sentences completely.

INCOMPLETE WORDING	COMPLETE WORDING
Their Atlanta office is at 423 Peachtree.	Their Atlanta office is at 423 Peachtree Street, NE.
Your flight reservation has been confirmed for 9:45 tomorrow.	Your flight reservation has been confirmed for 9:45 tomorrow night.
Just sign the enclosed card.	Just sign and return the enclosed card.

So far you have identified three communication criteria: accuracy, coherence, and clarity. Another criterion is conciseness.

THE FOURTH CRITERION: CONCISENESS

People often use many words to conceal a lack of information. But when knowledgeable people use mere brevity, they may omit data which their readers or listeners need. Conciseness does not sacrifice complete information simply for the sake of short sentences. Conciseness is the statement of complete, relevant data in as few words as necessary.

Notice that needlessly wordy terms can easily be condensed into their concise equivalents:

NEEDLESSLY WORDY	CONCISE
1. at all times	1. always
2. at the present time	2. now
3. at this point in time	3. now
4. at that point in time	4. then
5. costs the sum of	5. costs
6. despite the fact that	6. although, despite
7. due to the fact that	7. because, since
8. enclosed herewith for your information you will find	8. enclosed is
9. for the period of a year	9. for a year
10. for the month of June	10. for June
11. for the simple reason that	11. because, since
12. in conjunction with	12. with
13. in the event that	13. if
14. in the near future	14. soon
15. in the recent past	15. recently
16. in view of the fact that	16. because, since
17. it will be appreciated if you do	17. please do
18. to the effect that	18. that
19. until such time as	19. until
20. we would ask that you	20. please

Do such condensations omit data? See for yourself:

NEEDLESSLY WORDY	CONCISE
1. At all times be courteous.	1. Always be courteous.
2. Sales are rising at the present time.	2. Sales are rising now. (Or: Sales are rising.)
3. Sales are rising at this point in time.	3. (Same as #2.)
4. Sales rose at that point in time.	4. Sales rose then.
5. This camera costs the sum of $185.	5. This camera costs $185.
6. Despite the fact that sales are rising, we should economize.	6. Although sales are rising, we should economize.
7. Due to the fact that your work is excellent, you are being promoted.	7. Because your work is excellent, you are being promoted.
8. Enclosed herewith for your information you will find our current brochure.	8. Enclosed is our current brochure.
9. The Alaska assignment is for the period of a year.	9. The Alaska assignment is for a year.
10. Here are the cost figures for the month of June.	10. Here are the cost figures for June. (Or: Here are the June cost figures.)

11. I've phoned you for the simple reason that I don't understand your memo.	11. I've phoned because I don't understand your memo.
12. The sale begins in conjunction with the opening of our new store.	12. The sale begins with the opening of our new store. (Even more concisely: The sale begins when our new store opens.)
13. In the event that I'm not there, please wait.	13. If I'm not there, please wait.
14. Production will start in the near future.	14. Production will start soon. (Or: Production will start May 23.)
15. Production began in the recent past.	15. Production began recently. (Or: Production began May 23.)
16. In view of the fact that you've surpassed every quota, here is a bonus.	16. Since you've surpassed every quota, here is a bonus.
17. It will be appreciated if you reply immediately.	17. Please reply immediately. (Or: Please reply by August 30.)
18. They reported to the effect that sales had declined.	18. They reported that sales had declined.
19. Use that machine until such time as the new one is installed.	19. Use that machine until the new one is installed.
20. We would ask that you review this contract.	20. Please review this contract.

Be thrifty with your words. Economical word choice saves money and time for dictation, transcription, and typing; for reading and filing; for supplies, postage, telephone and telegraph services; for interview and conference resources. By combining complete information with brief statement, you can clarify your messages. By being concise, you can conserve your own and other people's resources. Remember: Of such things are bonuses and promotions made.

Having considered accuracy, coherence, clarity, and conciseness, you now approach another evaluation standard: courtesy.

THE FIFTH CRITERION: COURTESY

Probably the best advice for developing communication courtesy is this: Empathize, friend, empathize.

Courtesy Through Empathy

While recognizing your own needs and desires, constantly try to anticipate, to perceive, and to evaluate those of your receiver. Your time and effort are precious; so are your receiver's. You respond negatively to unjustified anger; so does your receiver. Empathize, friend. Whether you convey satisfying, disappointing, or neutral information, do so courteously.

DISCOURTEOUS	COURTEOUS
You don't need to keep reminding us about your claim.	Thanks for following up on your claim.
I'm too busy to talk to you about that refund now. Call back at 4:30.	Your refund request deserves my full attention. Please call back at 4:30.
There's no way for you to be promoted if you stay with us; so get a job elsewhere.	To advance your career, perhaps you should consider opportunities elsewhere.

Stereotyped Miscommunicators

The following stereotypes are models of *dis*courtesy. Minimize or exclude their influence as you develop your own styles of speaking and writing.

Information Hog. A common miscommunicator is the person who hoards data needlessly. Like a miser who enjoys acquiring rather than using money, Information Hog simply ingests data that co-workers can use. Information Hog seeks attention by implying only that he or she may have a secret. This stereotyped miscommunicator is a verbal tease. But co-workers eventually find ways of exposing information hogs. Few business people can work efficiently with noncommunicators.

Example: I have those specification reports you asked about, and some of those statistics would raise your blood pressure! However, that's not the purpose of my message.

Chatterbox. At least as harmful as Information Hog is the indiscreet person who, so far as business communication goes, is like a badly made sieve. Instead of determining what information should go to whom, Chattberbox rattles off virtually all data to almost everyone. Transmitting too much information to too many people, Chatterbox violates confidential matters by assigning equal importance (or lack of importance) to everything. Few business people can work efficiently with overcommunicators or with chronically deficient judges of information.

Example: The announcement won't be made for a while, but I know what goes on in the executive suite. Don't be surprised if Krug replaces McElroy now that Mac is retiring.

Vague Referencer. Another miscommunicator is the person who acts as if to avoid a noun is to earn a fee. Vague Referencer generates a fog of pronouns and of demonstrative adjectives without nouns. Vague Referencer names several persons or objects, then uses merely "he," "she," "it," or "they." For example: "I saw Lee, Lou, and Chris about this matter yesterday, and he said she'd send it to them tomorrow." Vague Referencer wastes other people's time, energy, and money.

Twister. Within this family of miscommunicators, a first cousin to Vague Referencer is the person who imposes inappropriate contexts upon a message. In effect, when using words, Twister shakes his or her head for "yes" and nods it for "no." If someone says "I was in the front office today," Twister is apt to announce, "It's a fact that Lee talked to the president this morning." The Twister is imaginative, unreliable, and dangerous.

Thunderer. This miscommunicator habitually substitutes emphasis for thought. Thunderer ignores the probability that when everything is stressed, little seems important. Instead of earning respect and cooperation, Thunderer is apt eventually to be ignored or isolated.

Example: The IMPORTANT thing *I must stress* is that we're upping the Lenz bid by TEN percent! Keep that fact to *yourself*. Furthermore, it's absolutely VITAL that you send your reports *immediately* AND IN TRIPLICATE!!!

Mumbler. This miscommunicator excludes emphasis that could help a receiver's understanding. By speaking inaudibly or by writing obscurely, Mumbler compels receivers to overwork themselves. Thereby Mumbler tries to elicit something that he or she ultimately loses: the receiver's attention.

Example: In oral communication, the italicized words of this example would be slurred or would lack vocal projection: Concerning *your suggestion*, have you *considered—you probably have*—that a *premature announcement* can put us in a *vulnerable* position? *On the other hand, of course.* . . .

Scarecrow. This miscommunicator distracts receivers by *irrelevant* words, data, gestures, facial expressions, postures, and the like. Scarecrow shifts attention *from* the message *to* his or her disorganized behavior. Scarecrow occasionally amuses, often exasperates, but rarely informs.

Example: The 1623 and 1650 packaging designs are *more or less identical. Well, not exactly the same, of course.* The latter has twice the capacity, as nearly as I recall, of the former. *The long and the short of it is* that the 1623 holds about half the amount of the

1650. (The italicized items do not convey significant data. In oral communication Scarecrows would also exhibit empty rather than significant gestures and movements.)

Laugher. This miscommunicator is a Scarecrow who specializes in irrelevant merriment. Laugher replaces information by a snicker (half-suppressed laughter), a giggle (silly laughter), or a yok (glutteral laughter resembling the cry of an ox). Laugher behaves as if chuckles and chortles could substitute for ideas or facts. When writing or speaking, Laugher jokes inappropriately about serious matters. Genuine humor can be a blessing, but people who misuse it can laugh themselves right out of a job.

Example: "Sales of our Safemade Door have plummeted. Let's make it ajar!"

Chronologist. This stereotype is more like a clock than a communicator. Chronologist habitually reports events according to time instead of importance. For example: Returning to the office after a conference elsewhere, a busy executive asks: "What happened while I was away?" And Chronologist replies: "At 10:15 we had the usual coffee break. At 10:25 someone phoned you but didn't leave a name. At 10:30 a fire broke out in the warehouse. At 10:35 the branch-office reports arrived." What would the executive's reaction be? Chronologist, like other miscommunicators, tends to change jobs often.

Wanderer. Chronologist does impose at least a time order upon a message. Wanderer, however, is a miscommunicator who ignores maps as well as timetables. Wanderer's message flits from Topic A to Topic B, returns to A, jumps to D, backtracks to C, and so on. Wanderer seems to lead (or rather to mislead) in several directions simultaneously. Wanderer may enjoy constant release of his or her impulses, pressures, and tensions. But Wanderer does not share information in useful, organized ways.

Example: The industrial exhibit opens June 20 in Chicago. By the way, Jason Stores of Detroit re-ordered yesterday. About that Chicago exhibit again: Jaffer will be in charge of our display there. As for the West Coast sales figures, I'll send you a summary as soon as they're tallied. I mean West Coast/Florida, of course, not West Coast/California.

Courtesy in Speaking and Writing

Information Hog, Chatterbox, Vague Referencer, Twister, Thunderer, Mumbler, Scarecrow, Laugher, Chronologist, and Wanderer have a common trait: They miscommunicate by distracting attention from a message *to themselves*. Their stereotyped behaviors affect their writing as well as speaking, because writing is a record of—or a substitute for—speech.

If you are advised to "write as you speak," consider this probability: Unless your oral communication accommodates the criteria cited in this chapter, your writing—like your speaking—may be negatively stereotyped. Especially concerning the fifth of those criteria, apply this insight: *Courtesy* involves genuine awareness of your receiver's needs, purposes, attention span, and time.

REVIEW AND TRANSITION

Effective communication standards include these five criteria: accuracy, coherence, clarity, conciseness, and courtesy.

Accuracy requires valid, reliable, complete data; proper message format; appropriate word choice, grammar, spelling, and punctuation. *Coherence* involves planning, emphasis, linguistic usage, transition, modification, and parallelism. *Clarity* is attainable by word choice, complete comparison, grammatical agreement, and suitable pronoun reference. But clarity may be blocked by sentence fragments, unnecessary connectors, and omitted words.

Conciseness is not brevity alone. Conciseness is the statement of complete, pertinent data in as few words as necessary. *Courtesy* results from empathizing with the receiver's needs, purposes, attention span, and time.

Part One of this book has described basic needs and responsibilities of business communicators. Chapters 1-3 have identified personal and organizational concepts, basic goals, fundamental skills, and criteria for communication effectiveness.

Part Two offers four chapters that focus upon multimedia values and behaviors in business communication.

DISCUSSION QUESTIONS

A. Within the context of Chapter 3, what are appropriate definitions and illustrations for these terms:

1. criteria
2. conventional
3. complement
4. coherence
5. contrast
6. comparison
7. subordination
8. compound sentence
9. independent clause
10. dependent clause
11. grammatical number
12. grammatical case
13. grammatical agreement
14. parallelism
15. clarity
16. pronoun reference
17. antecedent
18. sentence fragment
19. conciseness
20. courtesy
21. phoenetic
22. integral
23. personal pronoun
24. demonstrative adjective
25. stereotype

B. Chapter 3 refers to Part Nine of this book. What information does Part Nine present? In what ways does Part Nine complement Chapter 3? In what ways do you plan to use Part Nine as you study Chapters 4-19?

C. Based on your own observation, including work experience or class study, discuss the following:

   1. Cite actual examples of inaccurate, incoherent, or unclear communication. Why do those examples seem ineffective to you? Specifically, what would improve them?

   2. Cite actual examples of needlessly wordy or discourteous communication. What were their real-life effects? Specifically, what would have made those examples concise and courteous?

   3. Attack or defend this belief: "Probably the best advice for developing communication courtesy is this: 'Empathize, friend, empathize.' "

D. Chapter 3 describes Information Hog and nine other miscommunicators. What stereotypes should be added to that list? What are the traits of those additonal stereotypes?

E. Citing your own experience, discuss this probability: "Unless your oral communication accommodates the criteria cited in this chapter, your writing—like your speaking—may be negatively stereotyped."

APPLICATIONS

1. "Many people produce messages that may be understood. Effective communicators strive to produce messages that cannot be misunderstood." Using a business or an industrial context, compose three paragraphs of at least four sentences each that "cannot be misunderstood."

2. Write sentences that illustrate emphasis by each of these techniques:
   a. word order
   b. balance
   c. contrast
   d. comparison
   e. repetition
   f. restatement
   g. subordination of minor items
   h. typographical aids

3. Where necessary, rewrite the following items to illustrate conventional American English spelling, punctuation, and grammar:
   a. Metrico is hirng acountents, computor programors; and secretries.
   b. Ninty-to aplicants have intraview apointmants with the personel assistents.
   c. That departmant ordered fourty calcalaters, and recieved twenty one last Wedsday.
   d. Who's research on quaterly indicaters and, annuel trends were used for that report.
   e. The Precision Guage and Meter Company use these slogans: "Service with a Smile" and "Customer Stastifaction Guaranteed".

4. Where necessary, rewrite these items to illustrate the communication criteria discussed in Chapter 3:

    a. It can be estimated that it would cost the company much less than it costs it now.

    b. I just wanted you to keep this copy, the others are to be filed in my office.

    c. Every employee of this company can request the vacation period that they prefer which has been our policy for years.

    d. Precipitate action proliferates negation of economy.

    e. Enclosed herewith you will find a detailed statement showing your charges and payments through the month of December with the outstanding balance at $945.95, and will appreciate your noting we are not in receipt of your check No. 885 in the amount of $420.50 but look forward to recieving it in the near future.

5. Rewrite each of these items to illustrate coherence by transition. First, rewrite to demonstrate repetition of key words and key phrases. Secondly, rewrite to show use of link words and link phrases.

    a. Chronus has represented premier quality for almost a century. That name is on spring-wound clocks that have become heirlooms. It is on ultramodern timepieces today. Among them is the Model 2000 wristwatch at your jewelers now.

    b. The Metrico portable typewriter has these features: two-position line-space lever (up for typing, down for locking), variable line adjuster (for emphasis by special spacing), cylinder scale (for accurate tabulator settings) and four-position paper bail (to hold paper firmly even when you type near the bottom of a page). This performance-tested machine is efficient, durable, designed for personal use and for supplementing office equipment.

6. Rewrite the following items to demonstrate coherence by modification:

    a. I didn't spend $100 for those repairs; they only cost $79.50.

    b. Entering the machine shop, the lathes are to your right.

    c. Customers who pay their bills promptly receive discounts from us.

    d. Metrico builds storage elevators for grain of reinforced concrete.

    e. While repairing electrical circuits, wear gloves on your hands of insulated material.

7. Rewrite the following items to demonstrate coherence by parallelism:

    a. This program was designed to recruit salespeople and moving them into management positions.

    b. The XR Landau is built for passenger safety and to conserve fuel.

    c. Communicating is when you exchange the evidence of ideas and feelings.

    d. Agribusiness requires efficient systems to store, for transporting, and in distributing foodstuffs.

    e. This job requires mechanical aptitude and also that you should enjoy working with people.

8. Use business contexts for the following items:

    a. Write four sentences that demonstrate incomplete comparison. Then rewrite them to complete the comparisons.

    b. Write four sentences that are grammatically inconsistent. Then rewrite them to show grammatical agreement.

    c. Write four sentences that show unclear pronoun reference. Then write those sentences to clarify pronoun reference.

    d. Write two sentence fragments. Explain how those fragments may be clearly understood in oral-visual communication (e.g., as parts of a conversation or of a TV commercial). Then revise the fragments into unmistakably complete statements for a written message.

9. Rewrite the following items to eliminate unnecessary connectors:

    a. I arrived at 7:45 and finished the quarterly report but did not have time to collate the copies before 9:15, which was the time that the meeting began.

    b. Sign the original but initial both copies and keep a third copy for your file.

    c. Let's discuss the Russo account and also the Weiss or either the Ryan campaign.

    d. Those decisions must be made now, for we promised immediate delivery, and the buyers are counting on us, so we can't let them down.

    e. Also in addition we need equipment, supplies, and so forth and so on.

10. Rewrite the following items to supply necessary but omitted words:

    a. This product is as good or better than those others.

    b. You wish me success, and so do I.

    c. Just sign the enclosed form, and we'll authorize payment.

    d. This survey covers all of our employees—those who have been with us less than five years as well as six years or more.

    e. To park this vehicle, just depress the brake pedal, move the gear-shift lever to "P," and get out.

11. Rewrite these needlessly wordy items to concise equivalents:

    a. Despite the fact that Metrico was a new company at that point in time, it earned a substantial profit.

    b. Guided at all times by the principle of good quality at fair prices, Metrico has continued to expand services in conjunction with the opening of new facilities.

    c. In the event that you desire employment with us in the near future, it will be appreciated if you submit your application as soon as possible.

    d. Until such time as you complete your educational program, we would ask that you inform us periodically of your continuing interest in the possibility of employment with us.

    e. In the recent past this company had occasion to hire nineteen alumni of your fine school, and enclosed herewith for your information you will find a list of the positions to which they were assigned.

12. Rewrite the following items to demonstrate courtesy by empathizing with the receiver:

    a. [Telephone pick-up] "Beta, Inc.; hold on."

    b. Don't bother me now. I'm busy.

    c. You're wrong about that date; it's May 14.

    d. You failed to initial that memo.

    e. I can't do that now; I'm on my coffee break.

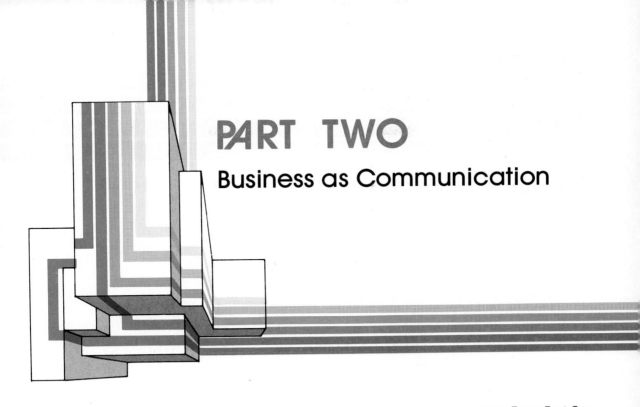

PART TWO
Business as Communication

Part One introduced your role as a person who ethically and profitably manages business resources by effective communication. You learned that communicative management requires efficient planning, organizing, activating, and controlling. You recognized these communication goals: to gain goodwill, to inquire, to inform, to persuade. You explored perception, interpretation, and application in terms of these communication skills: observing, reading, listening, analyzing, synthesizing, writing, speaking, performing. And you acknowledged these communication criteria: accuracy, coherence,

clarity, conciseness, courtesy. From Part One you derived basic insights for your profiting from the rest of this book.

Parts Two through Nine emphasize *applications* of business communication concepts, media, and techniques. In particular, Part Two presents these topics:

Planning, organizing, and developing messages

Conveying positive tone with written and oral messages

Designing and using message formats

Using nonverbal, oral, and multimedia communication

4

Message Planning, Organization, and Development

Your first message to the world was almost certainly a vocal and loud protest. You were reacting to eviction from nature's most protective, nourishing, and comfortable environment. Unaware of what you were doing, you nontheless communicated your loss of nearly perfect security by your birth cry.

Soon you added other sounds to your communication repertoire. Besides crying and weeping (which is crying with tears), you learned that smiles, gurgles, and chuckles could help you get what you wanted. You learned that people and things have names, that you could say those names, and that by saying them you could affect what happened to you. So you talked. Your nonsense syllables became words, phrases, sentences. Bit by bit, you learned to manage your new environment by what you did *and* by what you said.

Then you learned that what you thought, felt, or said could be written. You discovered that the letters of an alphabet stand for the sounds you had acquired. You began to print those letters. You began to write. Your writing pattern emerged also bit by bit: first, the alphabet; then words, phrases, sentences, paragraphs. Finally came the building of whole messages.

Because of your early learning experiences, are you still using that "building-block" approach to writing? When you now compose a message, do you as an adult still try to decide upon the first word, then the next? upon the first phrase, then the next? Do you consequently feel that you know what you want to say but just "can't" write or speak it? If so, Chapter 4 can be exceptionally valuable to you.

CONCEPTS OF MESSAGE PLANNING

Later chapters deal with detailed message structures; two basic planning concepts—"building block" and "whole into parts"—are presented here.

Building-Block Concept

Visualize a child playing with a set of brightly colored plastic bits. When fitted together in various ways, those plastic pieces produce larger objects of differing shapes. The child says, "I'll put this green-round thing here. Now I'll put this yellow-square thing next to it." The result pleases the child, who continues: "Those blue, wavy pieces are pretty, too. I'll put them *there*." And so the child goes on, placing and replacing pieces to construct a pattern.

But the pattern is made of pieces that *someone else* manufactured. The child's use of creativity is restricted, in this example, to *arranging* items that she or he did not design. After completing such an arrangement, the child may try to impose meaning upon it. He or she may present the pieced-together arrangement to someone else, who is apt to respond: "That's pretty. What is it?" And the child, disappointed by the response, replies: "Don't you see? It's a. . . ." Until that follow-up message is conveyed, the child may have *expressed*, but will not have *communicated*, his or her meaning.

Some people restrict themselves as adults by applying that kind of "building-block" approach to almost all of their communication efforts. Those people tend to produce pages of carefully "fitted-together" grammar, punctuation, spelling, and format, but do not provide pertinent corethoughts and supporting data. They soon earn this kind of response: "Your report looks good, Lou. Now tell me: what do you mean?"

Of course, like the child in this analogy, all of us use building blocks to some extent throughout our lives. We use bits and pieces of data that we ourselves did not discover, bits and pieces of language that we ourselves did not create. But as adults we often redesign and sometimes do invent our own communication materials. We adapt old word and linguistic styles, invent new ones, adapt messages already in a correspondence file, and create new ones. Unlike the child in this analogy, however, adults who are effective communicators strive *first* to determine the meanings they seek to convey; *then* select or create message patterns for those meanings. Effective *business* communicators, especially, formulate a design BEFORE choosing the bits and pieces that are to be its parts. They plan a message as a whole BEFORE choosing and fitting together its words, sentences, and paragraphs. Rather than being restricted only to the "building-block" approach, effective writers and speakers profit also from this "whole-into-parts" concept of communication.

Whole-Into-Parts Concept

Often you perceive the totality of a photograph, of a sculpture, or of a building *before* you notice its details. You can also determine the totality of a message *before* you plan its parts. Here is a technique for applying this whole-into-parts concept to message planning:

1. Instead of first deciding how to word your opening sentence, begin by determining the dual purpose (sender's and receiver's) which *the whole message* is to fulfill.
2. Determine the data *the whole message* should convey to support its purpose.
3. Decide upon the logical organization of that data within *the whole message*.
4. Decide upon the tone of *the whole message*.
5. Adapt Steps 1-4: Determine the purposes, supporting data, logical organization, and psychological tone of the *paragraphs* which will compose your message.
6. Adapt Steps 1-5: Determine the purposes, supporting data, logical organization, and psychological tone of the *sentences* which will compose your paragraphs.
7. Determine the wording, structure, grammar, punctuation, and spelling of those sentences. (If the message is to be oral, determine the wording, structure, grammar, volume, pitch, resonance, and pronunciation.)

Here is an example of the first four steps in whole-into-parts planning:

WHOLE-INTO-PARTS CONCEPT APPLIED TO PLANNING A COLLECTION MESSAGE

Step 1. *What is the dual purpose of the message that I plan to write or speak?* From the sender's viewpoint, the purpose is to collect an overdue payment. From the receiver's viewpoint, the purpose may be to continue enjoying credit privileges while paying off more than one debt.

Step 2. *What data should the whole message convey?* From the viewpoints of both the sender/creditor and the receiver/debtor, the data supports the message purpose:
   a. goodwill for continuing this business association
   b. specific payment obligations of sale and credit agreements
   c. assertion that a particular payment is overdue (How much? For what? Has a reminder been sent to the debtor? If so, when? Has any reply been received from the debtor?)
   d. legal and ethical recourse available for collecting payment
   e. advantages to the debtor when payment is made
   f. consequences for the debtor unless payment is made
   g. procedure for immediate payment

Step 3. *What logical or psychological organization should the data have?* For this example any of the following patterns is applicable:
   a. Use the sequence listed in Step 2.
   b. Begin the message with a reminder of needed payment; end by reinforcing buyer-seller benefits and requesting payment. Intervening paragraphs may include details listed in Step 2.

      c. Begin by stating that expected payment has not been received. Discuss data listed in Step 2. End by reinforcing goodwill while requiring remittance.

      d. Begin with a general summary of the situation. Proceed to the details listed in Step 2. End with a cordial but firm request for immediate payment.

      e. Begin with a statement that is apt neither to please nor displease the receiver. Proceed to the details of Step 2. Describe immediate payment as a logical consequence of those details. End with cordial but firm request for payment.

Step 4. *What tone should prevail throughout the whole message?* If your sentences constantly emphasize *I, me, my,* and *mine,* the whole message may convey a writer-centered (or speaker-centered) attitude which can prompt negative reaction. *You, your,* and *yours* suggest empathy through a reader-oriented (or listener-oriented) attitude that can prompt positive response. *We, our, ours,* and *us* show little empathy if they merely pluralize the sender; use them instead to convey a balance of tone that brings *sender and receiver* together. (Not my company and I = we, but you and I = we.) Chapter 5 discusses nuances of tone extensively.

Illustrations of steps 5-7 of the whole-into-parts concept are presented in the next section of this chapter.

TECHNIQUES OF MESSAGE DEVELOPMENT

The first time you hear a playback of your dictation, your reaction may be: "I didn't really say it that way!" Although you may acknowledge the need of improvement, your ego will have been involved in that dictation. Consequently you may find yourself clinging to your original words while you try to dictate the message again. That "clinging" tendency makes difficult the necessary revision of your sentences or paragraphs. But planning lists and message outlines make revision and development easy as well as effective.

Outlining: Lists, Purposes, Corethoughts, and Topics

Based upon the planning phase described earlier in this chapter, outlining can be invaluable for developing your messages. The outling techniques recommended here begin with simple lists.

Developing Lists into Outlines. As you apply your message-planning procedure (see pages 63-64 of this chapter), jot down any pertinent items that occur to you. At this point, do not try to decide whether one item is more or less important than another. Just be sure that they all relate to the message purpose, and list them.

Review your list. What other pertinent items should be added to it? Which redundant items should be consolidated or omitted? Be flexible as you adjust the list. Remember it is much easier to do *that* than to change a fully worded sentence or paragraph. Here is an example for the collection message mentioned earlier:

FIRST PLANNING LIST FOR A COLLECTION MESSAGE

Dual Purpose: To collect overdue payment and continue credit privileges

Items:
1. Send check today.
2. Amount due: $660
3. Reference: Contract 33190
4. Avoid losing credit privileges.
5. Continue mutually profitable transactions.
6. Payment was due two weeks ago.
7. Sent you a reminder one week ago.
8. No reply received.

Revision Notes: – Develop goodwill tone: Mention that this is the first time during our two year association that one of your payments has been late.
– Consolidate Items 2 and 3.
– Emphasize Item 5; relate it to Item 4.
– Consolidate Items 6, 7, and 8.
– End with Item 1; mention enclosed reply envelope.

Next, revise your list according to your notes. Group your items coherently and put them into a sensible sequence. Assign priorities to your items, as shown by the example on the following page.

REVISED PLANNING LIST (SHOWING PRIORITIES) FOR A COLLECTION MESSAGE

Dual Purpose: To collect overdue payment and continue credit privileges.

Priority 1: Reinforce goodwill and rapport.

Mention mutually profitable association during the last two years.

Acknowledge that this is the first time payment has been late.

Priority 2: State that the $660 payment on Contract 33190 is late.

Cite due payment date of two weeks ago.

Mention sending a reminder a week ago.

State that no reply has been received.

Priority 3: Emphasize receiver's need to continue credit privileges and therefore send payment now.

Mention enclosed reply envelope.

Request sending $660 payment for Contract 33190 today.

Test every item on your revised list: Do all of them pertain to the receiver's purpose and yours? Are all of them organized logically? Do they accommodate psychologically appropriate tone? When your listed items meet those criteria, you are ready to develop a detailed outline for your message. Here is a model for that development:

DEVELOPMENTAL MODEL FOR OUTLINES

Dual Purpose:
    I. First Paragraph Topic
       A. Supporting data for I.
          1. Item related to IA.
             a. Item related to IA1.
             b, etc. Items related to IA1.
          2. Item related to IA.
             a. Item related to IA2.
             b, etc. Items related to IA2.
          3, etc. Items related to IA.
       B, etc. Supporting data for I.
          1. Item related to IB.
             a.
             b., etc. } Items related to IB1.
          2. Item related to IB.
             a.
             b., etc. } Items related to IB2.
    II. Second Paragraph Topic
       (Develop as shown for I.)
   III, etc. (Develop as shown for I.)

Some business communicators prefer using this alternative model:

ALTERNATIVE DEVELOPMENTAL MODEL FOR OUTLINES

Dual Purpose:

1. First Paragraph Topic
  1.1 Supporting data for 1
    1.11 Item related to 1.1
      1.111 Item related to 1.11
      1.112 Item related to 1.11
    1.12 Item related to 1.1
      1.121 Item related to 1.12
      1.122, etc. Items related to 1.12
    1.13, etc. Items related to 1.1
  1.2, etc. Supporting data for 1
    1.21 Item related to 1.2
      1.211
      1.212, etc. } Items related to 1.21
    1.22 Item related to 1.2
      1.221
      1.222, etc. } Items related to 1.22
2. Second Paragraph Topic
  (Develop as shown for 1.)
3. etc. (Develop as shown for 1.)

Advantages of Using Outlines. *Flexibility* is a major advantage of using outlines. For most writers and speakers, outlining is more economical and more effective than trying, often unsuccessfully, to compose a "perfect" message at the outset of the communication process. Outlining has the major advantage also: It helps you build justifiable confidence in your ability to organize and develop messages. After becoming skillful with outlines, you can use them for extemporaneous oral delivery, for message dictation, and for writing complete drafts of messages that range from a few words to many pages.

Insights for Using Purposes, Corethoughts, and Topics. An essential requirement of effective outlining is to translate the dual purpose of your intended message into a corethought. For example, suppose you are trying to get a purchase order from someone preoccupied with maintenance costs. From your viewpoint the message purpose is sales promotion. From your receiver's viewpoint that purpose is satisfactory operation with minimal maintenance. The dual purpose translated into a corethought may then become: "Because it does the work you require and because it has a patented monitor to conserve energy costs, buy this machine." Or:

"Purchase this equipment because its sealed-in-steel construction mini-mizes maintenance costs to do the job you need."

As another example, suppose you are answering inquiries about Metrico Stereo Sound Systems. A completely stated corethought for one of your messages might resemble this: "A Metrico Stereo Sound System is an affordable investment in listening pleasure; buy Metrico." From your *message corethought* you derive pertinent *paragraph topics*. For example:

PARAGRAPH TOPICS FOR METRICO MESSAGE

Paragraph 1: You can afford to enjoy owning a Metrico Stereo Sound System.

(Develop this topic with supporting details in this paragraph and/or the following paragraphs. But keep Paragraph 1 relatively short.)

Paragraph 2: Metrico Stereo Systems are available as complete packages of superb sound-reproducing equipment.

(Develop this topic with supporting details of Metrico models, features, prices.)

Paragraph 3: The Metrico 1228 Package is the best seller in its field.

(Develop this topic with supporting details of the 1228.)

Paragraph 4: Enjoy an outstanding investment in listening pleasure at reasonable cost.

(Develop this topic with concise summary of previously mentioned reasons to buy. End with invitation to request sales catalog or brochure, visit showroom, order product, etc. Keep this paragraph relatively short.)

Again because outlines are flexible, you may easily develop Items 2 and 3 into more than one paragraph apiece. As a blueprint is to a building, so is an outline to a finished message. Keep revising your "blueprint"; it's more economical to do that than to alter the final architecture.

Outlining: Comprehensive Procedure for Organizing and Developing Messages

Use the following sequence to build your self-confidence as an effective communicator:

Step 1. Determine the dual purpose of your message.

Step 2. State that dual purpose as a message corethought.

Step 3. Support the message corethought with a list of relevant topics.

Step 4. Revise the list: Consolidate, delete, or add relevant items.

Step 5. Rearrange the list into an outline. Note: A *list* does not show relative importance or logical subordination of items. An *outline* does show importance and subordination by organizing items as topics, subtopics, sub-subtopics, etc. A logically developed outline is recognizable not only by its format but also by the grammatical parallelism of its items, as the examples in this chapter indicate.

Step 6. Revise the outline: Consolidate, delete, or add relevant items. Subordinate subtopics to topics. Subordinate topics to corethought. State items in grammatically parallel form.

Step 7. Write or dictate the message draft from the revised outline.

Step 8. Proofread the draft. If necessary, revise and proofread subsequent drafts.

Step 9. Transmit the final form of the message.

Develop the details of that sequence by answering these basic communication question-guides:

WHAT IS MY PURPOSE FOR WRITING OR SPEAKING THIS MESSAGE?

WHAT IS MY RECEIVER'S PURPOSE FOR READING OR LISTENING TO THIS MESSAGE?
Combine your answers and word them from the receiver's viewpoint as well as from your own. The result is your message corethought.

WHAT DATA SHOULD BE STATED? Your answer identifies items of relevance to your corethought, to your receiver, and to yourself. The result is a list from which you can develop a message outline.

IN WHAT ORDER SHOULD THE DATA APPEAR? Your answer becomes the organizational structure of the whole message, of the paragraphs which compose that whole message, and of the sentences which compose those paragraphs. The result is a detailed message outline.

HOW SHOULD THE MESSAGE BE UNIFIED? Your answer guides your applying those techniques of accuracy, clarity, coherence, conciseness, and courtesy which you studied earlier in this book. The result is a revised message outline to fulfill effective communication criteria.

For the following examples of list-into-outline development, this is the communication context: As spokesperson for Industrial Insurance Associates, Inc. (IIA), you are to organize and develop a reply to a prospective buyer's inquiry about employee hospitalization coverage. The inquiry comes from R.B. Ramos, Jr., general manager of Ramos Foods Corporation. Examples are on the following pages.

This discussion began with your formulating a corethought and has moved to your revising a complete message draft. The intention has been to give you an overall picture of the process involved in building your *message as a whole*. At this point, Chapter 4 presents special considerations for developing your *paragraphs* and *sentences*.

Special Considerations: Developing Paragraphs, Opening Sentences, Closing Sentences

You have considered applications of the whole-into-parts concept and of list-into-outline procedure for your entire message. Now focus your attention particularly upon the development of your *paragraphs* and of those *sentences* that begin or end your message.

Developing Paragraphs. Think of a paragraph not as a haphazard array of sentences but as an integrated unit. A paragraph may consist of a *single* sentence related to the message corethought. Or a paragraph may be a *group* of sentences related to themselves and to the message corethought.

Paragraph Placement and Length. To develop a paragraph, first determine a topic that supports the message corethought. To insure clarity, state the paragraph topic as a sentence. For variety and emphasis in paragraphs of more than one sentence, place the *topic* statement at the beginning or at the end of the paragraph. Finally build the paragraph with other sentences pertaining to its topic. Remember: As a whole message should be unified by its corethought, so should a paragraph be unified by the paragraph topic. Deliberately use your paragraphs to show your reader the step-by-step sequence of topics supporting your message corethought.

For ease of reading and for sustaining attention, business paragraphs often average fewer than a hundred words. Effective business writers intentionally use paragraphing to prevent formidable masses of words, to provide a change of pace in reading rate, to give a "breather" to the reader's mind and eye. But those expert writers know that, to be more than just a mechanical convenience, all of a paragraph should pertain to its topic; and the topic should pertain to the whole message corethought.

Sentences which open and close a *message* are usually better remembered than those in the middle of the message. Likewise, sentences that open or close a *paragraph* are in emphatic positions.

IIA MESSAGE: FIRST PLANNING LIST

Dual Purpose: Promote sale of hospitalization insurance to benefit Ramos Foods Corporation employees and their families.

Items:
1. Program proposal specifying cost and coverage
2. Outstanding features of coverage
3. General and maternity services
4. Services for children
5. Preferential identification of insured persons
6. Medical underwriting not required to join program
7. Additional feedback needed from prospective buyer
8. Toll-free telephone service available
9. Personal visit with IIA representative available

Revision Note: add acknowledgment of Ramos inquiry; establish goodwill.
- Consolidate items 1–6 in this order:
  -- 1 and 2
  -- 6, 5, 3, and 4
- Consolidate items 7, 8, 9.

IIA MESSAGE: REVISED PLANNING LIST

Dual Purpose: Promote sale of hospitalization insurance to benefit Ramos Foods Corporation employees and their families.

Priority 1: Acknowledge Ramos inquiry while establishing goodwill.

Priority 2: Enclose program proposal; refer to it while emphasizing these features:
--medical underwriting not required to join program
--preferential identification for insured
--general and maternity services
--services for children

Priority 3: Elicit additional feedback from Ramos
--reactions to enclosed proposal
--use of personal communication
--availability of toll-free telephone number for
--arranging visit with IIA regional representative

Test the List: Do all items pertain to the dual purpose? Are they arranged logically? Do they accommodate receiver psychologically & appropriately?

Notes for Outline: Translate technical medical & underwriting "words" into generally understood words.
- Use more "you attitude" to attract appropriate attention.
- Reinforce goodwill by "you" tone throughout.
- Use complimentary close that combines tone of reliability with tone of goodwill.

IIA MESSAGE: FIRST OUTLINE

I. What is the dual purpose of this message?

   A. Sender's Viewpoint: Promote sale of hospitalization insurance program

   B. Receiver's Viewpoint: Secure hospitalization insurance benefits for Ramos Foods employees and their families

II. What data should be stated?

   (See Priority Items 1-3 of Revised Planning List.)

III. In what logical and psychological order should the data appear?

   A. Acknowledge Ramos inquiry while establishing goodwill.

   B. Describe available services and costs; enclose program proposal with details.

   C. Emphasize outstanding features of coverage for employees and their families.

      1. medical underwriting unnecessary

      2. preferential identification

      3. general hospital services

      4. maternity services

      5. children's services

   D. Stimulate prospective buyer to request interview with IIA regional representative

      1. Emphasize personal communication.

      2. Make communication easy; supply toll-free telephone number.

      3. Use complimentary close to reinforce goodwill and to suggest IIA reliability.

IV. How should the message be unified?

   A. Establish and reinforce tone of interest, sincerity, capability.

      1. Personalize an innovative salutation ("Thank you, Mr. Ramos").

      2. Convey receiver-oriented interest.

         a. Emphasize "you" and "your" pronouns.

         b. Repeat receiver's name before closing message.

         c. Use a complimentary close that combines tones of goodwill and reliability.

   B. Repeat key words deliberately for coherence.

      1. State full name of seller, Industrial Insurance Associates, Inc., in letterhead; show "IIA" as its abbreviation.

      2. Repeat "IIA" in relation to "Ramos Foods Corporation." Reinforce tie between name of seller and name of buyer.

   C. Use a list for coherence, clarity, and emphasis in identifying outstanding features of program proposal.

   D. Refer (in the body of the message and by an "Enclosure" notation below signature block) to the enclosed program proposal.

   E. Elicit additional feedback

      1. Invite Ramos to use toll-free telephone number.

      2. Offer Ramos a personal interview with IIA regional representative.

   F. Summarize general tone of presentation by a complimentary close that combines goodwill with reliability ("Faithfully yours").

Note: Translate "medical underwriting unnecessary" into "no medical examination required, no health questions to be answered" when introducing Item IIICl.

IIA MESSAGE: REVISED DRAFT

May 23, 19—

Mr. R. B. Ramos, Jr.
General Manager
Ramos Foods, Inc.
125 East Lamar Road
Langley, SC 29834

Thank you Mr. Ramos:

Your inquiry about health-care protection for Ramos Foods employees and their families is welcome. IIA staff members are ready to serve your organization.

The enclosed proposal specifies many reasons for your considering IIA coverage, including these outstanding features.

1. No Medical Examination Required, No Health Questions To Be Answered—All of your employees and their immediate families can receive IIA policy coverage without medical screening.

2. Preferential Identification of Insured Persons—The IIA identification card guarantees admission of Ramos employees and their families to any general hospital in the United States.

3. General Hospital Services—IIA pays full cost of hospital rooms, operating facilities, medicines, x-rays, and the like.

4. Maternity Services—IIA places no limit on hospital charges for ten days, or less, of in-hospital care. That allowance applies to each pregnancy.

5. Children's Services—IIA Family Contracts cover unmarried dependent children from their birth to their twenty-first birthdays.

Mr. Ramos, please study the enclosed program proposal, which specifies the details of insured protection for your employees and their families. For an appointment to discuss this program personally with your IIA regional representative, please telephone me at this toll-free number: 800-555-1414.

Faithfully yours,

R. L. Valerian
Supervisor

Enclosure: Program Proposal

IIA MESSAGE: FIRST DRAFT

May 23, 19—

Mr. R. B. Ramos, Jr.
General Manager
Ramos Foods, Inc.
125 East Lamar Road
Langley, South Carolina 2983   *[handwritten: Check Zip Code]*

Thank you, Mr. Ramos: *[handwritten: Check Spelling]*

[handwritten: Revise tone to "you"]

I am glad to acknowledge your inquiry. We are ready to serve your organization. Here is a few reasons for your considering I I A coverage: *[handwritten: or—change tone to reach-centered—use "you" viewpoint]*

1. No medical examination required, no health questions to be answered:

2. Preferential identification of insured persons—our ID card guarantees admission to any U.S. general hospital;   *[handwritten: identification / Choppy term—use phrase instead / add other examples]*

3. General hospital services—we pay full costs of hospital rooms, etc.;   *[handwritten: Awkward—use two sentences]*

4. Maternity services—no limit on hospital charges for up to and including ten days of in-hospital care per pregnancy;

5. Children's services—unmarried dependent children included in coverage from birth through age 20)   *[handwritten: Clarify—does it mean through 20th or to 20th]*

Mr. Ramos, study the enclosure. It specifies details of the program we offer. Then discuss this with your IIA regional representative. Telephone me at 800-555-4414. We'll pay the cost of the call.

Faithfully yours,

R. L. Valerian
Supervisor

Enclosure: Program Proposal

[handwritten: 1. Last ¶—Revise tone to courteous request— Emphasize "you," "your IIA," "your employees and their families."]

[handwritten: 2. Revise Item 1—is not parallel with other items]

Expert business writers generally keep their opening and closing paragraphs relatively short. A one- to four-line opening paragraph, for instance, tends quickly to attract attention and interest. A counterpart closing paragraph tends quickly to summarize the message corethought and to elicit appropriate response.

An abundance of too-long or too-short paragraphs can distract your reader. For example, four paragraphs of five lines each, or five paragraphs of four lines each, are often easier to read than is one paragraph of twenty lines. Conversely, four paragraphs of six lines each are often easier to read than are twelve paragraphs of two lines each. But effective paragraph length is more the result of empathy for the reader than of arbitrary line quotas. The same is true of sentence length and whole-message length; empathy is a reliable, profitable guide.

Paragraph Coherence. Reminder: A *paragraph* is coherently unified when all of its sentences pertain to its topic. A *message* is coherently unified when all of its sentences pertain to the message corethought. For instance, one paragraph of a persuasive message may be intended to attract attention, another to stimulate interest, a third to develop desire, and a fourth to elicit response. *Each* paragraph should relate to its respective topic (attention, interest, desire, action). *All* paragraphs should relate to the whole message corethought (persuading the receiver to think, to feel, or to do what the sender intends). Sometimes you will use more than a single paragraph to develop a complex topic; sometimes you will use more than one message to accomplish complex communication.

Coherent message plans for orders, acknowledgments, inquiries, replies, and other specific types of business communications are discussed in later chapters. For now, stimulate your own awareness of the need to move your reader or listener from one part of your message to the next. And review these basic ways to improve coherence of paragraphs and of whole messages:

1. Use "link" words and phrases (*also, consequently, furthermore, however, therefore, for example, for instance, on the other hand*). But use them deliberately to connect the parts of your paragraphs and to connect the paragraphs of your message.

2. Repeat key words and key phrases (the names of your receiver and of her or his company, the name of your company, the name of the product or service being discussed, a phrase representing the message corethought, a phrase representing a paragraph topic). But repeat them deliberately for coherence and emphasis, taking care not to pad sentences, paragraphs, or whole messages.

3. Reinforce key data by presenting it in more than one way. Use examples, case histories, explanations, comparisons, contrasts, statistical tables, graphs, summaries, lists, or variations of spacing or typography. But do so deliberately in order to emphasize the data and make your message comprehensible.
4. Use inductive order for your data. Begin the whole message or begin a particular paragraph with specific examples or reasons. End with a general principle or observation derived from those examples or reasons.
5. Or use deductive order for your data. Begin the whole message or a particular paragraph with a general principle or observation. End with specific examples or reasons.

EXAMPLES OF LINK WORDS AND LINK PHRASES

TO SHOW:

ADDITIONS	also, and, another, as well as, besides, both . . . and, equally important as, finally, first (second, third, etc.), further, furthermore, in addition, lastly, moreover, not only . . . but also, not so obvious is, too
ALTERNATIVES	either . . . or, if, or, whether, whether . . . or not
CONCESSIONS	although, at least, despite, even though, still, yet
CONTRASTS	but, by contrast, from another viewpoint, however, in contrast to, nevertheless, notwithstanding, on the contrary, on the other hand, to contrast, in another way, unlike.
EMPHASIS	above all, especially, certainly, in detail, indeed, in fact, in particular, in truth, mainly, most importantly, particularly, principally, specifically, surely, urgently
EXAMPLES	as follows, for example, for instance, like, to illustrate
EXCLUSIONS	all but, all except, except, except that, neither . . . nor
PURPOSE	for, so, so that, to, to bring about, to effect, to result in
RESULTS	accordingly, as a result, consequently, for that reason (for this reason, these reasons, those reasons), hence, so, therefore, the outcome is, the results are, thus

SKETCHING PARAGRAPH PLACEMENT AND LENGTH CAN HELP YOU VISUALIZE YOUR FINAL MESSAGE FORM

Opening Paragraph: Welcome to _____.
Second Paragraph: As reported _____
_____
_____. Your _____
_____
_____.
Third Paragraph: The enclosed _____
_____. Other _____
_____. At your _____
_____
Closing Paragraph: Please _____.

This sketch is for a message announcing change of bank ownership. The message itself, addressed to depositors, is shown below.

First National Bank
of 1st
Beech Grove
POST OFFICE BOX 6830   BEECH GROVE, SC 29808

November 29, 19--

Dear Customer:

Welcome to the First National Family.

As reported last week by the news media, the First National Bank of Beech Grove has acquired all deposits and certain other assets of the Townson Bank and Trust Company. Your funds are secure, and full banking services are now available to you through First National.

The enclosed complimentary supply of checks replaces those that bear the Townson Bank name. Other complimentary items are available to you in our 1700 Broadway offices. At your convenience, let's share a cup of First National coffee and become better acquainted.

Please visit us soon.

Sincerely yours,

T. D. McCabe

T. D. McCabe
President

Developing the Opening Sentence. Use your opening sentence to get your reader's attention, keynote your message, signal your corethought, or prepare your reader for what follows.

Of all opening sentences, one that shows action favoring the reader is naturally the most welcome. Suppose, for example, that you are a retail employee who has requested time off during the peak winter shopping season. What positive feelings would the following reply give you?

> Your vacation request for the two weeks beginning December 9 has been approved.

Contrast that favorable-action opener with this one:

> I have compared your vacation request with those of our other employees and have decided to authorize your time off.

Here are two more examples of favorable-action openers that come right to the point:

> Yes, the St. Louis distributor will expedite your shipment.
> Your credit account is open and ready for your use.

The following left-hand paragraphs illustrate the effects of unnecessary wordiness. The concise paragraphs at the right attract attention.

(55 Words)	(7 Words)
We desire to acknowledge the receipt of your note of January 25, in which you inquire whether you are fully protected under our policy No. 2-40378. We wish to advise that an examination of our records shows that your policy is in force and that you are protected according to the terms and stipulations therein.	Your policy No. 2-40378 is still effective.

(51 Words)	(20 Words)
We wish to acknowledge receipt of your letter of the 15th and wish to state that we appreciate the interest you have shown in our present situation. In the matter of your inquiry relative to your illustrations, we wish to advise that they have had our attention and are enclosed herewith.	Here are the illustrations that accompanied your October 15 note. Thank you for letting us see examples of your work.

If you must refuse a request, reject a claim, or otherwise convey disappointing news, follow this suggestion: Begin with a relevant, neutral statement or one which is relevant and agreeable. That kind of opener will attract your reader's attention and interest, enable you to explain your reasons, and thereby prepare your reader for the disappointing news. The following left-hand examples are of openers likely to alienate a reader. The right-hand examples encourage the receiver to read on.

Your vacation request is denied.	Your vacation request has been carefully considered, Lou.
I regret to inform you that we won't release your St. Louis shipment, despite your explanation of non-payment for what is owed us.	Thank you for explaining the non-payment of your St. Louis invoice.
We cannot supply Metrico products to you.	Your interest in Metrico products is welcome.

Developing the Closing Sentence. Use your closing sentence to reinforce goodwill, to offer a counterproposal, or to stimulate action. For example, contrast the effects of the following:

Don't submit another vacation request until April.	Please resubmit your vacation request in April.
If you fail to send us at least a partial payment, you won't get that shipment.	As soon as payment, even partial, is received, the shipment will be on its way to you.
Because of a production mixup we don't know when those Metrico products can be sent.	Once the new production schedule is underway, we'll gladly supply you with those Metrico products.

Particularly concerning U.S. business correspondence, a participial closing (introduced, for example, by *thanking, trusting,* or other verbal adjectives ending in *ing*) is considered obsolete. As you contrast the following examples, notice that participial closings are in the left column:

Regretting our inability to comply, we remain ...	May we serve you in another way?
Trusting you will give this matter your prompt attention, we are ...	Please act promptly on this request.
Thanking you for your order, and assuring you of our careful attention, we remain ...	Thank you for your order. It is being expedited now.

"Thanking you in advance" is an especially trite, discourteous phrase because it implies that you take people for granted. Yes, thank people for their services. But do so *after* those services have been performed.

REVISING AND PROOFREADING MESSAGES

A quality-control inspector carefully examines products before they are shipped. Likewise, an effective communicator inspects and corrects messages before transmitting them. Revising and proofreading are the communicator's quality-control procedures.

Within the context of this discussion, *revising* is the updating, reorganizing, rewording, or other improvement of business correspondence, memos, reports, and publications. *Proofreading* is the actual marking of a page to correct errors. Once you have learned to use proofreaders' marks, you can save much time and energy in revising material that may range from a single sentence to an entire book. Examples of common proofreaders' marks and their application are shown below.

COMMON PROOFREADERS' MARKS

⊙	Use period.	⌐⌐	Move this item up.
⌃	Use comma.	⌐⌐	Move this item down.
=	Use hyphen.	⌐ or *tr*	Transpose these items.
:	Use colon.	*stet*	Let the original item stand; disregard changes already made.
;	Use semicolon.	ℐ	Delete this item.
?	Use question mark.	¶	Begin a paragraph here.
!	Use exclamation point.	*no* ¶	Do not begin a paragraph here.
˅	Open a quotation.	*Caps* or =	Capitalize this item.
˅	Close a quotation.	*lc*	Use lowercase letters (not capitals).
⌒	Close up; move these items together.	*ital* or —	Italicize this item.
⌐	Separate; move these items apart.	[/]	Use brackets here.
∧	Insert item here.	(/)	Use parentheses here.
#	Insert space here.		

BEFORE USING PROOFREADERS' MARKS

Product specifications in Comparisons and Ratings pages 312-859 of the

Mero Institute Data Book is especially helpful to designeers of towers, ski

lifts, etc   But since data book rarely provide all the answers to psefic

questions   please call on us fro technical assistance.   At your convenience,

visit our Atlanta office 621 Peachtree Plaza.   Or use our twenty four hour

toll-free telephone service   the number is 800-555-1212.

AFTER USING PROOFREADERS' MARKS

Product specifications in Comparisons and Ratings pages 312-859 of the

Mero Institute Data Book) is especially helpful to designeers of towers, ski

lifts, etc But since data book rarely provide all the answers to psefic

questions please call on us fro technical assistance. At your convenience,

visit our Atlanta office 621 Peachtree Plaza. Or use our twenty four hour

toll-free telephone service the number is 800-555-1212.

REVIEW AND TRANSITION

The "building-block" concept involves attempts to compose messages not by comprehensive planning but by selecting one word, then another, one phrase, then another, and so on. The "whole-into-parts" concept involves planning the total message before choosing and fitting together its words, sentences, and paragraphs.

Applied to message planning, the whole-into-parts concept requires a communicator to determine these features of the intended message: dual purpose (sender's and receiver's), data to support the dual purpose, logical organization of the data, and appropriate tone. Having decided those features for the message as a whole, the communicator next determines them for the paragraphs which will compose the message and then for the sentences which will compose those paragraphs. The communicator finally decides upon the wording, structure, grammar, punctuation, and spelling of each sentence. If the message is to be oral, the counterpart decisions are those of wording, structure, grammar, volume, pitch, resonance, and pronunciation.

Chapter 4 describes and illustrates methods of planning, organizing, and developing the following: message corethoughts and paragraph topics; lists, outlines, and message drafts; paragraphs, opening sentences, and closing sentences. Chapter 4 also discusses the revising and proofreading of messages.

After you complete the next set of discussion and application items, Chapter 5 will help you continue your development of appropriate message *tone*.

DISCUSSION QUESTIONS

A. Within the context of Chapter 4, what are appropriate definitions and illustrations for these items?

1. analogy	9. haphazard array
2. dual purpose of message	10. integrated unit
3. paragraph topic	11. inductive order
4. lists	12. deductive order
5. outlines	13. participial closing
6. redundant items	14. revising
7. pertinent items	15. proofreading
8. coherently	

B. In what ways does the corethought of Chapter 4 pertain to the corethoughts of Chapters 1-3?

C. In what ways does the "building-block" differ from the "whole-into-parts" concept of message planning? Why do *both* (rather than either) of those concepts merit the attention of communicators?

D. What evidence can you offer to support or to contradict this assumption: It is easier and more effective to revise lists and outlines than to change a fully worded paragraph or whole message?

E. In what ways are lists and outlines similar? In what ways do they differ? What are the advantages of using outlines to develop messages?

APPLICATIONS

1. Apply the whole-into-parts concept in planning messages for at least one of the following situations:

a. Assume that during an employment interview, you said something that misrepresented your education or work experience. On the following day, you telephoned the interviewer's office to correct the situation but were told that the interviewer would be on a business trip for the next week. You decide to write an appropriate message that will greet the interviewer's return.

b. (See Application 1a.) Put yourself into the role of the interviewer. You return from your business trip and read the goodwill message of explanation. You decide to write an appropriate reply.

2. Continue Application 1: Compose an appropriate planning list for your message. (Use page 63 as a guide for writing the list.)

3. Continue Application 2: In a written note to your professor, submit your planning list and request its evaluation. Also, share your list with several of your fellow students and ask for their comments or suggestions.

4. Continue Application 3: Using pages 64 and 69 as guides, revise your list. Submit the revision to your professor. Also, present the revision to your classmates. Request constructive criticism.

5. Continue Application 4: Use the criteria stated on page 64 to test your revised list. Then develop a detailed outline for your message. Apply the outline model shown on page 64 or the alternative model, page 65. Guide yourself by the illustration on page 70. Request your professor and your classmates to evaluate your message outline.

6. Continue Application 5: Revise the outline. Present the revision to your professor and classmates. Request constructive criticism.

7. Continue Application 6: Prepare to write the first draft of your message. Review pages 68-74 for techniques of paragraph development. Review pages 75-76 for techniques of developing your opening and closing sentences. Then write your first draft. Request constructive criticism from your professor and classmates.

8. Continue Application 7: Using pages 77-78 as a guide, revise and proofread your message draft. Then write the final form of your message. Request constructive criticism and evaluation from your professor and from your classmates.

9. Citing your experiences with Applications 1-8, explain how you applied the "comprehensive procedure for organizing and developing messages" (see page 67 of this chapter).

10. Plan, organize, and develop the following:

    a. a paragraph arranged in deductive order

    b. a paragraph arranged in inductive order

    c. a whole message arranged in deductive order

    d. a whole message arranged in inductive order

11. Write coherent paragraphs that use "link words" or "link phrases" to show the following:

    a. additions   f. examples

    b. alternatives   g. exclusions

    c. concessions   h. purpose

    d. contrasts   i. results

    e. emphasis

    You may use one paragraph to illustrate more than one "link word" or "link phrase."

12. Develop the following lists into appropriate message outlines:

    a. —Dual Purpose: To reconcile differences while maintaining goodwill

       —What accounts for the difference between my interim and my final grades?

       —I have received the evaluation report of my participation in the Mid-Management Seminar.

       —I enjoyed participating in the seminar and have already applied some of the information it provided.

       —You conducted the seminar last month as part of the Organizational Institute Program at our corporation.

—You required four written and two oral reports of each person enrolled in the seminar.

—The average of my grades for those six requirements was 94 points (equivalent to an "A" on your evaluation scale).

b. Dual Purpose: To reinforce goodwill of Metrico Mobile Home buyers by offering repair or replacement of engine parts.

—Despite extensive testing before Metrico Motors markets its mobile homes, unforeseen circumstances occur.

—For fifty years Metrico Motors Corporation has been known for its reliability.

—This announcement is being sent to purchasers of Metrico Challenger or Challenger II Mobile Homes that have been manufactured during the last fifteen months.

—Metrico has been, and continues to be, dedicated to customer safety and satisfaction.

—Recent reports indicate that the engines of some Challenger or Challenger II units manufactured during the aforementioned period may stall excessively.

—Metrico offers at no additional cost to the buyers concerned the repair or replacement of unsatisfactory engine parts in those Challenger or Challenger II vehicles.

—Concerned buyers are urged to visit their nearest Metrico dealers immediately.

13. Continue Application 12: Develop those outlines into message drafts.

14. Continue Application 13: Revise and use proofreaders' symbols to correct the message drafts.

15. Complete Application 14: Typewrite those messages in final form.

16. Plan, organize, and develop effective messages for the following situations:

a. Assume that you are applying for financial assistance to continue your education. Your school offers Vanover Foundation Scholarships, which pay the costs of tuition, books, supplies, and incidental expenses. To be considered for a Vanover scholarship, you must request written recommendations from three references (people other than members of your family) who will vouch for your intelligence, industriousness, and integrity. The recommendations are to be confidential messages sent directly by the references to M.A. Claussen, Director, Loans and Scholarships Office, at your school. Those recommendations must be received not later than two weeks from today. Ask your business communication professor to write a recommendation on your behalf.

b. (See Application 16a). Put yourself into the role of your business communication professor. Write the requested recommendation.

17. Copy the following paragraphs. Then use appropriate proofreaders' marks to correct them.

   a. Off All opening sentences, that which shows action favoring the reader is certainly the most welcome. Whenever such action is appropriate, your message should state it immediately.

   b. During your research did you consult authoritative publications for valid, and relible data. For example, K.G. Mobleys Marketing Patterns and Trends, Vols I and II probly would have ben useful.

   c. Consider for instance that HSR Corporation receives thousands of inquiries about it's patented designs for meters and guages. How would you answer such replies, would you emphasize ease and reliability of use, would you stress low-cost maintenance and repair. Those questions involve analysis of the inquiries and knowledge of the HSR policies concerning patented designs, as described by the following paragraphs of this memorandum. Cheyney and Ross have developed an innovative procedure for computerizeded analysis of incoming messages (see appended material for details). Here is a summary of their procedures and their findings;

18. In a written message to your professor, summarize and illustrate these Chapter 4 topics:

   a. Paragraph Placement and Length (pages 68-72 and 74)

   b. Paragraph Coherence (pages 72-73)

   c. Developing the Opening Sentence (pages 75-76)

   d. Developing the Closing Sentence (page 76)

CHAPTER **5**

Effective Tones for Business Messages

Continuing your study of message development, Chapter 5 focuses upon details of communication tone. Here are basic terms and definitions for this discussion: *Evidence* is that which tends to confirm or to prove something. *Attitude* is a mental/emotional disposition toward, or away from, someone or something. *Tone* is evidence of a communicator's attitude concerning a message and its receiver. *Verbal intelligence* is the deliberate use of written or spoken words as tools for solving problems, reaching decisions, accommodating changes, and achieving goals.

What kinds of communication evidence does tone provide? In what ways do verbal intelligence, attitude, data, and tone interact? What are the consequences for your career? Chapter 5 reinforces your awareness of those questions and guides you toward answers.

VERBAL INTELLIGENCE RELATED TO ATTITUDE

Your intelligence enables you to act and to communicate logically. But as emphasized in almost every chapter of this book, you are influenced by feelings as well as by ideas. The interaction of your thoughts *and* of your emotions disposes you to welcome some people and some circumstances, to avoid others, to have mixed feelings, or to remain fairly neutral. Those attitudes are conveyed by your applications of verbal intelligence; by your uses of words to plan, organize, and control actions; by your uses of language to communicate data and attitudes.

What are the ways in which verbal intelligence conveys attitudes as well as data? The process involves these communication factors: denotation, connotation, and context.

DENOTATION is direct statement of meaning; *to denote* is to point with your words instead of with your fingers. **CONNOTATION** is suggestion of meaning; *to connote* is to imply—to hint about but not to state directly—what you think and feel. **CONTEXT** is a communicative environment, a setting of words and other symbols, in which denotation and connotation function.

To illustrate these communication factors, think of a school graduation ring. As you visualize the ring, observe its parts: a gemstone, a setting for the gemstone, and an inscription on the setting. As the gemstone is a principal feature of the ring, so a corethought is a principal feature of a business message. As the setting of a ring safeguards and draws attention to the gemstone, so a context highlights a corethought. The inscription on the ring denotes; it identifies a school and a dated year. The inscription also *connotes*; it implies completion of an academic program at that particular school in that given year. Whereas the ring has a gemstone and an inscribed setting to convey meaning, a business message has words, numbers, and punctuation marks to denote data and to connote attitudes.

When the message setting—the *context*—changes, denotation and connotation also change. You can alter the interpretation of a sentence by substituting one word for another; you can also alter interpretation by changing the context but not necessarily changing the words. For example, assume that you receive this single-sentence message from your employer; notice how the meaning changes as the context shifts:

Your work on the Fedor contract is satisfactory.

Context A: Two ratings—"satisfactory" and "unsatisfactory"—are being used.	*Context B:* Several ratings—"excellent," "above average," "satisfactory," "below average," and "unacceptable"—are being used.
Denotation: Your Fedor performance fulfills the criteria set by your employer.	*Denotation:* Your Fedor performance fulfills some criteria, not all.
Connotation: Continue as you have done.	*Connotation:* Your work is neither good nor bad; consider improving it.

The words *Your / work / on / the / Fedor / contract / is / satisfactory* have not changed, but context has changed the meaning. As you see, *context* is essential to the functioning of your verbal intelligence.

Attitude also can restrict or enlarge your uses of words and of intellect. For example, if your attitude leads you to consider business communication as simply an addition to your "real" work, you restrict the range of your verbal intelligence. A negative attitude toward business communication prevents your profiting from this fact: Almost any business message, ranging from an informal note to a full-fledged research report, has potential value beyond itself. Your business messages provide opportunities for you to do more than inform. They enable you to improve conditions, enhance efficiency, enlarge rewards. Your business messages demonstrate your intellectual and emotional capabilities to your customers, your co-workers, and your employers. But an attitude of "I hate to write" will keep from you the personal and professional enrichment that effective communication can provide.

ATTITUDE RELATED TO TONE

Feelings sometimes influence behavior and communication far more than do ideas. For instance, you may admire, respect, and dislike someone. You may acknowledge that person's accomplishments but resent her or his power. Feelings often win or lose contracts and promotions. As you compose your business messages, therefore, be aware that they convey data *and* those *patterns of feelings* called "attitudes."

As a reader, you probably have a positive attitude toward business messages that transmit a conversational tone. Indeed, many communication experts share that attitude with you. They recommend that you write as you speak. Since writing is a substitute for and a record of speaking, their advice seems logical. However, the authors of this book caution you: "Write as you speak" can be helpful advice **IF YOU SPEAK EFFECTIVELY**; that is, if your oral communication accomplishes what you intend it to do. But if your speaking is not effective, "writing as you speak" is bound to be disappointing. For example, you may tend to misspell words that you mispronounce, thereby diverting attention from your message to your mannerisms; or you may write verbosely, because you use more words for speaking than you need for writing. Use the information presented throughout this book to help improve your oral *and* your written communication. Chapter 6, for instance, relates your application of verbal intelligence to formats of written messages; Chapter 7 relates your verbal intelligence to oral/visual and multimedia communication. All of the chapters are designed to help you convey pertinent data with appropriate tone.

DATA ORGANIZATION WORD CHOICE, AND TONE

Tone can be proved by at least two kinds of evidence—evidence of data organization and evidence of word choice.

Data Organization and Tone

To convey positive, constructive attitudes, an effective business message is organized for the convenience of its *receiver* rather than of its sender. If you make your receiver's reading or listening needlessly difficult, you defeat your message purpose. For instance, it is easy to organize sentences so that they all begin with the same kind of subject word followed immediately by a verb: "I have received your inquiry," "We wish to offer the following proposal," and so on. But half a dozen of those sentences, or several paragraphs of them, all organized for the sender's convenience, are apt to "tune out" the receiver. The attitude conveyed is one that nourishes the sender's ego at the expense of the receiver's. In this example, the sender's self-centered attitude is represented by the organization of data; the organization itself transmits a tone that interrupts rapport with the receiver.

Assume that you have news that is likely to please your receiver. If you postpone that news until the end of your message, your receiver may feel you have a "cat-and-mouse" attitude toward him or her. A person hungry for good news does not enjoy being teased. On the other hand, assume you have news which probably will disappoint your receiver. If you organize your data so that the bad news opens the message, your receiver may not forgive your lack of consideration for her or his feelings. As a result, your receiver may develop a negative attitude toward the disappointing data *and toward you* because of the way you organize the information. Struck by bad news at the beginning, your receiver may reject suggestions or counterproposals that you may offer later in the message. Again, the *organization* of your data contributes to the tone you transmit; and tone, as well as information, can influence a receiver's response.

Empathize with your receiver; which of the following messages would *you* prefer to receive?

GOODS NEWS BUT INAPPROPRIATE ORGANIZATION

Your loan application has been duly considered; I have been asked to notify you of the outcome.

Let me thank you for supplying all records necessary for a decision to be reached. That decision is in your favor, subject to the following terms.

Data Organization
1. Application considered
2. Decision reached
3. Cooperation acknowledged
4. Loan approved
5. Terms confirmed

Comments

Although this message is courteous, its organization teases the receiver by postponing welcome news. In this example the postponement is brief, but the receiver may be irritated by the "cat-and-mouse" attitude conveyed. If you have news likely to please your reader or listener, organize your message to convey that good news before supplying additional details.

GOOD NEWS AND APPROPRIATE ORGANIZATION

Your loan application has been approved; a confirmation of terms accompanies this note.

Thank you for supplying the documents that expedited this favorable decision.

Data Organization

1. Loan approved (This single item combines "application considered," "decision reached," and outcome.)
2. Terms confirmed
3. Cooperation acknowledged

Comments

Welcome news opens the message, immediately fortifying rapport. With this organization, the message avoids any connotation of a teasing, "cat-and-mouse" attitude. Having shared positive attitudes by tone as well as by data, the sender and the receiver can proceed easily to future transactions. Or the sender may develop the *present* message further; a proposal of other transactions could become Item 4 of the "Data Organization" list shown here.

BAD NEWS AND INCONSIDERATE ORGANIZATION

I regret to inform you that your loan application has not been approved.

Your request was given careful consideration, and we appreciate your interest in doing business with Midtown Bank. We suggest that you reapply when you have additional collateral.

Data Organization

1. Loan denied
2. Application duly considered
3. Interest in doing business acknowledged
4. Additional collateral needed before reapplying

Comments

Disappointing news opens the message, immediately stimulating negative feelings within the receiver. With this organization, the sender risks closing the receiver's mind to the courteous tone and to the constructive recommendation about additional collateral.

BAD NEWS BUT CONSIDERATE ORGANIZATION

Thank you for your interest in doing business with Midtown Bank.

Based upon careful consideration of your loan request, we offer this suggestion: additional collateral would improve the possibilities of approval. When it can be fortified with such collateral, please resubmit your application.

Data Organization

1. Interest in doing business acknowledged
2. Application duly considered
3. Constructive suggestion offered (connoting "no" and recommending a way of earning a possible "yes")

Comments

Neither positive nor negative news opens this message; the first sentence, courteous although noncommittal, avoids immediate disappointment that might have shut the reader's mind. With this organization, the message proceeds to reassure the receiver of careful attention to the request, thereby preparing the receiver's mind for the recommendation that follows. While *connoting* "no" to the request as it stands, the sender *denotes* the need of additional collateral. This message is organized so that the receiver can see how to change "no" into a possible "yes." The sender's positive attitude, conveyed by the data organization, is apt to elicit a reciprocal attitude (also positive) from the receiver.

As you have seen, data organization is an important ingredient of tone. An equally important ingredient is word choice.

To develop your communication ability, give deliberate attention to the words of people with whom you study or work, to the words you hear on television and radio broadcasts, to those you overhear in public places, and to those you read in books, newspapers, and magazines. Your goal is to acquire *vocabularies*. Why restrict yourself to "big" words or to "little" words, to technical or to general, to formal or to informal? As an effective communicator, you need to use all kinds. There will be times for you to use single and multiple syllables, times for formality and informality, times for technical jargon with those who understand it and for nontechnical language as well. Therefore decide first upon the tone that is appropriate to your message and its receiver; then choose your words to convey that tone. For example:

FORMAL TONE	INFORMAL TONE
approximately a decade	about ten years
ascertain an objective	set a goal
to explicate an occurrence	to explain what happened
unalterable conviction	firm belief
exercise caution	be careful

So far in this discussion, you have considered data organization and word choice—the ingredients of tone—separately. Now notice what happens when they are combined in various ways.

Combinations of Data and Tone

Business messages conveniently may be classified as those that say "yes," "no," or "maybe." But that classification usually summarizes what is conveyed by the message data rather than by the message tone. For instance, when you deny a request, your data *denotes* "no." Yet your tone can *connote* "yes," "maybe," or a reinforced "no" to the possibility of granting that request or a variation of it at another time. Whatever data you *denote*, you can organize your information and choose your words to *connote* positive, negative, mixed, or fairly neutral attitudes. You can deliberately use *tone* to convey your feelings toward your receiver, toward the request, toward the reasons for denying the request, and so on. Your data may say "no"; but your data *organization* and your word *choice* can safeguard your receiver's self-respect, thereby preserving rapport for future communication. Through *combinations* of data and tone you can influence your receiver's attitude and behavior. The diagram on page 92 indicates combinations of data and tone and their likely effect upon your receiver. Study the diagram before you read the examples which follow.

EXAMPLE OF A DATA ⊕ AND TONE ⊕ MESSAGE

Congratulations, Terry; you've earned a ten-percent raise in salary.

Since joining the Metrico organization last year, you have tackled hard-to-please accounts (Fedor, the Hahn Company, Joggerst Associates, among others); and you've succeeded in satisfying their requirements as well as Metrico's.

This note is an informal acknowledgement of your fine efforts, Terry. Clipped to it is the first of your increased paychecks.

Data Organization

1. Good news
2. Justification for good news
3. Acknowledgment of excellent work
4. Connotation of future rewards

Word Choice

Positive tone is conveyed by "congratulations," "you've earned a ten-percent raise in salary," "you have tackled hard-to-please accounts . . . and you've succeeded," "your fine efforts, Terry," "the first of your increased paychecks."

EXAMPLE OF A DATA ⊕ AND TONE ⊖ MESSAGE

It has come to my attention that your handling of the Fedor, Hahn, and Joggerst accounts, and others assigned to you, hasn't been unsatisfactory. You have not failed to fulfill our customers' requirements and our own during the twelve months of your employment with us.

Since your efforts should not go unrecognized, it is not without pleasure that I have authorized the ten-percent increase in your salary reflected by the enclosed paycheck, with the expectation that the quality of your work will not lessen.

DATA/TONE COMBINATIONS AND LIKELY EFFECTS

Notation: (+) = positive; (−) = negative; (+/−) = mixed; [0] = neutral

No.	Data as Perceived by Receiver	Tone as Perceived by Receiver	To Data	To Tone	To Message	To Sender
1.	(+)	(+)	(+)	(+)	(+)	(+)
2.	(+)	(−)	(+)	(−)	(+/−)	(+/−)
3.	(+)	(+/−)	(+)	(+) or (−) or (+/−)	(+) or (+/−)	(+/−)
4.	(+)	[0]	(+)	(+/−) or [0]	(+) or (+/−) or [0]	(+/−)
5.	(+/−)	(+)	(+/−)	(+) or (+/−)	(+) or (+/−)	(+/−)
6.	(+/−)	(−)	(+/−)	(−)	(+/−) or (−)	(−)
7.	(+/−)	(+/−)	(+/−)	(+/−)	(+/−)	(+/−)
8.	(+/−)	[0]	(+/−) or [0]	[0]	(+/−) or [0]	(+/−) or [0]
9.	[0]	(+)	(−) or (+/−) or [0]	(+) or (+/−)	(+) or (+/−)	(+/−)
10.	[0]	(−)	(−) or (+/−) or [0]	(−)	(−) or (+/−)	(−)
11.	[0]	(+/−)	(−) or (+/−) or [0]	(+/−)	(−) or (+/−)	(+/−)
12.	[0]	(+/−)	(−) or (+/−) or [0]	(+) or (+/−) or [0]	(−) or (+/−)	(+/−)
13.	(−)	(+)	(−)	(+) or (+/−)	(−) or (+/−)	(+/−)
14.	(−)	(−)	(−)	(−)	(−)	(−)
15.	(−)	(+/−)	(−)	(+) or (+/−)	(−) or (+/−)	(+/−)
16.	(−)	[0]	(−)	(+/−)	(+/−) or (−)	(−)

KEY
(+) = positive, affirmative
(−) = negative
(+/−) = mixed (positive and negative)
[0] = neutral (noncommittal, neither positive nor negative)

Data Organization

1. Acknowledgment of performance
2. Repeated acknowledgment of performance
3. Good news
4. Expectation of continuing quality

Word Choice

Negative tone is conveyed by "hasn't been unsatisfactory," "not failed to fulfill," "not go unrecognized," "not without pleasure," "will not lessen." Opening with "It has come to my attention that" suggests the sender's sense of self-importance but scarcely suggests the good news. The phrase "during the twelve months of your employment with us" momentarily suggests that the receiver may have lost his or her job.

EXAMPLE OF A DATA ⊖ AND TONE ⊖ MESSAGE

Although your handling of the accounts assigned to you during the past year has been competent, I regret to inform you that there is no possibility of a salary increase for you at this time.

Data Organization

1. Acknowledgment of competent performance
2. Bad news

Word Choice

Abruptly following recognition of accomplishment with words that denote disappointment is sure to stimulate negative feelings. Those negative feelings are reinforced by "regret to inform you . . . no possibility . . . ." The phrase "at this time" weakly connotes better possibilities later, but word choice and curtness combine to emphasize negative data by negative tone.

EXAMPLE OF A DATA ⊖ AND TONE ⊕ MESSAGE

You're right to review your salary prospects, Terry.

As you know, when you joined Metrico, you agreed to probationary terms for the first year of your employment. Those terms included the salary that you currently earn. Eight of the twelve probationary months have passed now, and you will be eligible for salary review in April. Continue your good work, and I'll gladly recommend a sizable increase in your paycheck then.

Data Organization

1. Mutually agreeable opening
2. Summary of reasons preparing receiver for temporary disappointment
3. Confirmation of present salary with reminder of possible raise soon
4. Recognition and encouragement of good work

Word Choice

Attention to receiver's needs and *you*-tone are highlighted by "You're right . . . Terry," "As you know, when you joined Metrico, you agreed," "you currently earn," "you will be eligible," "continue your good work," "increase in your paycheck then." The wording of the final sentence reinforces positive tone for the whole message. Data and word choice combine to remind the receiver of employment agreement, acknowledge receiver's performance, encourage continuing excellence of work, reaffirm possibility of increased reward when the probationary period ends.

As shown by the preceding examples, data organization and word choice are basic ingredients of message tone. Focus your attention more closely now upon the second of those basic ingredients: word choice.

Word Choice and Tone

Select your words; they stand for you. *Choose* your words; people take them as evidence of what you do, what you think, what you feel. That evidence is supplied abundantly by your choice of pronouns, of technical terms, and of words that convey criticism.

Pronoun Tone. This fact may be new to you: Few words affect the tone of business messages so often and so memorably as do pronouns. Business communicators generally should choose words with due care for content, denotation, and connotation. But pronouns require special attention; they particularly suggest a sender's self-concern or, much more profitably, a sender's ability to integrate self-concern with *receiver* needs.

To nourish your ego—and to risk losing rapport with your receiver—merely say *I, me, my,* or *mine* in almost every sentence you write or speak. You will thereby ventilate your sense of self-importance . . .and eventually alienate the most patient reader or listener. For example:

> I want to express my appreciation for the increase in sales reflected by the last quarterly report. I am pushing for even greater effort, but I want to emphasize that I'm pleased with last quarter's results. I expect the good work to continue; I want sales to keep increasing.

Notice that the sender's self-centered tone is scarcely changed by pluralizing *I* into *we, me* into *us, my* into *our,* or *mine* into *ours:*

> We want to express our appreciation for the increased sales reflected by the last quarterly report. We'll push for even greater effort, but we want to emphasize that we are pleased with last quarter's results. We expect the good work to continue; we want sales to keep increasing.

But *we, our,* or *ours* can bring sender and receiver closer together through occasional use of *you, your,* or *yours.*

Thanks for your help in increasing our sales last quarter. All of us need to push even more; but with efforts like yours, last quarter's results have pleased and encouraged us. Let's keep up the good work; let's continue increasing those sales.

The more often *you, your,* or *yours* is used, the likelier will the receiver become involved with the message. This "you-tone" can be reinforced by occasional use of the receiver's name, as illustrated in the following example:

Thank you, Lee, for your help in increasing sales last quarter. All of us need to push even more; but with efforts like yours, last quarter's results have pleased and encouraged us. You and I—all of us, Lee—need to keep up the good work. Let's continue increasing those sales.

Certainly *I, me, my, mine* are useful and often necessary words. The insight being stressed here is that when you use them, be aware of what you are doing, recognize their representation of your self-concern, and anticipate the attitudes they elicit as well as convey. Review these following probabilities:

1. Making *I, me, my,* and *mine* majority pronouns in your message will connote your self-centered attitude and may elicit a self-centered attitude from your receiver. Rapport can thereby be interrupted or blocked.
2. Simply pluralizing those pronouns into *we, us,* etc., will not change their egotistical tone.
3. Placing them in a context that includes *you, your,* and *yours* will connote an attitude of sender/receiver sharing.
4. Making *you*-words the majority pronouns of your message is the most likely way of attracting your receiver's attention and of developing your receiver's interest.

Pronouns also connote a sender's attitude toward sexism. If you believe in equal career opportunities for men and for women, choose pronouns that affirm your belief. For instance:

VERSION A: SEXIST BIAS

When you compose a business message, relate your words to your receiver's experiences and interests. Use terms familiar to him, terms that he will understand quickly. His response is likely to be: "Let's see what this man has to say."

VERSION B: SEXIST EQUALITY

When you compose a business message, relate your words to your receiver's experiences and interests. Use terms familiar to your receiver, terms that he or she will understand quickly. The response is likely to be: "Let's see what this person has to say."

Here are additional examples:

VERSION A	VERSION B
Dear Mr. Manager:	Dear Manager:
An executive knows the value of continuing education for himself and for his employees. He recognizes the need of updating information and modernizing office procedures.	Executives know the value of continuing education for themselves and for their employees. Executives recognize the need of updating information and modernizing office procedures.
Wanted: Teacher for new daycare center. Her credentials must include collegiate courses in educational psychology, and she should have had at least two years of child-care experience.	Wanted: Teacher for new daycare center. Required: Collegiate courses in educational psychology and at least two years of child-care experience.

A business firm contradicts itself when it announces equal-opportunity policies but conveys sexist bias through directives, instructions, correspondence, or reports. Word choice discloses such contradiction, and pronouns are an important part of word choice.

Notice that exclusion of male/female distinctions is not being advocated here. It is realistic and appropriate for feminine pronouns to characterize a message referring solely to women or for masculine pronouns to characterize a message referring solely to men. But freedom from sexist bias is realistic, appropriate, *and fair* for messages referring to people *as people*. Indeed, the choice of pronouns and other words tends to reflect personal and societal attitudes, not only toward human beings but also toward work specialization which increasingly affects our lives.

Technical Tone. As society becomes complex, those forms of specialized, technical, "insider's" vocabulary which are called *jargon* tend to multiply. Whether using technical or nontechnical terms, an effective communicator matches word choice to the people and the circumstances involved. For instance, your mentioning "cold-rolled steel," "capacitors," or "sintered carbides" is apt to be wasted effort unless you have reason to believe your reader or listener knows what those terms represent.

But specialized word choice—jargon—can convey a valuable and vivid tone when both the sender and the receiver understand it. "Insiders" of an occupation or a profession are often attracted to someone who "speaks their language," someone who uses "words of the trade." In fact, you may block communication if you choose common words to communicate with a person who expects specialized terms in your message. Conversely, if you use technical words with "outsiders," you can create rather than solve a communication problem. To be a successful communicator, fit your words to your reader or listener. Use terms that will be familiar to your receiver; explain your meaning of unfamiliar terms. As with almost every aspect of communication, empathy is a profitable guide to your choice of words. Let empathy guide your selection of pronouns, of technical and nontechnical language . . . and of words whereby you criticize.

Constructive Tone. These techniques of constructive criticism are useful:

1. Ask a question which implies the need of improvement and which guides your receiver toward the improvement.
2. Choose words that focus attention upon what is needed instead of upon your receiver's failure.

Here are examples of variations in critical tone:

DESTRUCTIVE TONE	CONSTRUCTIVE TONE	CONSTRUCTIVE TONE
You failed to type the second line of this memo.	Did I dictate the second line of this memo?	Please insert this second line and retype this memo.
I don't like your console design. You didn't put the control lever close enough to the power switch.	Would your console design be improved if you moved the control lever closer to the power switch?	Your console design would be excellent with the control level closer to the power switch.
You've ignored those instructions.	Have you followed those instructions?	Let's review those instructions; we need to follow them.

To develop a tone of constructive criticism, give praise where praise is due. Acknowledge accomplishments before focusing upon additional improvements. And whenever you can appropriately do so, word your criticism in the form of helpful questions, suggestions, requests, recommendations, or clear directives rather than as accusations.

REVIEW AND TRANSITION

Verbal intelligence, attitude, and tone are intimately related to successful communication through techniques of data organization and word choice. Those techniques involve empathy with the receiver as a basis for organizing information within a message, for recognizing pronouns as attitude reflectors, for using technical terms appropriately, and for conveying a constructive attitude when criticism is necessary.

Chapter 4 presented methods of planning, organizing, and developing business messages. Chapter 5 has emphasized evidence of a communicator's attitude toward the message and its receiver. Your study of

Chapter 6 will supply additional details for favorably impressing your receiver; Chapter 6 concentrates upon the physical appearance of a business message, particularly its format and layout.

DISCUSSION QUESTIONS

A. Based upon your study of Chapter 5, what are appropriate definitions and illustrations for these terms?

1. evidence
2. attitude
3. tone
4. verbal intelligence
5. denotation
6. connotation
7. context
8. verbosely
9. jargon
10. constructive criticism

B. In what ways is your attitude toward speaking like or unlike your attitude toward writing? What accounts for the similarity or difference of those attitudes? As a business communicator, which of those attitudes do you intend to change? What are your reasons for the change? Based upon your study of Chapter 5, what procedure will you use for making the change, and what results do you expect?

C. What was your attitude when you began reading the Chapter 5 section about pronouns and self-centered tone? about word choice and sexist equality? To what extent, if any, did your attitudes change as you continued studying those sections? What accounted for the change or the reinforcement of your attitudes?

D. What circumstances justify the use of jargon? When does the use of jargon block communication? What are examples of terms which once were jargon and now are generally understood?

E. What real-life incident elicited a negative attitude from you because of the tone with which you or your efforts were criticized? How have you overcome—or how do you plan to overcome—that negative attitude? What insights for constructive criticism have you derived from that real-life incident and from your study of Chapter 5?

APPLICATIONS

1. For each of the following sentences, write two paragraphs that illustrate change of meaning by change of context. For each of those paragraphs, identify denotation," "connotation," and "context" as illustrated by page 86.

a. Thank you for your interest in employment with Metrico, Inc.

b. Since joining this company two years ago, you have had several opportunities for advancement.

    c. The decision is based upon information that was submitted with your loan application.

    d. Payment on your account was received this morning.

    e. A refund check for $750 is enclosed.

2. Revise the following sentences to convey a conversational tone:

    a. I wish to take this opportunity of acknowledging your assistance.

    b. It is with pleasure that I inform you of your promotion to the position of assistant manager.

    c. You are urged to adhere to procedures prescribed in the manual.

    d. Should payment not be immediately forthcoming, it will be necessary to refer your account to a collection agency.

    e. This report is submitted with reference to the expansion of warehousing facilities in progress at the Moline plant.

    f. As regards the proposal to expand the Moline production facilities, please be advised that the decision is affirmative.

    g. Action has been taken to increase the amount of your salary by ten percent.

    h. A thorough study of available data discloses no basis for anticipating a downturn in the market at the present time.

    i. Increased sales volume in the order of magnitude of four percent is probable.

    j. It is requested that you submit your comments as regards the proposed packaging design.

3. Revise the following sentences to emphasize a "you-tone":

    a. I can't meet you Tuesday, but I'll be available Wednesday afternoon.

    b. We are pleased to acknowledge receipt of your inquiry.

    c. I checked and I found this answer to your question.

    d. We just want to say that we appreciate your business.

    e. We wish to acknowledge your recent order, and we promise shipment by February 7.

    f. We are happy to offer our Convention Center facilities for your industrial exposition; based on our past experience, we can provide the necessary display equipment.

    g. Our intention is to supply the best available merchandise for all of our customers, so be sure to shop with us soon.

    h. I want to take this opportunity to offer my congratulations and my best wishes to you.

    i. I'd like to acknowledge the excellent service that your field-catering staff made available to our construction crew at our Valdez Shoals site.

j. We are proud of our reputation; and, as has been our policy for the thirty years that we have been in business, we invite suggestions like yours for additional services that we might offer.

4. Revise these sentences to emphasize positive, affirmative tone:

   a. I don't mean to say that I disagree with you.

   b. Don't fail to submit that report by noon Friday.

   c. You probably won't receive that shipment before Monday afternoon.

   d. There's no way we can move our goods until the shipping strike ends, and we can't tell when that might be.

   e. No, I don't deny the merit of your idea.

   f. I haven't had time to locate that file yet.

   g. A salary increase is not unlikely.

   h. Don't neglect to repair that machine today.

   i. Didn't you tell them not to be late?

   j. If you need our services again, don't hesitate to call.

5. Revise these sentences to convey an attitude of sexist equality:

   a. A manager is supposed to be an idea man, and he must convey those ideas to other people.

   b. If someone has originality but does not transmit his ideas effectively, he limits his career opportunities.

   c. A verbose communicator often blocks rapport with his readers or listeners.

   d. Conversely, a communicator who uses only short, curt words may also lose the attention of his readers or his listeners.

   e. Unless you familiarize yourself with the goals of an employer, how can you relate your services to his needs?

   f. A buyer's personality and her roles in life determine sales strategy.

   g. A successful salesman not only expresses himself but also exchanges information with his customers based upon his awareness of their needs.

   h. Why should you communicate within the context of your *receiver's* self-concern? Why should you discuss your needs in terms of his needs, your proposals in terms of his benefits?

   i. Instead of asking a customer why she doesn't buy a certain product, market researchers sometimes ask her why she thinks other people buy it.

   j. An airline stewardess must be an expert communicator, especially with those of her passengers who are new to air travel.

k. These visual aids are designed to help every teacher with her classroom management.

l. The professional secretary is a vital member of the business team; she must be skilled in human relations as well as in office procedures.

6. Chapter 5 emphasizes the need of using *vocabularies* for effective communication. As an aid in developing your verbal intelligence and your word choice, "translate" these technical terms into nontechnical language:

a. abstract of title	**m.** computer "bit"
b. accounts payable	**n.** common stock
c. accounts receivable	**o.** condominium
d. acronym	**p.** consortium
e. actuary	**q.** debenture
f. ad valorem	**r.** escrow
g. amortization	**s.** fiduciary
h. annuity	**t.** loan co-maker
i. back order	**u.** par value
j. balance sheet	**v.** power of attorney
k. bill of lading	**w.** preferred stock
l. bona fide	**x.** surrogate

Now compose sentences that illustrate appropriate use of your "translations."

Effective Formats of Business Messages

Business communication involves various formats, or layouts, of written messages. The following are discussed in this chapter:

1. business letters
2. letter reports
3. office notes and message forms
4. memorandums
5. minutes of meetings
6. news releases
7. postal cards and reply cards
8. telegrams, mailgrams, cablegrams, and radiograms

Complementing this discussion, subsequent chapters provide details of visual/oral/multimedia communication. This book then focuses upon in-depth applications ranging from goodwill and order messages to more complex communications, including formal and informal reports.

BUSINESS LETTERS

The *appearance* of your message is the first stimulus your reader perceives. And first impressions endure.

What factors contribute to those impressions? Certainly those factors include stationery, letterhead design, layout style, and envelope selection.

Stationery

Unruled, firmly textured bond paper is normally used for business messages. The standard page size is 8½ by 11 inches. "Half sheets" of 8½ by 5½ inches sometimes are used for short messages; other sizes may be used occasionally for special purposes. Stationery colors may be pastels (light yellow, pale blue or green, perhaps tan or pink), but white remains most popular for business. To ensure a clear carbon impression, copies for office files are typewritten on onionskin or similar paper, thin but firm.

Letterheads and Envelopes

Letterheads are printed headings for business correspondence. A letterhead adds prestige to the business letter by its appropriateness and by its artistic quality in a simple design. Standard letterheads show the name, address, and telephone number of the sender's firm. Additional features may include the firm's identifying emblem, symbol, or logotype; a slogan or motto; cable or telex addresses; and branch addresses, often with their telephone numbers. The appropriate information for the letterhead usually occupies two to two-and-a-half inches at the top of the page.

Here are basic question-guides for evaluating letterhead effectiveness:

A LETTERHEAD RATING GUIDE

1. Is the data factually correct?
2. Are items clearly and quickly legible in an eye-pleasing arrangement?
3. If an emblem, a symbol, or a similar device appears, is it attractive and relevant to the firm's business role?
4. Are the addresses complete, including ZIP Code?
5. Are telephone numbers complete, including area codes for the convenience of out-of-town callers?
6. If colors are used, do they enhance legibility of data and visual appeal of the entire page?

Business envelopes customarily match their letterhead stationery in quality, texture, design, and color. Two common sizes of envelopes are designated No. 6 3/4 (which is 3 5/8 by 6 1/2 inches) and No. 10 (which is 4 1/8 by 9 1/2 inches). A No. 10 envelope accommodates multiple-paged letters or letters with enclosures. A No. 6 1/2 envelope (which is 3 1/2 by 6 inches) may be used for single-page letters on stationery of standard or of half-page size. Bulky mailings are sent in heavier envelopes of various sizes (commonly 6 by 9, 9 by 12, 10 by 13, or 10 by 15 inches).

The name and address of the *sender's* firm appear on the envelope as they do on the matching letterhead. Also, the *receiver's* name and address on the envelope are usually the same as on the letter itself. But the use of relatively new technology, involving Optical Character Recognition (OCR) equipment, requires special typing of envelope addresses so that

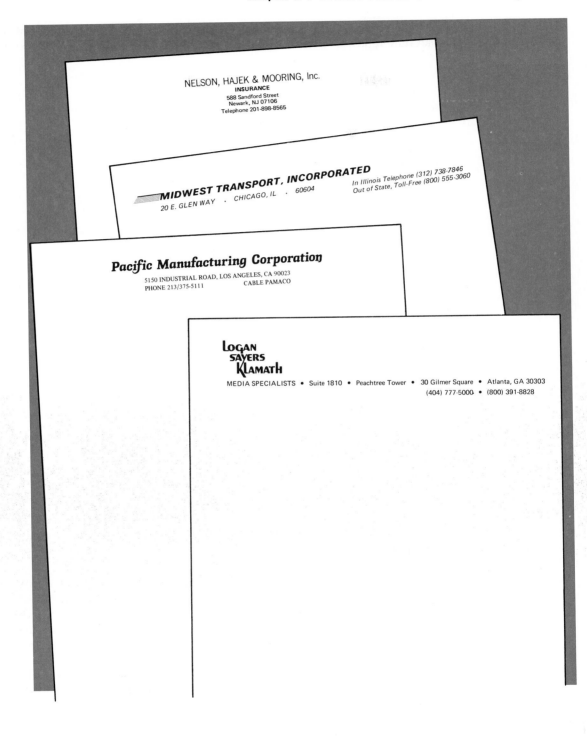

NELSON, HAJEK & MOORING, Inc.
INSURANCE
588 Sandford Street
Newark, NJ 07106
Telephone 201-898-8565

MIDWEST TRANSPORT, INCORPORATED
20 E. GLEN WAY · CHICAGO, IL · 60604
In Illinois Telephone (312) 738-7846
Out of State, Toll-Free (800) 555-3060

Pacific Manufacturing Corporation
5150 INDUSTRIAL ROAD, LOS ANGELES, CA 90023
PHONE 213/375-5111   CABLE PAMACO

LOGAN
SAYERS
KLAMATH
MEDIA SPECIALISTS ● Suite 1810 ● Peachtree Tower ● 30 Gilmer Square ● Atlanta, GA 30303
(404) 777-5000 ● (800) 391-8828

they can be sensed and processed by electronic machines. The table below shows OCR requirements for typical business-envelope sizes.

OCR REQUIREMENTS FOR ENVELOPE ADDRESSES

	No. 6¾	No. 10
Readable zone	2″ from top; 2½″ from left	2½″ from top; 4″ from left
Clear zone (no printing to appear)	½″ above, ⅝″ to the left of address; entire area below and to the right of address	Same as for No. 6¾
Return address (if type-written)	Block, single-spaced, Line 2 from top edge, 3 spaces from left edge	Same as for No. 6¾
Addressee notations (Hold for Arrival, Personal, etc.)	3 line spaces below return address, 3 spaces from left edge	Same as for No. 6¾
Mailing notations (Airmail, Special Delivery, Registered)	Below the stamp area, but at least ½″ above address	Same as for No. 6¾

Part Nine, which is a detailed reference section in this book, gives specific typewriting instructions for envelopes. Two examples are shown on page 108.

Correspondence Formats

For effective appearance of your business letters, use the following guides and those explained in Part Nine.

"Picture-Frame" Guide. Position your message so that the margins frame it evenly. Use side and bottom margins of about the same width so that your message, under its letterhead, resembles a picture placed in an attractive frame. Whatever the size of your stationery and whatever the length of your message, this "picture-frame" guide elicits reader attention and interest, as shown by examples on pages 113-114.

The "picture-frame" guide applies to stationery of standard or of unusual shape and design. Suppose, for example, that a column of printed data extends down the left margin of a letterhead sheet. In that column

Business Letterheads and Envelopes

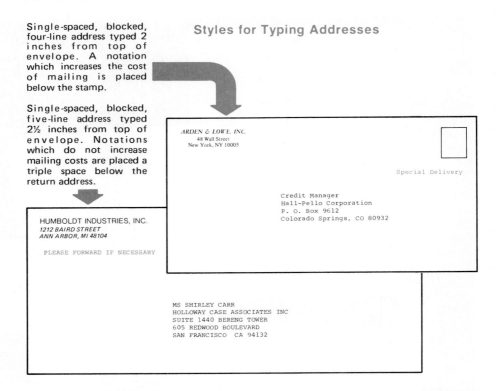

Styles for Typing Addresses

Single-spaced, blocked, four-line address typed 2 inches from top of envelope. A notation which increases the cost of mailing is placed below the stamp.

Single-spaced, blocked, five-line address typed 2½ inches from top of envelope. Notations which do not increase mailing costs are placed a triple space below the return address.

ARDEN & LOWE, INC.
48 Wall Street
New York, NY 10005

Special Delivery

Credit Manager
Hall-Pello Corporation
P. O. Box 9612
Colorado Springs, CO 80932

HUMBOLDT INDUSTRIES, INC.
1212 BAIRD STREET
ANN ARBOR, MI 48104

PLEASE FORWARD IF NECESSARY

MS SHIRLEY CARR
HOLLOWAY CASE ASSOCIATES INC
SUITE 1440 BERENG TOWER
605 REDWOOD BOULEVARD
SAN FRANCISCO CA 94132

may be branch-office addresses, lists of executive personnel, names of committee members, or the like. With such a format, simply move your message slightly to the right and frame it in the remaining space. Or if lines of printed data extend across the bottom of the sheet, just move your message upward, again framing it in the available space.

With a message too long for attractive framing on a single sheet, leave wider than usual margins for the "picture," use a second sheet with those same wide margins, and typewrite a heading for that second sheet (or, third, fourth, etc.), as shown here:

BLOCK STYLE

Mr. Daniel W. Binford
Page 2
March 12, 19—

(Note: Binford is the *receiver's* name.)

HORIZONTAL STYLE

Mr. Daniel W. Binford   2   March 12, 19—

Letter Parts. The following list of business-letter components shows their usual order of appearance in a message. Standard parts are identified here by *ITALICIZED CAPITALS*; special parts are identified here by parentheses ( ).

LETTERHEAD	Sender's company name, address including ZIP Code, telephone number including area code, cable address, company slogan, branch locations, etc.
MESSAGE DATE	Month, day, year
(Transmission or Classification Note)	"Special Delivery," "Confidential," "Personal," etc.
INSIDE ADDRESS	Receiver's name, job title, department, company name, address including ZIP Code
(Attention Line)	Used infrequently, this line shows the receiver's name if the inside address omits that name.
SALUTATION	The first line of the inside address governs the salutation. For instance, Mr. A. B. Ross would be saluted as "Dear Mr. Ross"; Mrs. A. B. Ross as "Dear Mrs. Ross"; Miss A. B. Ross as "Dear Miss Ross"; Ms. A. B. Ross as "Dear Ms. Ross" (*Ms.* stands for *Miss* or for *Mrs*); Dr. A. B. Ross as "Dear Dr. Ross," etc. If the first line of the inside address is a job title instead of a person's name, the salutation would be "Dear Sir or Madam" or, for up-to-date usage avoiding sexist discrimination, "Dear [Job Title]" as with "Dear Personnel Manager," "Dear Sales Supervisor," or the like. If the first line of the inside address is the name of a company or of a unit within the company, the salutation has traditionally been "Gentlemen" but is now being replaced by "Ladies and Gentlemen" as at the start of a formal speech to an audience.
	In private correspondence, the salutation ends with a comma; in private correspondence, the complimentary close (placed just above the sender's signature) also ends with a comma. But in *business* correspondence either of two punctuation

styles is used for those parts of a letter: *Open style* omits punctuation after both the salutation and the complimentary close. *Mixed* style places a colon at the end of the salutation and a comma at the end of the complimentary close. Remember: If you do not put a colon after a salutation, place no comma after the complimentary close. If you put a colon after the salutation, place a comma after the complimentary close.

(Subject Line)

This special part is a sentence fragment that states the message corethought or identifies the message reference. For instance:

SUBJECT: Your June 12 Request for Kopar Samples
Subject: Your June 12 Request for Kopar Samples

REFERENCE: Insurance Policy No. 188-66-0215
Reference: Insurance Policy No. 188-66-0215

MESSAGE BODY

Paragraphs between those parts already identified and the complimentary close constitute the message body.

COMPLIMENTARY CLOSE

"Yours truly," "Yours very truly," "Very truly yours," are now considered stereotyped and undistinguished. "Sincerely," "Sincerely yours," "Yours sincerly," "Cordially," "Cordially yours," "Yours very cordially," and the like, convey preferable nuances of tone. Word your complimentary close to suggest what you want your reader to recognize as the prevailing tone of your message. Participial wording like "Thanking you in advance, I remain" or "Hoping to receive your prompt reply, we are" were once popular transitions to the complimentary close; but such participial transitions are considered obsolete in U.S. correspondence today. Move your reader directly from the last paragraph of your message body to your complimentary close.

(Company Name)

This special part is seldom used today; the printed letterhead makes it unnecessary.

SIGNATURE BLOCK

This standard part consists of the sender's signature and usually the typed counterpart of that signature; also, sender's title and/or sender's unit within the company.

REFERENCE INITIALS

This line usually gives the initial letters of the transcriber's or typist's name.

(Enclosure Notation)

This special part is used to indicate material which accompanies the letter and may appear in these ways:

Enclosure
Enclosure: Price List
Encl.: Price List
Enclosures: 2
Enclosures: Price List
              Order Form
Encls.: Price List
        Order Forms
        Catalog Supplement

(Copy Notation)

Used to indicate message copies and their receivers, "cc" stands for "carbon copy" or "carbon copies"; the counterpart notation for photographic copies is "pc"—as in these examples:

cc Mr. D. L. Grey
pc M. O. Safie
   T. C. Wolsey

When such a notation appears on a copy but not on the original message, "bcc" for "blind carbon copy" or "bpc" for "blind photocopy" is used:
bcc Sara Fisher
bpc Security Office

Because "bpc" is a relatively new abbreviated notation, it is acceptable to write the full notation:
Blind Photocopy to Security Office.

(Postscript or P.S.)

Rarely used in business to add what probably should be part of the message body, a postscript *occasionally* conveys emphasis or a personal comment. For example:
This sale ends on September 5. Place your order now!

                   or

Almost forgot: Bring the Randall file with you.

Letter Styles. Examples on pages 113-114 explain and illustrate these four business-letter styles:

—block
—modified block
—modified block with indented paragraphs
—AMS Simplified

They are the correspondence styles most frequently used by U.S. business people.

Of the various formats for business letters, *modified block* is the most widely used. In *modified block*

the message dateline ordinarily is
—begun at the horizontal center of the page
—or typed to end at the right margin

paragraphs are typewritten
—with no indentation (except for lists)
—or with the first line of every paragraph indented five to ten spaces (and with additional indentation for lists)

complimentary close and signature block are started
—at the horizontal center
—or to end at the right margin

Because of its popularity, the *modified block* style is illustrated again on pages 116-117, with mixed punctuation and with a review of standard business-letter parts. This illustration also shows a printed letterhead which is begun at the top of a page and completed at the bottom.

Form Letters

Identical or nearly identical messages, based on a master draft and sent to more than one person, are called *form letters*. The number of copies to be mailed depends upon the task and the budget for each message. Form letters often are used for these purposes:

1. to represent single sales messages, series of such messages, and units in a follow-up system
2. to answer inquiries and requests
3. to acknowledge orders and remittances
4. to handle simple claims and adjustments
5. to serve as units in collection procedures
6. generally, to function as messages when personally dictated correspondence is not necessary

Block Style

Open punctuation is shown here; mixed punctuation may be used instead.

DAVIS, BECKWORTH & HINTON
Management Consultants

Suite 660, 1202 Sixteenth Street, NW   •   Washington, DC 20036   Telephone (202) 555-3700

February 1, 1978

Ms. Harriet Nicole Marais
Conference Coordinator
Center for Continuing Education
1803 Thibodaux Boulevard
New Orleans, Louisiana 70122

Dear Ms. Marais:

Subject: Your January 27 Request for Letter-Style Handout Materials

This letter and its enclosures are for your use at your Annual Communication Seminar. DB&H is glad to assist you by supplying four examples
of business-correspondence styles.

The letter you are now reading illustrates block style, which has these
features:

1. Every typewritten line--including message date line, complimentary
close, and signature block--begins at the left typing margin.

2. The salutation and the complimentary close may be punctuated in
mixed style (with colon following salutation and comma after complimentary close) or in open style (no punctuation after these parts except
for abbreviations, such as Jr., Sr., M.D., Ph.D., and the like).

3. This format facilitates typewriting speed. A visual disadvantage,
however, is that the letter appears to be "heavy on the left side"
rather than balanced "on the center" of the page.

Block style has gained favor, perhaps because its format saves typing
time. The first of the enclosed samples shows a popular variation of
this format.

Sincerely yours

Benjamin C. Hinton III

Benjamin C. Hinton III
Vice-President, Training Services

HBR

Enclosures: Format Illustrations

Modified Block Style

Open punctuation is shown here; mixed puncutation may be used instead.

DAVIS, BECKWORTH & HINTON
Management Consultant

Suite 660, 1202 Sixteenth Street, NW   •   Washington, DC 20036   Telephone (202) 555-3700

February 1, 19---

Ms. Harriet Nicole Marais
Conference Coordinator
Center for Continuing Education
1803 Thibodaux Boulevard
New Orleans, IA 70122

Dear Ms. Marais

This letter illustrates modified block style, which has the following features:

1. Message date, complimentary close, and signature block begin at the
horizontal center.

2. All other parts appear in block form (beginning at the left typing margin).

3. Salutation and complimentary close may have either mixed or open punctuation.

4. An advantage of modified block style is the appearance of "balancing" the
message for eye appeal.

5. Visual balance, however, does require the typist to use tab stops for message
date, complimentary close, and signature block, thereby slightly increasing
message-production time.

The next letter in this series illustrates still another format variation.

Yours for communication success

B.C. Hinton III

B. C. Hinton III
Vice-President, Training Services

hbr

cc R. E. Gould

DAVIS, BECKWORTH & HINTON
Management Consultants
Suite 660, 1202 Sixteenth Street, NW   •   Washington, DC 20036   Telephone (202) 555-3700

February 1, 19—

SPECIAL DELIVERY

Ms. Harriet Nicole Marais
Conference Coordinator
Center for Continuing Education
1803 Thibodaux Boulevard
New Orleans, LA 70122

Dear Ms. Marais:

This letter shows modified block style with indented paragraphs.

Please notice that, as with the preceding example, the message, date, complimentary close, and signature block begin at the horizontal center. In this illustration, a colon follows the salutation and a comma follows the complimentary close; mixed punctuation is being used here, but open punctuation is permissible instead.

This format resembles modified block except that paragraphs in the message body are indented five to ten spaces as shown here. Lists, also, are indented, as by this inventory of styles already shown:

1. Block Style

2. Modified Block Style

3. Modified Block Style with Indented Paragraphs

Modified block style with indented paragraphs provides visual variety for the reader while emphasizing the beginning of paragraph units. Its disadvantage is the slightly increased production time needed for indenting paragraphs.

The next, and final, letter in this series, written for you by Isabel Blair, Executive Vice-President, DB&H, shows an innovative format recommended by the Administrative Management Society.

                Cordially yours,

                Benjamin C. Hinton III

                Benjamin C. Hinton III
                Vice-President
                Training Services

hbr

The illustration you are now reading shows the use of a postscript and a transmission notation for special delivery.

DAVIS, BECKWORTH & HINTON
Management Consultants
Suite 660, 1202 Sixteenth Street, NW   •   Washington, DC 20036   Telephone (202) 555-3700

February 1, 19—

Ms. Harriet Nicole Marais
Conference Coordinator
Center for Continuing Education
1803 Thibodaux Boulevard
New Orleans, LA 70122

EXAMPLE OF AMS SIMPLIFIED FORMAT

As you see, Ms. Marais, the AMS Simplified format minimizes typewriting time and has these characteristics:

1. A subject line (typed in ALL-CAPITAL LETTERS) is required. The subject line is typed a triple space below the inside address. The first line of the message body is typed a triple space below the subject line.

2. Salutation and complimentary close are omitted.

3. Almost all lines, including the first line of numbered items in a list, begin at the left typing margin. But unnumbered items in a list are indented five spaces from the left typing margin.

4. The writer's name and title (or name and unit designation) are typed in ALL-CAPITAL LETTERS on one line at least four spaces below the message body.

Advantages and disadvantages of AMS Simplified include those of traditional block style. Additionally, AMS Simplified greatly facilitates typing speed. However, omission of the salutation and of the complimentary close may suggest an unintended curtness of tone. To offset some of that curtness, the receiver's name is mentioned in the first line of the message body.

You have now examined four business-letter formats:

        Block Style
        Modified Block Style
        Modified Block Style with Indented Paragraphs
        AMS Simplified Style

For additional details please consult Part Nine of Wolf, Keyser, and Aurner's Effective Communication in Business, 7th ed., South-Western Publishing Co.. Incorporated.

                Isabel Blair

ISABEL BLAIR, EXECUTIVE VICE-PRESIDENT

hbr

Modified Block Style with Indented Paragraphs

AMS Simplified Style

Mixed punctuation is shown here; open punctuation may be used instead.

Advantages. The form letter has these notable advantages:

1. *It multiplies skill.* An expert communicator can prepare master forms, adapt them to a specific situation, and give precise instructions for their use. Then less experienced communicators, guided by the originator's expertise and by proper supervision, can use the forms efficiently for numerous business situations.
2. *It widens coverage.* Many forms may be machine-produced and sent simultaneously over large geographical areas. The style of the form can be made to convey personalized attention to an individual reader, whose particular name and address can help to "personalize" the form.
3. *It saves cost.* One master draft of a form letter can be reproduced, virtually without limit, at relatively low unit cost. Individually dictated messages, as emphasized at the beginning of this book, are expensive.

Automated typewriters and electronic communication systems, fed by specially prepared cards or tapes, have increased enormously the business uses of form messages.

Types. Form messages involve use of these communication aids: guide forms, complete forms, and paragraph forms.

The *guide form* consists of a detailed outline and/or a model message based upon such an outline. The communicator uses the guide form as a reference for message content and format. For example, suppose you ask your professor to write an employment recommendation on your behalf. Yours may be one of many similar requests which your professor receives every year. To expedite communication, your professor may compose a message guide form identifying the teacher-student association, the length of that association, the number and nature of courses involved, your performance in each of those courses, and other appropriate data for recommending you to a prospective employer. Using the guide form would ensure that every recommendation written by the professor includes those categories of information, but the particular data used for the letter recommending *you* would apply to your circumstances specifically. In this example, your professor uses a guide form to organize a frequently recurring type of communication that he or she writes *but which can be adapted as needed* to personalize each recommendation message individually.

The *complete form*, however, is an entire message sent without adaptation or revision. The complete form may be imprinted on letterhead paper in a single impression by xerography, by multigraph, or by typewriter facsimile produced in a printing shop. If a complete form is to be reproduced as an individually typewritten message, the form often is given a key number. The communicator then specifies the key number, identifies the addressee, and the correspondence assistant produces the already prepared message.

The *paragraph form* consists of a group of related sentences that can be combined as units of a message. The paragraphs can be fitted so closely

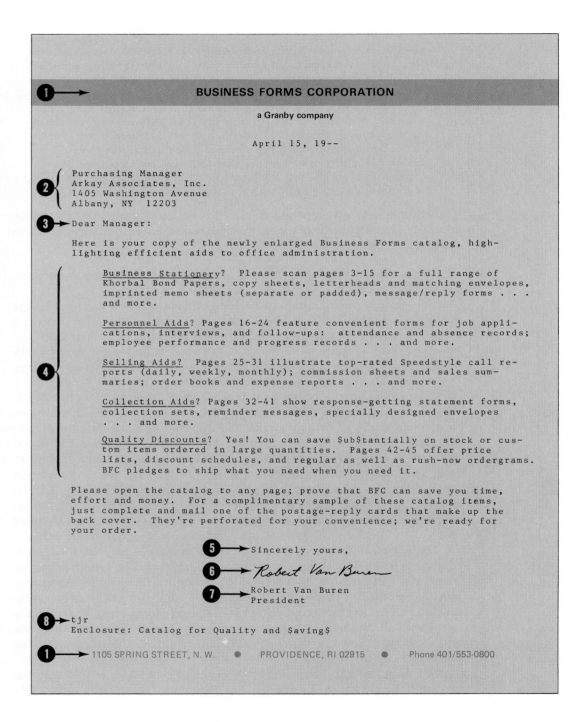

① → BUSINESS FORMS CORPORATION

a Granby company

April 15, 19--

② Purchasing Manager
Arkay Associates, Inc.
1405 Washington Avenue
Albany, NY 12203

③ → Dear Manager:

Here is your copy of the newly enlarged Business Forms catalog, high-
lighting efficient aids to office administration.

④

> <u>Business Stationer</u>y? Please scan pages 3-15 for a full range of
> Khorbal Bond Papers, copy sheets, letterheads and matching envelopes,
> imprinted memo sheets (separate or padded), message/reply forms . . .
> and more.
>
> <u>Personnel Aids</u>? Pages 16-24 feature convenient forms for job appli-
> cations, interviews, and follow-ups: attendance and absence records;
> employee performance and progress records . . . and more.
>
> <u>Selling Aids?</u> Pages 25-31 illustrate top-rated Speedstyle call re-
> ports (daily, weekly, monthly); commission sheets and sales sum-
> maries; order books and expense reports . . . and more.
>
> <u>Collection Aids</u>? Pages 32-41 show response-getting statement forms,
> collection sets, reminder messages, specially designed envelopes
> . . . and more.
>
> <u>Quality Discounts</u>? Yes! You can save ubtantially on stock or cus-
> tom items ordered in large quantities. Pages 42-45 offer price
> lists, discount schedules, and regular as well as rush-now ordergrams.
> BFC pledges to ship what you need when you need it.

Please open the catalog to any page; prove that BFC can save you time,
effort and money. For a complimentary sample of these catalog items,
just complete and mail one of the postage-reply cards that make up the
back cover. They're perforated for your convenience; we're ready for
your order.

⑤ → Sincerely yours,

⑥ → *Robert Van Buren*

⑦ → Robert Van Buren
President

⑧ → tjr
Enclosure: Catalog for Quality and $aving$

① → 1105 SPRING STREET, N. W.   ●   PROVIDENCE, RI 02915   ●   Phone 401/553-0800

AN ATTRACTIVE LETTER IN MODIFIED BLOCK STYLE

Arrange the parts so that they are framed evenly by margins in eye-pleasing proportion to sheet size.

1. **Heading.** The heading shows the place and date of message origin. On a printed letterhead, only the date is typed, usually from 12 to 20 lines from the top of the sheet, depending upon the length of the letter. With plain paper, the writer's complete mailing address and the date are typed from 1½ to 2 inches from the top of the sheet, starting at the horizontal center.

2. **Inside Address.** This address includes the receiver's name, title, company unit (if used); name of the receiver's firm; its street, city, state, and ZIP code number. All lines are blocked at the left margin, starting on the fourth line space below the date.

3. **Salutation.** The complimentary greeting that begins a letter is typed at the left margin a double space below the last line of the address.[1]

4. **Body.** Material between the salutation and the complimentary close is started a double space below the *salutation*, single-spaced with double spacing between paragraphs.

5. **Complimentary Close.** The complimentary close is typed a double space below the last line of the body.

6 and 7. **Signature.** The signature line may consist only of the name of the writer typed on the fourth line below the complimentary close [2] or may include the writer's official title. The title may follow the typed name and a comma; or it may be typed on the next line space, blocked with the name and the complimentary close.

8. **Reference Initials.** The initials of the typist or transcriber are typed at the left margin even with or two line spaces below the typed signature.[3] Some dictators prefer only a handwritten signature, with the typed name appearing at the left margin before the reference initials. The usual style for this practice is AJSmith/rs.

---

[1] Special letter parts, such as the *attention line*, the *subject line*, and the *reference line* are discussed and illustrated on pages 494 and 495 in Part Nine.

[2] Some firms still show the company name in all-capital letters a double space below the complimentary close. This practice is unnecessary when the company name appears in the letterhead.

[3] Variations in spacing and positioning letter parts are given on pages 489-505 of Part Nine.

to particular needs that they give the effect of personalized dictation. Using careful judgment, the communicator can join paragraph forms into almost limitless patterns that suit differing circumstances.

Paragraph forms (and complete forms) often are grouped in a book-like collection called a *dictaform*. Every paragraph is customarily keyed by the number of the page on which it falls and by an alphabetical letter. The paragraphs are grouped under subject headings—for example, headings for sales promotion, credit approval or rejection, collection, and so on. Every subject heading may have a certain number of pages reserved in the *dictaform*, as shown by this example:

DICTAFORM (OR FORM BOOK) INDEX

Subjects	Pages
Administrative Reporting	2-14
Acknowledging Customer Orders	15-20
Promoting Sales	21-33
Following Up on Sales	34-42
Responding to Credit Requests	43-52
Responding to Adjustment Requests	53-61
Enforcing Collections	62-75
Goodwill Messages for Special Occasions	76-85

Every page of the dictaform presents a group of paragraphs. Each paragraph is designated A, B, C, etc. The dictator scans the dictaform, selects the paragraphs needed, and constructs a complete message by jotting down the symbols; for instance, 7A, 9C, 11D, 12K, 14E. The secretarial assistant then copies the paragraphs in the order indicated.

Assume that you wish to construct a sales-promotion message from the dictaform indexed on this page. You would turn, in this illustration, to pages 21-33 ("Promoting Sales") of the form book. Pages 21-24 offer paragraphs for attracting your reader's attention; perhaps you select 21A (paragraph A from page 21):

To meet your requirements for rapid and reliable investment services, Foster & Schuyler offers you a new Commodity Section geared to prompt, personalized attention.

Pages 25-27 of the form book show a group of paragraphs designed to develop your reader's interest; may be you select 26F:

These Foster & Schuyler aids to decision are at your disposal:
   —detailed briefings on markets with notable potential
   —weekly summaries of trading patterns and price outlooks
   —modern telecommunication equipment for up-to-the-second data

Pages 28-30 present paragraphs for stimulating and reinforcing your reader's desire; you choose 29C, 30A, and 30E:

With Foster & Schuyler you can monitor Exchange developments as they occur.

With Foster & Schuyler you can share instantaneous reports from worldwide news services.

With Foster & Schuyler you can profit from the advice of professional account executives who have experience and insight.

Pages 31-33 provide paragraphs for eliciting favorable response, "action-getting" paragraphs; you select 31J:

Because speculation in commodity futures can be risky, you need sufficient capital to offset possible reverses. And you need *current* information, . . . which F&S is ready to supply. For that information, please visit our office or telephone (214) 717-0800.

Having chosen your paragraphs from the dictaform, you dictate their index symbols: 21A, 26F, 29C, 30A, 30E, 31J. Your transcriber turns to the dictaform, locates those paragraphs, and writes them in the order you indicated. An automated typewriter can be programmed to do the job in seconds. More extensive electronic systems also can be used for programmed production of such messages on a very large scale.

An example of the result appears below.

Dear Investor

21A To meet your requirements for rapid and reliable investment servies, Foster & Schuyler offers you a new Commodity Section geared to prompt, personalized attention.

26F These Foster & Schuyler aids to decision are at your disposal:
    —detailed briefings on markets with notable potential
    —weekly summaries of trading patterns and price outlooks
    —modern telecommunication equipment for up-to-the-second data

29C With Foster & Schuyler you can monitor Exchange developments as they occur.

30A With Foster & Schuyler you can share instantaneous reports from worldwide news services.

30E With Foster & Schuyler you can profit from the advice of professional account executives who have experience and insight.

31J Because speculation in commodity futures can be risky, you need sufficient capital to offset possible reverses. And you need *current* information . . .which F&S is ready to supply. For that information, please visit our office or telephone (214) 717-0800.

Sincerely yours

LETTER REPORTS

Business reports are oral, written, visual, or multimedia messages intended to convey information for decision and for use. This broad communication category includes reports as conversations, demonstrations, letters, memos, fill-in forms, many-paged documents, or other kinds of message formats. For convenience and for records management, reports may be classified according to their

—length (short, medium, long)
—tone (informal, semiformal, formal)
—subject matter (accounting, administrative, marketing, technical)
—timing (daily, weekly, interim)
—importance (routine, special, urgent)
—stylistic emphasis (narrative, descriptive, pictorial, statistical)
—intended distribution (interoffice, intracompany, public, private)

and in many other ways as well.

Many modern business reports are informal or semiformal. Examples would be reports in correspondence format, such as those on pages 121 and 122.

OFFICE NOTES AND MESSAGE FORMS

Perhaps the least formal kind of written business message is a brief note of information requiring no permanent record. Here is an example:

```
                                6/30/--
                                9:30 a.m.

        Gina, the personnel meeting is at

        2:30 this afternoon, Simm's office.

        Please be there.

                            FSW
```

LAMAR & LEONARD, INC.
INVESTMENT ADVISERS
SUITE 1127, FAIRFIELD BUILDING
19 SIMMONS SQUARE NORTH
BOSTON, MA 02115
(617) 833-7073

August 12, 19--

<u>Personal</u>

Mrs. Corrine V. Martin
220 Loraine Avenue
Orono, ME   04473

Dear Mrs. Martin

In accordance with your standing instructions, here is an informal
report of established firms offering attractive investment opportunities.
Supporting financial details concerning these companies, as well as the
relevant NYSE or AMEX closing quotations of this date, are enclosed.

   1. AMB CORPORATION, 659 MELLON PLAZA, PITTSBURGH, PA 15230

       Manufactures alloys, forgings, valves, oil-tool products. Has
       production and repair facilities in Erie, Penn.; Charleston,
       W. Va.; Gary, Ind.; Flint, Mich.; Tulsa, Okla,; Dallas, Tex.
       Has announced plans for new maintenance and repair installations
       in Valdez, Ala.

   2. ANCON, INC., 1010 MARKET STREET, WILMINGTON, DE 19898

       Produces industrial control systems and electronic components.
       Has plants in New Castle, Del.; St. Louis, Mo.; Long Beach,
       Calf. May establish branch operations in Waterbury, Conn.

   3. C&D CLARK COMPANY, INC., 211 BROAD STREET, PHILADELPHIA, PA
      19107

       Manufactures agricultural and industrial equipment. Has plants
       in Allentown, Penn.; Moline, Ill.; Louisville, Ky.; Negotiating
       for additional site at Omaha, Neb.

To discuss details of these issues, please call on me at your convenience.

Sincerely
R. A. Shaw
R. A. Shaw, Vice-President

lw
Enclosures

A Report in Correspondence Format

Mr. Douglas H. Campbell, Jr.   2   April 11, 19--

As you know, the schedule you assigned for this inspection tour will take me next to Oregon and then to Nevada. I plan to be back at the Memphis home office by April 19, which should allow sufficient time to prepare a formal, comprehensive report for your presentation at the next Executive Committee meeting.

Travel reservation have been reconfirmed as follows:

April 12-14, Speers Motel, Portland, OR 97202 (Tel. 503-555-8100)
    14-15, Van Fleet Inn, Reno, NV 89507 (Tel. 702-311-8501)
    17-18, Carr-Johnson Hotel, 4506 Maryland Parkway,
    Las Vegas, NV 89154 (Tel. 702-827-1145)

See you both on the 19th
Fran Frazier
Fran Frazier

En Route, West Coast
April 11, 19--

Mr. Douglas Campbell, Jr.
Assistant to the President
CMK Enterprises
969 Madison Avenue
Memphis, TN 33104

Dear Mr. Campbell

Your mailgram greeted my arrival here. Thank you for acknowledging my reports from Oklahoma City and Albuquerque. I'm happy to know that the Executive Committee has found the data useful.

This letter supplies preliminary information concerning the third potential franchising area which you instructed me to visit.

ORANGE COUNTY, CALIFORNIA

Population: Now approaching two million residents (contrasted to about 212,000 in 1950). Orange County encompasses 26 big cities, including Anaheim, Santa Ana, Huntington Beach, and Garden Grove.

Area: This 782-square-mile county extends 25 miles inland from the Pacific Ocean to Cleveland National Forest, with a 42-mile coastline from Long Beach to San Clemente and Camp Pendleton.

Money Picture: The median family income is $16,940 annually. Spendable is estimated at slightly more than $10.5 billion annually. Retail sales were $5.5 billion last year.

Transport: The area has six major freeways, countywide bus service, and a modern airport.

Educational and Cultural Facilities: Orange County has 2 tax-supported universities; 4 private colleges; 6 community colleges; 50 high schools; 52 city and county libraries; a symphony orchestra; light opera and ballet companies; 32 community theater groups; 4 art museums; numerous artistic and scientific expositions, exhibits, and displays at community centers.

Employment: Last year about 150,000 people worked at manufacturing; 14,000 at trade; 112,000, services; 94,000, government; 31,000, finance-travel-real estate; 24,000, construction; 19,000, transportation and communications; 12,000, agriculture.

WOODWYN HOTELS • California • Arizona • New Mexico • Texas • Louisiana

A Report in Correspondence Format

Although informal, such notes expedite intracompany communication. They may be typed or handwritten (legibly); they may be printed forms which the sender merely completes.

Do not treat office notes casually; write them accurately, clearly, and understandably, as you would other business messages in terms of communication effectiveness. Remember that although your notes may be informal, your reader will use them for decisions and actions.

To _____ LNA _____

Date __ 3/14-- _____ Time __ 11:05 a.m. ____

Caller/Visitor's Name __ Vera Weiss _____

Of ____ World Trade Associates _____

Phone No. ___ 666-5800, Ext. 1210 _____

✓	Telephoned	✓	Please Call
	Called To See You		Will Call Again
	Is Waiting To See You		Returned Your Call
	Wants To See You	✓	Rush

Message __ She needs the promo for _____

_____ International Business Week. _____

FROM THE DESK OF

R. K. DUMAS

Herb—   9/14--

Here are five sketches
for the Quenepa ads.
What are your
comments?

Rita

Interoffice messages often are on fill-in forms, asking and answering questions about administrative functions. For example:

1. **PERSONNEL ACTION**—Employee identification (name, address, telephone number, social security number)? Employment status (temporary, permanent, part-time, full-time, title or job classification, unit assignment)? Payroll status (pay rate, number of dependents, hospitalization and other special benefits)? Copies of such a message probably would go the personnel, payroll, accounting, and other offices concerned as well as to the employee.

2. **AUTHORIZED OVERTIME WORK**—Employee identification (name, department, sub-unit if applicable)? Circumstances of special work (job or project, location, duration, justification)? Copies of this message, also, would flow to and from the people concerned within the organization.

3. **ABSENCE REPORTS**—Employee identification and details of absence (dates and hours, with or without authorization)? Reasons for absence (injury, illness, personal matters)? Again, message copies would flow along multidirectional channels within the firm.

The illustration of a fill-in form below shows the use of check spaces for correspondence instructions.

```
┌─────────────────────────────────────────────────────┐
│   MARTCO, INC.    ·    Correspondence                 │
│                        Instructions                   │
│                      Date_____             │
│  Refer To _____         │
│          Indicate Purpose by Check Mark:              │
│  ☐  RUSH — Immediate action desired.                  │
│  ☐  Your comments, please.                            │
│  ☐  Please note and see me about this — —AM — —PM.    │
│  ☐  Please answer, sending me copy of your reply.     │
│  ☐  Please prepare reply for my signature.            │
│  ☐  To be signed.                                     │
│  ☐  For your information.                             │
│  ☐  Please note and file.                             │
│  ☐  Please note and send to main files.               │
│  ☐  Please note, initial, and return to me.           │
│  ☐  Please note, initial, and route to:               │
│      1 _____        2 _____            │
│      3 _____        4 _____            │
│  Remarks_____        │
│  _____         │
│           Signed_____          │
└─────────────────────────────────────────────────────┘
```

An Interoffice Message to Speed
Administrative Action

Careless treatment of forms can cause needless misunderstanding and expense. Like other business communications, completed form messages are judged by their accuracy, clarity, coherence, and conciseness. Therefore when you prepare form messages, be sure to insert all necessary information into appropriate blank spaces. Align your fill-in data as much as possible for easy reading. Choose your words carefully. For example, select concrete terms rather than vague expressions. Use jargon or specialized vocabulary only when it is likely to be understood by the reader of your form message. And be sure to write or type your fill-ins legibly.

The illustration of a purchase requisition is an example of a carefully prepared business form.

EVANS Corporation   **PURCHASE REQUISITION**

Deliver to: A. R. Fisher   Requisition No. **1042**
Location: Annex Office, Warehouse B Date   May 28, 19--
Job No: WB-A35   Date Required June 12, 19--

QUANTITY	DESCRIPTION
6	Grey, 4-tray, desk-top files (12x10")
500	Color-tab folders (letter-size)
500	Kraft envelopes, standard size, brown, gummed flap
250	Kraft envelopes, 9x12", brown gummed flap, metal clasp

Requisitioned by: _A. R. Fisher_____

A Company Unit Needing Supplies or Equipment Submits *Purchase Requisitions* Through Its Organizational Channels

MEMORANDUMS

Memorandums (also called memoranda or memos) are structured more formally than are notes. A memo has basically a four-part heading:

TO: (receiver's name)
FROM: (sender's name)
SUBJECT: (message corethought or file reference)
DATE: (month, day, year, even the time of day when appropriate to the message)

The order of presenting those heading parts may vary; "From" may appear before "To," for example. Courtesy titles for sender and for receiver usually are omitted, but job titles or department designations sometimes are used with sender and receiver names.

When the memo is intended as a routine message, the writer customarily does not sign or initial it. Memos that are to be perceived as moderately important (neither routine nor urgent) are initialled. Those which the writer wishes to be recognized as of great importance are signed.

Business people often place their initials, and sometimes their signatures, next to their typewritten names in the "From" space of a memo heading. But by initialing or signing at the *end* of the memorandum (as at the end of a business letter), the sender is likelier to review the message a final time and to correct errors before transmission.

THE KNUDSER CORPORATION

MEMORANDUM

TO   E. O. Brandt   FROM R. D. Davis

SUBJECT Neosho Mall   DATE August 29, 19--

Phone Duffy at Wichita: What's the status of Neosho Mall?

Ask Duffy to follow-up your phone call with a progress memo, including these items:

1. Issuance of construction permits

2. Leasing prospects and storefront-design agreements

Be ready to discuss the memo at next Thursday's meeting, please.

cbs   *RDD*

A Memorandum

OTHER BUSINESS MESSAGE FORMATS

You have studied the formats of letters and letter reports, office notes and message forms, and memorandums. Other formats commonly used in business include minutes of meetings; news releases; postal cards and reply cards; telegrams, mailgrams, cablegrams, and radiograms.

Minutes of Meetings

Minutes, which are written records of meetings or conferences, usually include these data:

1. Identification of the group that met.
2. Classification of the meeting (e.g., regular, monthly, quarterly, special, emergency).
3. Location, date, and time that the meeting began.
4. Identification of people in attendance and of the presiding officer (sometimes of other officers as well).
5. Identification of absentees and of reasons for their absence.
6. Reference to minutes of the previous meeting. (Were they accepted as read? Were they amended and then accepted?) An exception, of course, would be the case of a group which meets for the first time and therefore would have no previous minutes.
7. Reports of action on matters previously presented to the group; such matters sometimes are called "old business." In the case of a group which meets for the first time, the equivalent of "old business" would be statements of authorization for the group's existence and definitions of the group's role, scope, and administrative organization.
8. Reports of action on matters currently presented to the group ("new business").
9. Notation of when the meeting ended. (If the meeting is other than a regularly scheduled session, the place and time of the next session should be mentioned before this notation.)
10. Identification of the person responsible for preparing the minutes.

As with other effective communications, minutes should answer the following questions (not necessarily in this order): who? what? when? where? why? how? Here are additional suggestions for taking minutes:

1. Realize that you will not prepare the minutes themselves during a meeting. The minutes will be based upon notes that you take, so write those notes carefully as events occur during the meeting.
2. Note the name, location, time, and date of the meeting.
3. Note whether the meeting was properly called, with due notification to members.
4. Identify present and absent members (with reasons for absence if necessary); identify the presiding officer.
5. Note whether a quorum is present. (A *quorum* is the minimum number of members authorized for conducting the business of a meeting.)

Minutes of a Committee Meeting

MINUTES OF THE EXECUTIVE COMMITTEE MEETING

October 26, 19--

A regular meeting of the Executive Committee, Keuka Textiles, Inc., was called to order at corporate headquarters, New York City, October 26, 19--, at 10:30 a.m. Members present were Mrs. Chism, Ms. Dunn, Dr. Gratz, Dr. Green, Mr. Haneda, Mr. C. J. Smith, Ms. G. R. Raub, and Mrs. Hart who presided. Mr. Gomez was absent, representing the Company at the Fiber Technology Conference in New Orleans.

Minutes of the previous meeting were accepted as read.

Mr. Haneda reported that expansion of Keuka Mills at Charlotte and Winston-Salem, N. C., and at Greenville, S. C., was proceeding as planned. Production schedules are being maintained during this interim period; the expansion program is set for completion early next year.

Mrs. Hart distributed copies of a progress report from G. W. Hill, manager of Carolinas Division, for study and discussion at the next meeting of this committee.

Dr. Gratz and Dr. Green announced that, as authorized by the committee, Keuka Educational Grants-in-Aid, totaling $65,000 for the current fiscal year, have been made available to students at the following schools:

1. Atlantic School of Design, Providence, R. I. ($20,000)

2. Barstow Technical Institute, Roanoke, Va. ($15,000)

3. Boone A&M University, Durham, S.C. ($5,000)

4. Caycee Community College, Columbus, Ga. ($5,000)

     5. Muscogee Junior College, Columbia, S. C. ($5,000)

     6. Eufala Technical Institute, Troy, Ala. ($5,000)

Dr. Gratz presented a memorandum from J. M. Walsh, manager of Personnel Recruiting Department, suggesting that recipients of these grants be invited to visit Keuka headquarters. Mrs. Chism moved approval, with the stipulation that Keuka underwrite expenses for the visitors. Mr. C. J. Smith seconded the motion, which passed unanimously. Ms. Dunn will assign a member of the community services staff to plan the necessary arrangements for committee review at the next regular session, November 27, 19--.

The meeting was ajourned at 11:45 a.m.

                            Respectfully submitted

                            G. R. Raub

                            Secretary

6. Use an agenda (a list of topics to be discussed) as a guide form for your notes. Next to each of the agenda topics, note the actions concerning that topic.

7. If there is insufficient agenda space for your notes, write them on separate sheets. Number your notes to coincide with their listing on the agenda. For example, the third agenda item would also be No. 3 on your separate note sheet, thereby enabling you to correlate information easily.

8. If the meeting departs from or rearranges the agenda sequence, note the order in which discussion actually occurs. For instance, if the fifth agenda item is moved to third place, your note might be keyed this way:

    Item 5>   3.

In that example, 5 indicates *original* agenda placement of the topic; 3 shows its *actual* occurrence during the session.

9. Make orderly and legible notes. You may be required to read parts of them aloud as the meeting continues. And of course you will need to understand your note-taking when you prepare the minutes after the meeting.

10. Record corethoughts whenever possible. Summarize discussions, including reasons which the participants state for and against the views discussed.

11. Identify a formal motion exactly as stated at the meeting. Also identify the person who presents the motion and the person who seconds it. Summarize the ensuing discussion. Then record the outcome of the vote and the action taken for that motion.

12. To reduce possibilities of error, transcribe your notes as soon as you can do so after the meeting.

13. For the typewritten minutes that result from your note-taking, you may begin with a title put in all caps and centered as a heading. For instance:

PUBLICATIONS COMMITTEE

14. Capitalize the first letters of Board, Committee, Company, and the like, when those words refer to the group which the minutes represent. For example:

    The Committee considered four new publication proposals.

15. Although typewritten minutes sometimes are single-spaced, *double spacing* and *ample margins* (for readers' comments) are preferred.

16. Your minutes, as well as your notes, should record data and actions but not subjective generalities of your own. For example, if during a meeting the chairperson accepts a report as "splendid work" and authorizes those words to appear in the minutes, you would quote them directly, or the group would pass an official resolution of thanks, which you would record. But do not, of your own volition, emotionalize your minutes with *brilliant, superb, antagonistic*, or similar terms. Your job is to record, to report—but not to editorialize—the business of the meeting.

17. If a complimentary close is used for minutes, it customarily is either of these:

        Respectfully submitted
        Respectfully

18. Minutes usually are signed by the duly authorized officer(s) of an organization—for example, by the official secretary or by another officer.

19. A typewritten line at the end of the minutes is usually provided for recording the date of their approval.

News Releases

Another business-communication format is that of the news release intended for mass-media transmission by radio/TV broadcasts, newspaper stories, and magazine articles. Effective news releases do the following:

1. Identify the sender.
2. Indicate when the message should be publicized.
3. State the corethought as a journalistic headline.
4. Cite the information source when applicable.
5. Answer the basic communication questions: WHO? WHAT? WHEN? WHERE? WHY? HOW? The order for answering those questions may vary (for example, WHAT before WHO).

The message body of a news release is organized in what journalists call "inverted-pyramid form": Answers to the basic questions appear first; supporting details of the answers come later in the message.

FLORIDA – DE SOTO Broadcasting Group, Incorporated

7959 Holgate Rd., Pensacola, FL 32504
(904) 813-3055

June 16, 19--

FOR IMMEDIATE RELEASE

            FLORIDA-DESOTO TO SELL SIX TV STATIONS

     Pensacola television station WRZ and five companion De Soto
stations will be sold to an Illinois business firm, officials of
the Florida-De Soto Broadcasting Group, Inc., announced today.
Katherine Minton Korsky, vice-president and general manager of
Florida-De Soto, emphasized that the purchase is subject to approval
by the Federal Communications Commission and by the Securities and
Exchange Commission.

     The new owner is Affiliated Communications Corporation of Chicago,
which has television and radio stations in Illinois, Indiana, Missouri,
Kansas, and Nebraska. Besides WRZ this purchase includes TV stations
WBX in Tallahassee; WDZ, Daytona Beach; WGK, Ocala; WJB, Fort Pierce;
and WWG, Gainesville.

News Release

Postal Cards and Reply Cards

Among relatively fast and inexpensive business messages, postal cards and reply cards deserve attention. Their arrangement can be simple, allowing easy and speedy preparation. They save the cost and time of folding, sealing, and stamping a message; and, for postal cards, the mailing charge is less than that of a letter sent first class.

Heading and salutation appear on the message side of the postal card. The receiver's address need appear only on the stamped side of the card. When the heading on the message side gives the sender's address, you may omit that address from the stamped side of the card. When the sender's address is printed, you further reduce time and amount of message preparation. And to save space, the sender's address may be arranged in straight-line style, as shown in the illustration below.

EXPO Services, Inc. P. O. BOX 99175, TACOMA, WA 98499

WHO? 　　　You,　Your Family,　Your Friends

WHAT? 　　　AGRI-BUSINESS MOBILE EXPOSITION

WHY? 　　　For Information and Fun!

WHERE 　　　Oregon — 　　Portland Mall, July 12-15, 19—
& 　　　　　　　　　　Eugene, Lane Center, July 17-18
WHEN? 　　　　　　　　　La Grande, Alban Center, July 21

　　　　　　　Washington — Spokane Shopping Plaza, July 27
　　　　　　　　　　　　Tacoma Retail Mart, July 29-30
　　　　　　　　　　　　Pullman City Mall, August 1-2
　　　　　　　　　　　　Seattle Trade Center, August 5

● A PRESENTATION OF NORTHWEST MERCHANTS ASSOCIATION ●

A Postal Card Business Message

Reply cards, like postal cards, are convenient types of business messages, as illustrated by the following:

UNITED STATES POSTAL SERVICE
Washington, DC   20260
OFFICIAL BUSINESS

PENALTY FOR PRIVATE
USE TO AVOID PAYMENT
OF POSTAGE $300

CONSUMER AFFAIRS
U.S. POSTAL SERVICE
WASHINGTON, DC 20261

Date: _____
        mo   day   year
                        ,

CONSUMER SERVICE CARD   B0175290

Name	*Address*	*City*	*State*	*ZIP*	*Day Phone*

● Is this: Information request ☐   Suggestion ☐   Complaint ☐   Other ☐

● If this is a problem with a specific mailing, please complete following:

Was it:
☐ Letter
☐ Regular Parcel Post
☐ Air Parcel Post
☐ Newspaper/ Magazine
☐ Advertisement

Was mailing:
☐ 1st Class
☐ Airmail
☐ Special Delivery
☐ Certified
☐ Registered
☐ Insured

Did it involve:
☐ Delay
☐ Non-receipt
☐ Damage

Please give information on the other person involved in this mailing:

Name _____
Address _____
City _____
State _____ ZIP _____

Was the above person   ☐ Sender   ☐ Receiver

● If not specific mail problem, is it: ☐ Self Service Postal Equipment   ☐ Money Order   ☐ Postal personnel

● Please give essential facts: _____
_____
_____
_____
_____

PS Form 4314-July 1975   Thank you. You will be contacted soon.

A Reply Card

Telegrams, Mailgrams, Cablegrams, Radiograms

In the United States most telegrams are delivered by telephone or as mailgrams instead of by messenger. To send a mailgram, the sender dictates his or her message by telephone to a nearby telegraph office. The mailgram is transmitted to the post office near the addressee for delivery by the Postal Service, usually with the next day's mail.

Cablegrams and radiograms are used for overseas communication. As indicated by their names, *cable*grams are transmitted via transoceanic cable, and *radio*grams are wireless messages. Virtually all forms of modern telecommunication are greatly expedited by satellite relay systems for message transmission within and across national, continental, and hemispheric boundaries.

Full-rate cablegrams and full-rate radiograms provide fast service for messages in plain language, in code (an economical arrangement of words having not more than five letters each), or in cipher (a secret arrangement of letters or numerals to convey confidential data). For somewhat slower delivery of nonconfidential data sent in plain language, cable letters and letter telegrams provide reliable service.

				western union		**Telegram**	

MSG. NO.	NO. OF WDS. CL. OF SVC.	PD.-COLL.	CASH NO.	ACCOUNTING INFORMATION	DATE	FILING TIME	SENT TIME
				Charge the account of OEM Associates	8/13/--	A.M. P.M.	A.M. P.M.

Send the following message, subject to the terms on back hereof, which are hereby agreed to ☐ OVER NIGHT TELEGRAM

UNLESS BOX ABOVE IS CHECKED THIS MESSAGE WILL BE SENT AS A TELEGRAM

TO Miss I. A. Hammid, Gelatos Co., Inc.

ADDRESS & TELEPHONE NO. 2110 Lakes Drive   313-526-1129

CITY — STATE & ZIP CODE Detroit, Michigan   48212

New arrival time noon Friday BonAir Flight 1010.
S. K. Pakel, Sales Engineer

SENDER'S TEL. NO. 517-515-0317 NAME & ADDRESS OEM Associates 1060 Cupertino Place
(Area Code)   Canton, OH   (Zip Code) 44718

W.U. 5210 (3/73)

A Telegram

REVIEW AND TRANSITION

In Chapter 6 you studied message formats used with handwritten, typewritten, printed, telegraphic, and wireless media of business communication. You familiarized yourself with physical factors of appearance for business stationery, letterheads, envelopes, and correspondence formats. You were introduced to styles and functions of form letters, letter reports, office notes, message forms, and memorandums. You acquainted yourself with minutes of business meetings, with business news releases, with business uses of postal cards, reply cards, and telecommunications.

After you complete the following discussion questions and applications, you will discover in Chapter 7 that much of what you have learned pertains not only to written communication but also to effective oral, visual, and multimedia messages.

DISCUSSION QUESTIONS

A. Within the context of Chapter 6, what are appropriate definitions and illustrations for these terms:

1. "picture-frame" guide
2. open punctuation
3. mixed punctuation
4. signature block
5. "complete form" letter
6. "paragraph form" letter
7. business memorandum
8. minutes of a meeting
9. "inverted-pyramid" organization of a news release
10. dictaform

B. What information do standard letterheads convey?

C. What data appears in a heading for the second and additional pages of a business letter or memorandum?

D. What are appropriate salutations for these inside addresses:

1. Spence Corporation
   205 E. Amite Street
   Jackson, MS 39201

2. Personnel Department
   Silver Inns Corporation
   403 W. Second Street
   Reno, NV 89501

3. Office of the President
   Kenspar Industries
   One Miramar Road
   Salt Lake City, UT 84109

4. Purchasing Agent
   El Yunque Exporters, Inc.
   129 Coamo Plaza
   Rio Piedras, PR 00923

5. Mrs. O.A. Norstrom
   General Manager
   Capital Tours, Inc.
   225 Virginia Ave.
   Washington, DC 20061

6. Ms. L.C. Lucas
   Industrial Relations
   Prudhoe Oil Corporation
   P.O. Box 1905
   Anchorage, AK 99501

7. R.M. Lenz, Ph.D.
   Director, Aerospace Division
   Adams Laboratories, Inc.
   130 Morrissey Boulevard
   Milwaukee, WI 53211

8. Miss Matilde Vasquez
Customer Services Department
Sierra Enterprises, Inc.
2018 Menaul Street, NE
Albuquerque, NM   89107

9. Albin, Delst & Hart
Certified Public Accountants
332 E. Grace Street
Richmond, VA   23220

10. Mr. R.P. Hogue, Sr.
President
Hogue Foods Corporation
1619 Dodge Street
Omaha, NE   68102

E. In what ways are the following correspondence styles similar, and how do they differ from one another?

  1. block

  2. modified block

  3. modified block with indented paragraphs

  4. AMS Simplified

F. What kinds of communications are "business reports"?

G. Besides length and tone, what are five other ways in which business reports are classified?

H. The letter report shown on page 121 does not have a usual letterhead. What letterhead data is omitted from that illustration? What circumstances justify the omission? (Suggestion: Read that letter carefully to determine its context.)

I. What are the advantages and the disadvantages of using office notes and message forms in administrative communication?

J. What are the four basic parts of a memo heading? Which of the following are usually omitted from a memo heading?

  1. courtesy titles for sender and for receiver

  2. job titles

  3. department designations

K. Concerning degrees of intended importance for a memo, what do the writer's initials or the writer's signature imply? What is the advantage of placing the writer's initials or signature at the *end* of a memo (rather than near the "From" part of the heading)?

L. What communication advantages do postal cards and reply cards provide?

M. What are the format requirements of a business postal-card message?

N. What are the major similarities and differences in use of telegrams, mailgrams, cablegrams, radiograms?

APPLICATIONS

1. Obtain three different samples of actual business letterhead stationery. Evaluate those examples according to the criteria on page 104. Explain and illustrate use of the "picture-frame" guide with those samples. Explain and illustrate second-page headings, both block and horizontal styles, for business letters that exceed a single letterhead sheet.

2. Design letterheads which you believe would effectively represent at least two of the following firms. Then in a memorandum to your professor, explain why your letterhead designs would be especially appropriate to the firms. Request constructive criticism of your designs and of your memo.

a. Fairfax Corporation, 180 Piedmont Avenue, N.E., Chicago, IL 60622. In-state telephone: (312) 883-5604. Toll-free telephone: (800) 555-3636. Manufactures and markets resilient flooring materials, carpeting, and home furnishings. Has plants and branch offices at Gainesville, Macon, and Savannah, Georgia; Chattanooga and Knoxville, Tennessee; Oak Brook, Illinois; Dallas and Lubbock, Texas; San Jose, California. Established in 1885.

b. Fulton and Samuels, Inc., 1201 Michigan Boulevard, Racine, WI 53402. Telephones: (414) 209-7766, (800) 977-3800. Manufactures paper and cellulose products. Has plants at Charleston, South Carolina; Green Bay, Wisconsin; St. Paul, Minnesota; Portland, Oregon; Moses Lake, Washington. Motto: Quality You Can Trust.

c. Greater Yield Company, Inc., 1059 Sixth Avenue, Des Moines, IA 52802. Telephone: (515) 333-0870. Buys, transports, stores, and sells grain. Manufactures formula feeds. Processes oil-bearing seeds. Operates barges and boats for agri-business transportation. Has storage elevators, processing plants, and other facilities in Iowa, Illinois, Nebraska, Kansas, Tennessee, Alabama, Mississippi, and Louisiana. Uses GYC monogram as its identifying emblem.

d. HAF Stores Corporation, 175 Wyman Plaza, Spartanburg, SC 29304. Telephones: (803) 955-3900, (800) 444-2000. Cable address: HAFCO. Retailer with more than 2,500 general-merchandise stores throughout continental U.S., Alaska, Hawaii, Puerto Rico, and the Virgin Islands. Divisional and regional offices in New York City, Chicago, New Orleans, San Diego, Seattle, San Juan.

3. Page 113 shows a business letter in block-style. Appropriately adapt that illustration as follows:

   a. Include this cable address in the DB&H letterhead: DABHI.

   b. Change the letter style to modified block (either with or without indented paragraphs).

   c. Use mixed punctuation for the salutation and complimentary close.

   d. Note that carbon copies are being sent to these DB&H people: R.E. Gould, Director of Communication Services; Isabel Blair, Executive Vice-President.

   e. Revise the message body to reflect the changes you have made.

4. Page 114 shows a business letter in AMS Simplified style. Appropriately adapt that illustration as follows:

   a. Add this data to the letterhead: Established in 1958. Offices in major cities of the United States, Canada, and Mexico.

   b. Add a "special delivery" notation.

   c. Change the letter to block style; do not indent the beginnings of paragraphs.

   d. Note that copies are being sent to these DB&H people: R.E. Gould, Director of Communication Services; B. C. Hinton III, Vice-President, Training Services.

   e. Revise the message body to reflect the changes you have made.

5. Page 114 shows a business letter in modified block style with indented paragraphs. Appropriately adapt that illustration as follows:

   a. Change the letterhead in one of these ways:

      (1) Place the DB&H name at the top of the sheet, and move the rest of the letterhead to the bottom of the sheet.

> (2) Place the DB&H name along the left edge of the sheet, and place the rest of the letterhead at the top of the sheet.

   b. Change the letter to AMS Simplified style.

   c. Delete the postscript.

   d. Revise the message body to reflect the changes you have made.

6. (Reference: pages 112-114) Assume that you—not Ms. Marais—are conference coordinator at the Center for Continuing Education in New Orleans. You have received the DB&H illustrations of correspondence formats. Write separate "thank you" letters to Benjamin C. Hinton III and to Isabel Blair. Include at least the following items but not necessarily in the order given here:

   a. Acknowledge the prompt and helpful response to your request for the DB&H material.

   b. Emphasize potential uses of that material for your Annual Communication Seminar (e.g., as handout illustrations for discussion, as visual aids displayed by an opaque projector, or as models for you to follow in preparing your own examples of correspondence formats).

   c. Describe the number of people expected to attend the seminar and their educational or business backgrounds.

   d. Mention that DB&H will be given full credit for providing illustrations of letter styles.

   e. End the message by reinforcing the tone of goodwill.

   f. Use any of these three styles, with open or mixed punctuation, for your letter to Mr. Hinton: block, modified block, modified block with indented paragraphs.

   g. Use the AMS Simplified style for your letter to Ms. Blair.

7. Continue the assumption that you are conference coordinator at the Center for Continuing Education (CCE) in New Orleans. You have requested seminar material from many expert sources, including but not limited to DB&H. Compose a guide form acknowledging receipt of the materials you receive, describing how you plan to use them, pledging seminar program credit for your sources, and reinforcing goodwill.

8. Continuing your role as CCE coordinator, write a letter report to your employer, M. O. Goshen, Director of CCE in New Orleans. Pages 113-114 give the CCE mailing address. This is the context of your message:

   a. You need nine principal speakers for your Annual Communication Seminar. Five business communication experts, located in various parts of the country, have accepted your invitation by letters. Four others have sent interim replies but have neither accepted nor declined your invitation. M. O. Goshen has authorized your travel to confer personally with those four potential speakers and to secure their acceptance of your program invitation. They have agreed to meet you at their offices, which are respectively in New York City; Washington, D.C.; Chicago; and Los Angeles.

   b. This is the fourth day of your trip. Two hours are available before you leave the Midwest Center Hotel at which you have been staying in Chicago. You telephone your New Orleans office, intending to report that R. D. Atkins of the New York Management Academy, A. L. Briscoe of the Washington Administrative Institute, and Dr. T. Y. Valerian of the Chicago Communication Society have agreed to participate in your seminar. You will leave Chicago this evening, fly to Los Angeles, and meet tomorrow with M. I. Shen, head of the California Program for International Business.

   c. During your phone call to New Orleans, you learn that your employer, M. O. Goshen, has suddenly been called to a special meeting in Houston. Goshen's secretary relays Goshen's request for a report from you, summarizing what you've accomplished thus far on your trip.

   d. Address your special-delivery letter-report to Goshen at the Westheimer Towers Hotel, 5700 Belvedere Place, Houston, TX 77021. (Use any of the letter styles discussed in Chapter 6. Sketch a suitable letterhead for your Chicago hotel stationery.)

   e. Adapt the preceding exercise: You have a supply of CCE interoffice memorandum sheets with you. Write a suitable memo report to Goshen at Houston. (Be sure to show the appropriate memo heading.)

9. Prepare suitable minutes based upon these notes of a Publication Committee meeting:

   a. Group: Publications Committee, Dalton Savings & Loan Association. Place: headquarters office of the Association. Date: April 27, 19—. Time: Called to order at 9:45 a.m. by Committee chairperson, who presided at this regular meeting.

   b. Present: all Committee officers and members. Roll: Chairperson D. L. Pierce, Vice-Chairperson R. S. Devon, Secretary K. B. Verdery; also S. W. Kaplan, M. C. O'Connor, J. A. Silva.

   c. Minutes of the previous meeting were accepted as read.

   d. Old business: O'Connor and Silva presented revised cost estimates (copies appended to these minutes) for proposed monthly newsletters to Association members. Devon noted that the revised estimates included bids from only two printers (i.e., from Cole Associates and from NFB Company). Devon: additional bids should be solicited. O'Connor: Committee has been satisfied with previous contracts awarded to Cole Associates. Devon: other bids needed. O'Connor called for a vote on Devon's suggestion. Moved by Devon, seconded by Kaplan: "I move that O'Connor and Silva invite bids from Press Services Company and from Metro Printers, Inc." Motion passed by 3:2 vote, Pierce abstaining. O'Connor was instructed to report the new bids at the next regular meeting of Committee.

   e. New business: Pierce read a memo (dated April 25) from W. K. Darcey (State Street office manager) suggesting that the Committee include these items when publishing the next annual report:

      i. Association employees' participation in community projects (volunteer work, fund drives, etc.).

      ii. Summary profile of Association employees' education, work experience, and length of service with Dalton.

   Pierce asked whether the Committee wanted to discuss these suggestions personally with Darcey. Moved by Kaplan, seconded by Verdery: "that Chairperson Pierce invite Darcey to a Committee luncheon meeting, subject to concurrence of Darcey's supervisors, for discussion of Darcey's annual-report suggestions." Motion passed unanimously.

   f. No further business. Silva moved adjournment; O'Connor seconded. Meeting adjourned at 10:20 a.m.

10. From business or financial articles published in a newspaper, select an article that you believe to have been issued as a news release. Compose that news release. (Use one of the letterheads you designed for Application 2, or design another appropriate letterhead).

CHAPTER 7

Communication Media and Message-Dictation Techniques

Expert business communicators rarely limit themselves to one communication medium; they use *media*. This chapter examines basic media separately and in combination.

NONVERBAL COMMUNICATION

By definition, nonverbal communication is wordless. It may be transmitted by touch (the gentle pressure of a friendly hand on your shoulder can communicate encouragement). It can be conveyed by taste (flavors of food products can communicate fulfillment of recipes and proper operation of equipment) or by smell (fragrances, aromas, and odors can signify fulfillment of production, packing, or storage instructions). It can also be conveyed by hearing; for instance, a typewriter bell indicates the end of a line, and a horn may signify the approach of a vehicle. Most often, however, nonverbal communication is perceived visually and is transmitted by these means: appearances, timings and distances, postures, movements, gestures, and facial expressions.

Appearances, Timings, and Distances

The way that someone or something *looks* can create, or bridge, communication gaps. For instance, the appearance of a job applicant (or an employee already on the job) may be interpreted as evidence of personal values and attitudes. Soiled, crumpled, or ostentatious clothing; grimy hands or dirty face; improperly used cosmetics or colognes; superfluous jewelry or accessories—these and other facets of personal appearance can block career advancements. Rightly or wrongly, observers take appearances as cues, as indications of care or carelessness toward oneself, toward other people, and toward responsibilities of earning a living. Incorrect layout, poor corrections, repetitive paragraph beginnings, or wordy paragraphs in a business *message* can produce lasting, often negative, impressions. Clean, moderate, appropriate features of personal appearance and of message appearance tend to promote rapport between sender and receiver. You can improve the effectiveness of your own communication by being aware of this fact: Many employers, co-workers, and customers interpret *appearances* as realities.

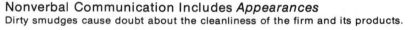

Rely on GOURMAND'S reputation for cleanliness, freshness, and flavor. Scan the enclosed catalog, please. Luscious fruits . . . delicious cheeses . . . creamy chocolates . . . juice-rich jams and jellies . . . all are guaranteed for their purity.

Nonverbal Communication Includes *Appearances*
Dirty smudges cause doubt about the cleanliness of the firm and its products.

Timings and distances also are parts of nonverbal communication. For example, when you deliberately place a telephone call so that it is received very early in the morning or very late at night, your timing may convey urgency. When you lean close to someone during a face-to-face conversation, you may imply that your message is confidential. But these nonverbal cues should be used judiciously. An unimportant telephone call received at dawn or at midnight will scarcely please your listener. And if you approach a face-to-face listener too closely, he or she instinctively will move away from you, thereby breaking rather than reinforcing rapport.[1]

Appearances, timings, and distances are powerful means of nonverbal communication. So are postures, movements, gestures, and facial expressions.

Postures, Movements, Gestures, and Facial Expressions

Your own experience may indicate that by assuming a posture of poise and by moving confidently you can communicate a sense of well-being to others. As you develop your own communication behaviors, observe other people's postures and movements also. For example, notice that when a

[1] Edward T. Hall's *The Silent Language* (New York: Doubleday & Company, Inc., 1959) describes behavioral patterns of timings and distances in many societies. Our discussion pertains to lifestyles in the United States primarily.

speaker is rooted rigidly to one spot for a long time, or rocks and swings constantly, you pay little attention to that speaker's words and much attention to his or her disconcerting stance. If speakers habitually place their elbows or forearms on lecterns, those speakers seem to diminish their body heights by protruding their hips. If speakers slouch constantly, they nonverbally communicate feelings of fatigue or stress to their viewers. If speakers shuffle aimlessly, they suggest a lack of organization that viewers may attribute to a lack of logic in what is being said.[2]

As we tend to be distracted by no movement or by too much movement of a speaker, so we may be distracted by too few or too many hand-and-arm gestures and facial expressions. But when gestures and facial expressions seem genuine rather than contrived, relevant to the message purpose, and integrated with the speaker's total body balance, nonverbal communication greatly enhances what is spoken.

As a business communicator you will use many languages—among them the languages of words, numbers, appearances, timings and distances, postures and movements, gestures, and facial expressions. Since your work will involve written, spoken, and nonverbal messages, focus your attention now upon oral, visual, and multimedia communication, including dictation of business messages.

ORAL COMMUNICATION

Picture yourself arriving at your office or plant. Your co-workers greet you. Your supervisor asks about a revised production procedure. Your secretary inquires about a dictation schedule. A customer telephones you. You participate in a decision-making conference. These circumstances are typical of your need to communicate orally. "So what?" you say. "I've been talking for years, and talk is easy."

You are right; talk is easy. Talk is casual, largely undirected, often expressive. But communication transcends expression. Many people talk. You need to *speak*—intelligently, clearly, informatively, and persuasively.

What is oral communication? How is speaking related to you and to your career? How do breaths become messages? Unless you appreciate and apply the answers to those questions, you risk misusing an instrument of personal fulfillment and of business prosperity.

Physiological Aspects: Breaths, Sounds, Messages

To communicate orally, you produce sounds that stand for meanings. Production of those sounds involves four physiological phases: inhalation, phonation, resonation, modification. Understanding these phases can help you consciously to control and improve your oral communication.

---

[2] The importance of postures and movements as nonverbal "action language" prompts modern business people to use videotape recorders for communication training and for actual transmission of some messages.

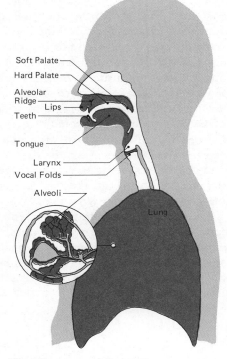

Soft Palate
Hard Palate
Alveolar Ridge
Lips
Teeth
Tongue
Larynx
Vocal Folds
Alveoli
Lung

The Organs of Speech

Phase One: Inhalation. To sustain your life and to obtain the "raw material" of speech, you introduce air through your nostrils and your mouth. That air proceeds to your lungs where it is temporarily stored in tiny sacs, called alveoli, which function as reservoirs. Consciously or unconsciously, you cause your stomach muscles and your diaphragm to act so that the air moves out of the alveoli.

Phase Two: Phonation. Moving upward along its escape route, the air that has become your breath now passes through your larynx ("voice box"). The larynx contains two membranous surfaces, the vocal folds, which impart *pitch* (highness or lowness of sound) to your breath. When your vocal folds vibrate quickly, the pitch of your voice is high. When they vibrate slowly, your vocal pitch is low. Your breath thus becomes voice but not yet speech.

Phase Three: Resonation. Continuing its escape, the breath imbued with pitch moves into your head. The cavities of your nose, throat, and mouth amplify and enrich that breath, which reverberates within them. The greater the reverberation, the richer the *timbre* ("quality" or "warmth") of your voice. In effect, your throat and head cavities act as natural echo chambers, or resonators, creating overtones that enhance your voice. You can control your use of those echo chambers. By swallowing to relax your throat muscles, by flaring your nostrils, or by slightly protruding your lips, you adjust the resonators to add warmth and richness.

Air has become breath in the alveoli of your lungs. Breath has become voice between the folds of your larynx. Voice has gained resonance in the cavities of your head. You have created sounds but not yet speech. Now you proceed to shape those sounds into recognizable symbols, into spoken words that represent meanings.

Phase Four: Modification. You shape sounds into symbols with your lips (as for *w*ish and *w*here), your teeth (*f*riend, tele*ph*one), the ridge just above and below your upper teeth (*h*ow, *wh*o), the hard palate above and behind the teeth ridge (*c*ool, *g*et), the soft palate extending in back of the hard palate (bri*ng*, thi*ng*), and your tongue acting with your teeth (*th*ere, *th*in) or acting with your teeth ridge (*t*o, *d*o).

The speech sounds you produce are classified as vowels, diphthongs, and consonants. They are the oral elements of syllables, words, and phrases.

The alphabetical letters *a, e, i, o, u,* and sometimes *y* are vowels in *written* communication. But *oral* communication has these definitions: A *vowel* is any sound which, if given sufficient breath, continues indefinitely. A *diphthong* is any combination of two vowels, rapidly blended into what seems to be one sound, with the first vowel stressed and the second vowel slighted. A *consonant* is any sound which, regardless of breath supply, seems to interrupt itself.

Examples of vowels, diphthongs, and consonants include these *sounds* represented by underlined letters in the list on the next page. Notice that almost every sound has more than one spelling. Say the listed words aloud until you recognize the particular sounds represented by the italicized letters.

Does the physiology of speaking concern you, a business communicator? Should you become consciously aware of the speech process?

Other people may take speech for granted. But as a business communicator you have responsibility of recognizing this fact: When you write or read, you use visible symbols (alphabets and numbers)—when you speak or listen, you use invisible symbols (sounds, postures, gestures)—to convey goodwill, to inquire, to inform, to persuade. The process of oral communication is especially remarkable: You transform air into breath. You give that breath pitch and resonance. Then using lips that obtain your food, teeth that chew your food, a tongue that moves your food so that your body may be nourished, *you speak.* You use your body to transcend itself, *to communicate.* Surely this wonderful process merits your awareness, your appreciation, and your care.

VOWELS

1. b*e*, b*ee*t, b*ea*t, p*eo*ple, k*ey*, p*ie*ce, perc*ei*ve, sk*i*, qua*y*, am*oe*ba.
2. *i*t, pr*e*tty, b*ee*n, w*o*men, b*u*siness, b*ui*ld, s*y*llable
3. *ah*, *o*n, *a*re, p*a*lm, h*ea*rt, know-ledge, s*e*rgeant, *ho*nest
4. *a*t, pl*ai*d, s*a*lve, l*au*gh
5. *ea*rn, *u*rn, h*e*r, s*i*r, c*o*lonel, w*o*rst, c*ou*rage, m*y*rrh
6. *a*bout, *o*ccur, probl*e*m, *u*pon
7. l*o*ve, d*oe*s (verb), fl*oo*d, m*u*ch, t*o*ngue, *u*s.
8. t*o*, t*oo*, tw*o*, st*u*dent, kn*ew*, li*eu*, que*ue*, tr*ue*, y*ou*
9. l*oo*k, w*o*man, w*ou*ld, w*o*rsted, f*u*ll
10. *a*ll, *aw*l, b*oa*rd, t*a*lk, v*au*lt, t*au*ght, *o*ffice, *ough*t
11. *e*gg, h*ea*d, d*e*bt, m*a*ny, *ae*sthe-tic, s*ai*d, w*ea*ther, h*ei*fer, l*eo*pard, b*u*ry, g*ue*ss

DIPHTHONGS

1. *ou*r, *hou*r, d*ou*bt, br*ow*, kr*au*t
2. *oh*, *owe*, s*o*, s*ew*, c*oa*t, r*oe*, r*ow*, d*ough*, b*eau*, y*eo*man, s*ou*l, br*oo*ch, aprop*os*
(When slighted or unstressed, this sound assumes the charac-teristics of a vowel.)
3. *I*, *aye*, *eye*, t*ie*, b*uy*, b*y*, h*igh*, a*i*sle, *i*sle, *eye*, gu*i*de, he*igh*t
4. *a*ble, m*ai*n, s*ay*, m*e*sa, gr*ey*, st*ea*k, th*ey*, n*eigh*, ga*u*ge, bouqu*et*
(When slighted or unstressed, this sound assumes the charac-teristics of a vowel.)
5. b*oy*, c*oi*n
6. *ai*r, *e'er*, c*a*re, th*e*re, th*ei*r, w*ea*r
7. *ea*r, p*ee*r, p*ie*r, h*e*re

CONSONANTS

1. *p*ay, ha*pp*y, she*ph*erd, hic-cou*gh*
2. *b*est, ri*bb*on, cu*pb*oard
3. *t*ip, le*tt*er, *th*yme, aske*d*
4. *d*esk, a*dd*
5. *k*iss, *c*ool, o*cc*ur, e*ch*o, clo*ck*, *kh*aki
6. *g*ive, ri*gg*ing, *gh*etto
7. *f*ive, sa*f*e, cu*ff*, so*ft*en, di*ph*-thong, lau*gh*
8. *v*ote, o*f*, fli*vv*er
9. *th*ink
10. *th*is, brea*the*
11. *s*ee, su*ccess*, *s*cience, *ps*ychology
12. *z*est, bu*zz*, a*s*, becau*se*, *x*ylophone
13. *sh*op, pa*ss*ion, *s*ugar, con*sc*ience, addi*ti*on, appre*ci*ate, *ch*ic
14. plea*s*ure, a*z*ure, re*g*ime, prestige
15. *ch*at, cat*ch*, righ*te*ous
16. *j*oke, mana*g*er, wa*ge*
17. *w*ear, q*u*iet, *ch*oir
18. *wh*ere
19. *m*ay, li*mb*, na*me*, co*mm*ent, hy*mn*
20. *n*ow, fu*nn*y, *gn*at, *kn*ow, *mn*emonic, *pn*eumatic
21. thi*nk*, si*ng*
22. *l*ike, wi*ll*
23. *r*ight, a*rr*ive, *rh*ythm, *w*rite
24. *y*ou, mill*i*on, halleluj*a*h (also combined with vowel in *u*se)
25. *h*ello, *wh*o

People who habitually mumble or shout, who elocute without saying, who chatter without communicating may exhale noises; but they rarely speak. The rest of this chapter would not interest them. *You* know, however, that oral communication can be an instrument of personal fulfillment and of business success. For you the following pages offer use and profit.

Psychological Aspects: Establishing Justification, Developing Confidence, Overcoming Stage Fright

Oral communication is more than a physical process. It also has *psychological* aspects, of which the following are fundamental.

Establishing Justification. Almost all of us enjoy occasional chatting. Social conversation can provide moments of relaxation, necessary to counteracting personal and business pressures. Even serious business messages often can be stated informally. But the effective business speaker, like the effective business writer, establishes definite reasons for exchanging messages. Those reasons involve answers to basic communication questions with which you are becoming familiar: What potential value does the oral message have for the speaker and for the listener? What results is the oral message likely to produce? Why does the communication merit the investment of time, money, and other resources? By determining appropriate need for your oral communication, you can begin building confidence in yourself as a business speaker.

Developing Confidence. Are you an applicant for an employment interview or a candidate for a fitness evaluation? Be confident: Business careers are built on such opportunities to communicate your achievements, your personality traits, and your prospects. Are you invited to a "brainstorming" session? Be confident: Such a session is a showcase for your ideas. Are you asked to participate in a decision-making conference? Be confident: The request enables you to advance your career by supplying needed data, insights, suggestions, and recommendations.

Develop justifiable confidence in yourself by maintaining a personal "achievement journal." Record in it the dates, descriptions, and results of your educational and occupational attainments. Summarize your successes. Also list less than satisfactory outcomes; even negative experiences can help you to learn, improve, and achieve. Keep your journal current. From daily notes, make a weekly or monthly summary. From those summaries, write quarterly and yearly accountings for yourself. By reviewing your achievement journal, you will give yourself an ongoing personal inventory of self-insight, performance, and future direction. You will have relevant data for documenting the development of your career. And you will have a communication aid for constantly developing justifiable confidence in yourself.

Overcoming Stage Fright. So-called "stage-fright" is often nothing more than a speaker's misdirected awareness. For example, when addressing groups, you may sense a "nervousness," a tensing of your muscles, a quavering of your voice. Such signs usually indicate that you are directing your attention excessively to yourself instead of to your message and its receivers. These few techniques are enormously helpful in overcoming stage fright:

1. Prepare yourself. Generally avail yourself of appropriate opportunities to speak. Those opportunities yield communication experience by which you can continue improving your oral communication. Justify your need to address a particular audience, and justify the audience's need for your message. Review evidence—including your achievement journal—to reinforce confidence in yourself and in what you say.

2. Design your presentation. Do your "homework." Listeners resent the inadequate researching or scanty planning of an oral message that wastes their time. Research your audience also; familiarize yourself with what is known about your listeners' traits, needs, desires, and behaviors. Adopt a positive attitude toward this preparatory work. Thorough preparation, including adequate rehearsal, can be a speaker's most effective safeguard against stage fright.

Here is a comprehensive rehearsal procedure:

a. To develop appropriate attitude, recognize rehearsals as advantageous opportunities for improvement and practice.

b. To establish self-confidence, first rehearse alone. Silently study your notes or text; familiarity with your material will reassure you. Then speak your message aloud several times to increase that reassurance. If a tape recorder is available, use it to study what you actually say and to determine what should be revised. Edit your notes or text to improve wording, timing, or emphasis. For vocal variety, use the techniques listed on pages 153-154. For memorizing material, use the techniques listed on page 154. Those techniques are valuable for your final presentation as well as for rehearsal.

c. To reinforce self-confidence, rehearse in front of a "tryout" group. Ideally, invite three kinds of judges to the tryout: (a) someone inclined to praise you, (b) someone likely to emphasize deficiencies, (c) someone apt to identify positive features *and* areas that need improvement. Consider their comments as you plan your subsequent rehearsals. (Use the tape recorder so that you and the judges can share evidence on which to base suggestions and revision. Remember to encourage comments concerning your verbal *and* nonverbal behavior, use of visual aids, etc. Parts A and B of the Rating Chart on page 174 list details of concern to yourself and your judges.

d. Invite the same (or a similarly constituted) group of judges to your final rehearsal. Consider their comments. But since your next step is your actual presentation to the full audience, make few if any changes following your final rehearsal. Ideally, your final rehearsal should be as nearly "perfect" as you can make it. Think of your actual performance as a faithful repetition of that final rehearsal.

Whenever possible and appropriate, insist upon sufficient time and and adequate facilities for all of your preparation, certainly including your rehearsal.

3. Deliver your message. Focus your attention where it belongs—not only upon yourself, but also upon your message and your listeners. Remind yourself of your listeners' need to receive data that only your message, at the moment of its delivery, can give them. If you make an error, correct it and continue the delivery. Everyone makes a mistake now and then; why should you be different? The important thing is to correct errors and go on. If you tremble, know that your body is just generating energy. *Use* that natural energy for appropriate adjustments of your posture or movements, for relevant facial expressions, for pertinent gestures. If you must remain at one spot because of microphone location, lectern positioning, or furniture arrangement, release the extra energy you feel. For instance, press your fingertips against the sides of the lectern momentarily. Or press your thumb against the reading surface of the lectern. Or if you are seated, just touch the side of your chair. Remember that your listeners are human beings, no more, no less. If you need to relax, notice their appearance as they listen to you. Imagine how they look when they first awaken in the morning. Mentally visualize every member of your audience with, or without, long underwear. Invent your own preposterous images if you need them to help you untense. Continue speaking confidently, but be careful: You may have so much fun that you overlook the serious business of your message. Use those techniques in moderation, please!

Preparing and Presenting Oral Communication

These suggestions concern communication ranging from informal chats to serious discussions and to dictation of business messages.

1. Determine purpose.
2. Analyze audience.
3. Evaluate situation.
4. Organize data.
5. Structure message.
6. Plan delivery.

What do those suggestions involve?

Determine Purpose. To economize and enhance your communication work, guide yourself by deciding upon a two-fold purpose for your message. Justify your conversation, conference, or oral report to yourself *and* to your listeners. Is your purpose mainly to transmit or receive information? to stimulate awareness, affect attitude, elicit feedback? What counterpart purpose do you provide your receiver? Is it fulfillment of an obligation? satisfaction of a desire or need? Determine the two-fold purpose of your message; then translate that purpose into listener as well as speaker contexts. One way of having people listen is to tell them about themselves and their needs in *relation* to whatever else you say.

Analyze Audience. Determining message purpose requires awareness of your receivers' traits. The number and nature of your listeners should influence your planning as well as your presentation. Are you to address one person during an employment interview, hundreds of people at a shareholders' meeting, or thousands at an industrial convention? Consider your listeners' needs as well as your own. Facial expressions and gestures which one person can detect in an office may be imperceptible to an auditorium group. Plan to accommodate the education and the experience of your listeners. Recognize occupational, social, and other influences that can block or aid your communication. In short, strive to *relate* your presentation to your listeners. Otherwise, you will be talking to yourself; and business success rarely is based upon echoes.

Evaluate Situation. Anticipate the circumstances of your communication event. In what ways are your timing, content, location, and presentation apt to affect your listeners' responsibilities, ideas, and feelings? Is the authority of your listeners subordinate, equal, or superior to yours? What other personal and organizational factors are likely to affect their responses? In what ways do you expect the acoustics, the lighting and furniture arrangements, or the size and shape of the room to affect your presentation? What kind, shape, and size of charts, tables, diagrams, maps, or models would reinforce your oral message? What type of microphone, public address system, lectern, chalkboard, or visual projection equipment should you use? Answering these and kindred questions can help you familiarize yourself with the psychological and physical situation for your message. You then can work toward uniting people and purposes in that setting.

Organize Data. Arrange your data according to your knowledge of particular *purposes* involving a specific *audience* in a given *situation*. Although objectives, people, and circumstances vary greatly, this organizational sequence is often profitable:

1. Attention
2. Interest
3. Discussion
4. Action

Attract audience attention by mentioning a subject, especially a problem, that affects your listeners, but do not yet describe it. Tell an anecdote, but relate it to the two-fold communication purpose in terms that your listeners are apt to appreciate. Say or do something that startles or puzzles, but which neither terrifies nor antagonizes your listeners. Begin with deliberate or emphatic silence. For a few seconds, without saying a word, look directly at your listeners. When appropriate, nod or smile during this initial pause. When you begin speaking amidst noise or confusion, say something relatively *un*important first but continue speaking. Your listeners' curiosity about what they may be missing is apt to help you establish rapport.

Develop audience interest by striving to involve your listeners in what you say and do. Emphasize those parts of your presentation that appeal to your audience's wishes and wants. Add variety by examples, comparisons, contrasts, statistics, testimonials, restatements, demonstrations, or audio-visual aids. Nourish your listeners' logical and psychological appetites for ideas *and* for feelings.

Reinforce audience attention and interest by *listener-oriented discussion*. Identify, explain, and describe your corethoughts and details; but do so while emphasizing their relevance to your listeners' concerns. Use transitions to move your listeners from the familiar to the new, from the simple to the complex. For persuading rather than merely informing, describe anticipated benefits of what you propose. Also describe negative consequences of rejecting your proposal. Use words that stimulate your listeners to visualize what you explain. Then summarize your discussion. This sequence of reinforcing audience attention and interest has three parts: forecast, descriptive explanation, and summary.

Stimulate audience action by requesting or requiring feedback. When you inform or instruct, elicit pertinent questions or comments. When you inform, instruct, or persuade, observe how your listeners *use* your information. In speaking as in writing, communication should elicit responses from receivers.

Considerations of purpose, audience, situation, and data have influenced your communication planning. In what ways do these considerations affect the structuring of your message and its oral delivery?

Structure Message. To compose your oral messages, follow these guides:

1. Simplify the message structure. Speakers sometimes try to use all of the previously listed techniques in every message. The sequence of attention-interest-discussion-action is productive, but you should select the appropriate device or devices for each of those phases. If you use too many techniques (or overuse a single technique) in one message, you can block rather than achieve communication.

2. Unify the total message by continually *relating* data to the dual communication purpose that integrates the listeners' needs and yours.

3. Emphasize key data with appropriate examples and comments. Stress teamwork, fairness, discretion, and empathy. Acknowledge your listeners' abilities and accomplishments. By suitable personal references, demonstrate your appreciation of individuals or of groups that listen to you.

You have explored these five general suggestions for oral communication: determine purpose, analyze audience, evaluate situation, organize data, and structure message. The sixth suggestion concerns techniques of oral delivery.

Plan Delivery. There are four general types of oral message delivery: impromptu, extemporaneous, textual, and memorized. By acquainting yourself with their advantages and disadvantages, you can appropriately develop your own presentation techniques.

Impromptu delivery is the only type that omits rehearsal. When you speak "on the spur of the moment," without text, notes, or memorized script, you are speaking impromptu. This type of presentation typifies conversations and casual meetings. Its advantages include timeliness, immediate pertinence, enthusiasm, and sincerity. But if you prolong impromptu speaking, you may tempt yourself into digressions. Also, because your statements are spontaneous and unrehearsed, you may risk miscommunication by wordiness, unconventional grammar, or distracting mannerisms. The other delivery types—extemporaneous, textual, and memorized—require preparation and rehearsal.

Extemporaneous delivery gives the appearance of spontaneity but involves the use of notes, often on cards. Reassured by the presence of your notes, you tend to be confident. With those notes on the lectern or in your hand, you can establish and maintain "eye contact" (visual rapport) with your listeners. You can adjust your physical position relatively freely. You can benefit from the outlined order of your presentation. But you must keep your notes in order and avoid impulses to flip or sort them as you speak.

Textual delivery is the reading aloud of complete sentences from a typescript, manuscript, or other verbatim material. An advantage of textual delivery is that the availability of every word in your message tends to bolster your confidence. Also, as soon as you complete this kind of delivery, the text itself becomes a record of what you have said. When you speak textually, however, your delivery runs the risk of becoming monotonous, mechanical, or obviously formal. That risk becomes great if you assemble your audience, distribute word-for-word copies of your complete text, recite the text, and expect your listeners to be attentive. They will read their copies faster than you can speak, and you will therefore disturb rather than promote rapport. Consider these alternatives instead: *Before* beginning your textual delivery, distribute concise summaries or condensed outlines to guide your listeners. Or first present your textual message orally and *then* distribute copies of the text, a summary, or an outline. Enable your listeners to use such hand-out material for discussion with you and among themselves as well as for their own future reference.

Memorized delivery is the oral presentation of statements learned by rote. When you use memorized delivery, you repeat what you have stored in your mind paragraph by paragraph, sentence by sentence, word by word.

Memorized delivery gives you maximum freedom for posture, movement, and eye contact. Another advantage is that you convey expertise; your audience sees that you need no notes or text to assist your communication. But anxiety or interruption may cause you to forget the words and the organization of your message.

Combinations of these oral delivery techniques are frequent in business communication. For example, imagine that you are a salesperson speaking to a prospective buyer. You have memorized statements that attract favorable attention, develop interest, reinforce desire, and stimulate action. You intersperse impromptu remarks based upon what the buyer asks or states. To emphasize key topics or to verify details, you read verbatim from a typewritten or printed text. You also use extemporaneous delivery by referring to notes taken from your research file or made during the present conversation with the buyer. The point made here is that you can enjoy the aforementioned advantages of these delivery types, separately or combined.

Moreover, you can minimize the disadvantages of these separate or combined techniques. For example, you cannot rehearse impromptu delivery; but you can—and should—anticipate *situations* that elicit your impromptu participation. Prepare by considering possible and probable messages for future situations. Benefit by recalling similar incidents from the past. Prepare yourself to recognize and to benefit from impromptu opportunities. Welcome those opportunities to speak when you have something valuable to say. The richer your speaking experience, the better your impromptu delivery can become. The disadvantages of extemporaneous, textual, and memorized deliveries can be overcome by ample, appropriate rehearsal and by these methods:

1. Thoroughly familiarize yourself with the data and with your *statement* of that data.
2. When you prepare to speak from notes or text, number your cards or pages consecutively.
3. Except for rehearsal or actual delivery, keep a rubber band around the cards; use a paper clip or a staple for the pages.
4. Before final rehearsal and actual delivery, verify the numbering sequence; be sure those cards or pages are in proper order. Then, just before you start to speak, remove the rubber band or paper clip.

Remembering that almost any kind of oral delivery can seem monotonous, try these techniques to improve your vocal variety, especially with extemporaneous, textual, or memorized presentations:

1. Underline the words and phrases you wish to emphasize. Stress those items with adjustments of volume and of pitch during rehearsal as well as delivery. Underline once for slight, twice for moderate, and three times for heavy emphasis.
2. Draw a rising arrow (↗) when you particularly want the pitch of your voice to go up, as at the end of a question. Draw a falling arrow (↘) where you want your vocal pitch to drop, as at the end of a declaration.

3. Place vertical or diagonal lines in your text where you want to pause. Draw one line for a brief pause, two lines for a moderate pause, and three for emphatic silence.

If you prefer using colors instead of repeating those line-cues, let one color (perhaps blue?) stand for slight or brief, a second color (maybe green?) for moderate, and a third color (red?) for heavy or long.

Particularly concerning memorized delivery, here is a method for offsetting mental blocks: Instead of rehearsing your message word by word or sentence by sentence, begin to memorize the text as a whole. At the beginning of your rehearsal, avoid trying to remember every bit. Rehearse by speaking aloud the *entire* message, straight through from start to finish, *frequently*. Each repetition will imprint more of the message upon your memory. By learning the message as a whole, you will reduce possibilities of forgetting a part. Finally, on a single page, summarize the entire message in outline form. Look at that page as if you were examining a photograph or a painting. Let the total appearance of that page impress itself upon your memory. Then if a lapse occurs during your memorized delivery, your memorized picture of the outline will help you complete your presentation.

Face-to-Face and Telephone Communication

The preceding comments have general application. However, there are special requirements for these categories of oral communication: conversing, interviewing, conferring, reporting, and telephoning.

Conversing. This category designates relatively informal and impromptu speaking that may range from a friendly chat to a casual discussion. Because it is usually spontaneous, conversing requires you to perceive and to interpret circumstances quickly. For proper relevance and timing of your remarks, you need to detect purposes and interests; to evaluate events, statements, and implications; to relate people, things, actions, and words. You may be expected to respond *and* to help direct the course of conversation by questions, explanations, descriptions, transitions, comparisons, or contrasts. By using your listening and speaking skills, you can encourage permissive, reciprocal conversation which especially enhances social gatherings and initial business interviews. If timidity or unfamiliarity blocks conversation, you can introduce topics of common interest dealing with mutual friends or acquaintances, with sports, travel, entertainment, or the like. When conversation lags, you can ask about the individual's interests, concerns, or attitudes toward current events. And you can respond to comments or reinforce your own remarks nonverbally as well as orally. A smile, a nod, or a gesture can be potent.

Face-to-face conversation easily accommodates these techniques, but telephone conversation requires special awareness and care. When you speak with someone by telephone, *visualize* the person. Instead of talking at a disembodied voice, converse with *a person*. Successful telephone conversation demands empathy. When your phone rings, answer promptly and courteously. Although you may be busy at the moment, resist the temptation to snap "Hold on" or "Just a minute." Begin by identifying your office *and yourself*, thereby personalizing the communication and promoting rapport. Let the caller identify himself or herself. Then if you must ask the caller to wait, do so pleasantly. When you resume the conversation, thank your caller for being patient.

Before you place a telephone call, gather pertinent correspondence, reports, or other references for the conversation. Have note-taking materials ready for your use. Allow at least ten rings at the other end of the line; some telephone companies recommend a full minute of time allowance for answering calls. When you speak into a telephone, place the receiver against your ear and keep the mouthpiece about an inch from your lips. That is the distance recommended for a regular telephone handset. For a headset, the distance between lips and transmitter should be about half an inch. Speak clearly; neither shout nor whisper. Speak slowly enough to be understandable, rapidly enough to be interesting. Strive to be as brief as thoroughness permits. And when you are the one to end a conversation, do so courteously but definitely.

Interviewing. Earlier in this discussion you were advised to develop your own "achievement journal." Besides reinforcing justifiable confidence in yourself, that journal can be a profitable data source for your employment communication. Chapters 11 and 12 deal with the writing of employment messages. This chapter focuses now upon nonverbal and oral aspects of employment interviews.

Suitable preparation for the interview can give you a competitive advantage over other employment candidates. Prepare yourself by researching your achievement record, the history of the company that may become your employer, and information about the business fields in which that company operates. Data sources include the company's annual reports, relevant brokerage-house reports, and publications listed in *How to Use the Business Library*.[3]

Anticipate having more than one interview to secure a job. For example, you may have several meetings with placement counselors at your school, campus representatives of the employer, personnel interviewers at the company offices, the department head for whom you may work, and an executive to whom the department head reports. Build a positive attitude toward the interviews. Remind yourself that they are opportunities for your success.

---

[3] H. Webster Johnson, *How to Use the Business Library* (Cincinnati: South-Western Publishing Co., 1972).

Expect your oral communication to be greatly influenced by nonverbal attributes. How you act and what you wear can affect judgments of what you say. Establish and reinforce eye contact with the interviewer. If amenities include handshaking, use a firm but not excessive grasp. When you enter and when you leave the interview room, walk confidently but do not swagger. When seated, square your shoulders to avoid slouching. Refrain from clasping your hands together. Avoid having one of your knees touch the other; avoid bringing your feet together. In short, use your body to communicate justifiable confidence, not timidity or boorishness. Wear relatively conservative clothing. If you like leisure suits, jeans, or other casual attire, wear them—but wear them at home or at play, not to a job interview.

Expect the interviewer to say something like "Tell me about yourself" or "Why do you want to work for our company?" Cite a few biographical details from your résumé (which the interviewer will have available for reference), but strive to relate those details to the prospective employer. For example, you can relate paid or unpaid work to the need of self-reliant, responsible employees. You can relate your participation in community projects to an employer's need of people-oriented workers. You can relate your academic program to the need of employees who keep learning.

Know that the interviewer expects you to ask as well as to answer questions. Pertinent topics include the role and scope of the organization, job and career prospects, performance requirements, salary scales, and fringe benefits. Permit the interviewer to initiate discussion; be ready to *participate* with your pertinent comments, replies, and questions.

The interviewer has the privilege and responsibility of ending the session. As long as you are permitted to do so, continue communicating genuine interest even if some of the early remarks about a specific job disappoint you. The longer the interview, the greater the possibility of finding more than one work opportunity within the organization.

When the session does end, state your gratitude for the interviewer's time and interest. As you leave, also thank those of the interviewer's assistants who greeted your arrival. Those assistants include the secretary and the receptionist. Within a business week after the session, telephone or write to the interviewer, reaffirming your appreciation. Other profitable suggestions for employment communication are presented in Chapters 11 and 12.

Conferring. Conferences are oral exchanges of data and opinions, intended to inform or to persuade, for purposes of agreement or decision. Complete planning of a conference involves preparation of an agenda and designation of a leader.

Preparing the agenda (a list of topics to be discussed and things to be done during a conference) involves these steps:

1. Determine the conference purpose. Is it to inform? whom? of what? why? when, where, and how?
2. Identify the conference topics, the people who will present them, and the amounts of time needed for discussion.
3. List the conference topics according to their significance for this meeting (#1, most important; #2, second in importance; and so on). Give priority to those items which need *immediate* attention.
4. Review the topic list. If necessary, adjust the priority of topics and the designation of speakers as well as times.
5. Determine the period anticipated for the entire conference.
6. Correlate the topic list with the total available time. Compose supplementary lists for use if the main agenda takes more time or less time than planned.
7. Place the items in logical sequence. For example, if a conference is to deal with personnel requirements of a revised production schedule, it would be logical to discuss the production timetables before focusing on personnel changes.
8. Separate main topics into their parts. For instance, "production schedule" may be discussed in terms of departments, of impact upon other units of the organization, of logistics and quality control, etc.
9. Predict probable responses from the conferees. Unlike a formal lecture, a conference needs conversational give-and-take to be effective. Allow time for questions, answers, and comments from the conferees.
10. Confirm availability of the conference room (including necessary furniture, note-taking supplies, and audio-visual equipment if necessary). Confirm availability of the conferees as well.
11. Edit and proofread the agenda into its final form.
12. Have the agenda and its proposed distribution approved by appropriate authority within your organization.
13. Reproduce copies of the authorized agenda.
14. Distribute the copies. Allow the conferees sufficient time to study the agenda before the meeting.

Organizing and controlling the discussion are responsibilities of the conference leader. As that leader, your tasks are to elicit participation, allow and often reconcile divergent opinions, bring people to agreement, and move people to propose actions or to accept decisions. These are your basic leadership duties and techniques:

1. Formulate the conference purpose.
2. Detect directions to which the discussion tends. Tactfully minimize irrelevant talk.
3. Identify significant ideas, and give due credit for them. Stress their relevance to the conference purpose.

Communication at the Conference Table

4. Emphasize elements of agreement. To achieve major agreement, you may decide to compromise on minor issues. Perhaps you will restrict or postpone controversial discussion that blocks the business of the meeting.
5. When leading discussions of alternative proposals, invite recommendations from the conferees. List all of the proposals on a chalkboard or other group-viewing aid. Encourage adequate discussion to reach unanimity or consensus. Remember that although you serve as conference leader, you may retain the privilege of other members in the discussion group. Like them, you may remain neutral, you may speak directly for or against a proposal, you may support conferees who advance a proposal you prefer, or you may support conferees who criticize a proposal you do not favor.

Oral Reporting. Formal or informal presentation of data, intended to inform or persuade, for purposes of goodwill, decision, or record, is categorized as oral reporting. Your report may be primarily informative, offering data without recommendations; or it may be analytical, offering investigation and recommendations for solving a problem. In either case, you are responsible for showing relationships between your research findings and management objectives. During oral reporting sessions, you may often need to convince your listeners that your findings are pertinent, valid, reliable, and useful to the organization and to the people it serves.

As in other forms of business communication, correlate your oral report with the interests and needs of your listener. You may wish to begin with a concise statement of transmittal and authorization. For instance: "On February 15 you authorized preparation of this report." Or: "Here is the XYZ report you authorized March 7." Clearly state the report subject and purpose. Summarize your findings. Relate them to the aims and resources of your company and to the responsibilities of your listener. As evidence of validity and reliability, describe the data sources and the research methods used. Basing your discussion upon your findings, state your logical conclusions. Also, when appropriate to do so, offer your recommendations. Invite pertinent questions and comments concerning your report; they can supply valuable feedback.

Again as with other forms of business communication, oral reporting procedures are flexible. Adjust your own to the perferences of your listener and to the policies of your company. Reinforce your data and your suggestions; show how the listener and the company can use them profitably and ethically. Concerning informative reporting or instructional presentations, follow the attention-interest-discussion-action sequence mentioned earlier in this chapter. Have your listeners restate your information or your instruction in *their own words*. Instead of asking "Do you understand?" or other questions answerable simply by "yes" or "no," begin your feedback questioning with *who, what, when, where, why*, or *how*. Evaluate and comment constructively on the answers you get. Then observe and discuss the listener's *application* of what you have said.

Audio-Visual Aids to Reporting. When appropriate to oral reporting, use disc, cassette, or reel-to-reel tape recordings (videotape as well as audio tape), motion pictures, filmstrips, slides, transparencies, models, chalkboards, chartboards, or demonstrations. To reinforce oral *or* written reporting, use appropriate photographs, charts, diagrams, graphs, tables, maps, or other aids. Experiment with colors for emphasis. Against a dark background, try white, light green, or light yellow. Against a white or grey background, try black, red, dark blue, or dark green.

As you study the following examples of visual aids, notice that the *tables* (columnar arrangements of words and numbers) have these features:

1. Identification
   a. A title summarizes the content of the table. If more than one table is used, the title is preceded by the word *Table* and an appropriate number. Traditionally, tables are identified by Roman numerals (I, II, etc.). But Arabic numbers (1, 2, etc.) are often used to identify tables today. Be consistent; use *either* Roman numerals *or* Arabic numbers for all tables in a single report.
   b. Traditionally, identification of a table is shown at the top of the visual aid. But modern practice permits that identification to appear at the bottom instead. Again, be consistent; place the identification *either* at the top *or* at the bottom of all tables in a single message.

2. Data Source

   a. The word *Source* (fully capitalized, underlined, or italicized, and followed by a colon) introduces acknowledgment of where or how information was obtained.

   b. If the data source is a book or other publication, identify it as for a footnote.
   Source: J. A. Lee, *Business Tomorrow* (New York: S-W Books, Inc., 1979), p. 40.

   c. If the data source is your own personal observation, give the circumstances, location(s), and date(s) of the observation.
   Source: Personal on-site observation, West Shopping Mall, Atlanta, Ga., noon to 2 PM and 5-7 PM, May 8-9, 19—.

   d. For conversations, speeches, and the like, also give circumstances, location(s), and date(s).
   Source: Keynote address by C. D. Stieg, National Convention of Business Communicators, Bergdorf Civic Center, Chicago, July 21, 19—.

   e. For interview surveys, give the name of the survey, the location(s), and the date(s).
   Source: MGA Marketing Survey, 335 Face-to-Face Interviews, Lawson's Supermarket, Westmont Shopping Mall, Bridgeport, Conn., March 12-15, 19—.
   Source: MGA Marketing Survey, 335 Telephone Interviews, Greater Bridgeport Area, Conn., March 12-15, 19—.

   f. For questionnaire surveys, give the name of the survey, distribution date(s) and area(s), and collection date(s).
   Source: Lopez and Lee Questionnaire Survey; 4,500 questionnaires mailed to residents of Stimmons County, N.J., February 29, 19—; 1,112 usable returns by due date of March 10, 19—.

Notice that the *figures* (graphs, diagrams, and other visual aids that are not tables) have these features:

1. Identification

   a. A title summarizes the content of the figure. If more than one figure is used, the title is preceded by the word *Figure* (or by the abbreviation *Fig.*) and an appropriate Arabic number (1, 2, etc.).

   b. Traditionally, identification of a figure is shown at the bottom of the visual aid. But modern practice permits that identification to appear at the top instead. As with tables, be consistent; place the identification *either* at the top *or* at the bottom of all figures in a single report.

2. Data Source
   Use the same procedure as for tables.

VISUAL AID RATING SHEET*

Place an X next to the word which answers the question (if applicable) for each item.

FIGURE/
TABLE

1. Was the Figure/Table given an identification number? (Applicable only if more than one visual aid was used.)   Yes_____ No_____ (−10)

DESIG-
NATION

2. If "Yes" to #1, did the word "Figure" or the word "Table" introduce the identification number?   Yes_____ No_____ (−2)

3. If "Yes" to #1, were Arabic or Roman numbers used consistently?   Yes_____ No_____ (−2)

TITLE

4. Was the Figure/Table given a title?   Yes_____ No_____ (−10)

5. If "Yes" to #4, was the title complete? Did it tell the viewer what information would be provided?   Yes_____ No_____ (−5) Partially_____ (−3)

SOURCE

6. Was a source line used?   Yes_____ No_____ (−10)

7. If "Yes" to #6, did it identify the person (or kinds of people) and/or organization providing the information? If a printed source, was a complete bibliographical reference given?   Yes_____ No_____ (−5) Partially_____ (−3)

8. If "Yes" to #6, was the date of data collection given? (If a printed source, was date of publication given?)   Yes_____ No_____ (−5) Partially_____ (−3)

9. If a survey was used and answer to #6 is "Yes," was the name (first name or two initials, plus last name) of the person conducting the survey given?   Yes_____ No_____ (−5) Partially_____ (−3)

10. If color *was not* used, would color have helped emphasize points in the aid?   Yes__(-5) No__ (−1) Somewhat_____ (−3)

11. If color *was* used, were the colors easily distinguishable from one another?   Yes_____ No_____ (−5) Somewhat_____ (−3)

LETTER-
ING

12. Was lettering (words, letters, and numbers) *large* enough for associates in last row of audience to read easily?   Yes_____ No_____ (−10)

13. Were words, letters, numbers, rows, and columns *separated* by lines or by enough space to be read easily?   Yes_____ No_____ (−5)

14. Did lettering on the aid give it a professional appearance?   Yes_____ No_____ (−5) Somewhat_____ (−3)

KEY

15. If the significance of colors or symbols had to be understood, was a key provided?   Yes_____ No_____ (−10)

16. If "Yes" to #15, did the key provide adequate information for understanding the aid?   Yes_____ No_____ (−5) Partially_____ (−3)

DESIGN

17. Did the design of the aid promote understanding of the data?   Yes_____ No_____ (−5) Somewhat_____ (−3)

Add the numbers next to the X's and subtract from 100.

SCORE_____

---

*Adapted with permission from a design by H. Karen Kincheloe, North Harris County Junior College (Texas).

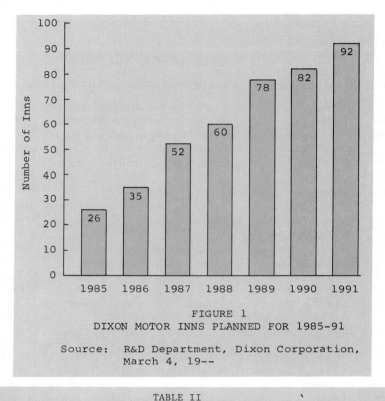

FIGURE 1
DIXON MOTOR INNS PLANNED FOR 1985-91

Source: R&D Department, Dixon Corporation,
March 4, 19--

TABLE II

AVERAGE WEEKLY SALARIES FOR

FIVE OFFICE OCCUPATIONS,

DISTRICT IV CITIES

	STATEVILLE	LAKE CITY	BROCKERTOM
Bookkeeping-Machine Operators	$178.50	$185.00	$168.50
Keypunch Operators	176.50	186.75	172.00
Secretaries	189.50	195.00	182.25
Stenographers	169.00	176.50	166.50
Typists	179.50	184.50	164.75

SOURCE: Bureau of Business Research, Central State College,
Employment Bulletin 80-1101, pp. 23-24.

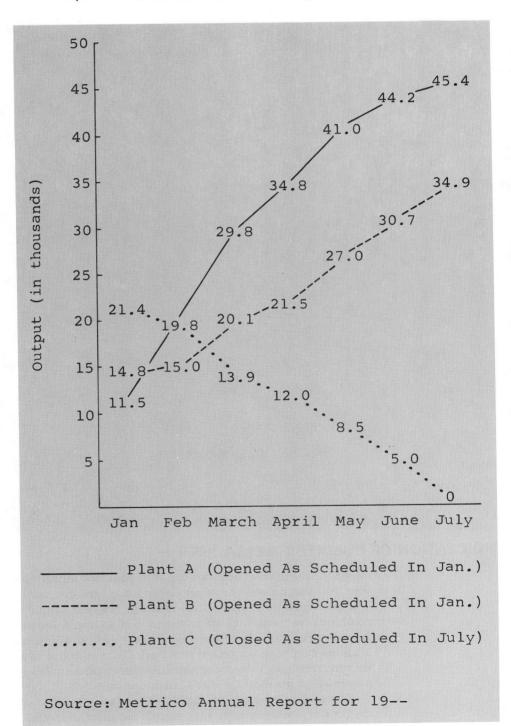

Source: Metrico Annual Report for 19--

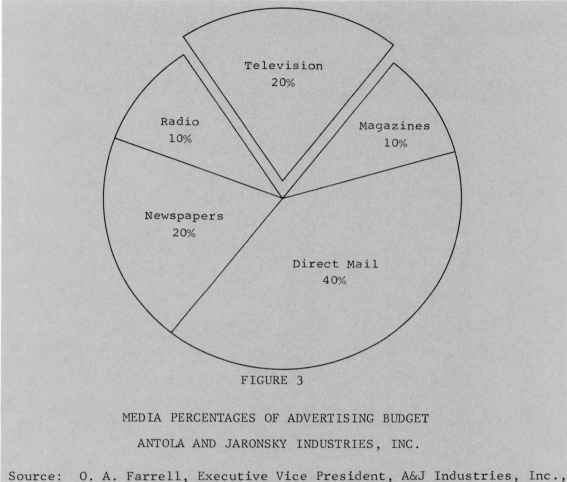

FIGURE 3

MEDIA PERCENTAGES OF ADVERTISING BUDGET

ANTOLA AND JARONSKY INDUSTRIES, INC.

Source: O. A. Farrell, Executive Vice President, A&J Industries, Inc.,
addressing the Fourteenth Annual Television Marketing Seminar,
Arista University, New York City, September 12, 19--

DICTATION OF BUSINESS MESSAGES

As your *nonverbal* behavior can contradict or confirm what you say, so can your *oral* communication offset or reinforce what you *write*—and vice versa. The nonverbal, oral, and written media of business communication are often combined for maximum effectiveness. For example, an interview or a conference usually involves "body language," spoken words, and documents. A business telephone conversation is basically oral; but it often involves use of written references, records, or notes. And nonverbal smiles, gestures, and even pauses affect the message that a telephone transmits.

Dictation of business messages also involves more than one medium. More than merely "writing with your voice," dictation is another example of multimedia communication: nonverbal, oral, and written.

Manager-Secretary Teamwork

A student majoring in secretarial science, office administration, or business education quickly recognizes the importance of efficient message dictation. Sometimes, however, a student whose major field is business administration or management science believes: "When I become an executive, I'll have a secretary to do my messages. Why should I study composition or dictation? I'll be concerned with more important matters."

But what is more important to business than its messages? Can an entrepreneur finance a project without communicating? Can raw materials be obtained, processed, stored, or distributed without communication? Can goods be produced, services provided, and profits earned without communication? Communication requires messages, and messages don't just happen. Their production requires teamwork among all members of an organization, certainly including managers, stenographers, transcribers, typists, professional secretaries. That teamwork is exemplified by efficient dictation procedures.

Pre-Dictation Phase. When you dicate a message, you simultaneously address two people: your stenographer and your reader. Consider their needs and your own as you adapt the basic communication guides that you have already studied.

1. *Organize your materials.* Whether planning to dictate a message that you originate or to answer one that you have received, decide upon the data and the message structure you will use. Consult or review the data sources you need. As you do so, correlate the data with the context of the message you are preparing to dictate. Use notes to help you remember your ideas.

2. *Write cues to yourself.* On your incoming mail, make marginal notes of your probable responses. Indicate items to be included, topics to be discussed, and points to be emphasized in your replies. (Caution: Most organizations approve that practice, but a few insist upon the use of separate notepaper which is later destroyed.) After making your notes, indicate a sequence for presenting them in your message. For instance, use circled *1*'s, *2*'s, and so on, to show the intended order. Written interoffice communication often involves marginal notation, as follows:

   a. An interoffice memo or similar message arrives.
   b. The reader replies with notes or comments along the margin of that message.
   c. A machine copy of the message is made, showing the original page with the marginal notations as responses.
   d. The annotated copy is returned to the original sender.
   e. The receiver keeps the original message, with its annotation, as a record of that communication.

3. *Visualize your reader.* As you prepare to dictate, try to *picture* the receiver of your message. Often you can learn about your reader from earlier messages, reports of field representatives or associates inside the company, available company files, occasionally even magazine or newspaper articles. Such data sources can help you visualize your reader as you approach actual dictation of your message.

Dictation Phase. Having reassured yourself by your planning, proceed confidently to use, or to adapt, the following suggestions for actual dictation.

1. *Number your messages.* During the dictation session, say "Message 1" (or whatever number is appropriate) to your secretarial assistant. What you say next will pertain to the message so numbered.

2. *Classify your messages.* Tell your stenographer that you are about to dictate a rough draft, a memo, a report, or another particular kind of message.

3. *Give special transmission introductions.* Tell your stenographer to send the message by special delivery, registered mail, certified mail, inter-office delivery, or the like.

4. *Identify special stationery requirements.* When appropriate, tell your stenographer to use a particular weight of bond paper, executive-size stationery, half-size memo form, or other type.

5. *State the number of copies necessary.* Tell your stenographer, for example, "an original and two copies."

6. *Just before you begin to dictate the message itself, revive your mental picture of the reader.* If necessary, pause momentarily; visualize your reader as clearly as you can. Then start dictating.

7. *Unless a special vocabulary is appropriate, use conversational language that is suited to your reader and yourself.* Even the salutation of a message can be made conversational. For example: "You're right, Ms. Salazar:" or "Thanks, Lou:" followed by the first sentence of the first paragraph.

8. *Convey a positive, constructive tone.* In almost every situation you can find something constructive to say. For example, a "complaint" may be an "adjustment request," "failed to ship yesterday but did so today" can be simply "shipped today," etc. Strive to communicate constructively, as in these examples:

   a. With definite rather than vague statement: "So that your refund request receives full attention, please complete Items 1, 5, and 9-11 of the enclosed form."
   b. With courtesy: "Thank you for requesting the enclosed brochure. When we can serve you further, please let us know."
   c. With clear-cut action: "Your credit account with us is ready for your use."
   d. With counterproposals if granting a request must be postponed or denied: "Please submit an updated credit request on July 15. Until then we gladly offer you the following discount privileges for cash transactions."
   e. With occasional, appropriate use of contractions and idioms: "We'll take care of it immediately." "You're in the home stretch now."
   f. With personal names when their use is appropriate: "Yes, Sal, that price is firm." "We're in the middle of year-end reports, Laurie. May I have a raincheck on your invitation?"

9. *Fully spell names and unusual words.* For instance, tell your stenographer "A. J. P-I-E-R-S-O-N" or it may be transcribed "A. J. Pearson." Spell a word like "A-L-V-E-O-L-A-R" or it may be typewritten as "Al V. Oller."

10. *Confirm special punctuation or special mechanics.* Say "open parenthesis," "close parenthesis," "ellipsis," "brackets, not parentheses," and the like.

11. *Announce the beginning of a paragraph.* Just say "Paragraph:"

12. *Indicate special indentations, subparagraphs, columns, etc.* For instance, say "Indent the listed items ten spaces instead of five" or "Set columns from left to right as follows:"

13. *Dictate fill-ins for printed forms from left to right and from top to bottom.* Guide yourself by using a blank copy of the form as you dictate the fill-in data.

14. *Speak clearly and use an even rate.* Pronounce your words clearly, but let your sentences fall into natural breath groups. Don't try to dictate a long sentence or a paragraph with a single breath. By mentally planning the corethought before you begin to dictate a sentence, you will tend toward clear pronunciation and even rate.

15. *Become your own constructive critic.* Ask your stenographer to read back—or have your dictating machine replay—what you have said. Clarify, reword, or otherwise edit the spoken draft of your message.

16. *At the end of the session, arrange your materials in the order of your dictation.* Give those materials to your secretarial assistant as reference guides for accurate transcription.

Post-Dictation Phase. When the messages are presented to you for signature (or for initialling, as with some memos), use these evaluation question-guides:

1. Appearance and mechanics—Does the message present an attractive visual impression? Are proper format and layout followed? Are there smudges or noticeable corrections that require retyping? Are the grammar, punctuation, and spelling appropriate to the image you are trying to convey?

2. Empathy—Are the data and tone suited to the reader's personality and purposes as well as to yours? Have you selected words that are likely to be understood? Ideally, have you chosen words that almost certainly will not be misunderstood?

3. Definitions—Have you stated what you mean by key, novel, or specialized words? Have you applied the semantic rule that words have no meaning? Do your definitions convey your meaning in terms that the reader is likely to understand?

4. Explanations—Have you used words that help your reader logically to identify, compare, contrast, remember, or apply what your message conveys?

5. Word Economies—Have you combined thoroughness with appropriate brevity and appropriate tone?

6. Instructions—Have your directions to your secretarial assistant been fulfilled?

7. Signatures—If the preceding steps are complete, have you signed or initialled the message? Customarily, business letters are signed. A routine memo need not be signed or initialled by its sender. A memo of moderate importance is initialled; one of considerable importance is signed.

Dictation Modes

The preceding suggestions are usable for face-to-face or for machine dictation. Each of those modes offers distinct advantages and disadvantages.

Face-to-Face Dictation. With this mode, the communicator dictates instructions and messages to a secretary or stenographer. If necessary, the dictator's assistant can ask immediately for clarification. Since a person instead of a machine is recording dictation, the communicator is free of microphone limitations.

These suggestions can help you with face-to-face dictation:

1. Be prepared to dictate, as described earlier in this chapter.
2. Arrange office schedules to avoid distractions during dictation.
3. Use the previously mentioned dictation techniques.
4. Speak clearly, evenly, and audibly. Keep pencils, paper clips, even your fingers, *away* from your lips as you dictate.

Face-to-face dictation has several disadvantages. For instance, sessions must be scheduled when both the dictator and the secretarial assistant are free from other tasks. Even with careful scheduling, however, telephone calls or unexpected visits may interrupt; and especially if the secretary has reception duties, the dictator's trend of thought may be broken. Also, face-to-face dictation is expensive. It is costly as well as inconvenient to employ secretarial or stenographic assistance for dictation when the communicator is traveling or when overtime pay is involved.

Machine Dictation. With machine dictation the communicator uses a recording element. The typist uses a transcribing or listening element to reproduce the spoken language. The dictating element usually has these basic parts:

1. motor—started and stopped by an on/off switch

2. microphone—to transmit the dictator's voice
3. reel, spool, or the like—to accommodate the recording medium
4. recording medium—tape, belt, or disc
5. recording head or stylus—to transfer the dictator's voice to the recording medium
6. volume control—to adjust loudness of the voice recording
7. playback control—to make audible what has been recorded

Various models of dictating elements have these supplementary features: tone control to adjust vocal resonance and pitch; volume indicator to show effects of volume control; index to mark the start and the end of a message, also to identify locations for corrections.

The transcribing element has an earplug instead of a microphone. Besides controls for speed, volume, and tone, the transcribing element may have a pedal that allows the transcriber to pace listening rate while typing the message.

Here are suggestions for effective machine dictation:

1. Familiarize yourself with the equipment. Make a test recording for audibility and clarity of playback.
2. Be prepared to dictate.
3. Resist being hypnotized by the sound of your own voice. Keep focusing your attention upon your message and its intended reader. Also empathize with your secretarial assistants; help them to detect from your recording *every detail* of what you want the typewritten message to be.
4. Use the dictation techniques discussed earlier.
5. Remain within the audio range of the machine as you dictate.

A major advantage of machine dictation is that is allows the secretarial assistant to do other work while the dictator records messages. Transcribing and typing can be scheduled flexibly. Also, since many up-to-date dictation machines are compact and battery-operated, dictators can use them conveniently during the business day, after business hours, or while traveling. A major disadvantage of machine dictation is that the communicator does not have immediate secretarial feedback and correction. The dictator must constantly anticipate and record answers to likely questions about the dictated material. Also, he or she must remain within the audio capabilities of the machine. As you see from this discussion, the nature and pace of modern business communication require expertise not with either but with *both* modes of dictation, face-to-face *and* machine.

Machine dictation is used frequently as organizations become complex, as data multiplies, and as technology advances. In their efforts to control the skyrocketing volume and cost of communication, business people are applying systems management (described in Chapter 1) to message production. "Word processing" is the term used for this integration of people, machines, and communication.

Besides dictation machines, modern word-processing systems include automated typewriters, electronic computers, and information-retrieval equipment. With word-processing systems, machines do the work of repetitive typing, of data recording and transmission, even of routine error correction. But word processing generates challenges. For example, schools and colleges need *constantly* to update their courses, teaching methods, and learning techniques so that students can cope successfully with the volume and pace of modern business communication. Educators and managers also share these concerns: What are the personal, societal, economic, and political effects of rapidly changing technology, particularly the innovative technology of communication? To what extent should human behavior be directed or otherwise influenced by computerized communication? To what extent should word processing be humanized?

REVIEW AND TRANSITION

Nonverbal communication includes actions and appearances, timings and distances, postures and movements, gestures and facial expressions. Inhalation, phonation, resonation, and modification are physiological aspects of oral communication. Psychological aspects involve establishing justification, developing confidence, and overcoming stage fright. These are basic steps for preparation and presentation of oral messages: determine purpose, analyze audience, evaluate situation, organize data, structure message, and plan delivery.

Categories of face-to-face and telephone communication include conversing, interviewing, conferring, and oral reporting. Often combined for maximum effectiveness, the types of oral delivery are impromptu, extemporaneous, textual, and memorized. Whether face to face or by machine, dictation of business messages is a multimedia process of nonverbal, oral, and written communication requiring manager-secretary teamwork.

Part One of this book established the need for—and introduced general concepts of—effective business communication. Part Two explained those concepts in greater detail and presented basic techniques for using them with written, oral-visual, and nonverbal communication.

Continuing this deductive order, from the study of generalities to the study of particulars, Parts Three through Seven will guide you toward expertise with specific business messages. Those messages include goodwill statements; inquiries, requests, and replies; orders and acknowledgments; explanations and instructions; employment communications; sales promotions; claims and adjustments; credit and collection series; research proposals and business reports.

DISCUSSION QUESTIONS

A. Within the context of Chapter 7, what are appropriate definitions and illustrations for these terms?

   1. media
   2. nonverbal communication
   3. rapport
   4. vowel
   5. diphthong

   6. consonant
   7. impromptu oral delivery
   8. extemporaneous oral delivery
   9. textual oral delivery
  10. agenda

B. In what ways have you observed or experienced nonverbal communication being used to promote sales of the following? Cite specific examples.

   1. automobiles
   2. clothes
   3. jewelry

   4. homes or apartments
   5. furniture
   6. foods or beverages

C. In what ways do the following aspects of nonverbal communication affect oral or written messages? Give particular illustrations.

   1. appearances
   2. timings
   3. distances

   4. postures
   5. movements
   6. gestures and facial expressions

D. What evidence from your readings, observations, and experiences tends to support or to challenge this assertion: Awareness of how air is transformed into spoken words can help you improve your oral communication.

E. Concerning psychological aspects of oral communication, what techniques seem especially useful to you in establishing justification for your message, developing confidence in yourself, and overcoming stage fright?

F. In what ways do preparing and presenting *oral* communication resemble—and differ from—preparing and presenting *written* communication?

G. What advantages and disadvantages are associated with these types of oral delivery: impromptu, extemporaneous, textual, memorized? In what ways can you minimize the disadvantages?

H. In what ways do these categories of communication resemble—and differ from—one another?

   1. conversing face to face
   2. dictating face to face
   3. conversing by telephone
   4. dictating by machine

   5. interviewing face to face
   6. conferring face to face
   7. reporting orally to one person
   8. reporting orally to a group

What are specific examples of communication effectively combining at least three of those categories? What are specific examples of effectively combining any of those categories with nonverbal or with written communication?

I. What is word processing? What are its advantages and disadvantages? What examples of word processing have affected you as a student? as a consumer? as an employer or an employee? In your opinion, to what extent should human behavior be directed or otherwise influenced by computerized communication? To what extent should word processing be humanized?

APPLICATIONS

(If audio/vido tape recorder is available, use it for playback of these exercises.)

1. As an application exercise for Chapter 1, you prepared a written introduction of yourself. Using that material for reference, introduce yourself orally now to your professor and your classmates. Limit your oral introduction to a maximum of three minutes. Invite written evaluations of your presentation; introduce yourself orally again.

2. Orally deliver any of the other material that you wrote for exercises in Chapters 1-7. Invite constructive criticism from your professor and classmates. Orally present the material again. (Ask your professor to assign a time limit for this activity.)

3. Adapt Applications 1 and 2: Include the use of at least one appropriate visual aid.

4. Here is a team application for an employment interview situation: Student 1 is the interviewee; Student 2, the office receptionist; Student 3, the interviewer's secretary; Student 4, the interviewer. This four-person team demonstrates what should happen between the interviewee's arrival and departure. The team then invites constructive criticism from its observers (the professor and classmates) before performing its second demonstration. This team approach may be used until all the class members have participated in demonstrating an employment interview.

5. With all members of the class as a team, say aloud the sounds represented by the underlined letters on page 146. Then have each student, individually, pronounce those sounds.

6. Form a six-student team to discuss these Chapter 7 topics of preparing and presenting oral communication:

   Student 1—Determine Purpose   Student 4—Organize Data
   Student 2—Analyze Audience   Student 5—Structure Message
   Student 3—Evaluate Situation   Student 6—Plan Delivery

   (a) Student 1 introduces the team and its topics. Student 2 ends the team presentation by inviting questions and comments from the audience. Students 1-6 communicate their assigned topics by textual delivery. Following constructive criticism by the other students in the class and by the professor, this team presents its textual delivery again.

   (b) Form a second team of six students. This team uses extemporaneous delivery of its topics, invites constructive criticism of its performance, and presents the extemporaneous delivery again.

   (c) Form a third team of six students. Each member of this team uses memorized delivery of at least one paragraph concerning the topic assigned to him or her. Following constructive criticism, present the memorized deliveries again.

7. Adapt Application 6: The teams design and use appropriate visual aids for their presentations.

8. Because successful dictation involves clear speech, practice aloud the following word-sets; request constructive criticism of your dictation from your classmates and your instructor.

steel-still	sell-sill	lips-lisps	tacks-tasks
deep-dip	pen-pin	gaps-gasps	tucks-tusks
bean-bin	real-rill	mitts-mists	peaks-speaks
seen-sin	heal-hill	boats-boasts	pacific-specific
head-hid	deal-dill		
bell-bill	feel-fill	ax-asks	grasp-grasps
		tax-tasks	asterisk-asterisks
caught-cot	flows-flaws		
court-cart	pose-pause	be in-being	cannon-canning
form-farm	rod-rode	see in-seeing	garden-guarding
store-star	con-cone	do in-doing	cash owed-cash showed
coal-call	on-own	bacon-baking	we'll own-we'll loan
bowl-ball	ah-oh	taken-taking	you'll end-you'll lend
			will buy-wheel by

9. Assume that you are to conduct a conference on improving dictation techniques within an organization. The other students are to be the conferees. If your class is large, separate it into several teams, each of which is to conduct a conference (with an assigned leader for each conference).

   (a) (Using Chapters 1-7 as data sources, prepare a suitable agenda.

   (b) With another student in the role of secretarial assistant, dictate the agenda as part of a message to the intended conferees.

   (c) You are the conference leader; conduct the meeting. After the conference, elicit constructive criticism from your professor and your classmates. Then write a summary of your own perceptions and evaluations of (a) the performances of the conferees and (b) the performances of the conference leader.

   An oral-visual communication rating chart appears on the next page.

AN ORAL-VISUAL COMMUNICATION RATING CHART

SPEAKER: TOPIC: DATE:

(Rating Scale: Excellent = 5 points   Good = 4   Average = 3   Fair = 2   Poor = 1)

		Scores	Comments
A.	Speaker's Behavior		
	1. Physical Appearance	_____	
	2. Visual Rapport	_____	
	3. Volume and Resonance	_____	
	4. Rate (speed of speaking)	_____	
	5. Pronunciation	_____	
	6. Facial Expressions and Gestures	_____	
	7. Postures and Movements	_____	
	8. Other Aspects (e.g., use of audio and/or visual aids)	_____	
B.	Message as Delivered by Speaker		
	9. Clarity of Corethought	_____	
	10. Logic of Organization	_____	
	11. Psychology of Organization	_____	
	12. Suitability to Audience	_____	
	13. Fulfillment of Purpose and Scope	_____	
	14. Language Usage (grammar, word choice)	_____	
C.	Discussion involving Conferees		
	15. Leadership of Discussion	_____	
	16. Stimulation of Audience Participation	_____	
	17. Attitude toward Conferees	_____	
	18. Relevance of Information	_____	
	19. Fulfillment of Purpose and Scope	_____	
	20. Language Usage (grammar, word choice)	_____	
	TOTAL SCORE:	_____	
	MAXIMUM:	100 points	

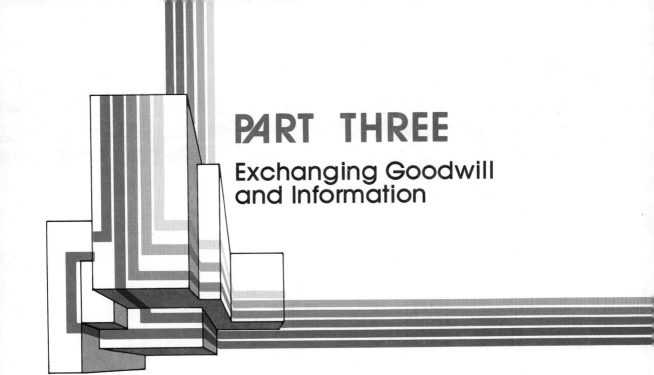

PART THREE
Exchanging Goodwill and Information

Part Three reinforces this concept: to communicate you need skills of perception, interpretation, and application, all of which involve goodwill.

To compose functional business messages, you need to know how to gain and to retain goodwill. Goodwill is the important thread which is used in all communication messages·to make them successful. Chapter 8 will help you convey appreciation and similar goodwill feelings through your understanding of empathy, ethics, and human behavior. You will use goodwill in saying yes or no to requests and in composing special human interest messages.

Chapter 9 pertains to goodwill in orders, remittances, inquiries, special requests, adjustment requests, and credit messages. And Chapter 10 discusses messages that help you inform, explain, direct, or instruct with goodwill. Tone, timing, and courtesy are also stressed in this chapter.

CHAPTER 8

Goodwill as a Business Commodity

Business success and strong personal relationships require a genuine interest in other people. To be genuinely interested in others, you must share their hopes, successes, and disappointments. From this sharing, you will be able to express in your messages a natural "you orientation," a sincere feeling of appreciation, and an unselfish helpfulness.

Unless you admit the importance of others to yourself and of yourself to others, how can you succeed as a human being or as a business person? And unless you use words and actions to establish and sustain beneficial human relations, how can you reap the profits of goodwill?

Your authors consider goodwill as more than the decision of a customer to return where he or she has been well served. Goodwill, in our opinion, is both an experience and a commodity. The "experience" factor is evident in the give-and-take relationships that are used in the business environment to work with and through people to accomplish particular goals. Characteristics such as the following are examples of the "experience" factor of goodwill: voluntariness, favorable humor, receptive frame of mind, cooperation, and compliance. The "commodity" factor is the confidence in, loyalty for, or satisfaction with the personnel, operations, and products of a business.

Goodwill is classified as a personal and professional asset—intangible but real—that profoundly affects your private life and your business career.

BEHAVIORAL INFLUENCES UPON GOODWILL

When psychological aspects of human behavior are examined, you discover how and why people do act. You soon identify psychological needs which are common to all human beings—belonging, self-esteem, personal fulfillment, etc. The need to belong involves acceptance and approval. Self-esteem embraces the need for status and self-respect, and personal fulfillment pertains to the development of one's potentialities and capacities. How individuals satisfy these psychological needs is reflected in their behavior.

Because psychological needs are related to behavior, interpersonal relations are affected. In other words, you react to and interact with other people based upon your psychological needs and your self-image. For example:

NEGATIVE SELF-IMAGE		POSITIVE SELF-IMAGE	
Mary:	You've done a good job in writing your January sales report, Bob. Your recommendations are good.	Mary:	You've done a good job in writing your January sales report, Bob. Your recommendations are good.
Bob:	Well, I did the best I could. I was hoping it would be better.	Bob:	Thanks, Ms. Smith. I really enjoyed writing it.
Jean:	Are you planning on applying for the office manager's position?	Jean:	Are you planning on applying for the office manager's position?
Lois:	No, why bother? Too many people are better qualified than I.	Lois:	Yes, and I think I'll have a good chance of being selected.
Dean:	I'll be able to recommend you for an assistant professor's rank as soon as you acquire a few more hours of advanced graduate work.	Dean:	I'll be able to recommend you for an assistant professor's rank as soon as you acquire a few more hours of advanced graduate work.
Teacher:	As much as I would like to take more graduate work, I just don't feel I can effectively teach and take courses at the same time.	Teacher:	I appreciate your advice, and I'll seriously consider what you've said.

Effective communicators *ethically* fulfill their own psychological needs. This means that the communicators use empathy, honesty, justice, and trust to advance their careers and the prosperity of their companies. Such ethical factors as these provide a foundation upon which communicators can effectively use goodwill to create positive attitudes and stimulate positive actions.

Communicating positive ideas and feelings, moreover, involves another ethical responsibility—the obligation of actually helping when you can. Resist the temptation to become what is called a "Pseudogoodwiller." Pseudogoodwillers are those often well-intentioned but usually deceptive people who busily TALK ABOUT but rarely PROVIDE genuine assistance, who invite you to call on them for help and then do not give it. Pseudogoodwillers, preoccupied with appearances rather than realities, are content to LOOK rather than to BE good. They depend upon the illusions of personal charm, of reliability, and of aid. But when you need them, you find that their goodwill, also, is an illusion. You ask for information they can and should supply; they promise to give you a report promptly and then "forget" to do so. You assign them responsibility for a task, and they accept the responsibility gladly (because it connotes prestige for them). Later, they tell you, in effect: "So many things were happening that I just didn't get around to it. I'll do it now." The pseudogoodwiller's *now* arrives late if ever, and the promises remain largely unfulfilled. Yet he or she will continue to TALK goodwill, to PROMISE cooperation, and to OFFER empathy with little or no results.

All of us may have a tendency toward pseudogoodwill, which, psychologically, is a use and, ethically, a misuse of communication to gain attention. Think of goodwill as an attribute that is other than superficial, decorative, or something "nice to have." Think of genuine goodwill as a human blending of ideas and emotions communicated by words or other symbols and provided by helpful, appropriate, productive action.

GOODWILL—A BUSINESS COMMUNICATION GOAL

Virtually every business message affords the opportunity to communicate goodwill. Use of that opportunity depends upon planning and organizing your message *before* writing. As discussed in Chapter Four, planning and organizing free the mind to concentrate on the attitudes and feelings which you wish to express in the written message.

By preparing messages which are reader-oriented, you can establish goodwill more easily. What is meant by "reader-oriented"? Simply stated, it means the message is composed with the reader in mind. The message is written in terms of the reader's interests, desires, and benefits. Therefore, your choice of words, phrasing, and psychological approach is designed to create a concerned, positive tone.

The tone of a message has a direct relationship to goodwill. Oral communications are supported by facial expressions and gestures. Written messages must depend entirely upon words and how those words are used. Therefore, a good writer avoids the use of words that are boastful, preachy, accusatory, or condescending.

Because goodwill is so essential to the success of a business message, examine and compare these two letter versions. Notice how the "well-written" message includes the following goodwill qualities:

1. A personalized expression of appreciation which refers to the reader's letter and interest;

2. A reader-oriented message which emphasizes benefits to the prospective customer;
3. A utilization of words which cannot be interpreted as boastful or condescending; and
4. A structuralization of sentences which convey a positive viewpoint.

A POORLY WRITTEN MESSAGE	A WELL WRITTEN MESSAGE
We received your letter concerning our mirrors. As you probably know, a well-constructed mirror will dramatize your walls and give added dimension to any room.	Thank you, Ms. Guevara, for your interest in furnishing your new apartment building with Clear Vision Mirrors. These mirrors will dramatize your walls and give a look of added dimension to each room.
Our Clear Vision Mirror is free from distortion because we construct them from high-quality glass and coat them with eight layers of silvering. And, of course, we give a fifteen-year guarantee on each mirror.	Clear Vision offers you the most distortion-free mirrors available. Each mirror is made of high-quality glass coated with eight layers of silvering to insure your satisfaction.
The enclosed brochure gives you additional information. After studying our brochure, you may wish to visit our display at the Allen Home Improvement Center. Their sales people will answer any questions you may have.	Every Clear Vision Mirror is guaranteed for 15 years against any defective material or workmanship. After examining the enclosed brochure, please visit our Clear Vision display at the Allen Home Improvement Center in your city.

Thus far, the discussion has centered around writing traits which are necessary in ALL business messages. To study the goodwill function of your messages in more detail, let us classify business messages into (1) those that help you say yes, (2) those that help you say no, and (3) those that demonstrate special "human interest" considerations.

Letters That Say Yes

When you can do what someone has asked of you—for instance, establish or renew credit, extend the period of an agreement, or grant a refund or other adjustment—you have a ready-made opportunity for gaining or retaining goodwill. To benefit from such an opportunity, write your letters in deductive order. This means your letters begin with general statements and are followed by supporting facts and details.

By writing deductively you are immediately providing your reader with the information he or she is hoping to receive—the favorable response. Stressing the favorable action in the first paragraph establishes a warm feeling between you and your reader; thus, goodwill is created. In addition, the final paragraph of your letter provides you with favorable conditions for concluding your message with a courteous goodwill closing.

By using comparisons, notice how the following "goodwill" messages are developed deductively. The first paragraph tells the reader what she or he is hoping to hear—the general statement. The succeeding paragraphs are concerned with details and explanations. And the final paragraph provides a courteous goodwill ending. In addition, these "goodwill" messages also have the following plus features:

1. A pleasant willingness to respond positvely to the reader;
2. A tone which is void of boastful, preachy, accusatory, or condescending words;
3. A concisely written message which avoids misunderstanding and curtness; and
4. A genuine interest in being of service to the reader.

BADWILL MESSAGE

We have received your letter of September 5 in which you requested four copies of our annual report. These copies are enclosed.

Please note, Professor Jones, the special reference section. Each topic and definition in the reference section is keyed to the report. By calling your students' attention to this section, they will be able to more fully understand the report.

We are also adding your name to our mailing list so you will be able to receive a copy of our company magazine, THE PRODUCTION DIGEST. We are sure you will find our magazine helpful and most informative.

If we can help you in other ways, please inform us.

GOODWILL MESSAGE

Four copies of our annual report are enclosed. We are pleased to supply this material for the use of your economics students, Professor Jones.

Although annual reports of various companies are similar, you will notice a special reference section in our report. By using this reference, your students will find explanations and definitions for comments and terms as they are used in the report. Moreover, these comments and terms appear in the same order as the items to which they refer and are keyed to the annual report's page numbers.

In addition to the copies of our annual report, your name has been placed on our mailing list to receive the monthly issue of our company magazine, THE PRODUCTION DIGEST. Should you wish additional copies or reprints of any of the articles, please let us know.

Best wishes for a successful academic year.

BADWILL MESSAGES	GOODWILL MESSAGES
This letter is to inform you that we have approved your credit application. As you probably know, a company as large as ours can purchase brand-named merchandise and offer it to our customers at reasonable prices. Additionally, we have a staff of sales people who have expertise in building and in home decorating. You may wish to take advantage of this service, also. Visit one of our stores soon. We are anxious to do business with you.	Your credit account is now ready for your use at all our Ware stores. Your reputation—both business and personal—is excellent, and we welcome this opportunity to establish a friendly relationship with you. When you visit one or our stores, you will find a pleasant atmosphere in which to browse and to shop for all your building and home-furnishing needs. A wide variety of brand-named merchandise is available from which to make your selections. Our sales staff includes experienced builders who can advise you on any building problems you may have. In addition, two interior decorators are available to assist you in the home decoration area. Come in soon, select your merchandise, and just say: "Charge it."
We were certainly surprised to hear that your portable electric heater was functioning improperly at the time you purchased it. The personnel in our receiving department carefully check each item before it is placed on the floor for sale. However, if the automatic thermostat is not maintaining its comfort selection as you claim, return the heater to us. We will certainly make whatever adjustment is necessary. Thank you for calling this to our attention. If we can help you in any other way, please let us know.	You're right, Mr. Bergstein. Your new portable electric heater is guaranteed within the terms of your purchase contract. And we're ready to justify your faith in our word. Please return your heater to us, and we will either correct the automatic thermostat so it will maintain its comfort selection or provide you with another heater. Thank you for calling this to our attention. Customer satisfaction is very important to us, and we value your patronage and your goodwill.

Letters That Say No

As a business person, you will receive requests to which you must say no. When these situations occur, your reply certainly needs to reflect goodwill. Some people, however, exploit the rejection of another person's request. For the sake of momentary pleasure because of someone else's pain, they risk losing ethical integrity, psychological fortitude, private peace of mind, and future business profit. If you detect within yourself a feeling of glee as you contemplate saying no to someone, try honestly to answer these questions:

1. Am I symbolically *substituting* this person for someone else who has injured me?
2. Do I mistakenly believe that I can *get back* at someone else by arrogantly rejecting this person?
3. Am I exposing myself to loss rather than gain by saying no antagonistically or viciously?

Truthful answers to these questions will prevent many foolish and costly errors that ruin personal relationships and destroy business careers.

In planning your written message, psychologically project yourself into your reader's situation. Recognize and accept the fact that your reader believes the request is justified. With this assumption you can carefully plan your message so that your reader can more easily understand and adjust to your decision.

Knowing HOW to say no is not enough; knowing WHEN to say no is equally important. For example, you may remember a past experience when you made a request which was denied. Did you receive reasons before the denial was made, or did the justifications follow the denial? Was justification or explanation omitted? What were your reactions?

To say no before explaining WHY usually closes the mind of your reader to anything you say thereafter. Giving well thought-out reasons prior to the rejection, you help the reader get a better understanding of the refusal. A carefully planned explanation of the reasons for the refusal will often help your reader surmise the rejection before it is explicitly stated or implied.

In using "the reason before refusal," you are writing in the inductive order—going from specific reasons to a general statement of refusal. Hopefully, this approach sets the stage for achieving a mutual and friendly relationship with your reader. Your opening statement or paragraph sets the tone for establishing goodwill; the tone and ideas are friendly and related to the gist of the message. The content is factual so as to avoid "losing your reader" before you present your reasons for the refusal.

The explanations for the refusal are stated positively. In other words, tell your reader what you can do—not what you can't do. For example:

NEGATIVE APPROACH	POSITIVE APPROACH
I will not be able to participate in your workshop on January 12, 19—.	I have previously agreed to conduct a workshop at the American University on January 12, 19—.
Therefore, we cannot repair your camera under the terms of the guarantee.	However, we will repair your camera for $10.50.

The closing paragraph of the "no" message is very important to goodwill. Remember, no matter how well you word the message, your reader will quite naturally experience some disappointment. For this reason the major thrust of the closing paragraph should be to regain any goodwill that you may have lost. Study the examples on page 185 to see how "no" messages can be effectively written in the inductive order.

When you use the inductive order in writing a "no" message, consider the words you use and the attitudes you communicate. Recognize—and so omit from *your* communications—the evidence of negative and often destructive attitudes.

ANTAGONISTIC MESSAGES

We are sorry, but we cannot give refunds on merchandise purchased during our January sale. If you recall, the conditions under which you bought your portable radio were explained to you at that time. Company policy dictates that we make no exceptions.

You agreed to make a definite payment on your account each month. An analysis of your account indicates you are in arrears in making your monthly payment. Inasmuch as we desire payment, we must insist that you give this matter your prompt attention. Please mail your remittance at once.

A message which implies good news and then, without preparation, disappoints your reader damages goodwill. By applying empathy you can avoid writing such disarming messages as the following:

DISARMING MESSAGES

Thank you, Ms. Miller, for writing us about the portable radio you purchased on January 10. Your satisfaction with our products and our services is important to us.

Your letter mentioned that you purchased the radio as a gift for your son who is in college. And after purchasing the radio, you discovered that your son already owned a radio. It is perfectly understandable how situations such as this can happen.

At the time you made your purchase we were offering the radios at a sale price. Therefore, we cannot issue a refund as you have requested.

Your September 10 credit application is sincerely appreciated, and it has been given prompt and careful attention.

Although you are new to our community, a routine investigation indicates you have already established an excellent personal reputation. Therefore, we are pleased you are interested in establishing credit with us. However, please resubmit your application when your business reputation has been established. In the meantime, your cash orders will be filled promptly.

If messages like these must be written, let your competititors send them! Let your competitors, if they insist upon needless injury through words, risk losing the goodwill—and the business—of potential or actual customers. When **you** must say no to people, inside or outside your company, use words that convey the reasons for the necessity of your action, words that preserve self-respect, and words that "keep the door open" for future transactions. Remember that the one whom you alienate today may be the very person whose goodwill you will need tomorrow.

Having these thoughts in mind is useful. *Applying* these thoughts to your "no" message is profitable.

MAINTAINING A CUSTOMER'S SELF-RESPECT

Your explanation for the lateness in making your June payment is appreciated, Mr. Oates. And the promptness with which you have always met your obligations in the past has been excellent.

If it were possible, your payment period would be extended. Like you, however, we too are debtors. And our creditors require a check from us, which in turn depends upon a check from you.

Let's continue our fine cooperation. Of course we'd prefer full payment of your current obligation; but, if necessary, we'll accept a partial payment. So please send your remittance by return mail.

ATTRACTING A POTENTIAL BUYER

Best wishes for the success of your new business—The Schear Office Supply Company. And thank you for considering us as a business with whom you wish to establish credit.

You can be assured that your credit application has been studied with care. You will also be pleased to know that the customary information sources have confirmed your excellent personal credit. Because this is your first business venture, we do believe your ratio of assets to liabilities should be stronger. Therefore, we hesitate to burden you with additional financial obligations. Please let us review your application in six months, Mr. Winters.

However, we do want to make our goods and services available to you. Avail yourself of our liberal cash discounts and our special sales, and let us help you achieve your anticipated success. Please send us your first cash order, and your merchandise will be shipped to you in ample time for your grand opening.

Letters That Demonstrate Human Interest

In addition to supplementing "yes" or "no" messages with goodwill contexts, you may design messages whose main function is to convey goodwill. Letters of welcome, appreciation, congratulations, and condolence are examples of messages which emphasize this function. As you study the remainder of this chapter, notice how a genuine interest in and appreciation for the reader is emphasized.

the Four Seasons Lodge

614 ERIE BOULEVARD
BARK RIVER, MI 49807

June 29, 19--

Mrs. Robert Hansen
United Retailing Association
525 Lincoln Road
Springfield, IL 62702

Dear Mrs. Hansen:

Your plans to hold your national retailing conference in Michigan during October will provide your members with a beautiful panorama of fall colors. And we appreciate your interest in using our facilities as your conference headquarters on October 25, 26, and 27.

During the fall season, many visitors are attracted to our area because of its geographical location. Several spring-fed lakes nestled in the surrounding forests are within minutes of our hotel. The brightly-hued colors of the season provide a spectacular background for the many families and civic groups who wish to take color tours of the area. And because this is a popular season of the year, our facilities are completely reserved for the dates you requested.

However, we do want to help you, Mrs. Hansen. May we suggest the dates of October 10, 11, and 12 for your conference? Your group can be accommodated at that time. We will place a "hold" on these dates until June 30. Please let us know your decision by then.

The fall colors should be at their brightest intensity during the dates we have suggested. And the members of your organization will find our hospitality and facilities designed with your comfort in mind.

Sincerely yours,

Charles Hempstead

Charles Hempstead
Conference Director

"No" Message with Goodwill

LONE STAR
LONE STAR SAVINGS & LOAN
2168 WEBSTER RD.
ABILENE, TX 79602

April 29, 19--

Professor Peggy Leeson
Department of Data Processing
City College
105 Williams Street
Abilene, TX 79606

Dear Professor Leeson

It will be a pleasure to have your advanced class in data processing
visit our computer center on Tuesday, May 19.

Mr. Mark Johnson, our systems analyst, will meet your class in the
main lobby of our corporate center at 9:30 a.m. Prior to the tour,
your students will then have an opportunity to discuss our operations
with Mr. Johnson. After the tour, arrangements have been made to meet
with your students in our conference room to answer any questions they
may have. As you requested, the entire program should end by 12:45 p.m.

We are looking forward to your visit.

Sincerely yours

Wilma J. Thompson

Wilma J. Thompson
Manager

art

"Yes" Message with Goodwill

Welcome. Welcome messages foster warm feelings between you and your readers. These messages express your awareness of their arrival, your pleasure in having them as new members of your community or your firm, and your good wishes for their success in their new environment.

By communicating these feelings, you help to alleviate loneliness or anxiety. Your recipient is grateful for your hospitality and fellowship; and this gratitude may produce a tie of lasting loyalty to you and to your company.

Although messages of welcome are basically greetings, they do accommodate *low-pressure* sales promotion or resale. Use them to establish a favorable relationship with you, your products, or your services (sales promotion). You can also assure the recipients of their wisdom in joining your community or your company and in trusting the people, the organization, and the goods that you represent (resale).

Notice how the following message conveys a feeling of genuine goodwill by subordinating the sales promotion to the element of greeting. The goodwill is achieved by emphasizing the welcome, providing useful information, and offering the company's services. The sales promotion is subordinated by simply introducing the company without giving additional information about the firm's operations.

WELCOME THE NEWCOMER

Your decision to make your home in Midland is pleasant news. We'll be happy to have you here!

While you are waiting for your company transfer, the enclosed booklet, *All About Midland,* should be helpful. If you have a particular question, however, just write or telephone our office . . . (517) 631-1400; and we'll supply the information you need.

As the letterhead indicates, our company is affiliated with a national real-estate network. Any of our sales staff will gladly describe the services we offer you . . . but that's enough about us. The purpose for writing this letter is to say:

Welcome . . . to YOUR city.

Welcome letters are also used for greeting new employees. They may reassure the newcomer of your interest in his or her welfare and of your expectations regarding fair play, helpful effort, and loyalty. Again, promotion or resale is subordinated and goodwill is emphasized. For example:

GREETING THE NEW EMPLOYEE

Welcome to Morrison's; we're happy to have you as a member of our staff.

You are joining a group of professionals who function as a team, and we know your cooperation and loyalty will be directed toward this teamwork. To help you become oriented to Morrison's the enclosed policy and procedure manual is for your use as a ready reference.

Your new position will offer you exciting challenges and opportunities for professional growth. You have our pledge of fair play in exchange for your helpful efforts. We're glad to know you and happy to have you with us.

Letters of welcome are important to the operation of successful businesses. And the opportunities for writing these letters are limited only by one's imagination. Other possibilities for using welcome messages may include the welcoming of (1) an employee who has been on an extended leave of absence, (2) potential customers to a grand opening or a special sale, and (3) a customer who has not transacted business with your firm for a long time.

Appreciation. To express appreciation is both good manners and good business policy. To do so strengthens interpersonal relationships with associates through recognizing the psychological needs for status and self-esteem. People need to feel accepted; they need to feel that they have the approval of others. And genuine expressions of appreciation are means through which businesses can convey their awareness of the reader's attainments, contributions, or special importance as a person.

The following are appreciative messages selected to illustrate typical occasions for use. Note the sincerity which these letters express:

APPRECIATION FOR A SERVICE

Thank you for conducting the two-day workshop on report writing for our management staff. Your presentation was both interesting and beneficial to our staff.

As a matter of fact, the materials you presented are being used as a guide in the preparation of our reports. We appreciate the help you have given us.

APPRECIATION TO AN EMPLOYEE

Your suggestion on how to reduce maintenance costs on office equipment is a good one. Thanks, Mary, for calling this to our attention.

You can be sure that we will begin to implement your plan next month. In the meantime, please accept the enclosed check as evidence of our appreciation.

APPRECIATION FOR A FAVOR

Your thoughtfulness in recommending our company to Mr. Alvarez is appreciated. You will be interested in knowing that we were able to find the kind of home for which he was looking.

You have our pledge of continuing customer satisfaction, Mr. Andrews, and our gratitude for your confidence.

APPRECIATION FROM A MANAGEMENT EXECUTIVE

Your thoughtful comments on our marketing study were excellent, and I sincerely thank you for your help. When I can return your courtesy, please count on me.

Congratulations. Genuine pleasure with the success or good fortune of others is expressed through messages of congratulations. These messages include incidents of professional or vocational distinction as well as celebrations of personal significance (marriages, birthdays, anniversaries, and the like). Congratulatory messages often are quite short. Here are several examples:

CONGRATULATIONS FROM AN EXECUTIVE

Congratulations are in order, Tom! Today marks your tenth year with our firm. The contributions and loyalty you have demonstrated are certainly appreciated. You have my best wishes for continuing success with National.

RECOGNITION OF A CUSTOMER

Your election as President of the American Marketing Association is certainly good news. With your expertise, experience, and personality, we know the Association will have a very successful year under your leadership.

Heartiest congratulations, and best wishes to you and AMA.

PRAISE ON PROMOTION

This short note is to tell how pleased I am to hear of your promotion to Personnel Director of your firm. Your promotion is well deserved, and I am glad to know that your company officials have recognized your fine services.

You've earned this advancement, Maria, and you have my best wishes for continuing success.

Although congratulatory messages emphasize your sincere pleasure in one's attainments or good fortune, many of these messages may lend themselves to low-pressure sales promotion. Bear in mind, however, that any sales promotion is subordinated to your main purpose—to congratulate your reader. For example:

BEST WISHES ON THE NEW ARRIVAL

Congratulations, Mr. and Mrs. Chiu, on the birth of your son, Kai-san. The enclosed birth announcement appeared in the *Starr* on January 12, and we thought you might like to have it.

To help you commemorate this happy occasion, we have selected a small gift from our infants' department for your baby. The next time you are in town, please stop in, present this letter, and receive your free gift.

Again, congratulations and best wishes to you and your new son.

CONGRATULATIONS ON THE ENGAGEMENT

The happy news of your engagement appeared in the *Gazette* on May 3. Please accept this copy of the announcement with our congratulations. Because the announcement is sealed in plastic, you will be able to preserve it with other mementos of that "special day."

You may also wish to know how we help future brides in planning their weddings. These services will be gladly explained to you when you visit the bridal department in our main store. But this is the end of our "sales talk," Ms. Smith. Our reason for writing is to congratulate you and to extend to you our very best wishes for a happy future.

Condolence. Condolence messages are written when you wish to express your concern over another person's grief. Various kinds of disaster such as illness, death, burglary, and fire are situations for which you may wish to communicate your sympathy. But to dwell upon unhappy circumstances may cause difficulty in composing your message. Therefore, the purpose of your message should be to encourage and to reassure the person.

Depending upon the situation, you may prove your goodwill by offering concrete aid such as temporary quarters, fill-in merchandise, extended credit, or financial loans. At the very least, instead of reminding the victim of the sorrow and despair, you should communicate moral encouragement and the prospect of improvement. Observe how the following messages encourage and reassure the reader and offer concrete aid.

LETTER OF ENCOURAGEMENT

You have many friends, Bill, who are looking forward to continuing their business relationships with your firm. Until you have new storage facilities, you are most welcome to utilize the available space in our warehouse on Second Avenue. Please let me know your decision.

LETTER OF REASSURANCE

Best wishes for a quick recovery, Bob. We know you will be following doctor's orders and will be out of the hospital in a short time. We're looking forward to seeing you back on campus.

REVIEW AND TRANSITION

Part Three continues to stress the application function of communication through relating the needs of the writer and receiver. Explanations are given regarding the composition of functional business messages that help to communicate rather than merely express.

Chapter 8 specifically stresses the importance of gaining and retaining goodwill. The psychological aspects of human behavior are examined to see how goodwill is affected. In addition the psychological approach to using goodwill in writing messages that say yes or no is analyzed. Messages that demonstrate human interest are also discussed in this chapter.

As you proceed to read and to study Chapter 9 of Part Three, you will be concerned with messages that help you search for information, assistance, products, or services.

DISCUSSION QUESTIONS

A. Explain the following statement:
"One must communicate rather than merely express ideas and feelings."

B. Goodwill is both an experience and a commodity. Describe a situation which demonstrates goodwill as (1) an experience factor and as (2) a commodity factor.

C. How are psychological needs related to human behavior?

D. Explain the following statement:
"How effectively you generate goodwill depends upon how well you have planned and organized your messages prior to writing."

E. Explain each of the following in terms of their effects upon positive tone:

  1. a. We are shipping your four-drawer filing cabinet today.
    b. Your four-drawer filing cabinet is being shipped to you today.

  2. a. Because of the superior rating given by the American Testing Laboratories, we handle the Tomlinson door chimes exclusively.
    b. We are sorry, but we do not handle the Zodiac door chimes.

  3. a. An electric cord for your new Western iron has been mailed today. Your complete satisfaction with our products is important to us. Thank you for writing.
    b. We received your letter of complaint regarding the frayed cord on your new Western iron. We'll check into the matter as soon as possible.

  4. a. We are very pleased to receive your order of January 12. It will give us the opportunity to demonstrate the excellent service that we give to all our customers.
    b. Thank you, Mr. Jones, for your order of January 12. We appreciate the opportunity to serve you.

  5. a. You must make your monthly payment now. It is two weeks late already.
    b. To insure your good credit rating, please send us your overdue payment today.

F. In what ways does your perception help and hinder your relationships with others?

G. In the context of Chapter 8, what letters are written in deductive order? Explain your answer.

H. Explain the effectiveness of the following closing paragraph of a "no" letter: "If there is any other way in which we can help you, please let us know."

I. Explain the following statement:
"Virtually every business message affords the opportunity to communicate goodwill."

J. Evaluate the following messages:

  1. We are sorry, Mr. Miller, but our company will not be contributing this year to your free medical clinic. Our management council decided at its last meeting to commit our contributions to the Bay County Community Chest. Perhaps we will be able to do better by you in another year.

  2. I am so sorry to hear that you are again in the hospital with the same old ailment. Get well soon, and let's hope you will not have another recurrence.

  3. As part of our routine investigation, we have checked your credit references, Mr. Watson. May we suggest that you make cash purchases of smaller orders at shorter time intervals. We can guarantee deliveries on short notice.

  4. I was very sorry to hear about the death of your partner. She was a very cheerful person whose dedication to the legal profession is unparalleled. I know you will have difficulty continuing your practice without her.

5. Your failure to supply us with a catalog number of the light fixture you ordered is causing the delay in shipment. Will you please supply us with the correct number so we can complete our transaction.

APPLICATIONS

1. Rewrite the following statements so they generate goodwill.
   a. It is against our policy to repair electrical appliances which are not purchased through our company.
   b. Because we are the leading manufacturer of electric typewriters, we will permit you to return your purchase for credit.
   c. It is now time for you to purchase your supplies for the new season.
   d. Your letter received. Adjustment to be made.
   e. We have investigated your complaint and find your claim to be legitimate.
   f. I'm sorry, but I cannnot accept your invitation to be a speaker at your conference on June 12. I will be busy at that time.
   g. We received your letter of April 4 concerning a request for our annual report. As you probably know, we appreciate the opportunity to distribute said reports to those who wish them. Therefore, we are sending you a copy as requested.
   h. We simply cannot extend credit to you when you are already overextended with financial obligations.
   i. It is not possible for us to sell our merchandise directly. We do have franchised dealers.
   j. If you wish, you can visit our ABC dealer and see our display.
   k. There is no way we can possibly extend credit. Please submit your payment immediately. We have creditors that must be paid, too.
   l. The vastness of our company permits us to work through dealerships only.
   m. We are unable to make shipment until next month; we are completely out of the merchandise you requested.

2. As a perceptual exercise, select a student who will orally describe an item or a picture. As the description is given, all students will draw the item as they perceive it. Then compare your drawing with the picture or the item described. How closely did you perceive the item to the description given? What prevented you from drawing the exact picture? What parallel can you see between this activity and the activity of writing a goodwill letter?

3. You are the Credit Manager of the Tidewater Petroleum Products Corporation, 55 Mercer Street, El Paso, TX 79910. Your company has received an application for credit from the Casper Auto Supply Company, 102 Buford Street, Casper, WY 82601. After careful consideration your company decides to grant credit. Write a deductive letter to Mr. Robert Sweet, President of the Casper Auto Supply Company, and grant the credit.

4. Adapt Application 3 so that you refuse to grant credit to the Casper Auto Supply Company. This letter is to be written in the inductive order.

5. As Personnel Director of the Saginaw Community Hospital, 820 North Washington Avenue, Saginaw, MI 48602, write a letter to Ms. Aline Lynch in response to her employment application. Ms. Lynch has applied for an accounting position, but none is available at this time. Address your letter to 452 Elm Court, Saginaw, MI 48604.

CHAPTER 9

Orders, Remittances, Inquiries, Requests

As a business person, you will be writing messages which seek products, services, and information. Within this category are orders and remittances, inquiries and special requests, adjustment requests (claims), and credit applications. When you compose these messages properly, they stimulate your reader to understand your needs and desires. And it is through such understanding that you earn favorable responses.

ORDERS

Order messages are written when appropriately printed purchase orders are not available. Like the purchase order form, therefore, the order message contains essential information such as the following:

1. ORDER NUMBER. Give the order number to facilitate records management as well as communication between buyer and seller.
2. QUANTITY. State number of units, sets, feet, yards, dozens, ounces, pounds, tons, reams, etc.
3. IDENTIFICATION. Cite the catalog number, which is a shortcut to exact identification of the article. When the catalog number is unavailable, describe the item in detail (size, color, material, weight, finish, quality, style).
4. PRICE. List the separate prices and their extensions (total for an item).
5. SHIPMENT. Unless you have a special agreement with the seller, specify the shipping method (parcel post, express, air freight, or other means) and, if necessary, the shipping route. For goods sent to an address other than yours, show the destination of the shipment. State whether the goods are to be delivered by a definite date. Designate "rush delivery" when you need especially speedy shipment.
6. PAYMENT. Describe the method of payment (unless you and the seller already have agreed upon such method).

GLENDON LIGHTING, INC.
1202 Grant Circle
Columbus, OH 43201

Purchase Order

Order No.   624

Date   June 30, 19--

To   Electrical Supplies Inc.
2200 Somerset Drive
Cleveland, OH 44141

Terms   2/10, n/30

Shipped Via   REA Express

Quantity	Cat. No.	Description	Price	Total
4	16J1912	Swivel Spotlights with 7-inch diameter, chrome-plated frames	8.96	35.84
1	16J2022	Five-light wagon wheel style chandelier, maple finish with brass components	41.50	41.50
3	16J2218	14-inch globe pendants, white components	12.25	36.75
				114.09

By _Kurt Sehenbach_
Purchasing Agent

Purchase Order

In completing a purchase order form or writing an order message, you must clearly arrange and accurately specify your requirements. To accomplish these objectives, use a separate line or a separate paragraph to describe each item you order. Tabulate all items ordered and show their total cost when possible. Also, carefully verify every detail of the contents so that delay, financial loss, or legal problems are not incurred.

Begin your order with a general statement and then follow it by facts and details (deductive writing). Remember to be specific when writing your general statement—"Please send the following equipment . . . ." Too often order messages become confusing when the general statement is written in the form of hinting such as, "I would like to order . . ." or "I would like to have . . . ." Notice how the following order message is written in the deductive order and includes:

1. A direct beginning (general statement)
2. A tabulation of all items ordered by quantity, catalog number, description and unit price, and total value
3. The shipping method and payment plan
4. The time shipment is expected

ORDER MESSAGE

Electrical Supplies, Inc.
2200 Somerset Drive
Cleveland, OH 44141
Ladies and Gentlemen:
Please ship the following lighting fixtures under my order number 624:

Qty.	Cat. No.	Description	Total
4	16J1912	Swivel Spotlights with 7-inch diameter, chrome-plated frames at $8.96 each.	$ 35.84
1	16J2022	Five-light wagon wheel style chandelier, maple finish with brass components.	41.50
3	16J2218	14-inch globe pendants, white components at $12.25 each.	36.75
			$114.09

Ship via REA Express. Payment is based on previous credit terms of 2/10, n/30, which have been established on past orders.
Please ship these fixtures so they will be received no later than June 25, 19—.
Sincerely,
Dale Stevens
Purchasing Agent

REMITTANCES

Businesses normally notify credit customers when an account payment is due. When credit purchases are made by an individual, the creditor usually sends a statement of account. However, an invoice is sent to a business which has made a credit purchase. By examining these forms you will notice that more detailed information is given on an invoice that on a statement of account. Because of the detailed information, state and federal auditors prefer the invoice as documentation when auditing business accounts.

Remittances are made by voucher check, duplicate invoice with an attached check, or remittance message.

The Voucher Check

Many businesses use the voucher check for remittances. When multiple purchases are made from the same vendor, the statement portion of the voucher check lists invoices for which the check payment covers. A copy of the voucher is then retained by the accounts payable department.

	Statement of Account
Date	August 1, 19--
	New Horizons Co. 333 Granville Drive Chicago, IL 60606
To	Mr. John Lucas 1300 Northville Street Chicago, IL 60608

Date	Items	Debits	Credits	Balance Due
July 1	Balance			23.10
10	Invoice #6775	32.50		55.60
15	Invoice #6823	15.25		70.85
20	Credit memo #123		5.50	65.35
25	Payment on account		50.00	15.35

Statement of Account

INVOICE

LUDWIG OFFICE FURNITURE
11515 Grandin Parkway
Reading, PA 19602

Sold To	MacArthur Manufacturing Company 1456 Industrial Avenue Reading, PA 19603	Date	May 2, 19--
		Our Order No.	16502
		Your Order No.	415673
Terms	2/10, n/30	Shipped By	Our truck

Quantity	Description	Cat. No.	Unit Price	Amount
5	Four-drawer, letter size file cabinets, Green	523J10	110.95	554.75
5	Two-drawer, letter size file cabinets, Green	523J20	72.95	364.75
				919.50

Salesman   Ormsby

Invoice

```
                                                              90-9000
                                                              ──────
                                                               1211

                         December 21 _____ 19-- _____ No. 165994

PAY to the order of  The Chemical Company of America          $545.20
──────────────────────────────────────────────────────────────────
Five hundred forty-five 20/100------------------------------------- Dollars


   Redwood Valley Bank                  ──────────────────────────
  ⑆1211⑆9000⑆ 143⑈0602⑈46⑈              Treasurer
```

─ ─

Detach This Stub Before
Cashing This Check

TO   IN PAYMENT OF THE FOLLOWING INVOICES:

    The Chemical Company of America
    1560 Hastings Road
    Sacramento, CA 95826

Date	Invoice	Amount
12/1--	5321	225.25
12/10--	5430	319.95

Voucher Check

Voucher checks are often prepared on computers. When the statement portion of the voucher check does not provide ample space for itemizing each invoice, a computer list is attached.

Duplicate Invoice with Attached Check

Many companies that do not use voucher checks prepare a check, attach it to a duplicate invoice, and mail it to the vendor. If a question arises as to the correctness of the invoice, a remittance message may also be enclosed.

Remittance Message

When composing your payment message, describe the amount and form of your remittance. Also specify how your money is to be applied; this is especially important when you have more than one account, owe a note, or are late in payment. Unless you specify how your payment is to be applied, it may be used as the creditor sees fit. Remember, also, that your remittance message should indicate enclosures by definite references—for example, "Enclosure: Check for $124.25."

You may wish to request information, assistance, or service in your payment message. In so doing, the following plan can be used:

1. Refer to your remittance by indicating the amount of payment and the invoice number.
2. State your inquiry or request.

The following illustration shows how this plan is applied:

Please credit the enclosed $124.25 check for Invoice No. 2301.

Your cosmetics have been well received by our customers. We therefore plan to offer a wider range of your products as soon as our building expansion is completed. Will you please have your sales representative call on us within the month to explain and to demonstrate the various counter displays you offer as a service.

Situations will often arise when you will respond to a creditor whose remittance shows that the amount of payment is incorrect or the terms of the payment are misunderstood. Should either situation occur, you need to compose a message which promptly, clearly, and tactfully results in the correction of the creditor's mistake.

Study this sample plan and the illustration that follows it:

1. Refer cordially to the reason for your message.
2. Indicate your belief that something is incorrect or misunderstood.
3. Explain the correction or proper interpretation.
4. Request appropriate action.

CLEAR, TACTFUL MESSAGE

Maintaining your goodwill, Mr. Miles, prompts us to clarify an apparent misunderstanding.

When crediting your account for the amount of your check ($441.30) in payment of our June 12 invoice ($450.30), we noticed a two percent discount had been taken. Because your cash payment was made after the ten-day discount period, we anticipated a payment for the full amount of the invoice.

Please send us another check ($9.00) so we may mark your account "paid in full."

INQUIRIES

When you seek information concerning the goods and services a business provides, you usually write an inquiry letter. Inquiries are also written when you request information of a reciprocal nature. For example, you will write inquiries when you ask for price quotations, payment terms, folders, catalogs, credit information, and employment recommendations. For these types of messages, the following plan can be effectively used:

1. State your request. (Often your statement will be a question.)
2. Give reasons for your inquiry.
3. Furnish pertinent facts and specific details.
4. Indicate when information is needed, if appropriate.
5. End your message courteously.

A CONSUMER'S INQUIRY

What is the estimated cost to a homeowner who wishes to insulate both ceilings and exterior walls as a do-it-yourself project?

Because your company manufactures a pure cellulose product which is nonsettling, fire resistant, vermin proof, and moisture resistant, I am particularly interested in your insulation. Here are pertinent details:

1. Structure: One-story, frame home
2. Dimensions: 28' × 50'
3. Insulation Depth: Walls—4 inches
                       Ceilings—6 inches

I am planning this project for my two-week vacation which begins on June 10. Please supply me with an estimate in ample time to make a decision concerning insulation costs.

INQUIRY TO AN APPLICANT'S REFERENCE

Please provide us, confidentially, the credit standing of Ms. Carol Cross, 1607 Jenkins Street, Brooklyn, NY 11208. Ms. Cross has applied for credit with us and has listed you as a business reference. We shall therefore appreciate your answers to the following questions:

1. How long has she had a credit account with you?
2. What are her buying habits (average purchases, seasonal fluctuations, annual volume)?
3. What are her paying habits (discounts, delinquencies)?
4. How do you rate her as a credit customer?

Your answers and other pertinent comments will be welcome. Please call upon us when we can reciprocate in exchanging credit information with you.

Requests for general information, catalogs, booklets, or samples may often be short letters. For instance:

Do you give discounts to educators on any of your business publications? If so, what are the titles and prices of these publications?

When the answer to your inquiry will benefit you rather than the respondent, enclose a stamped, addressed reply envelope. When an inquiry concerns something of mutual interest to you and the respondent or when you send an inquiry to a respondent with whom you deal often, you may omit the reply envelope.

SPECIAL REQUESTS

When writing a persuasive or favor-seeking request, you should be deliberately but tactfully forceful. These messages should create a logically and psychologically favorable impression no matter what favor is involved. To accomplish this, use a structured plan for your message.

The very beginning of your message should be reserved for the purpose of attracting attention. Attention can be obtained by referring to your reader's interests, responsibilities, or problems. Whatever method you use, however, relevance to the gist of your message is essential. Special request messages often begin by asking a question. If you use this approach, word your question so it requires more than a "yes" or "no" answer; this causes your reader to give some thought before answering and thus enhances interest.

Before making your request, give reasons why your reader should respond positively. Describe the details of your request within the context of the reader's self-concern. Use words that help the reader visualize mentally the positive results or qualities of cooperating with you. By using your creativity you can stimulate the respondent's desire to act positively to your request.

Ask your reader to accommodate your request, or tell the reader courteously and confidently what action should be taken. Be positive in making your request. You might say, for example, "Let us know which of the following two dates is more convenient for you." However, avoid statements such as, "Will you please let us know if either of the two dates is convenient for you." To write such a statement not only provides your reader with a ready-made excuse for refusing your request, but the statement itself may indicate that you are not confident of a positive answer.

When writing a favor-seeking message, be success conscious. Believe, and help your reader believe, the positive value of your request.

In summary, here is a useful structural plan for a special request.

1. Attract the reader's attention by referring to his or her interests, responsibilities, or problems.
2. Describe details of your request within the context of the reader's self-concern.
3. Ask the reader to accommodate your request, or courteously and confidently state the action that the reader should take.

PERSUASIVE REQUEST

How closely does the academic preparation of our retailing students match your business needs?

An evaluation of the retailing curriculum will be held during a luncheon meeting, November 10, in the Collegiate Room on campus. As manager of a leading department store in this city, Ms. Brown, you can provide valuable input to this discussion.

The administration and the business faculty invite your participation. Please sign and return the enclosed card to indicate you will be with us.

Notice how the writer of the persuasive request attracted attention by referring to the reader's concern; related that concern to the request; described pertinent circumstances that helped the reader visualize positive results; stated the request; and then specified, courteously and confidently, the action that the reader should take. The following special request also illustrates this structured plan:

SPECIAL REQUEST

Congratulations on the contract to test the feasibility of extracting gas and oil from Michigan shale deposits.

Because energy is of vital concern to all citizens, the American Travelers' Association has asked me to speak to their organization next September regarding energy for the future. Your recent announcement concerning your research contract has prompted me to include this information in my address.

Your assignment as research manager of the oil shale research group in the hydrocarbon and energy research laboratory makes your comments especially valuable. Answering the following questions will be most helpful:

1. What are the estimated chances of success?
2. What are the estimated barrels of oil in shale?
3. When will the feasibility test begin?
4. What are the major obstacles?

Your help in supplying this information will be appreciated. A stamped, addressed reply envelope is enclosed for your convenience.

Occasionally you will need to ask a favor from an associate. Notice how your structured plan for the special request message also applies to the favor-seeking request.

FAVOR-SEEKING REQUEST

The film strip on the free enterprise system that you and your students developed is very good. The method you used to extol the virtues of free enterprise is commendable.

As an educational institution, we are often called upon to provide speakers and to present programs for various professional and service organizations. By accepting these opportunities, we have created an excellent rapport with the community. And today, Bruce, the American Marketing Association requested a program for their April meeting. Your film strip would provide an excellent program for this organization.

May we count on your giving this presentation? Please call me (Extension 488), and I'll gladly make the necessary arrangements.

Notice how you can compose tactful yet forceful requests through the use of stimulating thoughts and feelings. Whether the favor is great or small, you should prepare each request as persuasively as possible to receive a favorable reception.

ADJUSTMENT REQUESTS

Business people sometimes receive unsatisfactory products or services. Shipments are occasionally incorrect, and misinterpretations of agreements—despite good intentions—do occur. Such situations are usually handled by writing an adjustment request.

When writing an adjustment message, show empathy toward your reader. Recognize that human beings are imperfect, and errors do occur despite precautions that are taken to avoid customer dissatisfaction. Also recognize that the company with whom you are transacting business needs your goodwill and wants you as a satisfied customer. With these thoughts in mind you will be able to write a courteous adjustment message which contains a minimum amount of irritating phrases.

The adjustment request also serves as valuable feedback to your recipient. Without such feedback your reader may not know that anything is wrong. And unless you communicate your dissatisfaction, how can it be corrected?

When you are dissatisfied and believe that a company is responsible for your dissatisfaction, write a direct request for adjustment. Here is a useful plan for structuring that request.

1. Identify the unsatisfactory product or service; state the date and conditions of purchase.
2. Describe the specific circumstances of your dissatisfaction. Use words that help the reader understand the facts you have determined, rather than the emotions that you feel.
3. Describe a suitable and fair adjustment (that is, correction or remedy).
4. Request prompt and appropriate action.

A DIRECT ADJUSTMENT REQUEST (MILD TONE)

Thank you for promptly processing our May 12 order, sent to you with our check No. 5233. When unpacking the order, we noticed the rib knit bottom of a man's cardigan contained a very noticeable construction flaw. The catalog number for this item is #5022.

Knowing your established reputation of complete customer satisfaction, we request an appropriate adjustment for this transaction. The cardigan was reshipped to you this afternoon. Please issue a refund for this part of our order.

AN ADJUSTMENT REQUEST (FIRM TONE)

A man's cardigan, Catalog 5022, arrived in unsatisfactory condition with our May 12 order. This order was accompanied with our check No. 5233.

When unpacking the order, we noticed the rib knit bottom of the cardigan contained a very noticeable construction flaw. An appropriate adjustment for this transaction is requested. Please issue a refund for the cardigan, which is being returned to you today.

More forceful adjustment requests should be written when both buyer and seller are responsible for error, when responsibility for error is uncertain, or when the seller tends to reject claims. Syllogistic reasoning, described in Chapter 2, is used in messages of this kind. This structural plan may be followed:

1. Describe, in terms with which the seller will agree, a general assumption that pertains to your claim. Bases for such a *major premise* are terms that identify the situation; facts about the transaction; the seller's reputation for fairness and customer service; the seller's need of goodwill.
2. Describe, in accurate and complete detail, the circumstances that have caused your dissatisfaction. Such *minor premises* should represent causes or effects that you, personally, can authenticate.
3. Relate the minor premises to the major premise. Show how the circumstances of your dissatisfaction pertain to the terms of the situation, the seller's good name, or the business association that you intend to continue with the seller.
4. State the logical conclusion: the seller should settle your claim equitably. Specify what you think is fair.
5. Request the seller to do what logical judgment dictates: grant your claim.

AN ADJUSTMENT REQUEST (FORCEFUL TONE)

Your desire to uphold your established reputation of complete customer satisfaction is certainly well known.

These circumstances pertain to that reputation:

1. Our May 12 order, accompanied by our check No. 5233, included a man's cardigan with rib knit cuffs and bottom.
2. When unpacking the order, we noticed the rib knit bottom of the cardigan had a construction flaw.

As a logical conclusion to this transaction, we have returned the cardigan to you and are requesting an adjustment that supports your reputation of customer satisfaction. Please refund our payment for this item.

Chapter 15 offers you additional examples of persuasive adjustment messages.

CREDIT APPLICATIONS

Messages that seek credit privileges fall generally into two categories: simple (routine or direct) and special. When you know the creditor probably will welcome your account, send a simple application. When approval requires concession, however, you should send a special credit-application message.

The Master Charge and VISA application which appears on page 206 is an example of a simple credit application. In this case, however, the banks advance payments to businesses from which you have made purchases. The customer then makes payments to the bank that issued the card.

APPLICATION FOR YOUR MONEY CARD

IMPORTANT: Read these Directions before completing this Application — Check Appropriate Box

☐ If you are applying for an individual account in your own name and are relying on your own income or assets and not the income or assets of another person as the basis for repayment of the credit requested, complete only Sections A and D.

☐ If you are applying for a joint account or an account that you and another person will use, complete all Sections, providing information in B about the joint applicant or user.

☐ If you are applying for an individual account, but are relying on income from alimony, child support, or separate maintenance or on the income or assets of another person as the basis for repayment of the credit requested, complete all Sections to the extent possible, providing information in B about the person on whose alimony, support, or maintenance payments or income or assets you are relying.

Are you applying for Master Charge ☐ **VISA** ☐ **Both** ☐

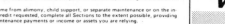

SECTION A – Information Regarding Applicant

NAME (FIRST, MIDDLE, LAST)	
STREET ADDRESS	
CITY	STATE	ZIP CODE
YRS. AT CURR. ADDRESS	HOME PHONE	DATE OF BIRTH
PREVIOUS ADDRESS (IF PRESENT LESS THAN 2 YRS.)	
SOCIAL SEC. NO.	DRIVER'S LICENSE NO.
NEAREST RELATIVE'S NAME (NOT LIVING WITH YOU)	
ADDRESS	RELATIONSHIP

EMPLOYMENT
- EMPLOYER | PHONE NO.
- ADDRESS
- SUPERVISOR'S NAME | YOUR POSITION | YRS. SERV.
- NET SALARY OR COMMISSION $_____ PER____

PREVIOUS EMPLOYER | YRS. SERV.

NO. DEPENDENTS   AGES

Alimony, child support, or separate maintenance income need not be revealed if you do not wish to have it considered as a basis for repaying this obligation. Alimony, child support, separate maintenance received under:
court order ☐   written agreement ☐   oral understanding ☐

Other income: $_____ per_____. Source(s) of other income

Is any income listed in this Section likely to be reduced in the next two years?
☐ Yes (Explain in detail on a separate sheet.)   ☐ No

Have you ever received credit from us?_____When?_____Office:_____

Checking Account No.:_____ Branch:_____

Savings Account No.:_____ Branch:_____

SECTION B – Information Regarding Joint Applicant, User, or Other Party

NAME (FIRST, MIDDLE, LAST)	
STREET ADDRESS	
CITY	STATE	ZIP CODE
YRS. AT CURR. ADDRESS	HOME PHONE	DATE OF BIRTH
RELATIONSHIP TO APPLICANT (IF ANY)	
SOCIAL SEC. NO.	DRIVER'S LICENSE NO.
NEAREST RELATIVE'S NAME (NOT LIVING WITH YOU)	
ADDRESS	RELATIONSHIP

EMPLOYMENT
- EMPLOYER | PHONE NO.
- ADDRESS
- SUPERVISOR'S NAME | YOUR POSITION | YRS. SERV.
- NET SALARY OR COMMISSION $_____ PER____

PREVIOUS EMPLOYER | YRS. SERV.

NO. DEPENDENTS   AGES

Alimony, child support, or separate maintenance income need not be revealed if you do not wish to have it considered as a basis for repaying this obligation. Alimony, child support, separate maintenance received under:
court order ☐   written agreement ☐   oral understanding ☐

Other income: $_____ per_____. Source(s) of other income:

Is any income listed in this Section likely to be reduced in the next two years?
☐ Yes (Explain in detail on a separate sheet.)   ☐ No

Have you ever received credit from us?_____When?_____Office:_____

Checking Account No.:_____ Branch:_____

Savings Account No.:_____ Branch:_____

SECTION C – MARITAL STATUS (Do not complete if this is an application for an individual account.)

Applicant: ☐ Married   ☐ Separated   ☐ Unmarried (including single, divorced, and widowed)
Other Party: ☐ Married   ☐ Separated   ☐ Unmarried (including single, divorced, and widowed)

SECTION D – CREDIT INFORMATION (If Section B has been completed, this Section should be completed giving information about both the Applicant and Joint Applicant, User, or Other Person. Please mark Applicant-related information with an "A". If Section B was not completed, only give information about the Applicant in this Section.)

Creditor	Type of Debt or Acct. No.	Name in Which Acct. Carried	Original Debt	Present Balance	Monthly Payments	Past Due? Yes/No
1. (Landlord or Mortgage Holder)	☐ Rent Payment ☐ Mortgage		$ (Omit rent)	$ (Omit rent)	$	
2.						
3.						
4.						

Everything that I have stated in this application is correct to the best of my knowledge. I understand that you will retain this application whether or not it is approved. You are authorized to check my credit and employment history and to answer questions about your credit experience with me.

Approved	Credit Limit Desired ☐ $300 ☐ $500 ☐ $700	Applicant's Signature	Date
Amount $_____	☐ $1000	Other Signature ☐ Joint Applicant ☐ Authorized User	Date

Credit Card Application

Chemical Bank and Trust Company, Midland, Michigan

Application for Personal Credit

You may request personal credit during a visit or a telephone conversation with a seller, but inconvenience or preference may prompt you to write a credit-seeking message. The corethought often is simply: "Please send me the required forms for opening a charge account with you." If you choose to submit detailed information, however, the following plan is helpful:

1. Request the opening of a charge account.
2. Identify yourself by name and address. (Mention your former address or addresses if you have relocated recently.)
3. Cite other credit affiliations (names and addresses of firms with which you have transacted credit business).
4. Describe your employment (your employer's name and address, your position, your salary).
5. Identify the bank with which you have a checking and/or savings account.

REQUEST FOR PERSONAL CREDIT

Please open a charge account in my name. I presently reside at 504 Post Street, Modesto, CA 95355. Until five weeks ago I lived in Muncie, Indiana, where my address was 630 West Elm Street.

Muncie firms with which I have credit accounts include Ardmore's Department Store, Jenkin's Hardware Co., and Jaye's.

As an accountant with the A.C. Reynold's Company, I earn about $19,500 a year. My checking and savings accounts are with the City Bank of Modesto.

I look forward to using and enjoying credit privileges with your firm.

Application for Business Credit

If a company seeking credit privileges is well known and has an excellent reputation, the message requesting credit need not be in detail. For example:

Please ship the enclosed order, on your usual credit terms, to our store at 150 East Main Street, Berkeley, CA 94709.

This company is listed in Dun & Bradstreet. We have done extensive credit business with major suppliers and look forward to a mutually profitable association with you.

Perhaps you have a new business and have not established credit, or you need a credit extension beyond the established credit policy. In such situations, you may use a special or persuasive application which follows this plan:

1. Attract the creditor's attention and interest by offering new business through a credit account.
2. Imply or state how your credit association can be one of mutual benefit.

3. Include the information usually expected in a routine credit application. (Emphasize the information that shows you merit the creditor's trust.)
4. State positively the action you wish to be taken.

A NEW BUSINESS CREDIT REQUEST

Another profitable market for Hetherwood China can be realized through featuring your fine products in my new gift shop in Northport, Connecticut. By extending credit to our company, you will be sure that Hetherwood China is available to this rapidly growing community.

In addition to our full-time residents, thousands of tourists are attracted to this scenic area for year-around activities. The results of a market research study indicated that both residents and tourists will constitute a strong buying public. And with my fifteen years' experience as manager of the Lewis Jewelry Company in Providence, Rhode Island, I feel the turnover of my inventory will be very significant.

Because my gift shop has just recently opened, I am enclosing personal credit references and a certified financial statement.

Please approve this credit request so that I may introduce Heatherwood China to our area of Connecticut.

Credit Terminology

The high standard of living that Americans enjoy is directly related to credit privileges that both individuals and businesses are granted. Because credit permeates almost all of American business today, all of Chapter 16 is devoted to a detailed discussion of credit. At this point in your study of business communication, however, familiarize yourself with the various classifications of credit and of credit terms.

Credit may be classified and defined as follows:

Type of Credit	Granted by	Granted to	Granted for
Personal	Merchant	Person or family	Buying ultimate-consumer products or services
	Consumer finance company	Person or family	Buying expensive ("big-ticket") consumer goods or paying bills.
	Credit union	Members	Buying consumer goods, paying bills, or making investments
Mercantile (Wholesale)	Company A	Company B	Reselling goods
Public	Miscella-neous	Nation, state, county, municipality	Financing governmental functions (public education, health, transportation, and the like)

| Banking (short-term loans) | Bank | Business person, professional person, family or individual | Starting, sustaining, developing, or expanding business operations, or buying consumer products or services |
| Investment | Noncommercial banking institution, estate trustee, private investor | Business firm, business person, or professional person | Buying land, buildings, equipment, special services |

Credit is either *secured* or *unsecured*. *Secured* credit usually involves the borrowing of large sums of money over an extended period. It also requires the debtor to furnish collateral such as stocks, bonds, mortgages, or promissory notes. If the debtor defaults in meeting the obligation, the creditor may, under certain conditions, satisfy the claim by disposing of the collateral. *Unsecured* credit does not require collateral. It is based upon the debtor's character and ability to pay.

Credit communications have a special vocabulary. Since the terminology for mercantile credit is especially common in business messages, learn to recognize and to use these words or expressions.

Bill of lading	A receipt given by the carrier to the shipper; in effect, it is a contract to deliver goods as well as evidence of title to goods. A bill of lading, properly endorsed, may be used as loan security.
Check	A written order signed by a bank depositor directing the bank to pay money as instructed.
Draft	An instrument drawn by A, ordering B to pay a definite sum to C on sight ("sight draft") or at a prescribed future date ("time draft").
Invoice	An itemized list, specifying quantitites, prices, date of shipment, and other pertinent data about goods shipped to a business.
Promissory note	A written promise given by a borrower to the lender stating that the loan will be repaid on a definite date.
Statement of account	An end-of-month report that shows a customer the monthly transactions.
Voucher check	A check with a detachable portion that shows the invoice numbers covered by the check.

Terms of sales vary with customers. When the seller is reluctant to extend credit, prepayment terms are applied to the sale. These terms can be C.B.D. (cash before delivery), C.O.D. (cash on delivery), or S.D.-B.L. (sight draft attached to negotiable bill of lading). When the seller extends credit to the customer, nonprepayment terms are applied. Because terminology is a basic tool for understanding and preparing credit messages, you should know the features of these particular terms:

Prepayment Terms:

C.B.D.	Relieves the seller of relative risk; the seller receives cash before delivering the goods to the buyer.
C.O.D.	Exposes the seller to virtually the same risk as do S.D.-B.L. terms. The buyer pays invoice amount to the carrier before the buyer receives the seller's goods. (The seller may require a deposit to avoid loss if the buyer does not accept the goods.). SPECIAL CAUTION: The buyer's check to the carrier may not be honored. (But the seller may instruct the carrier to accept only currency or a certified check and inform the buyer accordingly.)
S.D.-B.L.	Exposes the seller to the risk of having the buyer refuse the goods; thus the seller may lose shipping charges both ways. With S.D.-B.L. terms, the seller often follows this procedure: 1. Receives a negotiable bill of lading from the carrier 2. Draws a draft (bill of exchange) on the buyer (for the invoice amount) 3. Endorses and attaches the bill of lading to the draft (bill of exchange) 4. Sends the bill of lading, endorsed draft, and invoice to a bank 5. Notifies the buyer accordingly

Nonprepayment Terms:

Cash	Exposes the seller to some risk. Despite popular belief, cash terms permit the buyer ten days' credit to allow verifying the invoice and the merchandise received. Since payment is due at the end of the ten-day period, the seller should investigate the buyer's situation carefully. The seller, in effect, grants short-term credit to the cash buyer.
Consignment	Accommodates the seller who deals with a poor credit risk or with a buyer who cannot afford C.O.D. terms. The seller owns the goods until they are actually sold, whereupon he or she is paid from the

proceeds. Unsold goods may be returned; the consignee need not pay for them. If the consignee's business should fail before payment to the seller, the consigned goods belong to the seller instead of to the consignee's general creditors.

Individual Order

Accommodates the buyer who purchases goods from a particular seller once or twice monthly. The invoice date begins credit and discount periods. If payment is required in 30 days and no discount is allowed, the terms are stated simply "net 30" or "n/30." If a discount of 2 percent, for example, is allowed, the terms are stated "2/10/30" or "2/10, n/30." (This example shows that a discount of 2 percent is allowed for payment made with 10 days after the invoice date and that full payment is due 30 days after the invoice date.) SPECIAL NOTE: Invoices customarily bear the date that the goods are shipped, but—to avoid handicapping a distant buyer—the seller may date the invoice "arrival of goods" (A.O.G.) or "receipt of goods" (R.O.G.). Thereby, the buyer enjoys a discount period determined from the time that the goods are received.

End of Month (E.O.M.) or Lumped Order

Accommodates the relatively large buyer who purchases goods from a particular seller more often than twice monthly. The buyer enjoys a cash discount by paying on or before the tenth day of the month all bills of the previous month. The notation "10 prox." indicates that the credit and discount periods for one month are set from the tenth day of the very next ("proximate") calendar month after purchase. The notation "M.O.M." ("middle of the month") indicates that the periods are set from the fifteenth day of the proximate calendar month after purchase. (The buyer may specify that goods be shipped on the twenty-fifth day of a month to take full advantage of the credit period.)

Sources of Credit Information

As a responsible business person, you must use credit information with great care. Keep yourself current on federal legislation that prohibits discriminatory credit practices. With these principles in mind, you are better prepared to seek and to share credit information.

But with whom do you communicate about credit matters? Where is the credit information that you need? The following listing identifies customary sources of credit information:

1. Credit applicant
2. Credit applicant's business and personal references
3. Credit applicant's bank(s)
4. Companies that cooperate with yours in exchanging credit data
5. Mercantile agencies
6. Trade agencies
7. Credit publications

Although credit may be obtained in several ways—by written message, telephone, or personal visit—decisions concerning the credit privilege should be based upon investigation; and investigation often requires information that the applicant has omitted. When you, as creditor, request the needed information, avoid the suggestion that the applicant's financial standing is unstable. Simply state that you need information which all applicants provide as part of uniform credit requirements and routine credit procedures. Here is a useful and adaptable plan:

1. State appreciation for the applicant's interest.
2. Explain pertinent details of your credit policy.
3. Request the information that you need—credit references, a financial statement, or the like—but stress the fact that the information is required routinely.
4. Refer to an enclosed form for the applicant's completion and return.
5. Indicate how the applicant will benefit by supplying the required information promptly.
6. State cordial interest in serving the applicant properly.

The following message is a response to a customer who has applied for a charge account:

CREDIT INQUIRY ADDRESSED TO APPLICANT

Thank you for your interest in opening a charge account with us.

For customer convenience our credit policy makes it convenient to shop by simply presenting the customer credit card to one of our cashiers. And to keep the credit customer informed on the kinds of transactions made, each monthly statement indicates tax deductible charges, other charges, and total charges. Finance charges are based upon the previous balance less payments and credits. This amount is then multiplied by the monthly periodic rate of 1.5 percent. Additional finance charges may be avoided by paying the new monthly balance prior to the next billing date.

As part of our routine credit procedures, however, three credit references to whom we may refer are needed before a charge account can be established. Please supply this information on the enclosed form.

Your credit application will receive prompt attention as soon as the references have been supplied.

There are times when an applicant supplies enough information to indicate the extension of credit, but additional information is needed to complete the investigation. This situation is illustrated in the following example:

ANOTHER CREDIT INQUIRY

Your interest in establishing credit with us is certainly appreciated. We look forward to a pleasant business association with you.

For your information, the enclosed pamphlet will explain our credit policy and the services which are available to you. After you have read the material, we believe you will agree that every effort has been made to make your shopping through credit both a convenience and a pleasant experience.

So that we may give final approval to your credit request, please complete and return the enclosed form.

As part of your credit investigation, you will probably seek information from the applicant's references. Concisely and specifically ask for the confidential data that you need about the applicant's character, capital, and capacity for earnings.

Routine messages are often used to obtain credit reports from a credit applicant's references. These messages not only pose the inquiry but provide blank spaces for reply data. An example is located on the following page.

Often businesses are dues-paying members of their community credit bureau. When local residents seek credit, the business person telephones the credit bureau, gives an identification, and requests a credit rating on the applicant.

Since mercantile agencies, trade agencies, and credit publications may be new credit-information resources to you, here is a description of their purposes and methods:

1. Mercantile Agencies	Agencies that determine credit about business people and business firms. Credit information is communicated through books of ratings or through detailed and individualized reports. Credit information is given only to subscribers of the service.
2. Trade Agencies	"Mutual" and "private" agencies that determine data about a particular field of commerce (furniture, millinery, or textiles, for instance). The "mutual" trade agency, a voluntary association of manufacturers, jobbers, and wholesalers, collects and communicates credit data to its members, often through the operation of credit bureaus. The "private" trade agency, a profit-making enterprise for its owners, sells credit-information service to subscribers.
3. Credit Publications	Publications that describe companies' financial conditions, earnings, officers' and directors' names, and related data. This information is issued to subscribers.

SMART SHOES, INC.

947-957 Tenth Street
Omaha, NE 68102

March 26, 19--

Citizens National Bank
732-738 Racine Street
Terre Haute, IN 47803

Gentlemen:
    We shall appreciate information regarding the integrity, responsibility, capital, and promptness of
_____Mrs. Lee Rowe, 567 Maple Drive_____

    For this information, thank you. Enclosed is a self-addressed, stamped envelope for your answer.

C. L. Johns
Credit Manager

Please reply on this sheet

Credit information on:___Mrs. Lee Rowe_____

    We have the following credit information with which we are glad to

supply you: ___Integrity and responsibility are A-1.___
___Capital is adequate.___
_____

PLEASE SIGN THIS SHEET BEFORE YOU RETURN IT

Signed ___*Harvey Nichols*___
Title ___*Vice President*___

A Credit Inquiry

Probably the best-known mercantile agency is Dun & Bradstreet, Inc., with headquarters in New York City. Branch offices are located throughout the United States and abroad. Subscribers receive reference books and individualized reports. Dun & Bradstreet ratings represent the agency's appraisal of a person or a firm in terms of financial strength and credit position. Some of the frequently used credit publications are issued by Moody's Investors Service, Inc., and Standard and Poor's Corporation.

REVIEW AND TRANSITION

To bring forth favorable responses to your messages, you must use words which help your reader or listener visualize mentally the positive results or qualities of cooperating with you.

Messages that help you seek information, assistance, products, or services necessitate the use of adequate and appropriate explanation supported by specific evidence and fortified by appropriate tone. When such explanation is psychologically oriented to your reader or listener, you prepare your receiver to answer your messages as you intended.

In this chapter you studied messages for obtaining or receiving what other people can provide. As you read Chapter 10, you will study messages that are written to answer the requests and inquiries of other people.

DISCUSSION QUESTIONS

A. When writing an order letter, why is it advantageous to use a separate line or a separate paragraph for each item ordered?

B. Are the following statements effective openings for an order letter? Why or why not?

1. I'm interested in ordering the following items:
2. I'm wondering if I could order the following items:
3. I would appreciate having the following articles:
4. May I have the following order shipped to our Ohio warehouse?
5. Please ship the following order under our purchase order 2026:

C. Based upon your study of Chapter 9, constructively criticize the following order letter.

Please send me the following electrical supplies:

4 rolls of electric wiring for my house
1 electric service panel
2 table lamps—48 inches high

Please send these items so they will be received no later than April 6, 19—.

D. Should a direct inquiry message be written inductively or deductively? Explain your answer.

E. When asking a person to speak before your professional organization without remuneration, should your special request message be written inductively or deductively? Explain your answer.

F. Each of the following statements requests action. Analyze each statement and explain why you would or would not use it as written.

    1. Although you are a very busy person, would it be possible for you to be a participant in our meeting of January 12, 19—?

    2. Will you please let me know if you can supply the credit information that was requested?

    3. Please let us know which date you prefer—January 12 or January 13.

    4. Please sign and return the enclosed card to indicate which option you prefer.

    5. If possible, we would like to visit your offices on January 12. Is this date satisfactory?

G. As a business communicator, how can you use words to stimulate thoughts and feelings?

H. Business people often welcome adjustment messages from their customers. Why is this so?

I. When writing an adjustment message, why is it especially important to show empathy toward your reader?

APPLICATIONS

Order Messages

1. You own the House of Gifts at 1510 Downey Place, San Francisco, CA 94117. To replenish your stock, order these items from the Mayfair Leather Goods Co., 200 West Avenue, New York, NY 10008: zipper key cases, 3 dozen, #6873, $26.25 per doz., assorted colors and patterns; calfskin leather billfolds, 6 dozen, #6940, $85.80 per dozen., assorted colors and patterns; leather belts, 1 dozen, #42008, $61.20 per dozen, 1 3/4-inch wide top grain cowhide, brown; adjustable handbags, 2 dozen, #40105, $102 per dozen., textured vinyl in navy blue with removable zippered cosmetic case.

You want this merchandise for your sale which begins in three weeks. The merchandise is to be charged to your account with the usual 2/10, n/30 credit terms.

2. As purchasing agent for the Tri-City Paint and Supply Company, 1015 W. Main Street, Cheyenne, WY 82001, order the following items from the Universal Paint Company, 1321 West Richfield Road, Arlington, Virginia 22212: high-gloss Superguard enamel, 30 gallons, #3056, $8.50 per gallon., interior/ exterior latex, white; semi-gloss Superguard, 45 gallons, #3070, $7.25 per gallon., interior latex, white; Durabil flat., 60 gallons, #3001, $9.10 per gallon., interior latex, white; Hardcoat finish, 15 quarts, #2053, $2.15 per quart., polyurethane, clear.

Because you operate three stores, request the Universal Paint and Supply Company to ship directly (equal amounts of each item) to the following store addresses: 110 Center Avenue, Alvin, WY 82050; 1510 Brockway Avenue, Basin, WY 82410; and to your Cheyenne store. The merchandise is to be charged to your account with credit terms of n/30.

3. As a new business proprietor of Hammontree's Secretarial Services, 504 E. Park Drive, Kansas City, MO 64116, order the following equipment from Superior Office Equipment Company, 3030 Chester Street, Norman, OK 73069: one executive desk, #4J6624N, 60 × 30-inch top, walnut finish, contemporary style, $125.35; one executive chair, #4J5351N, padded Naugahyde vinyl back—walnut grained with padded 18 × 19-inch nylon seat and a nickel-chrome-plated steel base, $65.95.

Because your business is to open in four weeks, you will need the equipment before then. Since yours is a new business and you have not established credit, a check for the total purchase is to be enclosed with your order letter.

4. Order the following items from the T.A. Gasper and Company department store, 9771 Broad Street, El Paso, TX 79933: one repeat electric alarm clock with a woodgrained case, #1412, $9.99; one 36-prong tie rack, walnut finish with gold-color metal prongs, #1014, $5.99.

   The electric alarm clock is to be shipped directly to Mr. Bruce Leppien, 2825 Varsity Avenue, Urbana, IL 61801; it is a birthday gift that should reach him in ten days. You want a card with your name to accompany the gift-wrapped package.

   The tie rack is to be shipped directly to Mr. James Christensen, 2622 West Central Street, Wichita, KS 67203; it is a graduation gift that should reach him in twelve days. You want a card with your name to accompany the gift-wrapped package.

   Charge this order to your T.A. Gasper and Company account, which was opened in 1972.

Remittance Messages

5. You have made purchases under several invoices from the Apex Pharmaceutical Company, 51 Ridgeway Drive, Portland OR 97213. Send a remittance letter with a check for $152.95 to apply on Invoice No. 3185.

6. Send a $212.50 check to Aunt Jennie's Candy Factory, 615 North Sweetwater Circle, Worcester, MA 01610 in payment of Invoice No. 20068.

   Inquire whether a promotional sale discount on their Sea Breeze salt-water taffy will be forthcoming.

7. Send a check to the Sander's Sporting Goods Company, 115 Hill Road, Nashville, TN 37211. Your check is in payment of Invoice No. 7215 for $325.50. By sending the payment now, you are able to take a two percent discount. Ask if their company will be exhibiting at the national convention next December in Chicago, Illinois.

Inquiry Messages

8. You are the program chairperson for your state real estate conference. As one of your responsibilities, you are to inquire from various hotels and motels whether they can accommodate your organization on December 27, 28, 29, 19—. Prepare a letter and address including the following information:

   You expect approximately 450 people to attend the conference. You estimate you will need 100 single rooms and 175 double rooms for overnight accommodations. In addition, you believe you will need five large meeting rooms which will hold comfortably 80 people in each room. The noon luncheons are expected to attract 300 people each day. A banquet to handle 200 people is planned for the evening of December 28. Other evening meals will be planned individually by members of the organization, but eating facilities must be available. Inquire as to complimentary rooms for officers, a paid advertisement in your state bulletin referring to the conference, organizational costs, etc.

9. You are the business manager of a small intrastate trucking company. Due to the expansion of the company business, you have been asked to investigate the cost difference between purchasing or leasing two additional trucks. Write a letter to National Truck Leasing, Inc., 5400 Outer Drive, Springfield, IL 62704 and inquire about leasing policies and costs. Be specific in seeking the information.

10. You have decided to purchase an electric typewriter for your college work. Write an inquiry which can be sent to several office equipment suppliers. Inquire about the typewriter brand and its features. Ask about student discounts, trade-in allowances, and other special benefits.

11. You are a member of the School Employees Credit Union. You have (for the first time) a $4,500 loan with the credit union. Loan payments are automatically deducted from your pay checks. Upon receiving your first quarterly statement you notice that each weekly check deduction is credited to your shares. At the end of each month, the credit union then transfers a monthly payment from your shares to your loan. You do not understand why each deduction does not go directly toward your loan. Write an inquiry to the credit union manager, Mrs. Betty Roberts. The address is: 6230 Mission Bay Road, San Diego, CA 92120.

Special Request Messages

12. As program chairman of the Arizona Association of Business Teachers, write a letter to Dr. Robert L. Atkinson, University of Omaha, 11809 University Drive, Omaha, NE 68111. Ask Dr. Atkinson, author of *Effective Business English*, to deliver the keynote speech at your convention on Friday evening, September 6, 19—, at the Hotel Alexander in Tempe, AZ 85281. The executive board of your association authorized travel and housing expenses only.

13. You are the Dean of Instruction at Clinton Community College, 1223 N. Webster Street, Cincinnati, OH 45227. The board of trustees of your college has approved the construction of a 5.5-million-dollar vocational-technical building. Mr. Robert Wagoner of your city is President of the Wagoner Manufacturing Company. Write to Mr. Wagoner and ask him to serve on an advisory committee in the planning of this new building.

14. Your local chamber of commerce has decided to sponsor a festival which it hopes will become an annual event. As part of the festival, a large parade will be held the morning of May 1, 19—. As a member of the chamber, you have been asked to encourage all local businesses to enter attractive floats in the parade. Each float will depict some historical aspect of your city. To insure no duplication of historical themes and to determine the number of participants, write a letter with an enclosed entry form that can be sent to all businesses. Specify a final date for submission of the entry form.

15. You are the director of the Clear Water Camp for Teenagers. The camp is supported by the generous donations of individuals, organizations, and foundations. The sole purpose of the camp's operation is to provide a pleasant learning experience for boys and girls in your community who otherwise could not attend a summer camp. Clear Water Camp is located on a twenty-acre site bordering Clear Water Lake and the Pine Ridge State Forest. Dormitory housing is available for both boys and girls; house parents are provided for each dormitory. Swimming lessons, boating, nature-trail hikes, and horseback riding are a few of the activities available to the campers. A $50 donation will support one teenager for one week. Write to the Frances B. Gainey Foundation and request a grant for this worthwhile project.

Adjustment Messages

16. The House of Gifts has recently filled your order (see Application 1). When checking the shipment, you noticed that black belts were sent instead of the brown. Because you have plenty of black belts in stock, you cannot use more of them. Write to the House of Gifts and request an adjustment. You shipped the belts to them today.

17. As an owner of a new business, you have made a cash purchase of merchandise from the Hayward Merchandising Company, 632 North Sunset Street, Jacksonville, FL 32217. When your shipment arrived, two of the 6-foot fiberglass brass rods had defective ceramic guides. You have previously requested an adjustment but have had no response. Using a more forceful tone, write another adjustment request.

18. You purchased a woman's digital watch from the Southfield Jewelry Company, 110 Sixth Avenue, New York, NY 10017. When examining the watch upon its arrival, you discovered the face of the watch was noticeably marred. Because you planned to give the watch to your sister for her graduation in two weeks, you did not have time to return it for a replacement. Therefore, you purchased a gift locally. Return the watch to the Southfield Jewelry Company; request that your $55 be refunded.

19. As the manager of a women's apparel store, you returned two defective pullover tunics to the Fashion Center, 110 Fifth Avenue, New York, NY 10017. You asked the Fashion Center to credit your account. Although you did not receive a credit memo from the company, you assumed your account had been credited. Now you receive a statement from the Fashion Center requesting full payment. Write an explanation and request the adjustment.

Credit Messages

20. Since your employer, the South Dakota Gas Company, has transferred you to Rapid City, you are interested in establishing credit in your new community. Write the Westport Department Store, 110 Willow Street, Rapid City, SD 57701, and request personal credit. You maintain your savings account at the First National Bank of Sioux Falls, and you have established credit at the following businesses in Sioux Falls, SD 57101: Town and Country Fabric Shop, 103 Main Street; Jacobs and Bush Department Store, 406 Main Street; and the Oettmeier Building Supply Company, 2022 Third Avenue.

21. As purchasing agent for the Kiddy Toy Manufacturing Company, send an order to the Pembrook Paper Company, 2056 Gelncoe Road, Georgetown, MD 21930. Although the Kiddy Toy Manufacturing Company is listed in Dun & Bradstreet, it has not established credit with the Pembrook Paper Company. With your order, send a message seeking credit privileges.

22. You are the owner of a newly established business, the Powder Springs Mobile Home Park. You have decided to install an underground watering system for your park, but you need to purchase equipment on credit in order to install the system. Because you have no previously established credit, you decide to write a special credit application to the Wonder Plumbing Supply Company, 203 River Street, Athens, GA 30601 and apply for credit privileges.

23. You are the credit manager of the Women's Fashion Center, 6233 Topeka Avenue, Pinehurst, NC 28374. Ms. Florence Sampson of 206 Elmhurst Drive has requested credit. Ms. Sampson has listed the University Book Store as a credit reference. Write an inquiry to the University Book Store, 805 Wells Avenue, Pinehurst, NC 28374 concerning Ms. Sampson's request.

24. You have received a credit inquiry from Ms. Florence Sampson (see Application 23). Ms. Sampson has supplied enough information to indicate probable approval of credit. However, you need additional information to complete your credit investigation. Write a message to Ms. Sampson and request the additional information.

CHAPTER 10

Messages to Inform, Explain, Direct, or Instruct

Now that you have studied those messages that seek products, services, payments, and information, you are ready to study the functions of messages that inform, explain, direct, and instruct. Internally, management communicates on a daily basis with its employees on topics such as job instructions, policy statements, and procedural statements. Externally, communications with customers and other businesses include messages such as acknowledgments, replies, and general informational material. Whether you communicate internally or externally, you can specifically influence human behavior by using proper tone, correct timing, and demonstrated courtesy.

TONE

Tone is a demonstration of the speaker's or writer's attitude. How the receiver of the message interprets the tone depends largely on the sender's careful use of words, phrases, and linguistic conventions.

When you communicate, consider the attitudes that words can convey. Some words may be interpreted as condescending, boastful, or curt. Other words may be construed as sarcastic, preachy, or accusative. Effective business communicators use words that convey a considerate, sincere, and positive tone—words that indicate a straightforward, earnest, confident, courteous, and considerate approach to others.

Here are some examples of "poor" and "better" tones in word utilization:

POOR TONE	BETTER TONE
Evidently you are not aware of the high scholastic standing we require before we admit a student into this university. (condescending)	Factors such as citizenship, motivation, potential, and high scholastic standing in previous school work are some of the factors that determine college admission.
In a university as large as ours, we receive hundreds of applications each year from people who wish to be members of our outstanding faculty. (boastful)	Thank you, Ms. Muller, for submitting your application letter. We are pleased to know that you are interested in joining our faculty.
Complete the enclosed application. When returned, consideration will be given. (curt)	Please complete the enclosed application. Your materials will be evaluated as soon as we receive them.
I congratulate you, Steve, on being able to read your own notes—especially after they are a few days' old. No one else can! (sarcastic)	Clearly written orders will help us to efficiently serve our customers. We are asking all our salespeople to help in this endeavor.
It is now time for you to submit your Christmas orders. (preachy)	By placing your Christmas orders early, you will have a wide selection of merchandise from which to choose.
Although you claim to have supplied us with all the necessary materials, you failed to submit the three references that we require. (accusative)	As a matter of customary credit routine, please list your three references on the enclosed form. Your credit application will receive prompt attention.

Be sincere in what you say or write. To be overly humble in your expressions casts a doubt upon your sincerity and your honesty. Flattery and excessive personalization can seem suspicious to the recipient. So avoid making statements such as the following:

Only you can answer these questions for me.

Because you are the most outstanding authority in your field, will you please answer the following questions:

That little wife of yours will be happy with your purchase of the XYZ.

Whether the message communicates favorable or unfavorable action, strive to establish and to maintain a positive tone throughout your written or oral exposition. By "positive tone" we mean verbal evidence *from the recipient's viewpoint* of clear explanation, active interest, and genuine courtesy. Moreover, minimize negative terms even in positive contexts. For instance, instead of "Don't hesitate to call," use "Be sure to call" or simply "Please call."

Notice how the following negative statements have been transformed into positive statements:

NEGATIVE	POSITIVE
I am sorry, but I will not be able to attend your meeting on January 12, 19—.	I have accepted an invitation to participate in an AMA program in Dallas, Texas, on January 12, 19—.
The wiring booklet you requested is temporarily out of stock.	The booklet "How to Wire" will be sent to you as soon as additional copies can be reprinted.
We will not be employing any additional teachers for the coming year.	We will keep your credentials in our active file. Should a position become available, they will be reviewed.
Why don't you visit our store during our grand opening?	Please visit us during our grand opening.

TIMING

Your prompt response to messages will demonstrate courtesy and willingness to serve your prospective or actual customer. Such promptness will also convey efficiency in dealing with people, appreciation for their interest, and desire to continue a positive business relationship.

When you receive orders from customers, your prompt acknowledgments will win goodwill and realize profits for your company. For those replies that require time-consuming action—consulting files, tabulating figures, or preparing estimates, for example—send immediate acknowledgments with a statement of progress and an indication of the probable date on which you will send complete information. When booklets, catalogs, or similar purchasing information is requested, be prudent and also send a low-pressure sales message to sustain interest and to stimulate purchases.

You would be wise to answer promptly all orders and inquiries. Preferably, you should answer a message on the same day but surely within a business week (five days) after you receive it. In doing so, you demonstrate positive attitudes—attitudes of service, efficiency, cooperation, and eagerness to assist.

Here is an example of a late reply to a request. Notice that the tone of the message is negative, condescending, and boastful.

A LATE RESPONSE WITH POOR TONE

In reference to your letter of September 6, we cannot comply with your request for a copy of our catalog. As you are probably aware, the vastness of our business makes it practically impossible to keep a supply of these catalogs in stock. We are unable to state when additional copies will be available. Sorry this situation has occurred.

Let us now look at a revised version of the same letter. Note how it reflects courtesy through timely action and positive statements. It also demonstrates a willingness to help, and it conveys an appreciation for the opportunity to serve the customer.

A PROMPT RESPONSE WITH EFFECTIVE TONE

Thank you for requesting a copy of our catalog. You will receive your copy within two or three weeks. Because an unexpectedly heavy demand has depleted our supply, we are in the process of printing additional copies.

In the meantime, your name has been placed on our mailing list to receive all our promotional brochures of top-quality products that are offered at money-saving discounts.

We appreciate your interest in our company, and we look forward to serving you in an efficient and pleasant manner.

COURTESY

Tone and timing are elements of courtesy; so are considerate actions and remarks. For example, personalized "thank you" messages should be sent whenever a statement of appreciation is appropriate. To write appreciation messages demonstrates your respect for and consideration of others and helps to create and sustain goodwill. Messages of gratitude are frequently written to customers, employees, professional organizations, and service institutions to let them know that you value their efforts. The messages of gratitude may be either handwritten or typed; they are concisely worded, positively stated, and promptly written. The following are examples of such messages:

Thank you for reviewing our manuscript, *Interviewing Techniques*. We are pleased that you found the material to be valuable information for personnel directors to use in the interviewing process.

Your suggestion to include a checklist for evaluating prospective employees is also appreciated. Any other suggestions you may have will certainly be welcomed.

Thank you for participating in our career conference. As a panel member, your suggestion regarding the research phase of employment messages was excellent.

Your contribution to the conference's success is certainly appreciated by all involved.

Having explored these general considerations, let us now turn to the details of acknowledgments, replies, and other functional types of business messages.

ACKNOWLEDGMENTS

Acknowledgments are a form of feedback. They explain that a message has been received and that prompt action is being taken. The action, however, can be stated in several forms—formal, informal, personally written, standardized. Illustrations of informal or "card form" acknowledgments appear on page 226. A formal acknowledgment is illustrated by the following example:

Ms. Betty A. Montgomery
American Office Equipment Company
4056 Sauk Creek Road
Minneapolis, MN 55400

Dear Ms. Montgomery:

Thank you very much for your letter of April 3, expressing your interest in submitting bids for office furniture and equipment that we may purchase now and in the future.

Your name has been placed on our list of companies which will be notified of any purchases that we may be contemplating. We appreciate your interest in helping us meet our needs.

Sincerely,

Albert O. Lowe
Purchasing Director

sew

Acknowledgments should be answered promptly and should explain the action that is being taken. The structure of the content of the acknowledgment message will depend upon the specific type of acknowledgment written: interim, new or regular customer, large order, delayed shipment, or declined order.

Interim Acknowledgments

Despite your intention to be prompt, circumstances may cause delays in meeting the needs of your customer. While awaiting your action, the customer needs and deserves reassurance. Silence during a delay engenders doubt, suspicion, and even distrust. An interim acknowledgment or "meantime" message will help you keep the customer's goodwill. Following is an effective guide for an interim acknowledgment.

The enclosed material is in response
to your recent request. It is a
pleasure to supply this information
to you.

UNITED CHEMICAL SOCIETY
112 Rocky Drive
Estes Park, CO 80517

A Courteous, Printed Acknowledgment

Martine's

Sutter near Grant   *San Francisco*

To   Mrs. R. D. Bateman

*We acknowledge with pleasure the
opportunity to number you among our
friends and are placing your name on our
books today.*

*It is our sincere hope that we will
be able to assist you in all your home
furnishing needs. We especially welcome
any calls you may want to make on the
unusual services we are prepared to give
our patrons.*

Martine Sloane

A Formal Acknowledgment
and Welcome to a New Customer

Thank you. Your order is appreciated. Enclosed is your
invoice showing the items shipped, the date, and the
method of shipment. Large orders, shipped in more than
one package, may arrive in different deliveries. Please
allow reasonable time for your order to arrive. We look
forward to a mutually beneficial business relationship.

THE MERRIWEATHER MANUFACTURING COMPANY, INC.

A "Card-Form" Order Acknowledgment

1. Thank the customer for the inquiry, request, etc.
2. Explain reasons for delay.
3. Tell the customer what to expect.
4. Ask for additional or clarified data (if applicable).

Here in an example: Assume that you are a district sales representative of your company. While you are attending a sales manager's conference at the home office in another state, you instruct your secretary to answer promptly all incoming mail in your absence. You realize that prompt replies tend to create and sustain goodwill.

AN INTERIM ACKNOWLEDGMENT

Thank you for your November 20 inquiry, addressed to Mr. Charles Puterbaugh.

Mr. Puterbaugh, who is attending a sales managers' conference at our home office in Lexington, Kentucky, plans to be back in his office December 7. As soon as he returns, your message will receive his immediate attention.

Acknowledgments of Orders

When possible, send acknowledgments the same day that orders are received. Personalize your messages to new customers, to regular customers with large orders, and to new or regular customers whose orders contain incomplete information. Routine orders that can be filled completely and promptly may be acknowledged by filling in standardized forms to expedite customer service.

New Customers. Remember, a personalized, appreciative, and definite acknowledgment should be sent as soon as you receive a new customer's order. You may wish to use the following guide for writing this message:

PLAN A

1. Thank and welcome the new customer.
2. Identify (sometimes you may need to restate) the order.
3. Explain exactly how you are handling and shipping the order.
4. State your cordial interest in serving the customer.

NEW CUSTOMER ACKNOWLEDGMENT—PLAN A

Thank you for placing your order with us. We welcome you as a new customer.

Your order for twenty dozen carbon ribbons was shipped to you via Apex Freight Lines today. Whenever you need office supplies of fine quality, please let us serve you again.

Your order placed with our sales representative, Ray Stumpfig, on October 20, is certainly appreciated. We are pleased to welcome you as a new customer.

This merchandise is being shipped to you by express today. Retailers carrying our line of merchandise are reporting increased sales. Your comments about sales in your area will be especially valuable, since our objective is to continue assisting you with the expansion of your business volume.

A variation of the above plan is also used by many business people. Note the modification of this plan:

PLAN B

1. Explain what you are doing about the customer's order. (Be sure to identify the order.)
2. Thank and welcome the new customer.
3. State your cordial interest in serving the customer well through regular and special accommodations, extended hours of operation, unusual bargains, and other services.

Compare the letter versions in Plan B with those letters written under Plan A.

NEW CUSTOMER ACKNOWLEDGMENTS—PLAN B

Your order for twenty dozen carbon ribbons was shipped to you via Apex Freight Lines today. We appreciate the opportunity to welcome you as a new customer.

The enclosed brochure describes exceptional bargains for next month and contains a postage-paid order form for your convenience. Please give us the pleasure of serving you whenever you need office supplies of fine quality.

Your merchandise is being shipped to you by express today.

Thanks for your October 20 order, given to our sales representative, Ray Stumpfig. We welcome you as a new customer.

Other retailers who are carrying our line of merchandise are reporting increased sales. Your comments about sales in your area will be especially valuable, since our objective is to continue assisting you with the expansion of your business volume.

The enclosed brochure explains the many services that are available to you. Be sure to let us help you whenever we can.

Large Orders from Regular Customers. The preceding message plans for new customers can be adapted to acknowledge large orders from regular customers. When using either of the acknowledgment plans, emphasize your interest in the customer and in the customer's welfare. This can be accomplished through cultivating goodwill and focusing attention upon the selling points of the goods or services you wish to supply.

ACKNOWLEDGMENT OF A LARGE ORDER

Your decision to purchase eighty-five of our electric typewriters for your new corporate headquarters is certainly good news. Thank you for your confidence and your goodwill.

Your new typewriters are being shipped today in accordance with your purchase order. And when you receive your machines, our service representative, Mike Williamson, will be on hand to uncrate and personally locate each typewriter for you.

You can be sure, Mr. Ryan, that your new typewriters are constructed of the finest material and are designed to give years of exceptional service. The five-year guarantee on each typewriter insures that you will be completely satisfied.

You have our pledge of cooperation and our best wishes for a truly successful year.

Incomplete Orders. When acknowledging an incomplete order, never make the customer feel at fault. Tactfully ask for the additional information by concentrating your attention and your customer's upon the desire to fill the order correctly and promptly. Avoid destroying your customer's goodwill by such statements as "you failed" or "you forgot."

Here are effective guides for acknowledging incomplete orders:

PLAN A

1. Thank the customer for the order.
2. Explain that to provide proper service you need additonal information.
3. Ask courteously for the needed information.
4. Assure the customer that prompt attention will be given to the reply.

A much-used variation of this plan has the following steps:

PLAN B

1. Thank the customer for the order.
2. Emphasize your interest in filling the order properly.
3. Explain that to provide proper service you need additional information.
4. Ask for the required data.
5. Explain, politely and definitely, how the additional information should be supplied (for instance, by completing and returning a special form or a reply card that you enclose with your acknowledgment).

In the following messages, which illustrate acknowledgments of incomplete orders, notice the difference between accusations (negative) and tactful requests.

A NEGATIVE ACKNOWLEDGMENT

To comply with your February 3 order, we need complete information which you did not supply.

Evidently you do not realize that our electric pumps come in three sizes: 1/4 HP, 1/2 HP, and 3/4 HP. Each of these motors is designed for different uses, so you can understand why it is essential for us to know which size you really need.

Submit this additional information, and we will ship your pump as soon as possible.

A POSITIVE ACKNOWLEDGMENT—PLAN A

Thank you for your February 3 order.

To be sure that you receive exactly the kind of electric water pump you need, please tell us the size to send: 1/4 HP, 1/2 HP, or 3/4 HP electric pumps.

Just complete and mail the enclosed reply card for prompt, accurate processing of your order.

A POSITIVE ACKNOWLEDGMENT—PLAN B

Thank you for your February 3 order for an electric water pump.

Filling your order correctly as well as promptly is our chief concern. So that we may serve you properly, please complete the size-specification section of the enclosed reply card. Then just mail the card to us; as soon as we receive it, your electric water pump will be on its way to you.

Delayed Orders—Partial Shipment, Deferred Shipment, and Depleted Stock. Occasionally, only partial orders can be shipped or a complete order must be delayed. Unexpected demands may have exhausted the particular items ordered, or perhaps new merchandise is in production but has yet to be finished for shipping. In such cases, your acknowledgment should clearly explain the reason for delay. In wording your message, stress the positive—what you can do for the customer. Avoid using negative words such as *delay, disappointment, inconvenience.* The following plan can guide you.

1. Thank the customer for the order.
2. Explain the cause of delay, but stress what you can do.
3. Promise service as promptly as possible.
4. Request the customer's cooperation, or simply end the message cordially.

A POSITIVE ACKNOWLEDGMENT

Thank you for your January 5 Purchase Order No. 542. We appreciate your continued patronage, Ms. Siegle.

Now that our inventory of damask fabric has been replenished, we have begun production of Style No. 132. Complete shipment of your order can be made by February 15.

You will probably prefer to receive all the merchandise in one shipment. However, if you wish us to send by immediate express the 12 pairs of Style No. 140 and the 6 pairs of Style No. 58, just sign and return the enclosed card.

You have our best wishes for a profitable season.

Declined Orders. You redirect or decline orders when merchandising policies, exclusive agencies, or assigned territories place a restriction upon your making direct sales. For example, national manufacturers selling through exclusive dealers usually decline orders that are sent directly to the manufacturer. Also, local dealers with restricted territories are expected to accept orders only within their assigned areas.

When declining or redirecting an order, encourage your customer to complete the transaction through proper channels. Develop and maintain a positive tone—a tone that is courteous, informative, and service oriented.

The following plan will help both you and the customer.

1. Thank the customers for the order or the interest in your product or service.
2. Explain the regulations, practices, or circumstances that prevent you from accepting the order.
3. Decline the order, but indicate your willingness to help the customer obtain what is wanted.
4. Suggest, courteously and definitely, what the customer should do or what action you will take (for instance, referral of the order to a local dealer).

Contrast the following examples of declining-order acknowledgments.

AN IMPOLITE, NEGATIVE REFUSAL

We regret that we are unable to accept your April 18 order.

As you may know, our products are sold all over the world. Because of the vastness of our operations, we must of necessity restrict our sales to prescribed marketing channels.

If you wish, therefore, to purchase one of our chain saws, you will need to purchase it from our dealer, Wall and Hines Hardware Company, in your city. They will be glad to help you.

A TACTFUL, POSITIVE DECLINE

Thank you for your April 18 order. We are glad to help you get the heavy-duty electric chain saw you requested.

For your convenience, our products are sold through local stores. Wall and Hines Hardware, our dealer in Big Falls, will be happy to show and to demonstrate our products for you.

Will you give us the pleasure of serving you soon through Wall and Hines?

NOTICES, ANNOUNCEMENTS, APPOINTMENTS, AND INVITATIONS

Messages that conspicuously convey information—stockholders' meetings, committee conferences, business relocations, and new business ventures, for example—are communicated through notices, announcements, appointments, and invitations. Statements of data correction, personnel assignments, and requested attendance or participation are typical examples. The styles of such messages vary from extreme formality to refreshing informality. Study the examples on pages 233 and 234, and use them to stimulate your own imagination.

REPLIES TO INQUIRIES, REQUESTS, APPOINTMENTS, AND INVITATIONS

When responding to inquiries, requests, and invitations, your messages should be courteous, appropriate, and concise. These principles are essential to messages that supply or withhold information. Notice, for instance, this reply to the home-insulation inquiry mentioned in Chapter 9.

AN EFFECTIVE REPLY

Responding to your June 20 inquiry, we are pleased to supply an estimated cost of insulating your home with Cellulation. Because you are planning to make this a do-it-yourself project, the following information is based upon material only:

One-Story Frame Home
28' × 50'

	No. of Bags	R Factor	Cost
Walls (4-inch depth)	52	16.5	$161.20
Ceiling (6-inch depth)	70	25.2	217.00
			$378.20

The performance of insulation is measured in terms of R-values. The "R" stands for thermal resistance to heat flowing out in the winter and flowing in during the summer. The higher the R-value, the better the insulation performance. Cellulation guarantees that no cellulose insulation exceeds its efficiency.

Thank you for your inquiry. May we have the pleasure of serving you?

Observe how clarity and conciseness are achieved in the above message through a tabulation of the requested information. Clarity and conciseness can also be accomplished through the use of a numbered listing of answers, as shown on page 235.

DICK ROBINSON AND JIM AMES

TAKE PLEASURE IN ANNOUNCING THE FORMATION
OF A PARTNERSHIP UNDER THE FIRM NAME OF

AMES/ROBINSON

REAL ESTATE

JEFFERSON AT WHEELER
BOX 2063

(517) 636-0044
MILL VALLEY, MICHIGAN 48600

Announcing a New Partnership

AMES/ROBINSON

REAL ESTATE

CORDIALLY EXTENDS

AN INVITATION

TO

ATTEND OUR

OPEN HOUSE

SATURDAY, OCTOBER 5, 19--

2:00 - 7:00 P.M.

JEFFERSON AT WHEELER

A Business Open House

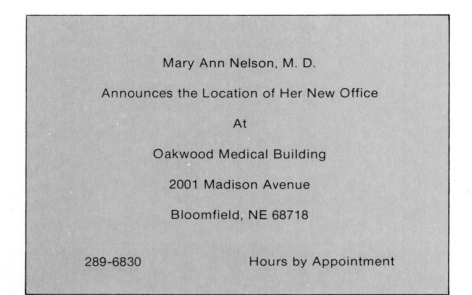

Mary Ann Nelson, M. D.

Announces the Location of Her New Office

At

Oakwood Medical Building

2001 Madison Avenue

Bloomfield, NE 68718

289-6830   Hours by Appointment

A Relocation Announcement

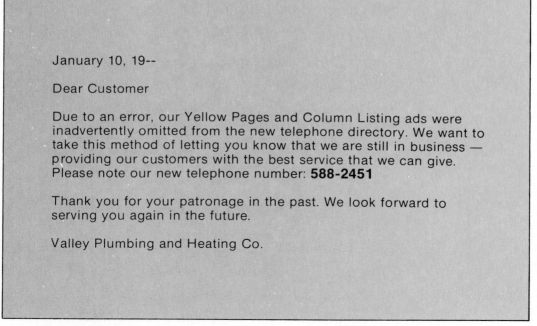

January 10, 19--

Dear Customer

Due to an error, our Yellow Pages and Column Listing ads were
inadvertently omitted from the new telephone directory. We want to
take this method of letting you know that we are still in business —
providing our customers with the best service that we can give.
Please note our new telephone number: **588-2451**

Thank you for your patronage in the past. We look forward to
serving you again in the future.

Valley Plumbing and Heating Co.

Postal Card Notice

ANOTHER EFFECTIVE REPLY

Durabilt steno chairs have these desirable features:
1. Sturdily built for years of use
2. Easily adjustable and cleanable
3. Ideally constructed to roll smoothly on carpeting
4. Remarkably comfortable

You have our good wishes for the success of your comparative study. Please let us know when we can help you again.

Favorable Response

Notice how the preceding messages begin by giving favorable responses. When you can respond favorably, follow the rule of beginning your message in this manner. An immediate favorable response creates goodwill with your reader or listener. Here are some examples of favorable-action openings:

The opportunity to participate in your study is appreciated. Here is the information you requested.

June 20 is an open date. I'm pleased to accept your invitation to address your organization.

The following is a suggested plan for composing replies which stress favorable action:

1. Begin with an "action-first" sentence or brief paragraph.
2. Explain pertinent details of the message.
3. Close with a courteous statement of goodwill.

Observe how the following message illustrates this plan:

FAVORABLE-ACTION REPLY

Here are your five copies of our college catalog. We are pleased to supply your counseling staff with this new edition.

The tab guides, which divide information into major divisions, are designed to help you find the information quickly. In addition to the general index at the end of the catalog, a special index precedes each major division. For any special information about Stillwell College, please use the prepaid postage cards inserted in the front of the catalog or call us collect 317-638-2305.

Providing this material for you is a pleasure.

Although "yes" should be easy to say, many messages are ruined by the sender's apparently grudging tone. When you grant requests, accept appointments, or say yes to invitations, remember to do so cheerfully and cordially. These favorable-action replies illustrate significant contrasts in tone:

GRUDGING	CORDIAL
The *Realtors' Code of Ethics* was published primarily for people engaged in the real estate profession. Because you wish to use this material in your classes, however, we have made an exception. Enclosed is a copy.	Here is your copy of the *Realtors' Code of Ethics*. It is a pleasure to supply you with this pamphlet. We are particularly pleased to know you plan to use this material in your Introduction to Business classes. Best wishes for a very successful year.
The recommendation in your March sales report seems good. Before we pursue your idea, however, I wish to discuss its feasibility with other members of the sales department. Expect me in your office Friday afternoon, April 10, about 3:15.	The recommendation you made in your March sales report is good. We should discuss its implementation soon. I'll be in your office at 3:15 Friday afternoon, April 10, to discuss your idea with you. You may wish to talk with other members of the sales staff for some additional input.
I might be able to attend your management-by-objectives conference on March 8. I have previously scheduled two meetings for that date. However, expect me unless you hear to the contrary.	Yes, Ms. Agostinelli, I'll be happy to attend your management by objectives conference on March 8. Thank you for asking me to participate.

Unfavorable Action

Empathy is an essential ingredient when the information communicated will probably disappoint the receiver of your message. Your reader must feel that you have given the message careful consideration. Remember that most people who write inquiries, requests, and invitations believe their messages should receive positive results. Therefore, you must prepare your reader or listener when the message you transmit is unfavorable.

When you must say no, therefore, assure your reader or listener that his or her message has received careful attention. Use words that explain reasons for your refusal. Develop a context that suggests your preference for saying yes except that valid circumstances compel you to do otherwise. When possible, offer acceptable alternative suggestions. In all cases maintain a tone of courtesy, thoughtfulness, and interest.

Avoid beginning your reply with "no" or its equivalent— "unfortunately," "we regret," or "we cannot." By doing so you risk closing your recipient's mind and create a negative attitude. Instead, reinforce courtesy and present a reasonable explanation before you inform another person of unfavorable action. Here is a plan for you to follow in composing unfavorable-action replies:

1. Begin with a cordial, relevant sentence or brief paragraph.
2. State—courteously, clearly, and definitely—reasons that logically lead to the news you must transmit.
3. Mention the unfavorable action *as a necessary consequence* of the reasons you have stated in Step 2.
4. Suggest, when possible, alternative and helpful actions.
5. End with a reaffirmation of your interest and goodwill.

As you follow this plan, maintain a positive tone by stressing what you can do (rather than what you cannot do). Almost every situation has some "yes" feature; your job is to discover that feature and to give it prominence.

Study the following versions of an unfavorable-action reply. Which message do you prefer?

NEGATIVE TONE

This is in response to your inquiry of March 8 in which you asked why you have not received the Life Style watch you ordered. If you remember, we told you that we would have to place a special order for it from Switzerland, and it would probably take several weeks before we received it.

Be assured, however, that we will forward the watch to you as soon as it arrives. We hope this will not inconvenience you.

POSITIVE TONE

Your new seventeen-jewel Life Style watch will be forwarded to you as soon as it arrives here for final inspection.

Your selection of a marquise-shaped watch with an accent diamond on each side expresses your appreciation for fine jewelry. And because these particular watches are hand-wrought by Swiss craftsmen on special order only, please be patient with us.

You have our assurance that you will be wearing your Life-Style watch very soon.

Here are additional examples of unfavorable-action replies:

UNFAVORABLE REPLY—DESIRE TO HELP

Thank you for your interest in the employer-employee human relations study that we are currently conducting.

The questionnaires that you wish to examine were developed by the American Human Relations Institute, 215 Whitmore Drive, San Pedro, CA 90731. Since the Institute is compiling and interpreting the data for us, all questionnaires—including the unused copies—had to be returned.

Although circumstances prevent us from complying with your request, you may obtain sample copies from the Institute. May we suggest that you write directly to the American Human Relations Institute?

When our study is completed, Mr. Miles, we'll be happy to send you a copy of the results. Please let us know if we can assist you further.

UNFAVORABLE REPLY—SUGGESTED ALTERNATIVE

Thank you, Mr. Caballo, for asking us to contribute a memo report for inclusion in your new edition of *Report Writing in Business.* Published materials of this nature are extremely important to young people who wish to pursue a business career.

As a professor of business, you know that management functions through reports related to all phases of operation; and for the sake of our stockholders, much of this information must be protected. For this reason our directors have passed a resolution prohibiting the distribution of operational materials for reprint.

However, we do want to help. We may be able to supply a memo report for your use providing our trademark and our company name are not included in your publication. Please visit my office at your convenience so we can discuss the matter further.

UNFAVORABLE REPLY—STRESSING THE POSITIVE

Your June 1 memorandum, requesting educational reimbursement, has received careful attention.

As you know, a large sum of money is budgeted each year to help employees further their education. However, the company policy stipulates that tuition reimbursement will be given for all academic courses in which a grade of "B" or better is earned. Since you received a "C" in your filing and records management course, the reimbursement policy does not apply.

Your personnel file shows that you have maintained a "B" average in your college studies, and that you have only fifteen more credits to earn before receiving your degree. Your perseverance, high-scholastic attainments, and work performance in our company are greatly appreciated. We wish you continued success in your academic work.

INTRODUCTIONS AND RECOMMENDATIONS

Your career in business will almost certainly be affected by introductions and recommendations. *Introductions* acquaint one person with another. *Recommendations* convey evaluation of a person's attributes. These types of communication draw attention to the person *who does* the introducing or recommending and to the person *who is being* introduced or recommended.

Introductions

When a company opens a new branch office in another city, the personnel who will be working there and the company itself must be introduced to the community. This can be done (1) by notifying the community's mass media of the company and its purposes, and (2) by sending messages of introduction to the community's civic leaders so they feel familiar toward the company, the new branch, and the new office's executives. Writing these introductions creates goodwill and permits productive work to begin almost immediately.

Relocation of personnel is quite common in business. During your business career, you may experience a company transfer to a city that is new to you but in which your employer has friends and business associates. When this occurs, you and your employer would be wise to see that messages of introduction precede or accompany you. On the other hand, you may be in a position to introduce another person properly. In either case, here is a useful plan to follow:

1. Identify the person being introduced.
2. Explain the reason for the introduction.
3. Describe the person being introduced.
4. Promise appreciation for courtesy or assistance.

A BUSINESS INTRODUCTION

It is a pleasure to introduce Mr. Donald McDermott who has managed our Springfield store since 1970.

Mr. McDermott has now been assigned as manager of our new Atlanta store which will open for business next December.

During his twelve years with Regency Department Stores, Inc., he has demonstrated qualities of cooperation and leadership. You will find him a capable business person and a fine citizen.

Your assistance concerning Donald McDermott's establishment in a community that is new to him will be very much appreciated.

The envelope containing a written introduction is addressed in the usual manner with a notation—for example: *Introducing Mr. Donald McDermott*—in the lower left corner. Occasionally, an annotated business card may substitute for a note of introduction. In either form, an introduction fosters goodwill and should be used.

Recommendations

At some point in your business career, you probably will write recommendation messages. An appropriate recommendation should emphasize professional and personal excellence, and it should also identify any serious deficiencies that the person being discussed may have. An effective recommendation includes the following points:

1. Identify the person.
2. Describe the person's work with you.
3. Explain the reasons for termination.

When you write a recommendation, use discretion. Remember: Unfounded rumors may destroy careers or cause lawsuits.

Consider carefully whether or not you wish to stress the deficiencies as well as the excellence of the individual about whom you are writing. A situation may be serious enough to require stressing. On the other hand, the person's shortcoming may not affect a specific position for which he or she has asked to be recommended. In either case, however, you are ethically bound to identify both excellence and deficiencies.

The General Recommendation. Recommendations intended for general use begin traditionally with "To Whom It May Concern." Such messages usually omit details that would interest a particular reader. Here are two brief examples:

GENERAL RECOMMENDATION

Ms. Mary MacFarland was our interior designer from September, 1972, to June, 1977. She performed her duties in a commendable manner and was well liked by both staff and customers.

Because her husband accepted a teaching position in another state, Ms. MacFarland resigned her position. We would be happy to have her on our staff again.

GENERAL RECOMMENDATION

While a member of our accounting department from 1973 to 1976, Mr. William Jaster performed all of his duties efficiently and cooperatively.

Because of his strong desire to pursue a teaching career, we reluctantly accepted his resignation. Should Mr. Jaster ever wish to return to industry, we would be pleased to rehire him.

The Specific Recommendation. Because it contains more detailed material, the specific recommendation is more effective than the general recommendation. It is more personalized and is often written in response to an inquiry from a prospective employer. For example:

SPECIFIC RECOMMENDATION

Ms. Mary MacFarland, for whom you requested an evaluation, was our interior designer from September, 1972, to June, 1977. In this capacity she was an extremely capable person.

Besides her knowledge of interior design, Ms. MacFarland's pleasant manners and communicative abilities made her a valuable staff member. Due to her efficiency and customer-service attitude, she developed an established clientele of very satisfied customers.

Because her husband accepted a teaching position in Des Moines, Ms. MacFarland resigned her position with the knowledge that we would be happy to have her back if the opportunity presented itself. From our experience the employer who secures Ms. MacFarland as an interior designer will be fortunate indeed.

Mr. William Jaster, about whom you inquired October 6, was employed in our accounting department from 1973 to 1976. Prior to joining our firm, Mr. Jaster attended City College where he graduated with a major emphasis in accounting. While on our staff, he developed into a very fine accountant.

Because of his desire to pursue a teaching career, Mr. Jaster resigned his position voluntarily. We regretted losing the services of this efficient and cooperative man, whose qualifications—especially in cost accounting—merit your favorable consideration.

JOB INSTRUCTIONS, STATEMENTS OF POLICY, AND STATEMENTS OF PROCEDURE

Education and training are continuous processes which move an individual toward fulfillment as an employee and as a person. Business recognizes the importance of education and training through the endorsement of academic courses of study, promotion of seminars and workshops, and sponsorship of technical programs and on-the-job training. Success in business is actually success in beginning and continuing the benefits of informal as well as formal learning.

Job Instructions

In business you will be expected to follow job instructions; moreover, you may have to compose instructional or directional messages so that others will learn through your words. How should you use your words to help people learn a job? Here are some suggestions:

1. Identify the subject in relation to the learner.
2. Describe the subject's components or features.
3. Explain how the components or features function.

As you apply these suggestions, use words and terms that the learner can transform into actions. Project yourself into the learner's situation. As you formulate instructions, determine what you *assume* the learner knows before reading or hearing your instructions. Keep challenging yourself: Are your assumptions about the learner's knowledge justifiable and correct? If they are, your message will be useful. It they are not, your message may be wasted.

Here is an example of effective job instructions:

HOW TO ERASE ON CARBON COPIES

1. Move the carriage to the extreme right or left so that the eraser crumbs will not fall into the machine.
2. Place a small card directly behind the original. Erase the error on the original copy.

3. Transfer the card behind the first carbon copy; erase that copy.
4. Erase all carbon copies in this manner, working from front to back.
5. On a manual typewriter, make the correction by striking the correct keys lightly. Repeat the stroking until the desired shade is achieved. On an electric, the touch-regulator setting will likely achieve the desired shade automatically.

Policy Statements

Policy statements are transmitted through various media such as letters, memos, handbooks, and conferences. Functioning as generalized instructions or directions, policy statements are management messages designed to unify employee behavior in recurring business situations. The following plan is suggested for these messages:

1. Identify the principles (basic beliefs) upon which the policy is founded.
2. State objectives that are related to the principles.
3. Describe methods of generally achieving the objectives.

A POLICY STATEMENT

TO: All Academic Faculty
FROM: A.J. Bristol, President
DATE: April 5, 19—
SUBJECT: Evaluation of Teaching Faculty

By mutual agreement between the Faculty Senate and the Board of Trustees, City College requires peer evaluations for excellence in teaching.

All faculty whom the College has employed for at least one academic year should participate in the evaluations.

For the benefit of each faculty member and the guidance of academic administration, the new policy—effective September 1, 19—, is to have annual peer evaluations. Each peer-evaluation team will be composed of three tenured faculty members who are selected by the teacher being evaluated. A written evaluation will be supplied to both the faculty member being evaluated and the academic dean.

When writing a change of policy, however, a slight modification to the above suggested plan is needed. Contrast the new or revised items (principles, objectives, or methods) with their predecessors and explain reasons for the change.

Procedural Statements

"Policies" are general; "procedures" are specific. When composing a procedural statement, you explain a particular way of completing a course of action. Using the following plan will help you in composing procedural statements.

1. State the objectives of the procedure.
2. Identify the company units that should follow the procedure.
3. Describe in sequence the functions to be performed by each person.

Statements of procedure should explain, clearly and concisely, the phases in a sequence of events. The following example is one format that can be used:

TRAVEL REIMBURSEMENT PROCEDURE

For prompt action and efficient control, all requisitioning units, Department Heads, Business Manager, and the Comptroller will process travel reimbursement requests in this sequence:

Requisitioning Unit	Department Head	Business Manager	Comptroller
1. Submit to Department Head the "Request for Travel" form (original and 2 copies, 1 yellow and 1 green).	2. Sign original and forward with all copies to Business Manager.	3. Approve or disapprove "Request for Travel." Send carbon copy 1 (yellow) to the requisitioning unit. Send carbon copy 2 (green) to appropriate department head. File original.	
4. Upon return from approved trip, submit to Business Manager the "Travel Expense Account" form in duplicate with attached receipts.	5. Process voucher. Notify Comptroller that payment is due. File original of "Travel Expense Account" form with attached receipts. Send carbon copy to requisitioning unit.		6. Authorize, issue, and record payment.

REVIEW AND TRANSITION

Tone, timing, and courtesy are essential elements of effective communication. How these attributes affect human behavior in messages which inform, explain, direct, or instruct, is stressed in this chapter. In addition to these attributes, you have learned how to plan and compose specific messages—acknowledgments, notices, favorable and unfavorable replies, introductions and recommendations, job instructions, policy statements, and procedure descriptions.

You have learned how to convey appreciation and similar goodwill feelings through your understanding of empathy, ethics, and human behavior. You have learned to plan and compose messages for obtaining and receiving information on products, services, and payments as well as messages that help you inform, explain, direct, or instruct.

Influencing human behavior through employment messages is covered in Part Four. As you read Chapter 11, you will be made aware of the necessity of research to insure your employment success.

DISCUSSION QUESTIONS

A. Give examples of sentences which illustrate the following tones:
1. condescension
2. boastfulness
3. curtness
4. sarcasm
5. accusation
6. consideration
7. sincerity
8. positiveness
9. negativism

B. Discuss why the composition of a favorable-action reply and an unfavorable-action reply are psychologically different.

C. Explain how a positive tone can be maintained when writing a "no" message.

D. Discuss the following statement: Introductions and recommendations draw attention to both the person *who does* the introducing or recommending and the person *who is being* introduced or recommended.

E. Explain how sentence structure can emphasize or de-emphasize a point being made.

F. When composing instructional or directional messages, why should you project yourself into the learner's situation?

G. In what ways does the writing of a change of policy differ from the writing of a policy statement?

APPLICATIONS

Acknowledgments

1. Mr. George Haskins, manager of Hillcrest Lodge, 238 River Front, Tillamook, OR 97141, orders 5,000 plastic-coated place mats depicting scenes (pictures enclosed) of his lodge. You can fill their order—the first that Mr. Haskins has given your company—in about three weeks. Acknowledge Mr. Haskin's order.

2. You are the secretary to Ms. Irene Waskevich, who is the buyer for Wear-well Clothing Company. You were asked to acknowledge all Ms. Waskevich's correspondence while she is away on a buying trip to New York. Ms. Waskevich will be back in her office on September 3, 19—. Send an acknowledgment stating her return to Ms. Ann Pepperhill, 5302 Ferndale, Kimberly, AL 35091.

3. You have received a new-customer order from Mr. Anthony Romano, manager of the West Side Hardware Store, 802 W. Court Street, Picqua, OH 45356. Mr. Romano's order consists of five variable-speed sabre saws and seven commercial-duty orbital sanders. You can fill the order immediately. Acknowledge Mr. Romano's order.

4. Mrs. Paula Martin, owner of Martin Furniture Company, 700 Main Street, Center Point, LA 71323, is a regular customer who purchases large orders with your firm. Her present order consists of dining room groups in the following quantities and styles: five French provincial, four Mediterranean, seven early American, and three colonial. Acknowledge Mrs. Martin's order.

5. Ms. Beverly Taylor, 306 Hill Drive, Morristown, IN 46161, has ordered a ten-foot, automatic roll-up awning for her house trailer. Before you can ship the awning to Ms. Taylor, you need to know whether she wanted the gold-and-white striped awning or the white-and-green striped awning. Acknowledge Ms. Taylor's order.

6. Mr. Richard Knapp, 804 Webster Street, Menlo Park, CA 94025, orders accessories for his van. You can immediately ship the mirrored sunroof and the two aluminum-framed bubble windows. The drink dispenser and the spare tire carrier are temporarily out of stock but can be shipped in three weeks. Acknowledge Mr. Knapp's order.

7. You are the sales manager for a large paint manufacturing company that sells its supplies through franchised dealers only. You receive an order for ten gallons of latex exterior house paint from Mr. Paul Best, 1062 W. Piedmont Street, Scooba, MS 39358. In your acknowledgment to Mr. Best, encourage him to purchase the paint through his local dealer, the Waverly Paint Company, 206 Ellsworth Street, Scooba, MS 39358.

Replies:

8. Ms. Mildred Whitman, a graduate student at City College, is writing a dissertation on career opportunity centers as a class requirement. Ms. Whitman has heard that you have done considerable research for your doctoral dissertation regarding career centers and asks you to share your research. Because you are just completing the writing of your dissertation and your research is vital to receiving your degree, write Ms. Whitman and decline her request. Address your reply to 208 Fort Street, Barney, FL 31625.

9. You have received a message from Ms. May Clare Sims, president of the National Association of Business Students. Ms. Sims asks you to be the membership chairperson for your state. This position requires the mailing of membership applications and messages to all college business students in your state. All mailing materials are supplied with an adequate budget allowed for postage. In addition, the position requires your attendance at three reimbursed meetings which will be held in Philadelphia, Pennsylvania, during the current year. Write Ms. Sims and accept the appointment. Her address is P.O. Box 1046, Philadelphia, PA 19122.

10. You have been invited to participate in a conference concerning affirmative action which is to be held at the Hotel Montpelier in Waukegan, Illinois, on March 20-22. As personnel director of your company, you have previously

committed yourself to interviewing prospective employees at City College in Georgetown, Maine, on those dates. Write to Mr. Robert Glyndon, 560 Echo Drive, Waukegan, IL 60085, and decline the invitation.

11. As president of Apex Company, Inc., you are invited to give the keynote address for the American Small Business Association convention in Ithaca, New York, at the Hotel Wolverine on August 20. Write Mr. Albert Townsend, 85 West Spencer Street, Steamburg, NY 14783, and accept the invitation.

Introductions and Recommendations

12. Ms. Donna Bailey, assistant manager of the Bellows Department Stores, has been promoted to manager of the new store in Freeport, Texas. Ms. Bailey will assume her new duties in six weeks. As general manager of the Bellows Department Stores, address a message of introduction to Mr. Dallas North, Freeport Chamber of Commerce, 820 North Ashman Street, Freeport, TX 77541.

13. Mr. Melvin McCloy is your new Midwest sales representative for the XYZ Publishing Company, 5020 Madison Road, Tipp City, OH 45371. As sales representative, Mr. McCloy will call upon all college business teachers in this area. Besides having earned a master's degree in business administration, Mr. McCloy has taught three years on the secondary level and five years on the college level. He has been an active member of his state and national business associations. Prepare an introduction message which is to be mailed to all college business teachers in the Midwest.

Job Instructions, Statements of Policy, and Statements of Procedure

14. Based upon your own course of study or work experience, select a specific job that you know well and compose a job instruction for it.

15. You are the manager of the A.W. Hendrick Company in downtown Memphis where parking is at a premium for both customers and employees. To provide adequate parking facilities, a new parking lot has been constructed and is to be used by the employees of your company. By providing the new employee parking lot (which is one block from the company), the company will assure store customers of convenient parking facilities in the parking area next to the store building. To be sure that all employees are aware of the parking regulations, prepare an appropriate statement of policy.

16. In your real-life role as a student, report orally (or in memo form to your professor) suggestions for improving the *actual procedures* involving students, faculty members, and administration related to one or more of the following:

   a. Admission to your college or university
   b. Course loads for full-time and part-time students
   c. Credit for work experience
   d. Registration for day and evening classes
   e. Academic probation
   f. Grievance procedures
   g. Cooperative education and apprenticeship requirements
   h. Changes in course programs—drops and adds and withdrawal from school
   i. Utilization of learning resources center
   j. Financial aid
   k. Counseling services
   l. Health services
   m. Housing

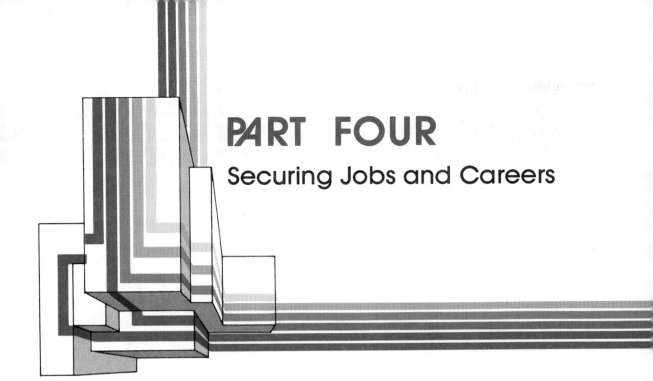

PART FOUR
Securing Jobs and Careers

Selecting a career is one of the major decisions you will make during your lifetime. As a matter of fact, modern technology may compel you to make modifications or complete changes in your job preferences during your working career. With much of your adult life devoted to employment, the work you choose should be enjoyable, challenging, and rewarding. How does one determine and obtain this type of work? Using a systematic approach including research and creativity will help you.

The *research phase* gives information about (1) yourself as a prospective worker, (2) other people as prospective employers or co-workers, and (3) circumstances likely to associate you with those other people. The *creative phase* based upon your research, yields words and actions whereby you fulfill yourself and your purpose through new or changed work that you desire.

Part Four explains how to combine research and creativity in planning your career profile and in applying for employment. Chapter 11 describes the research phase: analyzing yourself, your career potential, and specific jobs; analyzing the job market; and preparing a personal career history. The creative phase is presented in Chapter 12: the matching of your attributes to employment requirements through messages that are logically and psychologically effective.

CHAPTER 11

Employment Messages: Research Phase

Obtaining the right job—one that is interesting, challenging, and rewarding—depends upon (1) knowing yourself, (2) knowing your career potential, and (3) relating your knowledge to specific employment opportunities. This effort focuses upon the most exciting research subject imaginable: you.

UTILIZING RESEARCH TO INSURE EMPLOYMENT SUCCESS

Only through in-depth knowledge of yourself—your ambitions, attributes, abilities—can you effectively present your qualifications to a prospective employer. How well you relate specific qualifications to a likely employer depends upon your knowledge of the requirements and responsibilities involved.

To possess this information requires research: the digging for facts about yourself, your career field, and specific positions; the sifting, resifting, and organizing of those facts to fit a basic plan. This preliminary research is necessary for the preparation of your application message and for your success in the interview.

Many applicants handicap themselves by being concerned only with what the job can do for them. But this is a fact of life: Before you are hired, the employer must be convinced that your skills can serve the company.

Personnel executives often receive application messages which contain incomplete information and improper tone. These messages may imply that the applicant does not know himself or herself, does not understand the prospective employer's needs, or lacks those communication skills which are vital to business success.

Statements of facts alone may not be enough to win a job. Creativity in communicating those facts can give you a competitive advantage in attracting attention to your talents, arousing interest in your skills, stimulating desire for your services, and producing action. Therefore, recognize your research as a foundation for your communication.

ANALYZING YOURSELF, YOUR CAREER POTENTIAL, AND SPECIFIC JOBS

As you conduct your self-study, your analysis should become a rigorous examination of who you are and what you can do. Knowing yourself requires a truthful appraisal—strengths and weaknesses—of your personal characteristics and work abilities. Use this appraisal to guide the preparation of your application messages and the conduct of your interviews.

Self-Appraisal

What kinds of questions do you need to answer when examining who you are and what you can do? The New York Life Insurance Company's helpful booklet, *Your Job Interview*, reports 93 questions frequently asked during employment interviews in 92 companies. Here are samples of the questions, questions for which you should have appropriate answers.

1. What are your future vocational plans?
2. In what school activities have you participated? Why?
3. How do you spend your spare time? What are your hobbies?
4. In what type of position are you most interested?
5. Why do you think you might like to work for our company?
6. What jobs have you held? How were they obtained?
7. What courses did you like best? Least? Why?
8. Why did you choose your particular field of work?
9. What percentage of your college expenses did you earn? How?
10. How did you spend your vacations while in school?
11. What do you know about our company?
12. Do you feel that you have received a good general training?
13. What qualifications do you have that make you feel that you will be successful in your field?
14. What extracurricular offices have you held?
15. What are your ideas on salary?
16. How do you feel about your family?
17. How interested are you in sports?
18. If you could start college again, what courses would you take?
19. Can you forget your education and start from scratch?
20. Do you prefer any specific geographic location? Why? [1]

If you know the type of career you wish to pursue, begin *now* to assess your personal characteristics, your general knowledge and abilities, your specific skills and competencies as they relate to the type of career you wish to pursue. Use this research opportunity now to identify careers, their work requirements, and your ambitions.

---

[1] Frank S. Endicott, *Your Job Interview* (New York: New York Life Insurance Company, 1964).
New York Life Insurance Company also has a series of booklets on individual careers (public service articles on career opportunities) in separate reprints and a single paperback edition containing the entire list of articles on career opportunities.

Consider your accomplishments in all aspects of your life—for instance, in your academic work, full- and part-time experience, organizational activities, and sports or hobbies. Analyze those accomplishments to determine the skills and traits which are accountable for your success.

The following characteristics are listed as thought starters to help you begin your self-appraisal:

accuracy	leadership
ambition	neatness
communication skills	objectiveness
cooperation	perseverance
decisiveness	personal integrity
dependability	punctuality
efficiency	responsibility
enthusiasm	self-control
good judgment	tactfulness
initiative	

Additional data for your self-study may come from aptitude or achievement tests, from your performance in academic courses, and from your continued interest in particular areas of study.

For career information, visit your college library or your school placement center. An excellent source of information is the *Occupational Outlook Handbook,* which provides occupational briefs grouped into clusters.[2] Each occupation is described in these ways: nature of the work; places of employment; training, other qualifications, and advancement; employment outlook; earnings and working conditions; sources of additional information.

The *Dictionary of Occupational Titles* supplies excellent information for your self-study.[3] In addition to job descriptions, this publication summarizes occupational characteristics and abilities. For each job listed, the *Dictionary* identifies functions performed; significant aptitudes, interests, and temperaments for the job; critical physical demands; and working conditions. Qualification profiles are described in these terms: levels of general educational development, specific vocational preparation, intelligence, verbal and numerical ability, spatial discrimination, form and clerical perception, motor coordination, finger and manual dexterity, eye-hand-foot coordination, and as well as color discrimination.

---

[2] Published by the Bureau of Labor Statistics, U.S. Department of Labor; available from the U.S. Government Printing Office, Washington, DC 20402.

[3] Published by the Bureau of Employment Security, U.S. Department of Labor; available from the U.S. Government Printing Office, Washington, DC 20402.

For students pursuing a two-year college degree, the special volumes of *Career Opportunities* can be useful.[4] These publications identify specific occupational careers by type of work done, necessary personal qualities, educational requirements, performance requirements, and entry-level positions.

Many other resource materials are available, including the *Desk-Top Career Kit* by Careers, Inc., of Largo, Florida, and the *SRA Information Kit* by Science Research Associates, Inc., of Chicago, Illinois.

Also, computer-based aids like SIGI (Systems of Interactive Guidance and Information) can help you examine combinations of these factors: values, interests, abilities, perceptions, preferences, and plans in relation to specific occupations. SIGI was designed and developed by Educational Testing Service, Princeton, New Jersey.

With these and similar data sources, you can get to know yourself privately and discover how other people view that self. You can discover the ways in which your attributes and those of successful workers apparently coincide.

In your self-appraisal, include these categories of information:

1. Your own ratings of your personality traits, interests, and attitudes
2. Ratings of those attributes by vocational and psychological tests
3. Your education (completed, in progress, and planned)
4. Your work experience (completed, in progress, and desired)

From your research you can then identify, emphasize, or minimize facts and insights for your employment applications, resumes, and interviews. An example of such self-appraisal research is on page 254.

Career Appraisal

Having completed a *self*-appraisal, you proceed to the next phase of your employment research—the *career* appraisal.

Various careers require different preparations, attributes, skills, and interests. Also, job satisfactions—advancement possibilities, opportunities for personal growth, and professional and personal rewards—vary from one career to another. By comparing your *self*-appraisal with your *career* appraisal, you will guide yourself toward suitable employment decisions.

When preparing your career appraisal, consider the following factors:

1. Requirements, responsibilities, and rewards of the career field
2. Personal characteristics considered essential or highly desirable for success
3. Education and training (nature, cost, time, location)

---

[4] Published by the J. G. Ferguson Publishing Company, Chicago, Illinois, and distributed by Doubleday and Company, Inc., New York.

4. Model history of a person in this career (include your evaluation of this person's professional, social, and personal success; what the career has demanded; what limitations the career has imposed upon the person; satisfactions and disappointments of the career; stages of employment from initial job to top position)
5. Relation of career to your values, goals, and qualifications

Your career appraisal and your self-appraisal are private records. From them you can select information and insights for your messages to prospective employers. Make your appraisals truthful, candid, and detailed. Those appraisals are your messages to yourself and the basis of your messages to others. An example of a career appraisal is on page 255.

Specific Position Analysis

Your self-analysis has led to your career appraisal. The next step is to prepare a *specific position analysis*. Study the three examples of such analyses on pages 256 and 257. Case I is a specific adaptation of the data from page 255 passing from the business management appraisal to the specific position analysis for a sales management position. Case II represents a person seeking a position as advertising manager. Case III is that of someone seeking a position as fashion coordinator. Note that those examples refer to *specific* positions and provide needed data of characteristics, education, and experience.

ANALYZING THE JOB MARKET

After analyzing yourself, your career potentials, and specific position opportunities, your next step is to analyze the job market. To launch your job campaign successfully, conduct your job-market investigation in three phases: prepare a prospect list, research and analyze the prospect list, assemble position information.

Preparing a Prospect List

Instead of haphazardly collecting names of companies, research the particular markets. Seek out prospective employers by following this kind of systematic procedure:

1. Use the sources on page 258 to identify companies with increases in net earnings, expansion activities, or the like. Eliminate from your list those companies laying off workers.
2. Consult the local Chamber of Commerce for current business rentals, leases, and incorporations.
3. Communicate with bankers, business groups, and government agencies to determine industrial and commercial development.

From these sources you can get a valuable list of prospective employers with whose needs you can match your own.

A REALISTIC AND PRIVATE SELF-APPRAISAL

I. Personality

   A. Ambitious - I possess strong desires for personal advancement. At times, these drives interfere with my personal relationships. I make friends easily but sometimes lose them quickly. I admit my need of learning more about human relations.

   B. Conscientious - I strive to fulfill obligations but recognize a need for attending more carefully to details.

   C. Dominant - I enjoy influencing others but realize that influence can be reciprocal. I like to lead.

   D. Enthusiastic - My eagerness "comes on strong"; I can energize other people's efforts as well as my own.

   E. Gregarious - I enjoy meeting people and participating in social and service organizations. But I am sometimes more interested in making new friends than in helping old ones. I'm learning not to take people for granted.

   F. Self-Reliant - Holding a part-time job throughout my high school and college education has contributed to my independence. This self-appraisal shows I can study both sides of an issue and arrive at a relatively unbiased solution. However, I do welcome advice from qualified and experienced people in an effort to draw accurate conclusions.

II. Interests

   A. Social Interests - I enjoy these activities:
      1. Meeting people, associating with friends, and working with others.
      2. Attending social functions on campus and in the community.
      3. Participating in college activities. I am vice-president of the Business Administration Club on campus.
      4. Participating in off-campus activities.

   B. Academic Interests - My favorite study areas are these:
      1. Management   4. Accounting
      2. Psychology   5. Finance
      3. Communications   6. Mathematics

   C. General Professional Interests - I would enjoy a career that provides:
      1. Broad experience rather than specialization in one area
      2. Opportunity to work with top management
      3. Advancement to leadership
      4. Equitable financial rewards

   D. Other Interests - I enjoy:
      1. Traveling
      2. Water Skiing
      3. Swimming

III. Aptitudes - These seem to be my strong and weak points:

   A. According to academic achievement in college
      1. Excellent - Management, Public Speaking, Economics
      2. Good - Psychology and English
      3. Poor - Physical Science and Foreign Languages

   B. According to psychological tests
      1. Interests
        a. High - general problem solving
        b. Low - mechanical
      2. Aptitudes
        a. High - Quantitative
        b. Average - Verbal
        c. Low - Mechanical

IV. Education

   A. High School - was graduated June 3, 19--

   B. College - program in progress (sophomore year)
      1. Completing general education requirements.
      2. Plan to work for a Bachelor of Business Administration degree, with management major.

V. Experience

   A. Summer employment, during school, with the City Parks and Recreation Department.

   B. Entered the cooperative education program at City College. Employed in the accounting department of a large chemical company. As part of the co-op agreement, I am being rotated to various accounting jobs.

BUSINESS MANAGEMENT CAREER APPRAISAL

I. Requirements
   A. Education
      1. College degree--preferably in business administration
      2. Major emphasis in management courses
      3. Basic courses in finance, accounting, marketing, and production.
   B. Experience
      1. Familiarity with the general business environment
      2. Work in the specific area of interest

II. Personal Characteristics
   A. Creativity - develop new ideas applicable to specific business situations and recognize good ideas presented by others
   B. Decision-making ability - recognize facts, develop alternative course of action, foresee possible consequences, reach accurate decisions evaluate results
   C. Flexibility - adaption to changing circumstances
   D. Initiative - plan and execute ideas and programs within the framework of broad company policy
   E. Persuasiveness - influence others, directly and indirectly
   F. Verbal ability - communicate effectively, orally and in writing, with superiors, peers, subordinates, and people outside the organization

III. Observations of a successful person following a management career
   A. Brief history -- Mr. Arnold Babcock was graduated from City College with a business administration degree (management major, advanced courses in marketing).

   Upon graduation Babcock was employed as a management trainee by a national building supply company. During fifteen-month training program, Babcock received intensive training in major departments of the company.

   After the training program, Babcock was appointed assistant manager of the company retail outlet in San Jose, California. During Babcock's four years as assistant manager, profits of the San Jose store doubled.

   Babcock was then appointed manager of the Toledo store and is now completing his sixth year in this position. The Toledo store has markedly increased its sales volume and has been designated as a management training center for the company.

   B. Job demands -- Babcock's work requires long hours during peak work-load periods. Rewards have included advancement, opportunity, and financial success. A negative factor, however, has been occasional conflicts of time needed for career and for family responsibilities.

IV. My qualifications for a management career
   A. Education
      1. Expect to obtain a Bachelor of Business Administration degree two years from now (major in management)
      2. Have taken basic courses in accounting, finance, marketing and production
      3. Plan to continue study of accounting and marketing
   B. Ambitions
      1. To pursue a career offering opportunities for advancement
      2. To work for a large company that encourages and rewards individual initiative
   C. Work Experience
      1. In the cooperative education program, I am gaining experience as part of a business environment. Job assignments, however, now offer only initial exposure to a specific area of interest.
      2. After graduation, I plan to receive additional on-job management training.
   D. Other Experience
      1. To help pay for my college expenses, I've worked during summer vacations with the City Department of Parks and Recreation.
      2. As vice-president of a campus organization, I am developing my leadership ability.

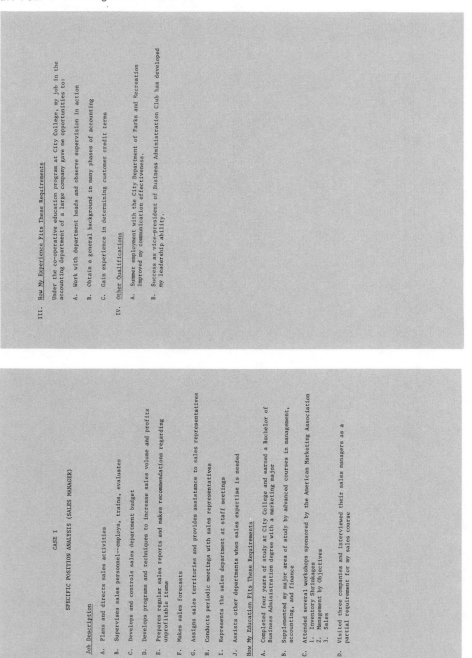

CASE I

SPECIFIC POSITION ANALYSIS (SALES MANAGER)

I. Job Description

A. Plans and directs sales activities

B. Supervises sales personnel--employs, trains, evaluates

C. Develops and controls sales department budget

D. Develops programs and techniques to increase sales volume and profits

E. Prepares regular sales reports and makes recommendations regarding unprofitable items

F. Makes sales forecasts

G. Assigns sales territories and provides assistance to sales representatives

H. Conducts periodic meetings with sales representatives

I. Represents the sales department at staff meetings

J. Assists other departments when sales expertise is needed

II. How My Education Fits These Requirements

A. Completed four years of study at City College and earned a Bachelor of Business Administration degree with a marketing major

B. Supplemented my major area of study by advanced courses in management, accounting, and finance

C. Attended several workshops sponsored by the American Marketing Association
1. Inventory Shrinkages
2. Management by Objectives
3. Sales

D. Visited three companies and interviewed their sales managers as a partial requirement for my sales course

III. How My Experience Fits These Requirements

Under the co-operative education program at City College, my job in the accounting department of a large company gave me opportunities to:

A. Work with department heads and observe supervision in action

B. Obtain a general background in many phases of accounting

C. Gain experience in determining customer credit terms

IV. Other Qualifications

A. Summer employment with the City Department of Parks and Recreation improved my communication effectiveness.

B. Success as vice-president of Business Administration Club has developed my leadership ability.

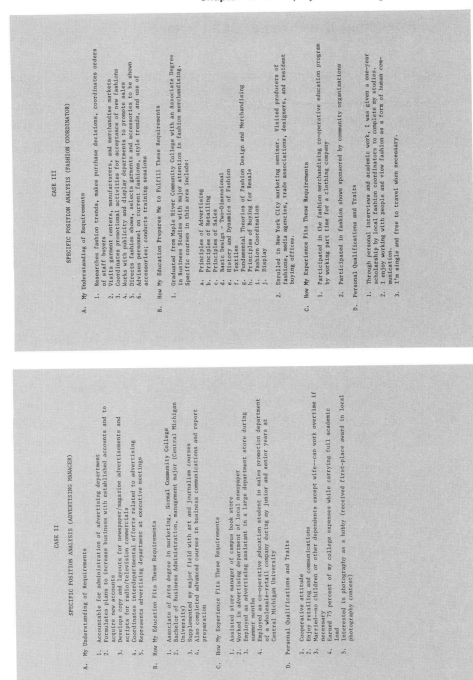

CASE III

SPECIFIC POSITION ANALYSIS (FASHION COORDINATOR)

A. My Understanding of Requirements

1. Researches fashion trends, makes purchase decisions, coordinates orders of staff buyers
2. Visits garment centers, manufacturers, and merchandise markets
3. Coordinates promotional activities for acceptance of new fashions
4. Works with publicity and display departments to promote sales
5. Directs fashion shows, selects garments and accessories to be shown
6. Advises personnel on current fashions, style trends, and use of accessories; conducts training sessions

B. How My Education Prepares Me to Fulfill These Requirements

1. Graduated from Maple River Community College with an Associate Degree in Business Studies with major attention in fashion merchandising. Specific courses in this area include:

   a. Principles of Advertising
   b. Principles of Retailing
   c. Principles of Sales
   d. Basic Design - Two-Dimensional
   e. History and Dynamics of Fashion
   f. Textiles
   g. Fundamental Theories of Fashion Design and Merchandising
   h. Principles of Buying for Resale
   i. Fashion Coordination
   j. Display

2. Enrolled in New York City marketing seminar. Visited producers of fashions, media agencies, trade associations, designers, and resident buying offices.

C. How My Experience Fits These Requirements

1. Participated in the fashion merchandising co-operative education program by working part time for a clothing company

2. Participated in fashion shows sponsored by community organizations

D. Personal Qualifications and Traits

1. Through personal interviews and academic work, I was given a one-year scholarship by local fashion coordinators to complete my studies.
2. I enjoy working with people and view fashion as a form of human communication.
3. I'm single and free to travel when necessary.

CASE II

SPECIFIC POSITION ANALYSIS (ADVERTISING MANAGER)

A. My Understanding of Requirements

1. Accountable for administration of advertising department
2. Formulates plans to increase business with established accounts and to acquire new accounts
3. Develops copy and layouts for newspaper/magazine advertisements and scripts for radio/television commercials
4. Coordinates interdepartmental efforts related to advertising
5. Represents advertising department at executive meetings

B. How My Education Fits These Requirements

1. Associate of Arts degree in marketing, Normal Community College
2. Bachelor of Business Administration, management major (Central Michigan University)
3. Supplemented my major field with art and journalism courses
4. Also completed advanced courses in business communications and report preparation

C. How My Experience Fits These Requirements

1. Assisted store manager of campus book store
2. Worked in advertising department of local newspaper
3. Employed as advertising assistant in a large department store during summer months
4. Employed as co-operative education student in sales promotion department of a wholesale-retail company during my junior and senior years at Central Michigan University

D. Personal Qualifications and Traits

1. Cooperative attitude
2. Enjoy retailing and communications
3. Married—no children or other dependents except wife—can work overtime if necessary
4. Earned 75 percent of my college expenses while carrying full academic load
5. Interested in photography as a hobby (received first-place award in local photography contest)

Analyzing the Prospect List

These sources will help you determine the history, character, products, and services of prospective employers. You can use such information profitably in services of prospective employers. You can use such information profitably in your job-seeking messages and interviews. Additional information may also be obtained by following these suggestions:

1. Use the employment-information resources of your library or your career information center.
2. Speak with people who know your field.
3. Visit a branch office of the company if feasible.
4. Identify the person who does the hiring.
5. Familiarize yourself with current business issues through publications and broadcast reports concerning your field.
6. Especially study relevant company publications and trade papers.

The following sources will help you to analyze your prospect list:

Accountants' Index
Ayer Directory of Publications
Bradford's Directory of Marketing Research Agencies and Management
College Placement Directory
Consumer Sourcebook
Directory of American Firms Operating in Foreign Countries
Directory of Corporate Affiliations
Encyclopedia of Careers and Vocational Guidance
Fairchild's Financial Manual of Retail Stores
Financial Market Place
Franchise Opportunities
Jane's Major Companies of Europe
Macmillan Job Guide of American Corporations
Moody's Handbook of Common Stocks
New York Stock Exchange Fact Book
Standard and Poor's Register of Corporations, Directors, and Executives
Statistical Abstract of the United States
Survey of Current Business (U.S. Department of Commerce)
Thomas' Register of American Manufacturers
U.S. Census of Manufacturers
U.S. Government Manual
Wall Street Journal
Who's Who in America
Who's Who in Commerce and Industry
World Almanac

Assembling Position Information

To assemble pertinent data for each position that interests you, follow these steps:

1. Appraise the company's position within its industry or field.
2. Consider the company's reputation among its employees, customers, and competitors.
3. Define the nature of the products and the type of services.
4. Note whether the company promotes from within its ranks.
5. Identify who really "runs the show" in your area of interest.
6. Define the qualities that the employer probably will seek in applicants: tact, conscientiousness, precision, ability, initiative, etc.
7. Determine the specific needs of available positions.
8. Request interviews with people who work at jobs for which you are preparing. Interview people who work in similar jobs but in different firms. Interview people who work in different jobs within your area of specialization. Ask your instructor or major professor to help you find people, perhaps recent graduates, who will talk with you about their careers.

But before you ask for interviews, plan your questions so that you will include these and similar topics:

Nature of the position
Duties and responsibilities
Usual entry-level position
Special training required
Favorable features of position
Unfavorable features of position
Opportunities for promotion
Places where this type of employment is likely to be found
General information about salary and other benefits

PREPARING A PERSONAL CAREER HISTORY

Executives may advise you to prepare a personal career history, adding to it as new experiences broaden your viewpoint and increase your qualifications for more responsible positions. This kind of record (sometimes called a *curriculum vitae* or "course of life") is valuable in preparing biographical summaries initially and as your career progresses.

To record data that you can supply now and that you can add as your experience and responsibilities grow, use this outline:

Personal

Your full name, address, telephone number.
Date and place of your birth.
Date and place of birth of nearest relatives with their present addresses.

Included might be your mother, father, grandparents, brothers, sisters, wife or husband, and your children, indicating any person deceased.

(This information may be needed if you are applying for a position involving national security or responsibility for large sums of money.)

Other personal details that are relevant to your career development:

Education

Names of institutions.

Degrees, diplomas, or certificates granted (with dates.)

Records of academic work.

Other records, such as vocational interest and aptitude test results, special awards, and honors.

List of extracurricular activities: services on committees, offices held, stating specifically what you did and any special programs in which you participated. Names of persons with whom you worked on special projects.

Work and Military Experience

Full name and address of each company, organization, or unit.

Detailed description of duties and responsibilities for each of your major assignments.

Dates for each job or assignment.

Salary increases, promotions and other recognitions.

Community or Social Group Participation

Activities or services that are important to you.

Church membership, leadership in groups, other services.

Avocational and Recreational Interests

Activities and hobbies you enjoy.

Clippings from Newspapers or Periodicals

Items describing your activities.

Copies of your writings that have been published.

Listing of People Willing to Recommend You

Names, addresses, and telephone numbers of persons who will vouch for your abilities if their names are used as references—persons who have observed your behavior with others at school, at work, in social activities, in community service, or with your family.

REVIEW AND TRANSITION

Chapter 11 has described research methods for prospective employment. You have learned how to prepare a self-appraisal which seriously examines your strengths, weaknesses, values, and goals. You have learned how to develop a general career appraisal which can be later converted to a specific position analysis, how to analyze the job market, and how to prepare a personal career history.

Chapter 12 describes the creative phase of employment communication, the composition of messages that direct attention and interest to you as a prospective employee. Besides composition of the application message and the data sheet, suggestions will be given to help you participate successfully in interviews and their followups.

DISCUSSION QUESTIONS

A. Explain the following statement:
"To be successful in acquiring the right job, you must first know yourself."

B. How can past and present accomplishments help you to determine those characteristics which are positive factors for employment?

C. What are several similarities between a "self-appraisal" and a "career appraisal"?
What is the value and what are the functions of a career appraisal?
What important factors should be included in a career appraisal? How will these factors help you in determining your career area?

D. Explain the importance of a "specific position analysis."

E. Are facts by themselves sufficient to help you get the job you want? (Explain your answer.)

F. What are the competitive advantages of preparing a "prospect list"?

G. What data sources and research methods can help you identify and locate prospective employers?

H. What are the advantages of your preparing and maintaining a personal career history?

APPLICATIONS

1. Prepare a self-appraisal which includes an assessment of your personal characteristics, interests, aptitudes, education, and experience. An example of such an appraisal appears on page 254.

2. Prepare a career appraisal within a career area in which you have an interest. Consider including the following information: general requirements, responsibilities, and rewards; personal characteristics considered essential; personal attributes considered highly desirable; education and training requirements; and relationship of career to yourself.

3. By using references in your library, prepare an annotated bibliography of sources which can be used to analyze companies. Examples of such sources appear on page 258.

4. Using the source material in Application 3, obtain the headquarters location, annual sales, principal product manufactured, approximate number of employees, and any additional information you think is essential regarding the following companies:
   - **a.** Bethlehem Steel Corporation
   - **b.** Chase Manhattan Bank
   - **c.** Continental Group, Inc.
   - **d.** Ford Motor Company
   - **e.** General Foods Corporation
   - **f.** General Motors Corporation

5. Prepare a self-analysis for a position in which you are interested. (Examples are given on pages 256 and 257.) In preparing your analysis, use the career appraisal you completed in Application 2.

6. Using the information on pages 259-260, prepare your own up-to-date personal career history.

12

Employment Messages: Creative Phase

The research phase of employment messages provides you with information about yourself, your potential, and the job market. The creative phase is used to fit your attributes to the needs of the prospective employer through messages that are logically as well as psychologically effective. In this chapter, you will learn how to plan and compose messages which help you to compete successfully for work opportunities.

CREATIVE EMPLOYMENT APPLICATION MESSAGES

Personnel directors report that many application messages they receive begin with the same time-worn, opening paragraphs which do nothing to attract reader interest; or the messages appear to be modified duplicates of well-known textbook models.

Your employment message must be creative; it must represent you as an individual; and it must gently persuade your reader by attracting favorable attention, arousing interest, stimulating desire, and producing action. These functions translate themselves into five systematic steps:

1. Establishing point of contact
2. Training for requirements
3. Identifying qualifications and human-interest images
4. Supplying references
5. Requesting the interview

Establishing Point of Contact

Structure your opening sentence, the point of contact, either with a fresh, imaginative statement or with a rhetorical question which will express your individuality as a superior applicant. Avoid the dull and trite expressions that are so often found in job-seeking messages—such as, "Please consider me an applicant for work with your firm," or "Are you looking for someone with ability and ambition?" To begin your message with a hackneyed statement or a question with an obvious answer creates little interest for the reader regarding your value to the company.

DULL AND TRITE	FRESH AND IMAGINATIVE
Please consider this letter as my application for a position in your marketing department.	Versatility is the name of the marketing field. With my proven experience in several areas of marketing, I am confident that my abilities can profitably serve your company.
Are you interested in a person who can effectively communicate in more than one language? If so, please consider me an applicant.	Does your world-wide company need an efficient trilingual secretary—one who can effectively communicate in French and German as well as in English? If so, I am that person.
I am writing regarding any openings you may have for an accountant. I am interested in any position you may have now or in the near future.	Are you in need of a reliable accountant who welcomes hard work and challenges? If so, please consider me as an applicant.

The preceding examples are opening sentences for the unsolicited or prospecting employment message. Such messages are written for seeking employment with companies where no particular position openings have been announced. Interest in these companies results from researching various firms who may require people with your specific training. Consider the employment possibilities available to you when writing an unsolicited message—wider selection of companies from which to choose, better geographical choice of employment opportunities, better possibility of creating a job where none previously existed, and less competition for the job you want.

As evidenced by the many employment advertisements which appear in such publications as newspapers, professional magazines, and placement notices, the solicited application plays an important role in bringing the applicant and the employer together. When writing a solicited application, mention who or what prompted you to send your message. Follow your opening sentence at once by a statement that you are applying; do not leave the matter to inference, implication, or oblique suggestion. Remember, also, to plan your "attention" opener so that it enables transition to a statement of your merits within the context of the employer's needs and desires. For example:

The excellent reputation and rapid growth of Packaged Homes, Inc., are indicative of an outstanding marketing division. Having a desire to be associated with your firm, I am applying for a position with your marketing team.

In your employment messages, you probably will find that using *I* seems natural and convenient. After all, you are describing *yourself*; your training, education, and experience; your personality and your individuality as they relate to your prospective employer's interests and needs. If *justifiable* confidence is the general tone of your message, there is nothing objectionable in using *I* when necessary. However, by choosing your words carefully, you will appropriately emphasize your *reader's* concern while relating your services to that person's interests and needs. Thereby, almost automatically, you will minimize *I*'s without straining to hide them.

Training for Requirements

Explain your education and experience in terms of the employer's needs. Through research you have discovered your success factors, and you have investigated the educational and job requirements for the position you seek. Equally important, you have investigated the company for which you wish to work. From this valuable information, use only those facts that relate your preparation and experience to the employer's concerns. Adapt highlights of your background to the activities or expectations of the employer.

At City College I earned a business administration degree with a marketing major. Related courses in advertising, management, and accounting increased my understanding of the marketing field. Courses in data processing showed me the techniques and procedures for gathering and effectively analyzing data. To help me in better understanding others, courses in psychology and sociology were also taken.

The experience factor is one of several qualifications that concerns employers. Perhaps your other qualifications far outweigh the experience factor. And perhaps you have had part-time experience with campus or civic groups which indicates characteristics such as initiative, responsibility, and integrity. However, to say "I lack experience in your type of business" or "I regret that I've had only part-time instead of full-time experience" is to put yourself needlessly on the defensive. Specifically and positively, describe your qualifications and leave the rest of the matter for discussion during the employment interview.

Identifying Qualifications and Human-Interest Images

Strange as it may seem, under certain circumstances, your most obvious accomplishments may not be rated the most important. Some item that you consider of little significance may, in the eyes of a certain prospective employer, set you off from the crowd. The winning item is often unpredictable. It could be one of your college activities, civic services, organizational memberships, hobbies, or summer employment.

For example, a college student financed his education by selling advertising space to business people in a small college town. The total revenue he collected in his venture not only paid for his overhead costs but also earned him a substantial profit. Emphasizing this enterprise as evidence of initiative highlighted his employment application.

In presenting your personal qualifications, tell why you are interested in the employer's business and why you feel you can do the work that needs to be done. Refer to a personal data sheet (a résumé) that accompanies your application message.

> Through City College's co-operative education program, I was employed by the Apex Company in Cincinnati, Ohio. This practical experience, reinforced by participation in college and city organizations which are listed on the enclosed data sheet, has developed my ability to communicate effectively and to fulfill responsibility. The opportunity to work with several department heads and observe supervision in action has reinforced my desire to work in a marketing department—especially yours.

Supplying References

References increase the employer's confidence in your ability. They should be given only with the permission of the persons named.

> Will you let me prove personally what my references will confirm?

Requesting the Interview

Your closing sentences should (1) suggest action and (2) make that action as easy as possible. Directly request an interview. Tell how and when the prospective employer may reach you.

> To arrange an interview at your convenience, please telephone me at 517-228-4512 or write me at the address given above.

PERSONAL DATA SHEET (RÉSUMÉ)

The personal data sheet outlines, tabulates, and summarizes the significant details of your personal history. In other words, the data sheet gives detailed evidence of what the application message describes. By performing this function, the application message then has the ability to

SALLY DETZEL
1600 Jefferson Street
Janesville, WI 53545
(414) 871-9087

EDUCATION

June, 19--   B.S.   Business Administration
                                    City College
                                    Fairchild, Wisconsin

June, 19--   Diploma   Northern High School
                                    Janesville, Wisconsin

Management Courses (College Level)

Introduction to Business   Operations Management
Quantitative Methods   Management-Union Relations
Marketing Principles & Policies   Organizational Structure & Design
Business Conditions & Forecasting   Production & Inventory Control
Behavior in Organization   Management Accounting

Related Management Courses (College Level)

Business Law   Business Communications
Corporation Law   Report Writing
Economics   Statistics
Corporation Finance   Credits & Collections
Money & Banking   Mathematics of Investment

EXPERIENCE

Summer Work   Accounting   Wilson's Department Store
19--   Janesville, Wisconsin

Two Years   Co-operative   Manaheim Plastic Company
19-- to 19--   Education   Janesville, Wisconsin

EXTRACURRICULAR ACTIVITIES

Marketing Club (President)   City College News (Advertising Manager)
City College Concert Bank   Varsity Cheerleader

REFERENCES

Supplied upon request.

Personal Data Sheet

quickly attract attention, motivate interest, identify you as a person whom the employer requires, and stimulate an invitation for an employment interview. Most employers expect to see a detailed data sheet attached to or enclosed with a concise application message.

The application message may be less than a page, but the carefully outlined and completely detailed data sheet runs often to two, sometimes to three, pages. Although data sheets, like application messages, are among the most personal of business communications, you will find the following organization guides useful:

1. Organize the data categories according to priority of interest for the employer rather than for yourself. List the categories in descending order of importance to *the employer* (that is, most important category first, next most important category second, and so on).
2. Organize the data items *within* categories according to descending order of importance for the employer (again, most important first).
3. List the names, addresses, and telephone numbers of references (people who will confirm your merits). Or mention simply that references are available upon request; then your references will be queried only by those employers who are seriously considering you as a prospective employee.

When preparing your data sheet, be sure to use your self-analysis record. From this material, select the facts you consider important enough to include on your data sheet.

SPECIAL PRECAUTIONS AND GUIDES

An interview is a privilege for which you must compete. Your application message and your data sheet can win that privilege for you. Since employers need information to decide about granting or refusing an interview, provide significant facts about yourself. Observe the following precautions to protect yourself against communication errors of content, organization, and tone that often lose instead of gain jobs.

Sending the Message

When you can identify the appropriate officer by name and title, direct your application to that person. If this is not possible, send your message to the "Personnel Director." Your message will then be routed to the appropriate office.

Discretion

As an ethical person, represent yourself truthfully and confidently. Create your own communication instead of copying models from this or any other book. The illustrations provided in this book are intended only to *guide* you as you create messages of your own.

1520 University Drive
East Lansing, MI 48823
June 1, 19--

Personnel Officer
Packaged Homes, Inc.
2226 Outer Drive
Springfield, IL 62704

Dear Manager:

The excellent reputation and rapid growth of Packaged Homes, Inc. are indicative of an outstanding marketing division. Having a desire to be associated
with your firm, I am applying for a position with your marketing team.

In preparation for a marketing career, a minor in economics was taken to
enrich my business background. Because a working knowledge of statistics is
important, I acquired the ability to use this skill in the preparation of
analytical reports. Communication courses were taken because the ability to
express oneself both orally and in writing is equally important to a marketing
career.

At City College I earned a business administration degree with a marketing
major. Related courses in advertising, management, and accounting increased
my understanding of the marketing field. Courses in data processing showed
me the techniques and procedures for gathering and effectively analyzing data.
To help me in better understanding others, courses in psychology and sociology
were also taken.

Through City College's co-operative education program, I was employed by the
Apex Company in Cincinnati, Ohio. This practical experience, reinforced by
participation in college and city organizations which are listed on the enclosed data sheet, has developed my ability to communicate effectively and
to fulfill responsibility. The opportunity to work with several department
heads and observe supervision in action has reinforced my desire to work in
a marketing department--especially yours.

Will you let me prove personally what my references will confirm? To arrange
an interview at your convenience, please telephone me at 517-228-4512 or write
me at the address given above.

                              Sincerely yours,

                              Charles Rotella

                              Charles Rotella

mco

Enclosure: Resume

Application Letter

Truthfully represent your education, experience, and references. Emphasize the extent and quality of your preparation. List your certificates, diplomas, or degrees. Use your data sheet to describe in detail your noteworthy work experience, including responsibilities, promotions, and attainments of vocational or professional recognition. Slighting your training, education, or experience is as wrong as claiming that you have done what you have not done.

Obtain permission before using the names of people as references. The names, addresses, and telephone numbers of your references may be listed on your data sheet. However, consider the advisability of simply mentioning that your references are available upon request. Then only those employers who are genuinely interested in employing you will communicate with your references.

Feedback

When you receive a response to your application message, acknowledge that response immediately. When you are invited for an interview, accept that invitation and confirm the meeting details. After the interview, send a goodwill message; thank the interviewer for her or his courtesy and restate your interest in the employment opportunity.

If your application elicits no response after a reasonable waiting period (generally at least two weeks), send another message reaffirming your interest in becoming an employee of the company.

THE INTERVIEW

An invitation to appear for an interview indicates that you have made a favorable impression on the employer. The interview provides you an opportunity to show that you are really the kind of person your application has represented you to be.

A personnel director may conduct the initial interview. Additional interviews may then be held with the prospective supervisor and possibly the supervisor's immediate boss. In most cases, however, the judgment of the immediate supervisor (the one who has the position to fill) weighs heaviest in the final hiring decision.

To overcome any anxieties you may have, remind yourself of what the interview signifies: the company's interest in you. Keep in mind that most interviewers make every effort to relax the candidate. Additionally, you have *prepared yourself* to demonstrate your ability to reason, describe, inform, or persuade orally.

How have you prepared yourself for the interview? You have conducted an intense self-analysis to determine your attributes and skills. You have investigated a job cluster which later was converted to a specific job analysis. You have matched your attributes and skills to a specific job—the position for which you are being interviewed. Furthermore, you have used library and other resources for information about the company for which you want to work.

With this wealth of information about yourself, the job, and the company, what else can you do to be prepared? Visit your college placement office for advice and materials regarding the interviewing process. Your placement officers will have valuable suggestions and guides for handling yourself during the interview. Also, talk with friends who have interviewed for similar jobs; but remember foremost—you are yourself, unique and individual.

The Interviewer and You

Since first impressions are important to your success, be sure to appear properly dressed and groomed at the time and place set for your interview. Prepare yourself for the interview as you would prepare yourself for a business photograph. Wear customary daytime attire which, rather than drawing attention to itself, encourages the interviewer to concentrate upon you and upon what you say.

Consider your physical mannerisms; they can consciously or unconsciously affect the impression the interviewer may have of you. When his or her hand is extended to you, look your interviewer straight in the eye and shake hands firmly. Be certain you know and correctly pronounce the name of your interviewer. If you are not sure, inquire before entering the interviewer's office. When offered a chair, sit down and assume a posture which reflects self-confidence and alertness. Square your shoulders; keep your hands in a relaxed position. Clenching your hands or placing your feet firmly together may give the impression of tenseness. Slouching or slumping may suggest carelessness. Try to give a relaxed impression.

Your interviewer may begin by chatting with you about topics of incidental or mutual interest in an effort to help you relax. In addition to questions related to your application message and data sheet, questions will be directed to determine your knowledge of the interviewer's company. Besides the Endicott list of common questions, sampled in Chapter 11, page 250, be prepared to answer the following classic question, a favorite of interviewers: "Why did you apply for a job with *our* company?" Also, expect opportunities for you to develop a topic of conversation. Remember that your interviewer has a double purpose in inviting you to pick up the discussion—to estimate your knowledge and to determine your proficiency in communicating that knowledge.

The Interview and Equal Employment Opportunity Legislation

Whether you are the interviewer or the applicant, it is important to understand federal and state legislation which pertains to the interviewing process. In the hiring process, it is not a violation of federal equal opportunity laws to make inquiries concerning race, color, religion, or national origin. However, the Equal Employment Opportunity Commission looks with extreme disfavor upon any inquiries of this nature. To ask questions related to race, color, religion, or national origin is suspect and may require validation by the individual company which persists in using this type of inquiry. Additionally, the Age Discrimination in Employment Act forbids discrimination because of age against anyone 40 years of age or older but less than 65 years of age.

Besides federal legislation, state fair employment practice laws vary. It is essential to know the specific laws of the state in which you live or in which your business is located. Inquiries into such topics as marital status, family planning, credit ratings, arrests, race, national origin, religion, or age can be in direct violation of state law.

The alert interviewer will avoid asking questions that violate laws regarding an applicant's race, color, religion, national origin, sex, age, or handicap.

The Follow-Up

Promptly send a follow-up message to the prospective employer immediately after your interview. In your note, state your appreciation for the interview, reiterate your interest in the position, and review points of special interest to the employer. If you were told to complete and return an application form, do so promptly and attach your follow-up note to the application form.

Sometimes a second follow-up is advisable, perhaps a week or two after the first. In your second follow-up message, remind the prospective employer of your having filed an application, express your continued interest in the position, and demonstrate your willingness to return for another interview.

The On-Campus Interview and Follow-Up

Many large firms send interview teams to discuss employment with students who are about to graduate. In these cases, the college placement center usually arranges the interview.

Although the interview is held on your campus, your preparation, your appearance, and your physical mannerisms are as important as they would be in the company office. The information described earlier applies to the on-campus interviews, also.

Only rarely are specially composed application messages required for the on-campus interview. However, the student may confirm the interview with a written follow-up message, or the interviewing team may ask the applicant to prepare such a message.

```
                                        1600 Jefferson Street
                                        Janesville, WI  53545
                                        November 2, 19--


        Mr. Robert Cleary
        Reardon Manufacturing Company
        812 Rust Drive
        Hibbing, MN  55746

        Dear Mr. Cleary:

            Thank you for the October 31 interview concerning a management-
        trainee position with your company.

            The opportunity to discuss my qualifications in terms of your
        firm's needs makes me confident that I can fulfill the requirements
        of your program.  With a bachelor's degree in management and with
        work-related experience as a student, I have acquired a solid foun-
        dation in preparation for management training.  Because Reardon offers
        challenges and opportunities to its personnel, I am very much inter-
        ested in a career with your firm.

            Please write me at the address given above or telephone me at
        (414) 871-9087 regarding your decision.  Because I am interested in
        a career with a vigorous, progressive firm, I look forward to an
        affirmative reply.

                                        Sincerely yours,

                                        Sally Detzel
                                        Sally Detzel
```

A Follow-Up Letter

REVIEW AND TRANSITION

Chapter 11 describes research; Chapter 12 explains how to use that research to create the employment application message, data sheet, and follow-up message.

Your application message should attract attention, arouse interest, stimulate desire, and produce action. Six steps are involved: establishing a point of contact, understanding the requirements, training for the requirements, identifying personal qualifications, supplying references, and requesting the interview. The data sheet, or résumé, gives detailed evidence of what the application message describes. Because the interview provides you the opportunity to demonstrate that you are the kind of person your application has represented you to be, preparation for the interview is essential. Following your interview, be sure to send a follow-up message. Such a message shows your appreciation for the interview and your continued interest in the position.

The next part of this book acquaints you with another category of informative-persuasive communication that also requires research and creativity; Chapters 13 and 14 deal with sales messages. Chapter 13 introduces you to the research phase of the sales message, including three common types of follow-up programs, product and market analysis, and campaign plans and organization.

DISCUSSION QUESTIONS

A. The following sentences have been used as opening statements in application messages. Discuss the effectiveness of each statement.
   1. This letter is in response to your ad in the *Mayville News* on August 22 for keypunch operator.
   2. In regards to your April 1 advertisement, I am interested in employment with your firm.
   3. I am responding to your search for an office manager.
   4. The ad in the *Freeland Press* appealed to my overall prerequisite for a challenging and growth-oriented business career.
   5. The job of programmer seems to be from all indications a job that I could be comfortable in most every respect.
   6. I would like to submit to you information that makes me believe I am qualified for the position you have recently advertised.
   7. I am interested in the possibility of a position in your company at the present time or in the near future.
   8. I am writing to inquire and apply for a position with your company.
   9. I have chosen to send this letter to see if you have any job openings.
   10. I would like this letter to be considered an application for employment.

B. From what sources can you obtain information concerning the employer's needs?

C. What process can you use in determining the relationship of your qualifications to the needs of the prospective employer?

D. If you have had no previous work experience, what should you emphasize in your application message?

E. The data sheet, as part of the employment message, performs a significant function. What is this function?

F. Why should references be used only with the permission of the persons named?

G. How does federal and state legislation on equal employment opportunities affect the information presented in the data sheet? How does this legislation affect the interviewing process?

H. How should the categories of the data sheet be organized?

I. What preparations should you make for an employment interview?

J. Why is it important for a follow-up message to be sent promptly after the first interview?

APPLICATIONS

1. Constructively criticize the following message; then revise it appropriately.

236 North Broadway
Bitter Creek, WY 82921
April 1, 19—

Mr. Robert Wallace
Bedford Insurance Company
1865 Willow Street
Bedford, WY 83112

Dear Mr. Wallace:

Please consider this message as an application for a secretarial position with your company.

I am presently employed in a non-challenging position and desire more utilization of skills. I also have a desire to relocate from this area.

If additional information or an interview is desired, I can be reached at the above address. References are available and will be furnished upon request.

Thank you for your attention.

Very truly yours,

Mary Alice Skooner

2. Write an application message to a company of your choice. When composing your message, request a position related to your major area of study. Follow the five steps outlined in this chapter.

3. Prepare a data sheet to accompany the application message you have written for Application 2.

4. Assume the personnel manager has responded to your message in Application 2. You have been invited to be in the personnel manager's office next week for an interview—Thursday at 10 A M. Prepare a suitable reply.

5. As a result of your interview (Application 4), you are very interested in a position with the prospective employer's company. Write a suitable follow-up message.

6. Visit your college library to locate major newspapers, magazines, and professional journals that advertise employment opportunities. Prepare a list of these resources. Select one advertisement that fits the qualifications you expect to have upon graduation and write an application message.

7. Using sources cited in this chapter, prepare a list of likely questions—and your answers—for an employment interview.

8. Prepare and present an oral-visual report on interviewing techniques.

9. Write a report summarizing highlights of federal legislation and your state's legislation concerning equal employment opportunities.

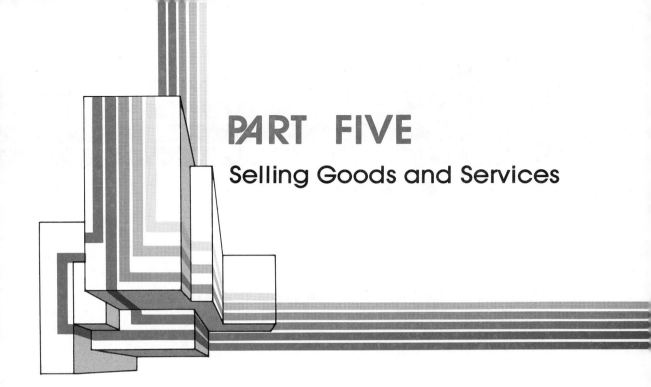

PART FIVE

Selling Goods and Services

In Part Four of your text, you studied one form of persuasive communication—the employment message. You are now going to study another type of persuasive communication which can help you influence human behaviors—the sales message.

The sales message is among the more important forms of persuasive communications. Its purpose is to promote the exchange of goods and services through effective communications. This requires an understanding of the nature, procedures, and techniques of sales messages. The carefully planned selling effort that you will study in Chapters 13 and 14 is sometimes called direct mail, often

classified as business promotion, and usually organized into a communication program or campaign.

The research phase of the sales message is discussed in Chapter 13. This phase includes analyzing products as well as markets for those products so that you can plan and create an effective campaign for a sales message. The creative phase of the sales message is discussed in Chapter 14. This involves psychological motivation, identification of the central buying point, and the design of the sales message. It is the combination of research and creativity that produces the effective sales message.

CHAPTER 13

Sales Messages: Research Phase

The selling function is a vital component in the successful operation of a business. Its purpose is to persuade a buyer to purchase the products or services of the company. In achieving this aim, those involved in sales must integrate information from facets of business, such as advertising, marketing research, marketing planning, and physical distribution. Because the sales function includes a wide variety of related business activities, common practice in large organizations is to place it as a responsibility of a marketing vice-president or a general sales manager.

Selling is part of the marketing function, and it is a generator of business activity. Because selling stimulates demand for products and services in the form of orders, a series of other management activities is created—for instance, extension of credit, processing of adjustments, control of contracts, and collection of payments.

How does the business message relate to the selling function? It is an integrated part of the communication mix which a company determines will maintain its share of the present market and, hopefully, increase its sales. A communication mix can be defined as the proportional share of the communicative methods—personal selling, advertising, and sales promotion—which a company selects for persuading buyers to purchase the organization's products or services. The sales message is the instrument through which sales promotion is conducted. Through effective sales messages, business communicators influence the behaviors of prospective customers by attracting the attention of those customers, impelling their interests, developing their desire, and activating their purchases.

ANALYZING THE PRODUCT AND THE MARKET POTENTIAL

Knowing your product and its sales potential is the first step in effective sales writing. Consulting with members in the marketing research and marketing planning departments is the logical action with which to begin acquiring this knowledge. Here new-product ideas are evaluated and analyzed in terms of potential market, growth rate, and competitive strength. Profitable ideas are then converted to products, tested, and refined. If the company chooses to test market the new product in a geographical area with a complete marketing campaign, this feedback from sampling is also valuable information to you.

By test marketing, we mean the selection (sample) of a geographical area—such as a specific city—which is considered to be typical of the total market. Within this geographical area, a total marketing campaign is introduced. The results of such test data aids management in estimating sales if the product is introduced to the total market.

Analyzing the Product

The success of your selling effort depends upon a systematic study of your product or service. Such a study provides basic facts you will need for stimulating your readers to purchase a particular product. Product analysis enables you to accomplish the following:

1. Determine, classify, and evaluate the basic features of your product.
2. Differentiate its features from those of competing products.
3. Key these basic facts to the prospective buyer's needs.

Basic Features. When preparing your basic study, you need to know important facts about your product and about competing products. Through comparisons, you will find characteristics that distinguish your product from others. In making your comparative study, include the following topics in the comparative analysis.

1. Materials and Construction
2. Method of Operation
3. Design and Appearance
4. Uses and Performance Facts
5. Differentiating Features
6. Service Facilities
7. Prices and Terms

Buyer Benefits. Once you have determined the product features you wish to stress, your next step is to translate these features into buyer benefits. Although a feature may suggest a benefit, do not assume that your readers will perceive it as such. For example, a chain saw may feature an all-position carburetor; but the benefit is that such a carburetor permits the user to cut from any angle. An automobile tire may feature a new tread design; but the benefits of the design are better traction, more safety, and increased mileage with gasoline economy. It is wise to remember that a buyer purchases a product or service because it meets the individual's needs or desires. You must translate product features into benefits for the purchaser.

Analyzing the Market

Management conducts market analyses to forecast sales potential. The results of these studies—combined with the basic data of the product—are used to determine the marketing strategy a company will use for obtaining maximum sales.

The two major alternatives available to management in determining its marketing strategy are product differentiation and market segmentation. *Product differentiation* is usually geared to a large marketing sector and emphasizes product differences, such as brand, quality, style, and reputation. Product-differentiation strategies are designed to promote identification and sale of something that usually has many similar competitors (e.g., soaps and detergents, household appliances, food products, and grooming aids); the message receivers are people in virtually all walks of life. *Market segmentation* recognizes individuals and groups of actual or prospective purchasers within the general buying public.

Management's decision to use differentiation, segmentation, or a combination of the two will influence your sales message. For example, product differentiation is a total market approach with sales messages directed to people in all walks of life with an aim at establishing the superiority or quality of a company's product over the product of a competitor. When market segmentation is used, the sales message is directed to a particular group of people—such as senior citizens, city dwellers, or middle-income segments of the population—with their particular needs and desires in mind. Therefore, the alternative selected by management will affect the choice of appeals or sales messages.

Three Kinds of Market Analyses. To determine potential markets for a product, market analyses can consist of several types of studies— geographic, demographic, and psychographic.

Geographic Market Analysis. Facts assembled in geographic market surveys may determine that a product can best be marketed by region, population density, climate, etc. The needs or wants of one area may differ from other geographical regions. For example, it may be more profitable for a company to market a particular type of home-heating product in one region of the country than in another, or it may be more economically sound to concentrate selling efforts in more densely populated areas than in less populated areas.

Demographic Market Analysis. Demography is defined as the science of vital statistics, such as births, deaths, and marriages of populations. Because consumer wants and desires are closely related to demographic variables, it continues to be management's most popular method of studying the market. The facts most often assembled are those concerned with

(a) buying power; (b) income distribution into rent, food, and clothing; (c) income groups; (d) age groups; and (e) other facts of population—family size and occupations. Such study is vital to planning production, distribution, and marketing procedures.

Psychographic Market Analysis. The psychographic market survey attempts to answer first the general question: What are the buying habits of the public? It then attempts to answer such specific questions as those shown in the following list:

1. What are the buying habits of the public in relation to a certain kind of product?
2. What are the possibilities of shifting the buying habits of the public in regard to a certain kind of product or in regard to a specific brand?
3. What are the chief barriers to be surmounted in altering fixed habits?
4. What types of appeals are likely to be most effective?
5. Why do so many more or so many fewer people use one kind of product or avoid one kind of product rather than other kinds?
6. How and where do people buy certain types of products?
7. What kind of distribution ought to be used in the light of this buying behavior?
8. How is the public likely to react when a new product is presented?
9. Will the new product be accepted?
10. What appeals will induce the greatest possible acceptance?

Examples of variables used in the psychographic market analysis are personality, life-style, buyer motive, usage rate, and brand loyalty.

Independent Market Research Agencies. Although many large companies have their own market research departments for conducting studies, use is also made of outside agencies when costs can be reduced or when specially trained personnel are required. Smaller companies which do not have research departments also utilize the services of independent market research agencies. Special areas that professional groups may investigate are (1) factors influencing brand choice; (2) consumer likes, dislikes, and opinions about what can be done to improve a product; (3) pricing; (4) public buying habits; (5) brand name and package selection; (6) people's opinions of store service; (7) discovery of new markets; (8) measuring effectiveness of appeals.

Many of these research agencies operate nationally and are equipped to obtain personal interviews with consumers, dealers, jobbers, and others. The research executives define the marketing problem, develop methods for getting the facts, and evolve a sound interpretation of the results. They then develop improved consumer relations, cut costs, and increase profit margins.

Collecting Data About Market Fluctuations

The market is dynamic and ever changing. The life cycle of populations creates new faces—new buyers—for products and services. From childhood to adulthood, a person's needs and desires change—from tricycles to bicycles to cars; from sleds to ice skates to skis; from living with parents to renting apartments to purchasing homes. Each time a need or a want is met, the market is affected. Breakthroughs in science and technology have not only saved more children at birth but also extended the life expectancy of the population and thus created new markets. Market research helps to find out when and where these sudden needs spring up in the ever-changing world. Among the data collection tools for such research are questionnaires and interviews.

Questionnaires. If results are to have value, questionnaires must be carefully prepared. Knowing what questions to ask so all pertinent data is obtained is essential.

Consideration should be given to the type of questions that will be used in the instrument—open-ended or close-ended questions. *Open-ended questions* allow the questions to be answered in the respondent's own words. The returns of your survey may be limited if all open-ended questions are used because many people do not like to write out answers. Also, these responses may be difficult to tabulate. *Close-ended questions* may supply all possible answers to each question, simply asking the respondent to make a selection. These responses are easier to tabulate, but the close-ended items tend to restrict the individuality of responses.

Sequencing of questions may also have significance to your study. Beginning your questionnaire with close-ended questions or questions which require easily-answered responses may insure a higher response than beginning your questionnaire with open-ended questions or questions which are considerably difficult to answer. Observe these three basic rules as you design your questionnaires to collect data:

1. Make items easy to answer.
2. Avoid leading questions.
3. Word the question so that answers can be easily tabulated.

Easy to answer: How often do you buy frozen orange juice?

Leading question: Don't you think the Majestic typewriter is the best you can buy?

Easily tabulated: Was your use of this product this year as compared with last year
                       _____(a) smaller?
                       _____(b) equal?
                       _____(c) greater?

Because of the many complex factors that must be considered in the preparation of the questionnaire, personnel skilled in research should be involved in developing the instrument. Pretesting the questionnaire on a pilot sample of persons should also be conducted prior to using the questionnaire on a large scale.

Cover Letters. Questionnaires should be accompanied by concise transmittal messages (cover letters) that establish rapport and elicit the respondent's cooperation. An effective cover letter is, in effect, a persuasive message that sells the idea of participating in the survey. The AIDA sequence of attention, interest, desire, and action—discussed in detail in Chapter 14—is particularly appropriate for cover letters:

ATTENTION:	Refer to your reader's interests, desires, ambitions, and basic needs.
INTEREST:	Reinforce your reader's motivation for physical and psychological satisfaction.
DESIRE:	Help your reader, mentally and emotionally, to sense advantages that will come through cooperation with you.
ACTIONS:	State politely, confidently, and clearly what your reader is to do.

Interviews. Another common method of collecting data is through personal or telephone interviews. However, strict supervision is required if bias in the interviewing process is to be avoided. For example, an inflection in the voice or accidental rewording may result in erroneously asking a leading question.

Personal interviews are more costly than mail surveys or telephone interviews. Although the personal interview is probably the most practical method of collecting data, its use in large surveys is not only expensive but also very time consuming. Besides using the personal interview as the primary method of collecting data, use it to follow up respondents who have not completed mailed questionnaires.

The telephone survey has several advantages. It is usually less costly and can be used for surveying large geographical areas, and the data can be collected in less time. Because telephones are not equally distributed among economic classes, however, care must be exercised in interpreting the data.

The foregoing pages have dealt with some of the phases of market research. Today electronic computers are playing a major role in analyzing research data. Because much of the burdensome work is done by the computer, successful managers are among the major users of market research. They know, however, that complete, accurate, and current data must be collected for their computers if the research results are to be meaningful.

PLANNING AND CREATING AN EFFECTIVE CAMPAIGN

Having matched the results of the product and market analyses, the marketing manager has a sound basis on which to plan and create an effective sales campaign. From the research, the groups of people more likely to want or need the product can be identified. Additionally, the benefits most sought in the product or service can be determined. Fortified with these facts, a procedure for bringing the buyer and seller together for their mutual benefit can be planned.

Stimulating Demand

An important part of an effective campaign is the stimulation of buying desire. This is especially important when your product is similar to a competitor's and you must stress differentiation; when a new product is introduced and requires the dissemination of information regarding its features and qualities; and when the sales volume of a product (maturity stage) begins to decline so that product differentiation and product improvements must be stressed.

Three major methods are used to stimulate buying desire: (1) use of the product or service, (2) personal selling, and (3) the written message. The written message, the most widely used method of stimulating demand, takes the form of direct mail, an advertisement, or related form of television, radio, or other media requiring the preparation of written script. For our purposes, this chapter will discuss the written sales message, the third of the three major methods for demand stimulation.

The Sales Letter

As a business person, you will discover that all messages sell. If you are not selling a product or a service, you will be writing messages that build a reputation for your company. Not only must prospective buyers be sought but also current customers must be retained through developing their goodwill and loyalty. Accordingly, all messages—replying to inquiries, acknowledging requests, responding to adjustments, reporting facts, etc.—provide an opportunity to turn people into friends and make them loyal customers.

Sales messages, however, are specifically designed to seek new customers. With this purpose in mind, you should at this point be aware of the advantages and disadvantages of sales messages, as well as the features of mailing lists.

Advantages. The mailed message has distinct advantages over the general media. The advertisement, for example, is a general message which is broadcast to many individuals over a general area. The sales message, however, is directed toward a specific group of people who have been determined—through the market analyses—to be prospective buyers. Because of its selectivity, the sales message can be more personalized and can present a more complete presentation.

Disadvantages. Certain disadvantages of mailed messages should be noted: (1) relatively high cost per unit; (2) mailing list deterioration; (3) list revision expense.

Mailing Lists. Ideally, a mailing list is a current inventory of correct names and addresses of people who are located in a given trade territory, and who, by reason of their careful selection, are prospective purchasers of a particular article or a particular service.

A company may purchase a mailing list from a list company or develop its own by using current source material. Here are some typical sources that are used:

Directories:
  Telephone
  City
  Trade
  Mercantile

General sources:
  Newspapers
  General advertising
  Sales representatives' reports
  Canvassing
  Social registers
  Rating books
  Contests

City records:
  Voting lists
  Tax lists
  License records
  Incorporations
  Auto licenses
  City employees
  County employees
  Permit records
  Labor records
  Real estate transfers

Organization membership lists:
  Club memberships
  Payrolls of firms
  Labor unions
  Church organizations

List companies can provide almost any type of listing requested. The more specifications required, however, the more expensive the listing may become. For example, you may want a special list of all hardware owners in Detroit, Michigan; all department stores with annual sales of $250,000 or more; or all shoe stores in Orlando, Florida.

Because mailing lists can be highly selective, management can direct its sales message appeals more specifically to the interest of a limited group. By so doing, the sales message is more personal than any other form of contact short of an actual visit.

Preliminary Plan for Writing

The creation of an effective sales message requires preliminary planning. As many experienced writers have discovered, the answers to the following questions have been most helpful:

1. *What do we have to sell?* The needed information is obtained through the basic data study. One must know what materials go into the product, how it is constructed, and what are its advantages and uses.
2. *Who will buy the product or service?* The market research must be analyzed. Study the people who will read your message. Where do they live? What are their buying habits? Are they old or new customers? Will your message answer an inquiry or stimulate inquiries?
3. *What action do you want to stimulate?* You must decide what you want the reader to do. Do you want to persuade the reader to visit 'your store? to order your product by mail? to try your product for a few days? or to take some other definite action?
4. *How interested is the reader in the product (service)?* The degree of interest your reader has in your product must be determined. How much does the reader know about your product? Knowing this information will guide you in determining how much you must say to develop interest and what product features you need to stress.
5. *Will the results justify writing?* This point must be decided by past records and experience. If a similar effort to a similar prospect under similar conditions has been successful, this one probably will be also.
6. *What is the central buying (selling) point?* The central buying point of the product is identical with the central selling point: the feature best designed to make the strongest impression and to make the product most wanted by your reader.
7. *What are the supporting facts?* Assemble all the facts. Choose those of strongest appeal to your particular group of readers.
8. *How do we organize selected facts?* Your facts should be organized according to an effective plan, as is outlined in later pages. In general, (a) begin "where the reader is"; talk about what he or she wants; (b) show how you can provide what is wanted; (c) close with a strong inducement for action.

Much of the information needed for answering the above questions has been discussed in this chapter. Additional material will be discussed in Chapter 14.

COORDINATING THE TOTAL SELLING SYSTEM

In planning and organizing an effective sales campaign, you have learned the importance of stimulating demand, gearing your messages to the right groups, and preparing a preliminary plan for writing. Let us now look at the campaign approach as a whole concept.

How may a total selling system be coordinated? As a basis for understanding, let us examine the nature of a full-scale follow-up program. A follow-up program is a planned system of sales messages or of sales messages and mailing pieces in combination. One unit follows another like links in a chain. The result is an interrelated system for accomplishing a defined sales objective. The parts of the system are integrated, mailed at calculated time intervals, and put to uses like these: (1) stimulating inquiries, (2) replying to inquiries about products or services, (3) selling by mail to a prospective customer, (4) bringing prospects to retail stores, (5) holding customers' goodwill, (6) introducing improvements and new models, (7) preparing prospective buyers for the sales representative's call.

While it is true that single sales messages are also based upon the preceding information in this chapter, it should be pointed out that most products and services require a series (follow-up program) of messages to give a complete sales presentation. The three common types of follow-up programs are (1) the campaign system, (2) the wear-out system, (3) the continuous system.

The Campaign System

The *campaign system* is fully prepared before the first mailing and is sent, piece by piece, during a definite period. The number of pieces, the time between the mailings, and the total length of the campaign are carefully scheduled. The campaign is based upon current market research, which is expensive, and follows a prescribed mailing schedule.

As part of the planning, the sales messages are carefully coordinated with one *central buying point*, the dominant value of the product, as the theme. Throughout the entire campaign, attention and interest are maintained through a variety of appeals. The change of pace in the appeals freshens the customer's interest.

Each message within the campaign is designed to progress from attracting attention and developing interest to creating desire and inducing action. In other words, the early messages attract attention and develop interest, and the later messages present powerful offers to induce action. Intervals between mailings may be a week, ten days, or two weeks. Action is invited at the close of each message in the series. The reader may be convinced and ready to buy long before the campaign is complete. Securing orders by early action economizes the rest of the expensive effort. Throughout the campaign the action urge increases until it reaches its most forceful persuasion in the final message.

The campaign system is used to promote relatively expensive products or services. The higher the price of the article, the wider the margin of profit, and the more selective the mailing list, then the larger the number of mailings that may be sent. For new and unfamiliar articles the system must be lengthy to develop confidence. For an article priced at a hundred dollars or more, a system of six to ten mailings with elaborate enclosures has proved profitable.

The Wear-Out System

In the *wear-out system*, each mailing piece carries its own complete message. One message after another is sent out until returns are no longer profitable. Each successive mailing may be either the same message or a different, complete presentation. The wear-out system is ordinarily used for selling inexpensive products, and the duration of the program is dependent upon when the mailing list is "worn out."

The wear-out system is less costly than the campaign but more costly than the continuous system. In determining the messages that will be used, several versions are usually composed for testing pulling power. This is done by mailing the messages to a sample of the mailing list to assess response.

The Continuous System

The *continuous system* is indefinite in length. Sales messages are sent at intervals, usually with monthly bills or weekly price lists. When sales messages are sent to established customers, a special mailing list is not necessary. When sales messages are included with other regular mailings, the postage costs are less. For these reasons, the continuous system is the least expensive follow-up program.

REVIEW AND TRANSITION

Before an effective sales message can be composed, research concerning the product or service must be conducted. For this reason, Chapter 13 is devoted to the research phase.

In Chapter 13, you learned the importance of analyzing the product or service through the preparation of a basic data analysis. In conducting such a study you know that your product or service is compared to the products or services of competitors' to determine differentiating features.

A second but equally important study is the market analysis. The three major approaches to conducting this study are geographic, demographic, and psychographic. In conjunction with the studies, the methods of collecting the data are discussed.

The coordination of the total selling system is important. The follow-up programs—campaign system, wear-out system, continuous system—are used for specific purposes. The appeals and emphasis for each follow-up program differ; these differences have been explained to you in this chapter.

In Chapter 14 you will study the concepts of psychological motivations and how to apply these concepts in planning, composing, and transmitting effective sales-promotion messages. You will also learn how to use specific techniques for attracting positive attention, developing interest and desire, and stimulating appropriate action.

DISCUSSION QUESTIONS

A. What is the meaning of the statement: "Selling is a generator of business activity"?

B. What is meant by a communication mix? Through the use of illustrations, how does the communication mix affect sales?

C. Some companies prefer not to test market a new product. Instead, the company proceeds with a full sales campaign. What is the reasoning behind such an option?

D. When preparing a basic data analysis, why is it important to determine the basic features of the product or service? Give an example of how a product feature can be converted to a buyer benefit.

E. What is the difference between product differentiation and market segmentation? Cite an example of each method in selling a particular product.

F. Considering the three types of market analyses, give examples of products or services that would depend upon each of the following methods: geographic, demographic, and psychographic.

G. Discuss the following statement: "The market is dynamic and ever changing."

H. "How one collects data for research studies may determine the response that will be received." Discuss.

I. Discuss the similar characteristics of the three follow-up programs: campaign, wear-out, continuous.

J. What are the differentiating characteristics of each of the three follow-up programs: campaign, wear-out, continuous?

K. What are the three major methods that are used to stimulate buying desire?

L. "In effect, all messages sell." What is meant by this statement?

M. Identify the advantages and disadvantages of selling products or services through these methods:

1. newspapers
2. magazines
3. television
4. radio
5. direct mail
6. outdoor advertising

APPLICATIONS

1. Using a format similar to the illustration given below, select two similar products or services and prepare a basic study. For example, you may wish to prepare such a study on two communication texts or two marketing texts which are published by different companies.

BASIC DATA STUDY CHART							
Product	Materials and Construction	Method of Operation	Design and Appearance	Uses and Performance Facts	Differentiating Features	Service	Prices and Terms
(Your Own Product)							
(Competing Products)							

2. From the results of your basic data study in Application 1, convert the differentiating features of your product into buyer benefits.
3. Present an oral presentation to your classmates regarding the pertinent information you have obtained in your basic data study in Application 1.
4. You are planning a sales promotion of a product which sells for more than $200 (you select the product). Before planning your promotion, you decide to survey the opinions of people in your community. Prepare a questionnaire with these characteristics:
   a. The respondent may remain anonymous.
   b. The respondent's personal traits need to be identified (for example: age, education, marital status, occupation or profession, and approximate yearly income).
   c. The respondent's reasons for buying the product need to be determined.
   d. The respondent's reactions to the product need to be described.
5. Prepare a suitable cover letter for your questionnaire in Application 4.
6. Using effective oral communication techniques, give a five-minute presentation on one of the following subjects related to marketing a product.
   a. Techniques used in marketing research
   b. Forecasting sales
   c. Marketing strategies
   d. Consumer behaviors
   e. Product life cycle
   f. Promotional strategies

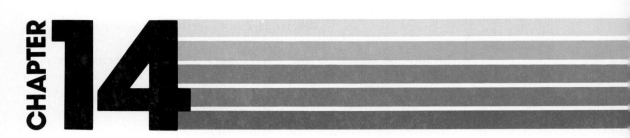

Sales Messages: Creative Phase

In Chapter 13 you were introduced to research methods for collecting, evaluating, and classifying data. You also learned how a total selling system can be coordinated through full-scale follow-up programs. The chapter you are now reading describes the aspects of the *creative* phase in sales: understanding the buyer's motivation, perceiving and evaluating the central buying point, and designing effective sales messages.

PSYCHOLOGICAL MOTIVATION

The human being is continually confronted with needs and desires such as health, admiration, love, success, and profit. Each of these has varying degrees of intensity for being satisfied. When a need or desire is aroused by a stimulus to the point of high intensity, however, the individual is motivated (moved) to take action to satisfy that particular need or desire. In successful sales presentations the stimulus that triggers the individual to act is the sales appeal. When correct appeals are used, the reader, viewer, or listener feels personally involved; and personal involvement increases the success of your message or presentation.

Human Drives

Needs and desires range from biological necessities to emotional preferences, from the satisfaction of physical requirements to the gratification of talents and abilities. The following list identifies needs and desires and presents a related grouping of drives that are often used in sales presentations. Within each grouping, possible selling points (appeals) are listed.

PSYCHOLOGICAL DRIVES

Human Wants	Selling Points
Activity (mental and physical)	Constructiveness, wanting to build or make things, wanting to handle things
Appetite, hunger	Taste, cleanliness
Body comfort	Warmth, coolness, rest, sleep, health, safety, fear, caution
Curiosity	Wanting to find out
Domesticity, having a home	Comfort, hospitality
Parental affection	Love of children, sympathy for, protection of, and devotion to others
Personal appearance, beauty	Style, attractiveness to others
Pleasure	Play, sport, amusement, humor, teasing
Possession, ownership, acquisitiveness	Efficiency, making things go well, saving time, effort, or material
Sociability, associating with others	Social distinction, approval by others, pride, imitation of others, group loyalty, cooperation, ambition, competition rivalry, managing others

The above listing is by no means complete. Use it as a thought starter and add additional wants and desires to your own listing with related selling points. In your sales presentation, however, do not be overly anxious to elect a single appeal to spark the motivation to buy; consider the possibility of dual appeals. For example a cloth coat may satisfy the biological *need* for warmth; but a mink coat may satisfy the *desire* for status. This may mean that the appeals selected may have to satisfy both the need and the desire if the object is to sell the mink cost.

Motivational Research

The modern sales communicator uses results of consumer-behavior studies which go beyond easily observable facts. It is relatively easy to determine who is buying what, when, and how. It is more challenging but sometimes more profitable to determine *why* people buy. Although questionnaire and interview surveys are popular, they require communication discipline if they are to yield valid, reliable data. Survey instruments should be worded and used with communication awareness of these facts: Respondents often report what sounds good rather than what is actual. And respondents themselves often are unaware of their own motives for buying.

Modern sales communicators therefore tend to base their messages upon a variety of research techniques rather than upon direct questioning alone. For example, indirect questions frequently are asked first and then followed by direct questions, by sentence completions, by word associations, or by cartoons for which the respondent supplies interpretations or captions.

Indirect Question: In your opinion, why do secretaries sometimes refrain from using transcription equipment although it is available in their offices?

Direct Question: What circumstances would cause you to refrain from using transcription equipment even though it is available in your office?

Sentence Completion: Please complete the following:
I wish that transcription machines had these improvements: ——————————

Cartoon Projection: What are the people in this cartoon thinking?

Determining what a buyer really wants can make the difference between sales success or failure. Is economy of operation really a major motive for purchasing a Model 23X automobile? Are dietetic foods purchased mainly for reasons of physical health? To what extent are CB radios bought for their entertainment rather than for their emergency values? Motivational research discloses answers to such questions and thereby guides the business writer or speaker toward creating timely, appropriate, and effective sales messages.

CENTRAL BUYING POINT

The features of your product or service that will make the strongest impression upon the prospective buyer are the *central buying point* (or, from the supplier's viewpoint, the central *selling* point). To find that point, avail yourself of the research techniques mentioned in Chapter 13, determine what the buyer wants and what your product or service offers, and then use your communication skills to bring the buyer and the product together.

Customer's Viewpoint

Project yourself into the customer's circumstances. If you were the buyer, what product benefits would help you motivate yourself to purchase? If you were the buyer, what service features would attract your attention, develop your interest, reinforce your desire, and move you to order? If you were the buyer, what other considerations would influence your purchasing decisions and behaviors?

Visualize the person who will receive your sales message. Before you plan the details of what you are going to write or say, *think about* and *feel for* that person. Associate the word "you" with that person and create attitudes like the following toward the recipient of your message.

1. You like to be accepted, perhaps even popular; you would rather be "in" than "out" of style. I understand; we can communicate.
2. You prefer safety and health to injury or illness. You dislike excessive heat and humidity or sub-zero weather and slush. At about the same time each night you yawn sleepily. At about the same time in the morning you wonder what the rest of the day will bring. I can recognize those feelings; I share them with you; we can communicate.
3. Several times a day you are hungry. You enjoy tasting delicious things, but somehow they taste even better in the company of other people. All of your physical sensations seem better when they are shared and appreciated. I understand; it's the same with me. We can communicate.
4. But you like to have things of your own—everyone has favorite possessions. Yet you want to save money and other resources for the future. That doesn't seem contradictory to me. I understand you; we can communicate.

5. Products and services help you to fulfill your wants. My messages can help to bring you and those products or services together. You and I need each other; we can communicate.

Such attitudes are essential to successful communication. But you need more than attitudes to make sales. You need adequate and appropriate knowledge of the product or service you offer.

Product Knowledge

In preparation for writing your sales presentation, you analyzed your product. You searched for facts about raw materials, manufacturing methods, construction, method of operation, design, appearance, and uses. In your search for product knowledge, you also discovered the differentiating features of your product. Armed with these facts and the knowledge of your prospective buyers, you can identify and support your central buying point.

Central Buying Point Selection

By empathizing with the buyer, you can discover an important need or desire that can best be filled by your product. Your object then is to relate that product feature to the buyer's chief need. When you select the central buying point in harmony with the buyer's chief want, you focus a verbal spotlight on that point.

Consider the purchaser's personality and roles in life when determining the central buying point. To the careful mother, for example, the central point in selling a portable electric heater may be the tip-over safety switch. For the electric appliance dealer, the central point is that since the heater uses fewer kilowatts per hour it will sell faster and increased profits are likely. Whatever the customer's classification, your goal in the sales message is to identify and satisfy as many of the customer's needs, wants, and preferences as possible.

SALES MESSAGE PLAN

Writing an effective sales message involves the use and the organization of human-interest words to stimulate and guide buying behavior. The AIDA plan is one successful way of designing a persuasive sales message.

A sales message will typically reflect four stages: ATTENTION, once favorably secured, arouses interest.[1] INTEREST, once aroused, leads to desire. DESIRE, reinforced with the belief that the product is valuable, leads to a growing acceptance and conviction that ignite enthusiasm. The merging of these factors leads toward ACTION.

---

[1] Most business people and home dwellers open their own mail. Hence the initial point of contact between sender and receiver is crucial. "The most critical and potentially decisive movement for a direct mail piece is the flick of time when its recipient's eye first rests on his/her own name." The *Curtis Courier*, Vol. XI, No. 3, p. 14.

AIDA

ATTENTION

Opening Paragraph: First sentence (headline) should get desire as well as attention. Five points to remember in planning headlines.

1. "Sell the sizzle" as well as the steak. Sell the scent as well as the rose. Appeal to the imagination.
2. Telegraph your thoughts. Cut the useless words.
3. "Say it with flowers." Avoid objectionable words.
4. Try to make it a "WHICH" proposition, not an "IF" proposition.
5. Watch your bark. Don't growl at your prospects.

Either ask a question or make a statement.

If a question—ask one which cannot be answered "yes" or "no," so reader can't brush you off quickly. If you cannot avoid it—make it a "yes" question.

If you make a statement, offer a fact which is (a) new, (b) different, or (c) interesting.

INTEREST

Make your messages interesting so they can compete with others for attention.

1. Appeal to the emotions.
2. Give a clear, concise description of the product or service.
3. Say what you mean positively and avoid unnecessary explanations.
4. Emphasize special features about the product or service.

Based upon a talk by Henry Hoke, Editor and Publisher of *The Reporter*, and other sources, and compiled by John J. Patafio, President of Ambassador Letter Service Co., New York.

DESIRE

Appeal to the emotions. Be dramatic. What customers feel about a product, a service, or a clause influences them to spend money. Few people spend money because of what they think.

1. Narrate a success story about the use of the product or service.
2. Use testimonials and endorsements.
3. Give a definite statement of value to reader.

ACTION

Tell the prospect what to do. When you get down to the most important part of the message (action closer), remember why you are writing. Tell the reader what to do . . . sign order blank, fill in reply card, send check, make reservation, etc.

P.S. The most important part of a successful message can be the postscript. The message with a P.S. usually outpulls others. The P.S. should rephrase the headline or first paragraph or highpoint some one important point of your offer.

Blue Pencil—Use freely on (1) Useless words that don't count toward final effect desired. (2) Dubious words ("I," "we," "our," "us," "me," "my," and phrases preceding and including "that"). (3) Incorrect expressions of thought. (4) Improper arrangement of words. (5) $20 or Sunday words—use everyday words—one-syllable words preferred. (6) Hackneyed expressions from horse-and-buggy days, "In reply to," "we beg to state," "we beg to remain," etc.

Suit the format to return-pulling copy—a. The message. b. An informative circular. c. An order form. d. A business reply envelope.

Attract Appropriate Attention

The opening paragraph of your message often influences the outcome of your sales effort. Will your reader's attention be drawn to what you have to say? How can you center your reader's attention upon your message in a way that will create an incentive to read it in its entirety? The following techniques have proven to be successful openers. Notice how each one either involves the reader in what is being described or arouses curiosity.

1. *Paint an Action Picture:* A snap of the wrist . . . the line sailed out over the stream, the reel hummed merrily . . . a strike! (For a letter on fishing rods and reels.)
2. *Refer to Current Events:* Three major airlines have slashed Florida fares.
3. *Describe a Situation:* While flying over the frozen landscape, where the highways were dotted with automobiles marooned in the deep drifts, my thoughts turned to the anticipated warmth of the Florida sunshine.
4. *Make a Pleasant and Agreeable Assertion:* Coming home is the best part of the day.
5. *Offer a Miniature Testimonial:* "My microwave oven saves me time, energy, and money," said one of our customers recently.
6. *Ask a Question:* How long does it take your secretary to type a one-page letter?
7. *Flash a "Short-Short" Story:* Her career zoomed—from attorney to the board of directors.
8. *Flash an Image:* A shampoo that makes your hair squeaky clean.
9. *Stimulate the Senses:* Do you long for a vacation spot, drenched in sunshine, where peace and quiet are penetrated only by the lapping of water against the shoreline . . .?
10. *Use a Quotation:* "Nothing great was ever achieved without enthusiasm," said Emerson—and we certainly agree.
11. *Use a "Power" Phrase that Compresses the Point:* The Mayville Company can save you thirty percent on your heating bills. (For a message stressing a reduction.)
12. *Strike a Parallel:* . . . as smooth as silk.
13. *Use an Allusion:* Andrew Carnegie's recipe for a poor man to get rich: Save $1,000 and then begin prudent investing.
14. *Supply a Startling Fact:* Only 2.3 per cent of management positions with salaries of $25,000 or more are held by women.

Attracting attention can be augmented by dramatizing the sales message. Such messages stress important buying features through unusual layout shapes and arrangements. Note that the dramatized features illustrated on page 301 clearly relate to the message theme. Remember, however: The use of human-interest words is the primary method for *attracting* attention while dramatization serves to *increase* attention.

Still another technique for attracting appropriate attention—and for economizing message-production costs—involves a departure from the usual inside address and salutation:

June 23, 19—

Suddenly you savor
silence
except for . . .
. . . the rustle of leaves . . . the murmur of brooks . . . the music of songbirds. Serenity is yours to enjoy at Greemont Village.

And here are more examples of attention-getters, distinctive in terms of their formats as well as of their wordings:

Your credit is good
at Smith's, Mr. Miller.

Mr. Robert Miller
1754 West Park Street
Unionville, IA 52594

Dear Mr. Miller:

Your excellent credit standing deserves the best there is. So, . . .

Memorandum from the Sales Manager

Dear Customer:

As a "preferred" customer, you are invited to a special sale . . .

April 1, 19—

For $1 a day
your child can have
a quality education.

How can such a nominal price provide . . . ?

February 19, 19—

Engineering . . .

Durability . . .

Dependability . . .
All these, plus many more features, are what you get when . . .

To generate and sustain attention, follow this advice:

1. Relate the attention-openers to the gist of your message.

UNRELATED	RELATED
Have you ever wondered how you will be able to recall past memories?	The Monarch movie camera captures those special moments in both film and sound.

"A thing of beauty
is a joy forever," said Keats; but
visitors to Michigan put it another way--"A
beautiful state for a memorable vacation." Travel
the 3,288 miles of sandy shoreline--a shoreline that
embraces four of the five Great Lakes--Erie, Huron
Michigan   and

Superior. And
try your luck at
skiing, fishing,
or boating on sev-
eral of the 11,000
inland lakes that pepper
the landscape. You will be
convinced that you are truly in a
water wonderland. Before driving to
the north, however, take a guided tour
of an automobile plant; spend a couple of
days visiting Greenfield Village and the
Ford Museum; and visit the Dow Gardens.
As you drive north, stop near Grayling   and
take a stroll through the Hartwick   Pines--
the last vestige of the great lumber   industry
that rocked the nation with tales of   the lumber-
jack. Now angle over to the west   and climb the
Sleeping Bear Dune. Experience the thrill of your
life by taking a dune-buggy ride across the dunes.
Head your car north and travel to the water's edge
and gaze upon the Straits of Mackinac. Park your
car and take a side trip by ferry to Mackinac Island
where you will be stepping back in time to the days
of the horse and buggy. Right ahead of you is
the five-mile-long Mackinac Bridge. Cross
over it into the Upper Peninsula--the land
of Longfellow's poem, The Song of Hiawatha.
Visit the beautiful upper and lower falls
of the Tahquamenon River. See the beautifully colored cliffs of Pictured Rocks.
Be spellbound by Lake of the Clouds in
the Porcupine Mountains State Park. And
experience the breathtaking view of Copper
Harbor. You, as so many others, will agree
with the State's motto: If you seek a pleasant peninsula, look about you.

Please turn page

Dramatizing with a "Map" Layout

2. Supply details rather than generalities.

GENERAL	DETAILED
We would like to tell you something about our product.	Discover a new suspended ceiling that does not look like a suspended ceiling.

3. Offer "protective" rather than "scare" openings.

SCARE	PROTECTIVE
Thousands of lives are lost each year through house fires!	Protect your family by installing a Smith Smoke Detector.

4. State novel rather than trite questions.

TRITE	NOVEL
Wouldn't you like to hear some good news?	Do you need to save on income tax—the annuity way?

Develop Interest and Desire

Having attracted appropriate attention, you continue your message by providing relevant details which develop interest. As you state your information clearly, vividly, and persuasively—relating it to *your receiver's* concerns—you help the prospective buyer to visualize your product or service, to "see" what it can do, and to recognize a need for it. With descriptive explanations, you then reinforce the receiver's interest until, almost imperceptibly, that interest becomes desire.

ATTENTION-INTEREST MERGING WITH DESIRE-ACTION

You relax. We do the work . . . at Timber Lodge.

Enjoy your full-comfort room with its private balcony overlooking the most beautiful part of Lake Huron. Relish the old-fashioned "home-cooked" meals served at our Lakefront Restaurant. Sunbathe and swim—indoor and outdoor pools as well as a sandy beach await you. Hike or bicycle through a hundred acres of woods hugging the shoreline. And top your daytime fun by dancing under the stars at our Outdoor Pavilion.

To develop interest and desire, the communicator uses factual as well as emotional persuasion. Factual material induces confidence in the worth of the product or service. Emotional persuaders create enthusiasm and eagerness for what is offered. By using both logical and psychological appeals, you can give a convincing answer to the customer's prevailing question: "What will your offer do for me?"

Factual (Physical) Description. Physical description represents objective details of a product: its length, breadth, height, size, shape, color, scent, sound, texture, and other specifications. Such factual description often stimulates initial interest. It may specify the stainless steel shafts and gears of a water-cooled outboard motor, the materials and operations of an industrial pump, the load-hauling capacity of a compound double-duty tractor, the acoustical range of an electronic organ, etc.

Psychological Description. The sensations, satisfactions, or pleasures your buyer will gain are represented by psychological appeals which translate the product or service into fulfillment of needs and desires. Successful selling is the ethical blending of cold facts with warm feelings.

Factually described, the electronic organ has an automatic rhythm unit; plays melodies in pre-set piano, banjo, mandolin, and harpsichord voices; is equipped with a twelve-inch speaker, a six-inch speaker, and a six-inch two-speed rotor horn for acoustic tremolo effect. Psychologically described, the same electronic organ is beautifully designed to accent the furnishings of the proud home owner who enjoys music and tranquility. Notice that the illustrations in this chapter synthesize objective and subjective images through both factual and psychological appeals.

Descriptive Evidence. To arouse attention, develop interest, stimulate desire, and induce confidence and belief in your product, you can use a variety of evidence: (1) facts and figures; (2) explanations of design or construction; (3) tests by manufacturer, independent laboratory, dealer, or customer; (4) records of the product in actual use; (5) testimonies of efficiency; (6) free demonstrations, trials, samples, and other means.

For example, an executive accustomed to methodical reasoning may become interested in automatic typewriters because of cost reduction or increased productivity. By presenting and reinforcing such evidence, you move the executive closer to a purchase decision. As shown by the following examples, concrete details stimulate those decisions.

A manufacturer of FM stereo radio and 8-track players describes the newest model in detail:

An 8-track tape player and stereo FM radio in one; beautiful wood-grained finish; modern integrated circuitry to assure years of stereophonic pleasure; volume, balance, and tone controls for tailoring sound to individual liking; pushbutton AFC control insures drift-free FM reception; program-select button changes programs manually or automatically; FM stereo light indicator shows which stations are broadcasting in stereo; fits 1¾ × 4¼-inch minimum dashboard opening.

A retailer gives details of a color television console:

Sharp, brilliant, 25-inch diagonal picture from negative matrix picture tube; solid-state chassis gives long-lasting operation; automatic color-tuning button; two 4-inch speakers; simulated woodgrain cabinet in high-fashion design; easy volume control; lighted channel selector; overall size: 30½H × 40½W × 19⅝ inches deep.

But notice the words "beautiful," "modern," "pleasure," and "high-fashion" in these descriptions. They have psychological appeal; the other words have logical appeal. And the combination of these appeals makes sales.

Enable your prospective buyer to justify the purchase through feelings and through logical reasoning. For example, provide logical as well as psychological evidence by authentic testimonials, test-if-yourself offers, reliable guarantees, free-trial offers, home or office demonstrations.

Testimonials can be extremely persuassive when delivered by competent, trustworthy people.

TESTIMONIAL WITHIN A SALES MESSAGE

How does Hikers' Backpack compare with similar products? Dr. Martin Koepler, President of International Hikers' Association, gives this assurance: "The anodized aluminum U-frame, padded shoulder straps, and adjustable polypropylene waistband make Hikers' Backpack the best that I have used."

TESTIMONIAL AS AN ENCLOSURE

The enclosed article is an excerpt of a recent *Outdoor Magazine* interview with Dr. Martin Koepler, President of International Hikers' Association. Read what Dr. Koepler says about Hikers' Backpack before you buy your new outdoor gear.

Another technique for intensifying desire is the *try-it-yourself* offer.

The enclosed material has the richness and softness of fine leather but requires less care. Polishing is a thing of the past; just wipe it clean with a damp cloth and see its luster return. Rub it against a rough surface and see how it resists scratches and scuff marks. Don't take our word; try it yourself.

Confidence in a product or service is also reinforced by performance tests and guarantees.

Grueling tests made by the Independent Testing Institute prove that the Beta electronic watch is the most dependable timepiece sold by fine jewelers. With this evidence, the Beta carries a five-year warranty of its precision workmanship and quality materials.

Free-trial offers are "clinchers" that motivate the prospective buyer to act.

See for yourself how these 100-percent-polyester dress slacks give you long-lasting comfort with good looks. For a thirty-day free trial, just complete, sign, and return the enclosed card to us.

Offering a home or office demonstration shows product confidence and enables the customer to see your product in the environment in which it will be used.

Showing you the easy operation and efficient performance of the Osgood will be a pleasure. For a demonstration in your home or office, please call us at 587-2641, or complete the enclosed card and drop it in the mail.

Stimulate Action

Spur a favorable response when the reader's interest and desire are keenest and when the buying impulse is at its peak. The effectively written "action close" offsets delay and urges appropriate decision or action.

To stimulate favorable action, (1) offer proper inducements, (2) make action easy, (3) stimulate prompt response.

*** *Aristo Corporation*   ★ *400 South Salina Ave*   ★ *Syracuse, NY 13202*

November 15, 19--

Ms. C. M. Sullivan
502 Greenhill Circle
Port Henry, NY 19297

Dear Ms. Sullivan

It's a cold, drizzly evening. You're late driving home. You step out of your car to open the garage door. The cold, damp air chills and drenches you.

But what if, sitting in your car, you simply push a button . . . and your door automatically opens to a lighted garage? "What if" is affordable. "What if" is Aristo.

The Aristo Garage Door locks automatically. It cannot be opened except by your own special key switch, button, or receiver. Talk about personal safety and property protection!

Paul Knapp of your community, who bought Aristo several years ago, says: "Aristo is the wisest investment I have ever made." You have the opportunity to make a similar investment now.

To have our representative visit you at your convenience, please fill out the enclosed card, and return it to us.

Yours for peace of mind

Anna Martino
Anna Martino

Attention, Interest, Desire, Action

Offer Inducements. These inducements often stimulate appropriate action:

1. Examine for (specify number) of days on approval.
2. Send no money in advance.
3. Pay by a certain date and get a premium or a discount.
4. Use a deferred-payment plan.
5. Be completely satisfied or payment will be refunded immediately.
6. Be reassured by a reliable guarantee.
7. This offer is available only until a given date.
8. Price will go up (specify amount) after (specify date).
9. A limited supply is available, so act now.

Make Action Easy. These are several "easy response" procedures:

1. *Enclose an order form.* Keep the form simple (for example, have the customer check squares or fill in spaces).
2. *Enclose a business reply card or business reply envelope.* Postage is due on business reply cards and envelopes only if they are returned.
3. *State exactly the form of payment* (cash, check, draft, money order, stamps). For instance: "Please send a check with your order."

Suggest Immediate Response. Many successful communicators use the following techniques:

1. *Imperative statement:* "Please sign and return the card now." "Just complete the order blank, and send it today."
2. *Persuasive Suggestion:* "To obtain your copy, sign and mail the enclosed card." "Let us send you a set; just mail the completed order blank now."
3. *Brisk Request:* (This popular technique combines the force of the imperative statement and the courtesy of the persuasive suggestion.) "Get *your* set promptly; please sign and mail the reply card today."

Provide Emphasis

Stylistic methods of stimulating response include (1) short sentences and paragraphs, (2) technical devices, (3) prominent postscripts.

Short Units. Occasionally, brief paragraphs can emphasize buying points. Also effective are relatively short sentences; when used for deliberate emphasis, they can move the buyer to decision and action.

Technical Devices. Occasional use of these mechanics can stress special sales features:

1. underlining
2. capitalization

3. exclamation points
4. dashes or dots
5. circles (encircled words), stars, other special marks
6. unexpected blank spaces
7. headings (capitals or small letters, sometimes a "running head" instead of a salutation)
8. Price will go up (specify amount) after (specify date).
9. A limited supply is available, so act now.
10. direct parallel: two short columns of contrasted facts, side by side
11. "split" paragraphing: breaking a sentence in the middle; showing the break by a dash at the end of the first paragraph and one at the beginning of the second
12. indention, special indention, or extension of first words of a paragraph
13. short double-spaced paragraph in single-spaced body (contrast)
14. check mark, handwritten words, or similar devices in the margin
15. colors for special words or sentences

Postscripts. As part of a *planned* sales presentation, a postscript may be used deliberately. Since it is separated from the message body, the postscript can convey emphasis. For this reason, an important sales point is often intentionally positioned as a P.S. For example, a special offer may be postscripted: "You can save ten percent by ordering before September 3."

Consider Word Processing

Electronic machines have enormously affected direct-mail selling. The automatic typewriter, for example, now plays an important role in message processing. Messages fed by magnetic card, cassette, or disk into computer memories can be retrieved and automatically typed with unprecedented speed. Besides the message itself, instructions for paragraphing, margins, and automatic stops are also recorded. As the automatic typewriter produces the messages, their margins are justified. Still another advantage: One employee can operate several automatic typewriters simultaneously.

Other word-processing machine systems range from "stand-alone" to "shared" minicomputers. With its storage capabilities and video display features, the stand-alone minicomputer expedites the reading and editing of data as well as the production of mailable messages. Shared minicomputers, which have even larger storage capacity and faster printers, are used by more than one processing station or terminal. Data for customizing messages (as with form paragraphs, for example) can be stored in and called from the computer memory, then inserted into a message as needed. Additionally, an automatic search capability permits customer addresses to be merged with the form letters.

FEEDBACK

To know whether your prospective buyer has associated your message with his or her own concerns, you need feedback. Sending a message is not enough. Feedback occurs when the customer acts in response to what you have sent.

Pulling Power

The degree of success with which a sales message elicits responses is called its *pulling power*. Be aware that pulling power varies widely, depending on the nature of the product or service, the character of the market, the kind of offer, and the particular action required.

Samples and Direct-Mail Programs

Preliminary small-scale tests are often run to determine the *potential* effectiveness of a sales message. A sales message—sometimes more than one version of it—may be mailed to a sampling of mailing-list names. An estimate of pulling power is then based upon the "test" feedback. For accuracy and reliability, pulling-power estimates are based upon records of many similar mailings used under similar circumstances. Even then, unpredictable influences on changing markets may invalidate the estimate.

An expert using a preliminary test on an appropriate sample, however, often can predict these factors: (1) approximate cost of the mailing in percentage of sales, (2) approximate volume of sales in dollars, (3) percentage of replies in relation to the total mailing list, (4) number of replies to be expected.

Experts expect direct-mail programs to produce sales of not less than five times, and an average of ten times, the cost of the effort. Direct mail succeeds best when used to sell, or to help sell, goods of high unit value.

REVIEW AND TRANSITION

Chapter 14 discussed planning and composing of sales messages in terms of logical and psychological motivation. You learned the AIDA sales-message plan: attracting attention, developing interest and desire, stimulating appropriate action. You also considered the impact of word processing related to sales-message production. Part Six discusses claim, adjustment, credit, and collection messages.

DISCUSSION QUESTIONS

A. Concerning sales communication, in what ways do "creativity" and "research" complement each other?

B. Discuss and illustrate these tools of projective research:

1. Indirect questions
2. Direct questions
3. Sentence completions
4. Word associations
5. Cartoon interpretations and captions

C. What factors help to determine the central buying points of sales messages?

D. What communication techniques are likely to attract appropriate attention for sales messages?

E. What communication techniques are likely to develop a prospective buyer's interest in and desire for a product or service?

F. What are the advantages and disadvantages of modern word-processing systems for direct-mail sales communication?

APPLICATIONS

1. Using an advertisement from a magazine or a newspaper, answer the following questions as though you were planning a direct-mail message about the product or service advertised.

   a. What buying points (or selling points) would *you* select? Why? What logical and psychological appeals would you use? Why?

   b. Using *one* of the fourteen techniques listed on page 299, write an opening paragraph to attract appropriate attention.

   c. In what ways does your attention-opener relate to the corethought of your message?

   d. Write two or three paragraphs to demonstrate how you would develop reader interest and how you would merge this interest into reader desire.

   e. Write a paragraph to stimulate appropriate action by the prospective buyer.

2. Based upon your experience with Application 1, write a complete sales message for another product or service. Compare and contrast your two messages; then report the insights you gained from Applications 1 and 2.

3. Write a message to promote sales of the Best cassette player-recorder. The Best has these features: built-in microphone, automatic-stop control, AC/DC operation, volume meter (and others which you believe appropriate). The Best sells for $75.95.

4. Write a sales message for an umbrella tent with these features: It is a lightweight, durable 10 × 10-ft. tent which easily accommodates six people. It weighs 9 lbs., folds to a neat 8 × 27 in., and has an outside aluminum frame. Center height: 7 ft. Wall height: 5½ ft. Material: 2.06-oz. green nylon, treated to resist moisture and flame. Two large side windows provide excellent ventilation. Price: $95.50.

5. You own the Outdoor Sports Center in your community and have just added Galaxy 10-speed bicycles to your inventory. Write a sales message to be mailed to residents of your area. Persuade your readers to visit your store so that your salespeople can demonstrate the Galaxy. NOTE: Galaxy 10-speed bicycles have disc brakes, a gear shift that prevents chain slipping, dual-position break levers, wide-range derailleur, welded-on cable stops, reflectorized tires, and 27 × 1¼-inch gumwall tires. The top-of-the-line Galaxy His or Hers sells for $155.

6. Compose your own appropriate examples for using these sales techniques:
   a. testimonials
   b. test-it-yourself offers
   c. guarantees
   d. free-trial offers
   e. home or office demonstrations

7. Examine a direct-mail message that you have received, and evaluate it in terms of what you have learned from your text.

8. Prepare a written or an oral report on the operation of a word-processing center. Data sources: inspection of such a center, interviews with word-processing personnel, pertinent literature.

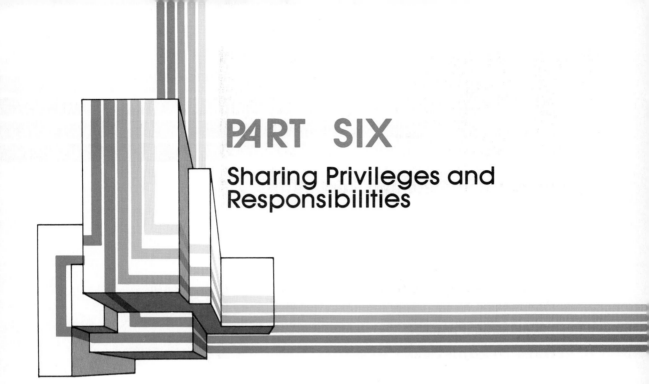

PART SIX
Sharing Privileges and Responsibilities

By integrating logic, psychology, ethics, and goodwill, Chapter 15 introduces you to message techniques for adjustment requests and for replies to those requests. Chapters 16 and 17 orient you to the twin functions of business finance: provision of credit for worthy customers and collection of payment when due.

Specifically, Chapter 16 describes the nature and function of credit, invitations and requests for credit privileges, the granting or refusing of those privileges, and their protection. Chapter 17 presents communication models for collecting owed payment through reminders, stronger reminders, discussions, and messages of urgency.

Whereas Part Five emphasized sales promotion, the following pages discuss values, behaviors, and messages which supplement the sale itself.

15

Adjustment Requests and Replies

Modern business firms use positive terms like "Customer Services"—rather than negative titles like "Complaint Department"—for units which process incoming adjustment requests. "Consumer Services" and equivalent phrases suggest that a buyer's dissatisfaction will be treated pleasantly, promptly, and fairly. This constructive customer-oriented attitude reinforces a vital business asset: goodwill. Also for these reasons, the phrase "adjustment request" is replacing the word "claim" in remedy-seeking communication.

Before responding to an adjustment request, management needs to determine causes and responsibilities for dissatisfaction. A seller may be accountable for sending a defective item; a carrier may be accountable for delivering goods late; a buyer may state an order incorrectly or may misuse a product. The buyer or the seller—sometimes both, sometimes neither—can be responsible for dissatisfaction.

People who request and people who process adjustment can profit mutually by empathizing with one another. Recognizing that business success requires customer satisfaction and that mass production involves degrees of error, the knowledgeable person who makes a request and the knowledgeable adjuster who receives it will use psychology as well as logic to reach an agreement.

ADJUSTMENT REQUESTS

Requests for adjustment should be written in a confident, positive tone. This suggests that your reader is fair and just and that customer satisfaction is the ultimate goal. Your message should reflect clearness, careful details, and avoidance of irritation.

When composing your message, include these three subjects: request for adjustment, statement of the problem, request for prompt action. The order in which these topics are included depends upon the message plan you use—chronological, logical, or psychoanalytical.

Chronological Plan

With the chronological plan, you state the causes of your dissatisfaction in the order of their occurrence. Chronological order can be advantageous in guiding your recall of events as they occurred, thereby helping you to compose your request according to a simple time-order sequence. Among the disadvantages of chronological order, however, are a tendency to include irrelevant details, rather than *significant* information, and to state data as though it is all equally important.

BUSINESS PERSON'S ADJUSTMENT REQUEST
CHRONOLOGICAL ORDER

Sequence
of
Events

The forty 48 × 53 inch awning window units, which our company ordered from you on June 10, arrived this afternoon at our construction site. Our supervisor, Mr. Charles Osborne, accepted the shipment and assigned two employees to unpack the order. We were quite pleased with your promptness in filling our request.

The units appeared to be in good condition. But when they were being installed, we noticed that crank locks on five of the windows did not function properly.

Adjustment
Request

We will gladly follow your directions about replacing the locks—at no additional cost to us, of course. With prompt replacement of these items, you will enable us to complete construction of the five homes we now have under contract by the promised completion date, July 15.

CONSUMER'S ADJUSTMENT REQUEST
CHRONOLOGICAL ORDER

Sequence
of
Events

The electric blanket, model #7891 queen size, has arrived, as promised, within two weeks of my mailing you the order.

However, in testing the blanket according to its enclosed instruction booklet, I find a hazardous defect. The electrical unit overheats even when set on "low."

Adjustment
Request

I have repacked the blanket in its original carton and will return it, upon request, for your inspection. Your prompt shipment of an identical blanket (but in proper condition, of course) will be appreciated.

Logical Plan

The logical plan consists of your describing causes of your dissatisfaction *inductively* (from specific instances to general conclusion) or *deductively* (from general assumption to specific instance), as you learned to do in Chapter 2.

BUSINESS PERSON'S ADJUSTMENT REQUEST
INDUCTIVE ORDER

Specific Instances

The excellent service you have given our firm prompted our recent transaction with you. Forty 48 × 53 inch awning window units were ordered for installation in five homes we now have under construction.

The units arrived at our construction site this afternoon via your truck. Upon installing them we discovered that five of the crank locks do not function properly.

General Conclusion

Please repair or replace these five window units immediately, at no cost to us—thereby continuing your reputation for customer satisfaction.

CONSUMER'S ADJUSTMENT REQUEST
INDUCTIVE ORDER

Specific Instances

On March 3, I placed an order with you for one battery-operated Dentalguard toothbrush kit; two Rena Mutron silk scarves, Model #312; and one Model 20 Airwave transistor radio.

The merchandise arrived March 12 in satisfactory condition except that the carrying case of the transistor radio was split.

General Conclusion

Please replace this defective carrying case at no cost to me.

BUSINESS PERSON'S ADJUSTMENT REQUEST
DEDUCTIVE ORDER

General Assumption

Your company's motto, "We *guarantee* our products and services," prompted our June 10 order of forty 48 × 53 inch awning window units.

Discovering that the crank locks on five of the window units were defective, we were unable to install them into homes we are now constructing.

Specific Instances

You agree, I'm sure, that the logical remedy in this situation is repair or replacement of the five units, at no cost to us. What are the necessary steps for this adjustment?

CONSUMER'S ADJUSTMENT REQUEST
DEDUCTIVE ORDER

General Assumption

Because your company guarantees its appliances against defects in material and workmanship, I ordered a 12-cup Monarch Coffee Maker, #KL390, from you a month ago.

Specific Instances

After carefully reading the accompanying booklet on proper usage and cleaning techniques, I have been trying to use the coffee maker as directed. But apparently there is a defect in the 1500-watt heating element. The water temperature will not exceed 70 degrees.

I'm sure you will agree that the unit is defective and should be replaced at your expense. Your prompt attention and appropriate action will be welcome.

Psychoanalytical Plan

The psychoanalytical plan is more direct—cuts faster to the point—than do the other plans. Directly or by implication, you state the desired adjustment; explain circumstances of the request; then restate your corethought.

SIMPLE REQUEST FOR ADJUSTMENT

Corethought First: Request

Please send us five new 48 × 53 inch awning window units to replace those we received from you today.

Details

When installing the units, we discovered that five of the crank locks are defective.

Corethought Restatement

So that we may meet the completion date of the five houses we have under construction, please send the replacements immediately.

More complex problems are adaptable to the psychoanalytical order. Notice how the following adjustment request begins by stating the request, explaining the details chronologically, and then restating the request at the end of the message. Notice, also, how care is taken to avoid any irritation.

PSYCHOANALYTICAL ORDER COMPLEX ADJUSTMENT REQUEST

Corethought

Please correct a $160 discrepancy involving my savings and my checking accounts.

My employer, City Suppliers, automatically deposits my salary in your bank every two weeks. When I selected this pay option, I authorized your institution to deposit forty dollars of each paycheck into my savings account; the remainder of my salary was to be deposited in my checking account. Until February 15, this arrangement was satisfactory.

Details

Knowing that additional money would be needed during the summer vacation, I notified your bank on March 1 that my entire salary was to be deposited into my checking account beginning March 15. Upon receiving

Restatement of Corethought

my April bank statement, I noticed this transaction had not been made.

You will be glad to correct this error, I'm sure. Please do so now.

REPLIES TO ADJUSTMENT REQUESTS

Whether an adjustment request is granted or refused, the reply message may be used to retain or to reinforce goodwill. A successful adjuster makes even bitter customers as pleased as they can be by using these and similar goodwill phrases:

"Thank you for telling us"
"Serving you is a pleasure"
"Let us help you in another way"
"May we ask"
"Thanks for this opportunity to prove our goodwill"

A successful adjuster avoids using the pronoun "you" in negative contexts, as shown below:

DESTRUCTIVE TONE	CONSTRUCTIVE TONE
You failed to specify which model you need.	Which model do you need?
You're wrong about the terms of our guarantee.	As indicated by the terms of our guarantee . . . .
The fault is yours, but we'll see what we can do.	We'll do our best to help you in this situation.
You are mistaken about your May 5 order.	As you see from the enclosed copy of your May 5 order . . . .

A successful adjuster avoids using terms which imply disrespect or helplessness.

RUDE OR HELPLESS TONE	HELPFUL, COURTEOUS TONE
You'd better read the instructions again. Then if you still insist on filing a claim, get your facts together and call me at this toll-free number.	Please follow the operating procedure described on pages 4-7 of your Owner's Manual. Then phone me at this toll-free number; I want you to be satisfied.
We are at a loss to know what has become of your order.	Yes, we'll try to trace your order immediately.
I can't do a thing about expediting your refund. Be patient; these things take time, you know.	Thanks for telling me of the delay; I'll do whatever is possible to expedite your refund.

"Your complaint" is a phrase which often breaks rapport. "If this is not satisfactory" and similar terms may suggest incomplete or inappropriate solutions; they may even connote incompetence of the adjuster and of the firm. When the firm seems doubtful about its services and its adjustments, that doubt is almost always communicated to the customer. On the other hand, it is foolish for a firm to insist that it never makes errors. In the real business world, mistakes do slip by now and then. That is why empathy is essential to adjustment communication.

Four Main Types of Adjustments

Replies to adjustment requests are classified according to responsibilities (1) of the seller alone, (2) of the buyer alone, (3) of the seller and the buyer mutually, (4) of a third party.

When the Seller Is Solely Responsible. When the seller is responsible, the adjustment should be granted at once. Here is a message guide for such a situation:

1. Approve the request promptly and courteously.
2. Explain reasons for the action.
3. Close cordially, inviting future business.

Consider the following exchange of messages:

AN UNHAPPY CONSUMER

Your food products have always been very popular in our home. However, I received quite a surprise this afternoon when I opened a can of your Reibold Kidney Beans. It contained a stone, small but dangerous.

Fortunately, the culprit was found before it was added to my chili. But what might have happened had a member of my family swallowed that concealed stone?

Enclosed is the label from the "guilty" can so that you can find out what went wrong. By the way, I'd like a replacement or a refund of 79 cents.

You may be thinking, "The sale is only 79 cents!" Yes, but the price has nothing to do with filing a rightful request for adjustment. And the request is certainly valid in this case.

A FAVORABLE ADJUSTMENT

Thank you for writing us on April 14 and for enclosing the label from the product you purchased. Please use the enclosed coupon to obtain six complimentary cans of Reibold Kidney Beans.

Because label codes identify our processing plants, we were able to perform an immediate inspection. Your thoughtfulness in supplying the particular label helped greatly.

Thank you for calling this matter to our attention. Every effort will be made to warrant your continued support of our products.

While unpacking a shipment of portable indoor/outdoor television sets, a store owner discovers three damaged sun shields. Here is the adjustment request:

A BUSINESS PERSON'S ADJUSTMENT REQUEST

Please send three new sun shields for the 19-inch Banner television, Model 206P, ordered from you September 3 (our purchase order 1760).

Upon arrival, three of the sets had sun shields that were badly marred. We have returned those shields to you today by air express.

Your prompt replacement of them will be much appreciated.

The request clearly tells what the trouble is and what the customer wants. The details, including the precise date and order number, help to achieve the desired result. Here is the reply:

A PROMPT ADJUSTMENT

Three new sun shields were shipped to you this morning via air express. You should receive them before this letter reaches you.

At the time we received your order, our supply of 19-inch Banner televisions was depleted. Knowing you needed these sets for your fall sale, we shipped them as soon as we received them from the manufacturer. Some of the cartons were evidently not opened for inspection.

Thank you for allowing us to correct the situation. Your next order will be filled promptly and properly.

When the Buyer Is Solely Responsible. Restoring the smooth relationship a customer has with a company requires diplomacy and tact. The customer may put incorrect data on an order. The size, color, quality, or catalog number may be omitted. Terms of a sale or of a warranty may be misinterpreted. What message plan does an effective adjuster use in refusing an adjustment request? Here is a guide:

1. Begin pleasantly.
2. Review relevant facts.
3. State the decision as a consequence of those facts.
4. Stress prospects of future satisfaction.

The following message is written in the above pattern. Notice how the adjustment refusal is strongly implied rather than absolute.

A REFUSAL

Your wide-angle Magnaview binoculars are among the finest made. Thank you for letting us reinspect them.

While examining your Magnaview, we discovered a dent to the left of the center wheel, indicating that an apparent jolt had damaged the focusing mechanism. As you know, your Magnaview is guaranteed to function properly with normal care and use. Because the damage occurred under unusual conditions, we must charge $15 for repairs.

Please sign and mail the enclosed repair-authorization card, so that your Magnaview can give you the top-quality performance you expect.

The following refusal was written to a business person who had made frequent and costly errors when placing orders for customers.

A BUSINESS SAYS NO

Your request for replacement of your February 26 order has received careful attention.

Our files indicate that the 300 wedding invitations for Miss Marlyn Jones were printed as ordered. Enclosed is a copy of the original order for your records.

Since no error has been made in following your directions, we are shipping the corrected invitations immediately and billing you at our usual wholesale prices. I'm sure Miss Jones will be pleased with her order and your quick action in making the correction.

When Seller and Buyer Share Responsibility. The effective adjuster searches for and emphasizes cooperation. Here is a message guide for the seller:

1. Admit your share of the responsibility.
2. Mention buyer's share of responsibility.
3. Explain what is appropriate for these circumstances.
4. State the adjustment.
5. Close courteously.

When you receive an adjustment request, often your writer will mention past and pleasant dealings with your company. Use such comments as cues for your opening statements when you respond to the customer. Your response might be: "Thank you for mentioning your many satisfactory dealings with us. You have made us even more determined to keep up the good work."

In the following case, the customer, a do-it-yourself installer of kitchen floor covering, did not follow directions. The adjuster tactfully reviews the situation and offers an appropriate adjustment.

RETAINING GOODWILL THROUGH A COMPROMISE

Your comments regarding your past association with us are certainly appreciated. Keeping your goodwill is of prime importance to us.

As you know, your new Superbia linoleum is guaranteed to give you years of excellent service when proper directions are followed for installing it. As stated in the written directions, the underlay for new floors requires a minimum of one-quarter inch plywood or masonite which is nailed two inches apart in every direction.

Mr. Toland, our representative, examined the warping effect of your floor. That examination and the following facts pertain to your adjustment request:

1. Your continuing goodwill is important to us.

2. Although written instructions for installation were provided, our salesperson did not follow our company policy of personally explaining those directions.

3. You used particle board instead of plywood or masonite for the underlay.

4. The underlay was nailed more than two inches apart in every direction.

In this situation, although we cannot reimburse you fully, we gladly offer to supply additional linoleum at cost and more adhesive at our expense.

So that the installation can be done to your satisfaction, please complete and return the enclosed form.

When a Third Party Is Responsible. An airline, a railroad, or a trucking company may be involved with loss of or damage to goods in transit. Before signing a receipt acknowledging that the shipment was received in good condition, the consignee (the one who receives the shipment) should take the following steps:

1. Make sure there is no shortage.
2. Examine shipment for apparent damage. Require freight agent to note on the freight receipt whether any damage has been done.
3. File an adjustment request against the carrier when damage or shortage exists. The consignee may then accept shipment if he or she so desires.

Even though they may not be legally responsible for the safe delivery of a shipment by the carrier, many sellers gain goodwill by making a prompt adjustment *themselves* and filing their own claim against the carrier. Here is a guide for writing the adjustment notice.

1. State the action taken.
2. Explain pertinent facts.
3. Close cordially.

A SELLER HELPS A BUYER

Another set of Portafiles (20K263) was shipped to you this morning, via air express.

The first shipment, as you reported, was damaged in transit by Midstates Railroad. Under such circumstances, the responsibility for adjustment normally falls upon the carrier. But railroad adjustments are sometimes slow. We have therefore duplicated your order to see that it gets to you as quickly as possible.

Please return the damaged set to the Midstates Railroad agent. We'll enter an immediate claim with the railroad.

Thank you for promptly notifying us of what happened. We are happy to help you in this matter.

In this example, knowing that the seller is not obligated to act, the buyer is almost certainly motivated to place future orders. Goodwill is good business.

Functions of Resale and Feedback

When a customer's confidence in an article or in a firm has been shaken, *resale* can preserve goodwill. A resale-oriented adjustment is a message which convinces the buyer of the wisdom of doing business with you. Words of resale are designed to freshen desire for your product or service and to sustain confidence in your firm. The messages throughout this chapter illustrate resale in contexts of adjustment communication.

Those messages illustrate another essential concept: When your customers tell you of dissatisfaction, they perform a valuable communication function. Buyers provide feedback which permits you to benefit from mistakes, yours or someone else's. Unless errors are exposed, how can they be corrected?

Adjustment requests do not deserve scorn or lack of concern. They help you to gain profitable insights. Therefore, they merit more than your tolerance. They justify your investment of empathy.

REVIEW AND TRANSITION

You have learned applications of logic, psychology, ethics, and goodwill related to adjustment communication. You have discovered that, for seller as well as for buyer, the smallest adjustment request can have great importance. And you have acquired message plans for adjustment contexts in which responsibilities of seller, buyer, or third parties may vary.

Chapter 16 will acquaint you with concepts and techniques of still another business activity which involves almost everyone today: credit communication.

DISCUSSION QUESTIONS

A. What human-relations insights justify the name-change from "Complaint Department" to "Customer Services Department"?

B. As applied to adjustment communication, what are the similarities and differences of these message plans: chronological, logical, psychoanalytical? To what other kinds of business communication do you believe those plans are suited? Why?

C. When an adjustment is granted, how can goodwill be lost? How can goodwill be regained? When an adjustment request is refused, how can goodwill be retained?

D. In what ways would previous experience as a salesperson be useful to an adjuster?

E. What are the functions of resale in adjustment messages?

APPLICATIONS

1. Appropriately revise the following:
   a. I do not understand how, with normal driving conditions, your Shur-Grip tire had ply separation as you claim.
   b. We cannot grant your request. The 83-5050 carpet squares had no guarantee.
   c. How could you have permitted that shipment to reach me too late for use despite my "rush" notation on the order?
   d. We have sold hundreds of those products, and yours is the first complaint received.
   e. Your failure to complete Form 1240 is what created the problem.

2. Three months ago, you bought four new Shur-Grip nylon tires for your automobile. These 7.50-16, 8-ply tires sold for $63 each. One of them now has a ply separation. Six months ago, your neighbor bought identical tires, which are still in excellent condition. A 12-month/12,000-mile warranty accompanied the tires, but the dealer who sold them to you says that they now are in short supply and that replacements are not available. Write an adjustment request to the Customer Services Manager, Shur-Grip Corporation, 37 E Market Street, Akron, OH 44308. Unless otherwise instructed, use the chronological message plan.

3. You are the Shur-Grip Customer Services Manager. Respond favorably to Application 2.

4. Two weeks ago, you purchased $75 worth of Wear-Well Indoor/Outdoor Carpet Squares (Catalog No. 83-5050) at a clearance sale. Although you carefully followed printed instructions for their use, these adhesive-backed carpet squares keep springing out of place. The store which sold them to you has gone out of business, but you feel that you're entitled to replacement or refund. Write an adjustment request to Wear-Well, Inc., 114 Eastbrook Road, Vicksburg, MS 39180. Unless otherwise instructed, use the logical message plan.

5. You are the Wear-Well Vice-President for Customer Services. Production of the 83-5050 Carpet Squares was discontinued two years ago. Since that time, their sales have not been accompanied by the usual Wear-Well guarantee. Respond as you see fit to Application 4.

6. As owner of the Greeting Card Haus, you ordered twelve dozen boxes of Mother's Day cards from the National Greeting Card Company, 824 Walnut Street, Kansas City, MO 64106. Your order was mailed eight weeks ago to insure delivery by May 1. But the shipment arrived on May 20—too late for Mother's Day. Return the shipment to National and request that your account be credited. Use the psychoanalytical message plan unless otherwise directed.

7. You are Marketing Vice-President for the National Greeting Card Company. Realizing the importance of properly timed shipments for your business, and having learned of the message from Greeting Card Haus, reply to Application 5 and offer not only the requested adjustment but also a special discount on the next order.

8. As purchasing agent for City College, you ordered ten electronic calculators from Majestic Office Equipment Corporation, 1016 Sycamore Street, Altoona, PA 16601. The calculators sell for $850 each, but a ten percent educational discount is usually provided. When Majestic billed City College, the educational discount was not given. Believing that this oversight was unintentional, write an adjustment request. Use whichever message plan you prefer, unless your professor directs otherwise.

9. You are District Manager, Central Insurance Company, 56 Circle Drive, Salem, MD 21860. You receive a message from Roberto Tonelli, 2056 Miller Avenue, Warren, PA 16365, protesting cancellation of his $15,000 life insurance policy. Although a premium notice had been sent to him, Mr. Tonelli states that he did not receive it. To guard against such circumstances, Central Insurance Company usually has a local representative telephone or visit policyholders during a 30-day grace period to remind them of the payment due. Mr. Tonelli says that this courtesy was not extended to him. Upon consulting the local representative, you learn that the Tonelli residence has no telephone and no one responded when the agent knocked at the door. Write an appropriate message to Mr. Tonelli.

CHAPTER **16**

Credit Messages

The granting of credit is a privilege that must be earned. And it is by far one of the most important privileges an individual or a business can possess. Because of its importance, credit ratings must be jealously guarded by insuring that good payment records are maintained.

Credit bureaus (consumer reporting agencies) collect individual credit histories and supply this information to subscribers who may use it only when considering credit, employment, or insurance for an individual. Because local credit bureaus are affiliated with national agencies, such as the Associated Credit Bureaus, Inc., an individual's credit history can be obtained from any region of the country.

With the advent of electronic data-processing equipment, computerized reports have expedited credit communication throughout this country and the world. Many local credit bureaus feed data to a local processing center—the data flowing in from banks, credit card operations, central charge headquarters, department stores, municipal license bureaus, utilities, and other sources that help to determine the bill-paying habits of a customer. A call to the computer center generates an instantaneous credit rating. Computer-to-computer networks are now being used for extracting a customer's credit-worthiness.

FEDERAL LEGISLATION

As a business person who extends credit or as a consumer who uses credit, you should be aware of federal legislation related to credit. Two major legislative acts are the Federal Fair Credit Reporting Act of 1971 and the Equal Credit Opportunity Act of 1976.

Federal Fair Credit Reporting Act of 1971

Under the Federal Fair Credit Reporting Act of 1971, individuals are guaranteed specific rights related to credit information that is collected about them. Basically, these rights are:

1. If a credit bureau has collected information regarding an individual, that person has a right to know the information collected.
2. If an individual feels that material in his or her file is erroneous or misleading, the credit bureau must reinvestigate and remove the questionable material from the file if it cannot be substantiated.
3. An individual whose credit file contains disputed material may place a statement of explanation in the same credit bureau file.
4. Individuals can request that notification of corrections made to the file be given to anyone who has asked for a credit report within the past six months.
5. If credit denial is based upon a person's credit report, the individual has the right to know the name and address of the credit bureau that supplied the report; the credit bureau in turn must let the person see his or her file without charge provided contact is made with the credit bureau within thirty days.
6. Negative material in an individual's file must be removed after seven years (14 years in the case of bankruptcy).

Equal Credit Opportunity Act of 1976

The Equal Credit Opportunity Act of 1976 prohibits credit discrimination based upon race, color, religion, national origin, sex, marital status, or age. Past practices generally made it difficult, if not impossible, for married women to open charge accounts in their own names or to borrow money from lending institutions.

Under this act, any information on an account that is used by both husband and wife must now be reported in both names. Any accounts opened after the enactment of the law automatically have dual reporting. Accounts opened prior to the act may necessitate a request for dual reporting. However, most lending institutions and creditors send notices like the one shown on the opposite page.

CREDIT BUREAUS

More than 2,000 credit bureaus are affiliated with Associated Credit Bureaus, Inc., the national trade association, and with Credit Bureau Reports, Inc., the national sales organization. In addition to these two organizations, many credit bureaus are subscribers to computerized reporting systems such as Credimatic, Trans Union Systems Corporation, and TRW, Inc. Membership affiliation and computer-service subscriptions

NOTICE
CREDIT HISTORY FOR MARRIED PERSONS

The Federal Equal Credit Opportunity Act prohibits credit discrimination on the basis of race, color, religion, national origin, sex, marital status, age (provided that a person has the capacity to enter into a binding contract); because all or part of a person's income derives from any public assistance program; or because a person in good faith has exercised any right under the Federal Consumer Credit Protection Act. Regulations under the Act give married persons the right to have credit information included in credit reports in the name of both the wife and the husband if both use or are responsible for the account. This right was created, in part, to insure that credit histories will be available to women who become divorced or widowed.

If your account with us is one that both husband and wife signed for or is an account that is being used by one of you who did not sign, then you are entitled to have us report credit information relating to the account in both your names. If you choose to have credit information concerning your account with us reported in both your names, please complete and sign the statement below and return it to use.

Federal regulations provide that signing your name will not change you or your spouse's legal liability on the account. Your signature will only request that credit information be reported in both your names.

If you do not complete and return the form below, we will continue to report your credit history in the same way that we do now.

When you furnish credit information on this account, please report all information concerning the account in both our names.

————————————	————————————————
Account number (You can find this number on your credit card or on your monthly bill.)	Print or type your name
	————————————————
	Print or type your spouse's name
	————————————————
	Signature of either spouse

provide local credit bureaus with complete national and international credit-reporting coverage.

With such complete coverage, in all probability, any person who has taken out a loan, used a charge card, or made purchases on the installment plan will have a credit file. And the information in that credit file will greatly influence whether or not new credit is granted. Because of computerized "on-line instant response," credit activity of an individual can be called up either by the terminal in a credit bureau or by the credit grantor's terminal.

What kinds of information are included in a credit report? Usually four types or categories of information are supplied to help determine whether or not credit is granted. These categories are:

1. Personal Data: name, spouse's name, current and former addresses, and social security numbers.
2. Employment History: past and present employment history on husband and wife, including years employed and salaries.
3. Public Record Information: bankruptcy, judgments, divorce, tax leins, and other related records.
4. Credit Profile: each item identified by firm number and name, dates involved, highest credit extended, balances and usual manner of payment, standard ratings, plus account history showing the number of times the individual was 30, 60, or over 90 days past due.

THE CREDIT PRIVILEGE

When an individual or an organization is extended credit, the grantor (the one extending the credit) is really saying, "I believe in this customer's dependability. On the basis of the credit information I have, I trust that the bill will be paid when it is due." The word *credit* comes from the Latin words *credo*, "I believe," and *credere*, "to trust."

The Function of Credit

The central function of credit is to enable a purchaser to take possession of goods now and to pay for them later. This privilege of deferring payments to a future date has in large measure influenced our standard of living, which is the highest in the world. Because people can enjoy using products or services while they are paying for them, much more than half of the products Americans buy are being paid for on credit. As a result, credit is the most powerful influence on the modern economy.

Multiplier Effect. The credit function carries with it the well-known multiplier effect. This means the extension of credit multiplies the volume of business that can be carried on with a given amount of cash, as illustrated in the following example.

Suppose a men's clothing store purchases twenty-five suits from a wholesaler for $2,500 on terms of 2/10, n/30 (two percent discount for payment within ten days, net amount due at the end of thirty days). Through efficient retail management, the owner sells all twenty-five suits at $150 each in twenty days and therefore takes in $3,750. But, as the net amount is not due the wholesaler until 30 days after the date of purchase, the merchant does not have to pay until the expiration of ten more days.

The above example shows how the clothier made a profit without spending a single dollar of capital. In the meantime the owner had the $2,500 of capital available for active use in many other ways. Remember, however, that the buyer usually has to have the cash capital before he or she can get the credit. The possession of the capital simply *multiplies*, through additional credit, the amount of business that the person can enjoy.

Discount Privilege. As a matter of good management, efficiently run businesses take advantage of credit-term discounts. With credit terms of 2/10, n/30, for example, the alert business person will make payment within ten days from the date of purchase. In so doing, a two-percent discount can be taken from the total amount of the bill with the balance being remitted. Thus a business makes money (by saving it) besides the normal margin on the retail sale of the goods. Taking advantage of discount periods results in a considerable saving over a one-year period.

Factors of Credit

Because selling is a generator of business activity, the credit manager has a responsibility to promote sales by judiciously granting credit to those individuals or companies who demonstrate the responsibility and ability for making payments within a prescribed period of time. This does not mean, however, that credit approvals are given to only those who are "sure bets." To operate in this manner would only restrict sales. The credit manager must carefully weigh all facts and possibly grant credit—perhaps a limited amount—to some applicants who are considered borderline.

Character, Capital, and Capacity. Since an account wisely opened is a collection half made, the credit officer appraises every application for three factors:

1. CHARACTER. Is the applicant's record that of a person who is steady and dependable? Does it indicate integrity? In negotiations with others does the applicant show a sense of obligation? Is the applicant honest, straightforward, aboveboard in business dealings?
2. CAPITAL. Does the applicant have enough money in his or her business to "turn around on"? What is the present ratio of the applicant's assets to liabilities? of assets quickly convertible into cash (quick assets) to liabilities that must be met in the near future? What is the applicant's general financial status?

3. CAPACITY. Does the applicant's record show that she or he can carry on a successful business? Is the applicant making progress or losing ground? Is the business location well chosen? Are there expanding opportunities in the business? Does the applicant show an aptitude for management and good judgment in meeting business situations?

Of the three credit C's, the most important is character. Many people have been known to lack capital and receive credit based upon character.

Sources of Information. Credit is granted only after the customary process known as credit investigation. Where does credit management get its facts? If an individual has had a previous credit, no doubt credit information is on file in one of the 2,000 or more credit bureaus located throughout the country. Affiliation with the Associated Credit Bureaus, Inc., and the Credit Bureau Reports, Inc., makes this information available. Additionally, subscriptions to computer-service systems permit almost instant access to an applicant's credit file. Information is also obtained through the credit application the person completes when seeking credit from a new grantor.

If an applicant has not had previous credit, information is gathered from sources such as references and from the credit application one completes. Typical information sought from a credit application includes:

1. Applicant's and co-applicant's names and social security numbers
2. Present address and length of time applicants have resided at current address
3. Previous address and length of time applicants resided at previous address
4. Occupation, present employer, length of time with present employer
5. Previous employer and length of time with previous employers
6. Mortgage balance, rent or mortgage payment per month, and gross income per month
7. Bank or credit union with which applicant is associated and whether applicant has a checking account, savings account, or both
8. Credit references including any loans, bank cards, travel cards, oil company cards, etc.
9. Previous applications for credit—where and when

Credit information regarding businesses that request credit may be obtained from the credit bureau's national trade association, mercantile agencies, and credit publications to which businesses can subscribe. Probably one of the best known mercantile agencies is Dun & Bradstreet which furnishes appraisals of firms in terms of financial strength and credit position. Subscribers receive reference books and individualized reports. Moody's Investors Service, Inc., and Standard and Poor's Corporation issue credit publications which are also frequently used.

Types of needed credit information vary according to the nature of the business. In general, however, such information should include answers to the following questions:

1. How long have you known the applicant?
2. How well does the applicant attend to business?

3. How good is the applicant's business location?
4. What kind of progress is being made?
5. What is the competition?
6. How does the applicant's management compare with that of competitors?
7. What real estate does the applicant own?
8. What is the applicant's degree of such ownership (equity)?
9. Has the applicant ever been in financial difficulty? If so, what were the circumstances and the outcome?
10. How do local bankers rate the applicant?
11. What characteristics typify the applicant's business and credit history?

Potential Credit and Actual Credit

Because more than half of all products sold in the United States are purchased through credit, it is evident that credit is vital to our economic well being. Credit has two important classes: potential and actual.

Potential Credit. Potential credit is the power to obtain present goods or services or money in exchange for a promise to render future payment. This power rests in the prospective purchaser or borrower; is based upon his or her character, capital, and capacity; and is sensitively influenced by business conditions. The amount of potential credit an applicant actually possesses depends upon the willingness and ability to pay and upon the length of the credit terms which have been allowed.

Actual Credit. Actual credit is created as potential credit is used. For example, suppose that the credit manager finds that the customer's income is considerably larger than the sum of his or her obligations and that the customer therefore possesses potential credit, or the power to secure goods by promising to pay for them in the future. The manager now allows the applicant to charge $75 worth of goods. Seventy-five dollars' worth of actual credit has been created by this transaction, and the customer's potential credit has been temporarily lessened by $75. This sum of actual credit, viewed through the customer's eyes, is a debt, an obligation to pay. Seen through the store owner's eyes, it is an asset on the account books and an equivalent right to demand payment.

To appraise a customer's potential credit, take into account the actual credit already in use. A customer who is involved in too much actual credit or outstanding debt may have little or no potential credit left. Clearly the credit manager, in controlling collections, must be concerned with the actual credit or outstanding debt of the customer. When faulty control allows noncash sales to people who have exhausted all of their potential credit, the so-called "credit" thus extended by the seller is pure fiction. The buyer, whose use of actual credit has steadily reduced and finally exhausted his or her potential credit, will not be able to keep the promise: a promise to pay in the future for goods secured in the present.

Thus the cycle of credit is:

Potential Credit———→ **Actual Credit** ———→ **Potential Credit**
converted into   *and reconverted into*   *once again*

Potential credit goes from actual credit back into potential credit as the indebtedness is paid.[1]

The Power to Buy Without Paying Cash. Credit represents the customer's power to buy without immediately paying cash. Part of the credit officer's job is to determine whether the customer really has this power or only an imitation of it.

CREDIT COMMUNICATION

With credit comes responsibility—responsibility for paying what is owed by the date the payment is due. If circumstances prevent payment on the due date, the credit user, or debtor, owes an explanation to the collector. In turn, the collector is responsible for maintaining goodwill whenever possible while insuring that the debt is paid. Credit policies and terms should be clearly communicated to the credit applicant before the debt is undertaken. If necessary, these policies should be restated so there is no possible misunderstanding on the part of the debtor.

Credit communication may take the form of inviting the use of credit, of granting credit, of refusing credit, of helping customers to develop systematic methods of protecting their credit privilege, and of other related forms. Let us examine some of these forms of communication activity.

Inviting the Use of Credit

To invite the use of credit is an important part of sales promotion. With instant computerized access to millions of individual credit files, credit invitations have skyrocketed. Businesses—banks, department stores, travel companies, oil companies, etc.—extend credit to prospective customers who have previously established excellent credit with some company somewhere in the country. Many such invitations require only the employer's name, address, and phone number; the applicant's home telephone number; and the signature of the applicant. On the opposite page is a suggested guide for extending an invitation for credit.

---

[1] This concept of the credit cycle is discussed in *Retail Credit Fundamentals* by C. W. Phelps (St. Louis: National Retail Credit Association), Chapter I, "Credit as a Business Force."

1. Use a goodwill opening.
2. Refer to credit advantages.
3. Courteously suggest action.

A CREDIT CARD INVITATION

Your excellent credit standing, Mr. Smith, deserves special recognition. So we have reserved an XYZ credit card especially for you. You now have approved credit with our company in the amount of $1,500.

You can now walk into any of our more than 3,000 stores any place in the country, purchase whatever you wish—from clothing to furniture to sports equipment—and simply present your credit card to one of our sales representatives. Or if you prefer, you may order items you wish from our large catalog. Give us your credit number, and your order will be on its way.

So be our guest. Return your reserved credit card application today and give us the pleasure of taking care of your shopping needs.

Cordially,

P.S.   Our large catalog will be sent to you as soon as we receive your signed invitation.

In addition to new customers, alert businesses also encourage past customers with excellent credit already established to make use of their credit privileges. The following message is an example:

CREDIT-PRIVILEGE REMINDER

Your promptness in paying your recent account is appreciated. Serving you is a pleasure.

Please visit us again very soon, browse around, and see the many striking values in merchandise that are being added to our store each day. While you are here, use your established credit for those items you want to purchase. You won't have to fill out any card again—just step over to the Credit Department and have it approve the payment plan on whatever you buy.

Please come in soon. We look forward to serving you again—SOON.

Granting Credit

Although credit-granting announcement cards and form messages consisting of one or two short paragraphs are often used, businesses which carefully compose credit-granting messages have a better opportunity to promote goodwill. Through such messages customers feel appreciated. Consider this guide when writing a credit-granting message.

1. Extend privilege courteously.
2. Assure cordial relations.
3. Explain credit terms.
4. Include sales promotion material.
5. Use a goodwill closing.

GRANTING CREDIT TO A CUSTOMER

Your established credit standing is excellent, Ms. Docham, and we are pleased to extend credit privileges to you here at Burton's.

As a credit customer, you can be assured that your association with our company will be pleasant. Every effort is made to make shopping convenient and to provide quality merchandise at reasonable prices.

When receiving your monthly statement, you may either pay the account balance before the next billing date or pay on installment according to the minimum payment indicated on your bill. With the installment plan a finance charge of 1¼ percent on the average daily balance will be added. Whichever option you choose, we know that you will be prompt in making your payments.

Visit our store soon and use your credit for purchasing those items you wish to have. You'll find a wide selection of quality merchandise in each department and a well-trained sales staff to assist you.

Thank you for giving us the pleasure of serving you. We look forward to taking care of your merchandising needs.

Many times well known companies will place first orders at the time they request credit. Since information about such companies is available through authoritative credit sources, the request may be simply this:

Please ship the enclosed order, on your usual credit terms, to our warehouses, 622 West Adams Street, Chicago, IL 60606.

We are listed in Dun & Bradstreet, have done extensive credit business with major firms, and look forward to a mutually profitable association with you.

By checking an authoritative credit source you find the firm's financial strength and credit position are such that credit can be extended. What kind of a guide should you use in responding to the request? You may wish to use this one:

1. Explain the order is being shipped (be sure to identify the order).
2. Thank and welcome the new credit customer.
3. Explain the credit terms.
4. State your cordial interest in serving the customer.

GRANTING CREDIT WITH A FIRST ORDER

Your order for fifteen air conditioners—19,000 BTU—was shipped this afternoon via Matrix Freight Lines. We sincerely appreciate welcoming you as a new credit customer.

Under our regular terms you are entitled to a two percent discount when payment is made within ten days of the date of our invoice. Full payment is expected, however, when payment is made between the eleventh and the thirtieth day.

Mr. Raymond Lewis, our sales representative for your area, will be calling on you within the next two weeks to explain the many services that are available to our customers. He will discuss with you the various ways we can help you in your sales promotion of our products.

We look forward to serving your future needs.

Refusing Credit

Perhaps the most challenging test of a credit officer is the ability to decline a request for credit and still keep the goodwill of the writer. Although the refusal itself is a disappointment, the way it is said can be devastating and cause irreparable harm to goodwill. And who knows? The person who is refused credit today may be the very person you would very much like to do business with tomorrow.

Messages that imply good news and then, without preparation, "drop the bomb" are as harmful as—and may be more so than—the message that says no in an opening statement. By applying empathy you can avoid writing such disarming messages.

How do experts say no and retain the goodwill of their customers? In general they have learned to say no in carefully planned ways. Here is what they suggest:

1. Instead of saying no, say yes to something else. Whenever you can offer an alternative, do so. And do it at the outset. Give the customer something positive to think about. Put your accent on what you can do.
2. State with unqualified, straightforward frankness the precise reasons for the refusal unless, of course, such reasons are confidential. State the explanation clearly and simply.
3. Assure the applicant that the request for credit has received thoughtful consideration.
4. Finally, strive to weave into your words those qualities of consideration, courtesy, and empathy that you, yourself, would appreciate if the positions were reversed.

How can we use the advice of the experts in writing our credit refusal? Here are some suggestions on how it can be done.

1. Open courteously.
2. Explain the situation (favorable facts first).
3. Offer temporary solution.
4. Close with goodwill ending.

REFUSING CREDIT TO A RETAIL CUSTOMER

Thank you for the compliment you pay us in expressing your interest in our store. Your wish to become one of our credit customers is appreciated.

You may be assured that your credit application has been carefully considered. You will also be pleased to know that the customary information sources have verified your excellent personal reputation. However, your credit file also indicates that you are somewhat overextended in obligations at this time. We are confident that, as matters develop, your situation will become generally more favorable for credit.

Please let us review your application in six months. Meanwhile we cordially invite you to let us serve you on a cash basis.

REFUSING CREDIT TO A BUSINESS PERSON

Thank you for thinking of our wholesale company as a supplier for your hardware needs. The promptness and completeness of the financial material you submitted for credit consideration is also appreciated.

You can be assured that your credit information has been studied with care. You will be pleased to know that complimentary comments about your personal character and ability show that you have developed an excellent reputation. Our study of your material, however, reveals aspects that might endanger your financial position. Your accounts payable and your notes payable seem to indicate that you are presently overextended because of the recent expansion of your business facilities. We hesitate to add to these obligations. Please let us review your application in six months.

You have our assurance of full cooperation in helping you attain a satisfactory future credit basis. Meanwhile, we'll gladly take care of your current needs with our most favorable cash items.

Protecting the Credit Privilege

The seller or the buyer may take steps to protect the credit privilege in the following ways:

Credit Education. Each message from the credit offices may convey information on the value of credit, of building up a credit reputation, of discounting bills, and of paying promptly. Obligations are treated seriously by those customers whose minds have been impressed with the importance of credit; they value their credit privilege. But even well intentioned people must become "educated," must be helped to understand the responsibilities that the privilege of credit entails. Often businesses help in credit education by using one side of their statement to print notations such as:

Your credit is one of your greatest assets. Protect it by keeping your credit record clear!

Customer Initiative. With enactment of the Fair Credit Reporting Act of 1971, individuals may find out what their credit files have to say about them by simply making a request at their local credit bureau. If any information in the person's file is vague, misleading, or in error, it is the responsibility of the individual to call this to the attention of the credit bureau officer and request that it be investigated and substantiated.

The customer, if the situation requires it, may also take the initiative of safeguarding his or her own credit record by vigorously calling attention to company error in recording payment or in handling of credit records.

A student with an excellent credit rating subscribed to a record club by mail. After the required number of records was purchased and proper written notification was given to discontinue sending records, the student continued to receive them. These additional records were promptly returned to the company. Today he receives the following message:

A FIRM (UNJUSTIFED) COLLECTION MESSAGE

Please note, Mr. Arthur, that payment on your account is now three months past due. Due to the expense of carrying accounts that are delinquent, we must make our position clear.

Because we were confident that you would meet your obligations promptly, we accepted your application to join our record club. Through August 5 you met your obligations. Since that date two records have been mailed to you, but your payments have not been received.

Consequently, we can do one of two things:

1. Wait one week for your account to be paid in full . . . or
2. Refer your account to a local collection agency and have them bear the expense and unpleasantness of collecting the amount due.

We hope to avoid the involvement of a collection agency by your sending your payment now.

This is an urgent matter. Please attend to it today.

This communication represents a small part of an involved situation comprising (1) credit extension and protection, (2) a long-drawn-out adjustment of error-correction, and (3) failure of the seller to coordinate intra-office procedures.

Since the company's credit manager signed the collection message, the customer's reply was addressed directly to him.

A CUSTOMER GUARDS HIS CREDIT

You will appreciate, Mr. Hughes, that it is something less than a pleasant surprise to receive today your demand for a payment that is not owed.

On July 15 I sent a letter explaining that I had purchased the required number of records from your company, and I did not want to continue my membership. Since that time I have received two records which I promptly returned by registered mail.

Your firm but inappropriate collection message has elicited an equally firm but quite proper reply. Please mark your records to show beyond any doubt that I do not want any more records mailed to me and that my account is paid in full and in excellent standing.

In this example (1) a person's valuable credit reputation is at stake, and (2) the company has made a serious operating error—that of sending a harsh and unjustified threat to an excellent credit customer. In effect the customer has rendered the company a priceless service in clearly revealing the urgent need of improving shipping operations and communications.

REVIEW AND TRANSITION

In Chapter 16 you learned that credit is a privilege that must be earned. Computer data banks now store credit information on any person who has ever had credit. This information can easily be obtained by a local credit bureau for transmission to a subscriber who is investigating a credit applicant. And, of course, recent federal legislation permits an individual to find out what types of information a credit bureau may have about him or her.

Chapter 16 also discussed the types of credit communication that most businesses handle—such as inviting the use of credit, granting credit, refusing credit, and protecting the credit privilege. Related to the granting or refusing of credit, you became familiar with the Equal Credit Opportunity Act of 1976 which prohibits discrimination based upon race, color, religion, national origin, sex, marital status, or age.

Chapter 17 will complete Part Six of your text. You will learn how human behavior can be influenced through collection messages. You will become acquainted with the classification of credit customers, the stages of collection management, as well as, the importance of timing and various types of psychological appeals that can be effectively used in collection messages.

DISCUSSION QUESTIONS

A. Completely automated credit reporting systems have been developed to provide an "on-line instant response" method of recording and dispersing information pertinent to the extension of credit as well as for other business and professional needs.

1. Discuss the advantages of these network systems.
2. Discuss the possible disadvantages of these systems.

B. The Federal Fair Credit Reporting Act of 1971 provides certain rights to the individual consumer. What are these rights?

C. The Equal Credit Opportunity Act of 1976 particularly affects married women. Discuss.

D. What kinds of information are usually included in a credit report which is obtained through a credit bureau? Discuss.

E. The credit functions carries with it the well-known multiplier effect. Explain the multiplier effect.

F. Through using an example, explain credit-term discounts.

G. Define the following three factors of credit:
  1. Character
  2. Capital
  3. Capacity

H. If an applicant has not had previous credit, from what sources is information gathered? Explain the sources and discuss the type of information obtained.

I. Credit has two important classes: potential and actual.
  1. What is potential credit?
  2. What is actual credit?
  3. How are the two related?

J. Credit-granting announcement cards, short form messages, and personal messages are used for granting credit to customers. If you were a business person, which would you use? Explain.

K. To write a credit refusal is probably the most challenging test of a credit officer. Why?

L. Give your opinions regarding the responsibility of business credit education. Is it a responsibility of business or not? Explain.

APPLICATIONS

Written Communications:

1. As credit manager of the East Coast Oil Company, you have obtained names and addresses of people who have previously established excellent credit ratings. Prepare a form letter (a letter that can be personalized) that offers them credit cards. A simplified form is to accompany the message.

2. Ms. Jennifer Castner is new to your city. Although she has not established credit locally, she has had credit in the previous city where she resided. On her credit application she mentions that she has had previous credit elsewhere. Through your local credit bureau you receive credit information that you believe warrants the granting of credit. As credit manager of the Style Shop, write Ms. Castner at 1607 Lincoln Drive, Hodgenville, KY 42748.

3. You are the credit manager of Nulite Products, Inc., 1010 Elm Avenue, Fairview, OK 73737. Robert S. Shaw, manager of the Office Supply Store (3210 N. Bellows Road, Nickerson, NE 68044) has asked that Nulite sell goods to the Office Supply Store on credit. You have verified the soundness of the Office Supply Store's credit rating. Using this opportunity to promote Nulite's merchandise, answer the credit application.

4. As the Nulite credit manager (see Application 3) you have learned that the Office Supply Store's credit rating is unsatisfactory. Answer the credit application; stress the advantages of cash sales.

5. As credit manager of the MacDonald Pharmaceutical Supply Company, 1010 Reading Road, Pleasant Lake, MA 02656, you receive a request for credit from Mrs. Andrea Goulette, proprietor of the West Dennis Drug Store (612 N. Easton Avenue, West Dennis, MA 02670). Mrs. Goulette opened her business just three weeks ago. As MacDonald's credit manager, you cannot accommodate her request until the West Dennis Drug Store proves financially reliable. However, you do want Mrs. Goulette to buy from you in smaller quantities on a cash basis. Write an appropriate message.

6. Mr. John Whitehead, 1631 N. Whetmore Place, Wellborn, FL 32094, requests a charge account at the Sanderson Men's Store (50 Woodville Circle, Winter Garden, FL 32787). As credit manager of Sanderson's, you review Mr. Whitehead's credit data and find that it is common practice for him to be slow in making payments. Write an appropriate message to Mr. Whitehead. Through the use of sales promotion, encourage Mr. Whitehead to purchase on a cash basis.

7. As credit manager of the Morrow Chemical Company, 3303 Lehr Road, Grand Forks, ND 58201, respond to an order received by the MacDonald Pharmaceutical Supply Company (1010 Reading Rd., Pleasant Lake, MA 02656). This is the first order MacDonald's has placed with your firm, and they are asking to have the order shipped in accordance with Morrow's usual credit terms. MacDonald's order letter states the following: "We are listed in Moody's and Standard and Poor's financial publications." Write a favorable reply.

8. Martin Green, a recent high school graduate, who lives at 1501 Troy Street, Twin Branch, WV 24889, has requested a credit card from the East Coast Oil Company. In Mr. Green's application he states that he does not have a job, has never established credit, and is planning on attending college in the fall. As credit manager, write Mr. Green and decline the credit request.

9. As the loan officer of City Bank (210 E. Main Street, Big Spring, TX 79720), you granted a mortgage loan to Robert and Alice Spencer, 612 Salina Street, Rockville, TX 84763. Since Mr. and Mrs. Spencer transact very little business at your bank, you feel that, if possible, they should direct more of their business with you in exchange for the loan privilege. Write to Mr. and Mrs. Spencer and emphasize the value of credit. Invite them to transfer their savings and checking accounts to your bank.

10. The West Dennis Drug Store has been in operation for one year (see Application 5). Mrs. Goulette, proprietor of the drug store, requests that you review her financial statements and consider her request for credit. As credit manager of MacDonald's, you believe the West Dennis Drug Store has proven financial reliability. Write Mrs. Goulette a favorable response.

Oral Communications:

11. As a communication student, obtain credit-policy information through interviewing a representative of one of the following organizations. From this information present an oral report.

    a. Bank

    b. Savings and loan company

    c. Credit union

    d. Department store

    e. Credit bureau

    f. Wholesale establishment

    g. Clothing store

    h. Public utility

Collection Messages

Finance management is a very sensitive area which requires insight, tact, and understanding on the part of the credit-collection manager. With responsibility toward the business firm, decisions must be carefully made regarding credit extension and collection procedures. To fulfill these responsibilities, the manager must (1) strive to protect the company's financial interest; (2) retain customer loyalty; and (3) help the company to make profitable sales, realizing that such sales are futile unless the customer ultimately pays in full for what was purchased.

Using careful selection criteria, the credit-collection officer extends the credit privilege to those who are rated as good risks. Through credit education customers are instructed in appreciating the credit obligation. Thus, selective credit extension and credit education are combined to minimize bad-debt loss. The wiser the credit extension, the fewer the deliquent accounts to be collected.

Although rigid standards for credit are applied, credit officers cannot detect all poor risks. Working with human factors, the credit officer cannot realistically be expected to make a perfect record. Situations can also arise to affect the financial status and credit stability of the debtor and cause him or her to fall behind in meeting financial obligations. To handle such situations, the collection system is put into operation.

COLLECTION PROCEDURES

Preserving friendly customer relations while securing past-due payments is the objective of a successful collection procedure. An effective collection officer knows that being too drastic drives away business; and, unless collection messages are handled with great care, steady customers who are good pay but slow may be alienated. On the other hand, a collection procedure which is too lenient can result in a reduction in the business' operating funds. Debtors, becoming familiar with lenient collection procedures, may let a business wait for their money while they pay others who are more strict. Accordingly, the collection officer must deal fairly but firmly with the several *credit classes* into which customers fall.

Classes of Credit Customers

Credit customers are normally classified as those who are good pay, those who are good pay but slow, and those who are uncertain.

1. *Those who are good pay* remit when notified; are eager to keep their credit unimpaired; cooperate with the credit bureau department when they delay a payment. This class is gilt-edged.
2. *Those who are good pay but slow* may be reliable in the long run, but they cause the collection department most of its work; may be careless but not dishonest; intend to pay—eventually.
3. *Those who are uncertain* will creep into the credit list in spite of the shrewdest precautions; their unreliability may at first fail to come to light, even under careful investigation. They pay only under pressure and in many instances are reduced to a cash basis. This class is a bad risk.

Most people are basically honest and eventually make their payments. Why do some procrastinate and pay only under pressure? Usually it is the result of bad habits—a lack of self-management ability, a lack of self-discipline, or just ordinary carelessness.

Stages of Collection Management

Collections are normally prepared in a series of four general stages, any of which under special circumstances may be modified:

1. Reminder
2. Stronger reminder
3. Discussion
4. Urgency

In each of the above stages, more than one mailing can be sent. Often the classification under which the person is listed determines how many mailings within a specific collection stage will be sent. For example, an individual classified as "good pay" may receive more than one reminder message; however, an individual classified as "uncertain" would not receive this treatment.

Reminder. The assumption is oversight. You assure in this first stage that the customer has overlooked the bill and will pay as soon as the reminder arrives. As a memory aid, the collection reminders keep the bills before the eyes of those who owe money. Sales material suggesting reorders, items introducing new goods, or news items of current interest may also be enclosed.

The following plan is an effective guide for a "reminder" message:

1. Re-establish rapport.
2. Mention obligation.
3. Use new data to stimulate payment.

A REMINDER TO A BUSINESS PERSON

Now that the "back-to-school" shopping rush is about over, you are probably planning for the introduction of your winter line of merchandise and the most effective way of displaying it. As we all know, success depends upon careful planning.

And while you are making your immediate plans, may we remind you to include us? Your July 10 order which was shipped under our invoice No. 621 on July 15 is now past due. Your promptness in sending us a check for $231.50 will be greatly appreciated.

Enclosed is information concerning special-priced merchandise that is now available to our customers. The excellent double knit dress slacks, the high-quality polyester leisure suits, and the colorfully knit crew-neck shirts will certainly be popular with your customers. When you send in your payment, why not include an order for these excellent buys and receive more quality merchandise BUT at an unusual savings?

A REMINDER TO A RETAIL CUSTOMER

The new Toddman, which you purchased from us on September 6, is one of the better suits that is on the market today. You will enjoy the satisfaction and the confidence of the well-dressed man as you wear it.

We also have confidence that this message will remind you to pay the balance due on your account. May we have a check for $50 so that we can mark your account—"Paid in Full."

A new shipment of some very fine dress shirts arrived this past week. Why not stop in and see them? We are sure you will want to purchase one or two of them to wear with your new suit.

As reminders, some businesses choose to send a duplicate of the original bill with a notation, "This is a reminder." Others will place reminder stickers on the duplicate bills. Still others prefer to send cards—some humorous—to jog their customer's memory. Examples of these appear on page 346.

Stronger Reminder. When a stronger reminder is mailed to the customer, the message is more firm in tone. And because attention is now directed solely toward receiving the amount owed, sales material is not included. Your assumption is still oversight. You assure that the customer has once more overlooked the bill and will pay as soon as the second notice arrives. Because the second memory jog is framed in stricter terms, the following guide will help you:

1. State debt.
2. Directly request payment.
3. Make it easy to respond.

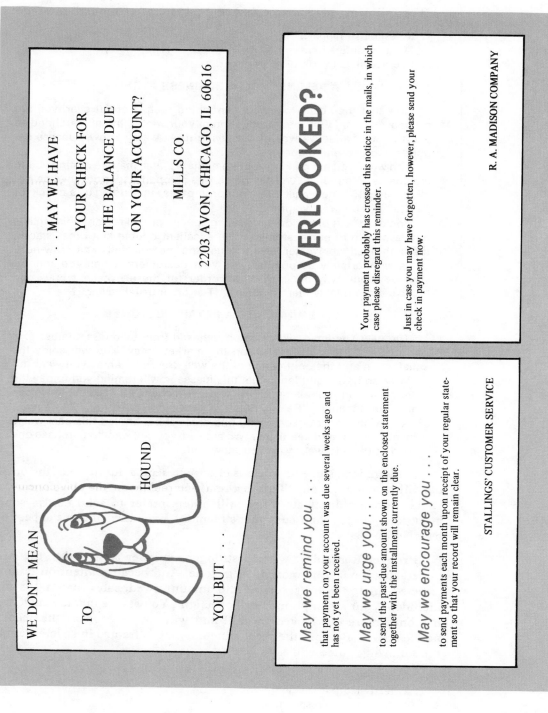

... MAY WE HAVE

YOUR CHECK FOR

THE BALANCE DUE

ON YOUR ACCOUNT?

MILLS CO.

2203 AVON, CHICAGO, IL 60616

WE DON'T MEAN

TO

HOUND

YOU BUT ....

OVERLOOKED?

Your payment probably has crossed this notice in the mails, in which case please disregard this reminder.

Just in case you may have forgotten, however, please send your check in payment now.

R. A. MADISON COMPANY

May we remind you ...
that payment on your account was due several weeks ago and has not yet been received.

May we urge you ...
to send the past-due amount shown on the enclosed statement together with the installment currently due.

May we encourage you ...
to send payments each month upon receipt of your regular statement so that your record will remain clear.

STALLINGS' CUSTOMER SERVICE

Effective Collection Form Reminders

A STRONGER REMINDER

The attached statement is a reminder that your July 10 order has apparently been overlooked. We're sure that we may rely on you to make payment now in order to avoid further correspondence.

Please mail us your check for $231.50 today. A stamped, addressed envelope is enclosed for your reply.

Discussion. Your aim in the discussion stage is to get the check or to draw a reply. The customer has not responded to a simple reminder and a stronger reminder of the obligation, and the account has run perhaps several weeks past the due date. The customer must be made to send a check or to explain what the difficulty is that prevents paying. It must be made clear beyond any doubt that the next move is up to the customer.

The appeal to friendly cooperation is now brought into play.

1. State facts.
2. Use psychological appeals.
3. Request payment or explanation.
4. Make responding easy.

The wording of your message is determined by the type of credit customer to whom you are writing. It would be sheer folly, for example, to alienate a good credit customer of long standing simply by sending the first letter in the discussion stage without recognizing that the customer has been a long and valued business associate.

DISCUSSION (TO A LONG-TIME CREDIT CUSTOMER)

Serving your business needs on a credit basis has always been a pleasure. You have been punctual in making your payments, and we have appreciated that effort. However, six weeks have now gone by since your last payment was due. We have had no answer to our notices of April 15 and May 1, calling attention to the evident oversight.

Knowing that you value your good credit reputation, the only conclusion we can reach is that some extraordinary circumstances have prevented you from making your payment. Is there anything we can do to help? Won't you let us know?

Of course, we would like to have full payment of your account; but, if this is not possible, perhaps a partial payment of $55 now and the balance paid next month will help you. We sincerely want to work with you in protecting your credit, but our hands are tied unless you let us know the problem.

Help us to help you in preserving your good credit by letting us hear from you now. Please use the enclosed reply envelope to do one of three things: (1) enclose your check for the full amount—$110; (2) enclose a check for $55—and we will assume the balance will be received next month; or (3) explain your situation and let us know what you can do to meet your obligation. Your immediate response is necessary.

Credit customers of short duration may not require the firm but understandable tone which is used for long-time credit customers. Your purpose is to make it clear that credit customers are expected to meet their obligations on time and that you expect an immediate response in the form of a check or an explanation of why payment has been deferred. In writing the letter, however, you must be courteous and tactful.

DISCUSSION (TO A CREDIT CUSTOMER OF SHORT DURATION)

Based upon your established credit standing, we were more than pleased to extend credit privileges to your company. And we have appreciated the timely payments you have made in the past. However, six weeks have now gone by since your last payment was due. We have had no answer to our notices of April 15 and May 1, calling attention to the evident oversight.

As you know, a sound credit reputation is a valuable asset. With it you are afforded many more business advantages than could otherwise be obtained on a cash basis. As you wish, we also want to see you continue to receive these credit privileges. But to make it possible for us to extend credit, we must have cooperation, in the form of prompt payments, from our customers.

Preserve your good credit reputation by explaining the extraordinary circumstances that have caused the delay in payment or by sending your check for $110 at once. A reply envelope is enclosed; please use it now.

As you have noticed in the preceding *discussion* messages, the communication to the customer usually takes the form of an inquiry. By *inquiry* we mean a message that drives for payment of the debt but, striving to keep the customer's goodwill and future patronage, requests at least an explanation. One of the purposes is to re-establish communication by showing the debtor that, although he or she has withheld payment past the due date, the company is still willing to cooperate.

When no response is received from the customer, the *discussion* stage then takes the form of appeals that trigger the self-interest of the customer by stressing the advantages that would be forfeited by nonpayment.

In the discussion stage credit information is reviewed, stressing the appeals of fair play and cooperation. Attention is called to the exact amount of the statement, the dates of previous notices, and the length of time during which the debt has been overdue. With a direct, imperative demand for explanation and payment, the message closes forcefully.

Urgency. At the urgency stage, your assumption is that the customer must be made to pay. Your message must be forceful, and it must issue an ultimatum which should promptly be followed by the action it threatens to take. The language or urgency is imperative. The keynote is finality, an insistence on immediate payment.

However, the insistence must be in a reasonable phraseology that avoids evidence of anger.

Here is an effective guide:

1. State facts.
2. Use psychological appeals.
3. Deliver ultimatum.
4. Make responding easy.

URGENCY (LEGAL ACTION INDICATED)

We have had no response to all our efforts of arriving at a mutually acceptable solution to your indebtedness, which is indeed unfortunate. The attached statement indicates the exact amount of your account and the full period of its delinquency. Justice to other customers prevents further delay of your payment.

Unless your check for full payment of your account is received by October 1, your account will be transferred to a collection agency. Such action—as you well know—will inevitably lower your credit rating.

To prevent this unpleasant action, your check must be in our hands by October 1. A stamped, addressed envelope is enclosed for your convenience in taking care of this matter now.

One insistent phrase after another emphasizes the necessity for fast action if unpleasant measures are to be avoided. Appeals are to self-esteem, community prestige, and fair play.

When no response is forthcoming from the urgency message and the threatening action that was promised has been taken, sometimes the creditor will send a message informing the individual that the action promised has taken place. In such a notification the writer reviews the complete situation—the credit agreement, amount of indebtedness and period of time the debt was past due, number of notices mailed, reasonableness of the creditor in attempting to collect the indebtedness, and the lack of recourse in which the creditor was placed.

Timing

In attempting to collect past-due accounts, the time interval between collection stages—also between messages within a collection stage—depends on several factors:

1. The credit standing of the customer on the basis of the original credit investigation and his or her past record
2. The nature of the business of the company—whether usual credit practice allows long or short collection periods
3. Business conditions

Credit Record. When a customer is known to have established a good credit record, the time intervals are liberal. However, for a customer who has earned the reputation of being slow or uncertain, the intervals are shortened. Often such customers may not be taken through the four general collection stages when their indebtedness extends beyond payment dates. The collection manager may, for example, begin with the stronger reminder and then conclude by sending the last-chance ultimatum.

Nature of Business. Accepted custom in the trade also dictates the usual period allowable for bringing in slow accounts. The farm-implement business may allow credit terms extending over months with a collection period running for months thereafter. At the other extreme a specialty manufacturer, selling a product in high demand and operating on small capital and fast turnover, may shorten the entire collection period to a matter of days.

Business Conditions. Prosperous times tend to make collections easy. When optimism prevails, collections are relatively prompt. In times of recession, on the other hand, money becomes tight because business is slow and little, if any, profit is being shown. Under such conditions collections become difficult. Therefore, collection policies must be modified to fit the situation.

PSYCHOLOGICAL APPEALS

Knowing what motivates people is not enough. One must know what appeals to use and how vigorously to stress them. Individuals are unique; selecting the correct appeal and stressing it sufficiently will result in accomplishing your full objective: It gets the payment and retains the customer.

Selecting Appeals

Select your appeals to match the collection stage that you have reached. In the first two stages your appeals are mild; in the second two they are vigorous.

Important appeals are timed as follows:

1. In all stages:	fairness, cooperation, self-respect
2. Helpful in every stage:	pride, self-interest, honor
3. Useful in any stage:	success, fair play, wish to avoid unpleasant things, force of habit

4. Useful when appropriate: self-esteem, community prestige, desire for comfort, acquisitiveness, family affection, imitation (of other good business people), loyalty (to a friendly house), competition, curiosity

5. Important in later stages: fear, threat, annoyance of legal force, ultimatum

After you have classified customers, your next step is to determine what motives are most likely to influence each to pay. For example, the motive of fear might be effective but inappropriate with good credit risks; it would antagonize people who pride themselves on paying bills with regularity. On the other hand, the motive of habit is a useful one for good credit risks but not at all effective for uncertain risks.

Pride Appeal. Because individuals need to feel good about themselves and to feel worthy of other people's respect, pride appeals are directed to the reader's self-esteem. The pride of maintaining a good credit rating is stressed in the following example:

> The landscaping you had us do for your new home is appreciated. The extensive use of high-quality shrubs and evergreens shows that you take pride in the appearance of your home.
> We are also sure you take pride in meeting your financial obligations. Although we've had no response to our April 10 and May 10 reminders, we are sure you will want to immediately take care of your past-due bill.
> Help us to avoid causing you embarrassment through further collection effort. Send us $450 by June 1, and we will mark the account "Paid in Full."
> Here is an envelope (postage paid) for your check.

Loyalty Appeal. When a long-time customer fails to pay and does not reply to any of the appeals, the credit officer may use the appeal to loyalty.

> Your usual promptness in paying your account makes us believe that some extraordinary situation has arisen to delay the payment which is itemized on the enclosed statement. Since we have had no response to our notices of September 10 and October 10, we cannot help but wonder what is wrong.
> Our business relationship goes back a good many years, Mr. Livingston. During this long association, your loyalty to our company and to our products has certainly been appreciated; and we certainly want to preserve the friendliness and cooperativeness that has existed between us.
> Ordinarily when payment is so long overdue, we place the account with our attorneys for collection. In the case of a loyal customer such as you

though, exceptional practice may be justified. However, an explanation and at least a partial payment are necessary now.

Please send us your check and your explanation, Mr. Livingston. Your reasons and your suggestion will be carefully considered.

Fair Play Appeal. The fair play appeal carries the theme that the seller has carried out his or her responsibilities to the buyer; therefore, the only self-respecting option the buyer has is to make payment in full.

When you requested credit, we were pleased to extend this service to you with the understanding that all credit privileges must be paid within thirty days. Contrary to this agreement, your account is long overdue.

As a criterion for selecting the wholesalers from whom you purchase your merchandise, you expect good credit terms, prompt service, and quality merchandise at competitive prices. You will agree, I am sure, that we provided these services to you. In return for services, however, we think it is only fair to expect our credit customers to pay their debts promptly.

You have already enjoyed an extension of time far beyond the usual. Justice to other customers prevents further delay.

To protect your credit rating, send your check for $115 today in full payment of your account. A reply envelope is enclosed for your convenience in mailing.

Psychological Tone

The collection officer's responsibility is not only to collect the overdue account but also to retain the goodwill of the customer. Therefore, all collection messages should be courteous.

When writing a collection message, remind yourself of its stage in the collection series. Because most overdue payments are collected during the reminder stages and because your assumption is that payment has been overlooked, the tone of your message should be friendly and cheerful. As your writing progresses through the discussion stage, your message should continue to be friendly but with an ever-increasing firmness in tone. The urgency stage uses a very firm tone with insistence that the debt must be paid.

RETAINING CUSTOMERS

When dealing with credit and collection, one must be aware that integrity is the cornerstone of both personal and corporate credit. Hence credit and collection presents challenging complexities that must be approached with tact, understanding, insight, and creative imagination. The collection officer of today plans collections as if they were sales messages. The customer's point of view is dominant in the collection officer's mind.

Hard-Pressed Customers

There are instances when some customers simply do not have the money with which to pay their accounts on time. These people are basically honest and are usually very sensitive regarding their predicament. Not knowing that anything can be done, they choose to remain silent to collection messages they receive.

This silence is what is most disturbing to the collection officer. When a debtor cannot meet a financial commitment, a frank and personal acknowledgment of the debt, stating the intention of making payment, is the best protection for a good credit rating.

Those Who Pay

Even though collection departments must concentrate on overdue accounts, the opportunity to reinforce the goodwill of those customers who pay promptly should not be overlooked. Notice how the following message expresses appreciation and, at the same time, welcomes the customer to make additional use of the company's services:

APPRECIATION TO THOSE WHO PAY

The prompt manner in which you paid your automobile loan is sincerely appreciated.

Because you are the kind of person who conscientiously honors financial obligations, we want you to know that you have established excellent credit with this bank. Whenever we can be of service to you again, please give us that opportunity.

After national news reported a section of the country was declared a national disaster area due to a severe winter storm, a well-known company sent this message to its credit customers who resided in that section of the country:

The severe weather that caused extensive damage in your area concerns us very much.

Hopefully, you and your family were not personally affected by this unfortunate incident. Please be assured that we will welcome the opportunity to extend additional time for paying your account should you need it.

Because you have demonstrated your promptness in meeting your obligations, your patronage is important to us. Please do not hesitate in letting us know if we can help.

A prepaid envelope is enclosed for your convenience.

FOLLOW-UP COLLECTION SYSTEMS

Collection-form messages ordinarily are developed by keeping copies of collection messages that have proven to be successful. Such messages are usually classified by collection stage—reminder, discussion, urgency. Additional breadkdowns can also be made—such as new customers, old customers, problem customers, stubborn customers.

From these files, the collection officer draws exactly the right master drafts upon which to base the "form" system. "Form collection messages are used over and over again, either in identical or modified versions, and are sent to debtors whose delinquencies—in terms of amounts owed, period of time overdue, etc.—are practically identical. Using imagination, the collection officer modifies or adapts highly successful message appeals previously put to test, and uses them through forms.

Form messages are normally used in 80 to 90 percent of all collection work. Individual messages—usually used in the advanced stages of the collection procedure—account for the remaining 10 to 20 percent. No "standard" collection-form procedure can be designed so that it can be switched from company to company. Each must work out the plan that best fits its needs.

Form Messages

Follow-up collection systems are designed to gradually increase psychological pressure on the debtor to pay the account. Each message within the series progressively uses stronger appeals and increased firmness to collect payment.

Larger organizations standardize the notices, reminders, and stronger reminders through form messages and form paragraphs to fit common situations. Using this method reduces the cost factor. When using form paragraphs, the collection manager also can insert personally dictated material into the message. For those situations that are not covered by form messages, personally dictated appeals are used.

To use a follow-up collection system, the form messages should be written as if they were to go to an individual instead of to many people. The test: When the appeal is read, does it have the impact of a personal message?

Timing

A set plan should be established when sending collection messages. The scheduling of mailings should be planned to prevent the thought of the debt from slipping from the debtor's mind. Customers gain a wholesome respect for the organization that, with courteous but decisive promptness, enforces collection within a regulated time frame.

Within the time frame, provisions should be made for flexibility. For example, an identical collection sequence sent twice in succession to the same debtor loses its effectiveness. Such a customer should be treated firmly at the first indication of the second delinquency. A different form of strong reminder should be sent immediately, or the collection officer should give the case personal attention with matters being concluded quickly.

To assure flexibility in collection procedure, it is the usual practice to indicate with simple code signs on the cards or in the accounts those customers who are most likely to violate their credit agreements, as proved by their past delinquencies. The number of times each customer has been delinquent is also recorded. The collection follow-up is then speeded up when applied to those customers with previous bad-pay records.

To explain how a follow-up collection system may operate, the following example which applies to an insurance company is given. Notice that this particular system includes 25 form messages. The numbering of the various sequences is designed so that the system can be expanded if needed. Although the system has 25 units, the entire sequence is not sent to one customer. The method is selective. Of the six "50-day appeals" (that is, appeals sent after the expiration of 50 days), *one* is chosen and sent; of the seven "60-day appeals," *one* is chosen; and so on. The appeals in each division vary in tone and phrasing to fit various classes of customers. Here is a summary of the units:

APPEALS

1 to 6	Reminders (50-day)
10 to 16	Stronger reminders (60-day)
20 to 25	Discussion stage with special appeals (70-day)
30 to 32	Urgency (80-day): Cancellations for new business, with notice of cancellation enclosed
40	Final urgency (90-day): Cancellation put into effect and return of policy called for
41	Last-chance appeal (90-day): For reconsideration after cancellation
50	Miscellaneous: To follow promise of payment

SPECIAL COLLECTION PROCEDURES

Collection departments sometimes use special procedures for collecting overdue accounts. The following approaches have proved successful:

1. *The Sporting Approach.* Messages in this category usually are more effective in the early stages of the collection series. Such messages use themes such as "Help me win my wager" or "Help me keep my promise."
2. *The Story Approach.* An anecdote may seize the customer's attention at the beginning of a collection message. However, caution must be taken to relate the story to the subject of the message—the overdue account.

3. *Half and Half Approach.* Used in the reminder stages, this approach is most effective. The format has two places for messages to be written. The left side is the space reserved for the typewritten message from the credit officer. The right side is reserved for the customer's explanation of delay.
4. *Turning the Tables Approach.* A deliberately emphatic appeal is used. When using this approach, the message carries the theme, "What would you do if our positions were reversed?"
5. *Telegram and Telephone Approach.* Telegrams and telephone calls are used for urgency stages as an effective method for collecting overdue accounts. Such a procedure adds the urgency of time to the message.

REVIEW AND TRANSITION

Preserving friendly customer relations while securing past-due payments is the objective of a successful collection department. To accomplish both of these requires insight, tact, and understanding on the part of management.

Based upon a classification of credit customers, Chapter 17 presented a comprehensive model of the collection procedure which includes the four communication stages—reminder, stronger reminder, discussion, urgency. Within the collection procedure you learned the importance of selecting the proper psychological appeals, developing proper tone, and enforcing standard timing.

In Part Six, Chapters 15-17, you have acquainted yourself with effective application of logic, psychology, and ethics to adjustment, credit, and collection messages. Part Seven, Chapters 18-19, will continue your study of business communications through the writing of reports.

DISCUSSION QUESTIONS

A. How drastic should a collection officer be in eagerness to collect overdue payments?

B. If we use the assumption that most people are basically honest, why don't some people pay their bills on time? Discuss.

C. Discuss some of the alternative methods that may be employed, other than the written message, during the reminder stage.

D. How do the reminder and the stronger reminder messages differ in content? Explain.

E. How do the discussion and the stronger reminder messages differ in content? Explain.

F. Suppose you have two collection messages in the discussion stage to write. One message is being sent to an established customer with whom you have been doing business for several years. The second message is being written to a new customer. Would the content of the two messages differ? If so, why? If not, why not?

G. How do the discussion and the urgency stages in the collection procedure differ? Discuss.

H. Explain the following statement: More than four mailings may be included in the four stages of the collection procedure.

I. Explain the selection of appeals for each of the four stages in the collection procedure.

J. Explain the use of tone in relation to each stage in the collection procedure.

APPLICATIONS

1. You are the credit manager of Nulite Products, Inc., 1010 Elm Avenue, Fairview, OK 73737. Robert S. Shaw, manager of the Office Supply Store, 3210 N. Bellows Road, Nickerson, NE 68044, has been purchasing supplies from you on a credit basis for several years. Although this business relationship has been mutually profitable, your invoice No. 2020 for desk calendars ($52.50) has not been paid. Previous reminders have elicited no responses. Write an appropriate message.

2. As credit manager of the MacDonald Pharmaceutical Supply Company, 1010 Reading Road, Pleasant Lake, MA 02656, you have been doing business for several years with Mrs. Andrea Goulette, proprietor of the West Dennis Drug Store, 612 N. Easton Avenue, West Dennis, MA 02670. Although it is very unusual for Mrs. Goulette not to meet her financial obligations, she has not paid her last statement—invoice No. 816 for $250. You have sent several reminders, some being strong. Write an appropriate message using the discussion level.

3. You still have not received payment from the Office Supply Company (See Application 1). Send a stronger reminder to Mr. Shaw.

4. As the credit manager of the Keenland Department Store, 2010 Bush Avenue, Cold Spring, MN 56320, write an appropriate collection message to Mr. John Williamson, 6403 Halstad Avenue, Glenville, MN 56036. From all indications, it appears Mr. Williamson is going to be late the second time in succession in paying his account ($50).

5. (See Applications 1 and 3) The Office Supply Company is still delinquent. You have not heard from Mr. Shaw in response to previous notifications. Write to Mr. Shaw using the discussion stage of the collection procedure.

6. (See Application 2) Mrs. Goulette has not responded to your previous message. Send another message on the "discussion" level. Use a different appeal from the one you used in application 2.

7. As credit manager of the City Lumber Company, 1020 Waldo Street, Union Springs, AL 36089, you have supplied building materials to Mr. Charles Arnold for his new home. Mr. Arnold still owes $352 on his bill. You have sent several messages—discussion stage—to Mr. Arnold but to no avail. Write an urgency message to him at 402 Plainfield Drive, Northport, AL 35476.

8. You are the credit manager of the Tilman Book Store, 2025 OceanviewDrive, Brunswick, ME 04011. You decided to use cartoon greeting cards as a means of collecting past-due accounts. Prepare a collection card that can be used at the "reminder" stage of the collection process.

9. Assume you work in the collection department of a local department store in your community. Prepare a set of form messages that can be used in the following collection stages:

a. Reminder
b. Stronger reminder
c. Discussion
d. Urgency

PART SEVEN

Developing Research Plans, Proposals, Reports

Parts One through Three of this book introduced you to concepts of successful management involving effective communication. Parts Four through Six acquainted you with typical business messages, ranging from simple orders and requests to complete collection series. Part Seven continues your applications of communication theory and practice in relation to business research and reports.

The formats of memo and letter reports were discussed in Chapter 6. Subsequent chapters identified research aspects of messages for employment, sales, adjustments, credit privileges, and collections. Completing this sequence, Chapters 18 and 19 explain methods of integrating research and reporting for effective business communication.

Chapter 18 describes plans and proposals for conducting research. Chapter 19 discusses development and presentation of reports which are products of research. Effective business research and reporting require excellence—excellence that you can achieve—in perceiving, in reasoning, and in related communication skills.

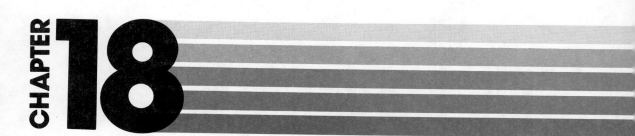

CHAPTER 18

Research Plans and Proposals

Research work plans and report outlines are related in these ways: A work plan represents the *process* which results in a report. An outline formulates the *product* of that process. The product, of course, is an oral, a written, or a multimedia message which conveys information for decision and use. The work plan serves as a guide for later developing the report outline. In turn, the report outline (which Chapter 19 discusses in detail) helps to develop and present the needed message.

As foundations for your business research and reporting, these communication factors require your attention:

1. Authorization
2. Identification
3. Purpose
4. Scope
5. Limitations
6. Design
7. Schedule and Budget
8. Justification
9. Additional Remarks

The following pages describe these factors individually and then illustrate their combination in a work plan (also called a "research proposal") designed ultimately to produce an effective report.

AUTHORIZATION

To avoid needless duplication of effort and resources, you and your co-workers need to know the source and the timing of a management request or directive for research activity. Knowledge of that authorization enables employees to keep work within proper channels of administration and communication. Moreover, you may be expected to state the authorization in the report which this planning process will produce. If you do not receive an authorization message with your research assignment, ask your superior to tell you for whom the project and its report are to be prepared.

IDENTIFICATION

You have learned that thinking requires the effective use of symbols, mainly of words and numbers. Therefore, early in your research plan—unless superior authority has already done so for you—you should determine the principal topic and the tentative title of your project. In the real world of business, a research *topic* may be so complex that paragraphs of concise wording are necessary to describe it properly. The *title*, however, summarizes the topic.

PURPOSE

As with every other effective communication effort, you need to determine the objectives which your proposed research project will accomplish. What do you intend to disclose? establish? describe? explain? prove? disprove? or recommend?

SCOPE

Having determined your research purposes, your next step is to decide upon the *range* of your research efforts. By analyzing your topic and purpose, you detect subtopics and issues. Then you can logically decide what to include within the scope of your research and of its product: the final report. Under the "scope" section of your proposal, you state where your research will begin, what it will include, and where it will stop—*all in relation to the purpose you have stated.*

LIMITATIONS

In research terms, "limitations" (also called "delimitations" or "restrictions") are statements that further reveal precisely what you plan to do.

Scope and *limitations* are related in these ways: Whereas *scope* is a commitment of what your research will include, *limitations* are statements of related aspects which you deliberately will exclude or which are beyond your control in conducting the project.

Scope represents the study items which your project will contain. Scope represents the proposed direction and extent of your investigation.

Limitations are inventories of pertinent factors which your project will omit or will contain only partially. Limitations include definitely set boundaries which keep the scope of a research project from becoming too broad to be significant.

DESIGN

Having determined authorization, identification, purpose, scope, and limitations, you are ready to plan your research design.

Except perhaps for a chronologically arranged project and message—like the journal accompanying a laboratory experiment—your research design for the work plan may not coincide with your later "content outline" for your report. Often, the research design may contain many more planning details than the final report requires. The design is a description of a logical pattern which connects (1) your assumptions and (2) your tentative conclusions through (3) your proposed study order for the research, leading to a work plan.

LIMITING A RESEARCH TOPIC

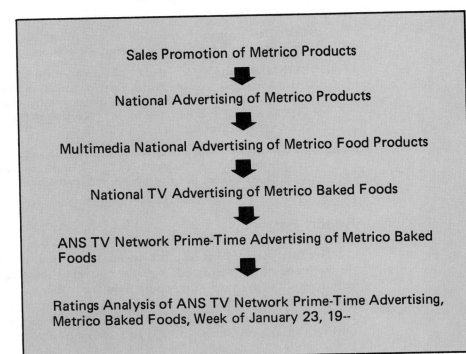

Sales Promotion of Metrico Products

National Advertising of Metrico Products

Multimedia National Advertising of Metrico Food Products

National TV Advertising of Metrico Baked Foods

ANS TV Network Prime-Time Advertising of Metrico Baked Foods

Ratings Analysis of ANS TV Network Prime-Time Advertising, Metrico Baked Foods, Week of January 23, 19--

Assumptions

Your design begins with statements of initial assumptions (beliefs or hypotheses that you present but which you have not yet proved).

Tentative Conclusions

Your design includes tentative conclusions ("guesstimates" of what your research may logically reveal). Remember that your tentative conclusions are *merely temporary conjectures*. Be sure to change them if they are contradicted or altered by the data you collect and process when your research is actually underway.

Study Order

Your design includes your proposed study order, which usually involves this procedure:

1. **IDENTIFYING** and **LOCATING** relevant data sources (people, publications, records, previous reports concerning your topic and purpose).

2. **SELECTING** from among all the available and appropriate sources *those which you will actually use for your project.*

3. **DECIDING** upon *methods* of collecting pertinent data (through readings, interviews, questionnaires, experiments, observations).

4. **REVIEWING** the collected data to discover what has already been *learned* from earlier studies which pertain, directly *or* indirectly, to your project. Usually you will report these insights under one of these headings: "Review of Previous Findings," "Review of Pertinent Sources," "Review of Relevant Literature," or the like.

5. **DETERMINING** techniques for data analysis, synthesis, and interpretation (as described in Chapter 2 of this book and as related to your own project identification, purpose, scope, and limitations).

Report Format

The final step of your research design is anticipation of the message to be produced: the report itself. You are not yet at the stage of outlining—certainly not of drafting—the report. You are still engaged in planning the complete research process. That process will culminate later with communication techniques explained in Chapter 19 to guide you through outlines, drafts, revisions, and the final version of your report.

At this point, however, part of your research design is to anticipate the format of that final report. Is the format to be written? If so, in what style? Is the format to be written and oral? Again, in what style? Is it to be primarily narrative? mostly explanatory? mainly persuasive? Will it include statistics? computer printouts? charts, graphs, tables, other exhibits? Will the format be that of a business letter, memorandum, semi-formal report, full-length research document, publishable article, oral-visual presentation? What message style, tone, and medium will be appropriate to *communicating* your research? As you see, the concept being advanced here is that research is not complete until it has been communicated.

So far, you have considered these communication factors in planning your research project:

1. Authorization
2. Identification
3. Purpose
4. Scope
5. Limitations
6. Design

There are three more factors to be included with your work plan:

7. Schedule and Budget
8. Justification
9. Additional Remarks

SCHEDULE AND BUDGET

Often the authorization message from your superior will indicate how much time, money, personnel, and other resources are to be invested in your project. But if schedule and budget are not specified, you need to set your own deadlines and determine the necessary resources for completing the entire project, including its final report.

We suggest that you initially plan your work schedule in reverse chronological order. Plan your project from the anticipated completion date to the starting date. Set intermediate "due dates" for completing phases of the work in this way:

1. Deadline for delivering final report:
   Resources required:
2. Due dates for revising and editing:
   Resources required:
3. Due dates for outlining and drafting:
   Resources required:
4. Periods for data analysis, interpretation, evaluation:
   Resources required:
5. Periods for data collection and tabulation:
   Resources required:

By scheduling your work in reverse chronological order, you can realistically pace your research efforts, step by step, without having to "race the clock" for the final deadline. Instead of submitting your report late, you can use this kind of timetable and budget guide to monitor your progress as you work. If one phase of your project requires more or less time and resources than scheduled, you can adjust other phases as you move along. Or well before the final deadline as originally set, you can request your superior to authorize additional time and resources if they become necessary.

JUSTIFICATION

Your research proposal—which is a blueprint for your proposed action—usually involves "selling" the value of your work plan in relation to your superior's purposes and functions. Therefore in the "justification" section of your proposal, be sure to identify people, units, or operations likely to benefit from the results of your project (and describe the nature of those benefits when appropriate to do so).

ADDITIONAL REMARKS

If your work plan, or research proposal, requires information which does not logically suit the preceding headings, state that information in a section headed "Additional Remarks," "Other Considerations," or the like.

THE WORK PLAN AS A UNIFIED MESSAGE

This nine-part work plan is summarized on the opposite page and illustrated on pages 368-370. Notice that the format is logically unified but flexible. You may rearrange its parts to accommodate your own stylistic preferences or those of your reader/listener.

The planning procedure described here has been and is being used successfully to propose and to guide research in business, education, government, science, and art. Applications of this comprehensive model have produced useful reports which range from letters, memos, and oral presentations to term papers, monographs, published articles, master's theses, as well as doctoral dissertations.

A WORK PLAN FOR EFFECTIVE RESEARCH AND REPORTING [1]

1. **Authorization**—What person, people, policies, regulations, or circumstances permit you to undertake your research project?

2. **Identification**—What is the topic of your study? the title of your project?

3. **Purpose**—What is (are) the objective(s) of your project?

4. **Scope**—What are the major areas of your study?

5. **Limitations**—How do you propose to confine your scope? What factors probably will modify or restrict your study?

6. **Design**—How do you intend to build and conduct your study?
   a. Assumptions: What ideas or concepts do you hypothesize initially without proof?
   b. Tentative Conclusions: What kinds of results are likely products of your study?
   c. How do you propose to separate your project into its related issues or subtopics? Concerning those issues or subtopics, what kinds of data do you seek? How do you plan to collect and evaluate the data?

   (1) Sources. What people, publications, records, and other references pertain to your study? Which of the pertinent references are available to you? Which of the available, pertinent references do you intend to use?

   (2) Data Collection. How do you intend to acquire information from the available, pertinent sources? Through readings, observations, interviews, questionnaires, experiments, other means? In what sequence do you expect to use the methods of acquiring information?

   (3) Previous Findings. What earlier work is related—directly or indirectly—to your project? What have earlier studies revealed?

   (4) Data Use. How do you plan to process the data that you collect? How do you propose to analyze, synthesize, and interpret the information?

   (5) Report Format. What kind of message do you expect to produce? Is your report to be written—a memorandum, a letter, a many-paged document, a publication? Is your report to be oral—an extemporaneous, a textual, a memorized message? What style and tone of writing or speaking do you intend to use? What method of report reproduction—typewriting, mimeographing, photocopying, printing, filming, tape recording, or other means—do you anticipate?

7. **Schedule and Budget**—What are the due dates for intermediate phases of your study? What is the deadline for presenting your final report? How much time, money, and other resources does every major phase of your proposal require? How much of these resources does your total project require?

8. **Justification**—Of what potential value is your project? Who is apt to benefit from your report? What kinds of benefits are likely to result? Why does your project merit the investment of time, money, and other resources?

9. **Additional Remarks**—What relevant considerations are omitted from the preceding categories of your work plan?

---

[1] According to writer and reader preferences, the parts of this plan may easily be rearranged while retaining logical unity. For example: Authorization, Identification, Purpose, Justification, Scope, Limitations, Design, Schedule and Budget, Additional Remarks.

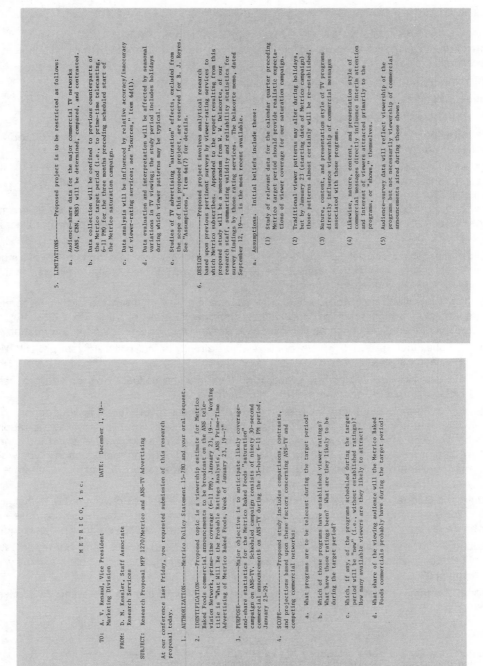

M E T R I C O ,   I n c .

TO: A. V. Renaud, Vice President　　　　DATE:　December 1, 19—
Marketing Division

FROM: D. M. Kessler, Staff Associate
Research Services

SUBJECT: Research Proposal MFP 1270/Metrico and ANS-TV Advertising

At our conference last Friday, you requested submission of this research proposal today.

1. AUTHORIZATION——Metrico Policy Statement 15-780 and your oral request.

2. IDENTIFICATION——Proposed topic is a viewership estimate for Metrico Baked Foods commercial announcements to be broadcast on the ANS television Network, prime-time coverage (6-11 PM), January 23, 19—. Working title is "What Will Be the Probable Ratings Analysis, ANS Prime-Time Advertising of Metrico Baked Foods, Week of January 23, 19—?"

3. PURPOSE——Major objective is to anticipate likely coverage-and-share statistics for the Metrico Baked Foods "saturation" campaign on ANS-TV. Scheduled campaign consists of ninety 30-second commercial announcements on ANS-TV during the 35-hour 6-11 PM period, January 23-29.

4. SCOPE——Proposed study includes comparisons, contrasts, and projections based upon these factors concerning ANS-TV competing commercial networks:

a. What programs are to be telecast during the target period?

b. Which of those programs have established viewer ratings? What have those ratings been? What are they likely to be during the target period?

c. Which, if any, of the programs scheduled during the target period will be "new" (i.e., without established ratings)? How many available viewers are they likely to attract?

d. What share of the viewing audience will the Metrico Baked Foods commercials probably have during the target period?

5. LIMITATIONS——Proposed project is to be restricted as follows:

a. Audience-share data for the major commercial TV networks (ANS, CBN, NBS) will be determined, compared, and contrasted.

b. Data collection will be confined to previous counterparts of the Metrico target period (i.e., to prime-time telecasting, 6-11 PM) for the three months preceding scheduled start of the Metrico saturation campaign.

c. Data analysis will be influenced by relative accuracy/inaccuracy of viewer-rating services; see "Sources," Item 6d(1).

d. Data evaluation and interpretation will be affected by seasonal variations in TV viewing; the study period includes holidays during which viewer patterns may be typical.

e. Studies of TV advertising "saturation" effects, excluded from the scope of this proposed project, are reserved for B. J. Reyes. See "Assumptions," Item 6a(7) for details.

6. DESIGN——Proposed project involves analytical research based upon previous pertinent surveys by viewer-rating services to which Metrico subscribes. Appended to the report resulting from this proposed study will be a memorandum from W. W. Delacorte, of our research staff, summarizing validity and reliability statistics for survey findings by those rating services. The Delacorte memo, dated September 12, 19—, is the most recent available.

a. Assumptions. Initial beliefs include these:

(1) Study of relevant data for the calendar quarter preceding Metrico target period should provide realistic expectations of viewer coverage for our saturation campaign.

(2) Traditional viewer patterns may alter during holidays, but by January 23 (starting date of Metrico campaign) those patterns almost certainly will be re-established.

(3) Nature, content, and presentation style of TV programs directly influence viewership of commercial messages associated with those programs.

(4) Likewise, nature, content, and presentation style of commercial messages directly influence interim attention and interest of viewers attracted primarily to the programs, or "shows," themselves.

(5) Audience-survey data will reflect viewership of the program but not necessarily viewership of commercial announcements aired during those shows.

DRAFT OF A RESEARCH PROPOSAL IN MEMORANDUM FORMAT

(2) Data Collection. This is the probable sequence for acquiring information:

    (a) Review target-period programing schedules of the ANS, CBN, and NBS television networks.

    (b) Review coverage/share ratings for established programs on that schedule.

    (c) Identify other than established programs scheduled for target-period telecasting on those networks; review industry forecasts of probable success for those programs.

    (d) Use findings derived from Steps 6d (2) (a)-(c) to compare/contrast probable drawing power for the ANS, CBN, and NBS target-period shows.

    (e) Determine in particular the probable coverage/share ratings for ANS shows contracted to carry Metrico Baked Foods commercial messages during the target period.

(3) Previous Findings. Delacorte concluded that both of the viewer-rating services to which Metrico subscribes tend to report generally valid and reliable statistics. The Neeiser Rating Service Reports are issued weekly; Viewtally Reports, monthly. Sampling techniques and survey methods differ, however, for those two services. Neeiser uses electronic recorders attached to selected television receivers whereas Viewtally uses logbooks which selected respondents complete in questionnaire form. Despite such differences of technique, the trend indicators reported by both Neeiser and Viewtally were almost identical in quarterly comparisons during the last calendar year. For week-by-week indices, Neeiser, of course, provided more nearly current data; details are discussed in the Delacorte memo previously cited by this proposal.

For the first, second, and third quarters of the current calendar year, Neeiser and Viewtally agreed upon the following:

ANS had seven of the ten "most watched" prime-time shows. CBN had two. NBS had one.

The ANS quarterly rating was 17.5, compared to 15.4 for CBN and 15 for NBS. Interpretation of survey analysts: In an average prime-time minute during the survey period, 17.5 percent of U.S. homes with television sets were receiving ANS programs. CBN and NBS each had two shows at the bottom of the ratings; ANS had none.

    (6) Nonetheless, program viewership is a basis upon which commercial messages attract viewers generally; therefore the proposed scope of this study seems appropriate to its research purpose.

    (7) "Saturation" effect of the scheduled Metrico advertising campaign is a major variable. Viewers are accustomed to a variety of sponsors and of commercial messages during the 35-hour broadcast period during which Metrico announcements are to be concentrated on ANS Television Network. As you instructed last Friday during our conference, that variable is acknowledged but excluded from further details of this particular work plan. My understanding is that B. J. Reyes of your office has your authorization to evaluate the planned Metrico commercials and the probable effects of their being presented in "saturation" campaign format.

b. Tentative Conclusions. This research project will probably yield the following conclusions about Metrico-ANS "target" telecast period:

    (1) ANS programs will attract more viewers than will programs on the other commercial TV networks.

    (2) Metrico commercial messages will have optimal opportunities for retaining a majority of the ANS-TV viewers.

    (3) These conclusions tentatively summarize effects for the total campaign period (January 23-29). Viewership statistics for time slots within that period probably will dip and then rise again between first and last nights of the the campaign.

c. Tentative Recommendations. Results of this proposed study should be consolidated with the Reyes' analysis of Metrico commercial messages and of probable "saturation" effects. Subject to your approval, these consolidated research efforts and those of the ANS-TV Network should be coordinated with our advertising agency operations for mutual benefit in present and future planning.

d. Study Order. Proposed project requires identification, evaluation, and projection of coverage/share programming probabilities on the three major television networks during the Metrico target period.

    (1) Sources. Relevant rating surveys, their evaluation and constructive critique as reported in the Delacorte memo, and industry forecasts for new target-period programs will yield data for this research. Survey administrators and Delacorte will be interviewed for complementary data if necessary.

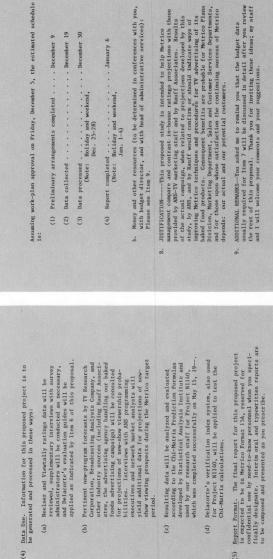

(4) _Data Use_. Information for this proposed project is to be generated and processed in these ways:

   (a) Neelser and Vieotally ratings data will be reviewed, supplementary interviews with survey administrators will be conducted as necessary, and Delacorte's evaluation guides will be applied as indicated by Item 6 of this proposal.

   (b) Pertinent new-program forecasts by TV Research Corporation, Broadcasting Analysis Company, and other industry sources (including Rauff Associates, the advertising agency handling our baked foods advertising campaign) will be consulted for projections of new-show viewership probabilities. Interviews with ANS programming executives and network market analysts will yield additional data for projections of new-show viewing prospects during the Metrico target period.

   (c) Resulting data will be analyzed and evaluated according to the Chi-Matrix Prediction Formulas developed by Statistical Analysis Institute and used by our research staff for Project N1140, which was completed successfully on May 15, 19—.

   (d) Delacorte's verification index system, also used for Project N1140, will be applied to test the Chi-Matrix calculations.

(5) _Report Format_. The final report for this proposed project is expected to be in Metrico Format 15A, reserved for confidential use by need-to-know personnel whom you specifically designate. Interim oral and typewritten reports are to be composed and presented as you prescribe.

7. SCHEDULE AND BUDGET——The following estimates are based upon resources normally available to this office.

a. _Time_ (for major phases, in weeks):

   (1) Preliminary arrangements following work-plan approval . . ½
   (2) Data collection, including interviews if necessary . . 1½
   (3) Data processing (analysis, synthesis, interpretation). . 1
   (4) Report production (outlining, drafting, revising, editing, presenting) 1

   Total 4

Assuming work-plan approval on Friday, December 5, the estimated schedule is:

   (1) Preliminary arrangements completed . . . . December 9
   (2) Data collected . . . . December 19
   (3) Data processed . . . . December 30
       (Note: Holiday and weekend, Dec. 25-28)
   (4) Report completed . . . . January 6
       (Note: Holiday and weekend, Jan. 1-4)

b. Money and other resources (to be determined in conferences with you, with budget director, and with head of administrative services): Please see Item 9.

8. JUSTIFICATION——This proposed study is intended to help Metrico management compare and contrast in-house ratings projections with those provided by ANS-TV marketing staff and by Rauff Associates. Results of the actual campaign, when related to projections developed by this study, by ANS, and by Rauff would confirm or should indicate ways of improving Metrico techniques and procedures for TV advertising of its baked food products. Consequent benefits are probable for Metrico Plans Division, Marketing Department, Sales and Customer Services Departments, and for those upon whose satisfaction the continuing success of Metrico depends: our actual and our potential customers.

9. ADDITIONAL REMARKS——You asked me to remind you that the budget data usually required for Item 7 will be discussed in detail after you review the rest of this proposal. Thank you for inviting these ideas; my staff and I will welcome your comments and your suggestions.

QUESTIONNAIRES AND INTERVIEWS

Questionnaires and interviews are data-collection tools for business researchers. The written questionnaire is usually less expensive to use than is its oral counterpart. The questionnaire is easy to administer, merely handed or mailed to intended respondents, and usually distributed to many people simultaneously. Face-to-face or telephone interviews require considerable time to conduct, and time is costly in business. But interviews have these advantages over questionnaires:

1. Because many people consider speaking to be easier than writing, they may respond more freely to an interview than to a questionnaire.

2. When a question or a response needs clarifying, interviews can permit such clarification immediately.

3. Especially during a face-to-face interview, not only the respondent's words but also the *behavior while responding* can be perceived, thereby enhancing evaluation of the information given to the researcher.

Like other data-collection instruments, questionnaires and interviews also share disadvantages. Respondents may provide inaccurate or unreliable data. For example, they may tend to recall an event as they *wish* that event had happened instead of as it did. Moreover, because people are apt to report their values and behavior favorably at the expense of accuracy, questionnaires and interviews rarely yield completely objective data.

But when designed and administered by communicators who are knowledgeable about people and words, questionnaires and interviews can elicit data that might otherwise be unobtainable or prohibitively expensive to collect.

The questionnaire procedure shown on page 372 can be used for interviews as well. Just substitute *interview* for *questionnaire* in Steps 1-9. Then follow those steps to produce a list of questions for each of your oral respondents. Finally, relate Step 10 to your oral presentation of the transmitted message as well as to the questions you ask.

TRANSMITTAL MESSAGE

To present the questionnaire or to introduce the interview, a transmittal message is usually arranged according to the familiar AIDA sequence of *a*ttention-*in*terest-*d*esire-*a*ction:

1. Attract the respondent's appropriate *attention* to the questionnaire or interview.
2. Impel relevant *interest*.
3. Develop *desire* to respond.
4. State confidently and courteously the appropriate *action* for the respondent (participation through the questionnaire or interview).

STEPS FOR DEVELOPING AN EFFECTIVE QUESTIONNAIRE AND TRANSMITTAL MESSAGE [1]

1. **IDENTIFY** the purpose of the questionnaire. (What is your objective for asking the questions? What is your respondent's objective for answering?)

2. **JUSTIFY** the use of the questionnaire. (Why should you prefer this kind of data-collection message rather than another instrument? Why should your respondent invest time and effort in answering?)

3. **ANTICIPATE** the kinds of data that the questionnaire should elicit. (What sort of information pertains to the purpose? What kind of data are you seeking? What kind of data is your respondent likely to give?)

4. **DESIGN** an appropriate questionnaire format. (How should you arrange the items so that they are convenient to answer? How should you word the items so that they are pertinent and clear? How should you logically and psychologically move your reader from simple to complex issues? How should you organize the items so that answers are easy to classify, record, and analyze?)

5. **DRAFT** the questionnaire and transmittal message. (What written statements should represent effective answers for Steps 1-4 in this procedure?)

6. **REVISE** the draft of your questionnaire and transmittal message. (What logical, psychological, and linguistic aspects of the draft should be corrected or refined?)

7. **PRETEST** the draft of your questionnaire and transmittal message. (What changes should you make after trying the revised draft with people who resemble your intended respondents but who are not to be included in your actual survey?)

8. **EDIT** the revised and pretested draft. (Which of the changes that Step 7 disclosed as necessary or appropriate should you incorporate with your materials?)

9. **PRODUCE** and **PROOFREAD** the edited, revised, and pretested materials. (What attributes, derived from Steps 1-8, should the copies of your final questionnaire and transmittal message convey?)

10. **DISTRIBUTE** copies of the final questionnaire and transmittal message. (What schedule should you follow so that your respondents can answer in time for you to use their information effectively? What postage medium—first class, special delivery, certified mail, registered mail—should you use? Or if you are not mailing the materials, when and how should you otherwise distribute and collect them?)

[1] This procedure can be easily modified for interview surveys.

metrico, inc.
Research Services Division • One Metrico Plaza • Chicago, IL 60602

February 4, 19--

Save your time and
Conserve your effort
Through Project CPM--

Dear Co-Worker

Your talents and skills have enabled all of us in Research Services
to meet increased work loads successfully. You have earned the admiration and respect of the entire Metrico organization for your
dedication and your expertise. Additional challenges are coming our
way. With them will be new opportunities for career advancement.

With your help we can plan now to make the best use of time and effort
in fulfilling those career opportunities.

You're right; I'm referring to the Critical Path Method surveys which
were discussed at our last staff meeting. And I'm requesting your
wholehearted cooperation with Project CPM, which begins this week.

Specially trained CPM analysts will be asking us to complete detailed
questionnaires and follow-up interviews about our work needs. Those
analysts recognize that only you and your colleagues in this Division
can supply the information and guidance necessary to develop a CPM
system which will help us all. Please keep that thought in mind as you
share your constructive insight through the questionnaires and interviews.

The first of those questionnaires--a preliminary personnel survey form--
accompanies this message. To be sure that your views do influence the
outcome of Project CPM, please complete and return the enclosed material
to your section chief by noon this Friday, February 8.

Yours for mutually profitable teamwork

V. J. Cioffi, Manager

jd

Enclosure

AN INTRACOMPANY TRANSMITTAL MESSAGE

Please help us know you better. By learning more about you and our other Metrico customers, we can economize advertising costs and pass the savings along for future purchases. Just take a moment to complete and mail this card. We'll pay the postage, and you'll have our thanks.

Mr. Ms. Mrs. Miss _____

(Last Name)   (First)   (Middle)

Address _____

City _____ State _____ Zip _____

Seller's Name _____ City/State _____

Date of Purchase _____ Product & Price _____

Your Occupation (check at least one, please)

Construction/Building Trades ☐   Communication Media ☐

Science/Technology/Research ☐   Educational Services ☐

Marketing/Advertising/Sales ☐   Government Services ☐

Management/Administration ☐   Other (please specify) _____ ☐

Your Annual Income   Under $4999 ☐ $5000-9999 ☐   Over $10,000 ☐

Your Age   Under 18 ☐   18-21 ☐   Over 21 ☐   Male ☐   Female ☐

CONSUMER QUESTIONNAIRE
(in postage-paid reply-card form)

Your answers will help provide articles and features of continuing interest to you and to your family. Please check the appropriate boxes.

1. Which of these hobbies interest you and your family?

    Cooking ☐   Gardening ☐   Home Repair/Redecorating ☐

    Arts and Crafts ☐   Other (please specify) _____

2. What kinds of music do you and your family enjoy?

    Big Band ☐   Country/Western ☐   Rock ☐   Classical ☐

    Other (please specify) _____

3. What subjects do you and your family like to discuss?

    Current Events ☐   History ☐   Philosophy/Religion ☐

    Performing Arts ☐   Science ☐   Sports/Athletics ☐

    Other (please specify) _____

CONSUMER QUESTIONNAIRE
(printed as part of a magazine subscription form)

Transcon
Airways Corporation

Flight No._____

DATE _____

I am traveling your Transcon Superjet Service from _____

to_____. Scheduled departure time:_____.

Actual departure time:_____. Estimated arrival time:_____.

Purpose of trip: Business ☐   Pleasure ☐   Other (please specify)

_____

I learned of your Superjet Service from: Travel Agent ☐   TV ☐   Radio ☐

   Newspaper ☐   Magazine ☐   Other (please specify)_____

I rate your Superjet Service as: Excellent ☐   Good ☐   Fair ☐   Poor ☐

My name and address:_____

_____. My telephone number:_____.

Additional comments:_____

_____

_____

(Please complete and give this card to your flight attendant.)

Thank You for Flying Transcon Superjet!

CONSUMER QUESTIONNAIRE
(handed to airline passengers)

CONSTRUCTIVE ATTITUDES TOWARD RESEARCH PLANNING

The temptation to begin composing a report without adequate research planning can be strong. But surrendering to that temptation may cause needless waste of time, money, and effort. Guide yourself with these insights:

1. Your research and your report are not identical. Each must be planned separately.
2. *Research* is an activity; *reports* communicate the nature and results of that activity.
3. Research *produces* reports. Plan the details of your research first. After your plan has been approved or modified, *apply* it to your phases of data collection, analysis, synthesis, interpretation, and evaluation.

Then—and, logically, not until then—will you be prepared to outline the first draft of your report. With this kind of detailed research planning as a foundation of your work, you can proceed to developing report outlines, drafts, and final presentations with proficiency and with confidence.

You may need to prepare several versions of your first work plan before your proposal is approved. Welcome opportunities for revision when necessary and appropriate. Improving a work plan is certainly better than having to rewrite—or to risk rejection of—your final report. You will discover that the more detailed your work plan becomes, the easier will be the phases of data collection, data processing, and final composition.

As you formulate your plan, be sure to anticipate *sources* of the data your research requires. Among those sources are the following:

1. Publications (books, magazines, newspapers, journals, pamphlets)

2. Company Records (correspondence, unpublished reports, policy statements, procedural descriptions, other documents)

3. Direct Observations of Behavior

4. Questionnaire and Interview Surveys

5. Scientifically Controlled Experiments and Discussions

Your work-plan statements of authorization, scope, limitations, schedule, and budget will help you decide upon the kinds and numbers of sources to use. And H. Webster Johnson's *How to Use the Business Library* (4th ed.; Cincinnati: South-Western Publishing Co., 1972) is a useful reference for your data-collection efforts.

By tapping appropriate sources according to your work plan, you will accumulate data. By constantly reminding yourself of authorization, purpose, scope, limitations, schedule, budget, and justification, you will process only pertinent data. The data processing for your project may include manual, mechanical, or electronic techniques. But whatever the techniques may be, your research requires these actions: analysis, synthesis, and interpretation.

When you *analyze*, you separate data into parts. When you *synthesize*, you arrange those parts into patterns which pertain to your research purpose, scope, and limitations. When you *interpret*, you relate your research discoveries to information that is already known. Whereas data *collection* will yield information for your entire report, data *processing* (analysis, synthesis, interpretation) will yield information particularly for the discussion, conclusions, and recommendations sections of your report. Composing that report is the topic of the next chapter.[1]

REVIEW AND TRANSITION

The research-planning *process* described in Chapter 18 involves development of a work plan for communicating details of your proposed project. You may be required to revise the initial plan. You may need to submit progress or interim reports as you collect and process your data or adapt your tentative conclusions. Your employer may authorize the work plan and subsequent reports to be presented orally, but you should keep written versions for your own file unless your employer forbids that practice. Such written versions can be useful as text or as notes for an oral report; they also provide a record of your work. After having collected, analyzed, synthesized, and interpreted the pertinent data that are related to your research purpose, scope, and limitations, you will be ready to compose and present your final report, as described in Chapter 19.

DISCUSSION QUESTIONS

A. In what ways are Chapters 6, 7, and 18 especially related to one another?

B. What are the communication relationships between a research work plan and a report outline?

C. In what ways are statements of "scope" and "limitations" related?

D. What are the advantages and disadvantages of using questionnaires and interviews as data-collection tools?

E. In what ways is the comprehensive model of a work plan, as presented in Chapter 18, applicable to your actual research assignments for an employer or a professor?

APPLICATIONS

The following study topics are clustered in two groups.

The first group is a sample of research projects which involve data sources

---

[1] Thanks to Dr. Zelda W. Jefferson, Texas Southern University, for her helpful comments concerning this chapter.

easily available to you at your school. Your selection or adaptation of a topic from this first group requires authorization by your professor and by other persons whom your professor may designate.

The second group is a sample of actual communication problems often confronting a real business firm (identified here as "XYZ Company"). If you are employed while attending school, consider using or adapting topics from this second group. Projects based upon this group require authorization by your professor, by other campus authorities concerned, and by your employer.

When you write your research proposal for a topic in either of the two groups, follow these suggestions:

1. Reword the topic to suit *your* circumstances. Because this book is used by many people in various situations, the topics are worded somewhat generally. As explained by Chapter 18, *limit* the scope of your topic so that your research will be valid and reliable but manageable.

2. For controlling data-source use, your professor may restrict you to published materials only. Otherwise, again as indicated by Chapter 18, consider using publications and other valuable aids, such as the following:
   a. unpublished documents—e.g., relevant master's theses, doctoral dissertations, records or reports supplied by your employer and which you get permission to use.
   b. interviews and questionnaires which you design, pretest, and, if necessary, revise before using—but only with permission of all people concerned.
   c. your own scientifically controlled observations or experiments—again only with permission of all people concerned.

Remember that Chapter 18 focuses your attention upon details of planning, proposing, and developing the research *process*. Chapter 19 focuses your attention upon the product of that process; that product is your research *report*.

GROUP A TOPICS

1. Specifically, how am I managing my time, effort, and other resources while attending school? What, if anything, should I do to improve that management? Why? What challenges to my communication abilities are disclosed by my answers to those questions?

2. In what ways should I improve my ability to perceive, interpret, recall, or evaluate my own and other people's communications?

3. In what ways should I improve my ability to observe, listen, read, speak, write, or communicate nonverbally?

4. What career should I follow after earning my diploma or degree? Why? What employment opportunities probably will be available to me then? What employment opportunities are available to me while I attend school? What placement services does my school offer me? What other forms of career assistance (aptitude tests, other psychological inventories, etc.) does my school provide? Which of these aids should I use? Why?

5. In what ways are academic needs similar and different for students who are unemployed, employed part time, or employed full time? To what extent do, or should, the needs of working students affect academic requirements at my school? What communications do I perceive as necessary among working students and their employers, professors, and academic administrators?

6. Of total costs for educating students at my school, how much is actually provided by tuition or student fees? What sources provide additional necessary funds? What effect does this information have upon my evaluation of my education? What changes of attitude, if any, does that evaluation produce within me?

7. In what ways does my study of business communications relate to my study of other business subjects? of liberal arts? of fine arts? of physical or social sciences? of theory-oriented courses? of skills-oriented courses?

8. Which campus organizations, if any, should I join? In what organizational programs or projects should I participate? To what extent? Why?

9. Excluding the people in my communications course, whom do I consider an excellent communicator? Why? Of the traits and techniques demonstrated by that communicator, which do I need to develop in myself? Specifically, how and why should I develop them? Which should I not develop? Why?

10. To what extent can I integrate the research-and-reporting requirements of my communications course with those of another course in which I am presently enrolled? For example, does my professor of accounting (or of finance, marketing, management, administrative services, etc.) require a research project? If so, to what extent may I work with that professor *and* with my business communication professor on a single research project? Will the business communication professor guide and evaluate my *communication techniques*—and will the other professor guide and evaluate my *research content*—for the single project? Will I thereby be permitted to earn credit for that project in both courses? What arrangements need to be made for forming such a student-and-faculty team? To what extent and why should I participate in making those arrangements?

GROUP B TOPICS

1. Who at XYZ Company are real-life models of success in my career field? What are their definitions of success? What is (or are) mine? In what ways are my traits, skills, education, and experience like and unlike those of my models? What circumstances account for the similarities and the differences between me and my models? What implications for my own career development does this research disclose? To what extent, if any, is it necessary or advisable for my qualifications to resemble or differ from those of my models?

2. What fringe benefits should XYZ Company provide for its employees? When ? Why?

3. Where should XYZ Company locate its plant? its offices? its other facilities? When? Why?

4. At XYZ Company where do responsibility and authority coincide? Where are they separated and what explains the separations? What are their consequences? What, if anything, justifies them?

5. At XYZ Company where, when, why, and how is unofficial communication more effective than official communication? What are the consequences? What communication changes, if any, should be made? By whom? Involving whom?

6. When and why should XYZ Company expand, add, reduce, or close organizational units?

7. When should XYZ Company introduce a new product or service to a particular market? How? Why?

8. Why did XYZ Company profits decline, rise, or remain stable during a given period?

9. Why should XYZ Company own rather than lease, or why should it lease rather than own, particular equipment or facilities?

10. Specifically, how should XYZ Company minimize its maintenance and repair costs? expand its customer services? improve its safety practices? its merchandising programs? inventory controls? sales promotions? collection procedures? purchasing procedures? production procedures? records management? administrative services? communication systems?

CHAPTER 19

Business Reports

What is a business report? In what ways are business reports classified? What are their uses and traits? Answers to these and to related questions are discussed in this chapter.

USE AND CLASSIFICATION

The basic use of a business report is to convey information for making decisions. Report styles and formats vary greatly; they may be written, oral, or multimedia messages. But whatever their manner or means of communication, business reports can be conveniently classified according to these traits:

1. **PREDOMINANCE OF WORDS OR OF NUMBERS.** *Narrative reports* use more words than numbers. *Statistical reports* use more numbers than words.

2. **INTERVALS OF TRANSMISSION.** *Periodic reports* are issued regularly (for example, weekly, monthly, annually). *Progress* (or *interim*) reports occur occasionally between start and finish of a project or of an operation. *Special reports* are sent irregularly in response to nonroutine requests or needs.

3. **DIRECTIONS OF TRANSMISSION FLOW.** *Horizontal reports* move among levels of equal authority within an organization. *Vertical reports* move between superior and subordinate levels. *Radial reports* cut across levels of authority and may move outside or within an organization.

4. **CONTEXTS.** *Technical reports* use specialized vocabularies to convey information among specialists with similar training and experience. *Nontechnical reports* use ordinary words to convey information to people with dissimilar training and experience. Classification by *field* or *subject* (for instance, "production report," "sales report") also characterizes the message according to its *context*.

5. **MESSAGE STYLE.** *Chronological style* presents information according to the sequence in which events occurred. *Logical style* arranges information in patterns of deliberate reasoning (for example, patterns of induction, deduction, comparison, contrast, elimination of alternatives). *Psychological style* accommodates the receiver's preferences or idiosyncracies by arranging information according to the receiver's special demands, needs, or wishes.

6. **MESSAGE FUNCTIONS.** *Informational* (or *fact-finding*) *reports* present data but omit comments. *Research reports* deal with the quest for knowledge ("basic" or "pure" research) and with practical uses of knowledge ("applied" research). *Analytical reports* (including "examination," "investigation," and "recommendation" reports) formulate an issue or identify a problem; analyze, synthesize, and interpret pertinent data; present logical conclusions; and often offer recommendations for appropriate action.

Here are examples:

SECTION OF A PERIODIC REPORT

The advancement of women and members of minority groups to positions of higher skill and higher levels of responsibility has shown an 8% increase over last year. These positions are primarily in the management, professional, and technical areas. Table I on page 3 shows the percentage of total female and minority employees in each job category.

Efforts to place male and female employees into nontraditional jobs are also progressing satisfactorily. Employment of males into office and clerical positions is 5 percent greater than last year. Additionally, an 8 percent increase of female employees into skilled and semiskilled positions previously held by males has been realized this year.

SECTION OF A PROGRESS REPORT

Valley Cablevision had a gain of about 2,500 new customers during the first six months of this year as compared with a gain of 1,452 during the first six months of 19—. During the second quarter of this year the gain was about 625, as contrasted with 500 for the corresponding period last year. The average number of Valley Cablevision customers during the first six months of 19— was 5.1 percent greater than for the corresponding period of 19—.

An Earnings Report of the Company for the three-month and twelve-month periods ending June 30, 19—, and for corresponding periods ending June 30, 19—, is appended.

SECTION OF A RESEARCH REPORT

Table II on page 8 compares the performance of materials used in home construction for insulating ceilings, walls, and floors. These results are measured in terms of R-value (thermal resistance to heat flowing out in winter and flowing in during summer). The higher the R-value, the more effective is the insulation.

Before June 15 most of the material used was blanket insulation with a value of R-22. After June 15, blanket insulation was continued for floor insulation, but loose-fill insulation (Cellulate) with a value of R-25 was used for ceilings and walls.

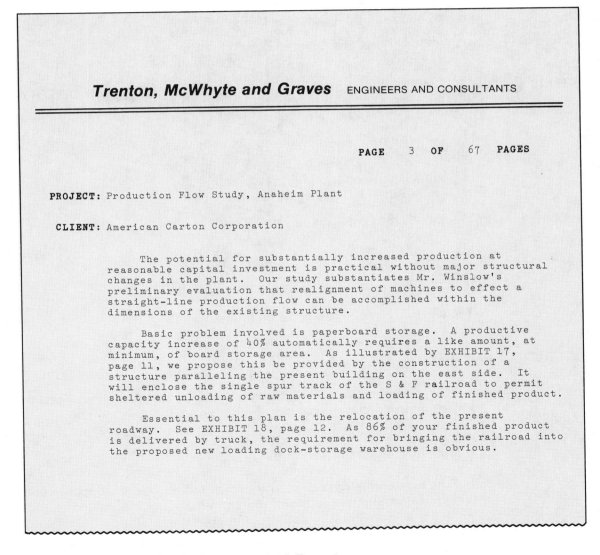

Trenton, McWhyte and Graves ENGINEERS AND CONSULTANTS

PAGE   3   OF   67   PAGES

PROJECT: Production Flow Study, Anaheim Plant

CLIENT: American Carton Corporation

The potential for substantially increased production at reasonable capital investment is practical without major structural changes in the plant. Our study substantiates Mr. Winslow's preliminary evaluation that realignment of machines to effect a straight-line production flow can be accomplished within the dimensions of the existing structure.

Basic problem involved is paperboard storage. A productive capacity increase of 40% automatically requires a like amount, at minimum, of board storage area. As illustrated by EXHIBIT 17, page 11, we propose this be provided by the construction of a structure paralleling the present building on the east side. It will enclose the single spur track of the S & F railroad to permit sheltered unloading of raw materials and loading of finished product.

Essential to this plan is the relocation of the present roadway. See EXHIBIT 18, page 12. As 86% of your finished product is delivered by truck, the requirement for bringing the railroad into the proposed new loading dock-storage warehouse is obvious.

Section of a Recommendation (Analytical) Report

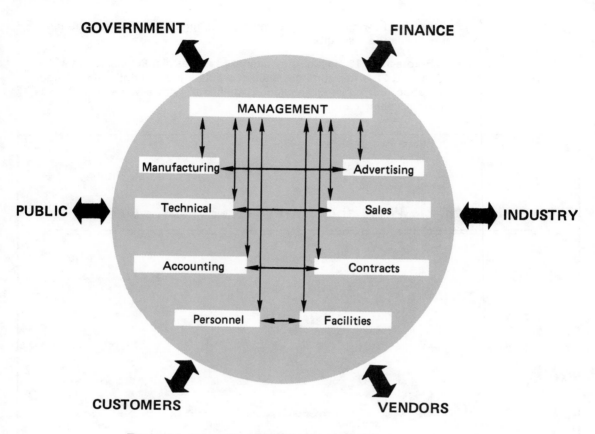

Typical Information Flow in Large Industry

DIRECTION AND FLOW

The communication flow of reporting, represented by the diagram above, merits special comment.[1]

Horizontal Information Flow

The *manufacturing* section of the large industry (inside upper left of the circle diagram) produces periodic reports dealing with materials and

---

[1] The discussion of horizontal, vertical, and radial information flow with the circle diagram is based on an analysis by Warren W. Wood, Aerophysics Section, Convair, Division of General Dynamics, Fort Worth, Texas.

processes. Some reports propose new procedures; others discuss current manufacturing methods and materials.

The *facilities* section (inside lower right of the circle diagram) produces reports that inform management and the other sections of the status of buildings, equipment, and space. On the basis of these reports, the rest of the industrial team can adjust plans and schedules to fit these controlling factors.

The *contracts* section issues reports interpreting or giving opinions on contracts and various other legal matters.

The *sales* department makes periodic reports of sales information and also may conduct market research, including customer surveys.

The *advertising* section produces similar reports about surveys of public opinion, of markets, of mass communication media, and the like. It also produces periodic reports (summarizing advertising costs and volume) for use by the accounting section and by top management.

When reports move within a single organizational unit, such as the personnel unit, or among units of equal status in the total organization, as in Personnel and Facilities, the direction of these reports is said to be horizontal. Think of horizontal reports, therefore, as flowing *along* one organizational level rather than *between* superior and subordinate levels. Senders and receivers of horizontal-flow messages often share similar backgrounds of education and experience. Their communications to one another include special vocabularies, symbols, allusions, and references that could be unfamiliar or even misleading if transmitted as parts of a vertical or a radial information flow.

Vertical Information Flow

Information that passes *between the functional sections* (the eight blocks within the circle) and *top management* is regarded as having vertical movement. The flow is both up and down, with most of the section reports ascending to the management executives and with directives descending to the sections.

During this vertical movement, there is a marked shift in how a report is read. For example, at the operating level on the factory floor, in the tooling sections, or at the assembly lines, a report is valued primarily for its technical content. But as it "ascends" through the various levels of administration, it is valued more for its financial and management information. A new production-design proposal, for instance, might be the subject of an enthusiastic report with favorable recommendations at the operating level, but could be thrown out at the top management level because the new design proves costly to produce or because its profit potential is small.

Radial Information Flow

Distributed around the outside of the circle diagram on page 386 are six important elements: government, public, customers, vendors, industry, and finance. These elements overlap, but they also express the need for outside communication.

The *government* is vitally involved in communication with business. Industry has had to devise methods of reporting wages and hours, unionization, strategic materials and equipment, taxation, and the issuance of securities. Reports flow both ways as industry supplies such information and as government agencies direct, interpret, and otherwise respond.

The *public* is the obvious source of sales revenue, of labor, and of investment capital. Hence, the annual report is as much intended to gain favorable response among the public as among financiers. Other reports cover charitable and educational efforts, human-interest situations involving people and products of the company, and the like.

Customers are prime receivers of periodic reports, policy statements, contractual material, production and design data, manuals, parts lists, specifications, and related technical material.

Vendors (manufacturing subcontractors and suppliers of such equipment as business machines and machine tools) participate in this information-and-report flow. For example, in a recent annual report, one company mentions dealing with 42,000 vendors. The reports supporting such a far-flung effort include technical documents, research data, specifications, design proposals, drawings, contracts, policy statements, and various periodic reports. Reports generate questions, modifications, revisions, additions, and comments which add to the flow of radial information.

Industry increasingly shares information concerning technological developments, manufacturing methods, accounting procedures, materials choice, and management techniques. Much of this information appears in service reports and in similar documents designed for circulation within industrial associations. Related industries issue joint policy reports concerning common problems.

Finally, *finance* participates in the communication flow through prospectus reports, production reports, and various other messages issued to stockholders, creditors, and other concerned persons or groups.

Look again at the circle diagram (page 386) to visualize the information-and-report flow inside and outside a major business enterprise. In the lower half of the circle, you see representative sections that are likely to share information among themselves through report exchanges (*horizontal distribution*). Above these sections is top management which in turn publishes for, and receives reports from, the subordinate sections (*vertical distribution*). Immediately outside the circle are representative and highly important areas that both receive and produce reports (*radial distribution*).

The "flow tracks" are interwoven throughout the diagram. Besides the indicated channels, reports may also flow between any other pair of elements shown on the chart.

As a business reporter, you will be expected to accommodate your receiver's needs and preferences. You may be asked for summaries, which are also called synopses, abstracts, epitomes, digests, or précis, to accompany or to circulate separately from your complete reports. You will realize that physical attributes such as mechanical layout, headings and subheadings, illustrations, colors, and other devices for attention, interest, and emphasis affect message reception. You will discover that oral reports in the forms of face-to-face and telephone conversations, interviews, conferences, forums, and other vocal exchanges are frequent. Often your reports will be *combinations* of oral and written messages. As an effective business communicator, you also will be concerned with information retrieval and records management involving the use, control, storage, reuse, retention, and disposal of your reports.

REPORT TRENDS

Although classifications are diverse, two trends are prominent in modern business reporting. Awareness of these trends can help you plan, produce, and use reports effectively.

Informalizing

Increasingly, modern managers require clearly understandable language rather than stilted language for reports. Many business firms send a special report to employees or give them a copy of the report sent to stockholders. Illustrating the "conversational" trend is the Mead Corporation Annual Report, Employee's Edition, which is shown on page 390.

Visualizing

Modern business reporters use charts, graphs, diagrams, and tables to picture ideas. Some companies enliven the pages of their reports with photographs of what is underway in manufacturing, sales promotion, and research. Other firms issue supplementary picture-surveys of operations. Pictures, graphs, bar charts, maps, tables, blueprints, drawings, rough sketches, diagrams, and other pictorial devices dramatize information for business reports. Illustrative examples are located on the following pages.

TO ALL MEAD EMPLOYEES AND THEIR FAMILIES

You did it again! You manufactured and sold almost $548 million worth of paper, paperboard, and converted products. That's 8% higher than last year.

Your efforts showed up even more in our earnings picture: up 15% to $20.6 million. And wages, salaries, and benefits for employees were up too, to a new high of $127 million. I'm proud of our record last year, and I want to thank all of you for your efforts achieving this excellent showing.

In previous progress reports, you were told where Mead stands and how each of us can contribute to its growth. This year we are going to tell you about our benefit program, our safety record, our efforts in air and water quality, and other important aspects of our company.

I SAW MY DOLLARS AT WORK

All shareowners wonder how the company is handling their investments. Here's one who investigated. The twist in this case: the shareowner is also an employee. *"Walking into No. 5 machine room was like going into tomorrow! I'd never seen such a big paper machine. I was told that this was just one of many new pieces of equipment and plants being built in the Corporation with money invested by shareowners like me. This is called capital expenditure, and it's necessary to keep our plants modern and efficient."*

WHEN YOU NEED IT, IT'S THERE

Last year the Mead group insurance plan paid $3,518,338 for employees and dependents who met medical and other emergencies, and the Mead Retirement Plan added 175 new names to make a total of 1,350 getting monthly checks. Here are a few who have learned when you need help, it's there. *"The operation I had last September put me back in good health, but it also ran up a lot of bills. The Mead group insurance came through in a big way to pay the expenses."*

ANYONE CAN UNDERSTAND A FINANCIAL STATEMENT

When Mead's treasurer and controller start talking about how the company is doing, what they have to say is lively, important, as well as easy to understand.

Sections of an Annual Report to Employees

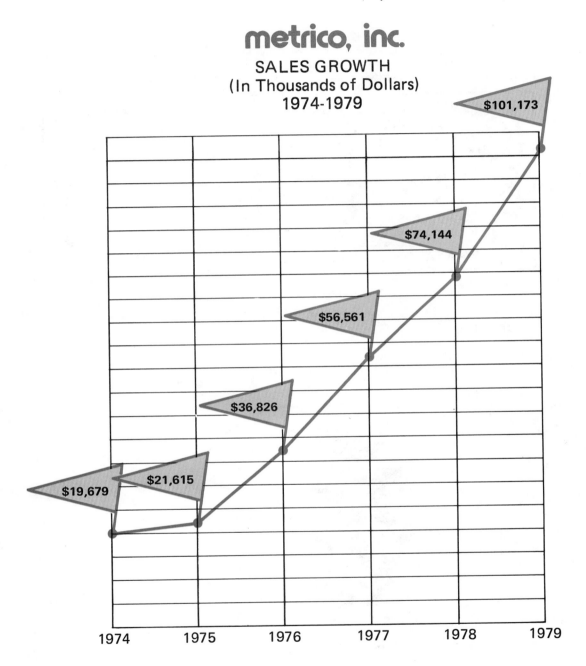

metrico, inc.
SALES GROWTH
(In Thousands of Dollars)
1974-1979

$101,173

$74,144

$56,561

$36,826

$21,615

$19,679

1974   1975   1976   1977   1978   1979

Charts, Graphs, and Diagrams are Often Called
"Figures" in Business Reports.

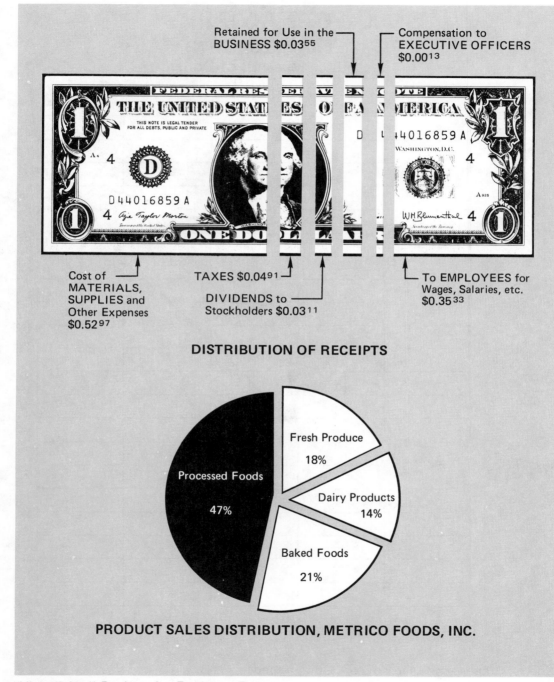

Retained for Use in the BUSINESS $0.03⁵⁵

Compensation to EXECUTIVE OFFICERS $0.00¹³

Cost of MATERIALS, SUPPLIES and Other Expenses $0.52⁹⁷

TAXES $0.04⁹¹

DIVIDENDS to Stockholders $0.03¹¹

To EMPLOYEES for Wages, Salaries, etc. $0.35³³

DISTRIBUTION OF RECEIPTS

Fresh Produce 18%

Dairy Products 14%

Processed Foods 47%

Baked Foods 21%

PRODUCT SALES DISTRIBUTION, METRICO FOODS, INC.

"Visualizing" Devices for Business Reports

FORMAL WRITTEN PRESENTATIONS

Although you may modify or adapt these guides, the comprehensive model of a complete, full-length report has the following parts:

A. Preliminaries

1. Cover or binder
2. Flyleaves
3. Title page
4. Authorization message
   Acceptance message
   Transmittal message

7. Receipt or approval message
8. Table of contents
9. List of tables or figures
10. Foreword or preface
11. Acknowledgments
12. Synopsis

troduction
cussion
lusions (and, when appropriate, recommendations)

nts

phy

items that supply a physical vehicle for the
xt for fully appreciating the body as well as

olds and protects the pages of the report,
le and the author's name. If the title is
sion may appear on the cover or binder.
ed.

pages and provide room for the
one blank sheet at the front and
rea   ort.
anot   report, identifies the principal
Th   submission of the report. A
reader   the front or back of the title
copyright
page.

The *autho*   dum) gives evidence of
permission for   authorization message
may be circulated   gives evidence of
The *acceptance*   the acceptance
agreement to underta
message may be circula

The *transmittal message* (letter or memorandum) presents the report and reinforces goodwill with the reader.

The *receipt or approval message* (letter, memorandum, or even a stamped notation on the front flyleaf of title page) gives evidence of the report's delivery or endorsement.

The *table of contents*, which occupies at least one page, represents the chapter or section titles, headings, and subheadings.

The *list of tables or figures* (including illustrations), which occupies at least one page, represents the visual aids that the report contains. Traditionally, Roman numerals are assigned to tables, while Arabic numerals represent figures as well as charts and graphs. Customarily, the list of tables precedes the list of figures. If your report contains relatively few visual aids, you may call this page a "List of Illustrations" and divide the list, with one part for tables and one part for figures.

The *foreword or preface*, which often is omitted when the transmittal message is bound with the rest of the report, supplies special details that may stimulate the reader's attention and interest.

Like the foreward or preface, the acknowledgments section, which gives credit to persons or groups that have particularly aided the researcher, is often replaced today by the bound transmittal message.

The *synopsis* (also called a summary, an abstract, a précis, a digest, or an epitome) recapitulates the purpose, results, and methods of the study. Although copies of the synopsis may be circulated separately from the full document, a modern business report also contains a synopsis immediately preceding the body. The synopsis allows recipients to develop a context for appreciating the complete report and to decide whether or when to read the entire document.

Body

The *body* of a report is that portion which supplies specific and definite details of the study's introduction, discussion, conclusions, and (when appropriate) recommendations.

The *introduction*, which may require at least a chapter in a long report or at least a paragraph in a short report, customarily states purpose, scope, limitations, design, methodology, and justification of the study. It may include definitions of special terms and a review of previous findings.

The *discussion*, which constitutes the bulk of the report, provides analysis, synthesis, and interpretation. If the introduction omits a review of previous findings, the discussion usually presents that review as well as description and explanation of the present project.

Conclusions, which are not merely "endings" but, rather, logical "sums," state the results of the study. *Recommendations*, which appear when they have been requested or are otherwise appropriate, state how the conclusions should be used and what other studies should be undertaken or continued.

Supplements

Supplements to the report are materials that identify data sources and provide exhibits which, although related to the study, are too cumbersome or less than essential to be included elsewhere in the report.

The *bibliography* lists the data sources upon which the study rests. Literally, a bibliography is a list of books; but this term is used in business reporting to designate all relevant sources, including published and unpublished materials as well as respondents to questionnaires and interviews. The more nearly accurate word "sources" may replace the traditional term "bibliography" for business reports.

The *appendix* presents comments, tables, figures, exhibits, and other relevant materials that are omitted elsewhere in the report. If the appendix contains more than one item, the items may be called Exhibit 1, Exhibit 2, and so forth. If the supplements contain appendixes, the first may be called Appendix A; the second, Appendix B; and so on. Special Note: Sometimes an executive will prefer that the appendix *precede* the bibliography.

The *index*, which is used especially in long and published reports, helps the reader to find specific data quickly. The table of contents does list names and page numbers of major sections, but the index lists names and page numbers of minor items as well.

DEVELOPING MESSAGE FORMAT

The illustrations on the following pages of this chapter depict major parts of a written report arranged in common formats. A business report may be as brief as a single sentence or as long as a complete book. Whatever the length or type of your report, try to discover and accommodate the preferences of your employer or instructor. Remember that your job in business communication is to inform or persuade your readers or listeners. By working with the message format that they prefer, you are likely to establish or reinforce *rapport* for acceptance of your message.

Physical Layout for Written Reports

Whatever style you follow for a particular report, be *consistent* in your use of that style. For informal business reports, use margins of at least an inch on all sides. If the report is to be bound, allow an extra half inch at the binding edge (left or top). Use white space liberally; it tends to emphasize chapter or section titles, main headings, and subheadings, thereby guiding your reader quickly to the content and relative importance of your message parts. You may place headings and subheadings in the center of the page, flush with the left margin, or otherwise; but be consistent. If you capitalize every word in the first major heading, do so with every major heading. If you underline the first subheading of a group, do so with every equivalent subheading. Reserve at least two single-spaced blank lines immediately below every major heading and subheading (except, of course, for subheadings that are set into the body of a paragraph itself). Remember that although single spacing permits effective display of text, many executives prefer the reading ease which double spacing provides. Use *your reader's preferences* as guides to developing your report.

Guide List of Headings for a Long Report. On the opposite page is a list of headings which commonly appear in corporate annual reports.

Paging. Traditionally, Roman and Arabic numerals are used to number the pages of a long report. A series of lowercase Roman numerals begins with the title page and ends with the last preliminary page. A series of Arabic numerals begins with the first page of the body and ends immediately before the back flyleaf.

Customarily, the first page of a major unit such as the title page, the table of contents, the list of tables, the beginning of a chapter, or its equivalent is *counted* but not numbered. Such a page is included within the numbering sequence, but a numeral is not typed on that page. According to this custom, if Chapter I ends, for instance, on page nine (Arabic-numeral series), the first page of Chapter II is counted as page ten; but 10 does not appear. The second page of Chapter II would be counted and numbered as 11.

An alternative custom is to center the first page number of a major unit at the bottom of the sheet which begins the unit. Generally, however, both the Arabic and lowercase Roman numerals are placed flush with the right margin, about four single-line spaces from the top of the sheet. (When reviewing a report, the reader can find a particular page more quickly if the number appears in the upper right corner instead of elsewhere on the page.)

Division Sheets. Occasionally, an executive may require separation pages, or division sheets, immediately before the first page of a bibliography and of an appendix. A division sheet, which is counted but usually not numbered, shows BIBLIOGRAPHY, APPENDIX, APPENDIXES, or APPENDIX A, APPENDIX B, and so forth, centered and completely captialized.

Direct Quotations. A direct quotation that takes fewer than four lines is usually identified simply by quotation marks. A direct quotation that takes more than three lines is usually identified by five-space indention from both margins (or nine-space indention from the left margin only), single spacing, and the *absence* of quotation marks. The source of a direct quotation should be cited by a parenthetical statement within the text or by documentation in a footnote.

Guide List of Report Headings

Year-to-Year Comparisons

Sales	Dividends	Reserves	Market value
Earnings	Taxes	Financial progress	of stock

The Financial Story

Sales	Changes in officers	Supplies
Earnings	Exports and imports	New policies
Dividends	Research and engineering	Employee relations
Taxes	Inventories	Dealer relations
Reserves	Unfilled orders	Customer relations
Net worth	Capital requirements	Community relations
Industry position	Capital structure,	Anniversary milestones
Expansion of plant	changes	Contract obligations
New equipment	Capital investment	Legal actions
Subsidiaries	Investment per employee	General economic
Branches	Fixed assets	comments
Sales offices	Intangible assets	Market prospects
Changes in directors	Raw material sources	Future outlook

Financial Statistics

Sales	Auditor's certification	Working capital
Earnings	Financial position	Payroll
Dividends	Earned surplus statement	Investments
Taxes	Capital surplus statement	Depreciation, depletion
Balance sheet	Reserves	Value of properties
Operating statement	Income distribution	Nonoperating income
Notes to these	Capital spending	Net worth

The General Story

Brief company history
Company growth
Product history, growth
New product development
Production process
Sales promotion
Trademarks
Distribution channels
Plant location, size
General offices
Divisions, subsidiaries

Stockholder Statistics

Number, total
Preferred, common, number
Distribution (men, women)
Distribution (geographical)
Average holdings

Management

Organization chart
Biographical briefs of directors and officers

General Information

List of directors and officers
Executive committee
Stock transfer agents
Registrars
Dividend disbursing agents
Attorneys; auditors
Proxy notice
Date of annual meeting
Company publications
Executive, corporate, and
general office addresses

Employee Statistics

Number of employees
Length of service
Age average
Honored veterans

Employee Benefits

Pension plan
Disability protection
Insurance protection
Tenure protection
Productivity bonus
Health provisions
Safety practices
Employee training
Personnel development

Visual Aids. Visual aids for business reports may be conveniently classified into two groups: *tables* (columnar arrangements of words or numbers) and *figures* (graphs, charts, diagrams, or other exhibits). Customarily, tables and figures are numbered consecutively throughout the report, including the appendix or appendixes. Uppercase Roman numerals are traditionally used to identify tables, Arabic numerals to identify figures. (Executives sometimes prefer, however, to use Arabic numerals for all visual aids in a report.)

This is an example of what usually appears at the *top* of a *table*:

TABLE VI

**PERCENTAGE OF RESPONSES TO ITEM 1,
QUESTIONNAIRES A, B, AND C**

Notice that the completely capitalized table designation and title are separated by a double space.

This is an example of what usually appears at the *bottom* of a *figure*:

FIGURE 6

**EPC PRODUCTION AND SALES OF MONITOR
CLOSED-CIRCUIT TV SYSTEMS**

Notice that the figure designation and title are separated by a double space.

Illustrations of simple but communicative tables and figures appear on pages 409-411.

Standard Abbreviations. Intended to save writing and reading time, the following abbreviations are widely recognized in reports:

c. or ca—about (from Latin *circa*; used in contexts of time—for example, *c.* 1900)
cf.—compare (from Latin *confer*)
Chap. or Chaps.—Chapter or Chapters (followed by numbers)
ed. or eds.—editor or editors
ed. or edd.—edition or editions
e.g.—for example (from Latin *exempli gratia*)
et al.—and other people (from Latin *et alii*)
etc.—and other things (from Latin *et cetera*)
f.—and the following page (for instance, p. 5 f.)
ff.—and the following pages (for instance, pp. 5 ff.)
ibid.—the same reference (from Latin *ibidem*—used, especially in footnotes, to repeat an immediately preceding source)
i.e.—that is (from Latin *id est*)
l. or ll.—line or lines
loc. cit.—place cited (from Latin *loco citato*)
n.d.—no date (used especially concerning details of publication)

n.n.—no name
n.p.—no place } used especially concerning details
n.pub.—no publisher } of publication
No. or Nos.—number or numbers
op. cit.—the work cited (from Latin *opere citato*)
p. or pp.—page or pages
par. or pars.—paragraph or paragraphs
passim—here and there (or throughout)
q. v.—which see (from Latin *quod vide*)
rev.—revised or revision
Sec. or Secs.—section or sections
sic—thus (usually placed within brackets, not parentheses, to indicate "thus it is in the original document or statement")
trans.—translator or translated
Vol. or Vols.—volume or volumes

Footnotes. Footnotes are used to acknowledge sources of information, to amplify or validate statements in the text, and to refer the reader to other parts of the report. A raised, or superscript, Arabic numeral usually is placed in the text immediately after the statement or the part of a statement to which the footnote pertains. (Asterisks, daggers, or other symbols are used instead of Arabic numerals occasionally, particularly in statistical tables.)

A footnote traditionally is placed at the bottom of the page to which it pertains and is separated from the text by a one-and-a-half-inch line beginning flush with the left margin. Variations, however, include placing the footnote in the text proper, separated by unbroken lines above and below the note, or placing all the footnotes at the end of the report. The first of these variations interrupts the textual continuity and, often, the readers' attention; the second compels readers to keep flipping pages as they study the report. However, any of these styles may be used consistently.

Footnotes may be numbered consecutively for each chapter of a very long report or numbered consecutively throughout the whole of a relatively short report.

When more than one source is cited for a fact, the several sources may be mentioned in a single footnote, with a semicolon separating one source from another.

Underline the titles of full-length works, such as books, magazines, newspapers, and other materials published in book form (plays, public records, and the like). *Place in quotation marks the titles of parts*, such as chapters of a book and articles in a magazine or newspaper. This practice helps your reader to locate quickly the sources that you cite. Remember, also, to cite interviews or other oral communications; they are major means of collecting information for business reports, and they should be duly accredited.

[1]Carl J. Stone, <u>Managerial Communication</u> (Chicago: Consolidated Book Company, Inc., 19--), p. 32.

[2]<u>Ibid</u>.

[3]<u>Ibid</u>., pp. 71-73.

[4]Sara Carlson and J. Robert Anders, <u>Industrial Tomorrows</u> (New York: Hamilton Press, Inc., 19--), p. 110.

[5]Stone, <u>op</u>. <u>cit</u>., p. 84.

[6]Patricia J. Hart (ed.), <u>Modern Managerial Practices</u> (Boston: Thomas Budding and Sons, Inc., 19--), pp. 5, 12, 18-20.

[7]Harold O. Allen, <u>et</u>. <u>al</u>., <u>Legal Aspects of Business Communications</u> (Richmond, California: Technibooks, Inc., 19--), p. 212.

[8]Leslie R. Montrose, "Cybernetics--Old or New?" <u>Administrative News</u> (June 10, 19--), pp. 33-37.

[9]"News and Notes," <u>Business Management Quarterly</u> (March 23, 19--), p. 41.

[10]"Business Reports," <u>Encyclopedia of Business Administration</u> (12th ed.; New York: University Publishers, Inc., 1964), Vol. III, pp. 429-432.

[11]George L. Sanders, Jr., President, Altomar Corporation, telephone conversation, April 2, 19--.

[12]Edith S. Nachman, Dean of Women, Atlantic University, keynote address to the national convention, Women in Administration, Gulf Coast Hotel, New Orleans, Louisiana, December 3, 19--.

Footnotes in Business Reports

CANADIAN SALES POTENTIAL AND
AGENCY AFFILIATIONS OF
ELECTRICAL PRODUCTS CORPORATION

An Examination Report
Prepared for
J. L. Griggs, Sales Manager
EPC Central Office

by

Evan R. Jacobs, Electrical Engineer
Business Research, Inc.

November 15, 19—

CANADIAN SALES POTENTIAL and
AGENCY AFFILIATIONS of
ELECTRICAL PRODUCTS CORPORATION

Prepared for
Electrical Products Corporation
Chicago

By
Evan R. Jacobs
Electrical Engineer
Business Research, Inc.
November 15, 19—

Two Examples of a Title Page

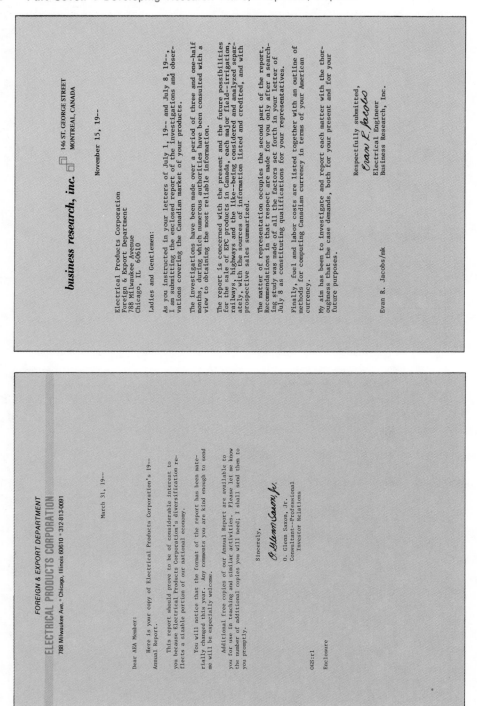

business research, inc.   146 ST. GEORGE STREET
MONTREAL, CANADA

November 15, 19—

Electrical Products Corporation
Foreign & Export Department
788 Milwaukee Avenue
Chicago, IL 60610

Ladies and Gentlemen:

As you instructed in your letters of July 1, 19-- and July 8, 19--,
I am submitting the enclosed report of the investigations and observations covering the Canadian market of your products.

The investigations have been made over a period of three and one-half
months, during which numerous authorities have been consulted with a
view to obtaining the most reliable information.

The report is concerned with the present and the future possibilities
for the sale of EPC products in Canada, each major field--irrigation,
railways, highways and the like--being considered and analyzed separately, with the sources of information listed and credited, and with
prospective sales summarized.

The matter of representation occupies the second part of the report.
Recommendations in that respect are made for you only after a search-
ing study was made of all the factors set forth in your letter of
July 8 as constituting qualifications for your representatives.

Finally, fuel and labor costs are listed together with an outline of
methods for computing Canadian currency in terms of your American
currency.

My aim has been to investigate and report each matter with the thoroughness that the case demands, both for your present and for your
future purposes.

Respectfully submitted,

Evan R. Jacobs

Electrical Engineer
Business Research, Inc.

Evan R. Jacobs/mk

FOREIGN & EXPORT DEPARTMENT

ELECTRICAL PRODUCTS CORPORATION

788 Milwaukee Ave. • Chicago, Illinois 60610 • 312 813-0091

March 31, 19—

Dear AEA Member:

Here is your copy of Electrical Products Corporation's 19—
Annual Report.

This report should prove to be of considerable interest to
you because Electrical Products Corporation's diversification reflects a sizable portion of our national economy.

You will notice that the format of the report has been mate-
rially changed this year. Any comments you are kind enough to send
me will be especially welcome.

Additional free copies of our Annual Report are available to
you for use in teaching and similar activities. Please let me know
the number of additional copies you will need; I shall send them to
you promptly.

Sincerely,

O. Glenn Saxon, Jr.

O. Glenn Saxon, Jr.
Consultant--Professional
Investor Relations

OGS:rl
Enclosure

Two Examples of a Transmittal Letter

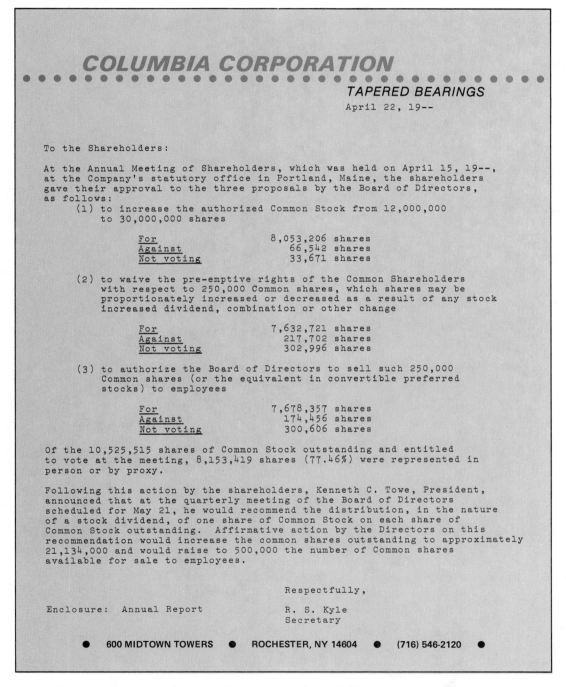

COLUMBIA CORPORATION

TAPERED BEARINGS
April 22, 19--

To the Shareholders:

At the Annual Meeting of Shareholders, which was held on April 15, 19--,
at the Company's statutory office in Portland, Maine, the shareholders
gave their approval to the three proposals by the Board of Directors,
as follows:
 (1) to increase the authorized Common Stock from 12,000,000
   to 30,000,000 shares

For	8,053,206 shares
Against	66,542 shares
Not voting	33,671 shares

 (2) to waive the pre-emptive rights of the Common Shareholders
   with respect to 250,000 Common shares, which shares may be
   proportionately increased or decreased as a result of any stock
   increased dividend, combination or other change

For	7,632,721 shares
Against	217,702 shares
Not voting	302,996 shares

 (3) to authorize the Board of Directors to sell such 250,000
   Common shares (or the equivalent in convertible preferred
   stocks) to employees

For	7,678,357 shares
Against	174,456 shares
Not voting	300,606 shares

Of the 10,525,515 shares of Common Stock outstanding and entitled
to vote at the meeting, 8,153,419 shares (77.46%) were represented in
person or by proxy.

Following this action by the shareholders, Kenneth C. Towe, President,
announced that at the quarterly meeting of the Board of Directors
scheduled for May 21, he would recommend the distribution, in the nature
of a stock dividend, of one share of Common Stock on each share of
Common Stock outstanding. Affirmative action by the Directors on this
recommendation would increase the common shares outstanding to approximately
21,134,000 and would raise to 500,000 the number of Common shares
available for sale to employees.

         Respectfully,

Enclosure: Annual Report   R. S. Kyle
            Secretary

  ● **600 MIDTOWN TOWERS** ● **ROCHESTER, NY 14604** ● **(716) 546-2120** ●

This Letter Serves a Dual Purpose of Reporting an Annual Share-
holder's Meeting and Transmitting the Annual Report

TABLE OF CONTENTS

TABLE OF CONTENTS

Two Examples of a Table of Contents

LIST OF TABLES

LIST OF ILLUSTRATIONS

Two Examples of a List of Visual Aids

Except for appropriately using *figures, figure,* and Arabic numerals (instead of *tables, table,* and Roman numerals), a list of figures resembles a list of tables.

Bibliographical Entries. Footnotes cite the exact location of evidence or authority for specific statements. Bibliographical entries cite sources as whole entities. A bibliography, therefore, should list at least the references cited in the body of the report; it may also list other pertinent references of potential benefit to the reader. An example of standard bibliographical format is on page 407. Notice how the bibliographical arrangement differs from the footnote style, especially in alphabetization and punctuation. Observe, also, that you should use "hanging indention" for bibliographical entries and you should avoid repeating an author's name by using a solid seven-space line instead (See page 407). The first two books are written by Martin O. Atkins, Jr.

When you compose an *annotated* bibliography, be sure to summarize each entry's content and relate that content to the purpose of your report, as in the following example:

Alton, Michael J., and Laura O. Madison (eds.). *Recent Studies of Marketing Procedures*. Cincinnati: Business Science Press, 19—.
A collection of research reports concerning projective data-collection techniques, new scaling procedures for survey responses, and related marketing themes. Used especially for current information of questionnaire construction and adaptation to various respondent groups.

Adapting the Comprehensive Report Model

The comprehensive report model is adaptable to "minireporting." When your company's policies, your recipient's preferences, or your own experienced judgments require reports that *represent but do not state in detail* all communication factors, you can easily abridge or modify the comprehensive model. The results will be informal or semiformal messages, often oral, sometimes in a letter or memo format.

Remember, however, that effective minireports, like their maxi counterparts, will elicit feedback. Therefore, have the data required by the comprehensive model ready for use even when your message is a minireport.

Contrasted with maxis, written *minireports* usually have these traits:

1. *Summarized contextual data.* However, specific details for statements of major ideas are expected.
2. *Condensed format.* Headings and subheadings, used to move the reader quickly while informing, are consistently positioned to minimize reading time. Consistent use of capitalization and underlining allows headings and subheadings to appear on the same lines as the sentences that those heads and subheads introduce. Spacing is condensed in other ways also. For example: Single spacing within a paragraph, double spacing between

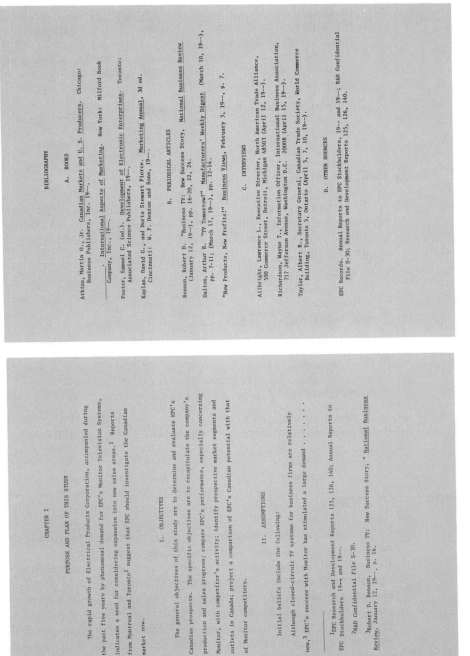

CHAPTER I

PURPOSE AND PLAN OF THIS STUDY

The rapid growth of Electrical Products Corporation, accompanied during the past five years by phenomenal demand for EPC's Monitor Television Systems, indicates a need for considering expansion into new sales areas.[1] Reports from Montreal and Toronto[2] suggest that EPC should investigate the Canadian market now.

I. OBJECTIVES

The general objectives of this study are to determine and evaluate EPC's Canadian prospects. The specific objectives are to recapitulate the company's Canadian prospects. The specific objectives are to recapitulate the company's production and sales progress; compare EPC's performance, especially concerning Monitor, with competitor's activity; identify prospective market segments and outlets in Canada; project a comparison of EPC's Canadian potential with that of Monitor competitors.

II. ASSUMPTIONS

Initial beliefs include the following:

Although closed-circuit TV systems for business firms are relatively new,[3] EPC's success with Monitor has stimulated a large demand . . . . . .

[1] EPC Research and Development Reports 125, 126, 140; Annual Reports to EPC Stockholders 19-- and 19--.
[2] R&D Confidential File S-30.
[3] Robert D. Benson. Business TV: New Success Story, "National Business Review, January 12, 19--, p. 16.

BIBLIOGRAPHY

A. BOOKS

Atkins, Martin O., Jr. Canadian Markets and U. S. Producers. Chicago: Business Publishers, Inc. 19--.

_____. International Aspects of Marketing. New York: Milford Book Company, Inc., 19--.

Foster, Samuel C. (ed.). Development of Electronic Enterprises. Toronto: Associated Science Publishers, 19--.

Kaplan, David G., and Boris Stewart Pierce. Marketing Annual, 3d ed. Cincinnati: W. P. Denton and Sons, 19--.

B. PERIODICAL ARTICLES

Benson, Robert D. "Business TV: New Success Story, National Business Review (January 12, 19--), pp. 16-20, 22, 24.

Dalton, Arthur B. "TV Tomorrow?" Manufacturers' Weekly Digest (March 10, 19--), pp. 7-11; (March 17, 19--), pp. 12-14.

"New Products, New Profits'" Business Views, February 3, 19--, p. 7.

C. INTERVIEWS

Allbright, Lawrence L., Executive Director, North American Trade Alliance, 500 Commerce Street, Detroit, Michigan 48503 (April 12, 19--).

Richardson, Wayne T., Information Officer, International Business Association, 717 Jefferson Avenue, Washington D.C. 20008 (April 15, 19--).

Taylor, Albert B., Secretary General, Canadian Trade Society, World Commerce Building, Toronto 5, Ontario (April 5, 7, 10, 19--).

D. OTHER SOURCES

EPC Records. Annual Reports to EPC Stockholders, 19-- and 19--; R&D Confidential File S-30; Research and Development Reports 125, 126, 140.

Bibliography (References)

Page of a Long Report, Showing an Effective Use of Footnotes

paragraphs in a single major section, triple spacing between major sections. *Lists* of words or numbers often replace narrative or expository sentences or paragraphs.

3. *Abridged visual aids.* Tables, charts, and other graphic aids appear mainly as visual summaries. Detailed visual aids and other pertinent exhibits, of course, may be appended to the minireport.

Examples of minireports are on pages 412-416.

FEATURES OF SHORT REPORTS

Like their longer counterparts, short reports, which are often in memorandum or in letter format, may be organized inductively, deductively, or psychologically. A basic pattern for short reports follows this sequence:

1. Identification
2. Authorization
3. Purpose
4. Discussion

That basic pattern may be expanded, as needed, to include these parts as well:

5. Conclusions and Recommendations (when appropriate)
6. Summary (often placed at the beginning rather than at the end)

Various formats and headings may be used to designate the parts of those patterns, as illustrated on pages 412-418 and 420-421.

ORAL PRESENTATIONS

Much of the information in this chapter applies to oral as well as to written reports. You would do well to review Chapter 7 at this point. Refresh your comprehension of what the planning, development, and presentation of oral reports generally will require you to do. Determine the report purpose from your standpoint and that of your listeners, analyzing your listener's needs as well as your own. Evaluate the situation that involves you with your audience. Organize your data psychologically as well as logically. Prepare a delivery that benefits from the advantages of impromptu, extemporaneous, textual, or memorized styles. If you use audio-visual aids for your oral report, be sure they can be heard and viewed appropriately by your receivers.

TABLE I

PORT OF GULFTON ACTIVITY IN MILLIONS OF TONS,
JUNE-DECEMBER, 19--

MONTH	INCOMING TONNAGE	OUTGOING TONNAGE	TOTAL TONNAGE
June	2.80	3.25	6.05
July	3.10	2.75	5.85
August	2.70	2.80	5.50
Sept.	2.20	3.30	5.50
Oct.	1.75	3.50	5.25
Nov.	2.25	3.25	5.50
Dec.	2.50	3.75	6.25

SOURCE: Gulfton Harbor Commission, March 10, 19--.

TABLE II

PROJECTED POPULATION OF PACIFIC STATES

STATE	1970	1975	1980
Alaska	290,000	335,000	381,000
California	21,463,000	24,748,000	28,440,000
Hawaii	763,000	823,000	887,000
Oregon	1,999,000	2,129,000	2,282,000
Washington	3,220,000	3,521,000	3,860,000
Totals	27,735,000	31,556,000	35,850,000

SOURCE: U. S. Bureau of the Census, January 15, 19--.

Illustrations of Tables

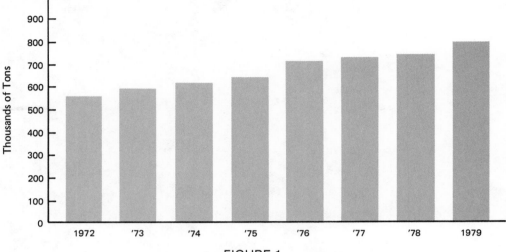

FIGURE 1
PRODUCT W PRODUCTION
Source: Metrico, Inc., R&D Files, April, 19--

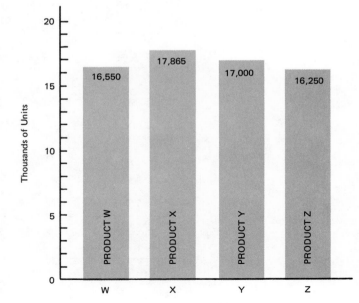

FIGURE 2
THE AVERAGE UNIT ORDER
FOR PRODUCTS W, X, Y, AND Z
(From Metrico, Inc., Files,
April, 19--)

Examples of Figures

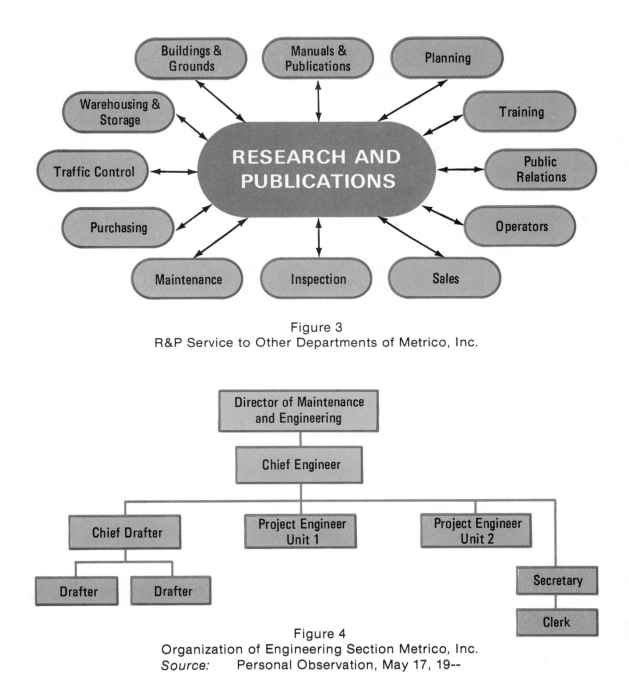

Figure 3
R&P Service to Other Departments of Metrico, Inc.

Figure 4
Organization of Engineering Section Metrico, Inc.
Source: Personal Observation, May 17, 19--

Sample Figures of a Metrico, Inc., Report

metrico, inc.

Petrochem Plant 5

TO: H. L. Shaw, Personnel Services

FROM: B. D. Whitney, Training Department.

DATE: January 17, 19--

SUBJECT: Training Department Load and Assignments, Revised

Thank you for requesting this revised workload report of current Training Department assignments. A detailed analysis of trainee enrollments, including names and ID designations, is attached.

AUTHORIZATION: Your January 12 memorandum.

SUMMARY: The department is training a total of 415 employees.

<u>Distribution</u>: "Basic Safety Education (BSE)," 85
"Advanced Safety Education (ADE)," 150
"Metrico Career Opportunities (MCO)," 180

<u>Staff</u>: The training staff is as follows:

metrico, inc.

March 30, 19--

Mr. H. L. Hennesy
Metrico, Inc.
Petrochem Plant
Rochester, NY 14620

Dear Mr. Hennesy

Here is the vehicle fleet report that you authorized May 5 for submission today. Your comments will be welcome.

<u>Purpose</u>   To recommend whether Metrico should continue
                   leasing rather than buying its automobiles and
                   delivery vans.

<u>Conclusions</u>   The enclosed cost comparison, based upon pertinent
                   records of the last five years, shows that Metrico
                   has saved an average of $19,000 annually by its
                   leasing arrangements. Data for this study indicate
                   probable continuation of this savings margin.

<u>Recommendation</u>   Continue leasing the S & L vehicle fleet.

Minireports Often Appear in Memo or Letter Format.

GIVE PROPER DISPLAY TO A SHORT REPORT

Importance of Effective
Use of Display

Display, which involves the liberal use
of white space, is essential to make the
captions, the section headings, and the
main divisions stand out and guide the
reader to the information wanted.

Specifications to be
Followed in Producing
Effective Display

Reserve a liberal margin at the left of
each sheet of the report. In ordinary
cases it is well to use white standard
stationery, measuring eight and one-half
by eleven inches. Somewhat better display
results from the use of single spacing
because there is a clearer contrast of
black and white masses. Some executives,
however, prefer double spacing. It is
advisable to determine in advance which
is desired.

Proper Use of Captions
and Subcaptions

Captions and subcaptions, which may also
be called headlines and subheadlines, may
be typewritten in the center of the page
or even with the left-hand margin.

Optional Positions
of Subheads

Subheads may be inset into the body of a
paragraph at the left or may be typewritten
in the margins opposite the sections to
which they refer. The matter is optional.

General Purpose of Display
to Assure Clearness

The general purpose of display is merely
to ensure and to increase clearness. For
this reason, a triple space precedes and
a double space follows display lines; and
the most important captions are typewritten
in solid capitals.

Illustrations

Illustrating the Contents
of a Report

The effect of a business report is often
made stronger by the use of pictures, graphs,
bar charts, maps, tables, blueprints, drawings, sketches, diagrams, and flat samples.
Such items are placed with the sections to
which they refer.

A Page From the Body of a Short Report (Notice the Use of Headings and Subheadings)

OPERATIONS REPORT
JONES PIPE COMPANY, INC.

This report summarizes the results of a survey of Jones Pipe Company, Inc., to determine what action should be taken to reduce costs and put the company on a profitable basis.

Current Condition. The possibilities for improving the operation of this company are many. This report outlines a plan that will enable you to realize the greatest returns on your investment. It is important to point out, however, that the company is now in poor condition. Rarely in our extended practice have we encountered a company that needed improvement on so many fronts. Facilities are antiquated, methods are high cost, labor is inefficient, and the existing management is unable to cope with the situation.

Fortunately, such weaknesses are at the same time opportunities for great improvement. By utilizing modern management know-how, you can correct these weaknesses, earn a handsome return on your investment, and demonstrate your keen judgment in buying a company that appeared destined for the auction block.

Recommendations. Listed below are the major changes we believe should be made very soon. There then follows an estimate of the profits that will result from these moves. These following

1

suggestions need considerably more refinement and development before they can be put into effect, but our experience with such problems will enable us to get the work done quickly and in a manner that will assure the greatest return. Briefly, here are the changes that should be made:

1. Major building alterations should be made. These are essential to provide adequate housing for modernized operations.

2. Pipe-threading equipment should be modernized. This is necessary to bring the plant efficiency and labor costs into line with those of other manufacturers who have modern equipment.

3. A general plant cleanup is needed. In connection with building alterations and installation of new equipment, all parts for old unused machines and other miscellaneous scrap in the warehouse and about the plant should be sold. In addition, the plant needs a new coat of paint and modern lighting fixtures should be installed.

4. The unloading and handling of pipe should be mechanized. A small electric hoist mounted on a rail running from the railroad siding across the pipe storage shed could eliminate most of the present unloading by hand.

5. Mechanical equipment for the movement of pipe and finished nipples is needed. If the lengths of pipe coming from the cutters are dropped into properly designed tote boxes, they could then be easily moved by a small fork-lift truck from the cutters to the threading machines.

6. A system of inventory control and production scheduling should be established. Such a system is needed to avoid partial shipment to customers, rush production orders, and an irregular volume of work in the shop itself.

7. Output standards and financial incentives for plant workers should be established. All the preceding steps will contribute to a lowering of labor costs. The setting of individual output standards with financial incentives will assure that these savings are realized.

2

Short Report in Standard Format

3

As a result of these changes, we are confident that your labor costs can be reduced to approximately 20 percent of the selling price of your product. At the same time, your service to customers should be improved and your employees will be receiving more take-home pay because of the bonuses they will be earning.

Investment Requirements. You will recognize, of course, that these important changes in company operations cannot be made without some additional investment of capital. While it is impossible at this time to make accurate estimates of the new investment required, we have prepared some approximate figures because we know you will want to face squarely whatever is needed to put the company on a sound basis.

Tentative Estimates of Capital Requirements

Building alterations		$ 5,000
Machinery		
6 automatic threading machines	$24,000	
Motors and installation	6,000	30,000
Plant cleanup		3,000
Material handling equipment-pipe		2,000
Material handling equipment-nipples . . .		4,000
Total		$44,000

Estimated Returns. If it were not for substantial improvement in operations that this capital investment will permit, we might hesitate recommending these moves. Our estimate indicates, however, that you will receive handsome returns from this additional expenditure. We have made some tentative estimates of the lowered operating costs that, on the basis of our experience, we are convinced you will enjoy when the plant is modernized as outlined above.

4

Estimated Operating Costs and Profits
Resulting from Modernization Program

(Yearly Figures in Thousands)

	$100	$200	$300	$400
Net Sales Income				
Operating Costs				
Materials	49	98	147	196
Labor	20	40	60	80
Depreciation	12	12	12	12
Heat & Light	2	2	2	2
Factory Supplies	2	5	7	9
Repairs	3	6	8	8
Office Salaries	8	8	8	8
Insurance, Taxes, etc.	2	2	2	2
Total	98	169	240	311
Operating Profit	$ 2	$ 31	$ 60	$ 89

Other Requirements. To reap these profits, improvement in sales effort will be necessary. You now have only one good sales agent and are completely unrepresented in your local market. By securing two new agents and by selling to manufacturers as well as to wholesalers, your sales should increase substantially. Moreover, the low operating cost that will result from modernization will permit you to make strategic price cuts on large orders and still gain a handsome profit.

One of my associates and I will do intensive work over the next three months to effect the improvements outlined above. We will also supervise the operation of the new setup for two years. Thus, you will continue to get the broad experience of our company and will obtain a much-needed supplement to your existing management personnel. At the end of two years, we can take another look at the arrangement to see what changes either of us may wish to make.

Short Report in Standard Format (concluded)

MARTIN J. LONGSTAFF ASSOCIATES
PUBLIC ACCOUNTANTS
567 W. WASHINGTON STREET, INDIANAPOLIS, INDIANA 46203

March 26, 19—

To the Stockholders and Board of Directors
of Siegman Manufacturing Company
2009 W. Hanna Avenue
Indianapolis, IN 46217

Ladies and Gentlemen:

We have examined the accompanying consolidated statement of condition of the Siegman Manufacturing Company and subsidiaries at December 31, 19—, and the related consolidated statements of earnings and retained earnings for the year then ended. Our examination was made in accordance with generally accepted auditing standards, and accordingly included such tests of the accounting records and such other auditing procedures as we considered necessary in the circumstances.

In accordance with the terms of our engagement, the customers were not requested to confirm their balances. The aggregates of the detailed balances were found to be in agreement with the corresponding controlling accounts. The accounts may be classified as follows:

Unsecured	$6,963,301
Secured by lien on property	221,220
Debit balances in accounts payable	97,800
	$7,282,321

The accounts were reviewed in detail and discussed with the credit manager. While some of the unsecured accounts are past due, it appears that adequate provision has been made for any losses that may be sustained.

Fixed assets are stated at cost less depreciation and amortization. Service building properties with a net depreciated cost of $950,862 are pledged as security for the 5% mortgage note. Depreciation in 19— amounted to $821,993. Depreciation rates were applied by the straight-line method.

In our opinion, the accompanying financial statements present fairly the consolidated financial position of Siegman Manufacturing Company and its subsidiary companies at December 31, 19—, the results of their operations, and the supplementary information on funds for the year then ended in conformity with generally

---

To the Stockholders and Board of Directors
of Siegman Manufacturing Company
Page 2
March 26, 19—

accepted accounting principles applied on a basis consistent with that of the preceding year.

The accounting system and methods employed by the Company appear to meet the requirements of the business. The books and accounting records are well kept.

Very truly yours,

MARTIN J. LONGSTAFF ASSOCIATES

Martin J. Longstaff

Martin J. Longstaff

rh

Minireport in the Form of a Letter

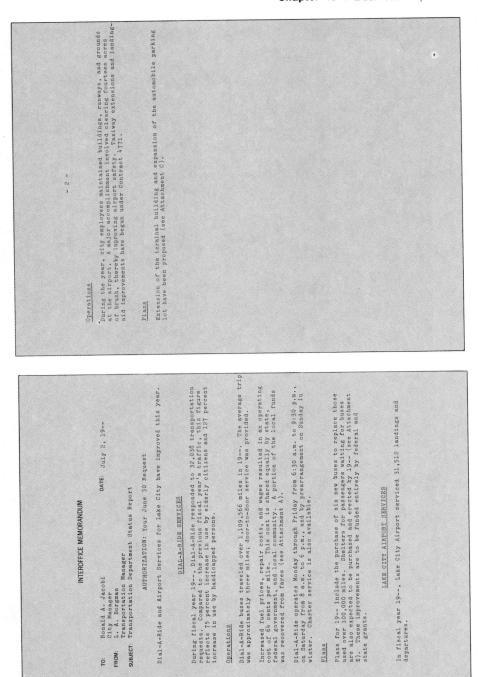

INTEROFFICE MEMORANDUM

TO: Ronald A. Jacobi
         City Manager
FROM: L. A. Borgman
         Transportation Manager
SUBJECT: Transportation Department Status Report
DATE: July 2, 19--

AUTHORIZATION: Your June 30 Request

Dial-A-Ride and Airport Services for Lake City have improved this year.

DIAL-A-RIDE SERVICES

During fiscal year 19--, Dial-A-Ride responded to 32,038 transportation requests. Compared to the previous fiscal year's traffic, this figure reflects 75 percent increase in use by elderly citizens and 127 percent increase in use by handicapped persons.

Operations

Dial-A-Ride buses traveled over 1,109,566 miles in 19--. The average trip was approximately three miles; door-to-door service was provided.

Increased fuel prices, repair costs, and wages resulted in an operating cost of 64 cents per mile. This cost is shared equally by state, federal government, and local community. A portion of the local funds was recovered from fares (see Attachment A).

Dial-A-Ride operates Monday through Friday from 6:30 a.m. to 9:30 p.m., on Saturday from 8 a.m. to 6 p.m., and by prearrangement on Sunday in winter. Charter service is also available.

Plans

Plans for 19-- include the purchase of six new buses to replace those used over 100,000 miles. Shelters for passengers waiting for buses are also expected to be purchased and erected by 19--. (see Attachment B). These improvements are to be funded entirely by federal and state grants.

LAKE CITY AIRPORT SERVICES

In fiscal year 19--, Lake City Airport serviced 31,512 landings and departures.

- 2 -

Operations

During the year, city employees maintained buildings, runways, and grounds at the airport. A major accomplishment involved clearing fourteen acres of brush, thereby improving airport safety. Taxiway extensions and landing-aid improvements have begun under Contract 4771.

Plans

Extension of the terminal building and expansion of the automobile parking lot have been proposed (see Attachment C).

INTEROFFICE MEMORANDUM

DATE: December 3, 19—

TO: A. J. Bowers

FROM: D. A. Phillips

SUBJECT: Monthly Progress Report, Southfield Office Building Project

November work was on schedule, as summarized here.

Work Completed

1. Concrete floors on the first and second levels were mixed and placed.

2. Mechanical room equipment was installed.

3. First floor conduit was installed.

Work in Progress

1. The concrete roof deck was begun on November 26; completion scheduled for December 7.

2. Exterior masonry was begun on November 12; completion scheduled for the week of February 19.

3. Installation of the second floor conduit was begun October 22; completion scheduled for the first week of December.

4. Switchgear and transformer installation is on schedule; completion set for the last week of December.

Anticipation Problem

Bricklayers are presently on schedule. However, new contract negotiations seem to be running into difficulties. Should a strike materialize, both exterior and interior masonry will be delayed.

Additional Remarks

The October progress report cited delay in delivery of air-conditioning equipment. But additional workers assigned to the mechanical room enabled installation to be completed on schedule.

NOTE: The "additional remarks" section of this illustration is used to notify management of how a previously reported problem was solved.

INTEROFFICE MEMORANDUM

DATE: November 2, 19—

TO: Y. O. Panella, Security

FROM: Edith Harrison, Industrial Relations

SUBJECT: Parking Facilities at Duval Corporation

REFERENCE: Policy Statement No. 20-155

SUMMARY: Corporate headquarters maintains one main parking lot for visitors and for company personnel. Although room is available to accommodate all vehicles, the parking spaces reserved for handicapped drivers.

RECOMMENDATION: To correct this situation, the Security Department should do the following:

1. Notify all personnel about this violation.

2. Assign security personnel to enforce the parking regulations, especially between 7 and 10 a.m.

DISCUSSION: During the last two weeks, I have observed 15 instances of these spaces being used by unauthorized staff members. Handicapped people have had to park far from the building because of these violations.

SOUTHFIELD OFFICE BUILDING

Item	June	July	August	Sept.	Oct.	Nov.	Dec.	Jan.	Feb.	March	April
	4 11 18 25	2 9 16 23 30	6 13 20 27	3 10 17 24	8 15 22 29	5 12 19 26	3 10 17 24 31	7 14 21 28	5 12 19 26	4 11 18 25	1 8 15 22 29
Building Excavation											
Conc. Ftg. & F'dn. Wall											
Structural Steel											
Metal Decking											
Conc. Lower Floor											
Conc. First Floor											
Conc. Second Floor											
Sprayed on Fireproofing											
Conc. Roof Deck											
Exterior Masonry											
Interior Masonry											
Roofing and Sheetmetal											
Aluminum Windows & Ent.											
Wall Finish Lower Floor											
Wall Finish First Floor											
Wall Finish Second Floor											
Acoustic Ceilings											
Hydraulic Elevator											
Rough in First Floor											
Rough in Second Floor											
Ductwork — Lower Floor											
Ductwork — First Floor											
Ductwork — Second Floor											
Plumbing Fixtures											
Mechanical Room Equipment											
Underground Conduit											
First Floor Conduit											
Second Floor Conduit											
Feeders											
Branch Circuits — Lower											
Branch Circuits — First											
Branch Circuits — Second											
Lighting — Lower											
Lighting — First											
Lighting — Second											
Switchgear & Trans.											

**Partial Graph Showing
Time Frames for Construction Phases**

Bay Electric Co.   Twenty Circle Drive   ■   Duluth, Minnesota 55801

April 19, 19--

Mr. James Stark
1020 Applewood Lane
Hibbing, MN 55746

Dear Mr. Stark

As you requested, your building plans have been reviewed to determine the electrical service capacity your cottage will require. These suggestions are based upon a floor area of 2800 square feet.

Service Entrance Panel

A 100-ampere fuseless service panel is suggested to provide these circuits for present and future needs:

1. Five 15-ampere general-purpose circuits to be used for bedrooms, bath, living room, basement, and kitchen lights.

2. Two 20-ampere circuits for kitchen appliances

3. One 20-ampere circuit for laundry appliances

4. One 15-ampere circuit for oil furnace

5. One 50-ampere circuit for electric range

6. One 30-ampere circuit for electric dryer and washer

7. One 30-ampere circuit for electric water heater

Mr. James Stark
Page 2
April 10, 19--

Wiring Requirements

The following suggestions will help you wire your cottage properly:

1. Convenience Outlets. No. 14 wire with ground can be used for all 15-ampere convenience outlets; however, No. 12 wire with ground should be used for 20-ampere convenience outlets.

2. Electric Range. Use a separate 3-wire No. 6 cable from a 50-ampere circuit to a heavy-duty wall receptacle.

3. Clothes Dryer. Use a separate 3-wire No. 6 cable from a 30-ampere circuit to a heavy-duty wall receptacle.

Additional Remarks

Although it is not essential in your area, you may wish to use conduit for wiring your home. You can notch the wall studs or place your conduit between your rough and final floors.

When you are ready to wire, please let us know. We will gladly supply you with a cost estimate.

Sincerely yours

Laurie Yetter

Laurie Yetter
Customer Services

SWIFT BUSINESS MACHINES INC.
1515 MADISON AVENUE/PORTLAND, OREGON 97204

May 5, 19--

Ms. Pamela Newton, Director
Purchasing Department
City of Munfordville
Munfordville, KY 42765

Dear Ms. Newton

Your interest in updating your office with Swift Electric Typewriters is certainly appreciated. We look forward to serving you.

As you requested, we have prepared two purchasing plans for your consideration. Plan A offers our 40-30-30 time-payment plan and will update your typewriters over a five-year period. Plan B provides the updating over a three-year period. These examples show trade-in allowances at current prices. Of course, prevailing market prices must be used when the machines are traded.

Plan A: the Five-Year Plan

You have the advantage of a time-payment plan extended over five budget years without interest. By using this plan, you will have no typewriter that is over five years old.

A. First Year
   1. Purchase 21 Swift Electrics:
      21 Swift Electrics @ $575 = $12,075
      21 trade-in machines @ $200 = 4,200
              Total Cost $ 7,875
   2. Payment first year: (40% of $7,875) $6,150.00
B. Second-year payment: (30% of $7,875) $2,362.50
C. Third Year
   1. Purchase 42 Swift Electrics:
      42 Swift Electrics @ $575   = $24,150
      42 trade-in machines @ $200 = 8,400
              Total Cost $15,750
   2. Payment third year: (30% of $7,875) = $2,362.50
                    (40% of $15,750)= 6,300.00 $8,662.50
D. Fourth-year payment (30% of $15,750) $4,725.00
E. Fifth-year payment (30% of $15,750) $4,725.00
          Total Cost over Five Years $23,625.00

Ms. Pamela Newton
Page 2
May 5, 19--

Plan B: the Three-Year Plan

You purchase twenty-one Swift Electrics each year for three consecutive years.

A. First Year
   1. Purchase 21 Swift Electrics
      21 Swift Electrics @ $575   = $12,075
      21 trade-in machines @ $200 = 4,200
   2. Payment first year $7,875.00
B. Second Year
   1. Purchase 21 Swift Electrics
      21 Swift Electrics @ $575   = $12,075
      21 trade-in machines @ $200 = 4,200
   2. Payment second year $7,875.00
C. Third Year
   1. Purchase 21 Swift Electrics
      21 Swift Electrics @ $575   = $12,075
      21 trade-in machines @ $200 = 4,200
   2. Payment third year $7,875.00
           Total Cost over Three Years $23,625.00

Under either arrangement, delivery can be made within thirty days after your order is received. Please let us know which plan you prefer.

Sincerely

Anthony S. Lister

Anthony S. Lister
Sales Representative

REVIEW AND TRANSITION

Whereas Chapter 18 explained how to plan a research process, Chapter 19 has described the product of that process: a useful business report. You have learned to identify the parts of a comprehensive, full-length report model, from preliminaries through body to supplements, and how to develop those parts effectively. Techniques for limiting the research topic; organizing data that have been collected, analyzed, classified, and synthesized; and transmitting the resulting message through written, oral, and visual means have been described.

By studying Chapters 1-19, you have learned the principles and purposes of business communicators. You have perceived applications of logic, psychology, and ethics to informing and persuading through written-oral-visual media. You have acquired techniques of planning, composing, transmitting, and evaluating messages that range from a simple inquiry to a fully documented report. You have examined numerous communication models and illustrations offered as guides to your own appropriate creativity and have participated in end-of-the-chapter discussions and problem-solving exercises.

To help you with your continuing progress toward successful communication, we ask you now to consider the basic question suggested throughout this book: Unless a person masters linguistic skills and make it possible to perceive, process, and react to the evidence of thoughts and of feelings, how can one expect—whatever the marvels of technology—to communicate effectively?

DISCUSSION QUESTIONS

A. In what ways (other than their lengths) are short business reports like and unlike their longer counterparts?

B. In what ways does the information presented by Chapters 18 and 19 pertain to oral as well as to written business reports?

C. Define and illustrate the proper uses of these standard abbreviations:

1. cf.	**7.** ibid.
2. et al.	**8.** i.e.
3. etc.	**9.** op. cit.
4. e.g.	**10.** passim
5. f.	**11.** q.v.
6. ff.	**12.** sic

D. Review the examples of footnotes on page 400. What do footnotes 2, 3, and 5 signify?

E. Review the examples of bibliographical entries on page 407. What categories besides "books," "periodical articles," and "interviews" could be appropriate to a business report?

F. Review the examples of tables and figures on pages 391-392. What other forms of visual aids would effectively convey their data?

G. What traits typify each of the following?

1. narrative reports
2. statistical reports
3. interim reports
4. periodic reports
5. horizontal reports
6. radial reports
7. technical reports
8. fact-finding reports
9. analytical reports
10. chronologically styled reports
11. logically styled reports
12. psychologically styled reports

Explain how a single report may appropriately 'fit' more than one of those message categories.

H. "Informalizing" and "visualizing" are two prominent trends of modern business reporting. What other report trends are gaining popularity because of improvements in communication technology?

I. In what ways are the following chapters especially related to one another?

1. Chapters 6, 18, and 19
2. Chapters 7, 18, and 19

APPLICATIONS

1. Based upon an approved work plan which you developed for any of your Chapter 18 exercises, conduct the research you proposed. Then present a written, an oral, or a multimedia report of your research.

2. As chairperson of your department's Safety and Health Committee, you discover that 85 percent of your associates have had no instruction in lifesaving skills of cardio-pulmonary resuscitation. Write a memorandum report to your department head, Mrs. R. W. Amhurst, recommending that a CPR workshop be conducted for all personnel.

3. Using the chart shown on page 419, write a progress report to A. J. Bowers concerning construction status of the Southfield Office Building during August. These data are pertinent: Heavy rains caused a two-week delay of work with concrete footings and foundation walls. Consequently, this construction phase cannot be completed before the second week of September. Underground conduit installation is on schedule, but an electricians' strike is pending and may cause additional delays.

4. The college or school you attend is engaged in a self-study research project. The purposes are to determine how the institution has changed during the past five years and to identify areas of needed improvement.
   Dean N. C. Steinbeck explains that all of the administrators and faculty are participating in the study but that, to be accurate and complete, the final report should include evaluations and recommendations by the students. "We are especially concerned," says Dean Steinbeck, "with student reactions to the academic program, including adequacy of course content and instructional methods; to the library materials and services; to the classrooms and equipment; to social and other extra-curricular activities."
   As president of the Student Association, you welcome this opportunity of involving the students in this important communication effort. Compose an appropriate work plan, perform the research, and prepare a suitable report.

5. Your employer, Miss K. M. Lee, general manager of Amalgamated Industries Corporation, is rightly concerned with "our keeping mountains of paper and too often being unable to find or to use a document that we have kept." Lee asks you to discover "what you can" about modern principles of records and control and information retrieval.

   Compose an appropriate work plan, perform the research, and prepare a suitable report.

6. You are employed by a retail firm that operates a store near your campus. Conduct a research-and-report project which enables you to accomplish the following:

   Study the local advertising practices of your firm as well as its chief competitor.

   Compare, contrast, and evaluate the effectiveness of these practices.

   Offer suitable recommendations to your employer.

7. Your employer must decide whether to advertise through local mass-communication media. Research and report the relative advantages and disadvantages of advertising by AM radio, FM radio, TV, and newspapers.

8. Using government publications and trade materials, as well as other sources, report how to establish a local business or service. (For example, a clothing store that will attract college students, an automobile service station or parking facility, a drive-in restaurant, a bookstore, an accounting or tax service, a secretarial service, a travel agency).

9. Appropriately revise these statements:

   a. The annuity plan was established by ABC Company to encourage employees to provide systematically for their own financial security in the years after requirement.

   b. This study examines one phase of the transportation crises involving our corporation. The first chapter is a lengthy chapter but is actually short when compared to the vast amount of pertinent data collected. The entire study involved participation of every key personnel in our organization. Chapter 2 reviews previous reports on the same subject, however those reports are briefly summarized.

   c. This procedure permits customers to be prepared to pay their bills with promptness at a fairly regular time each and every month. On the other hand it would be, practically speaking, impossible for us to bill all of our customers on any one day of a month. But the previously mentioned procedure merits attention. Especially in reference to the situation that recurs in some of the areas with very high delinquency which on a large scale requires firm collection methods.

   d. Some objections were voiced to the suggested labor pool. Most of these were voiced by those concerned, namely the section chiefs. The laborers themselves were interested in the idea. Besides section chiefs, however, the team supervisors objected.

   e. A purposive sample was used to select the stocks instead of a random sample. Using this method the research found nine industries to use in the study.

   f. A question in which the responses of the subject are limited to stated alternatives is called a "closed-end item." A tabulation of observed data into classes is referred to as a "frequency distribution."

g. The stability of earnings were measured for each stock over a four year period of time from 1966 to 1970.

h. By glancing at Table II, the trend can be easily determined.

i. Downtown merchants have solved the parking problem by building parking garages in close proximity to their stores. They have been especially successful as businessmen because they provide convenient parking.

j. Profits and losses on sales of securities illustrates how evenly divided accounting practices are. Although those practices may differ somewhat, there has been noticeable improvements in financial reporting.

k. The technician on the other hand is concerned with the performance and action of stocks, and the stock market for determining which stocks to buy, and when to purchase them.

l. Incoming calls are handled by pushing the blinking light asking the particular party who they want, push the hold button, push station or extention wanted, every thing else is automatic.

m. The reasons for this are many, but the most important reasons are two, which are the following:

n. In recent times the professions have been recognized and even acknowledged to accommodate profitable careers because of the limited access to the years of training required to qualify in them.

o. It was concluded that so long as the customer's order is satisfactorily handled it matters little to the customer the manner in which it is accomplished.

p. While conducting this survey customers were questioned in an indirect manner to ascertain the importance of secretary convenience in the dispatch of business.

q. The weight of the results of this study requires a recommendation that Metrico, Inc. forgo employment of another secretary at this time due to the simple reason that the cost does not justify the convenience.

r. In order to obtain production figures for the Hutchins plant careful observations were made by me of work done under the method now being utilized.

s. By connecting recording machines and Delayed voice Operated relays to the present PBX switchboard every telephone instrument can become a convenient dictating facility.

t. The present system of inventory control Metrico, Inc. utilizes is extremely inefficient, and adoption of a new system of inventory control cannot be over-emphasized sufficiently, because it serves as a guide to effectiveness of selling and ultimate maximization of profits.

u. This area will provide adequate floor space for the components of the system to be arranged to create maximum efficiency in using the machines.

v. This report shall commence with a generalized discussion of the parameters of the "problem." This discussion then shall delve briefly and in depth into the psychological aspects, both cognitive and affective, as it affects both management and the employee.

w. The tabular analysis will be presented in this chapter in five different groupings which, for the sake of simplicity, will be grouped according to the respondents present locations.

x. Although much information exists on real estate appraisal finance and law apparently little is available on the nature and scope of real estate brokerage in general, and in Seattle in particular.

y. After coming up with the cost of building the building a survey was made as to how the majority of the people would react to a business such as of this type.

z. Because a substantial segment of the responses were negative, it would not seem advisable to postpone discontinuing production of this product at this point in time.

PART EIGHT

Advanced Communication Exercises: Minidramas, Scenarios, Cases

Congratulations! By completing Parts One through Seven, which compose the body of this book, you have taught yourself basic concepts and uses of effective business communication.

But the development of lives and of careers is a *continuing* process. Part Eight, therefore, is the first of two supplementary units which provide communication practice and a review of basic language skills.

Advanced Communication Exercises: Minidramas, Scenarios, Cases

As you approach the end of this book, try to recall the ideas and feelings you experienced at the start of your communication study. Compare them, contrast them, with those you experience now. Using the communication awareness you have gained, consider this book itself as a message—a message intended to practice what it teaches. By reviewing even briefly the sequence and techniques of presentation, you can enlarge your insight to what has been happening while you turned these pages.

GENERAL REVIEW

Your learning experiences with *Effective Communication in Business* have involved six essential factors: identification, explanation, illustration, application, discussion, and evaluation.

Part One (Chapters 1-3) *identified* concepts, goals, skills, techniques, and traits of effective communicators. Part One thereby introduced you to the study of needs and responsibilities for exchanging the evidence of ideas and feelings.

Part Two (Chapters 4-7) supplied increasingly detailed *explanation*, *illustration*, and *application* of data introduced in Part One, particularly those data concerning media and formats of business communication. Whereas Part One emphasized values and behaviors, Part Two focused upon their desirable results. In Part Two you studied how to achieve those results through appropriate organization, development, tone, and related uses of your verbal intelligence. You learned to associate those uses with spoken, with written, and with multimedia communication.

Parts Three through Seven (Chapters 8-19) built upon previous information by providing in-depth *discussion* and *evaluation* of specific, functional, recurring kinds of business messages, ranging from goodwill notes to comprehensive research reports.

With this book you have proceeded gradually from general concepts to specific details, from overall principles to particular applications. The preceding chapters have focused your attention upon types and variations of business media and messages. Part Eight now challenges you to review what you have learned and to seek new opportunities for continuing your improvement as a communicator.

MULTIMEDIA EXERCISES

Part Eight provides eleven integrated exercises: three minidramas, three scenarios, and five case histories. Since the format of these materials may be new to you, here is an explanation of their functions: The *minidramas* supply word-for-word dialogue and step-by-step actions for classroom performance and evaluation. The *scenarios* are somewhat more challenging; they describe contexts only, leaving dialogue and actions for you to decide. Still more advanced tests of your communication abilities are the *cases,* which narrate communication problems for you to solve. These three kinds of exercises—minidramas, scenarios, and cases—offer a progression of communication challenges and opportunities.

Use these materials as vehicles for perceiving causes as well as consequences of communication and of miscommunication, as stimuli to reasoning about your own and other people's behavior. Use them as opportunities for applying your own communication insights and abilities. Use them as exercises in empathy.

All of these exercises may be "recycled," with you and your fellow students changing roles, circumstances, outcomes, or interpretations. You and your classmates may rewrite the exercises or improvise your own variations to demonstrate other aspects of their themes.

Three Minidramas

Research Reporting: A Multimedia Presentation

The scene is your business-communication classroom. FIRST STUDENT *has been presenting an oral report with the use of visual aids for group viewing. A stack of handout material, not yet used, is near* FIRST STUDENT.

FIRST STUDENT: (LOOKING AT PROFESSOR) That ends my formal report. (LOOKING AT CLASS) Is there any question?
SECOND STUDENT: Could be.
                            There is a long pause. FIRST STUDENT *becomes fidgety, looks at* PROFESSOR *again.*

FIRST STUDENT:	What do I do now?
PROFESSOR:	(SMILES ENCOURAGINGLY AND GESTURES TOWARD THE CLASS) Ask *them*.
FIRST STUDENT:	(TO THE CLASS) What do I do now?
SECOND STUDENT: (JOKING)	Quit while you're ahead!
	Chuckles and good-natured comments from the group break the tension; FIRST STUDENT *smiles*.
FIRST STUDENT:	I thought you were my friend.
SECOND STUDENT:	I am. We all are. (TURNS TOWARD OTHER STUDENTS:) Aren't we?
OTHER STUDENTS:	Right on! Right! On!
PROFESSOR: (CHUCKLING)	Just the word *yes* would have been concise.
THIRD STUDENT:	And emphatic???
PROFESSOR:	Right on.
	There is good-natured laughter again from the group.
FIRST STUDENT:	I appreciate what's happening. You're all trying to help me overcome my stage fright. But it's not easy, being up here like this. You'll find out when you give your own reports.
FOURTH STUDENT:	Is that a threat?
THIRD STUDENT:	I think it's a promise.
	Laughter again. FIRST STUDENT *relaxes*.
PROFESSOR:	*This* is the place to learn about "stage fright" . . . *and* how to control it.
FIRST STUDENT:	You're trying to build our self-confidence, aren't you?
PROFESSOR:	Am I? Can anyone but you build justifiable confidence in yourself? (TO CLASS:) You know, that's exactly what all of you are doing by presenting these reports.
FIFTH STUDENT:	I think it's more than that. Sure, the reports and the research behind them are important. But we're also presenting ourselves.
THIRD STUDENT:	And evaluating, too. Not just the communications but also the communicators.
PROFESSOR:	Let's look at what's been happening here. (TO FIRST STUDENT:) You've given your report orally, and you've reinforced your spoken words with nonverbal language. You've used gestures, facial expressions, postures, movements. You've established rapport. You've earned our goodwill. (TO CLASS:) What's next?
SIXTH STUDENT: (CONSULTING NOTEBOOK)	According to my notes, the assignment goes this way: Each of us reports his or her research. We use more than one communication medium for the reporting. That is, we prepare a version in prescribed typewritten format and submit it to the professor. We keep

a copy of what we submit. While the professor evaluates the type-written versions, we use class periods to present our material orally. And we can use visual aids (GESTURING TOWARD FIRST STUDENT'S VISUAL AIDS) like those up there.

FOURTH STUDENT: Or audio aids. (HOLDING UP A CASSETTE) Like this tape I've prepared. It's a sample of my interview survey.
There is a sprinkle of applause.

SECOND STUDENT: Where's your cassette player?

FOURTH STUDENT: Knew I forgot something!
Much applause now.

SIXTH STUDENT:
CONSULTING
NOTEBOOK AGAIN)   Then . . . after the formal presentation . . . the reporter is supposed to . . . quote *elicit group discussion* unquote.

FIRST STUDENT: Well, that's what I'm doing.

THIRD STUDENT: Right. But you're supposed to relate the discussion to your research topic.

FIRST STUDENT: I'm trying to. Didn't I ask all of you: "Is there any question?"

THIRD STUDENT: Sure. But "Is there any question?"—that's a yes-or-no kind of thing. You want a discussion, don't you?

FOURTH STUDENT: Ask us something that begins with "who" or "what"—

SECOND STUDENT: —"when," "where," "why"—

FIFTH STUDENT: Or maybe "how." Start your questions with those words, and you'll put the ball in our court. Next thing you know: you've got a discussion.

FIRST STUDENT:
(THOUGHTFULLY)   Who, what, when . . . where, why, how . . . . All right: What's your opinion . . . of my research methods?

SIXTH STUDENT: We don't remember them all.

FIRST STUDENT: Gotcha! (PICKS UP THE STACK OF HANDOUTS.) These are copies of my summary, including a description of my research methods.
The group applauds enthusiastically.

PROFESSOR: Good work. All of you did well today. (GLANCES AT WRISTWATCH.) Pick up your copy of the summary before you leave. Study it, please, for next time. We'll be reviewing the research process, the report, and the communication techniques that all of us have used here.

As the group disperses amid adlib conversation, PROFESSOR *and* STUDENTS *take copies of the summary. Several people, including* PROFESSOR, *congratulate and chat briefly with* FIRST STUDENT. *Only* FIRST STUDENT *and* SECOND STUDENT *remain in the classroom, to collect the visual aids and extra handout copies.*

FIRST STUDENT: Thanks for helping with these; I'll do the same for you. (GESTURES TOWARD THE HANDOUT COPIES IN SECOND STUDENT'S HAND) How many extras?

SECOND STUDENT: (COUNTING QUICKLY)	. . . . four, five . . . six here.
FIRST STUDENT:	And three here. Nine extras; that's about right.
SECOND STUDENT: (HANDING THE SIX TO FIRST STUDENT)	How come?
FIRST STUDENT:	Well, who was absent today?
SECOND STUDENT:	Let's see . . . Foley and Davis—
FIRST STUDENT:	Esposito . . . Binford . . . anybody else?
SECOND STUDENT:	Just those four.
FIRST STUDENT: (HOLDING UP FOUR COPIES OF THE HANDOUT)	These'll be waiting when they get back.
SECOND STUDENT:	What about the other five copies?
FIRST STUDENT:	Replacements . . . a few always get lost.
SECOND STUDENT:	That's what I call planning!
FIRST STUDENT: (GRINNING)	Me, too. (SECOND STUDENT IS ABOUT TO TAKE DOWN THE LAST OF THE VISUAL AIDS.) Should've made that one larger. I don't think everyone could read it properly.
SECOND STUDENT: (STEPPING BACK TO VIEW THE VISUAL AID)	Maybe a little larger. And maybe more contrast with the colors?
FIRST STUDENT:	Good idea. (SHAKES HEAD) I need to remember not to block a visual aid while I'm using it. I did stand directly in front of it, didn't I?
SECOND STUDENT: (GIVES REMAINING MATERIAL TO FIRST STUDENT)	Just once, only for a second or so.
FIRST STUDENT: (LOOKS AROUND TO BE SURE THAT ALL THE MATERIALS HAVE BEEN COLLECTED)	Well, m'friend, that does it. Thanks again. .
SECOND STUDENT:	No charge; I've got a "free" period.
FIRST STUDENT:	Funnn-eeee.
SECOND STUDENT: (AS THEY LEAVE)	Glad you agree.

INSIGHTS

1. Unless you are accustomed to many kinds of message formats, the minidrama "script" may have challenged your study discipline and your patience. However, role playing is now common in advanced management training, with contexts drawn from actual business and personal experiences. Role playing is provided here so that you will not be a stranger to its format. An additional benefit of this practice is that you can learn to analyze real-life communication problems by occasionally writing them down and studying them in minidrama form.

2. Try to recall your attitudes, your feelings, and your ideas as you first began reading this minidrama. Initially, what pleased or displeased you about the minidrama format? In what ways, if at all, did your reactions change as you used this material? What communication insights did you gain from the minidrama? Report them as part of a classroom discussion or as an informal memorandum to your professor.

3. Now consider the minidrama as a message. What is its corethought? What are its supporting topics? Which of the communication media studied in this book are involved in the presentation of that message? How, if at all, did those media reinforce, or how did they block, transmission of that message?

4. The minidrama has dialogue and stage directions, often not as complete sentences but as fragments. Identify the fragments; then rewrite them as complete sentences.

5. In business memo format, convey the minidrama's corethought and its supporting details. Use your memo to explain basic techniques of presenting a research report orally with audio or visual aids. Address the memo to your professor; request constructive criticism.

Khamco Isn't Kirby's

Cast: Caller Switchboard Operator
Voice on First Tape Recording Salesperson
Voice on Second Tape Recording Answering Service Operator
Directory Assistance Operator

Seated at a table or desk on which there is a telephone, CALLER studies a wrinkled bit of note paper.

CALLER: Hmmm, let's see now . . . Comco Industries, 555-1010. (DIALS THE TELEPHONE NUMBER.) 5-5-5 . . . one-oh . . . one-oh.

VOICE ON FIRST
TAPE RECORDING: The number you have reached is not in service. We cannot complete your call as dialed. Please consult your telephone directory before placing the call again. The number you have reached is not in service. We cannot complete your call as dialed. Please consult—
CALLER *hangs up the telephone, looks at note again.*

CALLER:	Comco Industries . . . 555-1010. (LOOKS MORE CLOSELY AT NOTE:) Or is that *seven*-oh, *seven*-oh? (RUBS EYES, LOOKS AT NOTE ONCE MORE:) Whoever wrote this was in some kind of hurry. Well . . . . CALLER *dials Directory Assistance. There is a long pause before we hear:*
VOICE ON SECOND TAPE RECORDING:	If you have consulted your telephone directory for the number you need, please hold on. A Directory Assistance Operator will be with you shortly.
CALLER:	Okay, tape recording—I'll hold on.
VOICE ON SECOND TAPE RECORDING:	If you have consulted your telephone directory for the number you need, please hold on. A Directory Assistance Operator will be wi—
D. A. OPERATOR: (OVERRIDING THE RECORDING)	Your telephone number, please?
CALLER:	I'm trying to reach—
D. A. OPERATOR:	What number are you calling from, please?
CALLER:	I know *my* number; I'm trying to reach—
D. A. OPERATOR:	I must have the number you are calling from before I can assist you. *Your* telephone number, please . . . .
CALLER:	It's 555-1010 . . . no, that's the one I'm trying to *get*. I mean—
D. A. OPERATOR:	Your. Telephone. Number. Please.
CALLER: (STARING AT TELEPHONE)	393-62-24.
D. A. OPERATOR:	393-6224? Thank you. Now, may I help you?
CALLER:	Maybe. I'm trying to reach Kahmco Industries.

D. A. OPERATOR:	Kahnco Industries?
CALLER:	Did you say "Kah*nnn*co"?
D.A. OPERATOR:	"KHANCO" . . . *N* as in—
CALLER:	No!
D. A. OPERATOR:	Yes, *n* as in "no."
CALLER:	Not *n* as in "no." *Mmmmm* as in KhaMco. (SPELLING) K-H-A-
D. A. OPERATOR:	One moment, please. (AFTER A BRIEF PAUSE:) The number for Kha*m*co Industries is listed in your directory. Please make a note for future reference. It is . . . 5 5 5 . . . seven-oh, seven-oh.
CALLER:	Oh!! *Seven*-oh.
D. A. OPERATOR:	No, not oh-seven-oh. Please make a note: 5 5 5—
CALLER:	7070?
D. A. OPERATOR:	That is correct.
CALLER:	*Thanks*. (HANGS UP THE TELEPHONE, TAKES A DEEP BREATH, SIGHS WHILE EXHALING, DIALS AGAIN. THE CALL GOES THROUGH, AND WE HEAR:)
SWITCHBOARD OPERATOR:	Hold, please. (PUTS THE CALL ON "HOLD.")
CALLER:	I don't believe this. Hello? Helloooooh!
SWITCHBOARD OPERATOR:	Thank you for holding. I can connect you with Housewares now.
CALLER:	Connect me with what?
SWITCHBOARD OPERATOR:	Aren't you the party who wants Housewares? That line is clear now; I'll connect you.

CALLER: Don't connect me!

SALESPERSON: Housewares. May I help you?

CALLER: Is this Khamco?

SALESPERSON: This is Perkins. Ms. Pat Perkins, in Housewares.

CALLER: What's your phone number?

SALESPERSON: I beg your pardon?

CALLER: What telephone number have I reached?

SALESPERSON: This is Extension 1214.

CALLER: I mean, what's your *company* telephone number?

SALESPERSON: 555-7060.

CALLER: Seven-oh-SIX-oh? Aren't you Khamco Industries?

SALESPERSON: I'm Pat Perkins. And this is Kirby's.

CALLER: Kirby's what?

SALESPERSON: Kirby's Department Store.

CALLER: Wrong number.

SALESPERSON: We have some bargains in Housewares today.

CALLER: I'll . . . call back . . . some other time . . . .

SALESPERSON: We're open 'til nine tonight.

CALLER: Goodbye.

SALESPERSON: *Good* buy? our kitchen utensils are a *great* buy. They're on sale today—20% off! And we're open 'til nine.

CALLER: I'll remember; thank you. (HANGS UP THE PHONE.) One more time . . . (DIALS AGAIN.)

ANSWERING
SERVICE OPERATOR: Kahmco Industries . . . .

CALLER: Listen, I'm returning an important call from (LOOKS AT
                          NOTE) J. B. Dorsey, or Darcey, or—

ANSWERING SERV-
ICE OPERATOR: It's after five o'clock; the offices have just closed for the weekend.
                          They'll open again at 8:30, Monday morning . . . . Excuse me;
                          Monday's a holiday; They'll be closed until Tuesday. This is the
                          answering service. Would you care to leave a message?

CALLER: Yes. But I'd better not.

OPERATOR: Say what?

CALLER: Nothing. Have a good weekend. (HANGS UP THE PHONE,
                          STARES AT IT, THEN REDIALS.)

SWITCHBOARD
OPERATOR: Kirby's . . . .

CALLER: Housewares, please.

INSIGHTS

1. Precisely at what points in this minidrama did miscommunications
   occur? Which of the miscommunications were primarily oral? Which
   written? What were their causes and consequences? What techniques
   would you use for preventing or resolving them? Revise the minidrama
   script to demonstrate your recommendations.
2. What insights does this exercise provide for using skills of perception,
   interpretation, criticism, and empathy? Which of those insights pertain
   mainly to your own communication needs? to the communication
   needs of other people? to your needs *and* those of other people?

Is Mabry Hiring?

This minidrama is a variation on the theme of communicating by telephone. If a tape recorder is available, use it for playback, evaluation, and
constructive criticism of the presentation.

CAST: Switchboard Operator, Caller, Shaw

SWITCHBOARD OPERATOR:	Good morning. Mabry Corporation . . . .
CALLER:	I'm phoning about job opportunities with your company.
SWITCHBOARD OPERATOR:	Thank you; I'll ring Dale Shaw's office for you. *The call is transferred.*
SHAW:	Personnel Recruiting.
CALLER:	Mr. Daleshaw, please. Or maybe it's *Miss* Daleshaw?
SHAW:	This is Dale Shaw.
CALLER:	Oh. Well, I'm inquiring about possible employment with Mabry.
SHAW:	Do we have a file on you? Have you contacted us before?
CALLER:	No.
SHAW:	What kind of work are you interested in? What's your background? Tell me something about yourself.

INSIGHTS

1. What communication deficiencies does this brief dialogue illustrate? Although the dialogue takes only a few seconds to occur, what communication problems, if any, do you recognize as developing between Caller and Shaw? Rewrite the dialogue to minimize or to prevent misunderstandings between Caller and Switchboard Operator—also, between Caller and Shaw. Include directions concerning the tone which you believe these speakers should use. In what ways is your revised version superior to the original minidrama as an illustration of effective telephone communication? To what extent do your fellow students and your professor share your judgments of the original minidrama and of your revision?

2. To illustrate additional telephone skills, write (or improvise) the rest of the minidrama using these data:
   a. Mabry Corporation has mail-out materials for job seekers. Besides application forms, these materials include descriptions of Mabry's history, scope, organization, work classifications, and job requirements. The materials are costly; usually they are not sent in response to merely casual inquiries.
   b. As the telephone conversation continues, Shaw should begin to determine whether Caller's qualifications and Mabry's needs coincide. With this initial "screening" by phone, elicit answers to *unspoken* questions, including these:
   (1) Is Caller's inquiry legitimate?

(2) Should Mabry invest time and money in having Caller complete an employment application form? in reviewing the completed form and perhaps an accompanying résumé? in interviewing Caller? Should Mabry mail its recruiting materials to Caller? If so, which of those materials should be sent?

3. Write or improvise the rest of the minidrama to demonstrate each of these possibilities:

   a. Caller impresses Shaw favorably. Shaw decides to mail appropriate materials and to schedule an interview appointment for Caller.

   b. Shaw determines during the initial telephone conversation that Mabry's needs and Caller's qualifications do not match. Both Shaw and Caller know, however, that goodwill is good business. And Mabry may need Caller's services in the future.

   c. Shaw has mixed feelings about Caller's qualifications; but as the telephone conversation continues, Caller persuades Shaw favorably.

4. What communication insights have you derived by writing or improvising the rest of "Is Mabry Hiring?" In what ways do you plan to use those insights for your own continuing development as a business communicator? Discuss your insights with your classmates; what additional benefits does that discussion provide? In a memo report to your professor, summarize your experiences with "Research Reporting: A Multimedia Presentation," "Khamco Isn't Kirby's," and "Is Mabry Hiring?" Identify the communication benefits you have gained from those experiences. Identify the needs that you now recognize for your continuing improvement as a communicator. Compare and contrast your current needs with those you recognized at the beginning of your communication course. Explain how you propose to continue meeting your communication needs after completing the course.

Three Scenarios

The minidramas gave you specific dialogue and actions to perform and to evaluate. These scenarios, however, are merely *descriptions of contexts* for dialogue and actions. The responsibility for details of their application is left largely to you. *You* supply your own multimedia communication for these exercises.

Discuss with your classmates and your professor the communication insights you gain from using these three scenarios as related to the purposes and scope of your communication course.

Scenario for Demonstration, Discussion, and Constructive Criticism. In a memo or a business letter addressed to your professor, you describe a real-life example of effective (or of deficient) business communication which you believe pertinent to your own and to your fellow student's needs. You explain why your example is pertinent, and you propose methods of communicating through a multimedia classroom presentation.

After reviewing your memo or letter and those collected from your fellow students, your professor authorizes several of the proposals for classroom presentation. If your proposal is among those authorized, you request other students to portray roles which you assign. You organize those people into a working team for planning, rehearsing, and presenting your real-life example. Then you lead classroom discussion of your team's presentation; and you request appropriate, constructive criticism. If your proposal is not among those authorized by your professor, you participate as a member of someone else's team or as a constructive critic of the presentations. Your professor may require your criticism to be written or oral. You should be prepared to justify your comments and your suggestions.

Scenario for Constructive Criticism Through Teamwork. Every student in the class selects two business messages that he or she has written during the course but which the professor has not graded. A code number or code name known only to the student and the professor is assigned to each student. *The sole identification of who wrote the various messages is the code name or code number.*

This communication procedure is then followed: Professor collects the two messages from each student. Professor organizes the class into teams of three or four students each. Professor distributes the messages to the teams; no team is to receive material written by any of its members. Each team constructively criticizes the messages given to it, justifying the criticism by citing pertinent classroom instruction and information from this book. Each team reports its constructive criticism informally (perhaps by memo or by fill-in form which the team designs), addressed to the code numbers or code names. The original messages, accompanied by the team reports, are returned to the professor, who uses them as a basis for full-class discussion. (An opaque projector would be useful for this multimedia exercise if the professor wishes to have the class present the materials for group viewing.)

Following the discussion, the professor privately returns the original messages to their authors. That material is accompanied by the team report concerning it. A full-class discussion has evaluated the messages, but the identity of the authors has remained confidential.

In a memorandum or a letter addressed to the professor, each student responds to the team criticism and full-class discussion by revising his or her material or by writing an explanation of why that material should be revised. The written revisions or explanations, the team criticism, and the two original messages are collected as a set, which the professor then evaluates. Finally, professor and class discuss the communication experiences and insights derived from this scenario.

A Multimedia Learning Situation Involving Committees. Professor organizes class into committees (five to seven students per committee). Each committee elects (or the professor appoints) a chairperson, a vice-chairperson, and a secretary as officers. The chairperson is responsible for all committee work but may delegate tasks. In case of the chairperson's absence, the vice-chairperson has that responsibility; otherwise, the vice-chairperson functions as the chairperson's administrative assistant. If both of these officers are absent, the committee secretary heads the group and appoints other aides as needed; otherwise, the secretary functions as recorder/reporter of committee activities.

The chairperson leads the committee in establishing a work atmosphere of productivity and goodwill and guides the committee in selecting, from previous chapters of this book, three communication topics for possible presentation to the entire class. The committee designates its most preferred topic as Topic 1, its least preferred as Topic 3; Topic 2 would represent intermediate preference. For example, a committee topic list might resemble the following:

Topic 1: Nonverbal communication aspects of an employment interview
Topic 2: Techniques for personalizing business-form messages
Topic 3: Methods of improving face-to-face and machine dictation

Having determined three topics, the committee proposes a scope of discussion for each of those topics. For instance, with what aspects of each topic does the committee intend to deal? Which committee member(s) will be accountable for developing and communicating those aspects to the class when the committee makes its final presentation? Since the committee officers are involved in administration, to what extent should those officers also participate in other work of the committee?

Answers to the foregoing questions are included in the committee's first report to the professor. That first report, written in memorandum format, also identifies the committee officers, provides minutes of the initial committee meeting, and offers an agenda for the next committee meeting.

The professor reviews the memos, then invites officers of all the committees to an administrative conference. (The conference may be held with other class members as observers and as resource persons.) If audio or video tape-recording equipment is available, it should be used for playback and evaluation of this administrative conference. During the conference, officers of all the committees present their written minutes to the professor and summarize them orally. The conference proceeds to a discussion of the proposed topics (three for each committee), elimination of duplicated topics, revision of topics where necessary, and final assignment of one appropriate topic per committee.

Following the conference, the officers report to their own committee members, announce the assigned topic, and schedule a series of meetings to do this work:

1. Review textbook information concerning the assigned topic; consult additional authoritative sources if needed.

2. Select data for the final committee presentation to the class.

3. Set specific data-and-presentation responsibilities for individual committee members.

4. Plan, organize, and rehearse the final presentation, which is to include at least two of the following: appropriate use of visual and/or audio aids; demonstration of data applications; use of extemporaneous, textual, or memorized oral delivery; use of typewritten handouts or other supplementary materials.

All the committees follow this procedure for their final presentation to the entire class:

1. Chairperson is responsible for introducing committee officers and other committee members, providing appropriate transitions among parts of the presentation, eliciting relevant discussion that involves the committee with its audience, and summarizing the whole presentation. (Note: The chairperson is responsible for these tasks but, in the role of an administrator, may delegate their performance to other officers or members of the committee.)

2. Chairperson also is responsible for timing the final presentation. Suggestion: Determine the number of minutes judged adequate and available as minimum and as maximum time quotas for each speaker. Multiply that number of minutes by the number of persons on the committee. The result will be the amount of time allocated to each committee for its final presentation to the class. For example, assume that there are thirty students in your class. Six committees (five students per committee, in this example) may be formed. Time limits for the final presentation may be set at a minimum of three minutes and a maximum of five minutes per speaker. Multiplying the number of people by those time limits, you derive these guides: 5 people × 3 minutes = 15 minutes, 5 people × 5 minutes = 25 minutes. Thus the prepared committee presentation, for this example, ranges from at least 15 minutes to not more than 25 minutes. Your professor may allot additional time for the whole-class discussion, which is to follow each committee presentation.

If available, video or audio tape-recording equipment can be used for playback and evaluation of what this entire scenario produces. Otherwise, when a committee gives its presentation, other class members may be assigned the roles of observers and constructive critics.

Five Cases

The following case histories are narratives of communication and miscommunication. The cases may be presented in class and then discussed, or they may be studied as reading assignments for classroom discussion.

First Day on the Job

On this first morning of Lee Waley's job with Consolidated Products, Inc., Lee skips breakfast to be sure of getting to work on time.

The morning's activities go well. Shortly before noon, Lee's new employer says: "Take your lunch break now, but be back by 12:45. We're shorthanded today, and I'll need you when the Collins Company buyer comes in. Make it a quick lunch this time, Lee. Try Dory's on Washington Avenue; their turkey-and-cheese sandwiches are pretty good."

A portion of Washington Avenue, between Industrial Road and Interstate Highway 20, is known as "Hamburger Alley" because of the many fast-food businesses located there. Surrounding the Alley are manufacturing plants, office complexes, and a junior college; so lunchtime traffic is heavy every weekday.

Dory's Quikserv is a recently opened franchise unit of a six-state chain operation. Upon entering Dory's, the customers go to a counter, place their orders, pay the cashier, and move alongside the counter as food and beverages are placed on their trays. Then the customers carry the trays to tables in the dining area. This pattern is designed for fast service, but today Dory's and the other Alley places are overcrowded.

It is 12:15 when Lee Waley joins the waiting line that extends to the parking lot at Dory's. Fifteen minutes later, Lee reaches the order-taker's position at the counter, and the following conversation takes place.

ORDER-TAKER: Your order, please.

LEE: I'll have . . . let's see . . . I'll have a turkey-and-cheese sandwich on rye . . . lettuce and tomato . . . no mayonnaise but extra relish. Better make that two turkey-and-cheese. And an order of fries. A large order of fries.

ORDER-TAKER: Anything to drink?

LEE: A large cola, please.

ORDER-TAKER: Is that a large cola and two orders of fries?

LEE: One order of fries.

ORDER-TAKER: You said an order of fries *and* a large order of fries.

LEE: One. Large. Order. Of. Fries. Andonelargecola.

ORDER-TAKER: Thank you.

LEE: Don't forget the sandwiches.

ORDER-TAKER: Two Jubilee Combos, extra relish, no mayo—right?

LEE: I want two turkey-and-cheese sandwiches—

ORDER-TAKER: That's our Jubilee Combo. See, it's right here on the order tickets. I just mark "2" in this little box, and you get your Jubilees at the end of the counter. Pay here, please; that's $2.89.

LEE: I've never heard of Jubilee Combos; I want—

ORDER-TAKER: That's what we call them.

LEE: Look, I'm hungry—no breakfast and it's a busy day. I need a good lunch. But if that food isn't what I want, I won't pay for it.

ORDER-TAKER: You pay here; you pick up the food down there.
The Dory's manager appears.

MANAGER: What's holding up the line?

LEE: In plain English, I want two turkey-and-cheese sandwiches.

MANAGER: Sorry, we're out of Jubilees.

Exasperated, Lee mutters "Cancel the order!" and turns away from the counter. A crowd of impatient customers blocks the entranceway. Really fuming now, Lee turns again, stalks alongside the serving counter, and moves through the packed dining area, looking for an exit. Passing around and between tables and people, Lee hears one seated customer say to another: "These Jubilees are delicious." Almost groaning, Lee locates the exit door. Above it is a poster with Dory's motto: *Good Food, Fast Service, Customer Satisfaction.*

Although managing to get a snack somewhere else on the "Alley," Lee is further delayed by a traffic jam and returns to work at 1:15. "The Collins buyer couldn't wait," says Lee's new employer. "This is your first day on the job, and you get back late. Why?"

INSIGHTS

Test your awareness of empathy and oral/visual/nonverbal communication factors by answering these questions:

1. What communication problems did you detect during Lee's visit to Dory's? In what ways were those problems likely to be perceived and interpreted by Lee Waley? by the order-taker? by Dory's manager?

2. What oral/visual/nonverbal factors apparently influenced the behavior of those three people during Lee's visit? Specifically, how would you have tried to control those factors if you had been Lee? the order-taker? the Dory's manager? Why?

3. If you were Lee, how would you respond to your new employer's statements? Why? If you were Lee's new employer, what would you have said when Lee returned from lunch? Why?

4. What insights to empathy and to oral/visual/nonverbal communication do your answers to these questions disclose?

Media Selection at Bauer

As part of its public communications program, the Bauer Corporation, a large agribusiness firm, occasionally conducts tours of its headquarters facilities in Minneapolis. At this moment a group of students and educators is being greeted by Miss Laurie Moore, assistant manager of Bauer's Communication Services Division.

"Welcome to Bauer," says Moore; "we're glad you're here. Some of what you see and hear this morning may be new to you, but a good deal will seem familiar. You'll have an opportunity to notice applications of communication concepts and techniques in actual business situations here."

During the tour, representatives of production, training, and administration departments are introduced to the group. Each of the representatives emphasizes communication aspects of the work being done. The theme of the tour is that effective communication is essential to every kind of job.

The tour ends with a question-and-answer session conducted by Moore, who states: "As you've seen, Bauer Corporation uses many kinds of communication media and message formats. We stress selection as well as use here."

"Selection?" a student asks.

"Yes. Communication involves choices. Of all the alternatives available to you in a particular business situation, what will you choose to do or write or say? How will you transmit your actions and your messages? What media will you choose?"

"Letters and memos mostly, I guess," says the student. "They're basic to business communication, aren't they?"

"If you have any doubts," Moore replies with a smile, "just ask the people in our Mail Room. But this is the kind of thing I mean by choice: We deliberately select the business letter as a format when our message, although important, is not extremely urgent. We select that format also when the Bauer letterhead and an official signature will reinforce the message."

"When do you choose a memo format instead?"

"Again when the message, although important, is not extremely urgent," Moore replies. "Also, mainly when the message is intended for our own people within the Bauer Organization."

"What about telephone communication?"

"It's another mainstay," says Moore, "particularly for brief, uncomplicated messages which must reach people quickly. At Bauer we rely on the telephone when voice communication is needed to fortify or expedite what otherwise might be written. For example, we usually telephone when we want to convey special emphasis for explanations, persuasive messages, requests, or apologies. Phoning is our choice, also, for reinforcing a written message or for alerting someone about receiving such a message when it has unusual importance. But Bauer uses other communication formats and media as well."

"You mean mass media for advertising?"

"Yes, certainly. But I was thinking also of mailgrams, teletypewriter networks, and the like."

"Mailgrams would convey urgency for a message," says the student.

"Right," continues Moore; "they tend to get attention when a phone call or a letter hasn't done so. We also use them for transmitting one message relatively fast to many people."

"You mentioned teletypewriter networks, too."

"Yes. Telex and TWX, for instance, are like the telephone in terms of speed. But they also provide documentation—the *evidence* of communication—as a business letter does."

"What are Telex and TWX?"

"They're interconnected teletypewriter networks operated by Western Union. You know," Moore observes, "teletypewriters can transmit and receive written messages at any time, day or night. That factor can be critical when different time zones affect business transactions. You see, Bauer Corporation has branch offices in just about all of the major cities, and timing is essential to us."

"What do you mean?"

"Well," says Moore, "suppose you're managing our Atlanta office. At 10 a.m. Eastern Time, you teletype an important message to the branch at Fresno, California. Your message is transmitted instantly, but it is 7 a.m. out there on the West Coast. Although unattended at that hour, the teletypewriter in the Fresno office receives your message; and when that branch office begins its business day, your message receives immediate attention. The teletypewriter provides an exact copy of the message for your receiver's file as well as your own. Also, Telex and TWX can transmit a single message very rapidly to people in various locations."

"What other kind of telecommunication does Bauer use?"

"Facsimile machines; they're called 'fax' for short and are profitable for our business. We use fax to transmit complicated materials. I mean messages which are extremely difficult to explain or describe by telephone, to set up on a typewriter, or to redraw. For instance, photographs, charts, diagrams, and so on—which need to be received in a matter of minutes. But fax has a disadvantage at its present stage of development. Material transmitted by fax does not always reproduce clearly on office copying equipment."

"You seem to be saying that every communication medium has advantages and disadvantages. Is that why you've been emphasizing *selection* during this discussion?"

Moore replies with a grin: "Pardon the pun, but you get the message."

INSIGHTS

Test your awareness of business communication media and message formats by answering these questions:

1. Specifically what media and formats are described in this case? What are their basic advantages and disadvantages for business communicators?
2. What other media and formats are described in Chapter 6 of this book? What are their basic advantages/disadvantages?
3. Concerning the career field that interests you most, with which communication media and formats do you need to be familiar? To what extent? Why?
4. What opportunities does your school provide for familiarization with media and formats? In what additional ways, if any, do you propose to gain communication expertise? Why? When?

Communication Teamwork at Bauer

C. W. Brenner is marketing vice-president of Bauer Corporation (the company mentioned in the preceding case). Recognized nationally as a knowledgeable and an effective communicator, Brenner accepts about thirty speaking engagements annually on behalf of the Bauer organization.

Ordinarily Brenner schedules adequate preparation time for those important addresses. But there are unexpected circumstances on this occasion. At 11 a.m. today, Brenner concludes a marketing staff conference. Scheduled to leave Minneapolis at 11:45 and to address the National Farmers and Bankers Convention in Chicago at 2:30 this afternoon, Brenner hurries from the conference room. A staff assistant, Leslie Taro, is at Brenner's side.

"You've just enough time to get to the airport," Taro remarks.

"Right," says Brenner as they approach the elevators. "Thanks for pitching in, Les."

"Glad to do it," Taro replies, "especially since your regular assistant is ill. Now, here's the typewritten text for your Chicago speech."

Quickly leafing through the pages, Brenner says, "They're not here."

"What's missing?"

"Those pages with comparative data for 1976 and '77. I need them as historical facts to clinch my recommendations at the convention."

Brenner continues: "I made longhand notes of those statistics. Akins was going to edit the notes and add a summary chart—something I can use for quick reference at the convention. But Atkins' illness came on so suddenly that—"

An elevator door opens as Taro says, "If you miss your plane, there'll be no speech at all in Chicago. Let me see what I can do."

Stepping into the elevator, Brenner urges Leslie Taro to locate the missing materials. "Get them to me through our Chicago branch as soon as you can, Les. I need that part of the speech and the summary chart."

The elevator door closes. Returning to the Marketing Department suite of offices, Taro locates these notes with the help of a secretarial assistant:

Corethought: On October 19, 1977, the U.S. Department of Agriculture published this finding: Rising land values continued to increase farmers' assets despite a slump in farmers' net incomes between January 1, 1977, and January 1, 1976.

Details:

1. As of Jan. 1, 1977, U.S. farm assets had reached a then-unprecedented total of $670.9 billion, up 13% from the $592.8 billion recorded on Jan. 1, '76.

2. Net farm income (what remained after farmers had paid their bills) dropped from $21.9 billion (Jan. 1, '76) to about $20.1 billion (Jan. 1, '77). *Important:* Net farm income had risen to a record high of $29.9 billion in 1973.

3. Farm debt was reported on Jan. 1, '77 as $102.1 billion, up 12.5 per cent from $90.8 billion (Jan 1, '76).

4. On Jan. 1, '77, farmers owned $568.8 billion of their assets outright, a 13.3 per cent gain from equity of $520 billion reported Jan. 1, '76.

5. Farm real estate accounted for about 87% of total farm assets reported Jan. 1, '77. But money owed on farm real estate accounted for 55 per cent of the farm debt reported Jan. 1, '77.

6. Average value of farm land nationally was $456 per acre (Jan. 1, '77), up from $390/acre (Jan. 1, '76).

"Well," Taro muses, "we need to edit these notes for oral presentation, do the visual aid, get the results to Brenner in Chicago—and all in less than three hours. No problem; here we go."

INSIGHTS

In the role of Taro, test your communication skills by answering these questions:

1. Specifically what communication challenges and tasks do you face? What sequence do you propose to follow in meeting them? Why? What teamwork, if any, do you expect from other Bauer employees? Specifically, from whom? Specifically, how do you expect to elicit and manage that necessary teamwork?

2. Knowing that Bauer has innovative as well as traditional communication equipment at its home office in Minneapolis and at all of its branches throughout the nation, what media will you use to do this job for Brenner? Why?

3. What is your revised version of the notes for Brenner's speech? In what ways does your revision fulfill effective communication criteria? Timing is critical in this case; how long did you need to complete the revision? What, if anything, would have expedited the revision?

4. What is your visual aid for Brenner's speech? Specifically, how is your visual aid likely to be appropriate and effective for Brenner's use at the Chicago convention?

5. What transmission medium or media will get your written and visual materials to Brenner in time for presentation at the Chicago convention?

Injuries: The Markel Company

Implementing its affirmative-action policy, Markel Company has hired Fran Belize. Young and unmarried, Fran lives at home, contributing to the support of two pre-teen sisters, a widowed mother, and an elderly aunt.

Fran Belize's home is one of many multiple-unit dwellings in a city neighborhood with a high incidence of crime. Although the residents have very small incomes, they are often the victims of burglars and vandals, despite conscientious police efforts. Fran hopes that employment with Markel Company will enable the Belize family to move to a safer neighborhood.

Fran has been working at Markel for two months now. At 11:45 yesterday morning, an office employee reported that a set of company keys was missing from a desk drawer. About an hour later the keys were found, wedged between the desk and the adjacent wall.

The office worker was told: "You just dropped them and became excited."

"I looked there, thinking they might have fallen off the desk somehow. But believe me, those keys were gone."

"They're right where you dropped them," was the reply. "We're all a little jumpy; too much overtime, I guess."

Just before dawn today a security guard startled someone who had unlocked a side door and had entered the Markel Building. The intruder fired a pistol, wounded the guard, and escaped. The guard's injury was painful but minor.

"Guess I could have been killed," the guard said later. "It happened so fast I didn't even get a good look at the guy. But whoever it was didn't break in. He—or, maybe, she—had a key to the lock on that door."

Although the report of that incident certainly has disrupted morale at Markel Company, the employees are trying to do business as usual today. A police investigation is underway. One of the focal points is the temporary disappearance of the office keys. Someone could have taken them, have had them duplicated during the lunch hour, and then could have put them where they were later found. The Markel grapevine is buzzing. "It's an inside job," everyone agrees.

S. M. Markel, president of the company, has called department heads and other executives to a special meeting. "We've been in business for twenty years," says Markel. "Sure, we've had some pilfering in that time. But never anything like this incident."

"Times change," the personnel manager remarks. "We need to be more careful these days about the people we hire. We need better security."

"You're right," Markel agrees, "we'll be more careful. But I'm not thinking entirely about possible property loss, although it could have been considerable. What concerns me most is that our guard could have been seriously hurt, and all because of carelessness with some keys."

The conference continues. "It has to be one of our own people," a department head named Royce emphasizes. "Everything points in that direction. And you know we've been hiring newcomers from some tough neighborhoods lately."

"I'd say that most of us started out in tough neighborhoods," Markel observes. "I didn't come from a rich family. Did you?"

"It's different today," Royce insists. "We've lifted ourselves by our bootstraps. But kids have everything handed to them now. What they don't earn, they just take."

"What makes you think it was a kid?" Markel says. "We don't know who shot the guard."

"As the conference continues, suspicions are voiced about several recently hired employees, including Fran Belize. Finally Markel says: "All right, you've given me five names. The police have the job of solving this thing, but I can't help wondering now about those five people. Are they all here today?"

"Yes," the personnel manager replies, "they're here: Jordan, Holmes, Greene, Carr, Belize—all of them came to work today as usual. In fact, we had no absence reports at all this morning."

Markel concludes the conference a few minutes later but asks the personnel manager to remain. After the others leave, Markel says quietly: "Tell me in confidence; who do you think it really is?"

"I don't want to accuse an innocent person," the manager replies. I'll get you those five personnel records, if you wish."

"We'll go over the records together. But tell me now whatever you can."

The personnel manager sighs before replying: "Jordon, Holmes, and Greene were hired at the same time, during our expansion program about three years ago. Their work has been good; they've received raises regularly. But Jordan and Holmes have mentioned family problems a lot lately. Jordan's children were badly injured in that traffic accident a month ago, and insurance isn't covering the medical bills."

"What about Holmes?"

"Holmes' children were in the same accident. You know, Holmes and Jordan are cousins; their children were together when the accident happened. Holmes and Jordan were working overtime; we had a rush of orders that day."

"And Greene?"

"Greene, Carr, and Belize have similar backgrounds. They're young, ambitious, competitive. They want to get ahead as fast as they can. Carr is married; no children yet. Greene and Belize are single but help to support their relatives. All three worked at temporary jobs until we hired them. We gave them their first real opportunities."

"I understand what you're saying," Markel replies. "But which one of those five people do *you* think did this thing?"

Several weeks have passed. Because of insufficient evidence, the case remains unsolved. Markel Company morale now is at rock bottom. Efficiency is seriously impaired; suspicions are rampant.

At another meeting in the president's office, Royce declares: "There's just one logical thing to do. We've got to fire Belize and those other four, or we won't get any work done around here."

"Maybe you're right," Markel replies. "Our business is suffering."

"Enough to terminate those five jobs!" Royce emphasizes.

There is a knock at the door; Markel's secretary enters. "Excuse me. Detective Verdry has telephoned twice and is on the line again."

Markel sputters: "Why didn't you tell me right away?"

"You said to hold your calls," answers the secretary, "but Detective Verdry has an urgent message for you."

Markel picks up the telephone. "Markel here. Yes . . . where? At Grace and Company? Posed as a job applicant . . . and just lifted the keys? Confessed to doing the same thing here! Thank you . . . thank you very much for letting us know."

Markel hangs up the telephone, stares at it, then turns to the others.

"It wasn't one of our people."

"Good," says Royce, "I'm glad it wasn't. But you mentioned Grace and Company. Was anybody hurt over there, too?"

There is a long pause before Markel responds: "Not so many as have been hurt here."

INSIGHTS

Test your knowledge of logic, of fallacies, and of their effects upon communication by answering these questions:

1. In what ways, if at all, were inductive and deductive reasoning used appropriately in this case? Specifically how, if at all, were they used inappropriately? What were the consequences of their use and misuse?

2. What fallacies (errors of reasoning) occurred? Who made them? Of what did they consist? What were their consequences? How should those fallacies and their effects have been corrected? By whom? When? Why?

3. Reread the last two paragraphs of the case; what *were* the "injuries at Markel Company"? Specifically how, if at all, were these people hurt:
   a. Fran Belize?
   b. the office worker who reported loss of the keys?
   c. the security guard?
   d. S.M. Markel?
   e. the personnel manager?
   f. Royce?

4. What evidence from the case confirms or contradicts your answers for Item 3? To what extent, if any, are those answers based upon your own suppositions and inferences rather than upon evidence stated in the case?

5. What insights to your own use of perception and interpretation are disclosed by your responses to Items 1-4? In what ways are those insights related to your continuing improvement as a business communicator? Specifically, how do you propose to benefit from your experience in analyzing this case?

Spahr's Monologue to Biscoe

Stacy Spahr, a junior executive at Tolby Associates, returns from a staff conference and beckons Cass Biscoe into a private office. Looking pale and harassed, Spahr rapidly says all of the following to Biscoe. The statements are presented here as a single paragraph to simulate Spahr's manner and rate of speaking.

Am I glad *that* meeting's over! Tell me, Cass; why do some people use so many words to say so little? Never mind; we're way behind schedule now, aren't we? First thing: You'd better take these notes I made on the conference. Type them for our reference file. If you have trouble deciphering my scribble, let me know while they're still fresh in my mind. Handle them yourself, Cass; don't give them to the typing pool. A few of those items are confidential, okay? I've also got a bunch of letters and memos to dictate as soon as possible. They need to get out right away, Cass. Say, did Crandell phone? I'm expecting calls from Crandell and

Breen; be sure to put them right through. And tell Ross and Yates I'll be in their office today about the Sima Imports deal. About 2:30. No, better make it 2:15, will you? Now, *this* goes to Doyle at Salt Lake City. Make it a memo. Tell Doyle we must have those sales summaries by the 15th of every month. Make it clear, Cass; the 15th is the date for delivery here, not the date for mailing them to us. But don't make it sound harsh; firm but not harsh. You know, Doyle's a little sensitive about that kind of thing. Say the sales volume is good, but we've got to have those things when they're due—and that's by the 15th of every month. This next one I want to dictate personally. It goes to Ortega at Albuquerque. Start with "Congratulations on landing the Roswell account. I want you to know we're impressed by your efforts." Guess that's all I really want to say, Cass, but it's too short. Add a few words of your own. Make it personal, but use executive letterhead. Which reminds me: I'm not satisfied with some of the letters and memos our people have been sending. Here are some samples; look them over and see what you can do with them, will you? I mean, see if you can come up with some models, maybe some guide forms, for routine correspondence, you know? Got another meeting now; I'll be in Bethune's office if you need me.

Here are the unsatisfactory messages which Spahr gives to Biscoe for revision:

Unfortunately we are unable to grant your request for a refund with reference to the Tolby Industrial Marine products which you purchased seven months ago.

The enclosed literature covering Tolby products, including the Industrial Marine line, is for your reference. It behooves you to notice that the period of time for the guarantee is six months, not seven months, from the date of sale and that, under the terms of our agreement, we are not required to provide refund, repair, or replacement of our expense beyond that date.

We solicit your interest in ordering new Tolby products to replace those concerning which you expressed dissatisfaction.

Your failure to answer our previous reminders of your long overdue payment disappoints us.

We are entitled to full settlement for your July 15 order or to at least an explanation of why your account remains delinquent and a definite indication of when you will make payment.

Here is my memo on justification of expansion of our Engineering Services. The purpose of this proposal is to justify the hiring of additional personnel needed to increase the efficiency and productivity of that department and to enable the department to render faster and better service to other units of our organization. Briefly stated, the current workload cannot be handled adequately and effectively with the present number of engineering personnel and supporting staff. We need more people as soon as they can be hired. Space requirements for the additional personnel can be handled without additional offices being assigned at this point in time.

INSIGHTS

Test your communication knowledge and skills by answering these questions:

1. What evidence in this case indicates that communication improvements are needed in the working relationship between Spahr and Biscoe? Specifically, what improvements should be made? Why? Who has responsibility for achieving them? Why?

2. Exactly what tasks did Spahr give Biscoe? What priorities did Spahr assign to each of those tasks? As Biscoe, in what sequence would you perform those tasks? Why?

3. If Spahr returned to find that those tasks had not been done as quickly as desired, what would you as Biscoe say to Spahr? Why? If Spahr then became disappointed or angry, how would you renew rapport in the working relationship? If Spahr demonstrated empathy instead of disappointment or anger, what constructive suggestions would you as Spahr offer at that moment? Specifically, how would you word those suggestions? Why?

4. Prepare the memo to Doyle and the letter to Ortega. What are the positive features of the Doyle and Ortega messages you prepare? What are the positive and negative aspects of the three additional messages given to Spahr for revision? What would be appropriate revisions of those messages? Why?

ADDITIONAL CHALLENGES AND OPPORTUNITIES

In a memorandum addressed to your professor, propose an original minidrama, scenario, or case history of your own design. Relate your proposal specifically to one of the following topics:

1. Ways to develop skills of perceiving, reasoning, interpreting, or empathizing

2. Kinds and consequences of nonverbal communication in business

3. Methods of improving reading or listening skills for business

4. Methods of improving oral and visual communication skills for business

5. Suggestions for improving dictation of business messages

6. Recommendations for improving use of multimedia communication in business

7. Techniques for developing accuracy and clarity of business messages

8. Techniques for developing and using conciseness and courtesy in business messages

9. Effects of tone upon data in business communication

10. A relevant topic of your own choosing

Then do the following:

1. Obtain your professor's authorization of the proposal.

2. Develop the proposal into a suitable minidrama, scenario, or case as a classroom presentation.

3. Ask your professor and fellow students for constructive criticism of your presentation.

4. Report communication insights that you derive from this experience.

TRANSITION

Even the most advanced communicator sometimes benefits from a review of basic language skills. The next unit of this book, Part Nine, is a reference section intended to help you refresh those skills.

PART NINE

Reference Division:
Review of Language Skills

Almost every communicator benefits occasionally from a review of basic language skills. Part Nine provides such a review, geared to communication standards which U.S. managers generally expect career employees to use. Striking a middle ground between extremes of formality and informality, Part Nine summarizes the major aspects of American English grammar, sentence structure, punctuation, and style for business writing.

This reference section and all the chapters preceding it have been prepared with your needs in mind. The authors and the publisher invite your comments about this edition—and your constructive suggestions for the future editions—of *Effective Communication in Business.*

Reference Division: Review of Language Skills

NOUNS, PRONOUNS, AND ADJECTIVES

Nouns, or name words, are classified as follows:

1. **Proper nouns** are capitalized to show that they are particular names (Jan Jones, Miami, Concorde).

2. **Common nouns** are not capitalized (person, city, aircraft); they are general names.

3. **Concrete nouns** identify what our physical senses can perceive (rocket, typewriter, fragrance).

4. **Abstract nouns** identify qualities beyond physical sensing (courage, honor, initiative).

5. **Collective nouns** identify groups (committee, company, family). In American English, collective nouns usually take singular number, as with "The committee *is* deciding" or "Yates and Rawls *is* an advertising agency."

6. **Verbal nouns** are discussed on page 467.

Pronouns are noun substitutes. Like a noun, a **pronoun** may be used as a subject (nominative case), object (objective case), or possessor (possessive case), as shown here:

NOMINATIVE CASE	OBJECTIVE CASE	POSSESSIVE CASE
I	me	my
we	us	our
you	you	your
he	him	his
she	her	her
it	it	its
they	them	their
who	whom	whose

A pronoun functioning as subject usually takes the nominative case. (Exception: A pronoun immediately following "to be" takes the case of the preceding noun or pronoun. Example: "I know *you* to be *him* who outbid us." Such a sentence is grammatically correct but awkward. A more businesslike version would be "I know you outbid us.")

The pronouns *yours, mine, ours,* and *theirs* often take the nominative case ("*Yours* is the better proposal") or the objective case ("Of all those offers, I selected *yours*.").

To indicate ownership, pronouns take the possessive case, as with these examples: *Your* proposal is better; *my* proposal is too costly." "*Our* offer was accepted; *their* offer was declined." A pronoun is the possessive case functions as an adjective.

Adjectives contract or expand the scope of nouns and pronouns, thus, **adjectives** are said to *modify* nouns or pronouns.

Proper adjectives are derived from proper nouns and therefore are capitalized.

PROPER NOUN: We sell silverware made in *Denmark*.

PROPER ADJECTIVE: Do you sell *Danish* silverware?

PROPER NOUN: This style of furniture is named for Queen *Victoria*.

PROPER ADJECTIVE: That shop sells modern as well as *Victorian* furniture.

The basic form of an adjective is called its **positive degree. Comparative degree** is used when an adjective modifies one of *two* items. **Superlative degree** is used when an adjective modifies one of *more than two* items.

Adjectives with only one syllable in their positive degree generally add -*r* or -*er* for the comparative and -*st* or -*est* for the superlative.

POSITIVE   COMPARATIVE   SUPERLATIVE

close....... closer....... closest
near .... nearer....... nearest

Adjectives with more than one syllable in their positive degree generally use *more* or *less* for the comparative and *most* or *least* for the superlative.

POSITIVE   COMPARATIVE   SUPERLATIVE

efficient ....more efficient ....most efficient
            less efficient .....least efficient
profitable ..more profitable ...most profitable
            less profitable ....least profitable

A few adjectives have special comparative and superlative forms.

POSITIVE   COMPARATIVE   SUPERLATIVE

good ....better ....best
bad ....worse ....worst
little..........less ....least
much ....more ....most
some..........less ....least
many..........more ....most

And several adjectives have only the positive degree.

POSITIVE   COMPARATIVE   SUPERLATIVE

excellent   — — —   — — —
unique   — — —   — — —
full   — — —   — — —
empty   — — —   — — —

Logically, nothing can be "excellenter" than *excellent*. Logically, something may be "less than unique" or "not quite unique"; it cannot be "less unique" or "more unique," because *unique* is "one of a kind." Logically, if something could be "fuller" or "fullest," it would not be *full*; it would be *overflowing*. And how can something logically be "emptier" than *empty*?

This and *that* are the only English adjectives with plural forms; the plurals *these* and *those* should modify only plural nouns. For example, instead of "these kind," "those kind," or "them kind," say or write "this kin*d*," "these kin*ds*," or "those kin*ds*."

Either is used with *or. Neither* is used with *nor*.

Either you *or* I will attend.
    (NOT   You or either I will attend.
    NOT   Either you nor I will attend.)
I don't believe that *either* you *or* I can accept that order.
Neither you *nor* I shipped those goods.

This, that, these, those, either, and *neither* are adjectives when they modify nouns or pronouns. *This, that, these, those, either* and *neither* are pronouns when they do not modify other words.

EXAMPLES AS ADJECTIVES

This plan looks good. *That memo* is incomplete. *These people* are industrious. *Those ideas* are good.
Either applicant probably would be an effective employee. *Neither applicant* has been interviewed yet.

EXAMPLES AS PRONOUNS

This is exactly what I wanted. *That* looks good. *These* are good; *those* are better. Of the two purchase requests, *either* can be approved quickly; *neither* is extravagant.

A, an, and *the* are adjectives which sometimes are called by a special name: **articles**.

A and *an* are indefinite ("*a* memo," "*an* interview"). The indefinite article *a* is used immediately before words which begin with a consonant (*a b*argain, *a s*ale). *A* is usually pronounced "uh"; only for extraordinary emphasis is it pronounced like the name of the first alphabet letter ("ayy"). The indefinite article *an* is used immediately before words which begin with a vowel or diphthong (*an o*ffice, *an ai*sle).

The is definite ("*the* memo," "*the* interview"); it is used to particularize a reference ("*the* memo you dictated this morning," "*the* interview scheduled for 3 p.m."). *The* is pronounced "thuh" immediately before words beginning with consonants ("thuh" *b*argain, "thuh" *s*ale). *The* is pronounced "thee" immediately before words beginning with vowels or diphthongs ("thee" *o*ffice, "thee" *ai*sle), immediately before intentional pauses in speaking, and for extraordinary emphasis before any word.

VERBS

Verbs represent actions or states of being.

ACTION	STATE OF BEING
do	is
communicate	seems
produce	appears

Verbs are controlled by their grammatical *subjects*. By composing a sentence with a grammatical subject that *originates* action or *asserts* a state of being, you put the accompanying verb into "active voice." By composing your sentence so that its grammatical subject *receives* action, you put the accompanying verb into "passive voice."

ACTIVE VOICE	PASSIVE VOICE
Pat wrote that memo. Subject (Pat) originates action.	That memo *was written* by Pat. Subject (memo) receives action.
They shipped the merchandise. Subject (They) originates action.	The *merchandise was shipped* by them. Subject (merchandise) receives action.

Besides having active or passive voice, **verbs** possess grammatical *tense*, grammatical *number*, and grammatical *person*. **Tense** communicates timing. **Number** distinguishes between one (singular) and more than one (plural). **Person** distinguishes among sender (first person), receiver (second person), and others (third person).

The charts on pages 462-463 show tense, number, and person in typical verb forms. The first chart is for active voice; the second is for passive voice.

The past tense of most verbs is formed by adding *-d* or *-ed* to the simple verb form; for example, the past of *use* is us*ed*, the past of *add* is add*ed*. However, the half-million words of English do include verbs with irregular formation of past tense, as shown in the chart on pages 464-465.

Most verbs may be used with or without grammatical objects.

Hoyt *telephoned.* (No grammatical object)
Hoyt *telephoned* early. (No grammatical object)
Hoyt *telephoned* that *order* early. (Object: *order*)

They *will deliver.* (No grammatical object)
Certainly they *will deliver.* (No grammatical object)
Certainly they *will deliver it.* (Object: *it*)

When used without a grammatical object, a verb is said to be "intransitive." When used *with* a grammatical object, a verb is said to be "transitive." *T*ransitive verbs *t*ake objects; intransitive verbs do not.

Note: Grammatical agreement of subjects and verbs is discussed on page 476.

ADVERBS

Adjectives modify nouns and pronouns; but **adverbs** modify verbs, adjectives, and other adverbs.

ADVERBS MODIFY VERBS

We *must decide* **here** and **now**.
(verb)
Our employees *work* **efficiently**.
(verb)
That shipment *has been sent* **east**.
(verb)

Time Guide for Verbs Active Voice				
TENSE	NO.	SIMPLE	PROGRESSIVE	EMPHATIC
Present	*Singular*	1. I pay 2. you pay 3. he (she *or* it) pays	1. I am paying 2. you are paying 3. he is paying	1. I do pay 2. you do pay 3. he does pay
	Plural	1. we pay 2. you pay 3. they pay	1. we are paying 2. you are paying 3. they are paying	1. we do pay 2. you do pay 3. they do pay
Past	*Singular*	1. I paid 2. you paid 3. he paid	1. I was paying 2. you were paying 3. he was paying	1. I did pay 2. you did pay 3. he did pay
	Plural	1. we paid 2. you paid 3. they paid	1. we were paying 2. you were paying 3. they were paying	1. we did pay 2. you did pay 3. they did pay
Future	*Singular*	1. I shall pay 2. you will pay 3. he will pay	1. I shall be paying 2. you will be paying 3. he will be paying	1. I will pay 2. you shall pay 3. he shall pay
	Plural	1. we shall pay 2. you will pay 3. they will pay	1. we shall be paying 2. you will be paying 3. they will be paying	1. we will pay 2. you shall pay 3. they shall pay
Present Perfect	*Singular*	1. I have paid 2. you have paid 3. he has paid	1. I have been paying 2. you have been paying 3. he has been paying	
	Plural	1. we have paid 2. you have paid 3. they have paid	1. we have been paying 2. you have been paying 3. they have been paying	
Past Perfect	*Singular*	1. I had paid 2. you had paid 3. he had paid	1. I had been paying 2. you had been paying 3. he had been paying	
	Plural	1. we had paid 2. you had paid 3. they had paid	1. we had been paying 2. you had been paying 3. they had been paying	
Future Perfect	*Singular*	1. I shall have paid 2. you will have paid 3. he will have paid	1. I shall have been paying 2. you will have been paying 3. he will have been paying	
	Plural	1. we shall have paid 2. you will have paid 3. they will have paid	1. we shall have been paying 2. you will have been paying 3. they will have been paying	

Time Guide for Verbs (Continued) Passive Voice			
TENSE	NO.	SIMPLE	PROGRESSIVE
Present	*Singular*	1. I am paid 2. you are paid 3. he (she *or* it) is paid	1. I am being paid 2. you are being paid 3. he is being paid
	Plural	1. we are paid 2. you are paid 3. they are paid	1. we are being paid 2. you are being paid 3. they are being paid
Past	*Singular*	1. I was paid 2. you were paid 3. he was paid	1. I was being paid 2. you were being paid 3. he was being paid
	Plural	1. we were paid 2. you were paid 3. they were paid	1. we were being paid 2. you were being paid 3. they were being paid
Future	*Singular*	1. I shall be paid 2. you will be paid 3. he will be paid	
	Plural	1. we shall be paid 2. you will be paid 3. they will be paid	
Present Perfect	*Singular*	1. I have been paid 2. you have been paid 3. he has been paid	
	Plural	1. we have been paid 2. you have been paid 3. they have been paid	
Past Perfect	*Singular*	1. I had been paid 2. you had been paid 3. he had been paid	
	Plural	1. we had been paid 2. you had been paid 3. they had been paid	
Future Perfect	*Singular*	1. I shall have been paid 2. you will have been paid 3. he will have been paid	
	Plural	1. we shall have been paid 2. you will have been paid 3. they will have been paid	

Examples of Irregular Verbs

PRESENT	PAST	PERFECT PARTICIPLE (have, has, had)
am	was	been
arise	arose	arisen
bear	bore	born, borne
beat	beat	beaten
become	became	become
begin	began	begun
bend	bent	bent
bid [command, invite]	bade	bidden
bid [make an offer]	bid	bid
bind	bound	bound
bite	bit	bitten
blow	blew	blown
break	broke	broken
bring	brought	brought
burst	burst	burst
buy	bought	bought
carry	carried	carried
catch	caught	caught
choose	chose	chosen
come	came	come
cost	cost	cost
dig	dug	dug
do	did	done
draw	drew	drawn
drink	drank	drunk
drive	drove	driven
eat	ate	eaten
fall	fell	fallen
fight	fought	fought
find	found	found
flee	fled	fled
fly	flew	flown
forbid	forbade	forbidden
forecast	forecast	forecast
forget	forgot	forgotten
freeze	froze	frozen
get	got	got
give	gave	given
go	went	gone
grow	grew	grown
* hang [suspend]	hung	hung

* The verb *hang* (a death penalty) is regular: *hang, hanged, hanged.*

PRESENT	PAST	PERFECT PARTICIPLE (have, has, had)
hide	hid	hidden
know	knew	known
lay [put into place]	laid	laid
lead	led	led
leave	left	left
lend	lent	lent
let	let	let
lie [recline]	lay	lain
lie [falsify]	lied	lied
make	made	made
pay	paid	paid
put	put	put
ride	rode	ridden
ring	rang	rung
rise	rose	risen
run	ran	run
see	saw	seen
set [put into place]	set	set
shake	shook	shaken
show	showed	shown
shrink	shrank	shrunk
sing	sang	sung
sink	sank	sunk
sit [take a seat]	sat	sat
slay	slew	slain
sleep	slept	slept
speak	spoke	spoken
spring	sprang	sprung
steal	stole	stolen
strike	struck	struck, stricken
strive	strove	striven
swear	swore	sworn
swell	swelled	swelled, swollen
swim	swam	swum
swing	swung	swung
take	took	taken
teach	taught	taught
tear	tore	torn
think	thought	thought
throw	threw	thrown
wake	waked, woke	waked
wear	wore	worn
weave	wove	woven
win	won	won
write	wrote	written

ADVERBS MODIFY ADJECTIVES

This agreement is **altogether** *legal.*
                    (adjective)
Our employees are **quite** *courteous.*
                    (adjective)
Your meaning is **really** *clear.*
                    (adjective)

ADVERBS MODIFY ADVERBS

They filled those orders **very** *fast.*
Our employees work **quite** *efficiently.*
Can anyone write **too** *clearly?*

As shown by those examples, adverbs are modifiers which answer these questions: when? where? which kind? how much, how?

Many adverbs end in *-ly*; others, like the following, do not:

also, too, quite, very, here, there, where, how, then

Some adverbs function also as adjectives:

a fast car	("car" is a noun; "fast" modifies that noun; since nouns are modified by adjectives, "fast" functions as an adjective in this example)
move fast	("move" is a verb; "fast" modifies that verb; since verbs are modified by adverbs, "fast" functions as an adverb here)

To determine whether a modifier should take adjective or adverb form, identify the grammatical job of that modifier in what you plan to write or speak. For instance, if you want to modify a noun or pronoun, use an *adjective* as modifier. If you want to modify a verb, an adjective, or an adverb, use an *adverb* as modifier.

Quick (adjective) or *quickly* (adverb)?

That's **quick** *service.*	(noun modified by adjective)
That *service* is **quick**.	(noun modified by adjective)
It is **quick**.	(pronoun modified by adjective)
They *work* **quickly**.	(verb modified by adverb)

This service is **usually** *quick.*	(adjective modified by adverb)
It can be done **very** *quickly*.	(adverb modified by adverb)

PREPOSITIONS AND CONJUNCTIONS

Prepositions and **conjunctions** are connectors; they join individual words and groups of words. A **preposition** requires a grammatical object; a **conjunction** has no grammatical object. *Subordinating* **conjunctions** make one grammatical element depend upon another for meaning; *coordinating* **conjunctions** do not.

The next two sentences have common prepositions printed in boldface type; the objects of those prepositions are italicized here:

Among the *messages* you prepared **for** my *review* was this summary **of** a *report* **from** *Davis* **to** *Cory.*

Concerning this *contract* **with** *Jay Company*, please verify the totals **by** *noon* today.

The next sentence shows three common *subordinating* conjunctions:

Although those totals seem correct **because** you updated them, verify them again **since** they are so important.

And this sentence shows three common *coordinating* conjunctions:

I received the Davis **and** Cory reports **but** have not finished editing **or** summarizing them.

INTERJECTIONS

Interjections are sounds of emotion in written form. **Interjections** are grammatically independent of other words or word groups. Examples: *ah, ha, 0, oh, ho, uh, huh.*

Ah, I certainly enjoyed that discussion.
Oh, did you?
I—**uh**—I'm not too sure now.
Ha! I thought so!

VERBALS

Verbal nouns (also called **gerunds**) end with the letters *i-n-g*. Like ordinary nouns, **gerunds** do the jobs of subject, complement, or object. But being *verbal* nouns, **gerunds** can take objects (as transitive verbs do).

Communicating is essential to business.
(verbal noun
functioning
as subject)

Writing *reports* is common in business.
(verbal   (object
noun as   of verbal
subject)   noun "writing")

What media does XYZ Company use for **communicating** market *quotations*?
(verbal noun as   (object of
object of prepo-   verbal noun
sition "for")   "communicating")

Verbal adjectives (also called **participles**) end with *i-n-g* or a past-tense sign; like ordinary adjectives, **participles** modify nouns or pronouns. But being *verbal* adjectives, *participles* can take objects (as transitive verbs do).

Hurrying, they reached the airport just in time.
(verbal adjective
modifying subject
pronoun "they")

Written reports are common in business.
(verbal adjective modifying subject noun "reports")

The display case, **swept** clean and **shined** to a luster, attracted buyers.
(verbal adjectives modifying subject noun "case")

When did Acme Company build the bridge **spanning** *Grand River*?
"spanning" = verbal adjective modifying common noun "bridge"
"Grand River" = proper noun functioning as object of verbal adjective "spanning"

Karen Dana is the person **directing** this *project*.
"directing" = verbal adjective modifying common noun "person"
"project" = common noun functioning as object of verbal adjective "directing"

Gerunds and present participles are verbals which end with *i-n-g*. **Infinitives** are verbals which begin with the word *to* and which do not end with *i-n-g*. An **infinitive** is versatile; it can function as noun, as adjective, or as adverb. And being a *verbal*, the **infinitive** can take an object (as a transitive verb does).

To succeed is our general objective.
(infinitive "to succeed" is being used here as subject; therefore it is a verbal *noun*)

We want **to improve** our efficiency.
(infinitive "to improve" is being used here as direct object of transitive verb "want"; therefore this infinitive is functioning as a verbal *noun*)

The need **to succeed** is common in business.
(infinitive "to succeed" modifies "need"; "need" is a common noun; nouns are modified by adjectives; therefore the infinitive "to succeed" functions as a verbal *adjective* here)

These notes seem ready **to transcribe**.
(infinitive "to transcribe" modifies "ready"; "ready" is used here as an adjective modifying the noun "notes"; adjectives are modified by adverbs; since "to transcribe" modifies "ready," the infinitive functions as a verbal *adverb* here)

SENTENCE COMPONENTS

A verb and those sentence elements tied directly to it compose a **complete predicate**; the main verb of a complete predicate is called the **predicate verb**.

Sentence elements *not* in the complete predicate constitute the **complete subject**. The main nouns or main pronouns of a complete subject are called the **subject words**.

Complete subjects grammatically control *complete predicates*. **Subject words** grammatically control *predicate verbs*.

These press and lathe operators generally work late.

complete subject =   "these press and lathe operators"
subject word: "operators"

complete predicate = "generally work late"
predicate verb: "work"

Jan, Lee, and the other supervisors sent their reports to Lou's office.

complete subject = "Jan, Lee, and the other supervisors"
subject words: "Jan," "Lee," "supervisors"

complete predicate = "sent their reports to Lou's office"
predicate verb: "sent"

Subject words take these grammatical forms:

> common nouns
> proper nouns
> pronouns
> gerunds
> infinitives functioning as nouns

A **complete subject** consists of subject word(s) plus any or all of these companions:

> modifer(s)
> conjunction(s)
> preposition(s)

A **complete predicate** consists of predicate verb(s) plus any or all of these:

> modifer(s)
> conjunction(s)
> preposition(s)
> complement(s)

Examples:

Those press and lathe operators generally work late.
"those press and lathe operators" = complete subject
"those" = modifier of "operators"
"press" = modifier of "operators"

"and" = coordinating conjunction joining "press," "lathe"
"operators" = subject word
"generally work late" = complete predicate
"generally" = modifier of "work"
"work" = predicate verb
"late" = modifier of "work"

Jan, Lee, and the other supervisors sent their reports to Lou's office.

"Jan, Lee, and the other supervisors" = complete subject
"Jan," "Lee," "supervisors" = subject words
"and" = coordinating conjunction linking the subject words
"the" = modifier of "supervisors"
"other" = modifier of "supervisors"

"sent their reports to Lou's office" = complete predicate
"sent" = predicate verb
"their" = modifier of "reports"
"reports" = direct object of transitive verb "sent" (complement)
"to" = preposition linking "reports," "office"
"Lou's" = modifier of "office"
"office" = object of preposition "to" (complement)

Consider this version of the last example:

The supervisors sent their to Lou's.

What missing words are needed to make sense? "Reports" and "office" complete the intended meaning. Words and word-groups used that way are called *comple*ments because they *comple*te the intended sense of verbs.

Complements are of these types: subject complements, direct objects, indirect objects, objects of prepositions, and objective complements.

1. Subject complements are so called because although they are part of a complete predicate, they refer to a *subject word*. There are basically two kinds of subject complements: **predicate adjectives** and **predicate nominatives**.

Predicate adjectives follow a special group of *in*transitive verbs, called *linking verbs* (e.g., "appears," "becomes," "seems," "am," "is," "was," "were," "looks," "hears," "smells," "tastes," "feels," "sounds").

Your *decision* seems *appropriate.*
Our bakery *products* smell *good.*
That *fabric* feels *rough.*

(predicate adjectives = "appropriate," "good," "rough," as used here)

Predicate nominatives (sometimes called **predicate nouns** or **predicate pronouns**) also follow linking verbs. Although part of the complete predicate, **predicate nominatives**—like predicate adjectives—refer to *subject words.*

Chris is the marketing *manager.*
Pat, Lee, and *Lou* are our *supervisors.*
You asked for the manager; *I* am *she.*

(predicate nominatives = "manager," "supervisors," "she" as used here)

Note that predicate nominatives, as implied by their name, take *nominative* case, not objective case: "I am she" instead of "her"; "I am he" instead of "him"; "good friends are we" instead of "good friends are us"; etc.

2. Direct objects have these traits:
   a. Direct objects are nouns or noun-equivalents (pronouns, gerunds, infinitives, or word groups functioning as nouns).
   b. Direct objects complete the intended sense of *transitive* verbs.

Finish those **reports** before you go.
(t.v.)   (d.o.)

/noun as d.o./

Who *dictated* **them**?
(t.v.)   (d.o.)

/pronoun as d.o./

They *require* careful **editing.**

/gerund as d.o./

I *intend* **to edit them.**
/infinitive as d.o. of "intend"; pronoun "them" as d.o. of the infinitive "to edit"/

Send **whoever is available.**

/word group as d.o. of t.v. "send"/

3. Indirect objects have these traits:
   a. Indirect objects are nouns or noun-equivalents.

   b. Indirect objects are placed between transitive verbs and direct objects.
   c. Indirect objects imply the sense of "to" or "for."

Send   *Harit*   that   report.
(t.v.)   (i.o.)   (d.o.)
They've bought *us* new typewriters.
       (t.v.) (i.o.)   (d.o.)
We mailed *whoever inquired* a copy of that
   (t.v.)   (i.o.)   (d.o.)
news release.

4. Objects of prepositions have these traits:
   a. They are nouns or noun-equivalents.
   b. They complete the connection which prepositions begin.

You asked for the *manager.*
            (obj. of prep. "for")

With *whom* did you speak about it?
   (obj. of   (obj. of prep.
prep. "with")   "about")

Ship these goods to *them* by the fastest
                  (obj. of
means available.   prep. "to")
(obj. of
prep. "by")

Note that as their name implies, *objects* take *objective* case, not nominative case: "With whom did you speak," not "with who did you speak"; "send those goods to them," not "to they"; etc.

5. Objective complements are adjectives or nouns used with—and placed immediately after—direct objects.

We painted the storefront
   (t.v.)   (d.o.)

green.
(adj. as o.c. to "storefront")

The committee members have elected you
chairperson.   (t.v.)   (d.o.)
(noun as o.c. to "you")

They named the company
   (t.v.)   (d.o.)

"Metrico."
(noun as o.c. to "company")

PHRASES AND CLAUSES

Phrases and clauses are word *groups* which do the jobs of individual words. What is the basic difference between phrases and clauses? A **phrase** does not contain a verb *and* subject. A **clause** does contain a verb *and* subject.

At the bottom of the page is a list of phrases, their ingredients, and their functions. Conjunctions, if used, are also considered parts of a phrase or of a clause.

Examples of **prepositional phrases**:

Various kinds of phrases are used **in business writing**.

"of phrases" functions as an adjective modifying the noun "kinds"
"in business writing" functions as an adverb modifying the verb "are used"

Impressive **in their size and design**, these engines are known **for reliability**.

"in their size and design" functions as an adverb because it modifies the adjective "impressive"
"for reliability" functions as an adverb because it modifies the verb "are known"

Examples of **participial phrases**:

Your memo **summarizing the new sales campaign** is well written.
(adjective modifying noun "memo")

Having considered the data carefully, I endorsed the merger proposal.
(adjective modifying pronoun "I")

Examples of **gerund phrases**:

Succeeding in business often requires skill with **writing messages**.
(noun as complete subject)
(noun as obj. of prep.)

Business success involves **communicating thoughts and ideas**.
(noun as direct object of t.v. "involves")

Communicating is **exchanging the evidence of ideas and feelings**.
(subjective complement; a predicate nominative; specifically, a predicate noun following the linking verb "is" and referring to the subject "communicating")

Examples of **infinitive phrases**:

We are beginning **to understand the interaction among words and word groups**.
(direct object of transitive verb "are beginning")

Note: The prepositional phrase "among words and word groups" functions here as an adjective because it modifies the noun "interaction." The noun "interaction" functions here as object of the infinitive "to understand."

TYPE OF PHRASE	INGREDIENTS	FUNCTIONS
1. prepositional	preposition + its object (and modifiers, if any)	adjective or adverb
2. participial	participle + its object (and/or modifiers)	adjective
3. gerund	gerund + its object (and/or modifiers)	noun
4. infinitive	infinitive + its object (and/or modifiers)	noun, adjective, or adverb
5. absolute	noun or noun-equivalent + participle (and modifiers, if any)	grammatically independent unit separated from the rest of a sentence by a comma
6. appositive	usually noun, pronoun, modifier, verb, or verbal (with or without modifiers for itself)	reidentifies, explains, or elaborates the immediately preceding sentence element

To communicate is **to exchange the evidence of ideas and feelings**.
(subjective complement/predicate nominative)

Note: "To communicate" is an infinitive but not an infinitive **phrase**, because it shows no grammatical object here. The basic ingredients of an infinitive phrase are infinitive + object. Also notice that "to exchange the evidence of ideas and feelings" is an infinitive phrase which contains a prepositional phrase. The prepositional phrase ("of ideas and feelings") functions here as an adjective because it modifies the noun "evidence." The noun "evidence," in turn, functions as a direct object of the infinitive "to exchange."

It is easy **to understand management's need to communicate a proper image**.
(adverb modifying subjective complement/predicate adjective "easy")

Note: The long infinitive phrase contains another infinitive phrase; "to communicate a proper image" functions as an adjective because it modifies the noun "need"; "need," in turn, functions as object of the infinitive "to understand." Also notice that this example shows a noun in possessive case ("management's"), which modifies a common noun ("need"). Insight: Nouns and pronouns in possessive case function as adjectives.

Examples of **absolute phrases**:

The conference having ended, we returned to our own offices.
Reminder: The elements of an absolute phrase are a noun or noun-equivalent plus a participle. Absolute phrases are grammatically independent; they do not perform the functions of nouns, adjectives, adverbs, etc. Notice also that an absolute phrase is separated from the rest of a sentence by a comma.

The session being longer than anticipated,
(absolute phrase)
we revised our travel plans.

I believe the future looks really right, **everything considered.**
(absolute phrase)

Note: In the last example, "considered" is a past participle. Also notice that the first of these three examples contains a prepositional phrase ("to our own offices"). That prepositional phrase modifies the intransitive verb "returned" and therefore functions as an adverb.

Examples of **appositive phrases**:

This letter is offered on behalf of Emily Doyle, **a former student of mine**.

Reminder: An appositive immediately follows and reidentifies another sentence element. Note: An appositive has the same grammatical function as the element which it follows. In this example, the proper noun "Emily Doyle" functions as object of the preposition "of"; so does the appositive phrase "a former student of mine.")

Management's purposes—**to decide and to achieve**—are themes of this book.

The common noun "purposes" functions as subject here; so does the appositive phrase "to decide and to achieve."

Three employees **(Kenada, Brandt, and Adams)** have been promoted.

Note: As these examples indicate, appositives often are set off by commas, by dashes, or by parentheses. *Exception*: An appositive which is absolutely necessary to the intended meaning of a whole sentence is not set off by punctuation. Examples of such "restrictive" appositives:

My brother **John** works with me.
Theories of the economist **Keynes** have been influential.
The colors **red, white, and blue** are on our corporate emblem.

Additional comment: Besides the six kinds of phrases already described, the term "verb phrase" is sometimes applied to a verb plus its modifiers or helpers. "Helpers" include "shall," "will," "has," "have," "had," etc., as in these examples:

I **shall gladly share** my opinions with you.
If you **had arrived** earlier, you **would have enjoyed** meeting Yates.

Reminder: A clause contains a verb and a subject. If it is equivalent to a completely stated sentence, the clause is said to be **independent.** Otherwise, the clause is said to be **dependent.**

Examples of **independent clauses** used as sentences:

1. You telephoned me.
2. You telephoned me at noon last Friday.
3. I was busy.
4. I was busy with employment interviews on that day.
5. You probably could tell.
6. You probably could tell interesting stories about your experiences.

As shown by the second, fourth, and sixth of those examples, independent clauses may contain phrases ("at noon last Friday," "with employment interviews on that day," "about your experiences").

Examples of **dependent clauses**:

When you telephoned me at noon, I was busy, **as you could probably tell**.

Although employment interviews are often brief, I find **that they often reveal interesting stories about work-related experiences.**

Dependent clauses need other sentence elements to make sense. **Independent** clauses, by themselves, would make sense as complete sentences. Like independent clauses, **dependent clauses** may contain phrases ("at noon," "about work-related experiences" in preceding examples).

Independent clauses often are linked by *coordinating conjunctions* ("and," "but," "or," etc.). **Dependent clauses** also may be linked by those conjunctions. But **dependent clauses** are *introduced* by *subordinating* conjunctions ("as," "after," "although," "because," "before," "despite," "if," "since," etc.). Reminder: **Independent** clauses are equivalent to completely stated sentences. BUT: **dependent** clauses function as nouns, as adjectives, or as adverbs.

What you recommend determines **which policy we follow**.

"What you recommend" has "you" as subject word, "recommend" as transitive verb, and "what" as direct object of that verb.

Since this word group has subject *and* verb, it is a clause (not a phrase). Because the word group functions as complete subject of the sentence and because functioning as a subject is the job of a noun, we have a **noun clause** here (instead of an adjective clause or an adverb clause).

"which policy we follow" has "we" as subject word, "follow" as transitive verb, "policy" as direct object of that verb, and "which" as modifier (adjective) for the noun "policy." Since this word group has subject *and* verb, it is a clause. Because this clause functions as direct object of the transitive verb/predicate verb "determines," and because being a direct object is one of the jobs of a noun, we have a **noun clause** here.

Other examples:

Tell me **why you want to market that product**.
(direct object of "tell"; therefore, a noun clause)

You are someone **who has a bright future with this company**.
(modifier of predicate pronoun "someone"; pronouns are modified by adjectives; therefore, we have an adjective clause here)

That's the office **where I work**.
(modifier of noun "office"; nouns are modified by adjectives; therefore, this is an adjective clause)

The customers returned **after you had left**.
(modifier of verb "returned"; verbs are modified by adverbs; therefore, this is an adverb clause)

Clauses can contain not only phrases but also other clauses.

What you recommend when you submit this report will determine which of the policies we adopt for this organization.

The basic formula of that long sentence is *complete subject + predicate verb + complement.*

The complete subject is a noun clause (consisting of all the words before "will determine"). That noun clause contains a smaller noun clause ("what you recommend"); the subject of that smaller clause is "you"; the verb of that smaller clause is "recommend"; the complement of that smaller clause is "what," functioning as direct object of "recommend."

The *predicate* verb ("will determine") is transitive. Transitive verbs take indirect objects and direct objects as complements. The long clause beginning with the word "which" and completing the sentence does the job of complement (direct object) for the transitive verb/predicate verb "will determine."

This is the structure of that ending clause:

which of the policies we adopt for this organization

"we" = subject of the clause

"adopt" = verb of the clause

"which" = direct object of transitive verb "adopt"

"of the policies" = prepositional phrase modifying "which"; "which" function as direct object of this clause; direct objects are nouns or noun-equivalents, and "which" does the job of a noun-equivalent (pronoun) here. Pronouns are modified by adjectives; the prepositional phrase "of the policies" functions here as an adjective modifying the pronoun "which."

"for this organization" = prepositional phrase modifying "adopt."

"adopt" is a verb; adverbs modify verbs; the prepositional phrase "for this organization" functions as an adverb because it modifies a verb ("adopt").

Reminder: "for this organization" is a *phrase* because it does not have subject and verb. It is a *prepositional* phrase because it consists of a preposition ("for"), the object of that preposition ("organization"), and an adjective ("this") modifying a noun ("organization").

Phrases and clauses provide clarity, variety, emphasis. For *conciseness*, however, phrases and clauses often can be condensed into single words. Examples:

PHRASES	SINGLE-WORD EQUIVALENTS
in the event that sales increase	if sales increase
in all probability	**probably**
provide them **with an explanation**	**explain**
starting **at this (that) point in time**	starting **now (then)**
stopping **at this (that) point in space**	stopping **here (there)**
with reference to requirements **of the job**	**concerning the job** requirements
in the order of magnitude of 2 percent	**about** 2 percent

CLAUSES	CONCISE EQUIVALENTS
the policy **that is recommended**	the **recommended** policy
a person **who has responsibility for**	a person **responsible** for
shipments **which are delayed**	**delayed** shipments
When seasonal trends are in effect, sales volume reflects them	**Sales volume reflects seasonal trends**
a message **which is completely informative but which is briefly stated**	a **concise** message
While you are at the Chicago office, telephone me.	Telephone me **from** the Chicago office.
What I want to know is whether you have received that shipment.	**Have you received that shipment?**
Your business messages should be accurate, complete, clear, and courteous; **and you also need to write or say them concisely.**	Your business messages should be accurate, complete, clear, courteous, **and concise.**

CLAUSES AND SENTENCE STRUCTURES

A **simple sentence** has not more than *one* independent clause but *no* dependent clause.

A **compound sentence** has *at least two* independent clauses but *no* dependent clause.

A **complex sentence** has *not more than one* independent clause *and at least one* dependent clause.

A **compound-complex sentence** consists of a compound sentence *and at least one additional* independent clause.

Knowing those patterns will help you vary your sentence structure, thereby providing interesting changes of pace for your readers and listeners.

SIMPLE SENTENCES

Simple sentences need not be short; the *quantity* of words does not determine the *kind* of sentence structure. But **simple sentences** must have *not more than one* independent clause and *no* dependent clause.

1. Stop! (The subject is "you," not stated but clearly understood.)

2. We start and stop machinery. (Subject: "we"; predicate verbs: "start," "stop"; coordinating conjunction for predicate verbs: "and"; direct object of the two predicate verbs: "machinery." "We start and stop machinery" is an independent clause functioning here as a **simple** sentence.)

3. Garcia and Duval start the machinery at 8 a.m. and stop it at 4 p.m. daily.

   Complete subject: "Garcia and Duval"
   Complete predicate: (the rest of the sentence)
   Subject words: "Garcia," "Duval"
   Predicate verbs: "start," "stop"

   The entire sentence consists of a single independent clause; the example is a **simple** sentence.

4. Garcia, Duval, and Claussen start the machinery at eight in the morning and stop it at four in the afternoon.

   (Again we have a single independent clause that functions as a **simple** sentence.)

COMPOUND SENTENCES

1. Garcia starts; Duval stops.
2. Garcia starts the machinery; Duval stops it.
3. Garcia starts the machinery, and Duval stops it.
4. Garcia starts the machinery at 8 a.m., but Duval stops it at 4 p.m.
5. Garcia and Phillips start the machinery at 8 a.m.; Duval and Ryan stop it at 5 p.m.; all of them leave by 5:15.

Note: Each of those five sentences consists of at least two independent clauses but no dependent clause. Therefore, they are **compound** sentences.

COMPLEX SENTENCES
(Dependent clauses are italicized here.)

1. We *who write* need insight.
2. We *who write business messages* need to develop insight.
3. Writing effective business messages requires insight *which is extraordinary.*
4. The writing of effective business messages requires people *who develop extraordinary insight to the patterns of human behavior and to the uses of language as a tool for influencing those patterns constructively.*
5. The writing of business messages *which are effective* requires people *who can develop extraordinary insight to the patterns of human behavior.*
6. We *who bring people and goods together* need messages *which are effective.*

Note: Each of those six sentences contains at least one independent clause *and* at least one dependent clause. Therefore, they are **complex** sentences.

COMPOUND-COMPLEX SENTENCES
(Dependent clauses are italicized here.)

1. At 8 a.m. Garcia starts the machinery *that laminates these products,* and at 5 p.m. Duval stops it.
2. At 8 a.m. Garcia starts the machinery *which laminates these products,* at 5 p.m. Duval stops it, and at 5:15 the shop closes for the day.
3. The machines start at 8 a.m.; they stop at 5 p.m.; the shop closes at 5:15 p.m. *after the guards have reported for duty.*

4. The machines start at 8 a.m., and they stop at 5 p.m.; the shop closes at 5:15 p.m. *after the guards have reported for duty*.
5. *Because we are business communicators*, we need extraordinary insight; and sometimes we need exceptional patience, too.
6. *Because we are business communicators*, we need insight; often we need patience, too.
7. Business communicators need insight *which is extraordinary*, and they need patience *which is exceptional*.

Note: Each of those seven examples consists of a compound sentence plus *at least one additional independent clause*. (In other words, each of those seven examples contains *at least two independent clauses* and *at least one dependent clause*.) Therefore, they are compound-complex sentences.

REFERENCE OF PRONOUNS

The noun for which a pronoun substitutes is called an **antecedent** (from Latin "that which comes before"). A pronoun should refer unmistakably to its antecedent; otherwise, the antecedent should be repeated, or the entire sentence should be rewritten for clarity.

VAGUE REFERENCE

I saw Bette, Lucy, and George today; she mentioned her being recognized as Executive of the Year.
  (Is "she" Bette, or is "she" Lucy?)

CLEAR REFERENCE

I saw Bette, Lucy, and George today; Bette mentioned Lucy's being recognized as Executive of the Year.
  /or/
Lucy mentioned Bette's being recognized as Executive of the Year.
Bette told me that Lucy is Executive of the Year.
Lucy told me that Bette is Executive of the Year.

"Lucy is Executive of the Year," Bette said.
Lucy said, "Bette is Executive of the Year."

VAGUE REFERENCE

We successfully closed that deal, which pleased us.
  (What pleased us? the deal? or the successful close?)

CLEAR REFERENCE

Successfully closing that deal pleased us.
Our success in closing that deal pleased us.
That deal, which we closed successfully, pleased us.

AGREEMENT OF PRONOUNS AND ANTECEDENTS

A pronoun and its antecedent need to share the same grammatical **gender**, **person**, and **number**. Grammatical **gender** is masculine (as with "son"), feminine ("daughter"), or neuter ("home"). Grammatical **first person** "speaks," **second person** "is spoken to," **third person** "is spoken about." Grammatical **number** is either singular (one) or plural (more than one).

The noun "typewriter," for example, has neuter gender (neither masculine nor feminine), third person (it neither "speaks" nor "is spoken to"), and singular number (one). A pronoun substituting for "typewriter" also must have neuter gender, third person, and singular number; the pronoun therefore would be "it."

A pronoun and its antecedent should agree in gender, person, and number—but need not share the same grammatical case. Example: "That typewriter is new; take good care of it." (The subject noun "typewriter" is in nominative case there, but the pronoun "it" is in *object*ive case because that pronoun is *object* of the preposition "of.")

PRONOUNS AND ANTECEDENTS

Disagreement	*Agreement*
This shopping mall just opened; isn't she a beauty?	This shopping *mall* just opened; isn't *it* a beauty?
I tried to stop that truck before he smashed into the loading dock.	I tried to stop that *truck* before *it* smashed into the loading dock.
When someone communicates, it is exchanging evidence of ideas and feelings.	When *someone* communicates, *he or she* exchanges evidence of ideas and feelings.
Whenever an executive dictates a message, you should speak clearly.	Whenever an *executive* dictates a message, *she or he* should speak clearly.
Either Sam or Jim can change their own schedules.	*Either Sam or Jim* can change *his* own schedule.
Neither Sue nor Marie is casual about their own work.	*Neither Sue nor Marie* is casual about *her* own work.
Both Sue and Marie take her own work seriously.	*Both Sue and Marie* take *their* own work seriously.
Do you judge a message by their length?	Do you judge a *message* by *its* length?
Do you judge messages by its length?	Do you judge *messages* by *their* length?

AGREEMENT OF SUBJECTS AND VERBS

A verb and its subject need to share the same grammatical person and number. (Grammatical gender and case do not apply to verbs.)

NOT You instead of Lynn is scheduled for overtime work.
BUT *You* instead of Lynn *are* scheduled for overtime work.

NOT Salaries has been rising.
BUT *Salaries have* been rising.

NOT Either Evans or Ross are concerned.
BUT *Either Evans or Ross is* concerned.

NOT Neither Evans nor Ross are concerned.
BUT *Neither Evans nor Ross is* concerned.

NOT One of our employees have a master's degree.
BUT *One* of our employees *has* a master's degree.

NOT Where is the supervisors' offices located?
BUT Where *are* the supervisors' *offices* located?

NOT Each of us hope to succeed.
BUT *Each* of us *hopes* to succeed.

NOT All of us tries to succeed.
BUT *All* of us *try* to succeed.

SELECTION AND PLACEMENT OF MODIFIERS

Choose and position modifiers (words and word groups functioning as adjectives or as adverbs) so that their intended effect is clear.

UNCLEAR MODIFICATION

That machine whirred as I tried to transcribe loudly. (Transcribe loudly?)

The executive who dictated that memo efficiently manages this department.
   (Dictated efficiently? Manages efficiently?)

I ordered a new typewriter for my secretary with all the latest features.

(Does your secretary have half-spacing?)

Walking into this office for the first time, that furniture looks impressive.

(Although desks and chairs have legs, can furniture walk?)

I almost used a ream of paper for that report.

(If you "almost used," you did not use.)

Before submitting this report, two months were spent in research.

(Did those months submit the report?)

CLEAR MODIFICATION

That machine whirred loudly as I tried to transcribe.
As I tried to transcribe, that machine whirred loudly.

The executive who dictated that memo manages this department efficiently.
The executive who efficiently dictated that memo is manager of this department.

I ordered a new typewriter with all the latest features for my secretary.
I ordered my secretary a new typewriter with all the latest features.

That furniture impresses people who walk into this office for the first time.
Walking into this office for the first time, people are impressed by that furniture.

I used almost a ream of paper for that report.

Before submitting this report, I spent two months in research.
Two months of research preceded submission of this report.

Suggestion: Place adverbs between the parts of an infinitive only for unusual emphasis. Otherwise, do not "split" the infinitive.

REGULAR INFINITIVE

I intend **to work** efficiently.
We seem **to agree** absolutely.

The purpose is certainly **to improve** this process.

SPLIT INFINITIVE

I intend **to** efficiently **work.**
We seem **to** absolutely **agree.**
The purpose is **to** certainly **improve** this process.

PARALLELISM

Parallelism indicates equality of ideas and of words which represent those ideas. To achieve parallelism of individual words, *balance* nouns with nouns, adjectives with adjectives, verbs with verbs, adverbs with adverbs, prepositions with prepositions, conjunctions with conjunctions, and verbals with verbals.

NONPARALLEL: This job requires skills in management and also communicating.

PARALLEL: This job requires skills in both management and communication.
This job requires skills in both managing and communicating.

NONPARALLEL: I enjoy learning to write and speaking effectively.

PARALLEL: I enjoy learning to write and speak effectively.
I enjoy learning to write effectively and to speak efficiently.

NONPARALLEL: I expect the next shipment to be as big or bigger than this one.

PARALLEL: I expect the next shipment to be as big as or bigger than this one.

NONPARALLEL
  I. Two Sending Skills
    A. Writing
    B. To speak
  II. Two Skills for Receiving
    A. Observing
    B. By reading
      1. listening

PARALLEL: I. Sending Skills
                A. Writing
                B. Speaking
          II. Receiving Skills
                A. Observing
                B. Reading
                C. Listening

PUNCTUATION

A subsystem of language, **punctuation** consists of cue marks for joining or separating words, phrases, clauses, and sentences. The purpose of punctuation is to clarify what otherwise would seem vague or confusing to a reader.

Punctuation marks function as traffic signals controlling the flow of written language. Except for experimental or deliberately unconventional purposes (as, occasionally, with innovative advertisements), punctuation of business messages is systematic rather than impulsive or decorative. Punctuation is an integral part of—not merely an addition to—effective writing. As competent highway engineers incorporate traffic designs into their roadbuilding plans, so should you incorporate punctuation within, not after, the flow of your written composition.

Notice that punctuation itself can change a message even though the words of that message remain constant:

Pat Jones
{
said you're correct.
said you're correct!
said you're correct?

said, "You're correct."
said, "You're correct!"
said, "You're correct?"
}

Pat, Jones said you're correct.
Pat, Jones said: "You're correct!"
"Pat," Jones said, "you're correct?"
"Pat? Jones said, 'You're correct.' "

As you see from those examples, **punctuation** is not an ornament but a tool for writing effectively. This section of Part Nine is designed to help you use that tool skillfully.

Period .

As a red light signifies "full stop" in traffic, so a **period** signals full stop for the following:

1. Declarative sentences (as in ordinary assertions)

   Our central office is in Milwaukee.
   Your order was filled yesterday.

2. Mildly imperative sentences (as in routine commands)

   Issue the refund.
   Make two copies of this memo.

3. Most personal initials as well as most abbreviations

   R. G. Davis, Jr.   B.B.A., M.Ed., Ph.D.
   Mr. L. N. Travis   a.m., p.m., A.M., P.M.
   Ms. Foster   f.o.b., c.o.d.
   Foster, Inc.

   But **acronyms** (abbreviated names consisting entirely of initial letters) often are written in all-capitals and without periods.

   ABCA (**A**merican **B**usiness **Co**mmunication **A**ssociation)
   HUD   (Department of **H**ousing and **U**rban **D**evelopment)
   NABTE (**N**ational **A**ssociation for **B**usiness **T**eacher **E**ducation

   And initials of exceptionally famous personalities sometimes are written in all-capitals without periods.

   FDR (**F**ranklin **D**elano **R**oosevelt)
   JFK (**J**ohn **F**itzgerald **K**ennedy)
   LBJ (**L**yndon **B**aines **J**ohnson)

4. Decimal point for dollars-and-cents amounts stated in figures

   The invoice totals $87.50, not $8.75.

   Notice that a dollars-*without*-cents figure does not require the period as decimal point.

   This $875 invoice needs correction.

Question Mark ?

The **question mark** punctuates *direct* queries.

How many pages have you revised?
I asked, "Where has the Wesco report been filed?"

The question mark does *not* punctuate *indirect* queries.

We asked if they will finish this work today.

When a sentence seems to be a query but is actually a request or a command, the question mark need not be used; a period replaces it.

Will you report to my office at once.

To convey emphasis, a question mark may punctuate each item in a series.

What is our market segment in Iowa? in Kansas? in Nebraska?

Exclamation Point !

The **exclamation point** punctuates an urgent command, extraordinary emotion, or exceptional emphasis.

Stop! Look! Listen!

Special Note: Sentences normally end with only *one* of these punctuation marks: period *or* question mark *or* exclamation point.

Comma ,

The **comma** is used for these purposes:

1. To introduce a short or informal quotation

   Pat said, "Meet me in Jensen's office."
   Kim asked, "When can you ship those goods?"

2. To punctuate a dependent clause that precedes an independent clause

   If your report is accurate, we should buy those shares.

3. To set off a *non*restrictive clause (i.e., to set off a clause which may be omitted without changing the corethought of the sentence)

   This stock, which has a good dividend record, is highly recommended.

4. To set off a *non*restrictive appositive (but not a restrictive appositive)

   Boise, **the capital**, is our headquarters city for Idaho.
   (*non*restrictive appositive)
   Business leaders **Ryan and Biggs** are quoted in this article.
   (restrictive appositive)

5. To punctuate independent clauses joined by a coordinating conjunction

   They have met our terms, and we should sign the contract.

6. To punctuate a long introductory phrase or an introductory phrase containing a verbal

   With the comprehensive survey completed well before that due date, the contractor had time to develop detailed cost estimates.
   After completing the survey, the contractor had time to develop detailed cost estimates.

7. To punctuate parenthetical terms

   Consider, for example, the Patel offer.
   As you know, the work is on schedule.

8. To punctuate a series of at least three words or word groups which *do not already have* a comma

   Essential commodities include oil, coal, and steel.

9. To imply (but not state) the word *and* between two adjectives modifying the same noun

   Metrico is a strong, progressive firm.
   Ortega is an honest, industrious employee.

Note: Do not use a comma if the word *and* would seem awkward or illogical.

a new jet aircraft
a former advertising executive

10. To punctuate terms of direct address

Margaret, this information is confidential.
This information, Margaret, is confidential.

11. To clarify sentence elements which otherwise might be misunderstood

NOT   This branch opened in 1957; ever since it has been our most profitable unit.

BUT   This branch opened in 1957; ever since, it has been our most profitable unit.

12. To imply omitted words

Ruth and Jay attended the sales meeting; Ann and Bill, the marketing session.

We plan to inspect Plant A this month, Plant B in July.

Semicolon ;

The **semicolon** is used in these ways:

1. To punctuate independent clauses of a compound sentence when no coordinating conjunction links those clauses

The inspectors have been here; they will return tomorrow.

2. To punctuate transitions, a semicolon is often used before—and a comma is used after—terms such as "that is," "i.e.," "for example," "e.g.," and the like

Bartok is an auditor; i.e., someone who verifies accounting records.
I've requested three people to attend; namely, Lucas, Kaplan, and Griggs.
Nonverbal messages have many aspects; for example, gestures, postures, timings, distances.

3. To separate independent clauses of a compound sentence if at least one of those clauses already contains a comma

That policy, my friend, is official; be sure to follow it.
However, this report is confidential; handle it carefully.

4. To separate items of a series when at least one of those items already contains a comma

The crew members are Smythe, not Smith; Halsey; and Ruiz.
Our branch offices are in Los Angeles; Chicago; and Columbus, Georgia.
Those reports were filled on June 30, 1976; June 29, 1977; and July 1, 1978.

5. To emphasize every item in a series of at least three independent clauses

We perceive; we interpret; we apply.

For less emphasis, the comma replaces the semicolon—

We perceive, we interpret, we apply.
Effective communicators notice, they read, they listen.

Colon :

The **colon** is used for these purposes:
1. To present a sentence element emphatically

I have just one word to say to you: Congratulations!

2. To introduce a series or a list

These are traditional management functions: to plan, to organize, to activate, and to control.

3. To introduce a long or a formal quotation

The certificate reads as follows: [long quote]
The second paragraph of our agreement states: "You are obligated under this contract to return unused items."

4. To separate hours, minutes, and sometimes seconds when time is stated in figures instead of in words

The conference began at 8:30 a.m.

5. To punctuate the salutation of a business letter or the heading of a memo

Dear Ms. [Miss, Mrs., Mr., Dr.] Rossi:

TO: L. A. McNair SUBJECT: Project 1422
FROM: B. R. Ming   DATE: April 3, 19—

Apostrophe '

Use the apostrophe for these purposes:

1. To indicate possession—except for words which are already shown in possessive form

We need to protect our patent rights.
         (NOT our's patent rights)
This steel mill is operating at its peak capacity.
         (NOT it's peak capacity)
These reports are his; those, hers; these, yours; and the rest, ours.
         (NOT his's, her's, or hers'; not your's or yours'; not our's or ours')

Note: The firm's patent rights are those of one firm.
      The firms' patent rights are those of more than one firm.
      Hotchkin's office is where Hotchkin works.
      Hotchkins' office is where Hotchkins works.
      Adele's and Dale's reports are more than one message.
      Adele and Dale's report is one message.

2. To indicate omitted letters of a contraction (i.e., to indicate omissions which occur when two words are combined into one word)

I am . . . I'm
I should, I would . . . I'd
I shall, I will . . . I'll
you are . . . you're
you could, you would . . . you'd
you will . . . you'll
he will . . . he'll
she will . . . she'll
it will . . . it'll
he could, he would . . . he'd
she could, she would . . . she'd

it could, it would . . . it'd
we are . . . we're
we should, we would . . . we'd
we shall, we will . . . we'll
they will . . . they'll
they could, they would . . . they'd
are not. . . aren't
cannot . . . can't
could not . . . couldn't
did not . . . didn't
do not . . . don't
has not . . . hasn't
have not . . . haven't
is not . . . isn't
it is . . . it's
shall not . . . shan't
was not . . . wasn't
were not . . . weren't
will not . . . won't
would have . . . would've
would not . . . wouldn't

3. To show the plurals of abbreviations, figures, letters, and words

Ph.D.'s head our research programs; Ed.D.'s supervise our training programs.
The 4's, 6's, and 8's on this typewriter are clogged.
Too many *and*'s, *but*'s, or *also*'s may needlessly lengthen a message.

Quotation Marks " " ' '

Use quotation marks for these purposes:

1. To enclose direct quotations

I asked, "Who is the manager of the Collection Department?"
"Who," I asked, "is your manager?"

If a direct quotation has more than a single sentence and is not interrupted, use opening quotation marks only at the beginning and closing quotation marks only at the end.

I asked, "Who are your managers? What are their names?"

For double-spaced typewriting of a quotation that has more than one paragraph, use opening quotation marks to begin each paragraph but closing quotation marks to end only the last paragraph.

The transmittal memo was worded as follows:

"Here is the report you authorized May 12 for submission today.

"Both historical and current data support recommendations to lease rather than to purchase Site 43. Cost figures are itemized on the following pages and summarized in the appended charts.

"Your response to this report will be welcome."

For a message that is otherwise double-spaced, you may typewrite a quotation of more than three lines this way: with single spacing, with double indention, but with no beginning or ending quotation marks.

The transmittal memo for the Site 43 recommendation report was prepared by O. A. Rashad and worded as follows:

Here is the report you authorized May 12 for submission today.

Both historical and current data support recommendations to lease rather than to purchase Site 43. Cost figures are itemized on the following pages and summarized in the appended charts.

Your response to this report will be welcome.

To enclose a quotation within a quotation, use single instead of double marks.

The minutes of the Executive Committee contain this statement:

"Evans proposed and Roswell seconded a motion 'to accept with regret the resignation of Chairperson B. K. Schuyler.' The motion passed unanimously."

For a message that is otherwise double-spaced, you may type a quotation within a quotation of more than three lines this way:

—with single spacing
—with double indention
—and with double quotation marks at the beginning and at the end of the second quote

The transmittal memo for the Site 43 recommendation report was prepared by O. A. Rashad and worded as follows:

Here is the report you authorized for submission today.

Our research confirms this statement in Marley's September 25 letter to you: "Both historical and current data support recommendations to lease rather than to purchase Site 43." Cost figures are itemized on the following pages and summarized in the appended charts.

Your response to this report and to Waley's urging "immediate action on this matter" will be welcome.

2. Use quotation marks to enclose titles of book **chapters**, magazine **articles**, newspaper **items**, and other **named parts** of complete works. But *italicize* the titles of complete works (i.e., italicize the titles of books, magazines, newspapers, etc.). Titles of parent or of full-length works are italicized; titles of their parts are quoted. In typewritten messages, italics are represented by underlining.

Have you read "Financial Forecasts" in today's *Manhattan Journal*?

"Ten Top Firms," the first chapter of Cory's newly published book, includes a history of Metrico, Inc.

3. Use quotation marks to enclose slang terms in an otherwise formal message, unusual words, or words used for special effect.

In personnel jargon of the entertainment industry, a "gopher" is someone whose job is to "go for" coffee and to do other errands. "gophering" is sometimes a way of "getting a foot inside the door" of that industry. As you know, jargon and slang change quickly; "gopher," for example, is becoming "gofer." This example shows how "old" words are given "new" definitions as well as "new" spellings.

Hyphen- and Dash—

1. Use the **hyphen** to divide a word at the end of a line. Rules for word division are given on pages 488-489.

2. The **hyphen** often follows these prefixes: *anti, ex, pro, self, vice.*

anti-progressive, ex-mayor, pro-diversification
self-centered, vice-chairperson (also: vice-chairperson)

3. A **hyphen** is often used between two adjectives which modify and which *come before* a noun (they are called compound adjectives).

first-class work, five-room suite, up-to-the-minute report

But when such adjectives *follow* a noun, they usually are not hyphenated.

The quality of your work is first class.
This office suite has five rooms.

Usually, a hyphen does not appear between an adverb and an adjective.

a highly effective presentation
their quite profitable undertakings

4. A **hyphen** is used in compound numbers written as words.

ninety-eight, one hundred and twenty-nine, seventy-seven, etc.
However, a one-third share is one third of the total.
　　　　↑　　　　　　↑
　　(hyphen)　　(no hyphen)

5. The hyphen can be used to clarify intended meanings.

VAGUE: They are junior high school students.
CLEAR: They are junior high-school students.
(in their third year)
CLEAR: They are junior-high school students.
(not in their third
or fourth years
of high school)

To typewrite a **dash**, strike the hyphen key twice without spacing. Use the dash for these purposes:

1. To show a sudden interruption or shift of thought

They should arrive at the Denver office by 2 p.m.—better make that 2:30, to be sure.

2. To convey momentary suspense for emphasis.

Congratulations, Lee—you've been promoted!

3. To emphasize an appositive

That important document—the Bramco contract—is in the safe.
I was asked to safeguard an important document—the Bramco contract.

4. To replace commas for emphasis

Those who first opposed us—and they were many—supported our ideas later.
Consider the probable consequences before you decide—not just afterwards.

Caution: If you overuse the dash, you will lose its quality of emphasis and suggest that you are unfamiliar with other punctuation marks. Use the dash sparingly and deliberately; reserve it for the purposes stated here.

Parentheses ( ) and Brackets [ ]

The functions of dashes (listed above) also are those of **parentheses. Parentheses,** however, are less emphatic than dashes and are used more often than dashes for supplementary explanations.

They should be at the Denver office about 2:30 this afternoon. (Better make that 2:45, to be sure.)
Legal documents (contracts, etc.) often show money amounts in words and in parenthesized figures; e.g., one hundred and fifty dollars ($150).

Use **brackets** to enclose material already in parentheses.

This parenthetical reference is directly quoted from our agreement: "The hourly rental (one hundred and fifty dollars [$150]) may be applied toward purchase of said machine."

Use **brackets** to identify material which you insert into a direct quotation made by another person.

"Official protests against that regulation were filed by five corporations [the actual number was six] on April 10."

The Latin word *sic* ("thus") is bracketed to identify but not to correct an error in a direct quotation; [*sic*] stands for "thus it is in the original statement."

"Official protests against that regulation were filed by five [*sic*] corporations."

Ellipses . . .

Ellipses, or "omission marks," signal deletions from quoted material. An **ellipsis** consists of three dots with intervening spaces . . . plus a period, a question mark, or an exclamation point when the ellipsis ends a sentence.

ORIGINAL QUOTATIONS	ELLIPSES
"For the time being, delete from this confidential statement the names of Croyden and Sklar; but mention that negotiations are still in the preliminary stage."	"For the time being . . . negotiations are still in the preliminary stage."
"Their purchase offer is $20 million."	"Their purchase offer is . . . ."

Placement of Punctuation

1. Periods for abbreviations are placed before any other punctuation mark. When an abbreviation occurs at the end of a declarative sentence, the period is not doubled.

   Metrico needs two Ed.D.'s and a Ph.D.
   Will you send that shipment C.O.D.?

2. Follow these American English rules of order for closing quotation marks:
   a. Place the period or the comma *inside* closing quotation marks.

      Gomez wrote "Economic Trends of Tomorrow."
      When you speak of "improving the sales picture," do you mean in terms of volume or, rather, of net profit?

   b. Place the colon or the semicolon *outside* closing quotation marks.

      Gomez emphasized in "Economic Trends": "P/E ratios are the key."
      You mentioned "improving the sales picture"; did you mean in terms of volume or, rather, of net profit?

   c. Place the question mark, exclamation point, or dash (1) *inside* when it is part of a quotation but (2) *outside* when it refers to the entire sentence of which the quote is a part.

      Should your slogan simply be "Buy now"?
      The investor asked, "Buy now?"
      Walters ordered 750 copies of the magazine containing "We Should Invest"!
      "Cancel that order!" she insisted.
      "I'm so busy that—" is all she said as she rushed by.
      Two words—"Please wait"—were all she had time to say.

   d. Punctuate a quotation within a quotation according to the preceding rules. Notice the sequence of single and double quote marks:

      She said, "I've read 'Economic Trends of Tomorrow.' "
      I asked, "When did you read 'Economic Trends'?"
      I asked, "Have you also read 'Should We Invest?' "
      He exclaimed, "Cancel that order for 'Economic Trends'!"
      " 'Buy now!' is Jay's idea of a slogan," I remarked.

3. Use parentheses with other punctuation as follows:

   a. If punctuation applies to the entire sentence and not just to the parenthetical material, the punctuation mark goes *outside* the closing parenthesis:

      This research confirms our prediction (see Formula 32).
      When I was introduced to Gomez (who wrote "Economic Trends of Tomorrow"), I was tempted to ask for an autograph.

b. If a question mark or an exclamation point applies only to parenthetical material, place the punctuation *inside* the closing parenthesis.

That slogan ("Buy Today!") is overused. Those people (are they shareholders?) have been waiting to see you.

Spacing for Punctuation

Space once after a punctuation mark— except for the following:

1. Do *not* space immediately before or immediately after

   a. A period inside an abbreviation

   Kenneth Lowry, M.B.A., will join us at 3 p.m.

   b. A period used as a decimal

   That percentage should be 3.15, not 3.51.

   c. A hyphen or a dash

   Can you build an up-to-date model of that process?
   Yes, we can—but not by the date you mentioned.

   d. An apostrophe

   Tyler's design is unique, isn't it?

2. Do *not* space immediately after opening or immediatly before closing quotation marks, parentheses, or brackets.

He announced: "We have been awarded the contract."
That price is firm (see page 37 of the catalog).
"This advertisement has typographical errors; for example, it mentions Frankln [Franklin] stoves."

3. Space *twice* for the following:

   a. Immediately after a colon

   The messages began with this formal statement: "When signed by you and by us, this letter will constitute a contract."

   b. Immediately after a period used with itemized numbers or letters

1. Traditional Management Purposes
   a. to decide
   b. to achieve
2. Traditional Management Functions
   a. to plan
   b. to organize
   c. to activate
   d. to control

   c. Between the end of one sentence and the beginning of another sentence typed on the same line

   Please transcribe this message now. It's a special directive.
   That's good news! Thanks for telling me.

NUMBERS

Many writers are sometimes puzzled by whether a number should be written in words or in figures. With business forms such as invoices, sales tickets, or purchase orders, figures are used almost entirely. But with messages written in paragraph form, numbers are sometimes expressed in figures and sometimes in words.

General Rules

1. Write a number at the beginning of a sentence as a word. If the number is very large, rewrite the sentence so that the number appears later as a figure.

   Fourteen dozen pairs of gloves were ordered last month.
   Twenty thousand dollars is the goal of the drive.
   The goal is $20,000.

2. Use figures for numbers greater than 100 except in the case of isolated round numbers.

   They registered 375 at the first convention, 1,237 at the second, and 2,119 at the third.
   They shipped nine thousand carloads in the first month.

3. Round numbers (numbers in even units, such as tens, hundreds, or thousands) should be spelled in full, except when they are used with other numbers expressed as figures.

We saw him ten days ago.
These machines range in price from $10 to $23,500.

Large round numbers may be written in words or figures or both according to the writer's preference or the nature of the copy. For example, if only one large round number is used, it may be written in words. But if many figures are used in other sentences or paragraphs, a large round number should be written in figures.

fifteen million dollars
$15,000,000
$15 million

4. If several numbers are used in parallel construction, write them in figures, unless all are small or are round numbers that can be written easily in words. A number at the beginning of a sentence should be written out even though later numbers are written in figures. You may improve the sentence by rewriting it so that the first word is not a number.

She ordered 45 typing books, 125 economics books, and 68 law books.
He bought three ties, six shirts, and ten handkerchiefs.
Seventy-seven men, 725 women, and 196 children were called in the poll.
In the poll 77 men, 725 women, and 196 children were called.

When a small number is used with a large number but not in a similar context, the small number may be written as a word.

I asked the two auditors about the $652,890 deficit.
Those three men use a $750,000 machine.

5. When one number immediately follows another, spell out the smaller number and express the larger one in figures.

She purchased 75 four-cent stamps.
He bought four 25-cent notebooks.

6. When one unrelated number immediately follows another, separate the two numbers by a comma.

In 1965, 654 new charge customers were granted credit.

Addresses

1. Write house numbers in figures, except for house number *One*.

Roberts lives at One Riverside Drive; Marshall, at 2185 Sutton Avenue; and McKie, at 8 Maple Terrace.

2. Spell out a number naming a street if the number is *less* than eleven. When a street has a number as its name, you may separate the building number from the street number by a hyphen preceded and followed by a space. The letters *d*, *st*, or *th* may be added to the number that represents a street name.

He moved from 438 West Fifth Street to 867 - 66 Street.
Our office is located at 104 - 131st Street.
Deliver the equipment to 210 West Tenth Street.

Dates

1. After the name of a month, use figures to express the day.

Your inquiries of June 2, 6, and 9 were answered in full on June 14.

2. When the day of the month stands alone or when it precedes the month, it may be written in figures with *d*, *st*, or *th* added, or it may be spelled out.

In your inquiry of the 6th, you asked for our catalog.
In your inquiry of the sixth, you asked for our catalog.
We sent a check for $200 on the 3d of August.

Amounts of Money

1. Sums of money, whether in dollars or in cents or in foreign denominations, should be typed in figures except for legal documents.

The total amount of the equipment recently purchased was $769.33.
The British firm may invest £ 50,000 in our project.

2. In legal papers spell out sums of money; write figures in parentheses.

   I agree to pay the sum of Five Hundred Sixty Dollars ($560).
   I agree to pay a weekly rental of One Hundred Ten (110) Dollars.

3. Even sums of money are written without the decimal and zeros.

   She mailed a check for $45 in full payment of her bill.
   Is that service charge $15?

4. When stating cents, use the figures without the decimal and spell out *cents*.

   The little girl purchased a small toy for 89 cents.

NOTE: The ¢ sign often appears on orders, invoices, and the like. Two doz. @ 98¢ per doz.

Fractions and Decimals

   Simple fractions that stand alone are usually written in words. Mixed numbers and decimals are written in figures. When a decimal fraction is not preceded by a whole number, a zero may be used before it.

   He bought one-half dozen erasers.
   The average age of secretaries in our department is 24½.
   The average age of secretaries in our department is 24.5.
   The quotient, 0.758, was obtained swiftly on the calculator.

Quantities and Measurements

   Quantities and measurements should usually be written in figures, as in the following examples:

   a. Age (*exact*)

      He is 37 years old.

   But use words in expressing *approximate* age:

      Richard is about twenty years old.

b. Balloting results

   There were 6,756 votes in favor of the amendment and 3,310 votes against it.

c. Dimensions

   They bought bond paper of a standard size, 8½ by 11 inches.

NOTE: Spell *by* in full, except in technical matter where x is used for *by*.

d. Distance

   It is 13 miles from my office to my home.
   It is 2,098 miles from San Francisco to Honolulu.

e. Financial quotations

   They bought Monarch Utilities at 100⅝.

NOTE: In financial quotations it is customary to express the plural of figures by adding the *s* without the apostrophe.

f. Mathematical expressions

   We found the total as follows: 125 plus 68 minus 38.

g. Measures

   We produced 200 bushels on every 4 acres.
   The chart showed that 231 cubic inches equal 1 standard liquid gallon.

h. Percentages—

   Interest on the note was computed at 9 percent.

NOTE: In business writing the % sign is often used to express percent:

   She purchased three 5-year, 4% bonds.

i. Serial Numbers

   Policy No. 622147, a new life insurance policy, is discussed in Bulletin No. 3.

j. Temperature

The highest official temperature record for this city is 110°.

k. Time

The plane leaves at 11:45 p.m.

BUT spell the hour in full when *o'clock* is used in starting time:

The office closes at five o'clock.

l. Weights

It takes 2,240 pounds to make a long ton.

DIVISION OF WORDS

When a word is divided at the end of a line, the division is indicated by a hyphen at the end of a syllable. Sometimes it is necessary to separate the parts of dates, names, and addresses even though these sentence elements are expressed as units. Such separations, however, should be avoided when possible.

Rules for dividing words and separating other sentence elements are given here. The dictionary is the authority for dividing words into syllables.

Guides for Dividing Words

1. Divide words only between syllables. Do not divide one-syllable words (*through, filed, missed*).

2. Write more than one letter with the first part of the word and more than two letters with the last part of the word.

above	*not*	a-bove
steady	*not*	stead-y
teacher	*not*	teach-er

Thus, no four-letter word should be divided. And it is preferred that five- and six- letter words not be divided.

infer	*is preferred to*	in-fer
little	*is preferred to*	lit-tle
inform	*is preferred to*	in-form

3. A syllable that is separated from the rest of a word must contain a vowel.

| con-trol | *but not* | could-n't |
| doc-trine | *but not* | does-n't |

4. When a final consonant, preceded by a single vowel, is doubled before adding a suffix, divide between the two consonants.

| step-ping | *not* | stepp-ing |
| run-ning | *not* | runn-ing |

BUT when a root word ends in a double consonant before a suffix is added, divide between the root word and the suffix.

| tell-ing | *not* | tel-ling |
| assess-ing | *not* | asses-sing |

5. A single-letter syllable within a word should generally be written with the first part of the word.

| sepa-rate | *not* | sep-arate |
| busi-ness | *not* | bus-iness |

Exceptions:
(a) When two one-letter syllables occur together within a word, divide between the one-letter syllables.

| gradu-ation | *not* | gradua-tion |

(b) When the single-letter syllable *a, i,* or *u* is followed by the ending syllable *ble, bly, cle,* or *cal,* join the two ending syllables to be carried over to the next line.

de·pend·a·ble	*divided*	depend-able
a·gree·a·bly	*divided*	agree-ably
di·vis·i·ble	*divided*	divis-ible
mir·a·cle	*divided*	mir-acle
cler·i·cal	*divided*	cler-ical

Note that this rule applies only when the vowel is correctly written as a syllable by itself. In the following examples the vowels *a* and *i* are *not* single-letter syllables.

du·ra·ble	*divided*	dura-ble
pos·si·ble	*divided*	possi-ble
mu·si·cal	*divided*	musi-cal

6. Divide hyphened words and compounds—such as *three-fourths, record-breaking, self-explanatory,* and *brother-in-law*—only at the hyphen that connects the words.

7. Put on the first line enough of the divided material to suggest what the complete word will be.

THIS	NOT THIS
clearing-house	clear-inghouse
diffi-cult	dif-ficult
gentle-men	gen-tlemen
recom-mend	rec-ommend
stenog-rapher	ste-nographer

8. Avoid dividing a surname. Separate titles, initials, or degrees from the surname only when it is impossible to avoid such separation.

Cunningham	not	Cunning-ham
John A. Link	not	John
		A. Link
Mr. Link	not	Mr.
		Link

9. Try to avoid dividing: words at the ends of more than two or three successive lines, the final word on a page, or the word at the end of the last complete line of a paragraph.

10. Avoid the division of figures and abbreviations.

$3,500	not	$3,-500
A.T.& S.F.	not	A.T.-& S.F.

11. Separate the parts of an address only when unavoidable and then as illustrated here.

2143 Market	not	2143
Street		Market Street
987 North	not	987 North Bridge-
Bridgeport		port
1741 - 16th	not	1741-
Street		16th Street
New York,	not	New
New York		York, New York

12. If separating the parts of a date is unavoidable, separate the day of the month from the year, not the month from the day.

August 20,	not	August
1979		20, 1979

STYLES AND PARTS OF A BUSINESS LETTER

Layout Styles

Letters may be arranged in a variety of styles, the most common of which are the block, the modified block, and the AMS.

In the **block style** (page 491) each line begins at the left margin. This style interferes with picture-frame symmetry but saves time for the typist.

The **modified block style** (page 491) takes a little more typing time but gives a more nearly "balanced" appearance.

AMS Simplified Style (page 492) differs from block style in the following details:
1. The salutation is omitted.
2. The subject heading is typed in capital letters a triple space below the address.
3. Questions, listings, or like items in the body of the letter are indented five spaces from the left margin except when they are preceded by a number or a letter.
4. The complimentary close is omitted.
5. The name and title of the dictator are typed in capital letters at the left margin at least three blank spaces below the end of the letter.
6. The names of persons to receive carbon copies are typed three spaces below the typed signature.

The **official letter style**, illustrated on page 492, is used in (a) messages of an official character, (b) formal messages to persons of prominence, and (c) nonbusiness messages to individuals not personally known. This style differs from the ordinary only in the position of the inside address, which is placed flush with the left margin from four to six spaces below the complimentary close. The reference initials are placed on the second line below the final line of the inside address.

Punctuation Styles

Open punctuation permits the omission of the colon after the salutation and the omission of punctuation after the date, address, and complimentary close, unless a line ends in an abbreviation requiring a period. Modern usage tends toward open punctuation.

Mixed punctuation, the punctuation style most used in business, is illustrated in the letter on the right of page 491. Mixed punctuation requires a colon after the salutation and a comma after the complimentary close. No other end-of-line punctuation is used in the opening and closing lines except for periods required by abbreviations.

Spacing

Business people prefer single spacing for the body of a message. More words can be put on a page typed with single spacing and less stationery may be required. Paragraphs have greater visual unity when typed in single-spaced blocks with double spacing between paragraphs. Their darker mass is better displayed against the light background of the letterhead.

Double spacing is sometimes used for the body of a message of under fifty words. Even when double spacing is used, however, the lines of the address are single spaced.

The Introductory Parts of the Letter

Heading. The heading (also called the return address) shows where the message comes from and when it was written. The longest line of the heading should not run into the right margin of the letter. Normally the heading should not extend to the left of the center of the sheet. The preferred order of information is: room and building (if they are included) on the first line, otherwise number and street on that line; city, state, and ZIP Code on the next line; date on the last line.

Block Heading

25 Standish Hall
201 College Place
Des Moines, IA 50308
May 1, 19—

Dateline. Write the date in full: *August 23, 19–*. Upon the accuracy of the date may rest a legal decision. Figures alone, like *8/23/79*, 8-23-79, 8:23:79, invite misunderstanding. Avoid their use except in office

memorandums. Avoid also the needless additions of *st, d, nd, rd,* and *th* after the day of the month.

Letters are usually dated the day they are dictated, not the day they are transcribed.

Armed Forces Dateline. The Armed Forces favor writing the date with the number of the day in Arabic numerals first, the name of the month second, and the figures for the year third—23 August 19--. This procedure is logical, and it has come into civilian use as an approved form.

Preferred Positions for the Dateline. The date of a message is a part of the reference material, much of which is supplied by the printed letterhead. The date gives information in terms of *time*, while the address printed on the letterhead gives information in terms of *place*. As time and place information are related, it is a good practice to place the date on the second line below the city and state names printed on the letterhead. In block and AMS styles the dateline is started at the left margin; in the modified block style it is acceptable practice to begin the date at center or type it so that it ends at the right margin. If the letterhead is unusual in arrangement, the dateline may be placed in relation to the body of the letter so as to achieve an impression of balance.

Address. The address (also called the inside address), states (1) the name of the person or the business to which the message is to be sent, (2) the street address, (3) the city, state, and ZIP Code. Each line of the address is typed even with the left margin. At least three lines are normally used. When a title or a descriptive phrase is used with the name of the person or the business, four or more lines may be necessary to prevent the use of a long line that would mar the layout.[1]

Ms. Janice McKinsey
South Ft. Mitchell
Kentucky 41011

Mrs. Edward Andrews
1521 Bond Avenue
Flint, MI 48506

Mr. Ralph Johnson
Executive Secretary
Automatic Processes, Inc.
204 Woodlawn Avenue
Flushing, NY 11311

[1] See pages 500-503 for further discussion of address layout and placement.

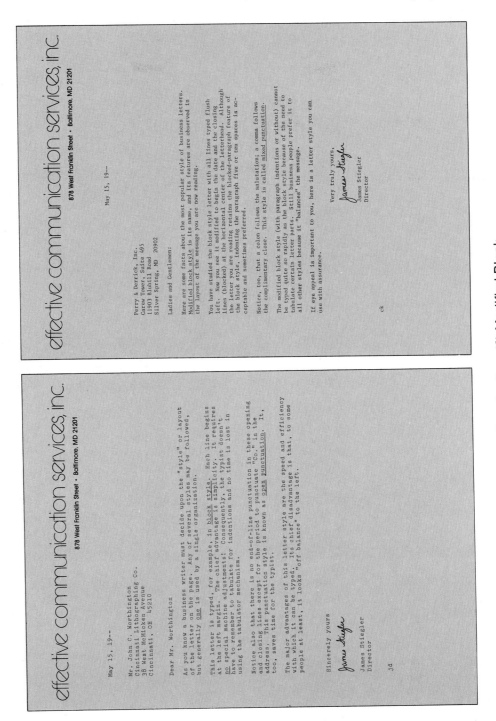

Two Styles of Layout (1) Block Style—Open Punctuation, (2) Modified Block Style—Mixed Punctuation

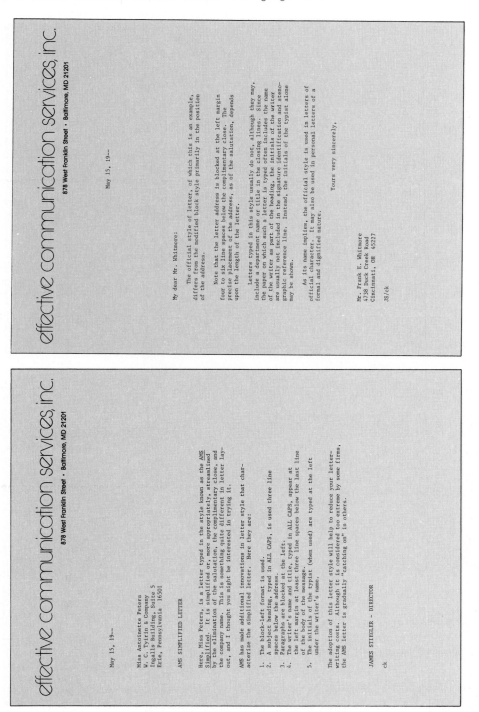

effective communication services, inc.

878 West Franklin Street · Baltimore, MD 21201

May 15, 19—

Miss Antoinette Peters
W. C. Tyirin & Company
Ingalls Building, Suite 5
Erie, Pennsylvania 16501

AMS SIMPLIFIED LETTER

Here, Miss Peters, is a letter typed in the style known as the AMS Simplified. It is simplified or, more appropriately, streamlined by the elimination of the salutation, the complimentary close, and the company name. This is something quite different in letter lay-out, and I thought you might be interested in trying it.

AMS has made additional innovations in letter style that characterize the simplified letter. Here they are:

1. The block-left format is used.
2. A subject heading, typed in ALL CAPS, is used three line spaces below the address.
3. Paragraphs are blocked at the left.
4. The writer's name and title, typed in ALL CAPS, appear at the left margin at least three line spaces below the last line of the body of the message.
5. The initials of the typist (when used) are typed at the left under the writer's name.

The adoption of this letter style will help to reduce your letter-writing costs. Although it is considered too extreme by some firms, the AMS letter is gradually "catching on" in others.

JAMES STIEGLER - DIRECTOR

ck

effective communication services, inc.

878 West Franklin Street · Baltimore, MD 21201

May 15, 19—

My dear Mr. Whitmore:

The official style of letter, of which this is an example, differs from the modified block style primarily in the position of the address.

Note that the letter address is blocked at the left margin four to six line spaces below the complimentary close. The precise placement of the address, as of the salutation, depends upon the length of the letter.

Letters typed in this style usually do not, although they may, include a department name or title in the closing lines. Since the paper on which such a letter is typed often includes the name of the writer as part of the heading, the initials of the writer are usually not included in the signature identification and steno-graphic reference line. Instead, the initials of the typist alone may be shown.

As its name implies, the official style is used in letters of official character. It may also be used in personal letters of a formal and dignified nature.

Yours very sincerely,

Mr. Frank E. Whitmore
4738 Duck Creek Road
Cincinnati, OH 45227

JS/ck

Two Additional Layout Styles: (3) AMS Simplified, (4) Official

Mr. J. R. Newcombe, Vice-President
Evan K. Menninger Company
312 Crescentville Road
New Orleans, LA 70108

The address is typed four to ten single spaces below the date, depending on the length of the message. Double spacing is used between the last line of the address and the salutation.

In messages to prominent persons and to others for whom a formal or official style is desired, the address is often typed below the signature, as illustrated on page 492. This style is also frequently used when a letter is addressed to a friend of the writer. The complete address may be desired so that it will show on the carbon copy and thus be available for filing purposes, but the message sometimes seems a bit more personal if the address is given at the bottom rather than in its usual position at the beginning.

If window envelopes are used, the address must be arbitrarily positioned so that it will show in full through the envelope window when the sheet is folded and inserted.

Handling Numbers in the Address.
1. Express house numbers in figures, except for house number *One*.

   Harold lives at One Cedar Drive: and Mark, at 2015 Bedford Street.

2. Spell out a number naming a street, if it is ten or below. When a street has a number as its name, you may separate the house number from the street number by a hyphen preceded and followed by a space. The letters *d, st,* or *th* may be added to the number that represents a street name.

   He moved from 721 Fifth Street to 864 - 37th Street.

Selecting the Correct Title. Use the correct title before the name of the person addressed, both in the address on the letter and in the address on the envelope. The correct general titles for the first line of the address are:

Individual: *Mr., Miss, Mrs., Ms.* [2]

---

[2] *Ms.* (pronounced "MIZ") is a form for both *Miss* and *Mrs.*

Messers. (the abbreviated form of the French *Messieurs*) is used in addressing men, or men and women; *Mmes.* (the abbreviated form of the French *Mesdames*) is used in addressing women. Modern usage tends to omit these two titles and to use instead the name of the firm as it appears on the letterhead.

To determine whether to use *The*, the sign "&" (called the *ampersand*), or the word *and* in the corporation name, follow the exact style used on the letterhead of the company to which you are writing.

Punctuating Titles. The period is used with each of the following abbreviated titles:

Mr.	man
Messrs.	more than one man
Mmes.	more than one woman
Mrs.	married woman
Ms.	married or single woman

The period is not used with the following forms:

Miss	unmarried woman
Misses	two or more unmarried women
Mesdames	two or more married women

Special Titles. Certain titles, in addition to those already given, often occur in written correspondence.

Doctor (Dr.) is the title of one who holds a doctor's degree, whether in philosophy, law, literature, theology, education, or medicine.

Professor (Prof.) is usually written in full; its abbreviation is becoming common.

The Reverend (Rev.) is a title for clergy.
1. *The*, as an article preceding *Reverend* or *Honorable*, is traditional usage, but the growing practice in America (as distinguished from that in England) is to use the title *Reverend* or *Honorable* alone.

Traditional examples:

The Reverend Dr. C. E. Frederick
The Reverend Mr. Bradshaw
The Reverend J. J. Bowen
The Honorable Georgia Sherwood
The Honorable Mr. Sherwood

In the case of direct *oral* address *The* is dropped.

2. Although abbreviation is common, many prefer to write and to read such titles in full.
3. When preceded by *The*, such titles should *not* be abbreviated.
4. Conventional addresses do not use *Reverend* or *Honorable* with the last name alone. Avoid *The Reverend Crane*, *The Honorable Towne*.
5. When *the* is not the only word used before *Reverend* or *Honorable*, *the* should not be capitalized.

We sent this suggestion to the Reverend Nicholas Towne and to the Honorable N. W. Johnson.

The Honorable (Hon.) is a title for someone who holds, or who has held, a prominent governmental position. It is used with the names of cabinet officers, ambassadors, members of Congress, governors, mayors, and judges. Courtesy often extends it to others. As in the case of *Professor* and *Reverend*, it is conventional to write *Honorable* in full, but abbreviation is common. When preceded by *The*, the title *Honorable* should not be abbreviated. Do not address *Honorable* with the last name alone. Avoid *The Honorable Wiley*.

Double Titles. Double titles are justifiable when the second title adds new information or distinction and does not merely duplicate the first.

Appropriate:
Mr. Richard E. Crawford, Manager
Dr. W. L. McGregor, Director
The Honorable K. L. Cameron, Chairperson
The Reverend H. H. Davenport, Moderator
Mrs. M. J. Anders, Superintendent
Inappropriate:
Dr. Steward R. Jones, M.D.
Dr. R. N. Barnes, D.D.

Typing the Official Title. The official title in an address may be typed on the first line with the personal name to equalize line lengths or placed at the beginning of the second line followed by a comma and a space. This title indicates the official position in relation to the company named in the second line.

Ms. Janice Harrison
Manager, Ross Company
399 King Avenue
Camden, NJ 08108

Mr. C. F. Wells, Vice-President
Petroleum Refining Corporation
899 Kearny Road
San Francisco, CA 98104

If the title itself is rather long, it may be typed on the second line by itself.

Mr. C. D. Nelson
Chairman of the Board
The Donovan Corporation
315 Randolph Street
Chicago, IL 60610

Handling Names Properly. Do not alter names. In the address of the letter and elsewhere, write a name exactly as it is written by its owner.

Attention Line. If you know only the last name of your receiver, you may address his or her firm and follow that address with an attention line. The attention line is typed two spaces below the last line of the address. It usually begins at the left margin (but may be indented in a modified block letter style).

Michaels and Cox, Inc.
General Contractors
6300 Decatur Place
Dallas, TX 75206
Attention Mr. Cox
Ladies and Gentlemen

On the envelope, type the attention line a triple space below the return address. (See the styles illustrated on page 502.)

A letter carrying an attention line will often be opened at once, along with general correspondence. If the person specified is absent and a prompt answer is required, the letter is referred without delay to another member of the staff. In larger companies, however, *all* letters—except those marked *Personal* or *Confidential*—are usually opened regardless of the address format.

Subject Line. The subject of a message is sometimes emphasized with a subject line, thus: *Subject: Unions* or *Subject: Order No. 3572*. If the printed letterhead does not indicate the place for the subject line, the subject may be centered or blocked on the second line below the salutation. In the latter case the body of the message begins on the second line below the subject line. The word *Subject* should be followed by a colon. The word is not necessary if the position of the subject line makes its nature clear.

Watson Corporation
2913 Drexel Road
Austin, TX 78703

Ladies and Gentlemen:

Subject: Unions

Watson Corporation
2913 Drexel Road
Austin, TX 78703

Ladies and Gentlemen:

                          Order No. 3572

Attention and Subject Lines Used Together. If the same message has subject and attention lines, follow this procedure: (a) Type the attention line on the second line below the last line of the address. (b) Type the salutation on the second line below the attention line. (c) Type the subject line on the second line below the salutation, placing it as you did the attention line—blocked to the left or centered.

Watson Corporation
2913 Drexel Road
Austin, TX 78703

Ladies and Gentlemen:

Subject: Unions

Watson Corporation
2913 Drexel Road
Austin, TX 78703

Attention Office Manager   Subject: Unions

Ladies and Gentlemen:

Reference Line. Occasionally at the top of a letter a request like this appears: "In your reply please refer to File 586." You should then respond with the following reference line, typed at the same point as the subject line.

Reference: Your File 586

          or

Your File 586

Salutation. Type the salutation on the second line space below the address and flush with the left margin. If there is an attention line, type the salutation on the second line below the attention line. Double-space between the salutation and the first line of the message body.

In order of decreasing formality, common salutations are:

FOR MEN

Sir
My dear Sir
Dear Sir
My dear Mr. Brock
Dear Mr. Brock
My dear Brock
Dear Brock
My dear Paul
Dear Paul

FOR WOMEN

Madam
My dear Madam
Dear Madam
My dear Mrs. Adams (Miss Adams, Ms. Adams)
Dear Mrs. (Miss, Ms.) Adams
My dear Ruth
Dear Ruth

Plural salutations are:

Gentlemen—This salutation is for addressing an organization made up entirely of men.

Mesdames—This salutation is for addressing an organization made up exclusively of women. *Ladies* is an alternate salutation.

Ladies and Gentlemen—This salutation is gaining popularity for addressing an organization consisting of men and women.

How Well Do You Know Your Correspondent? Choose the salutation that represents the person addressed and that matches the tone of your message. For those whom you have never met, the formal *Sir* or *Madam* may be used, although in such instances the less formal *Dear Mr. Brock* (or whatever the name may be) is much more popular.

How to Capitalize a Salutation. Capitalize the first word of a salutation. The word *dear* is not capitalized unless it is the first word. The following words are always capitalized for salutations:

Sir
Mr.
Every surname (Jones, for example)
Every first name (John, for example)
Madam
Mrs.
Ms.
Miss

All titles (President, Superintendent, Director, Doctor, and the like)

How to Punctuate a Salutation. In the mixed punctuation style, the colon punctuates the salutation of a business letter.

Dear Mr. Morris:

Do not use a comma to punctuate a business salutation. (The comma is for personal correspondence.) If open punctuation is used, the colon is omitted.

Special Salutations Involving Familiar Titles. It is permissible to abbreviate these titles in a salutation, but many people prefer them written in full:

Doctor (Dr.)
Dear Dr. Sterling
Dear Doctor Sterling:

Professor (Prof.)
Dear Professor Bell:
Dear Prof. Bell

The Reverend (Rev.)
Dear Reverend Father:
Dear Rev. Father:

Omitting Salutations. The AMS Simplified style drops the salutation (see illustration on page 492) and puts a subject heading in its place.

A few firms have also experimented by dropping the salutation and substituting such forms as:

Mr. Rand, Please
Greetings, Ms. Randolph

Good Morning, Mrs. Rankin
How Do You Do, Mr. Rand

A variation lifts the opening words of the first paragraph into the salutation position:

Here, Ms. Randolph,

is our idea of how you should proceed. Schedule your shipments for the first month (etc.)

or

So You May
Get Acquainted
With An Extraordinary New (etc.)

Still another variant launches the message abruptly without using the introductory words:

Mrs. Roberta Rankin
987 Waverly Drive
Louisville, KY 40209

Here, Mrs. Rankin, is the brochure which you recently requested (etc.)

The Body and the Concluding Parts

Body of the Letter. The paragraphs in the message are indented or are in block form according to the layout style used. No paragraph indention is used for block or AMS style. Indention may or may not be used for modified block or official style. When indented paragraphs are used, the first line of each paragraph is commonly indented five or ten spaces.

Paragraphs are usually typed single-spaced with double spacing between paragraphs. In very short messages with indented first lines of paragraphs, however, the entire body of the message may be doublespaced.

Paragraphs. As a rule, paragraphs in business messages are shorter than those in other forms of writing. An opening paragraph of two to five lines, for example, is easy to grasp. It is easier to read four paragraphs of six lines each than one solid paragraph of twenty-four lines. It is easier to read four paragraphs of six lines each than twelve paragraphs of two lines each. But do not overparagraph. Strike a happy medium. In general, vary later paragraphs from four to eight lines or so.

Abbreviations. Use abbreviations sparingly. To write names, titles, and expressions in full is a courtesy that many well-known firms thoughtfully extend. Certain abbreviations should be especially avoided in business letters.

USE	AVOID
account	acc't, acct., a/c
amount	am't, amt.
received	rec'd
Philadelphia	Phila.
San Francisco	S. F.
Dear Sir	D'r S'r
Gentlemen	Gents
Secretary	Sec'y
and Company	& Co.
Yours	Y'rs
March 6, 19—	3/6/—

But in routine communication when the addressees are familiar with the terms used, shortened forms are permissible. In such cases communicators often standardize their abbreviations according to the *Style Manual of the United States Government Printing Office.*

Second Sheets. Contrasted to pica, elite type permits more copy on a single page and makes possible more one-page messages. *But do not crowd one page merely to avoid the use of a second.*

Top and side margins on the second page should match those on the first. The heading of the second page is preferably written in one of the styles illustrated below, approximately one inch (or 6 spaces) below the top edge of the sheet.

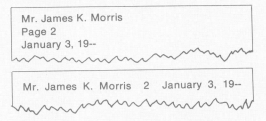

Leave three lines between the second-page heading and the continuation of the message.

Stationery used for second pages should *exactly match* the first sheet in quality, weight, color, and size.

Complimentary Close. Like a salutation, the complimentary close is controlled by (1) good taste, (2) the practice of leading business organizations, and (3) the degree of acquaintance you have with the reader.

Match the Complimentary Close to the Salutation. Note the direct link between the salutation and the complimentary close. The most commonly used closes in business messages are:

Very truly yours
Yours very truly
Sincerely yours

The close *Yours truly* is less often used in modern correspondence because it sounds too routine.

Choose the complimentary close to match the salutation and the message body in tone. If the salutation is familiar because of a long-standing acquaintance, the complimentary close should be so. If the salutation is directed to a person of high position or to someone with whom you have not previously corresponded, the complimentary close may be relatively formal.

Form of the Complimentary Close. (1) Type the complimentary close on the second line below the last line of the body. (2) Begin it (a) flush with the left margin in the block style; (b) at a point even with the dateline; or (c) at the center point, if the dateline has been started at the center. (3) Capitalize only the first word of the close. (4) When the colon is not used after the salutation, omit the comma after the complimentary close. If the comma is used after the salutation, put the comma after the complimentary close.

Signature. In its usual form the signature of a business letter has three parts:
1. Dictator's signature (penwritten)
2. Dictator's name (typed)
3. Dictator's title in the organization (typed)

Company Name. The company name, if used, is typed in all-capital letters on the second line below the complimentary close. If the company name is long, it must begin far enough to the left so that it will not extend noticeably into the right margin.

An Approved List of Complimentary Closes

Faithfully yours,
Yours faithfully,
Faithfully,

{ Close personal friendship
with or without business
Close confidential relations
involving business

Cordially yours,
Yours cordially,
Cordially,

{ Daily business contacts
Close business friendship
Informal business relations

Very sincerely yours,
Yours very sincerely,
Sincerely yours,
Yours sincerely,

{ Semiformal
Ordinary business matters
Business acquaintance
Ordinary business friendship

Very truly yours,
Yours very truly,

{ Formal, but widely used

Respectfully yours,
Yours respectfully,
Respectfully submitted,

{ Severely formal or for use
in official messages, reports,
or communications to
indicate special respect

Penwritten Signature. Standardize your signature for business matters. In legal disputes signatures are scrutinized, so sign consistently.

Dictator's Name and Title. The dictator's name is typed on the fourth line below the company name or on the fourth line below the complimentary close when a company signature line is not used. An acceptable optional arrangement is to type only the dictator's official title on the fourth or fifth line below the company name or the complimentary close and to combine the full name of the dictator with the stenographic reference initials.

If the name of the signer appears on the letterhead in such a line as *Office of A. B. Horton, Executive Director*, it is unnecessary to type an identification; initials are sufficient.

If only the dictator's name appears in the typed signature position, the official title is usually placed on the line below the dictator's name. When both the name and title are short, combine these two items on the same line.

GOODNER ARMS, INC.

Henry J. Erickson

Henry J. Erickson
Vice-President

ILLINOIS GLASS COMPANY

L. V. Simms

L. V. Simms, Manager

Indicating the Status of Women. Women may identify their marital status as shown here:

Sincerely yours

Kathryn D. Lynn

Mrs. Kathryn D. Lynn

Sincerely yours

Carla M. Vargas

Miss Carla M. Vargas

Signature Identification and Stenographic Reference. If the name of the dictator is typed in the closing lines, the stenographic identification is typed after the dictator's initials, which appear at the left margin, thus: *SFL:jc.* Otherwise the name of the dictator is typed flush with the left margin, followed by the initials of the stenographer. The preferred form is that which identifies only the stenographer.

The reference line is typed on the second line space below the signature block, flush with the left margin.

Sincerely yours
TRI-STATE, INC.

P. A. Leeds

Vice-President
PALeeds/ld

Special guide lines for mailing and carbon copy instructions are placed below the reference line, flush with the left margin.

Enclosures. Call attention, in the body of the letter, to enclosures. Add a notation (usually the word *Enclosure*, or the abbreviation *Enc.* or *Encl.*) at the left margin, on the second line below the stenographic sequence.

Enclosures 2

or

WFK:jao
Encs. 2

Double-spacing below the identification line causes the word *Enclosure* or the abbreviation *Enc.* to stand out clearly for the attention of the mail clerk. When the letters have been signed by the dictator and are being folded and prepared for the mail, the enclosure reference guards against failure to include the required enclosure.

Separate-Cover Negotiations. When the letter refers to items sent in a separate envelope or package, an appropriate notation should appear at the left margin below the last enclosure line (or below the reference line if there is no enclosure line). The notation should indicate the method of transportation used in sending the separate-cover material and the number of envelopes or packages.

Separate Cover—Express
Separate Cover—Mail 2

Mailing Instructions. When a special postal service is to be used (airmail, special delivery, registered mail), a notation to that effect should be typed in all-capital letters even with the left margin midway between the date line and the first line of the address.

SPECIAL DELIVERY
REGISTERED MAIL

Carbon Copies. A carbon copy of each typewritten letter is usually filed for reference. Additional copies are sometimes made for special purposes, such as conveying information to others interested in the correspondence. In such instances it is correct to sign the carbon copy. If the carbon copy is used under circumstances that make a personal tone desirable (for example, an identical message to several committee members), the signature should be placed on each as if it were an original.

If you wish to indicate, on the original letter, those to whom copies are being sent, you may write *Copy to* or *Copies to* (optionally *cc*) on the second line below the reference, enclosure, or separate-cover notation (whichever is last) flush with the left margin, with the names of the copy recipients on the spaces immediately following, thus:

MVH/as
Copy to John C. Halterman

or

MVH/ac
cc Mrs. Mary Robertson
     Dr. W. G. Sprague [3]

If the information regarding carbon copies is not for the benefit of the addressee, this notation may be placed on the carbon copies only. If this is the case, it may be placed at the top of the sheet rather than at the bottom.

Postscripts. A postscript may be used to cover a point thought of after the message has been typed or to give special emphasis to some particular point. The postscript is seldom used in business. Logical construction of the message makes most postscripts unnecessary, except for those few cases in which deliberate special emphasis is wanted.

---

[3] When carbon copies are sent to a number of persons in an organization, the names may be arranged (a) alphabetically, (b) according to rank (highest on down), or (c) according to the relative degree of interest in the particular subject. The alphabetical arrangement is used most often.

A postscript is the last item to be typed on the letter. It is typed on the second line below the last notation in the same form as any other paragraph of the message. The postscript should not be preceded by the letters P.S. (abbreviation for *post script*) or N.B. (abbreviation for *nota bene*, "Note well"). Position and format identify a postscript as such.

Addressing the Envelope. On envelopes, the return address is typed a double space from the top edge and three spaces from the left edge. Address placement is as follows:

Envelope	From Top	From Side
Small envelope	2"	2½"
Large envelope	2½"	4"

The United States Postal Service recommends these guides:

a. Block all lines of the address.
b. Single space all lines.
c. Place city, state, and ZIP Code (in that order) on the bottom line. The Postal Service prefers the use of two-letter state abbreviations with the ZIP Code.

Special Lines on the Envelope. When an attention line is a part of the address, it may be typed either on the line immediately following the company name or on a separate line a triple space below the return address.

Other special lines, such as *Hold for Arrival* and *Please Forward*, are usually typed a triple space below the return address.

Styles of Envelopes. The illustration on page 502 shows various styles of envelope addresses:

1. Single-spaced, block-form, four-line address.
2. Single-space, block-form, three-line address. Note the use of capital letters and no punctuation. This is the format preferred by the Postal Service.
3. Single-space, block-form, four-line address. Note placement of *Hold for Arrival* notation.
4. Single-spaced, block-form, four-line address, showing one placement of the attention line.

Why Some Mailings Never Arrive. Millions of pieces of mail each year are undeliverable, delayed in delivery, or returned to the sender because of:

1. No street or number in the envelope address.
2. Not putting the complete return address in the upper left corner of the envelope.
3. Errors in typewriting or handwriting addresses.
4. Omission of North, South, East, or West (N., S., E., W.) street directions.
5. Not placing necessary postage on the envelope.
6. Not wrapping parcel-post packages securely.

Window Envelopes. The window envelope has a transparent pane of cellophane or similar material at or near the center of its face, permitting the address typed on the letter itself to show through. The advantage of the window is that it cuts the cost of addressing the envelope by letting the address on the letter serve the purpose. This kind of envelope is popular for sending checks, invoices, bills, and similar items. Its chief disadvantage for use with letters is that it requires special framing, spacing, and folding which, in turn, may unbalance the letter layout.

LAYOUT GUIDES

Guides for the Illustrated Letter on Page 505:

1. Make the layout look like a picture in a frame.
2. A ZIP Code appears on the same line as the names of the city and state. Leave one to two spaces between the name of the state (or the two-letter state abbreviation) and the ZIP Code. Do not place parentheses around the ZIP Code or a comma before it.
3. Place the dateline so that it conforms to the letter style used or to the letterhead itself. The dateline may be blocked at the left margin, typed at center, or placed so that it ends even with the right margin.
4. Spell names of months in full, both in the dateline and in the body of the letter.

TWO-LETTER STATE ABBREVIATIONS

Alabama	**AL**	Montana	**MT**
Alaska	**AK**	Nebraska	**NE**
Arizona	**AZ**	Nevada	**NV**
Arkansas	**AR**	New Hampshire	**NH**
California	**CA**	New Jersey	**NJ**
Colorado	**CO**	New Mexico	**NM**
Connecticut	**CT**	New York	**NY**
Delaware	**DE**	North Carolina	**NC**
District of Columbia	**DC**	North Dakota	**ND**
Florida	**FL**	Ohio	**OH**
Georgia	**GA**	Oklahoma	**OK**
Guam	**GU**	Oregon	**OR**
Hawaii	**HI**	Pennsylvania	**PA**
Idaho	**ID**	Puerto Rico	**PR**
Illinois	**IL**	Rhode Island	**RI**
Indiana	**IN**	South Carolina	**SC**
Iowa	**IA**	South Dakota	**SD**
Kansas	**KS**	Tennessee	**TN**
Kentucky	**KY**	Texas	**TX**
Louisiana	**LA**	Utah	**UT**
Maine	**ME**	Vermont	**VT**
Maryland	**MD**	Virginia	**VA**
Massachusetts	**MA**	Virgin Islands	**VI**
Michigan	**MI**	Washington	**WA**
Minnesota	**MN**	West Virginia	**WV**
Mississippi	**MS**	Wisconsin	**WI**
Missouri	**MO**	Wyoming	**WY**

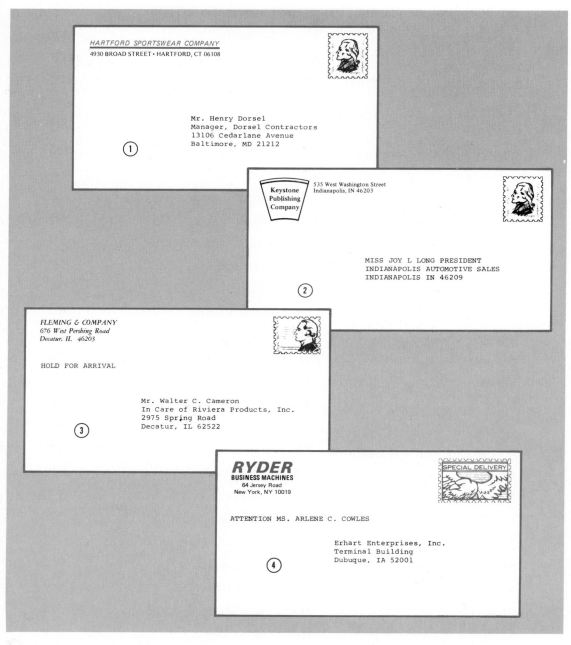

Styles of Envelope Addresses

5. Use *st, d,* and *th* after the number of the day only when the month is not mentioned.
6. Place a comma between the day of the month and the year.
7. Omit punctuation after the year except within a sentence, in which case insert a comma.
8. Type the address in block form even with the left margin; leave three to nine spaces between the date and the address, depending on the length of the letter.
9. Make the lines of the address as nearly equal as possible. For this purpose you may place the addressee's title:
    (a) on the same line as the addressee's name,
    (b) on the next line, preceding the name of the firm; or
    (c) on a line by itself.
    Base your decision on the length of the title, the length of the addressee's name, and the length of the firm's name.
10. Place a comma between the addressee's name and official title.
11. Capitalize the principal words of titles and the names of departments (Credit Department, Sales Promotion Department).
12. Use no punctuation after the lines in the address except after permissible abbreviations.
13. Write the firm name as it appears on the firm's own letterhead.
14. Use the ampersand (&) only when the firm itself uses it.
15. You may abbreviate *Incorporated (Inc.)* and *Limited (Ltd.).* Precede *Incorporated* and *Inc.* with a comma, but omit the comma before *Limited* and *Ltd.* When *Incorporated* or *Inc.* occurs within a sentence, use a comma immediately after it. Write in full the words *Company* and *Corporation.*
16. Write in full the words *North, South, East,* and *West* in street directions.
17. Spell out the number naming a street if it is ten or below; for eleven or above, use figures.
18. For postal sections of a city (N.E., S.E., N.W., S.W.; e.g., 711-14th Street N.W.), initials include periods; avoid abbreviating *Avenue, Boulevard,* or *Street.*

19. Type the name of the state on the same line as the name of the city in the address. Place a comma between the names of the city and state.
20. Use two-letter abbreviations for identification of the state. Type the abbreviation in capital letters with no punctuation.
21. If an attention line or a subject line is used, place it a double space below the inside address and double space above the salutation. The placement may be even with the left margin or centered. Capitalize only the principal words.
22. The first word of a salutation is capitalized.
23. Type the salutation even with the left margin two single spaces below the last line of the address or two single spaces below the attention or subject line if one is used. The salutation is followed by a colon in mixed punctuation.
24. Begin the body of the letter two single spaces below the salutation. Indent the paragraphs five to ten spaces. For the block style, begin the body even with the left margin.
25. An even right margin may require occasional hyphenation. Avoid frequent hyphens. Divide a word only when necessary.
26. Leave two spaces after a colon, exclamation point, a question mark, or period (one space after a period following an initial or abbreviation used *within* the sentence). Leave one space after a comma or semicolon. Leave two spaces between sentences.
27. Use a comma to point off words or word groups used in a series of at least three items. Place a comma before *and, or,* or *nor* in a series of at least three items. Exception: Semicolons replace commas in this usage if at least one of the series items already contains a comma.
28. A dash (—) is made by typing the hyphen twice, without spacing.
29. Double-space between paragraphs.
30. The hyphen (-) is used to link compound words.
31. Capitalize the first word of a fully stated direct quotation.
32. Use figures and write in full the word *cents.* (In tabulating work *75¢* is preferable to *$.75.*)

33. A comma or a period should precede closing quotation marks. A semicolon or a colon follows closing quotation marks. A question mark or an exclamation point is placed inside closing quotation marks when a part of the quoted matter, outside when not a part.

34. Set off nonrestrictive appositives with commas, parentheses, or dashes.

35. Within a sentence a title following a name is preceded and followed by a comma.

36. When referring to articles and books, place in quotation marks the titles of articles, short monographs, and chapters; underline or type entirely in capitals the titles of books, magazines, and other full-length works. Such titles are preceded and followed by commas only when the titles are in apposition.

37. Use a colon after words that introduce an enumeration, a long quotation, or a formal quotation. Use a comma before a short or an informal quotation.

38. Block in and center enumerations and long quotations. Double-space between paragraphs.

39. Place a period after a point number of an enumeration, and space twice after the period.

40. Begin the second and following lines of centered material directly under the first letter of the first word of the first line.

41. A quotation within a quotation is enclosed in single quotation marks (' '). Double quotation marks are placed with relation to other punctuation marks according to Guide No. 33. Examples:

    He said, "This job transfer gives me more 'weight.' "
    He said, "This job transfer gives me more 'weight'!"
    He said, "Will this job transfer give me more 'weight'?"

42. Seasons of the year are capitalized only when they are personified. For example:

    Will your family be warm when Winter brings his ice, snow, and frigid winds to your house?

43. Express even sums of money without the decimal point and zeroes.

44. Express percentages in figures; many business people prefer to spell *percent* rather than use %.

45. Use a hyphen to connect compound adjectives *before* a noun.

46. Begin the complimentary close two single spaces below the last line of the body of the letter. In block style begin the complimentary close flush with the left margin of the letter. In modified block style, begin the complimentary close at center or so that the longest line in the complimentary close and signature ends even with the right margin.

47. Type the firm name (if used with the signature) in solid capitals on one line, two single spaces directly below the first-letter of the complimentary close.

48. Type the dictator's title four or five single spaces below, and even with the first letter of the company name (if the company name is typed in).

49. Type the signature identification and stenographic reference flush with the left margin two single spaces below the dictator's official title.

50. Type the word *Enclosure*, or the abbreviation *Enc.* or *Encl.* (if this notation is necessary), flush with the left margin two single spaces below the signature identification. More than one enclosure may be indicated by *Enclosures* followed by the number of items:

    Enclosure 2
    Enc. 2
    Encl. 2

51. The phrase *Copy to* or *Copies to* or the letters *cc* or *CC* may precede the name or names of those to whom carbon copies are being sent. The phrase is typed two single spaces below the item it follows, flush with the left margin.

metrico, inc.

Administrative Services Division ● Post Office Box 6606 ● Brooklyn, NY 11210

February 1, 19--

Mr. M. B. Cory, Jr., President
Sales & Production Company, Inc.
2000 East Seventh Street, N.E.
Easthampton, MA 01021

Subject: Cost Efficiency

Dear Mr. Cory:

Your interest in communication efficiency is welcome. Experts who have made a special study--in the practical research laboratory of the small, medium, and large business office--can give you some surprising cost figures discovered through the use of cost control.

In the difficult art of maintaining consistent quality for communications output, some otherwise ultramodern executives seem to be self-trained. What is commonplace knowledge to the expert is to some of them shocking fact and startling news: a letter is often more expensive than a comparable telegram or a long-distance telephone call!

"Business letters are expensive production tools which may cost you more dollars and cents than necessary," writes a communication consultant, W. W. Kay, president of Kay and Associates, in Effective Communications. Chapter 1, "Can You Slash Letter Costs?" describes an effective business message this way:

1. It extends the personal power of the executive. Says one manager, "It enlarges my business field, gives me greater 'weight and stature'!"

2. In summer and winter, spring and fall, it can be made to win business friendship.

If every dozen of your letters costs you about $50, only a 10 percent rise in dictator-stenographer efficiency can put an "extra" $5 in your corporate pocket.

Sincerely yours,

METRICO CORPORATION

Terri J. Roth

President and Director

TJRoth: kd

Enclosure

Copy to Communications, Inc.

Illustrated Letter
The numbered items on this letter are discussed on pages 500, 503-504.

QUICK PUNCTUATION GUIDE

Period

●

Page 478

1. To end a declarative or mildly imperative sentence.
2. For most initials and abbreviations (*C.O.D., Inc., A. B. Hyer, but SEC*).

Question Mark

?

Page 479

1. After a direct question.
2. After a question in abbreviated form (Who is the employment interviewer? the advertising manager? the marketing vice-president?).

Exclamation Point

!

Page 479

To indicate strong emotion or heavy emphasis.

Comma

,

Pages 479-480

1. For a subordinate clause preceding a principal clause.
2. For a nonrestrictive clause.
3. For a nonrestrictive appositive but not a restrictive appositive.
4. To separate clauses joined by a coordinating conjunction.
5. For an introductory phrase containing a verbal.
6. For parenthetic words, phrases, clauses.
7. For words or word groups used in a series of at least three items that have no commas.
8. For words used in direct address or in explaining other words.
9. For sentence elements that might be misunderstood if there were no commas.
10. To indicate the omission of words that are clearly implied.
11. To separate numbers (*7,892,000*).
12. To introduce a short quotation.

Semicolon

;

Page 480

1. Between the clauses of a compound sentence if no coordinating conjunction joins those clauses.
2. Before *as, that is, namely, i.e., eg., to wit, viz.,* when introducing a complete clause or a series of several items.
3. To separate the clauses of a compound sentence when at least one of those clauses has a comma.
4. To punctuate a series of items which have at least one comma.

---

¹ References are to pages in this book.

Colon

:

Pages 480-481

1. To introduce a series of items.
2. To introduce a long or formal quotation.
3. To separate hours and minutes in figures (*10:15 a.m.*).
4. To punctuate the salutation of a business message.

Apostrophe

'

Page 481

1. To indicate possession.
2. To show omission in a contraction.
3. For the plural of abbreviations, letters, figures, and words.

Quotation Marks

DOUBLE

" "

SINGLE

' '

Pages 481-482

1. To enclose direct quotations.
2. To show titles of subdivisions of published works and titles of magazine articles, reports, lectures, and the like.
3. To indicate unusual terms, words used in a special sense, slang, or jargon.
4. To position closing quotation marks and other punctuation, the following rules apply:
   (a) Place the period or comma inside the quotation mark.
   (b) Place the colon or the semicolon outside the quotation mark.
   (c) Put any other punctuation mark inside when it is part of the quotation and outside when it refers to the entire sentence of which the quotation is only a part.

Hyphen

-

Pages 482-483

1. To divide a word at the end of a line.
2. To join the parts of compound words.

Dash

—

Pages 481-483

1. To show a sudden break or transition in thought.
2. To emphasize an appositive.
3. To replace a comma for heavy emphasis.

Parentheses

( )

Pages 483-484

1. To enclose figures following amounts in words.
2. To enclose numbers or letters in enumerations, series, or lists.
3. To set off nonrestrictive appositives.

Brackets

[ ]

Pages 483-484

1. To enclose items that you insert into a direct quotation.
2. To enclose a parenthetical item within material already in parentheses.

Ellipses

● ● ●

Page 484

To signify omissions from quoted material.

Index

514